Thinking

Readings in Cognitive Science

Thinking

Readings in Cognitive Science

Edited by
P. N. Johnson-Laird and P. C. Wason

Cambridge University Press
Cambridge
London   New York   Melbourne

Published by the Syndics of the Cambridge University Press
The Pitt Building, Trumpington Street, Cambridge CB2 1RP
Bentley House, 200 Euston Road, London NW1 2DB
32 East 57th Street, New York, NY 10022, USA
296 Beaconsfield Parade, Middle Park, Melbourne 3206, Australia

© Cambridge University Press 1977

First published 1977
Reprinted 1979

Phototypeset by Western Printing Services Ltd, Bristol
and printed in Great Britain by The Pitman Press, Bath

Library of Congress Cataloguing in Publication Data
Main entry under title:
Thinking: readings in cognitive science.
Bibliography: p. 581
Includes index.
1. Thought and thinking.   2. Artificial intelligence.
3. Psycholinguistics.   I. Johnson-Laird,
    Philip Nicholas.   II. Wason, Peter Cathcart.
BF455.T534   153.4   77–78887
ISBN 0 521 21756 3 hard covers
ISBN 0 521 29267 0 paperback

Contents

Preface

The aim of this book is to answer the question: what can cognitive science tell us about the intellectual processes of the mind? It brings together a set of readings ranging over the psychology of thinking and reasoning, Artificial Intelligence, and psycholinguistics.

It has become something of a fashion among experimental psychologists to wonder whether their discipline is making progress. A revolution occurred in the 1950s which might crudely be summarized as the overthrow of Behaviourism by Information Processing. A generation later, some psychologists are wondering whether the revolution was successful: certain Behaviourists do not seem to have realized that it has occurred, and certain Information-Processing psychologists are disenchanted with the new style. Strangely, the revolution has taken a long time to reach the study of thinking. Cognitive psychologists have focused nearly all of their efforts on such topics as perception, memory, and attention. Cognition proper has been relatively neglected. Yet, there has been a marked growth in understanding the psychology of thinking. Moreover, with the increased attempts to understand the mind by workers in other fields, particularly Artificial Intelligence, there are distinct prospects for some exciting developments in the future. The readings in this book have been brought together to try to capture explicitly this potential. They are intended to be comprehensive and, together with the introduction to each Part, to provide a detailed guide to those aspects of thinking currently under active exploration. Our goal was to provide an anthology that could help researchers in Psychology and Artificial Intelligence to understand each other's work on thinking, that would make a useful accompanying text to courses on Cognitive Psychology, and that might provide an interesting survey of the study of higher mental processes for workers in other disciplines. The introductions to each of the seven Parts describe the context to the problems, explain any potential sources of difficulty, and often incorporate material for which no suitable reading exists.

The selections in a book of readings are always to some extent arbitrary – a compromise between what the editors want to include and what they are able to obtain – and there are inevitably many excellent papers for which there is no room. The criteria that we followed in selecting a reading for inclusion in the book were: excellence, interest, and relevance. We have been fortunate in obtaining the rights for nearly all the papers we wished to include and in persuading some of our contributors to write papers specially for this volume. We thank all the authors for their efforts, directly or indirectly, on our behalf.

Some of the papers were too long to be included in their entirety. The presence of three dots '. . .' indicates an omission of more than a few words, but we have avoided, in the interest of the reader's fluency, a more elaborate system which could convey its extent more precisely. We have also made a number of minor stylistic changes which are unmarked in the text. On the rare occasion where we have introduced material into a reading, it occurs within square brackets. The provenance of each article is given in a footnote to its title. There is a single consolidated bibliography (and citation index) at the end of the book.

We would like to express our gratitude to the staff of Cambridge University Press; particularly to Dr Jeremy Mynott for providing us with encouragement, editorial wisdom, and tactful mediation with recalcitrant publishers; and to Penny Carter for the meticulous care which she devoted to our manuscript. We are also grateful to Professor Judith Greene and Dr Marc Eisenstadt of the Open University, who generously provided their advice and helped us to produce a book of readings suitable, we hope, for their students. Many friends, colleagues, and anonymous referees, provided us with ideas about the contents and organization of the book. We are especially grateful to Eve Clark, Herb Clark, Margaret Donaldson, Kate Ehrlich, Larry Erlbaum, Roger Goodwin, Jane Hughes, Sheila Jones, Stanley Jones, Annette Karmiloff-Smith, Barbara Lloyd, David Lowenthal, George Miller, Keith Oatley, Tom O'Brien, Tim Shallice, Catherine Weir, Til Wykes. We should like to thank Stella Frost and Valerie Nunn for the indispensable service of converting our indecipherable handwriting into clear typescript and for numerous other vital chores.

Finally, we owe a debt to our respective wives, Mo and Ming, for understanding our preoccupation with the problems of this book.

P.N.J.-L.
P.C.W.

March 1977

Acknowledgments

The full provenance is given in the first footnote to each reading.

The editors acknowledge with gratitude the contributors to this volume who have generously given permission for their material to be used. Acknowledgment is also due to the following writers and publishers for quotation of copyright material: Academic Press (London) (*Readings 9, 20*); the American Association for the Advancement of Science (*Readings 11, 21, 31*); the American Psychological Association (*Readings 5, 6*); Elsevier Sequoia (*Reading 18*); Lawrence Erlbaum Associates (*Readings 8, 23, 24, 29, 30*); Hemisphere Publishing Corp. (*Reading 12*); Hermann, Paris (*Reading 17*); S. Karger AG, Basle (*Reading 10*); the Merril-Palmer Institute (*Reading 14*); Sir Karl Popper (*Reading 16*); Sage Publications (*Reading 28*); Third International Joint Conference on Artificial Intelligence (*Reading 34*); The University of Chicago Press (*Reading 27*); John Wiley and Sons (*Reading 15*).

Contributors

R. P. ABELSON	Yale University
H. J. BERLINER	Carnegie-Mellon University
M. BOWERMAN	University of Kansas
J. D. BRANSFORD	State University of New York at Stony Brook
H. H. CLARK	Stanford University
M. COLE	Rockefeller University
M. E. DOHERTY	Bowling Green State University
M. EISENSTADT	Open University
I. M. L. HUNTER	Keele University
J. HUTTENLOCHER	University of Chicago
B. INHELDER	Geneva University
P. N. JOHNSON-LAIRD	Sussex University
D. KAHNEMAN	Hebrew University of Jerusalem
Y. KAREEV	Hebrew University of Jerusalem
A. KARMILOFF-SMITH	Geneva University
T. S. KUHN	Princeton University
A. S. LUCHINS	State University of New York at Albany
E. H. LUCHINS	State University of New York at Albany
N. S. MCCARRELL	Vanderbilt University
J. METZLER	Stanford University
G. A. MILLER	Rockefeller University
M. MINSKY	Massachusetts Institute of Technology
C. R. MYNATT	Bowling Green State University
K. NELSON	Yale University
A. NEWELL	Carnegie-Mellon University
K. G. OATLEY	Sussex University
J. PIAGET	Geneva University
K. R. POPPER	London School of Economics

E. ROSCH	University of California, Berkeley
R. C. SCHANK	Yale University
S. SCRIBNER	Rockefeller University
R. N. SHEPARD	Stanford University
R. A. SHWEDER	University of Chicago
R. R. SOKAL	State University of New York at Stony Brook
A. TVERSKY	Hebrew University of Jerusalem
R. D. TWENEY	Bowling Green State University
P. C. WASON	University College London
T. WINOGRAD	Stanford University
P. H. WINSTON	Massachusetts Institute of Technology

Introduction

An introduction to the
scientific study of thinking

Is it possible to study thinking from a scientific standpoint? The answer to the question is by no means obvious. There have been a number of thinkers who have been prepared to deny the possibility on theoretical grounds. There may well be many people who, confronted with a history of the attempts to study thinking, would join the chorus of sceptics. However, no matter how great their number or volume, other psychologists, computer scientists, anthropologists, linguists, and sociologists are likely to go on trying to study cognition scientifically. There are no overwhelmingly convincing arguments about the futility of the exercise. Indeed, the possibility of a cognitive science seems particularly auspicious at present. It is this sense of readiness – manifest in different disciplines concerned with human thinking – that we have tried to capture in this book of readings. We sense it most notably in the convergence on a number of fundamental ideas within theories proposed from totally disparate backgrounds. If, as we suspect, cognitive science is gaining in impetus, then it is natural to wonder about the underlying causes of this development and about the long period of its stagnation during the era of Behaviourism in which the subject was so neglected. Our aim in this introduction will be to look into some of these historical matters, and to survey recent developments in order to explain the particular contents of this book.

One of the striking aspects of psychology, revealed by a cursory consideration of its history, is how it has freely imported *theoretical* ideas from other disciplines but seldom reciprocated by exporting its own theories elsewhere. In recent years, for example, psychologists have made use of information theory, signal detection theory, control theory, holography, transformational grammar, and concepts from computer programming; yet it is very difficult to compile a comparable list of theories developed within psychology that have had an impact on other disciplines. A cynic might suppose that psychologists are, in Jane Austen's phrase, lacking in 'strength of understanding' in comparison with scientists from whom they borrow. Maybe. But we suspect that there is another more decisive reason for the discipline's failure to balance its intellec-

1

tual books. It has an Empiricist obsession with experiments – with designing, executing, analysing, reporting, and criticizing them. In psychology, one experiment is worth a thousand theories. Indeed, this ratio is apt if one compares the number of purely theoretical papers in the literature with the number of papers reporting experimental results. It is no surprise that psychology is not noted for its theoretical expertise. Unfortunately, an understanding of human mentality is not to be achieved merely by carrying out experiments – no matter how exemplary they are – and developing theories to account for their results. That is a hard truth, and one that is only just beginning to be learnt. We certainly do not advocate abandoning the use of experiments: they often yield illuminating phenomena that can be uncovered only in the laboratory. Our point is simply that the explanation of experimental results has often been taken as the actual goal of psychology. It is a poor substitute for understanding human behaviour and mentality.

Why is there a methodological obsession with experimentation in psychology? The answer lies in the origins of the subject. Although a number of physiologists in the first half of the nineteenth century carried out investigations which these days would be considered as psychological experiments, the real founder of the discipline was Wilhelm Wundt (1832–1920). Wundt opened the first laboratory of experimental psychology at the University of Leipzig in 1879, and most of the major figures in the early history of the subject went there to receive their training. The basis of Wundt's method was to examine the contents of consciousness during perceptual or associative tasks by precise and controlled *introspections* carried out by trained observers. As Miller (1966, p. 31) remarks:

What Wundt did was to look at the psychological problems posed by the British philosophers [Empiricists such as John Locke] with the eyes of a man trained in the traditions of German physiology. The notion that psychology could become a science of observation and experiment had been stated clearly and explicitly by the British philosopher John Stuart Mill in his *Logic* as early as 1843, but it required a person who really knew how observation and experiments are made to bring it off. Wundt was that person.

Wundt's eschewal of casual anecdotal observation in favour of laboratory experimentation was to set a stamp on psychology that has lasted down to the present day. However, Wundt considered his experimental methods unsuitable for investigating thinking and problem solving. It was his successors at Würzburg who first applied the 'introspective' method to such higher mental processes. The members of this school, led by Karl Marbe and Oswald Külpe, claimed that their subjects often reported a kind of conscious but unanalysable experience that was neither an image nor an awareness of an act of will. These experiences were dubbed *Bewusstseinslagen*, or 'imageless thoughts' (see Humphrey, 1951, for a scholarly account of the movement; Boring, 1953, provides a briefer description; Mandler and Mandler, 1964, have translated excerpts of some of their works). Imageless thoughts were important because they ran counter to the Empiricist view of thinking as associations between ideas. Other members of the school, such as Messer and Ach, argued that much of thinking goes on below the level of consciousness, thus giving rise to imageless thoughts, as the *results* of such processes emerge into consciousness. However, it was a strategic mistake to base theoretical arguments on the introspective contents of consciousness. Wundt himself challenged the movement from a methodological standpoint; other observers, notably Titchener, argued that images were always present in consciousness. Titchener (1909) himself seems to have had remarkable imagery. The concept of a triangle produced in him the following image:

It is a flashy thing, come and gone from moment to moment: it hints two or three red angles, with the red lines deepening into black, seen on a dark green ground. It is not there long enough for me to say whether the angles join to form the complete figure, or even whether all three of the necessary angles are given.

Although later commentators such as Humphrey have decided in favour of the Würzburgers, the controversy between them and other psychologists proved fatal. It could hardly have been settled by experiment.

After the demise of the Würzburg school, thinking was studied in psychology under the guise of 'problem solving'. Human beings are, of course, not alone in their ability to solve problems: animals are capable of exercising this sort of intelligence. In America, studies of animals had led to the belief that problems are solved by trial and error (Thorndike, 1911). Such views formed the basis of Behaviourism, which abandoned introspection as scientifically disreputable and relied exclusively on objective observations. Thinking came to be identified with subvocal speech, and mental activity was investigated by recording tongue movements or motor nerve potentials. The theoretical language of Behaviourism was, indeed, unsuited to the analysis of internal events: the terminology of 'stimuli' and 'responses' was an unpromising repertoire for exploring what is purported to mediate between them, even when it later was enriched by unobservable 'fractional anticipatory goal responses' giving rise to internal stimuli. Likewise, the methodological assumptions of the movement reinforced the Wundtian experimental 'imperative'.

During the years between the world wars another school, Gestalt psychology, flourished in Germany. It had arisen in opposition to Associationism, and its leading members, Wertheimer, Köhler and Koffka, stressed the importance of structural relations in perception. They also argued that it was a full grasp of the structure of a problem which led to an *insight* yielding its solution (Köhler, 1917). As Bertrand Russell (1927, p. 33) remarked, animals tended to display the national characteristics of the experimenters:

Animals studied by Americans rush about frantically, with an incredible display of hustle and pep, and at last achieve the desired result by chance. Animals observed by Germans sit still and think, and at last evolve the solution out of their inner consciousness.

The truth of the matter was, of course, that workers from the different traditions tended to set their animals different sorts of problem.

Trial and error is, in fact, a rather limited procedure for solving problems, and the Behaviourist tradition in problem solving is now virtually dead; even its defenders are unlikely to maintain that it was an important aspect of the school or that it led to any great advances in understanding human mentality. The reader will find little of the Behaviourists' undoubted contribution to psychology in the readings devoted to problem solving in this book (Part I). That contribution was made primarily to the study of animal learning. The Gestalt psychologists, however, conducted investigations of thinking that have retained some interest down to the present day (see Reading 1). But, the price they paid was a theoretical one. Behaviourism may have been an oversimplification but, at least in its early days, it offered a clear and explicit theory. Gestalt psychology, on the other hand, tended towards obscure formulations in its attempt to define the role of structure. When a member of the school talked, for example, of 'grasping the inner relations of a problem', it was natural to wonder quite what he had in mind.

Since many problems involve an element of deduction in their solution, it might seem that formal logic would provide psychology with a prescriptive account of reasoning in much the same way that linguistics offers a description of language from the standpoint of an ideal speaker or hearer (Chomsky, 1965). A very great deal has been discovered in this century about logical systems and about what can, and cannot, be proved within them. It is natural that psychologists should have studied deductive inference with an eye on logic. Indeed, a standard experimental practice is simply to select a set of inferences, valid and invalid, and to test intelligent but logically naive adults on them. A major theme of this book, which emerges from the readings on deduction (Part II), is that this research strategy is shortsighted, if not mistaken. The actual *content* of an inference matters, whether it is a simple three-term series problem, or a complicated propositional deduction. This phenomenon creates considerable difficulty for any theory such as Piaget's that is modelled on formal logic; it is heartening to see that Piaget (Reading 10) has come to appreciate this weakness of his theory. The development of the higher-order programming language, PLANNER, reflects a similar concern to couch rules of inference in terms of their specific contents (see Reading 4).

The question of content arises elsewhere in an unexpected quarter. One of the dogmas of nineteenth-century anthropology was that the contrast between the scientific and technological world of 'civilized' cultures and the technically primitive world of 'uncivilized' cultures reflected a difference in thought processes. The thesis that there are psychological differences between cultures received a further impetus from the notion of 'linguistic relativity': languages, which differ manifestly from culture to culture, determine the habitual patterns of thought and the way the world is perceived and categorized. In fact, it now seems that underlying the superficial variety of languages there are some universal principles, and as the readings on language, culture, and thinking (Part VI) illustrate, there is no robust evidence in favour of 'linguistic relativity'. However, experimental results have revealed that the reasoning ability of people from unschooled populations is markedly at variance with those from our own culture (see Reading 29). There is little reason to suppose that performance in the laboratory is a valid reflection of the competence brought to bear on problems in daily life: subjects are often capable of making the required deductions with a more realistic content. But even when such factors are taken into account there remains a considerable mystery. Perhaps one consequence of literacy is that it leads to an awareness of (the power of) inference. This awareness makes voluntary deductions feasible, and with them there comes a concomitant growth of logical, mathematical, and scientific thinking. A major component of the 'hidden curriculum' of school may be the growth of conscious deduction as a consequence of literacy.

The distinction between conscious deductions and everyday inference is probably a reflection of a more general contrast that can be drawn between *explicit* and *implicit* inferences. The inferences that underlie problem solving are often slow, voluntary, and at the forefront of awareness: they are explicit. The inferences that underlie the ordinary processes of perception and comprehension are rapid, involuntary, and outside conscious awareness: they are implicit. When one attempts to think about thinking, or to formalize deduction, there is an inevitable tendency to postulate explicit theories. Pascal writing in the seventeenth century makes the following observation in his *Pensées* (see the translation by Krailsheimer, 1966, p. 211):

It is rare for mathematicians to be intuitive or the intuitive to be mathematicians, because mathematicians try to treat intuitive matters mathematically, and make themselves ridiculous, by trying to begin with definitions followed by principles, which is not the way to proceed in this kind of reasoning. It is not that the mind does not do this, but it does so tacitly, naturally and artlessly, for it is beyond any man to express it and given to very few even to apprehend it.

Pascal was right; it has taken psychology a long time to grasp the importance of implicit inference. Yet, it is plausible to suppose that for most aspects of daily life, an individual can make do with purely implicit inferences.

A striking instance of a radical confusion between the two modes of thought has occurred in the study of concepts. When people attempt to formulate an explicit concept, they generally seek to define it in terms of some feature(s) common to all of its instances. Psychologists have studied the acquisition of such concepts in the laboratory, and a number of these studies are considered in the introduction to the readings on conceptual thinking (Part III). Yet, as we argue there, the implicit concepts of daily life turn out to have a very different structure. They often lack a common defining element, and their boundaries are usually fuzzy. It makes better sense to conceive of their mental representation in terms of *prototypes*. There is, for instance, a prototypical bird that sings, flies, nests in a tree, and so on. A robin is close to the prototype, but a penguin is not. The idea of a prototype seems to be a special case of the traditional idea of a 'schema', which Bartlett (1932) brought to the attention of psychologists. What is remarkable is the convergence between the intuitive deployment of prototypes in order to explain psychological phenomena (see Readings 13, 15, 30) and the independent development within Artificial Intelligence of an explicit representation for various sorts of prototype (see Readings 12, 22, 26).

The machinery of concepts and inferences presumably allows an individual to cope with the mundane problems of life. What it leaves unexplained, however, is the origin of a truly imaginative or creative idea. There are many fascinating studies of the personalities of gifted individuals. These sometimes take the form of (auto-)biographical accounts of artists or scientists (e.g. Hadamard, 1945; Gruber, 1974), and they are sometimes studies of the test performances of groups of subjects (e.g. Getzels and Jackson, 1962; Hudson, 1966). (This work falls outside our purview, and is in any case available in anthology, see Vernon, 1970, and Hudson, 1970.) There are also a number of popular accounts of how to increase your creativity (e.g. Gordon, 1961; de Bono, 1967). To what extent it is really feasible to do so is open to doubt: it would be extremely difficult to demonstrate that someone had genuinely become more imaginative – as opposed to merely scoring higher in a test of 'creativity'.

Unfortunately, psychology remains almost entirely ignorant about the mental process of creation. However, there is a considerable body of knowledge about the ways in which new ideas are submitted to test. This work is considered in the readings on hypotheses (Part IV). A scientific hypothesis ought, of course, to be given a potentially falsifying test (see Popper, Reading 16). However, people often fail to meet this criterion, and what emerges from this Part are a number of psychological principles underlying their failure. For example, in seeking to make sense of the world, it is better to have a theory – even a false theory – than no theory at all. But, in order to develop such a theory, it may initially be necessary to ignore counter-examples to it (see Reading 18). One has to start somewhere, and a simple-minded theory will be highly selective about what facts it takes into consideration. Once such a theory has become entrenched, and its implications fully understood, it is time to reconsider the counter-examples and to attempt to recast the theory in order to cope with them. This process of thought is likely to apply both to scientific theories and to their common-sense counterparts in general knowledge.

The mental representation of general knowledge is an enduring problem in cognitive science. The Behaviourists attempted to sidestep the issue; the Gestalt psychologists uttered recondite incantations about it. The first decisive step towards a solution was probably Kenneth Craik's book, *The Nature of Explanation*, published in 1943. In this work, Craik put forward the essential idea of an information-processing psychology of thinking. He wrote that there are three essential processes in reasoning:

1. A 'translation' of some external process into an internal representation in terms of words, numbers or other symbols.
2. The derivation of other symbols by a process of inference.
3. A 'retranslation' of these symbols into external processes (as in building a bridge to a design) or at least a recognition of the correspondence

between these symbols and external events (as in realizing that a prediction is fulfilled).

What Craik wrote has a distinctly contemporary sound to it:

This process of reasoning has produced a final result similar to that which might have been reached by causing the actual physical processes to occur (e.g. building the bridge haphazard and measuring its strength. . .); but it is also clear that this is not what has happened; the man's mind does not contain a material bridge. . . Surely, however, this process of prediction is not unique to minds, though no doubt it is hard to imitate the flexibility and versatility of mental prediction. A calculating machine, an anti-aircraft 'predictor', and Kelvin's tidal predictor all show the same ability. In all these latter cases, the physical process which it is desired to predict is *imitated* by some mechanical device or model which is cheaper, or quicker, or more convenient in operation. Here we have a very close parallel to our three stages of reasoning. . .

My hypothesis then is that thought models, or parallels, reality – that its essential feature is not 'the mind', 'the self', 'sense-data', nor propositions but symbolism, and that this symbolism is largely of the same kind as that which is familiar to us in mechanical devices which aid thought and calculation. . .

If the organism carries a 'small-scale model' of external reality and of its own possible actions within its head, it is able to try out various alternatives, conclude which is the best of them, react to future situations before they arise, utilize the knowledge of past events in dealing with the present and future, and in every way to react in a much fuller, safer, and more competent manner to the emergencies which face it.

(Craik, 1943, ch. 5)

The most notable of internal representations is visual imagery. An image is undoubtedly an introspective correlate of what Craik called a 'small-scale model' of reality. The power of an image, particularly one that can be modified over time, is precisely that it enables an individual to make predictions about the course of events. The readings on imagery and internal representations (Part VII) make this point for both theoretical and practical tasks. Although imagery is once more a respectable topic after decades of neglect, there remain considerable difficulties in understanding its exact nature. It is all too easy to think of an image as a 'picture in the head', but this formulation implies that there is a homunculus there too in order to scan the mental picture. This supposition leads on to the slippery slope of an infinite regress. Moreover, the evidence from the study of board games, which is reported in this Part, establishes conclusively that many images are not isomorphic with a simple visual field. The way in which a chess player represents a position on the board may be both considerably more abstract and symbolic than a visual field.

When the programmable digital computer was invented, some years after the publication of Craik's book, one might have supposed that the way was clear for the development of a cognitive science. An undisputed virtue of the computer is that it provides a metaphorical solution to the traditional dichotomy between the brain and the mind. A computer is an organized physical system, but from a logical standpoint it does not matter whether it is built from relays, valves, transistors or microchips. If its circuitry is appropriate, then it can imitate the behaviour of *any* other computer. What is crucial is not its physical realization but the logic of its operations. What it does on any occasion depends on the signal that is put into it. Computers are built to receive signals made up of sequential patterns of electrical impulses, and their power derives from the fact that different patterns trigger different computational operations. Complex computations can be elicited by a whole sequence of signals, and such sequences are known as 'programs'. The brain, too, is an organized physical system, and perhaps mental operations are merely its 'computations', depending not so much on the physiology of nerve cells as on the logic of their operations. In order to understand human mentality it may be more fruitful to discover the 'programs' and 'plans' that underlie it rather than their underlying physiological representation.

The resemblance between mind and machine is, indeed, a suggestive one. Yet, the computer has turned out to be singularly difficult to encompass within psychological theorizing. Almost from the start, we can discern a distinction between those theorists who wished to treat the computer as no more than a metaphor, and those who wished to take it more literally. This division resulted in a number of spurious debates. The most notable was on the question of whether a computer could think. Alan Turing (1950), one of the mathematicians who pioneered the theory of computing, argued that a stringent test would be whether an observer could judge that responses typed on a teletype, in answer to any question, were generated by a computer or a human being. If no such discrimination could be made, then one should conclude that a computer can think – it was certainly simulating human performance to a remarkable degree.

The earliest substantial attempt to simulate human thinking with a computer was a program written by Newell, Shaw, and Simon (1958b) for proving logical theorems. They were particularly concerned with comparing the performance of their program with that of human subjects in the laboratory – a feature of their work that continues to the present day (see Reading 3). However, it has generally proved to be extremely difficult to make such comparisons in a way that indicates how the program should be modified in order to improve its simulation. Turing's test is too easy to satisfy (see Weizenbaum, 1976, for a description of his program ELIZA that often fooled people into thinking that they were exchanging messages with a human being).

At about the same time that Newell and his colleagues were developing their program, other theorists were devising programs simply to prove theorems in an economical way (see Wang, 1960). This work was a starting point for a new discipline, Artificial Intelligence (or AI). Here the aim was, not to simulate human performance, but to develop programs capable of solving complicated problems by any means that happened to work.

Computer simulation takes computers rather literally as devices for imitating human beings; Artificial Intelligence is not concerned with human behaviour except insofar as it throws light on how to solve such problems as the analysis of visual scenes, or the proving of theorems in an intelligent way. The use of computers as a metaphor for mentality was explored most fully in Miller, Galanter, and Pribram (1960). This book undoubtedly had a liberating effect on psychology; but it did so without releasing the discipline from its obsession with experimentation. Had it done so, it is entirely possible that psychologists would have overwhelmingly opted for developing theories within the new metaphorical framework, and that the current division between psychology and AI would not have grown so large. In our view, it is important to achieve a rapprochement between the two disciplines. However, before such a meeting can be effected, it is necessary to consider carefully their respective weaknesses. We have already indicated a major problem within psychology, so let us turn to AI.

If we ignore the ethical problems raised by computers taking over erstwhile human tasks, then the most obvious criticisms of AI are that it is expensive, and that its protagonists often make promises that they fail to fulfil. Perhaps the most rash promise was Simon's prediction in 1958 that in ten years a computer program would be the chess champion of the world (for an account of what actually happened in chess programming see Part VII). A more debatable notion is that there may be psychological phenomena or mental skills that cannot be captured in a computer program. Dreyfus (1972) suggests that certain sorts of intuitive thinking fall into this category; Weizenbaum (1976) argues that human emotions cannot be engendered in a machine. They may both be right, but neither of them has advanced an irrefutable *a priori* argument to clinch the mattter. It may turn out to be singularly instructive to discover in what ways, if any, computers fail to have human-like cogitations.

A more damaging criticism of AI is that programs are often very large and very complicated. Weizenbaum claims that they sometimes become so involved that no one really understands how they work. Certainly, it can be very hard to evaluate them: it is often difficult to distinguish the central theoretical ideas from *ad hoc* assumptions inserted to ensure that a program works. There may be no obvious way for a psychologist to test the central ideas against human performance.

Of all the spurious criticisms of AI, the most dangerous and misleading one was advanced to us by an experimental psychologist: 'AI practitioners often work on problems to which the answer is obvious.' In cognition, there are no problems so difficult to solve as those to which the solution is 'obvious'. Indeed, one virtue of AI from the standpoint of psychology is that it has revealed many deep problems lurking under the deceptively simple surface of a mundane mental process. A pertinent example is the role of inferential mechanisms in understanding natural language. Ten years ago when we edited our first book of readings (Wason and Johnson-Laird, 1968), we would have been considerably surprised by the idea that inference was ubiquitous in comprehension. We would have taken the view that comprehension was largely a matter of syntactic and semantic processing. Much of the credit for laying bare the fallacious nature of this belief must go to Winograd, Schank, and Charniak, and to their colleagues on this side of the Atlantic, Isard and Longuet-Higgins. In trying to write computer programs to understand discourse, they inevitably discovered that inference is indispensable. The readings on inference and comprehension (**Part v**) reflect the importance of this work.

The contempt in which AI is held by many psychologists is reciprocated: there is incomprehension on both sides. Members of the artificial intelligentsia often declare that experiments are a waste of time, that psychologists spend most of the time pursuing phenomena rather than a genuine understanding of mentality, and that the subject is 'paradigm-ridden' – it revolves around a number of well-known experimental paradigms. A succinct statement of this case, expressed rather more politely than one is wont to hear it in private, can be found in Newell's (1973b) engaging paper, 'You can't play 20 questions with nature and win', and in Allport's (1975) thoughtful discussion of it.

Whether AI has need of psychology is a topic on which we shall not comment. But a case can definitely be made for psychology to absorb some aspects of AI. An obvious advantage of expressing a theory in the form of a computer program is that it is rendered entirely explicit and its logical coherence is put to a stringent test. If the program works and does what it is intended to do, then the theory it embodies is at least internally consistent. This truth leads naturally to the central imperative of AI: express your theories in the form of programs. This is an admirable ideal, but it must be rejected as impractical for psychology. Any plausible psychological theory of thinking would require a massive program embodying a large number of *ad hoc* assumptions. Since the theory would almost certainly be wrong, and the program almost certainly incomprehensible, it would be foolish to invest so much effort in this way. A preferable approach rests on the distinction between a *theory* and a *model*. Scientists and engineers are familiar with building models to represent only certain aspects of their theories. However, the practice is rare in psychology. An approach that may be worth trying is for psychologists to develop large-scale theories in the usual informal way, and then to implement small-scale models of important components of them as computer programs.

What is the point of the exercise? In fact, it is twofold. First, an attempt to develop an explicit model – even if only of part of a theory – leads in our experience to an almost inevitable reformulation of the theory itself (see, e.g. Steedman and Johnson-Laird, 1977). The struggle to make an intuitive idea explicit is a truly dialectical process. Second, the development of a small-scale model often leads to insights about how the general theory may be tested empirically. The reader will note that we place no great stress on the program providing a simulation of human behaviour, or of behaving in a particularly intelligent way. Those are not the aims of an exercise in *computer modelling*; the point is to learn from the experience of building the model, not from what it accomplishes once it is complete.

It is our belief that the scientific study of thinking demands the development of general theories, the construction of specific models, and the continued use of experimentation. This conviction lies behind the selection of the present set of readings.

Part I

Problem Solving

Introduction to problem solving

How do people solve problems? The short answer is that psychologists do not know. There is no comprehensive theory of problem solving, only a number of models and hypotheses about different aspects of the process. Part of the difficulty is that problems come in all shapes and sizes from nursery riddles to deep scientific puzzles, but there is no substantial taxonomy for them. There can even be a problem in recognizing a problem in the first place, whether one is trying to define the notion or is a practising scientist looking for something worthy of investigation. It is difficult to talk about such elusive entities in general terms, and so let us concentrate our minds on a specific instance:

Problem no. 1. You are in a hotel room in Tibet, and you want to have a wash. You go to the wash-basin and discover indecipherable symbols on the taps. Which tap do you turn on for hot water?

Obviously, the solution to this problem is a matter of trial and error. You try one tap and, if that fails, then you try the other. Thomas Edison, the inventor of the electric light bulb, similarly tried out thousands of different substances as potential filaments until he hit on something feasible. However, as a general technique for solving problems, trial and error is of restricted use. It is plainly inefficient, and there are psychological studies suggesting that if it becomes too costly, in terms of time or the consequences of error, subjects try to develop more insightful methods (see Galanter and Gerstenhaber, 1956; Galanter and Smith, 1958). If you have any sort of knowledge, then unless the problem is a trivial one you will attempt to develop a more efficient procedure. Trial and error is the last resource of a resourceless individual.

An alternative conception of problem solving was initiated by the Gestalt psychologist, Max Wertheimer. He studied the way in which children solved problems using a method that was partly experimental and partly 'clinical' observation. In many ways, his technique resembled that of Piaget, and it may be no accident that both men seem to have reacted adversely to Binet's test of intelligence. They were interested, not in whether a child got a test item right or wrong, but in the mental processes that led to the response. Of course,

Wertheimer recognized that the discovery of a solution to a problem could be the result of a routine application of rote learning, or of a happy chance in a series of trial-and-error responses. But, in his view, sensible thinking transcended such impoverished techniques. He reports in his book, *Productive Thinking* (Wertheimer, 1961), that children who have blindly learnt to work out the area of a parallelogram according to a formula often fail to grasp what they have been taught. They may be shown how to construct the perpendiculars given in figure 1, and told that the area equals the base times the perpendicular; they may perform entirely satisfactorily in conventional tests. Yet, when Wertheimer confronted them with the parallelogram depicted in figure 2, many of the children were truly perplexed. Their learning failed to transfer to the novel figure. However, a real insight into the underlying principles transferred naturally: some children produced one or other of the constructions shown in figure 3. On another occasion, a child called for a pair of scissors, snipped off one end of the parallelogram, and placed it at the other end in order to make a rectangle.

Figure 1. The area of a parallelogram = base × altitude

In order to convey the flavour of Wertheimer's work both as a researcher and as a teacher, we have chosen as our first reading an account by one of his students, A. S. Luchins, of a seminar in which Wertheimer discussed the use of his methods in studying subnormal children. The reader may care to compare this reading with Wertheimer's own more accessible account of the work (Wertheimer, 1961, ch. 2). The influence of these methods on both the clinical assessment of brain-damaged patients and on educational theory emerges clearly from Luchins's account. Although schools no longer rely so exclusively on teaching by drill, the relevance of Wertheimer to current practices can be established by consulting Holt (1969).

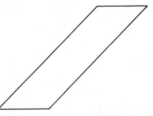

Figure 2. Wertheimer's parallelogram for testing a child's grasp of how to compute its area

The Gestalt theory of problem solving hinged on two notions: insight and structure. Insight into a problem occurs, not as a result of trial and error, but following a period of cogitation. It reflects the ability of the problem solver to perceive the structure of the problem, to centre his attention on its essential inner relations, and to reorganize these relations in order to fill in the missing informa-tion. (There is, of course, a close resemblance here to the Gestalt theory of perception.) A response based on insight tends to be well retained even without practice, and transfers to a new situation as in the case of Wertheimer's test parallelogram. There is a further aspect of insight, brought out quite nicely by a quotation from Bartlett who, although he worked in the more empirical English tradition, sometimes writes in a vein curiously reminiscent of the Gestalt school.

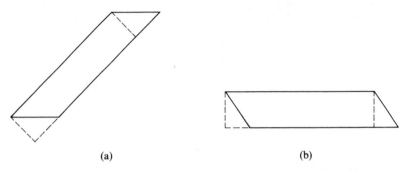

(a)   (b)

Figure 3. Insightful responses to Wertheimer's test parallelogram

He, too, regarded thinking as an extension of the available evidence in order to fill the 'gaps' in it. In discussing the solution of crossword puzzles, he writes:

Every cross-word addict will be familiar with the experience of getting required words, or groups of words, in what seems to be a single jump. The most curious instances are those in which the disguise is successfuly penetrated, but at the same time the solver is completely unable to say why the result is correct.

(Bartlett, 1958, p. 64)

Sometimes the 'flash' of insight is so fast that it seems to precede understanding.

Wertheimer's students extended his work in a variety of ways. Duncker (1945), for example, set his subjects the following problem:

Problem no. 2. Given a human being with an inoperable stomach tumour, and rays which destroy organic tissue at sufficient intensity, by what procedure can one free him of the tumour by these rays and at the same time avoid destroying the healthy tissue which surrounds it?

Duncker kept a record of what his subjects said as they attempted to solve this problem. When he compared tentative solutions in the protocols one with another, they fell into certain groups. Figure 4 presents the resulting 'family tree' of such solutions. Duncker characterizes a typical subject as moving down a particular branch of the tree, i.e. reformulating the problem into a subproblem, attempting to solve that by breaking it down into a subproblem, and so on until he can make no further progress. At this point, the subject is likely to try another branch of the tree in a similar fashion, until ultimately he either gives up the problem or comes up with a practical solution (e.g. directing a number of weak rays from different directions through the tumour). In solving such a problem,

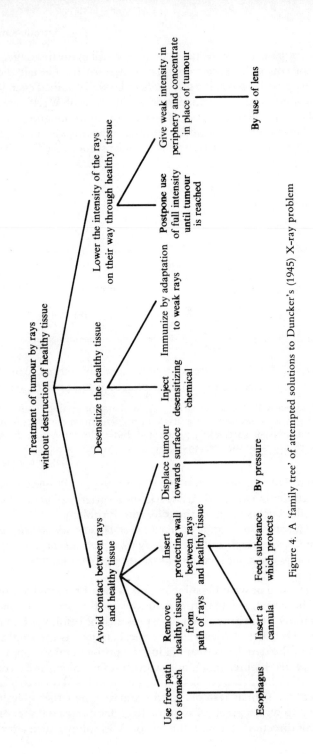

Figure 4. A 'family tree' of attempted solutions to Duncker's (1945) X-ray problem

past experience is invoked by what Duncker calls the principle or 'resonance'. Hence, if you want to hang a picture, then resonance suggests that you need a hammer and nail. If there is no readily available hammer and nail, then you have to reorganize your perception of the available materials and see new functions for them. Duncker attributes much of the failure to solve problems to 'functional fixity', an inability to reorganize perception in this way. Such difficulties have been abundantly confirmed in the laboratory: if a subject uses a gimlet to make a hole, he is unlikely to use it in lieu of a missing hook (Duncker, 1945; Adamson, 1952); if a piece of string is holding up a mirror as opposed to merely hanging on a nail by itself, a subject is much less likely to use it to tie two objects together (Scheerer, 1963).

Functional fixity is related in many ways to the rather older idea of 'set' (Einstellung), the state of preparedness for a particular task that is brought about by instructions, previous experience, general circumstances, and so on. One aspect of set is that a problem solver may assume that the solution to a problem lies in a certain direction, literally or figuratively. A simple riddle illustrates this factor:

Problem no. 3. How can one construct four equilateral triangles out of six matches, where each side of a triangle is equal in length to the length of the matches?

The solution of this problem turns out to be surprisingly difficult as the reader may discover. If the answer is not immediately forthcoming, then it may help to bear in mind that since there are only six matches, each of them must form the side of two triangles. But even this hint may not suffice to lead to the solution, as Reid (1951) discovered in an experimental investigation.

The real trouble is that most people make an implicit assumption that the triangles are to be constructed lying flat on the table. Such an assumption is, indeed, a case of setting out in the wrong direction for the solution to the problem. One makes it, presumably, as a result of past experience in playing with matches on table tops. This experience, invoked by the presentation of the problem, creates a misleading set, whose potency is probably all the greater because the whole process is implicit and outside conscious awareness. The solution to the problem is to construct a three-dimensional configuration of matches, as shown in figure 5.

Figure 5. How to make 4 triangles out of 6 matches

A 'classic' experimental demonstration of the way in which subjects can fail to solve a problem because they start off in the wrong direction is to be found in an experiment conducted by Maier (1930). The task was to construct two pendulums so that they would swing over two specified places on the floor. Most subjects assumed that the available materials – lengths of wood, wires, clamps, etc. – would have to be used in conjunction with a table in the room, or its walls. Unless the experimenter gave them clues that put them on the right direction, they were unable to come up with the correct solution. A subsequent replication (Weaver and Madden, 1949) yielded four lines of attack on the problem, as shown in figure 6. Structures A and B were unstable, structure C failed to meet the specifications since the pendulums were not long enough, and only the two D structures were satisfactory. One fascinating aspect of Maier's work (Maier, 1931) is the extent to which subjects are consciously aware of how they come to solve a problem. In one experiment the task was to tie together the ends of two strings hanging down from the ceiling of a room. If a subject grasped the end of one string, and walked towards the other, he soon discovered that he was unable to reach it. A variety of simple solutions were easily discovered, e.g. tying one string to a chair, and then bringing the other string over to it. However, what Maier was really interested in was the ability of the subjects to discover a more elegant solution in which a pair of pliers is tied to one string in order to convert it into a pendulum, which can then be set in motion and caught by the subject standing with the other string in his hand. The experimenter gave a hint to this solution: he 'accidentally' set one of the strings in motion by brushing against it as he walked about the room. If this hint failed, then the experimenter gave the subject the pliers and said, 'With the aid of this and no other object there is another way of solving the problem.' Some subjects got the solution in a single step, whereas other subjects first hit on the idea of swinging the cord and only later thought of attaching a weight to it. In the former case, subjects claimed that the experimenter's brushing against the rope had *not* helped them. Maier argues that the sudden experience of the complete solution to the problem dominates consciousness, and the effective role of the clue is not consciously experienced. It is as though the solution acts to mask the very clue that led to it – an idea reminiscent of Bartlett's observations about crossword puzzles.

A misleading set can be created within an experimental context. Luchins and Luchins (1950) set their subjects a series of problems of working out how to measure a given quantity of liquid using only three containers of given sizes. For example, with jars that hold 21, 127, and 3 quarts, how would one measure out exactly 100 quarts? The desired formula is clearly: $127 - 21 - (2 \times 3)$. If a subject is given a whole series of problems that can be solved by the same general formula: $b - a - 2c$, then the resulting set blinds him to discovering a simpler method of solution with a problem such as measuring out 20 quarts with vessels holding 23, 49, and 3 quarts. The effect was not eliminated if the subjects used actual jars to measure out real quantities of liquid. Similar results of the effect of set have been obtained where the task is to solve anagrams (Rees and Israel, 1935; Maltzman and Morrisett, 1953); and the extent to which subjects persist with a fixed procedure has even been used by Rokeach (1950, 1960) to define a personality trait of 'rigidity'.

The investigation of the effects of such variables as functional fixity and set

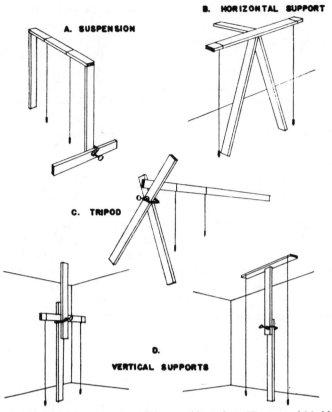

Figure 6. Solutions to Maier's two-pendulum problem (from Weaver and Madden, 1949)

can elucidate only certain aspects of problem solving. In order to understand the mental processes leading to a solution, psychologists need some way of classifying them. A first step towards this goal was taken by the mathematician, George Polya, in a series of publications designed to improve students' ability to solve mathematical problems (see especially Polya, 1957). Mathematicians distinguish between algorithmic and heuristic methods: an algorithm is a 'mechanical' procedure that always yields the answer to a problem in a finite number of steps, whereas a heuristic procedure is one which offers a useful shortcut but which does not guarantee a solution. With certain problems, it is altogether too costly to utilize an algorithm, e.g. searching every possible continuation in a game of chess. With other problems, there is no known algorithm. Indeed, in certain branches of mathematics and logic, it has been proved that there can be no algorithm. In all of these cases, it is necessary to resort to heuristic methods, rules-of-thumb that may yield a solution in a relatively economical way. Certain deductive processes appear to be essentially algorithmic (see Part II), and one clear case of an algorithmic psychological process is mental arithmetic. A numerate person has been taught, for example, an algorithm for multiplying any two numbers together. Few people, however, are capable of executing this algorithm without an aid to memory.

The second of these readings (with its two additional comments) is Ian Hunter's account of a distinguished mathematician, who was also capable of prodigious feats of mental arithmetic. The secret of his success was partly the incredible repertoire of arithmetical facts that he had amassed with years of experience, but it was also in part a reflection of his knowledge of a variety of unusual algorithms not normally taught in school. In particular, he had an algorithm for multiplication that places much less of a load on short-term memory than the usual method.

There is no algorithm for choosing which method to adopt in trying to solve a problem, a fact which Polya recognizes in distinguishing four phases of work on a problem:
1. Understanding the problem: you have to determine the goal, the data that you are given, and any general constraints or conditions.
2. Devising a plan: you have to find some method of connecting the data to the goal. Here, useful heuristics may be to consider any related problems with which you are familiar, to try to reformulate the problem, or to try to solve part of the problem. Often, there will be many related problems, in which case it can help to concentrate on those with the same, or similar, unknowns.
3. Executing the plan: you carry out each step, checking its correctness as you go.
4. Looking back: when you have solved the problem, you should check the result and reconsider your method. You may be able to discover a simpler procedure, or a more effective one.

One of Polya's non-mathematical examples may clarify these four steps:
Problem no. 4. Find the word that is the solution to the anagram: DRY OXTAIL IN REAR.
1. The goal (or unknown) is a word.
   The data are four words: DRY OXTAIL IN REAR.
   The constraint is that the desired word should be made up from the data.
2. In devising a plan, you should draw a figure, marking out 15 blank spaces corresponding to the number of letters in the word. It may also help to restate the problem, e.g. you have to make a word out of the following letters:
       Vowels: AAEIIOY Consonants: DLNRRRTX
   Indeed, now you can see another aspect of the unknown word: it has seven syllables unless there are some diphthongs in it. It may also help to solve part of the problem. The desired word is a long one, and hence is probably a compound word made up with a common ending. What endings could it have? One such ending is plainly, . . .ATION. Another partial problem is to think of a beginning to a long word that contains an X and a Y.
3. The reader may try to execute this last part of the plan.
4. With each attempt, the putative answer should be checked against the data.
   One extremely useful heuristic emphasized by Polya is 'working backwards'

from the desired state of affairs towards the data. This strategy is often attributed to Plato, and it can be illustrated by considering the following water-jar problem:

Problem no. 5. How do you measure 6 quarts of water using only a 4 quart and a 9 quart jar?

You might try filling the 9 quart jar and then pouring it into the 4 quart one. This would leave 5 quarts in the larger jar, but then what do you do? An alternative strategy is to start again using the 'working backwards' heuristic. Imagine you have solved the problem and have 6 quarts in the 9 quart jar. Now, consider what could have preceded this desired state of affairs. The answer is plainly that you have just poured out 3 quarts into the smaller container. But, for this manoeuvre to be possible, there must already be 1 quart in the 4 quart container. And how could this state of affairs be created? Obviously, you have to fill the 9 quart jar, then pour it into the 4 quart jar once (leaving 5 quarts), and then again (leaving 1 quart). This solitary quart can then be transferred to the 4 quart vessel. The solution of the problem is simply a matter of carrying out this sequence of operations in the opposite order.

The exploration of heuristics has proved to be an extremely fruitful one, especially with the aid of the computer and programming languages for non-numerical computation. The most sustained study of problem solving in the light of computational concepts is the work of Newell and Simon (1972). They have implemented a theory of general problem solving, GPS, that resembles in several ways an explicit version of Duncker's views. Its basic heuristic is what they call a 'means–ends' analysis, which in essence involves breaking a problem down into a series of subproblems. We can illustrate it by considering a specific algebraic problem (see Minsky, 1967, for a discussion of such problems whose simplicity belies their mathematical importance):

Problem no. 6. Given a calculus in which you can rewrite symbols according to the following rules:

i.   b ⇒ acc (i.e. b can be rewritten as acc)
ii.   ca ⇒ accc
iii.   aa ⇒ nil (i.e. aa can be deleted)
iv.   cccc ⇒ nil

show that the string bb can be rewritten as cccc.

Your task is clearly to transform the given, bb, into the goal, cccc, using the rewriting rules. Since you presumably do not immediately see how to solve the problem, consider first the nature of the difference between the given and the goal, and then set up a subgoal to reduce this difference. Obviously, one major difference is that the goal has a lot of c's, whereas the given string has none. The subgoal requires you to find some way of reducing this difference: rule (ii) is an obvious way of introducing c's into a string. However, as often happens, you cannot immediately apply this rule to the given string, and so it is necessary to set up a new subgoal of finding a way to apply it. Once again, you must determine the difference between what is given and what is required (for applying rule (ii)), and then seek to reduce the difference. In fact, rule (ii) requires the string ca, which differs from the given string in that it contains no b's. Such a difference can be reduced by applying rule (i), and this rule can be applied immediately to yield: accb. Rule (ii) still cannot be applied, but another application of rule (i) yields: accacc, and now rule (ii) can come into operation. The problem has been reformulated: the new goal is to transform the resulting string, acacccc, into cccc. The difference is now smaller than the one before since the b's have been eliminated, but you must start all over again with the means–ends analysis.

The heuristic can be applied to a variety of problems and the three main components of GPS, the general problem solver, are summarized in figure 7.

Goal: Transform object A into object B

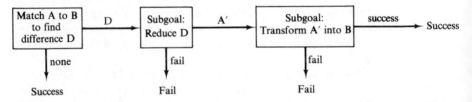

Goal: Reduce difference D between object A and object B

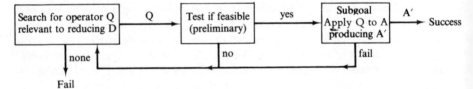

Goal: Apply operator Q to object A

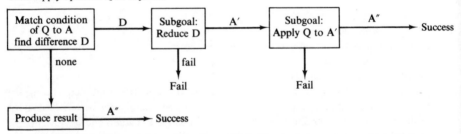

Figure 7. The three main components of Newell and Simon's 'means–ends' analysis (after Newell, see Reading no. 3)

Any system that actually operates such procedures requires considerable information about the problem domain, and the relevant objects and operations. Some way must be introduced of relating operations to the sorts of differences that have to be reduced. And, most importantly, the creation of subgoals must not be allowed to occur *ad infinitum*. Newell and Simon have introduced methods for handling these matters. However, their theory applies only to problems whose elements and operations can be spelt out in this way, such as cryptarithmetic, the Tower of Hanoi puzzle (Simon, 1975), the missionaries and cannibals problem (Ernst and Newell, 1969; but cf. Thomas, 1974; Greeno, 1974), and proofs in logic. The importance of the work lies not merely in the theory of problem solving, but in the revival of the tradition of having subjects 'think aloud' as they attempt to solve problems. Newell's paper, which we have included as the third reading, gives an account of Problem Behaviour Graphs – a sort of explicit version of Duncker's 'family tree' diagram, and of the way in which a subject's protocol can be interpreted in terms of the 'means–ends' analysis. The last section of his paper introduces the notion of a *production system*, a set of rules that from a formal standpoint are closely related to the rewriting rules of problem 6 but whose function is to model mental processes. They are analogous in some ways to the traditional learning theorist's bond between stimulus and response except, of course, that they are resolutely mentalistic in function and apply to the contents of short-term memory. Some of the psychological consequences of modelling problem solving with computer programs composed of production systems have been explored in Newell and Simon (1972), Newell (1973a), and Anderson (1976).

Psychologists have often studied the ways in which people solve difficult puzzles, but there are also lessons to be learned from more mundane problems. Here, for example, is one that requires no great logical expertise, though it does require a certain amount of information:

Problem no. 7. Make an approximate estimate of how much Brighton Pavilion cost the Prince Regent (George IV) to build.

A way in which people often tackle this problem is to estimate how much it would cost to build the Pavilion today. They then attempt to work out the amount of inflation that has occurred since the early nineteenth century. Finally, they carry out the appropriate arithmetic. A typical subject in an informal study (carried out by Johnson-Laird) argued that to build the Pavilion today is analogous to building the new Brighton Conference Centre. The Conference Centre is much larger but on the other hand it is much less lavish; it is going to cost about £8 million. He used as a datum for estimating the amount of inflation the fact that in the middle of the nineteenth century, police constables were paid a guinea a week. Since they are now paid something like £50 a week, a reasonable estimate of inflation since the beginning of the nineteenth century would be a ratio of 1:60. Finally, a sixtieth of £8 million is about £130,000. This is a very plausible estimate, which leaves out of account only the Prince Regent's expensive tastes. The Pavilion actually cost about half-a-million pounds.

The general procedure for solving such problems is of course to break them down into subproblems by ways reminiscent of the means–ends heuristic. But the solution of the subproblems raises some interesting psychological matters. In the solution above, the subject made use of an analogy – he thought of the Brighton Conference Centre as analogous to the Brighton Pavilion. He also thought of a representative fact – he took the wage of a policemen as a useful index of the cost of living. Analogies and representative facts can be misleading (see the reading by Tversky and Kahneman in Part IV), but the crucial psychological question is how knowledge is represented in such a way as to allow them to be established in the first place. Psychologists have, of course, investigated analogies but usually only extremely simple ones that occur in such questions as: a dog is to a bear as a cat is to a . . .? (see, e.g. Rumelhart and Abrahamson, 1973). However, as Beveridge (1950, p. 55) remarks, 'Originality often consists in finding connections or analogies between two or more objects or ideas not previously shown to have any bearing on each other.' We need a more powerful model of analogical thinking – one which might establish a connection between a falling apple and a falling moon, or between a roasting spit and Duncker's X-ray problem. The main clues, at present, are to be found in work in Artificial Intelligence, and the fourth reading in this Part is a discussion by Terry Winograd of some of the alternative theories about how knowledge is best represented for use by 'intelligent' computer programs. He describes various sorts of pattern matching, which is a procedure for retrieving relevant facts and is an explicit version of the sort of notion Duncker presumably had in mind when he used the term 'resonance'. Winograd illustrates how one form of pattern matching can be used to model analogical thinking. He also describes the higher-order programming language, PLANNER, which is a particularly important tool in the analysis of inference.

Higher-order programming languages similarly provide several ways of making explicit such hitherto vague notions as 'structure' and 'reorganization'. For example, one way of specifying explicitly Wertheimer's arch-like structures, discussed in the first reading, is illustrated entirely co-incidentally in Winston's paper, Reading 12. Another way of characterizing a structure is to specify a procedure that if executed would produce it. Such a definition of an equilateral triangle is given in the following procedure written in the language, LOGO, developed by Papert (1973):

```
       TO TRI   :SIDE
    1. FORWARD   :SIDE
    2. LEFT    120
    3. TRI   :SIDE
       END
```

The procedure can be used to control a little mechanical 'turtle' which draws the specified figure. The meaning of the procedure is straightforward: TRI is the name of the procedure; :SIDE is a variable denoting the length of the triangle's side, which has to be specified before the procedure can be executed; FORWARD is an instruction that causes the turtle to move a specified number of units (in whatever direction it happens to be facing); and LEFT is an instruction that causes the turtle to change its heading by turning left about its axis through the specified number of degrees. The reader may care to check that the program above will make the turtle describe perpetually an equilateral triangle. (It is a simple matter to stop the process.) It will be noted that instruction 3 requires the whole procedure itself to be executed again and again *ad infinitum*. Such 'recur-

sive' calls are an extremely important part of sophisticated computer programming. Thus, an apparently simple recursive procedure, which we can call
POLYSPI and which requires three variables to be specified:

```
TO POLYSPI    :SIDE         :ANGLE      :INCREASE
   FORWARD :SIDE
   LEFT        :ANGLE
   POLYSPI    :SIDE + INCREASE      :ANGLE      :INCREASE
END
```

can with appropriate values for the variables (40, 173, 6 respectively) produce
the dazzling figure 8.

Figure 8. A geometrical design produced by the LOGO procedure POLYSPI
(from Winograd, 1973)

Papert claims, much in the spirit of Wertheimer, that children learn to think
mathematically from acquiring control over the turtle. One discovery that they
soon make is how to eliminate the 'bugs' that occur in their programs, i.e. small
conceptual errors that may have disastrous effects for the achievement of the
desired goal. A program intended to produce the stick man shown in figure 9 (a)
may contain bugs and so in fact produce figure 9(b) (see Goldstein, 1974). It is
interesting to compare the distorted stick man with the sorts of spatial dis-
turbances caused by lesions in the right cerebral hemisphere. Figure 10 shows
the way in which a 'manikin' figure is assembled by a patient suffering from
such a lesion.

The view that certain aspects of problem solving are akin to 'debugging' a
computer program has been explored most notably by Sussman (1973). He has
written a computer program which in turn devises programs for solving simple
problems involving the manipulation of blocks. A simple and often successful
strategy in all sorts of problem solving, as we have seen, is to break it down into
subparts and to try to achieve them separately. However, there are often

unexpected interactions between the solutions to the separate parts (as is illustrated in figure 9(b)). Sussman's program classifies such 'bugs' by comparing what was intended with what would actually happen. A typical bug is one in which establishing a prerequisite for one procedure destroys a crucial state of affairs just established by another procedure. One of Köhler's chimps climbed onto a box to reach a banana without first having moved the box under the

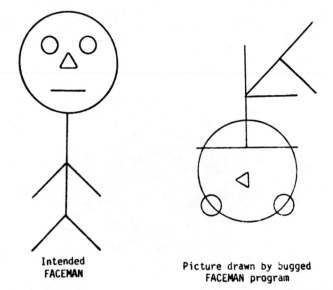

Intended
FACEMAN

Picture drawn by bugged
FACEMAN program

Figure 9. Stick men drawn by LOGO programs (from Sussman, 1973)

banana (Köhler, 1957, p. 46). In climbing down from the box, as a prerequisite for moving it, he cancelled out the effect of his previous action. Similar errors occur when small children attempt to nest cups in serial order (Greenfield, Nelson, and Saltzman, 1972). Such 'bugs' are, of course, easily rectified: the two procedures merely have to be reordered. Other 'bugs', however, may lead to a direct conflict of goals and can be rectified only by acquiring more knowledge about the situation. An example of such a conflict would be a putative solution to Maier's string problem that involves taking hold of one string and walking over to reach the other one.

Recent work on problem solving has been noteworthy for the exploitation of novel experimental techniques, especially measures of eye movements. There is evidence to suggest that people tend to avert their gaze more to the left when solving spatial as opposed to verbal problems, perhaps as a function of the different specializations of the two cerebral hemispheres (Kinsbourne, 1972). Their pupils tend to dilate during an intense mental effort such as in mental arithmetic (Kahneman, 1973, p. 24). They make more frequent eye movements during tasks calling for verbal rather visual imagination, perhaps because a changing visual input would interfere with visual imagery (Weiner and Ehrlichman, 1976). A more direct relation between eye movements and solving certain sorts of problems has also been established. Kapland and Schoenfeld (1966) observed that the number of fixations involved in solving anagrams goes down as subjects get used to a particular pattern of anagram. Explorations of the eye movements of chess players evaluating positions have been carried out by

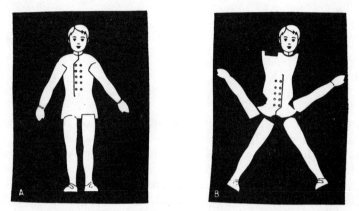

Figure 10. The assembly of a 'manikin' figure by a patient suffering from a right occipito–parietal lesion: (A) correct assembly; (B) assembly by patient (from McFie, Piercy, and Zangwill, 1950)

Tichomirov and Posnyanskaya (1966) and Simon and Barenfeld (1969): players tend to scan between pieces that are attacking or defending one another. Rather than select a reading representative of this work for this Part, we have emphasized the development of theories of problem solving, and especially ideas from Artificial Intelligence, because in the past brute empiricism has led to periods of long stagnation in the area. However, we have not entirely neglected recent experimental developments: the reader is referred to the account in Part vii of Eisenstadt and Kareev's studies of the board games of Go and Gomuku, using an ingenious technique analogous to recording eye movements.

1. Wertheimer's seminars revisited: diagnostic testing for understanding of structure[1]

A. S. Luchins and E. H. Luchins

The session started with a student saying that a few weeks ago Wertheimer had remarked that the children's education was the main reason for their failure to realize the structure of the problems which he had given to them. But he seemed to have overlooked the fact that a certain level of mental maturity or intelligence was needed to understand geometrical and arithmetical concepts. An elementary school teacher supported the student's argument by saying that Wertheimer had not tested the IQ's of the children. Perhaps his results were a function of IQ. Another teacher, however, objected to the assumption that the children did not solve the problems because they had low IQ's, saying, 'I'm tired of educators and teachers who hide behind the IQ and argue that they cannot provide for what God did not endow. We seem to spend more time working on methods to test intelligence than devising methods that will create intelligence.' The first teacher said that before intelligence tests were created it was assumed that all children could learn. If a child did not learn it was thought to be because of lack of concentration and diligence, etc. Children were beaten and tortured in order to force them to learn. It was also assumed that the child was a miniature man, that a child thought and felt just like an adult, but could only do less of it, just as his stomach could hold less food than an adult's stomach. This assertion sparked a discussion in which intelligence testing was defended as the modern approach; the idea that a child could learn if only one could find a way to teach him was called old-fashioned.

When the discussion ended, Wertheimer described his experience in the Neuropsychiatric Institute of the University of Vienna where he conducted research between 1905 and 1912. The director of the children's clinic asked him to find out whether or not certain children were really as stupid as the psychologists and pediatricians claimed them to be. The children had been tested and it was concluded that they were so feebleminded that they could not learn to

[1] A slightly edited version of chapter 10 of *Wertheimer's Seminars Revisited, Problem Solving and Thinking*, vol. II by A. S. and E. H. Luchins (State University of New York Faculty – Student Association, 1970), pp. 183–94.

speak (some were deaf mutes who were having difficulty learning to communicate in sign language). Wertheimer asked the class what they would have
done in such a situation. In response to a student's answer he said that he did not
retest them, nor did he read their charts.

He decided first to watch the children play and afterwards to give them some
interesting tasks. After some preliminary testing with various kinds of tasks, he
proceeded to examine these children, one at a time, in the following manner.
After putting the child at ease, Wertheimer built a bridge out of three blocks as
shown in figure 1. He then walked a little doll over it or under it. After this he
knocked the bridge down and motioned to the child that he should build a
bridge. Some did not wait to be told; they picked up the blocks and rebuilt the
bridge. Although some children required a few hints, all of the children eventually built stable bridges. He asked the class, 'What was the process that led to the
response? Did the child merely repeat blindly what I had done or had he grasped
what was involved in creating a stable structure?' No one answered. Wertheimer said that he gave the children three different types of tasks to test what
they had learned. In the first task he laid down before the child on the table two
large blocks and one small one as in figure 2(a). Some children immediately
picked up the two large blocks and placed them upright. They then placed the
smaller block over the two upright blocks as the crosspiece. The other children,
after a few failures, successfully built a stable structure.

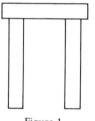

Figure 1

When a child finished the first test task, Wertheimer set before them two small
blocks and one large one as in figure 2(b). In order to build a bridge now, the
larger of the three blocks had to be used as the crosspiece and the smaller ones
had to be used as the columns. Again, all children successfully made a bridge.

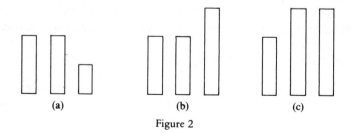

(a)   (b)   (c)

Figure 2

After the second task, he presented the child with the three blocks shown in figure 2(c). In this case the crosspiece was the same size as the blocks which had been previously used as columns, and the columns were the same size as the blocks which had been previously used as a crosspiece. All the children built a bridge; some did it immediately and some after a few trials.

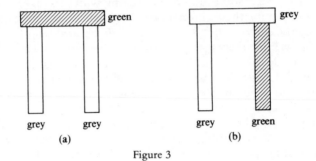

Figure 3

Wertheimer said that these results seemed to indicate that the children had not merely learned that a particular block was the upright and that a particular block was the crosspiece. They did not learn the absolute qualities of the stimuli, but had grasped certain relations which were inner necessities for building the bridge. They had learned that symmetry of the uprights was necessary for the bridge's stability. He added that the children did not repeat a conjunction of responses, but were guided by the inner necessity of the structure which had to be built.

When he invited counter arguments, no one spoke. Wertheimer continued, 'Someone might say that the child had learned the parts and the relation between the parts, that he was merely repeating the relations that he had learned.' He asked the class to devise a test for this hypothesis and, after a pause, said that he varied the task by using blocks of different colours. In one condition the colours were congruent with the required structure: the block for the crosspiece was green and the blocks for the columns were grey. In the other condition, the colours were incongruent with the required structure: one upright was green, the other upright was grey, and the crosspiece was also grey (see figure 3). The congruent task was carried out first and then the incongruent task. Both of these test tasks were given to a child after he had succeeded in building the bridge. The children readily succeeded in building bridges in both tasks. After a pause for students' comments, Wertheimer asked, 'Why did they not attempt to repeat in the second task the colour relations they had used in the first task?' In response to a student's comment he said, 'To say that the children followed structural relations is to presuppose that such relations exist', and thus actually to agree with Wertheimer's thesis. After a pause he added, 'The colours (the relations between the blocks in terms of colour) are peripheral for building the bridge . . . the relations as well as the parts get their meaning from the structure' that has to be built.

Some students wanted to know whether he had tested the children with more complex structures in order to see whether they really understood what was involved in making a stable structure. He then briefly described these test tasks. He erected, in front of a child, two blocks of equal length to serve as columns of a bridge and put on the table near them a third block which was too short to span the distance between the columns. He asked the class, 'What did the child do?' Wertheimer said that the children usually looked at the third block which was on the table and at the two blocks that served as the bridge's columns. After some hesitation they pushed one column closer to the other so that the columns could be spanned with the third block, i.e. in order to use the third block as a crosspiece they moved the columns closer to each other. When they did this, Wertheimer demonstrated to them that the doll could not walk between the two columns because the columns were too close to each other. He then put the blocks back to their original positions. Some children thereupon looked in the box full of blocks, which was near them, for a suitable crosspiece but could not find one. Some children resolved the problem by picking out from the box a small block which they put on one end of the crosspiece in order to counterbalance it (see figure 4(a)). After this response, Wertheimer put the columns still farther apart from each other so that the third block could not be used in this way. Some children then took two new blocks from the box to serve as crosspieces but the structure collapsed. Some of these children took from the box two small blocks which they used as counterbalances (see figure 4(b)) in order to keep the crosspieces in place, but the bridge usually collapsed at first. After a child had succeeded in making a stable structure in which the two crosspieces were kept

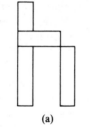

(a)

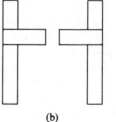

(b)

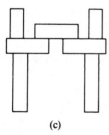

(c)

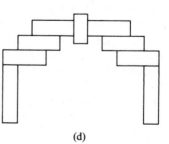

(d)

Figure 4

up by counterbalancing blocks, Wertheimer pushed the columns still farther apart. He indicated that the doll could not walk over the bridge because of the gap between the two crosspieces. A few children then took an additional block and used it to cover the gap and carefully counterbalanced the two end crosspieces so that they sustained the new middle piece (see figure 4(c)). A few children were eventually able to build a corbelled arch when the gap was further increased (see figure 4(d)).

A student sitting near to the present author whispered that Wertheimer had not really tested the children. He did what some inexperienced psychologists do when they administer the Binet intelligence test: he gave hints in order to help the children to get the right answer. Thus, one remains in the dark about the children's true intellectual ability. Someone else remarked that Wertheimer's method of testing the children left too much to the examiner's judgment and was unstandardized. However, another student said that Wertheimer's procedure reminded him of procedures considered in his course on remedial and diagnostic teaching of reading and arithmetic. It was a kind of clinical approach, but it was not an experimental one. This led a visitor (a German refugee psychologist) to say that the clinical approach was an experimental one. He went on to say that in giving an intelligence test one could merely obtain an IQ or one could try to discover the processes that led to the response. He then commented that . . . it was possible to present problem situations or tests in such a way that children and patients would or would not grasp their structural requirements. When one examined children or patients one should not merely judge whether their response was right or wrong, but one should find out just what were the processes that led to the response. One should present the problem or the question again in different ways, or should give hints so that the individual would be helped to realize the correct answer. Instead of just grading the person's intelligence, the examiner should find out under what conditions the person could or could not solve the problem. . .

Wertheimer seemed to agree since he went on to say that in studying behaviour and in evaluating it by examinations, the main question should not be whether the person gave the correct response but what were the processes that led to the response, because one might give the correct answer for the wrong reasons and one might give incorrect responses for the right reasons. Furthermore, the social atmosphere, other conditions of the school, and the test situation itself, might bias the results. When some students asked for more examples, he described some methods that he had used in the same clinic to examine patients with alexia and aphasia. These methods indicated that under certain conditions of testing, such patients were able to recognize pictures and were able to read. The session ended with comments by students on these findings. To the students who had been doing diagnostic testing and remedial teaching of reading and arithmetic, what Wertheimer had said not only made sense, but it gave them a feeling of security in what they were doing because it was in line with Gestalt theory. However, to the students who had taken courses in testing, individual differences and differential psychology, Wertheimer's statements seemed outlandishly unscientific and showed how 'naive he was about tests and measurements'. A few years later David Rapaport visited one of Wertheimer's lectures in which Wertheimer described his work in the Vienna clinic. It seemed from Rapaport's remarks that Wertheimer's clinical work had influenced Adhémar Gelb, the psychologist who had collaborated with Kurt Goldstein in extensive and prolonged studies of brain injured soldiers of World War I. Incidentally, Rapaport's own ideas (1945) about diagnostic testing reflected the work of Adhémar Gelb and Kurt Goldstein.

After class discussion

After the class some of the members of the seminar met in the cafeteria where they were joined by Martin Scheerer, who described to them the research he was doing with Kurt Goldstein. In this research they were interested, among other things, in the conditions under which a patient could and could not make a certain response in certain tests of abstract thinking. The author remarked that Scheerer's conception of testing intellectual functioning differed from the then current view. It was not really testing as it was known in America but more like an experiment in which one tried to maximize a certain phenomenon in a particular person's behaviour. Someone pointed out that such an approach did not deal with the problems for which tests had been constructed. Tests were made to find out the probability that someone would be able to make a certain response in a certain task. . . The author agreed that the methods advocated by Wertheimer might not be relevant for this aspect of mental testing; it was more like an experimental study of a single individual *per se* rather than a means of assessing his ability relative to a tested population. But subsequent experience in US Army hospitals a few years later led the author to realize the usefulness of Wertheimer's methods for clinical practice (see Luchins, 1959, p. 285, for references which reflect Wertheimer's approach to clinical phenomena).

It is interesting to note how a practical problem suggested by the director of a clinic led Wertheimer to devise methods and concepts that have influenced clinical practice in neurology and clinical psychology. Wertheimer, however, did not focus on the clinical aspects of his work. It led him to formulate several theoretical hypotheses concerning perception, thinking and methodology that eventually became Gestalt psycholgy. The consequences of his work in the clinic between 1905 and 1912 illustrate what Wertheimer had said in the intro-duction to the seminar, namely, that the solution of simple, concrete and practical problems may lead to theoretical developments of general significance. Wertheimer's assertion is relevant to the controversy about the relation of theory to practice in psychology. There are psychologists who believe that theory must come before practice, or that a solid theoretical foundation is necessary before practice. In opposition to them are those psychologists who see little or no relevance of the foundational problems of psychology to the prob-lems of the clinic and market place.

On the way to the subway station, the author asked Wertheimer whether it might be said that the Gestalt psychologists were using the Galileian as opposed to the Aristotelian approach towards science or philosophizing, since he had made some passing reference to Galileo's *Discoursi*. Wertheimer replied that although he found much to agree with in Kurt Lewin's paper on the Galileian versus the Aristotelian approach to science (1935, pp. 4–42) he did not think that such sharp distinctions could be made in all cases. It was fashionable to be against Aristotle but even those who claimed to be opposed to Aristotle actually showed the influence of his ideas in their work (see Beth, 1959, and Toulmin and Goodfield, 1966, for a summary of Aristotle's influence on scientific thought). He said that we must avoid adhering to a view to such an extent that we were unable to see the evidence before us. After a pause, he said that men like Galileo had asked different kinds of questions about the nature of motion than the questions which the Aristotelians had tried to answer. This illustrated that to formulate the right question, or to see what is the real or crucial problem, may be more important than its solution. What we need, perhaps, is to reformulate some of the problems in psychology instead of persisting in attempting to solve them in terms of existing formulations. This approach was what Gestalt psychology had been proposing.

2. Mental calculation[1]

I. M. L. Hunter

During 1961, I had the rare privilege of studying a man with exceptional ability in rapid mental calculation. He is the distinguished mathematician, Professor A. C. Aitken (born 1895) of Edinburgh University. His unusual powers may be illustrated by two examples. He is asked to express as a decimal the fraction 4/47. He is silent for four seconds, then begins to speak the answer at a nearly uniform rate of one digit every three-quarters of a second. 'Point 0851063829787234042553191914, that's about as far as I can carry it.' The total time between the presentation of the problem and this moment is twenty-four seconds. He discusses the problem for one minute and then continues the answer at the same rate as before. 'Yes, 191489, I can get that.' He pauses for five seconds. '361702127659574458, now that is the repeating point. It starts again at 085. So if that is forty-six places, I am right.' The second example concerns a more difficult problem. He is asked to give the square root of 851. After a short silence, he gives 29·17. Then, at irregular intervals, he supplies further digits of the answer. By the time fifteen seconds have elapsed, he has given 29·17190429. His ability is clearly remarkable. Indeed, he is probably the most expert mental calculator on whom detailed records exist . . .

Professor Aitken solves any given numerical problem in a sequence of steps. First, he examines the problem and decides the plan or method by which he will calculate the answer: in doing this, he typically recasts the problem into a form which he can more easily handle. Then he implements his chosen method and, step by step, generates the answer. This step-sequence pattern is evident in the following report. He has just solved the problem of expressing the fraction 1/851 as a decimal.

The instant observation was that 851 is 23 times 37. I use this fact as follows. 1/37 is 0·027027027, and so on repeated. This I divide mentally by 23, 23 into 0·027 is 0·001 with remainder 4. In a flash I can get that 23 into 4027 is 175 with remainder 2, and into 2027 is 88 with remainder 3, and into 3027 is 131 with remainder 14, and even into 14,027 is 609

[1] Excerpt from the original English version of 'Kopfrechnen und Kopfrechner', *Bild der Wissenschaft* (April 1966), pp. 296–303.

with remainder 20. And so on like that. Also, before I ever start this, I know how far it is necessary to go before reaching the end of the recurring period: for 1/37 recurs at three places and 1/23 recurs at twenty-two places, and the lowest common multiple of 3 and 22 is 66, whence I know that there is a recurring period of 66 places.

This report suggests the analogy of a traveller who undertakes a cross-country journey on foot. First, he surveys the ground to be covered and plans a route which will involve the smallest number of manageable steps; then he follows the route, step by step. The report also illustrates two of the most basic features of Aitken's ability, namely, his large repertoire of number facts, and his repertoire of ingenious calculative plans.

For most people, there is a limited repertoire of numerical questions which they can answer rapidly and without any awareness of having to work anything out. What is twelve divided by two? The answer come automatically. For people who do a lot of number work, say accountants or teachers of mathematics, the repertoire of such questions is larger. For Aitken, the repertoire is vastly more extensive than normal. For example, if he is given any number up to 1,500, he can automatically say whether it is a prime number or, if it is not prime, state its factors. Once, during discussion, the year 1961 was mentioned and he immediately commented that this is 37 times 53, or alternatively 44 squared plus 5 squared, or alternatively 40 squared plus 19 squared. So, he is able automatically to recognize many properties of numbers and to answer many numerical questions. Furthermore, he is able to recognize, and to think of, quite large numbers as distinctive, unitary items: this is comparable to the ability of literate people to deal with a word as a unit rather than as an unwieldy collection of letters or sounds. In solving a problem, this extensive repertoire of number facts is deployed to advantage. It enables him to recognize useful properties of the problem, for example, that 851 is 23 times 37, and that 1/37 is 0·027027 repeated. It also enables him to pursue his chosen method in a succession of large steps, to leap rather than walk. His extensive repertoire of number facts is clearly advantageous. However, it is also necessary that, during calculation, only the appropriate facts should be produced, and, furthermore, that they should be produced in appropriate sequence. The production of these facts must be governed by an overall plan of calculation.

Most, perhaps all, skilled activities involve step-sequences. Ability to carry out the component steps is necessary for skill, but it is not sufficient. The expert typist requires more than ability to strike any required key on the board; the master violinist requires more than ability to produce any required note from his violin; the fluent orator requires more than a large vocabulary. In all cases, it is necessary to organize component steps into an appropriate sequence. So also in calculating. When Aitken tackles a problem, his first priority is to decide a calculative plan. This is the key decision for it governs everything else which follows, and final success depends heavily on it. It is true that his activities at each successive moment will have to adapt to the changing circumstances of the moment, that the accuracy of his working will have to be assured and occasionally verified, and that advantage may be taken of some minor short-cut in working. But all this is subordinated to the plan decided at the outset. This plan preselects what is to be done at each step: it also ensures that each step will follow smoothly out of the steps which have gone before, and will lead smoothly into the steps which are to follow. It sometimes happens that, after he has selected and launched a plan, he becomes aware of another and better plan: but he does not change to this other plan because such a change would greatly disrupt his working. This fact, that one plan cannot easily be changed for another in mid-course, is further evidence for the central, and continuing, role of the plan in governing calculation.

Aitken has a large variety of calculative plans at his disposal, and he can solve the same problem in several different ways. So why should he choose one plan rather than another? The answer is: economy of effort. He searches for that plan which will carry him to the solution in the shortest time and with least difficulty. This may be illustrated by considering two problems which have already been mentioned. The problems are to express as decimals the fractions 4/47 and 1/851. Both problems could be done by straight division. But, for Aitken, there are other and more economical ways of working. In the case of 1/851, he factorizes 851 into 23 times 37, then expresses 1/37 as 0·027027027 repeated, and then divides this by 23 in a succession of large steps. The main economy here is that he can now divide by 23 instead of 851. In the case of 4/47, there is a similar economy. He transforms the problem so that he can divide by 8 instead of 47. He first recognizes that, since 47 is prime, he cannot proceed by factorizing. So he transforms 4/47 into 68/799, and this enables him to launch a plan which is familiar to him. He divides 68 by 800, in effect by 8, and makes certain corrections to allow for the fact that if he divides by 800 instead of 799 his answer will be in error by an 800th. The steps of this plan are represented in figure 1. These two examples illustrate that an appropriate plan can economize effort by reducing the difficulty and/or the number of steps required to solve a problem. A more familiar example of such economic planning occurs when a person is asked to divide a number by 25, and proceeds to multiply the number by 4 and then divide the outcome by 100.

Economy of effort is centrally important for Aitken's calculating, as it is for a great many human accomplishments. He, like anyone else, can only do so much at any one time. Within any period of time, there are limits to the amount which anyone can observe or say or think or remember. In brief, it is a universal property of human beings that they have limited capacity for concurrent activities. One consequence of this central fact is that many tasks must be done in a succession of steps rather than all at once. Another consequence is that, in carrying through any task, speed can be gained by excluding any activities which are not strictly necessary for the task in hand. Aitken does just this: he concentrates on minimum essentials. Some exclusions concern obvious irrelevances, such as reacting to events in his surroundings or thinking about other matters: when calculating, he is physically relaxed and inattentive to everything but the calculation. Other exclusions are made possible by his large repertoire of number facts and by his use of ingenious calculative plans. His ability to take large steps reduces the total number of steps required, and adherence to a chosen plan reduces his moment-by-moment activities of deciding what he should do next. Yet other exclusions concern speech movements and imaging. Just as people can learn to read silently instead of speaking or mouthing words, so Aitken calculates without speaking numbers or muttering instructions to himself. Likewise, he need not think of numbers in terms of visual or auditory symbols or, indeed, of any form of clearly conscious awareness. In brief, Aitken is able to exclude from calculating many activities which, for most people, are indispensable. He solves a problem with concentrated and streamlined effort. . .

Dividend	Answer	Remainder	Next dividend
680 ÷ 8	0·085	none	85
85 ÷ 8	10	5	510
510 ÷ 8	63	6	663
663 ÷ 8	82	7	782
782 ÷ 8	97	6	697
697 ÷ 8	87	1	187
187 ÷ 8	23	3	323
323 ÷ 8	40	3	340
340 ÷ 8	42	4	442
442 ÷ 8	55	2	255
255 ÷ 8	31	7	731
731 ÷ 8	91	3	391
391 ÷ 8	48	7	748
748 ÷ 8	93	4	493
493 ÷ 8	61	5	561
561 ÷ 8	70	1	170
170 ÷ 8	21	2	221
221 ÷ 8	27	5	527
527 ÷ 8	65	7	765
765 ÷ 8	95	5	595
595 ÷ 8	74	3	374
374 ÷ 8	46	6	646
646 ÷ 8	80	6	680

680 which is the original dividend

Figure 1. A representation of the unconventional step-sequence followed by an expert calculator. The problem is to express the fraction 4/47 as a decimal. First, he transforms 4/47 into 68/799. Then he proceeds to divide 68 by 800 (in effect, by 8) with a recurring correction to allow for the difference between 799 and 800. Each line represents the same cycle of events. The dividend is divided by 8 to give two digits of the answer and a remainder; then the next dividend is formed by combining this answer and this remainder, e.g. from answer 10 and remainder 5, the next dividend is 510. Repetition of this cycle generates the answer to 4/47, two digits at a time.

Let us leave Aitken for the moment, and consider a general question. What happens whenever a person, by whatever means, increases his calculative ability? Broadly, the answer seems always to be the same. He acquires a system of calculative techniques which has two general properties. First, when he solves problems in terms of this system, he saves effort. So he can solve in less time, and solve problems which were previously beyond his ability. Second, this effort-saving system can only be acquired through effort, that is, work must be expended to establish the system which saves him work. These two aspects of increased ability are of such general importance that they merit a few examples. Consider a person who increases his calculative ability by learning to use a slide-rule, or a table of logarithms, or an electric calculating machine. He has now mastered a calculative system. He translates numerical problems into this system and works them in terms of this system so as to generate the solution. And the system enables him to solve these problems with reduced effort. In such cases, part of the system is external to himself, embodied in the apparatus he has learned to use; and most of the work of establishing the system was done by the men who invented and made this apparatus. Consider the person who increases his skill in mental calculation. Again, he has mastered a calculative system which enables him to solve problems with reduced effort. But this system is entirely within himself and has no physical existence outside his own body. Further, almost all the work of establishing the system was done by the individual himself . . .

Throughout history, there have been reports of people with exceptional ability in mental calculation. What can be learned from these reports? Perhaps the most striking thing is that they concern such a diversity of people with such widely different accomplishments. There are reports of young children, of gifted mathematicians such as Gauss and Ampère, of illiterates, and of people who are almost mentally defective. Some of those people solve a wide range of numerical problems by highly ingenious procedures and with great rapidity; others are specialists who excel only in some limited range of problems; others tackle only fairly simple problems by slow and conventional techniques, and are remarkable merely for their willingness to work without external aids; others show modest calculative accomplishments which would be unremarkable except for the person's lack of ability in any other direction. Even among those with moderately high calculative ability, there is diversity. Some rely heavily on visual imaging, some on auditory imaging, and some use little imaging of any kind. They also vary in their characteristic speed of working and in their techniques. For example, at the end of the last century, the French psychologist Binet examined two men who had some renown as mental calculators. He gave each of them the same problems, written on paper, and required them to write the answer but nothing else. One problem was: multiply 58,927 by 61,408. One calculator (Inaudi) completed the answer in 40 seconds, the other (Diamandi) in 275 seconds; and I have recently met a professional accountant who completed this problem in 55 seconds. Inaudi produced the digits of his answer in the left-to-right order, whereas Diamandi produced these digits in the right-to-left order; my accountant also produced the digits in right-to-left order, but he used a calculative plan quite different from that used either by Inaudi or by Diamandi. Different calculators clearly have very different calculative systems.

Reports on mental calculators also show that these different calculative systems are, in every case, built up by experience with calculating. Exceptionally able calculators have usually had years of intensive practice and some have commented that, with lack of practice, their skill deteriorates. For example, Aitken has described how he became interested in numerical problems at the age of thirteen and how, until his mid-thirties, he continued to explore increasingly complex problems with intense fascination. In doing this, some routine of calculation would be evolved; this would be extended to further examples and, thereby, give rise to the discovery of new numerical relationships which, in their turn, would provide fresh problems for exploration and new plans for calculating. Through these cumulative achievements, he learned to solve hitherto unmanageable problems and to solve old problems in more economical and rapid ways. Even after his mid-thirties, his experiences of calculating were considerable, partly because of their utility in his mathematical work and partly because of their intrinsic interest . . .

From all the fascinating details contained in reports on mental calculators, we can draw two general conclusions. The first has already been mentioned: each individual builds up, through his own numerical experience, a distinctive calculative system which enables him to solve this or that type of problem with reduced effort. The second conclusion, to which we now turn, is this: the accomplishments of mental calculators are restricted by limitations of temporary memory.

Consider the problem of multiplying 234 by 567. When asked to solve this, most people reach for paper and pencil, and pursue a calculative plan which they learned at school (figure 2).

$$
\begin{array}{r}
2\ 3\ 4 \\
5\ 6\ 7 \\
\hline
1\ 6\ 3\ 8 \\
1\ 4\ 0\ 4 \\
1\ 1\ 7\ 0 \\
\hline
1\ 3\ 2\ 6\ 7\ 8 \\
\hline
\end{array}
$$

Figure 2. A representation of a conventional paper-and-pencil calculation.
The problem is to multiply 234 by 567. The two numbers are written as shown. Then 234 is multiplied by 7, then by 6, and then by 5, to give three products. These products are then added to generate the final answer in right-to-left sequence. In this way, the working is decomposed into a sequence of small steps and, because of the written record, nothing much needs to be remembered at any one time. However, if the answer is to be written, but nothing else, this procedure is not feasible because there is too much data to be held in temporary memory.

The person writes the two numbers and progresses through an ordered succession of steps: 7 times 4 is 28, write 8, carry 2; 7 times 3 is 21, add the carried 2 to the 1, write 3, carry 2; and so on. In this way, he obtains three written products, and then he adds these products together to generate the answer in right-to-left order. Now, suppose we ask the person to solve this problem without writing anything except the final answer. If he pursues the same plan as before, but without jotting down the intermediate steps, he soon finds that there is too much to hold in temporary memory. He must remember the four digits of the first product, the four digits of the second product, and the four digits of the third; then he must recall these digits, in a different order, so as to add the three products; and all this must be done at the same time as he carries out the component calculative steps. Most people cannot complete this calculation, and the main reason is the limited amount of data which can be held in temporary memory.

Any mental calculator, however accomplished, has this difficulty of limited temporary memory. The difficulty becomes especially acute when he is required, at any one time, to hold a large amount of data in temporary storage. This restricts the range of numerical problems which he can profitably solve without external aids. In particular, it excludes most multiplication and division problems which contain large numbers. This restriction was clearly stated in 1856 by G. P. Bidder, a well-documented English calculator of considerable accomplishment.

The exercise of (temporary) memory is the only real strain on the mind, and which limits the extent to which mental calculation can be carried . . . In proportion as the numbers increase, so the (temporary) registration by the mind becomes more and more difficult, until at last the process becomes as slow as registration upon paper. When that point is arrived at, it is clear that the utility of mental calculation ceases, and the process ought to be carried upon paper.

The restriction is all the more evident nowadays with the advent of powerful electronic computers. For example, Aitken reports that when, in 1923, he first used a calculating machine, even of the antiquated kind then available, he

saw at once how useless it was to carry out for myself any mental multiplication of large numbers. Almost automatically, I cut down my ability in that direction, though I still kept up squaring and reciprocating and square-rooting, which have a more algebraic basis and a statistical use. But I am convinced that my ability deteriorated after that first encounter.

So, the utility of mental calculation is restricted to problems which can be done without, at any juncture, having to hold a large amount of data in temporary memory.

Despite what has just been said, many mental calculators give the appearance of being able to hold an impressively large amount of data in temporary memory. In Aitken's case, there is little doubt that he has a greater than normal capacity for holding data in temporary store, whether the data is numerical or verbal or musical or diagrammatic. This may also be the case with some other calculators. However, quite apart from such above-normal capacity, there are two general ways in which calculators can reduce the amount which they need to hold in temporary memory. The first way is to devise calculative plans which lighten the required memory load. The objective here is, as Bidder said, 'to bring all calculations, as far as it may be practicable, into one result, and to have that one result alone, at a time, registered upon the mind'. The literature refers to a variety of such plans. One is exhibited (figure 3): this plan was much used by

Bidder and by Inaudi, and gives the digits of the answer in left-to-right order. Another plan is shown (figure 4): this gives the digits of the answer in right-to-left order and was often used by Diamandi. This plan is especially interesting when we ask how it differs from the plan represented in figure 2. The multiplication steps are identical; what differs is the sequence in which these steps are taken. This altered sequence greatly reduces the amount which needs to be held in temporary memory at any one time.

$$
\begin{array}{rcl}
200 \times 500 &=& 100,000 \\
200 \times 60 &=& 12,000: \\
200 \times 7 &=& 1,400: \\
30 \times 500 &=& 15,000: \\
30 \times 60 &=& 1,800: \\
30 \times 7 &=& 210: \\
4 \times 500 &=& 2,000: \\
4 \times 60 &=& 240: \\
4 \times 7 &=& 28:
\end{array}
\qquad
\begin{array}{rcl}
12,000 + 100,000 &=& 112,000 \\
1,400 + 112,000 &=& 113,400 \\
15,000 + 113,400 &=& 128,400 \\
1,800 + 128,400 &=& 130,200 \\
210 + 130,200 &=& 130,410 \\
2,000 + 130,410 &=& 132,410 \\
240 + 132,410 &=& 132,650 \\
28 + 132,650 &=& 132,678
\end{array}
$$

Figure 3. A representation of a step-sequence which reduces the strain on temporary memory.
    The problem is to multiply 234 by 567. The problem is treated as $(200 + 30 + 4) (500 + 60 + 7)$ and the nine multiplication steps are taken in the order shown. The answer from each multiplication is added to the cumulative product obtained so far. This cumulative product is all that needs to be carried forward into the next line: all previous results can be forgotten. In this way, the cumulative product is built up, step by step, until it becomes the final answer. Note that the digits of the answer are generated in left-to-right order.

Problem: 234 multiplied by 567

Sub-problem		Write	Remember
$7 \times 4 = 28$		8	2
$6 \times 4 = 24$: $24 + 2 = 26$			
$7 \times 3 = 21$: $21 + 26 = 47$		7	4
$5 \times 4 = 20$: $20 + 4 = 24$			
$6 \times 3 = 18$: $18 + 24 = 42$			
$7 \times 2 = 14$: $14 + 42 = 56$		6	5
$5 \times 3 = 15$: $15 + 5 = 20$			
$6 \times 2 = 12$: $12 + 20 = 32$		2	3
$5 \times 2 = 10$: $10 + 3 = 13$		13	

Figure 4. A representation of another step-sequence which reduces the strain on temporary memory.
    The problem is to multiply 234 by 567 and, usually, these numbers would be written down. However, the calculator writes nothing else except the final answer. Each digit of one number is multiplied by each digit of the other number and these multiplicative steps are taken in the order shown. Note that the digits of the answer are generated in right-to-left order.

The second general way in which calculators reduce the memory load derives from their economic ways of detailed working. Consider the working shown in figure 3 as it would be carried through by Bidder. For him, the strain on temporary memory is less than might be supposed. For one thing, he is familiar with the step-sequence involved, and so he knows precisely what to do at each moment. Again, he can think of numbers as distinctive qualities. He tried to express this by saying that, for him, every number up to a thousand was but one idea, and every number between a thousand and a million was, to his regret, two ideas. So, he does not remember a six-digit number as a string of six digits but, rather as two items. This lightens the load because it reduces the amount to be remembered: to give a familiar example, it is easier to remember 'mental calculation' as two words than as a string of seventeen letters. Then again, the very rapidity of working reduces the memory load because whatever must be remembered has to be kept in store for a shorter time. A number which is laid aside for future use is brought into that use before much forgetting can take place. It is no accident that mental calculators work as rapidly as they can. In summary, there are various ways in which calculators are able to reduce both the amount of data which they need to keep in temporary memory and also the length of time during which they must hold it. However, there are limits beyond which this cannot be done. When these limits are reached, the mental calculator must admit the superiority of certain other calculative systems, notably those involving the use of an electronic computer.

The most important general conclusion to be drawn from the study of mental calculation is probably this. Increase in ability concerns the development of techniques which enable the person to make more effective and economic use of his basically limited capacities for handling information. This increasingly effective use of limited capacities is evident in the many qualitative changes which bring about more rapid and accurate working. It is most evident of all in the apparently simple fact that the person can solve problems, that is, he can answer questions correctly even though he has never learned the specific answers to these specific questions. Life is too brief to permit the rote learning of each particular answer to every possible question.

Nevertheless, a novel question can be answered if the person can decompose it into several familiar questions and answer these in an appropriate sequence. Such problem-solving activity is a class of technique which makes vividly effective use of limited resources.

Within recent years an increasing amount of detailed study has been devoted to the techniques by which people acquire their many and varied abilities. What are the characteristics of such techniques in this or that sphere of accomplishment? How are they acquired? How can their development be facilitated? These are intriguing questions for scientific research, and their answers have significance for human well-being.

Two additional comments[1]

The first comment concerns psychological method. The above paper inquires into one class of complex, knowledge-handling skill, i.e. mental calculation, but the method of inquiry noticeably differs from the methods conventionally used in experimental psychology. The method is clinical and comparative. It starts

[1] Specially written for this volume, by I. M. L. Hunter.

with a naturalistic survey of one person's skill as observed under real-life conditions that are as free as possible from artificial constraints and preconceived theories. It observes what the person characteristically does and how he does it, and has regard for subjective commentaries as well as the objective properties of performances. An attempt is made to grasp how all these observations relate together to reflect a coherent cognitive *system*, i.e. an organized body of knowledge, techniques, and ways of comprehending and dealing with numerical problems. This clinical survey deals with only one individual and there is no expectation that it will necessarily resemble surveys of other people's calculative skill. However, when several case studies are available, comparisons can be made between the cognitive systems of different people.

In computer science, comparisons are made between the cost-effectiveness of different data-processing systems; in economics, between the cost–gain balance of economic systems; in biology, between the strengths and weaknesses of systems of adaptation to the environment. Likewise, in psychology, comparisons can be made between different systems of calculative skill and, more widely, between different systems of representing, organizing, and using knowledge. Differences between systems show what they variously require in the way of cognitive resources, and what they variously enable, and do not enable, their users to accomplish. Persisting similarities between systems suggest the existence of constraints inherent in the human constitution – constraints which somehow limit the variety of ways in which it is humanly possible to organize and use knowledge. In conclusion, the clinical-comparative method merits explicit recognition among the methods available to psychological investigators.

The second comment concerns A. C. Aitken who died in 1967. He was outstanding, not only as a mental calculator, but also as a mathematician and as a man with exceptional powers of memory. In his lifetime, he became legendary for the range, tenacity, rapidity, and precision of his memory. Hunter (1977a) reports a case study of Aitken's memory and compares it with the exceptional memory of S. V. Shereshevskii – the 'S.' studied by Luria (1969). The two men, although similar in some respects, were strikingly unlike. They differed in the kind of information they committed to memory, the way this information was organized in memory, and the use they could make of information stored in memory.

Aitken was an erudite scholar whose greatest accomplishments lay in creative mathematical thinking. He learnt and retained new information by being interested in its meaning, and able to discern in it a richly meaningful pattern of conceptual relations. He was consequently able to recall the information in much of its original detail, and also use the information selectively in the service of flexibly novel thinking. By contrast, S. was a professional mnemonist whose greatest accomplishments lay in memorizing strings of haphazardly presented items. He used the classical Method of Loci (see Hunter, 1977b) in his professional work and also in everyday life. He learnt and retained new information by treating it as a succession of isolated fragments. He translated each fragment into a rich, perception-like image which he linked, again by mental imagery, to the adjacent fragment. He was consequently able to recall the information in serial detail. But the information lacked meaning in any conventional sense and he was unable to deploy it in creative thinking.

Aitken and S. were both highly exceptional and it is informative to survey with some care their characteristic ways of working and to see how they compare with people of more average accomplishments. Direct comparison between the two men is also informative because it shows clearly that different human beings can organize their knowledge in radically different ways. Aitken organized his knowledge in terms of 'conceptual maps', while S. organized his in terms of 'perceptual chains'. Each man's mode of cognitive organization was pervasive and far from trivial in its effects: it moulded the very way he comprehended and dealt with the world in which he lived.

3. On the analysis of human problem solving protocols[1]

Allen Newell

The Newell and Simon theory of problem solving

. . . The theory assumes an underlying information processing system like that shown in figure 1. This system comprises a large memory of symbolic structures, an essentially serial processor for accessing and restructuring this memory, and some input-output mechanisms. The organization is familiar enough, differing from existing computers primarily in that its memory organization is a network of labelled associations between symbols . . .

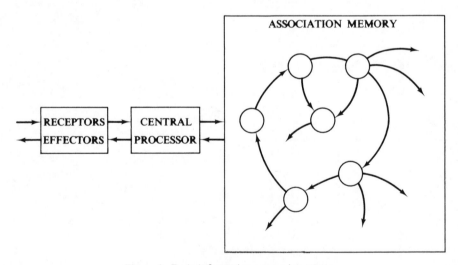

Figure 1. Basic information processing system

[1] Edited excerpts of the paper in J. C. Gardin and B Jaulin (eds.), *Calcul et formalization dans les sciences de l'homme* (Paris: Editions du Centre National de la Recherche Scientifique, 1968), pp. 145–85.

The theory is concerned with the methods, organization of processes, knowledge, etc., that constitute the program that a given system follows when problem solving. This viewpoint is clearly oversimplified. Limitations on immediate memory, on the rate at which reaction can occur to new data, and on the rate at which relatively permanent memory can be built up all pose boundary conditions within which the problem solving organization must operate. Additional limitations exist on perceptual and motor processes, but can be avoided in setting up experimental situations. Not so the former, and our excuse for ignoring them is our ignorance of how they affect problem solving, together with the fact that humans solve problems in such a way that these boundaries are not especially evident.

Problem solving takes place in a *problem space*. The elements of this space consist of *states of knowledge* about the problem . . . Both the *initial situation* and the *desired situation* are represented as elements of this space. A problem space also has associated with it a set of *operators*, which, when applied to an element of the space, produce new elements. Thus, these operators are the means by which new information about the problem can be obtained from old.

Problem solving is always a matter of search – of starting from some initial position (state of knowledge) and exploring until a position is attained that includes the solution – the desired state of knowledge. The behaviour of a problem solver is not fully determined by the problem space. Figure 2 shows the range of considerations that are relevant when the problem solver is at a position in the space . . . They do not form a program for behaviour at a position, since a

    Evaluate the position:
        Is it the desired state?
        Should it be remembered, so that either it can be returned to later, or it can be recognized if encountered again?
        Is there some new information that should be extracted and remembered independently of position?
        Is progress being made, so that search should be continued; or are there difficulties?
    Select new operator:
        Has it been used before?
        Is it desirable: will it lead to progress?
        Is it feasible: will it work in the present position if applied?
    Apply operator to present position:
        If it works, then it produces new position.
        If it does not work, what is the difficulty?
    Evaluate difficulty:
        Should a subgoal be set up to overcome this difficulty?
        Should the position be rejected?
            Return to prior position?
            Return to initial position?
            Return to a remembered position; if so, which one?
    Evaluate old position, just returned to:
        Should it be used, or rejected?

Figure 2. Considerations at a position in problem space

problem solver may organize them very differently, perhaps ignoring some altogether. Nor is the list necessarily complete, although it seems to encompass many of the considerations used by both artificial and human problem solvers.

Search in a problem space is *constructive*. The elements of the space, although they exist abstractly, do not exist for the problem solver unless he generates them, or remembers them for later retrieval once generated. This gives the search a different character from that through a world that exists independently of the problem solver – e.g. a forest. In essence, problem spaces are always exponentially growing trees: two independent paths cannot end up at the same element of the space. One cannot do in a problem space what one does in a forest: put marks on trees to recognize the same place if it is returned to. In the problem space an element may be generated that is identical in structure and content to another – but it will not be the identical one, and hence will not contain any 'tree mark'. Only if the problem solver remembers each new element as it is constructed, and determines if each new one is identical with any of those kept so far, will he be able to simulate the tree marking scheme.

. . . The problem solver is not limited to a single problem space. He may obtain a new one after finding the initial one inadequate. More importantly, he may make use of more than one simultaneously. An example is provided by a program for proving theorems in plane geometry (Gelernter, 1963a), which uses both a space of symbolic expressions, representing theorems, and a space of coordinates, representing the diagram. This latter provides much of the problem solving power of the system, since operations of direct measurement of angles and length are available in it to check the assertions of the theorems. . .

The Problem Behaviour Graph (PBG)

Let us see what this theory implies when applied to protocol material. If we knew what problem space the subject was working in, then we could view his behaviour, as revealed through the protocol, as a search in this space. More precisely, we would be able to (1) state the kinds of information that make up the states of knowledge of this space; and (2) specify a set of operators, such that each change in the state of knowledge corresponds to an application of one of the operators.

. . . The actual problem space used by the subject is unknown. Indeed, it is even unknown if the subject is behaving in accordance with the theory. Consequently, the appropriate data analysis procedure is to posit a problem space and see if the subject can be analysed as searching in this space.

In case the subject is wandering in more than one space, of course, the two must be unravelled simultaneously. If we are successful, we shall know it by getting a reasonably complete picture of the search (it will not be perfect in any event due to ambiguity and incompleteness in the protocol). Then, we can go on to consider what other information about the remainder of the subject's program can be obtained.

Search trees published in the literature of problem solving programs show mostly the total extent of the search – what positions were ultimately visited (Gelernter, 1963b; Newell, Shaw, and Simon, 1963). Often, if the search strategy is simple, the actual path of search can be inferred from the total tree. However, we need a way of tracking the search that lets us reconstruct its actual history. The scheme we adopt we call the *Problem Behaviour Graph* (PBG). We give the conventions below; referring to figure 3 for an example.

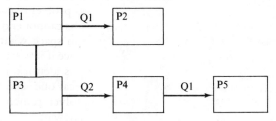

Figure 3. Problem Behaviour Graph (PBG)

Rules for Problem Behaviour Graph (PBG)

A state of knowledge is represented by a node (the labelled boxes in the figure).

The application of an operator to a state of knowledge is represented by a horizontal arrow to the right; the result is the node at the head of the arrow (Operator Q1 to position P1 gives position P2).

A return to the same state of knowledge as node X is represented by another node below X and connected to it by a vertical line (P3 results after abandonment of P2; it constitutes the same state of knowledge as P1).

Time runs to the right and down; thus the graph is linearly ordered by time of generation (from P1 to P5).

The problem solver is viewed as always being located at some node in the PBG, and having available exactly the information contained in its state of knowledge. The act of search itself generates information in addition to that represented at the node: in particular, *path information* about how the node was arrived at; and *past attempts information* about what else has been done when in this state of knowledge. Both these kinds of information are viewed as being associated with a node; in fact, this sort of information is what distinguishes node P3 from P1.

With this much apparatus, we are ready to consider an example.

Crypt-arithmetic

The top of figure 4 shows a version of a familiar puzzle, called a crypt–arithmetic problem. Each letter is to be assigned a distinct digit between 0 and 9 such that when the letters are replaced by their assigned digits a legitimate sum is obtained. As a starter, it is given that D is 5; thus, no other letter can be 5 and a 5 must replace all three occurrences of D in the figure. A college student was given the task to solve, with instructions to 'think aloud'. The initial segment of his protocol is shown in figure 5. It has been broken into short phrases, which have been labelled. The expressions on the right side of figure 5 will be discussed later.

Problem: DONALD   D ← 5   Each letter assigned to one and only one digit
         + GERALD   Each digit assigned to one and only one letter
          ROBERT

Terms: entities that can be referred to in problem space

  l   is any letter, A, B, D, E, G, L, N, O, R, T
  d   is any digit, 0, 1, . . . , 9
  ds is any set of digits, *d, d, . . . , d*
  c   is any column, c1, c2, . . . , c7 (c1 is the right hand column)
  t   is any carry *to* a column, t1, t2, . . . , t7
  v   is any variable, either a letter, *l,* or a carry, *t*

Elementary expressions: relationships and properties among terms

  $v \leftarrow d$ *v* has been assigned the value *d*
  $v = d$ *v* has the value *d* by inference
  $v = ds$ *v* has one of the values in the set *ds*
  $l > d$ ⎤
  $l < d$ ⎟ *l* has the respective constraint
  l even ⎟
  l odd ⎦
  l free   *l* can take any value (in an implied domain) without constraint

Expressions: an elementary expression or term, *ee,* followed by a suffix:

  −*p*   it is not possible or can take no possible value, e.g. $(R = 5) - p$, it is not
       possible that R = 5
  ?   its truth or value is unknown
  !   its truth or value is critical to the inference

States of knowledge: any conjunction of expressions (need not be consistent)

Operators

  PROCESS (*c*)   Process the column *c*. The input is all the information about the column and the letters and carries in it; the output is some information that can be inferred from the column, which may include specification of something as critical (!) or unknown (?).

  GENERATE (*v*)   Generate the values of variable *v*. This takes into account the constraints known to hold for *v* (e.g. *v* odd), but not the exclusion of values due to assignment to other variables.

  ASSIGN (*v*)   Assign a value to the variable *v*. The output is in form $v \leftarrow d$. This value will be selected from the set generated by GENERATE (*v*).

  TEST (*l, d*)   Test if *l* can take the value *d*. Failure is due to *d* being assigned to another letter, or to *d* lying outside the permissible range for *l*.

Goals

  get *v*   Get a value for *v*; determine something about the value of *v*.
  get *ee*   Determine whether expression is true.
  check *ee* Determine whether expression, believed to be true, is in fact true.

Figure 4. Crypt-arithmetic: definition of problem space

B1	Each letter has one and only one numerical value - -	?:	(ask Exp. about rules)
B2	Exp: One numerical value.		
B3	There are ten different letters		
B4	and each of them has one numerical value.		
B5	Therefore, I can, looking at the two D's - -	S1 : D ← 5	→ Find-column (D) ⇒ cl; Process (cl) ⇒ T = 0
B6	each D is 5;		
B7	therefore, T is zero.	T1 : T = 0	→ Test (T,0) ⇒ Yes
B8	So I think I'll start by writing that problem here.		
B9	I'll write 5, 5 is zero.		
B10	Now, do I have any other T's?	S1 : T = 0	→ Find-column (T) ⇒ fail
B11	No.		
B12	But I have another D.	S1 : D ← 5	→ Find-column (D) ⇒ c6; (no Process (c6))
B13	That means I have a 5 over the other side.		
B14	Now I have 2 A's	G4 : get 1s	→ Find-letter (1s) ⇒ R; get R
B15	and 2 L's		
B16	that are each - -		
B17	somewhere - -		
B18	and this R - -		
B19	3 R's - -		
B20	2 L's equal an R - -	S2 : get R	→ Find-column (R) ⇒ c2; Process (c2, R) ⇒ R odd
B21	Of course I'm carrying a 1.		
B22	Which will mean that R has to be an odd number.		
B22.1		R1 : Process unclear	→ Get R; repeat Process
B23	Because the 2 L's - -	↑ :	Process (c2, R) ⇒ R odd
B24	any two numbers added together has to be an even number		
B25	and 1 will be an odd number.		
B26	So R can be 1.	S4 : get R	→ Generate (R) ⇒ 1,3,5,7,9
B27	3,		
B28	not 5,	T1 : R = d	→ Test (R,d) ⇒ (R = 5) is not possible
B29	or 7,		
B30	or 9.		

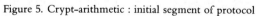

Figure 5. Crypt-arithmetic : initial segment of protocol

The first step in the analysis after obtaining the protocol is to construct a problem space. The simplest one, of course, is defined directly from the rules of the puzzle. The elements are sets of assignments; the operators are the acts of assigning a new digit to a new letter. The initial position is that one where no assignments have been made; and the final position is the one where all ten have been made, such that the three constraints have been satisfied. In fact, this problem space would be used by someone who wanted to build a simple search program for the task. Clearly, our subject is more sophisticated. He makes inferences using the column constraints; he uses the carry; he works with concepts such as even-oddness; he attends to the columns in variable order.

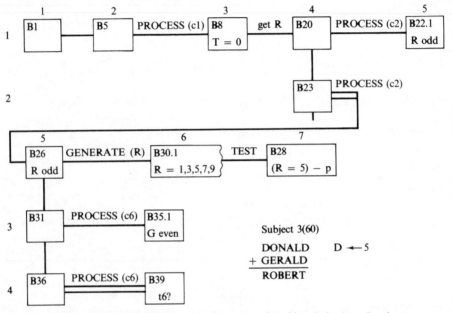

Figure 6. Crypt-arithmetic: initial segment of Problem Behaviour Graph

The bottom part of figure 4 provides a definition of a problem space for this subject. The element, corresponding to the state of knowledge, is a conjunction of elementary expressions, each of which deals with some relation between variables (letters or carries) and digits. Neither path information nor past attempts information is stated explicitly. Actually, we would hope to infer from the PBG what information of this kind is being kept.

There are four operators. Each is defined with reasonable precision in terms of input–output characteristics, which are the features necessary to identify whether the operator was evoked in the protocol. Whether all occurrences so identified constitute a single operator, in the sense of being produced by a consistent subroutine, is a matter for later analysis. The initial part of the PBG, extending much less than the segment of protocol reproduced in figure 5, is given in figure 6. The double lines indicate that an operator is being repeated from the same state of knowledge. A condensed version of the complete PBG is given in figure 7.

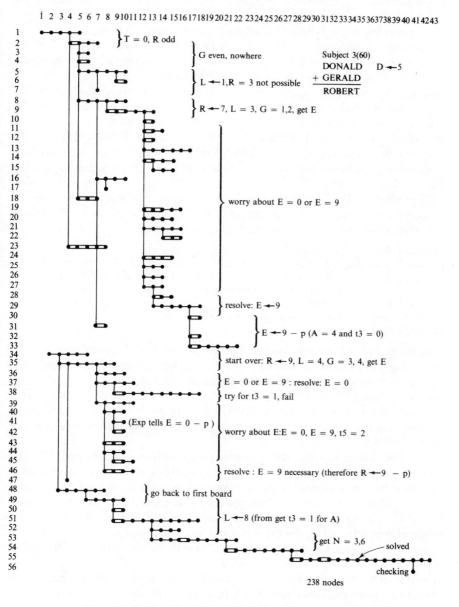

Figure 7. Crypt-arithmetic: total Problem Behaviour Graph

Let us consider briefly how the coding goes. Starting at the beginning (B1) we have an exchange that is really outside the problem space, since it involves clarification of the rules. Therefore, no operator is indicated. In the second box, B5, we have a clear statement of considering the two D's, asserting their value, and concluding that T is zero. The coding of this as the operator PROCESS (c1) is clear. Some open questions are (1) when did the inference actually occur; (2) why did column c1 get considered; (3) was it desired to find the value of T before processing column c1; and (4) was it also concluded that the carry to column 2 = 1? About some of these questions we do not need to have the answers. As to the first, we require only the approximate ordering. As to the second, the selections of columns is internal to each box and thus irrelevant to the problem graph. The third question is relevant, but we adopt the view that unless specific information is available on the variable desired, we will not record it. Finally, although it is plausible that the carry to column 2 = 1 is inferred since 5 + 5 = 10, there is no immediate evidence. However, later behaviour (B21) shows that in fact this information was retained.

The next box, B8, should be considered in conjunction with box B20. In this latter we clearly have a consideration of column 2 with the inference of R odd. If we write down what happens before this we have:

B8–B9   Writing prior result.
B10–B11 Searching for a next step with no result in terms of our problem space.
B12–B13 Another writing step, when D of c6 is noticed; conceivable that new information obtained, but certainly no evidence for it.
B14–B19 Consideration of c2, c3, A, L and R in the apparent search for a next step. No new information obtained in our problem space.
B20–B22 Processing of c2.

The concern with R, clearly indicated in B18 and B19, leads to the inference that the decision to process column c2 is based partly on the decision to obtain some information about R. Thus we code B8 with the goal of getting R. Those things occurring prior to B18 all belong within a box: the operations of writing and the (attempted) selection of columns on which to work. If the inference to get R were less clear, we would have only a single box for B8 to B22, whose operator would be PROCESS (c2).

It is clear that in B23–B25 the reasoning used in B20–B22 is repeated. Why the repetition occurred is not as clear. It might be to check the processing – to assure that the inference is correct. That a correction can occur the second time around is shown by the sequence B32–B35, yielding G even, and the immediate repeat, B36–B38, leading to the realization that no such inference is possible. Repetition might also be affected by the experimental instruction to get the subject to talk. In any event, we need to create a box, B22.1, for the result of the first PROCESS (c2) and then back up one for the second at B23.

In B26–B30 an explicit generation of the odd digits follows immediately upon the (confirmed) conclusion that R is odd. Thus the inference that GENERATE (R) occured is not problematic. The generation does not take into account what values are already used, since the already used digit, 5, is generated and explicitly rejected. This supports the inference that TEST was applied to the output of GENERATE. It is not as clear, of course, that TEST was applied to 1, 3, 7 and 9, since these were 'OK' and no special indication of their acceptability is provided. However, if TEST was applied sometimes and sometimes not, then a process must have existed to make the decision; but this process would have had to perform (uniformly) the same function as TEST namely, to determine if a digit were used. Consequently, it is simpler to assume that TEST was applied uniformly.

. . . We have only given the first bit of a very long (and dull) argument. What do we learn from the PBG for this subject? First, his problem solving can be described as search in a well defined problem space. Second, from the definition of the problem space, we obtain information about the intellectual tools he is capable of using. This is revealed most clearly by the kinds of situations in which PROCESS is able to provide new information – e.g. to take as inputs R odd and D← 5 and produce G even. Third, we have taken a preliminary step to asking if there exist regularities in his search behaviour. This does not follow from the existence of the search tree. The encoding has been done entirely on a local basis. Whether the subject has consistent modes of behaviour for carrying out the considerations of figure 5 remains an open question. The PBG does provide a segmentation of the total stream of behaviour into a set of units (238 of them in this case) that now permit inquiry into further regularities. . .

Production systems

At each node of a PBG the subject makes a number of decisions (or selections), already summarized in figure 6 . . . We need language to express the decision and selection processes. We would like a scheme that facilitates inducing these processes, rather than requiring the invention of the complete program all at once. One that appears to have some of the desired virtues is the *production system*. This consists of a set of *productions*, each of which consists of a *condition* expression followed by an *action* expression:

condition→action

The production is to be considered in the context of the state of knowledge at a node. If the condition is true of the state of knowledge, then the action part is evoked; otherwise the production has no implication for the behaviour of the system at that node. In applying a production system (i.e. a set of productions) to a node, some doctrine of conflict resolution is necessary to select a unique action if the condition of more than one production is satisfied. The simplest such scheme is a priority ordering of the productions, so that the one of highest priority always wins out.

. . . The advantage of a production system for the task of program induction lies in the fact that at each node one of the productions is evoked. Therefore its condition is true of that state of knowledge and its action occurs at that point.

Thus, an hypothesis formed by the analyst at a node takes the form of a proposal for one of the productions that exists in the system. This can be specified independently of what other productions exist in the system. Thus, the total system can be put together piece by piece from a consideration of what happens in each local situation.

The system is not actually as free as the above paragraph indicates. Once a production has been specified, it should be evoked in any situation where its condition is satisfied. Since the states of knowledge are already given in the PBG, the set of nodes where a production is theoretically evoked is determined. Whether it is in fact evoked, as indicated by what action takes place there, is an empirical matter to be answered by an inspection of the PBG. To the extent that the production does occur where predicted, we get confirmation of a regularity in the subject's behaviour.

Some extensions to the above picture must be introduced before the scheme for the analysis of regularities is complete. The nodes provide a first segmentation of the protocol. Thus, there will be at least one production per node whose action includes the operator that is evoked at the node. But it is possible to have additional productions whose output is some intermediate information used by another production that leads to the selection of the operator. This intermediate information will not be such as to change the state of knowledge in the problem space, of course. For example, it might be the discovery that all operators had been tried at the node, which would lead to the cessation of the attempt to select an operator and to the evocation of a production leading to the selection of what node to return to. Thus, the total population of observables may increase somewhat as productions are defined.

Secondly, defining the productions locally and in isolation only partially specifies the total production system. Many productions may be predicted to occur at a node. The evidence will indicate which one (or perhaps none) of the predicted set occurred. A conflict resolution rule, such as a priority ordering, needs to be added to complete the production system in a way consistent with the actual occurrences.

. . . We are now ready to examine these ideas concretely. We will do this for the crypt-arithmetic example, and even here we will have to be sketchy, considering how much detail is necessary to describe fully a production system and its coordination with the full protocol. . .

Crypt-arithmetic

Figure 8 shows the production system for the PBG of figure 7. The condition part of a production occurs on the left side of the arrow ($\rightarrow$) and the action part on the right. The condition is sometimes composite, with separate disjunctive alternatives. The letters indicate both variables and the class to which the variables belong, as defined by the problem space. Thus, v is a variable which is a letter or a carry. The square brackets are used to identify something or state an additional condition. . . . . The action part may consist of a sequence of actions (separated by ;). The double arrow ($\Rightarrow$) is used to indicate the output of a process.

There are four types of productions. S1–S5 lead to the selection of an operator of the problem space: PROCESS, GENERATE, ASSIGN. In doing so they may require intermediate information about a column, provided by processes that are not operators in the problem space, e.g. FINDING a column.

S1 reflects the use of newly achieved information by trying to find some place where it can yield still other information. S2 is just the opposite; given the goal of getting something, it tries to find a place where something about it can be found out. S3 is an indirect form of assignment; instead of assigning an arbitrary value to l directly, it backs off to something that determines l, assigns a value to it and then derives the value of l. This tends to assure that one more relationship will be taken account of. S4 is a reaction to obtaining partial information by generating the possible values and assigning one of them as a trail. However, if the generation is complex and there are many of them (more than two) no assignment is made. S4 is the only production with a conditional action sequence. S5 provides for checking an answer by iterating through the columns and adding up each successively; it occurs only once during the course of the protocol.

The second type of production, G1–G5, leads to setting up a goal, either to get something or to check something. G1 says: if the value of something is unknown, then set up the goal of getting it. This will arise, of course, only in the context where the value of that thing has occurred in some other processing. That is, the knowledge state does not contain an expression, *ee ?*, for everything the system does not know. G2 says: if a given statement has been found out not to be true of something, then set up the goal of finding out what is true of that thing. G3 says: one way to check something is to get its value. G4 reduces the goal of getting the members of a set to the goal of getting one of them. G5 says: if some fact, *ee*, becomes critically important, as symbolized by *ee!*, then it should be checked. Such items can arise from TEST in causing something to be impossible, or from PROCESS.

The third type of production, T1 and T2, is concerned with terminating lines of search. T1 evokes TEST, the problem space operator that can declare something not possible; T2 is the backtrack operator that concludes that if something implies an impossibility, then it is, itself, not possible.

The final type, R1 and R2, is concerned with repeating paths already trodden. R1 repeats processes that were unclear. R2 says: to check an item that has already been produced by some processes, repeat that process. It implies that the subject remembers something about paths already taken, and has this path information accessible as a function of the results produced.

There is not space to discuss fully the psychological implications of this system; they are examined in Newell and Simon (1963, 1965a, b, 1972) and Simon and Newell (1964). Note that productions jointly accomplish most of the functions given in figure 2, but that they are not organized entirely as that figure would suggest. Notice also that the productions are neither novel nor cryptic.

Selection

	Condition		Action
S1	$v = d$ by inference $\Big\}$ $v \leftarrow d$	→	FIND-COLUMN involving $v \Rightarrow c$; PROCESS (c)
S2	get v $\Big\}$ get $v = d$	→	FIND-COLUMN involving $v \Rightarrow c$; PROCESS (c) to determine something about v
S3	get l	→	FIND-ANTECEDENT relationship that detemines $l \Rightarrow$ column in which v is constrained; ASSIGN (v); PROCESS (c) to determine something about l
S4	get v, where its value is constrained	→	GENERATE (v) i.e. possible values of v; if only a small number of possible values, ASSIGN (v)
S5	check the set of columns, cs	→	GENERATE-COLUMNS $(cs) \Rightarrow c$; PROCESS (c)

Goal setting

G1	ee? i.e. the truth or value of ee is unknown	→	get ee
G2	$(ee\ [v]) - $ p, i.e. a statement about v is not true	→	get v
G3	check ee	→	get ee
G4	get ls, i.e. goal of obtaining values of a set of letters, ls	→	FIND-LETTER $(ls) \Rightarrow l$; get l
G5	ee!	→	check ee

Terminating

T1	$l = d$ $\Big\}$ GENERATE $(l) \Rightarrow d$	→	TEST $(l,d) \Rightarrow$ Yes, or else not possible $(!)$
T2	$(ee)-$p, i.e. a statement, ee, is not possible	→	FIND-ANTECEDENT $(ee) \Rightarrow ff$; $(ff)-$p.

Repeating

R1	An operation Q constraining the value of v was unclear	→	get v; repeat Q
R2	Check ee		RECALL production, P, used to generate ee; get ee; repeat P

Definitions of additional processes

FIND-COLUMN (v)	Find a column that involves v. For l, the column includes l, but for t it may be either the carry-out-of column or the carry-into column
FIND-ANTECEDENT (ee)	Find the antecedent that generated ee or, if a variable, a relationship that determines v
GENERATE-COLUMNS (cs)	Generate the columns in the set of columns, cs

FIND-LETTER (*ls*)   Find letter in the set of letters, *ls*
                                            that is still undetermined and occurs a
                                            maximum number of times
RECALL (*ee*)   Recall production, P, that was used to
                                            generate the expression *ee*

Figure 8. A production system for crypt-arithmetic

Each expresses a meaningful unit of action that is rational at a local level – that is, adapted to the task at hand. This does not imply that when put together the system adds up to highly rational or effective total behaviour. In fact a global judgment on the subject's behaviour would be that, although he appeared to know what he was doing, it still took him three or four times as long as it would a really good problem solver.

Given the production system of figure 8, one can go back to the protocol and determine just what productions occur at each point. The right-hand side of figure 5 gives a sample of this. In general there is only one production per node, although occasionally more than one (B8), and sometimes a single production covers several nodes (B22. 1 and B23). A judgment is clearly involved in whether a particular production occurs or not. However, it is rare for there to be uncertainty between two or more productions. Where it has not been possible to determine what production occurred, either because none of the defined productions fits or because the protocol is too obscure, a question mark (?) has been put down.

. . . To finish the specification of the production system a conflict resolution rule is required. We have used a priority scheme, although it is not entirely satisfactory. Thus, for each pair of productions we want to put higher in the order of priority the one which was chosen most often when there was a choice between the two... With this priority ordering added, the production system of figure 8 uniquely determines the production that occurs at each node, except for the ?-nodes . . .

Let us summarize where we have come. Technically any production system is a program. If presented with an initial state, it will evoke a sequence of productions, executing their actions and modifying the information state accordingly. This will continue until either the system loops, or a state is reached where no production is evoked, at which point the system stops. The system of figure 8, although a program in this sense, is not yet a full program either for simulating the subject or even for solving crypt-arithmetic tasks. If set loose on a new task,

SEND

MORE

———

MONEY

it would not know what to do with the fifth column, which has blanks in it. That is, the productions have all been built around one episode and have not been extended to form a complete system. They have not even been extended to cover the ?-nodes, so that as a system it will not keep going for the DONALD + GERALD task. Instead, figure 8 represents the regularities found in the protocol and has expressed them in a form in which any program that is built can take them into account. Such final programs can be made by extending the system by additional productions until it is complete, say, over all crypt-arithmetic tasks of the simple type used here. Indeed, this seems the natural way to proceed. But one could also proceed using more conventionally organized programs with a more constrained flow of control, or trying to embed the process into a structure such as GPS [General Problem Solver]. In these latter cases, the production system, along with the summary of how well the various productions fared, provides strong statements about what has to go into the simulating system. . .

We have been concerned with making protocol analysis into a useful tool. This has led to a methodological emphasis with, however, the focus on improving the technology for developing theory, rather than for validating theory. We introduced a series of steps in the data analysis whose function was to make evident the important regularities in the protocol, and pave the way for constructing process models of the subject's behaviour. Briefly summarized, these steps are:

Divide the protocol into phrases. Each phrase represents a single assertion about the task or a single act of task oriented behaviour. Although trivial, this step is worth noting, since it represents the limit of precoding of the verbal behaviour.

Construct a problem space. Both the operators and the information constituting a state of knowledge are set down. There may be more than one problem space, of course. The problem space is a hypothesis about the subject's behaviour.

Plot the Problem Behaviour Graph (PBG). Proceed through the protocol phrase by phrase. The key constraint is that all changes in knowledge state (as defined for the problem space) that are detectable in the protocol must come about through application of one of the operators of the problem space. The PBG segments the protocol into a population of occasions for action.

Create a production system. This system attempts to capture the regularities in the search behaviour. It can be viewed (with some literary licence) as proceeding in several steps:

Conjecture individual productions. At each node of the PBG conjecture a production that responds to features in the knowledge of that node (essentially known through the construction of the PBG) and yields the action taken. This leads to a large collection of individual productions.

Consolidate the production system. Rewrite as many productions as possible as variations on a few, thus reducing the total number of productions in the system. This is analogous to subroutinizing a large program, and yields the same dividends in permitting the essential organization of the system to emerge.

Plot the production system against the PBG. Proceed through the PBG node by node. For each determine not only what production occurred, but what others could have occurred, but didn't.

Determine a conflict resolution rule. This may be a simple priority system, as used here, but it may involve quite different distinctions. For example, it may lead to elaborating the conditions of some of the productions.

This analysis scheme is still incomplete, as we have not carried it through the final steps of getting a running program. These latter steps are not superfluous. They provide the verification that we have a sufficient set of processes for carrying out not only the immediately present task, but others of similar character as well. In addition, the hand codings engaged in during the preliminary steps described in this paper always leave something to be desired by way of accuracy. The final system as a running program provides much stronger guarantees.

In our emphasis on the methodology, we have slighted the psychology. Production systems carry additional psychological implications beyond those already apparent in the problem solving theory we laid out explicitly. We have not discussed them, nor have we discussed the nature of the particular production system we derived. Finally, even assuming we accept a production system as an appropriate way to express the microtheories, we have not explored how these contribute to the more general information processing theory of problem solving.

A final note should be made about the scope of the techniques. Although it is reasonably clear that they apply to tasks involving the exploration of consequences, it is unclear how far they stretch. For example, no evidence is available yet for concept formation tasks, even though some of these have made good use of protocols (Duncker, 1945; Gregg, 1967; Johnson, 1964).

4. Formalisms for knowledge[1]

Terry Winograd

Basic issues of representation

In designing a system for representing knowledge in a computer program, there are a number of issues we must face.

First, we must be concerned with how the system will make use of the representation in *operation*, and in particular we want it to be efficient. We must be concerned with the way the efficiency changes with the amount of knowledge in the system. Some representations are good for small amounts, but explode in an exponential way as more information is added. Other representations are less sensitive to size, and large systems run as efficiently as small ones.

The next issue is *learning* – the addition of new knowledge. It is important that the knowledge be *modular*. We should be able to add new facts without worrying in detail about how they connect with others. The easiest form of learning would take place in a completely independent system where each fact served as its own module. Learning would then be a simple process of accumulation. In any realistic system this is not the case, since we have to be concerned with the interactions between the new piece and the ones that were functioning before. We also want the representation to be *natural*, so that it is easy for a person to add new knowledge. If the format is difficult for people to work with, it makes it harder to put knowledge into the system.

Finally we must be worried about *building* the system. We must choose between complex structure of many parts, or a structure operating in a simple uniform way. There is a trade-off between the complexity of structure and the generality of the system. We would like it to be able to handle as many different kinds of knowledge activities as we can. . .

---

[1] An edited extract of lecture 3 of *Five Lectures on Artificial Intelligence* by Terry Winograd (AI Laboratory, Memorandum AIM no. 240, Stanford University, 1974).

Using a representation

A number of Artificial Intelligence (AI) representations have been developed for use in a variety of problem tasks. This paper will present a number of them and discuss the ways in which they give useful methods of operating on knowledge structures. Figure 1 lists some of the different operations a representation must support to be useful in a system.

> Control:
> > What should I do next?
> Retrieval:
> > What knowledge might I try using?
> Matching:
> > Does it apply? How?
> Application:
> > What can I conclude from it?

Figure 1. Operations of a knowledge-using system

The first question is that of *control*. Given a set of facts and procedures, how does it decide what to do next at any point. There is an obvious trade-off between tight control (which gives efficiency) and a flexible control structure which gives more generality. The more freedom there is in deciding what to do next, the more likely the system is to be able to handle situations not directly anticipated in building it. But this also may involve doing a lot of searching and looking around.

The *retrieval* process involves sorting out large quantities of knowledge to decide which ones are relevant to what is being done. In ordinary programs, this is not an issue. A subroutine is called explicitly, so there is no need to look around at others, or decide whether it is the one to use. In heuristic search, on the other hand, it becomes important to be able to choose a particular set of methods to be tried on a problem. When we try to decide which methods will possibly work, we must use some sort of retrieval mechanism.

The *matching* problem involves looking at a particular method and seeing how it actually fits with the problem. It is more specific than retrieval, which generates plausible choices, in that it is concerned with understanding just how the one chosen interacts with what is being done – how does this program fit with the job at hand, or how does this particular fact answer the question which is being posed.

Finally, we must *use* the resulting match to draw a conclusion or have an effect. This, like the terms above, will become more clearly defined as we go through some examples.

Predicate calculus

Let us begin with a representation from mathematics and formal logic – the predicate calculus. In this system, a small number of possible structure types are used in a very general way to describe knowledge without regard to the particular domain. I will not describe here the details of the formalism, which are available in many places [see Introduction to Part II; McCarthy and Hayes, 1969; Sandewall, 1973].

Simple facts, like 'Fido is a dog', or 'Kazuo owns Fido', are expressed in *atomic* statements like Dog(Fido) and Own(Kazuo, Fido). Quantifiers make it possible to express more complex facts like 'A dog is an animal', or 'Every dog has an owner', as:

$(\forall x)\text{Dog}(x) \supset \text{Animal}(x)$: For any x, if x is a dog then x is an animal.
$(\forall x)\text{Dog}(x) \supset (\exists y)\text{Own}(y,x)$: For any x, if x is a dog then there exists a y such that y owns x.

Through use of a small set of logical manipulations, these facts can be combined to answer questions and solve problems. If we know that Fido is a dog, then the question 'Does anyone own Fido?' might be answered directly if information about his ownership were in system, but, if not, it could still be answered 'Yes', by deducing from the general fact above that he must have some owner. We could derive this in the form of a logical proof of the owner's existence.

There is a straightforward connection between asking questions and finding solutions to problems. It is so simple as to be a trick. Faced with a problem, such as building a certain structure out of blocks, I can phrase a question like 'Is there a series of possible actions whose end result is the desired arrangement?' In order to answer this, the system will usually operate by actually figuring out what the sequence of steps must be. This is not a logical necessity, as it could know that there is a possible sequence on more abstract grounds. However, due to the way the axioms are put into such systems, they can generally only find the proof by constructively working out the sequence of operations. I will use the phrases 'solve problems' and 'answer questions' interchangeably to represent a kind of reasoning operation which begins with a set of facts and procedures, and ends with a desired result.

In using predicate calculus, we must have some way to generate a proof. The system must have some way to decide which fact it should apply, and to see how that fact applies to the question. Faced with 'Does anyone own Fido?' it must decide that the general fact $(\forall x)\text{Dog}(x) \supset (\exists y)\text{Own}(y,x)$ is relevant. It must match the 'x' in that fact to Fido, and must use rules of logic to combine this with the fact Dog(Fido) and draw the necessary conclusion.

In most systems using predicate calculus, this is all done by a *uniform proof procedure* [see Introduction to Part II]. This is a method built into the system for taking a group of axioms and looking for a proof. The methods used can be shown to be complete: if there is enough knowledge in the system to prove something, most theorem provers will eventually get to it. But this is a significant 'eventually'. The demands of generality make these systems inefficient in a combinatorial way. If the number of facts is doubled, the running time is squared.

Retrieval – the decision of what facts to look at next – is not dealt with as a separate problem. Those things which are tried include any facts which might fit in accordance with the rules of logic. There may be heuristics which involve choosing shorter facts first, or the like, but there is nothing in the basic principles of predicate calculus or in the implementation of current systems, corresponding to the human decision of 'What kinds of things seem likely to be most relevant?'

Matching is handled by a process called *unification* which matches objects to variables, in a purely syntactic way.

Finally, the application of any particular fact is to deduce a new fact or to establish a truth or falsity. Each 'step' involves combining some old facts according to rules of logic, either to establish a new one or to find a contradiction.

The advantages of predicate calculus systems are along the dimensions of modularity and generality. Each fact is valid, independent of whatever else is in the system. The notation is explicitly general, not tailored to any particular sort of knowledge. The main problem with this approach is efficiency. All of the systems which have adopted it have been limited to very tiny sets of facts, usually on the order of less than a hundred, and often less than ten. The complexity of such a system depends on how much concern there is for efficiency. In principle, theorem proving could be done with a very simple system, but the ones which have been designed are quite complex due to needs of reducing some of the gross inefficiency.

Along the dimension of naturalness, it is a matter of taste. Some people (usually trained in mathematics) find predicate calculus a very natural way of expressing things, while others find it quite difficult.

Simple programs

A very different sort of representation is the simple form of what we think of as *programs*. In programming there is a separation between *program* and *data*, as opposed to the more uniform representation of predicate calculus. The knowledge of a specific domain will be a combination of special procedures, and specific data. A program which calculates astronomical orbits will contain much of its knowledge about astronomy in the program which performs the calculation, while other knowledge will be in the form of data.

This form of representation implies very different trade-offs. The control is completely explicit. Which piece of knowledge will be called at any particular time is determined in advance by the programmer. If a procedure requires some question to be answered, it contains a specific call to the subroutine which can generate that answer. This is very different from the general sort of retrieval in predicate calculus where any fact which matches the one being looked for may be used by the system, and may be added without explicit programming to call it.

The binding of arguments can be viewed as a kind of matching procedure, where the particular case is put in correspondence with a general formula. A routine says 'For any number x, I know how to square it.' To answer the specific question 'What is the square of 3·14158?' the system *binds* the value 3·14158 to the variable x, then runs the procedure. As a result of applying a procedure, a specific sequence of further procedures might be called as subprocedures.

One of my main goals is to show the ways in which activities like predicate calculus theorem proving and numerical calculation are really doing very much the same thing. Although knowledge that 'All dogs are animals', and 'To square a number multiply it by itself', are represented very differently, they have much in common, and in AI, we are looking for the right specific trade-offs to handle as many kinds of knowledge as possible.

The efficiency of programs is the greatest we could expect. There is no time wasted in deciding what to do next, or trying different possibilities. As programs get larger, as long as they are well structured, they do not lose efficiency, and can include great amounts of specific knowledge. On the other hand, their modularity is often bad. Structured programming is an attempt to get away from this, but in general a change to one subroutine can have far reaching effects on the others that use it. If I have a program which calls a subroutine, and change that program, then when the subroutine is called, the environment may be different from what was anticipated, and this may cause it to fail. Whenever I make changes to one thing, I must worry how it interacts with others.

. . . We can look at programs and formal logic as being at two opposite poles. Programs are efficient at the cost of low generality, while representations like predicate calculus are very general at the cost of low efficiency.

PLANNER-like languages

One of the main developments in AI has been the invention of programming languages which give us some of the benefits of a more flexible representation (see Bobrow and Raphael, 1974). They want to keep the efficiency and runnability of programs, avoiding the problems of general search, while breaking loose from some of the rigidities of program control. One such language is PLANNER (Hewitt, 1972). There is a whole set of PLANNER-like languages, such as: MICRO-PLANNER (Sussman, Winograd, and Charniak, 1972), an implementation of a subset of its ideas; CONNIVER (McDermott and Sussman, 1972) a close descendant of MICRO-PLANNER, and QA4-QLISP (Rulifson, Waldinger, and Dirksen, 1968), a very similar approach developed at the Stanford Research Institute.

The basic idea of these languages includes having a data base of primitive *assertions* much like the simple assertions in a predicate logic system. A simple fact like 'A is on B' is represented in a data structure like: (ON A B). There is then a set of *theorems* representing more complex knowledge, like those in figure 2.

The first theorem says that in order to establish that an object X is on an object Y, establish that X is on some object Z and Z is on Y. This same fact might be represented in a simple logic formalism as:

$$(\forall\, x,y,z)(On(x,z)\ \&\ On(z,y))\ \supset On(x,y)$$

Rather than simply stating that fact, the PLANNER *consequent* theorem states a particular sequence of actions to be taken if there is a goal of establishing the fact (ON X Y). In a natural way, this can be used to describe complicated sequences of actions, as in the second theorem of figure 2. It says that to put X on Y, we need to clear the top of Y, then grasp X, move it to a location on top of Y and let go. I have included this simplified example to illustrate how PLANNER tries to bridge the gap between the program world and the logic world. The first theorem is much like a logical statement – 'If A is true and B is true then C is true.' The second theorem is much more like a program with calls to sub-routines.

```
(CONSEQUENT (X Y Z) (ON ?X ?Y)
    (GOAL (ON ?X ?Z))
    (GOAL (ON ?Z ?Y)))

(CONSEQUENT (X Y) (ON ?X ?Y)
    (GOAL (CLEARTOP ?Y))
    (GOAL (GRASP ?X))
    (GOAL (MOVE-TO ?Y))
    (GOAL (LET-GO-OF ?X)))

(ANTECEDENT (X Y) (ON ?X ?Y)
    (ERASE (CLEARTOP ?Y)))
```

Figure 2. Some theorems in a PLANNER-like language

PLANNER-like languages use *pattern-directed invocation:* rather than calling a subroutine by name, a PLANNER theorem specifies a pattern of the result to be achieved, like (ON A B). The theorems are stored with a special index which can decide which ones match the goal pattern. When a particular goal is set up, the system automatically tries the various theorems which are indexed as being useful for this goal. The theorems of figure 2 would be called for any goal of the form (ON ? ?) where the question marks indicate arbitrary elements. PLANNER also allows explicit recommendations to be added to a goal. They can specify a particular routine, or provide heuristics for choosing among several. If you give specific recommendations, PLANNER operates like any other programming language. If you don't, it provides a very general procedure for searching through all the theorems.

PLANNER also contains *antecedent theorems* which are automatically triggered by the addition of certain assertions to knowledge. The theorem at the bottom of figure 2 says 'If you ever add a fact saying that some object X is on an object Y, then also erase the fact that Y is clear on top.' An antecedent theorem can specify an entire sequence of actions, and call any other sort of theorems in doing it.

. . . The retrieval system for these languages is straightforward. In deciding what theorems are relevant to a goal or new assertion, the system calls on a syntactic pattern–matcher, comparing the form of the new item with the patterns stored in the index. . .

Production systems

Another pattern-based representation is the *production system* developed by Newell and Simon [See Reading 3]. A body of knowledge is represented by a linearly ordered set of rules called *productions* which operate on a *short-term memory* of patterns. These correspond in a loose way to the theorems and assertions of PLANNER. A production rule is very much like a PLANNER antecedent theorem. The action of a production is essentially 'If the patterns in the short-term memory match the indexing pattern of the production, then do the actions specified in the production.' Figure 3 shows the possible contents of short-term memory for a simple blocks world, and a set of productions to work with it. The patterns on the left of the arrow are those that trigger the production, those on the right represent its action.

Short-term memory
(ON A B) (ON B C) (GOAL (ON A C)) (LOCATION C (100 200 100))

Productions
(ON X Y) (ON Y Z) → ADD-TO-STM (ON X Z)
(GOAL(ON X Y)) (ON X Y) → ADD-TO-STM (GOAL-COMPLETE (ON X Y))

Figure 3. A hypothetical production system for the blocks world

There are some important differences between the operation of a production system and a PLANNER-like language. First, the production patterns match against the entire contents of short-term memory, not just a single assertion. Therefore a production can be triggered by a combination of facts in a way which is very awkward for PLANNER. Another important difference is in the way of deciding which production to apply. In PLANNER there are mechanisms for explicitly naming the theorems, for making recommendations for selecting them, and a mechanism which applies by default for doing a complete search. In a production system, there is an ordering built into the productions, and the system uses this permanent ordering to decide which production should be applied in the case that more than one is possible. Most of the work that has been done has used a simple linear ordering of all the productions. Newell and Simon have tried to show how this sort of ordering can explain many aspects of human problem solving. It remains to be seen how it will work for complex problems involving large amounts of knowledge. If it does, it provides a specific compromise between an efficient but inflexible call and a general search.

There is no separate mechanism for retrieval in a production system. The decision of what to try is based on a syntactic match between the patterns in short-term memory and the patterns of the productions. Matching is done in a very simple way (intentionally avoiding the complexities of other matchers in order to remain more plausible as a psychological model). The action of a production is an explicit sequence of operations on the contents of short-term memory. This is different from a PLANNER-like language, in that a production does not directly call another production in the same way that a theorem can call another theorem. All it can do is leave the contents of short-term memory modified in such a way that they will cause other productions to be called when the next round of pattern matching is done.

MERLIN

Another system being developed by Newell is MERLIN (Moore and Newell, 1973). It is in a very early stage of development, and only one paper has been published on it. . . The primary data object in MERLIN is a *beta-structure* like those in figure 4. The first says that a man is an animal, further specified as having a house and a nose. We view each object as an instance of some more general class with some *further specification*. A pig is also an animal, but with different further specification. The basic operation is something called *mapping*. It can be thought of as 'Try to view this object as an instance of that object.' If we ask 'Try to view a man as an animal', MERLIN will answer 'It is one, with a house and a nose.' If we ask 'View a pig as a man', it says 'I can only do that if I view a sty as a house and a snout as a nose.' It then recursively asks 'How can I view a sty as a house.' Presumably sty will have been defined as a 'house for a pig', so this mapping succeeds, and so on.

MAN [ANIMAL: HOUSE NOSE]

PIG [ANIMAL: STY SNOUT]

Figure 4. Beta-structures (Newell)

The details of this operation leave much to be worked out in terms of the selection of elements in the beta-structure for mapping, the control of which will be tried when, and what level will be taken as satisfactory, etc. But what is important is the basic idea that we should think of controlling a problem solving procedure in terms of mapping. We should look at a particular set of facts as an instance of some more general object, and the basic reasoning process involves trying to establish the correspondence in this mapping.

. . . MERLIN says that the fundamental operation is a kind of analogy. One pattern is viewed as representing another pattern, and the analogy must be established between the internal elements of them. The thought process is driven by a kind of inference based on trying to apply a stock of general descriptions to the specific data on hand, and as a result coming out with further specific facts. . .

Semantic nets

Another type of representation used in natural language programs is the *semantic net* (e.g. Quillian, 1968; Rumelhart and Norman, 1973; Simmons, 1973). Nets have been formulated and used in a variety of ways, and I will just try to point out the basic emphasis. They are used to express much of what we might call 'common-sense knowledge'. They are not designed like symbolic logic to express complex formulae and connections, but rather are a natural way of expressing simple relationships. Figure 5 shows a simple net. There is a node for 'dog', and one for 'animal' connected by a link called 'is-a', indicating that a dog is a kind of animal. In the predicate calculus formalism, this fact would be started in a quantified formula: $(\forall x)Dog(x) \supset Animal(x)$. For certain kinds of information, such as the class–subclass hierarchy for types, the net notation is a natural and simple way to describe things.

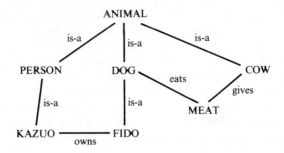

Figure 5. A semantic net

Once the information is in this form, these are two basic operations that can be done on it. One is a simple kind of deduction. If we ask 'Does Fido eat meat?' a system could have a set of procedures for looking at the net, and seeing the two connections 'Fido is a dog', 'Dog eats meat', and answering 'Yes.' The system would have built into it the deduction rules appropriate to the different kinds of links. This sort of mechanism has been proposed as being close to human deductive mechanisms.

The other operation is a kind of search, using intersection in the net. It is used for deciding which links are relevant to what is being asked. If I say something about 'Fido' and 'meat' in the same sentence without explicitly mentioning any connection, this network could be used to find one. We can imagine sending out signals from those two nodes, spreading through the net one link at a time. When two signals intersect, the path between them will be the shortest set of links connecting the two objects – in this case we would find the two link connection 'Fido is a dog', 'Dog eats meat.'

One problem with this search is that it explodes very quickly as the number of links goes up. If the search must extend farther than one or two links, there will be a host of connections, some relevant and others irrelevant. For a node like 'dog' or 'meat', the number of connections may be very large. The ones which will be found depend strongly on the kinds of links allowed, and it is not clear how far a simple network algorithm can be extended into complicated domains.

The other problem is that of expressing more complex facts, like those involving quantifiers [see Woods, 1975]. The fact that 'Every dog is owned by some person' cannot be simply expressed by linking the nodes for 'dog' and 'person', since that would not distinguish it from 'Every person owns a dog' or 'Some people own dogs.' In order to use nets well, we will need to combine their naturalness and simplicity for simple cases with the more extended power of other representations, including the equivalent of variables and quantifiers.

Semantic networks are the only representation I have described which concentrate on the problem of retrieval – how to find the set of facts relevant to a given problem. The others have concentrated much more on how to apply the facts when they are found. The two ideas might well be combined, since the strength of network systems is more in finding connections than in making use of them.

Conclusion

I hope it is clear by this point that there are many issues to be dealt with in choosing a representation for knowledge. We would like to combine the benefits of all of the current approaches. The uniformity or generality of some approaches needs to be combined with the efficiency and simplicity of others. . . . The system must be able to handle both those things whose general nature is best thought of as a procedure and those which are better thought of as a set of independent facts which must be worked on and put together. There are currently many people looking into formalisms which they call *frames* [see Reading 22]. It is important to point out that this does not involve an actual working system, or even a coherently worked out set of ideas. . . The idea is to provide a system with enough facilities to do the things which other representations allow, but to do it within a coherent framework for putting things together. Simple facts are represented in a straightforward declarative way. If specific procedures are called for, there is a way to attach them which allows the control structure to move back and forth between more general and more specific processes without having to pre-decide just how each piece of information will be stored or used. . .

Part II
Deduction

Introduction to deduction

One very special technique in trying to solve certain sorts of problem is deductive inference. A valid deduction is one in which the conclusion follows logically from the premises: if the premises are true, then the conclusion is necessarily true. Logicians from the time of Aristotle have been concerned to formalize deduction, that is, to develop systems of logic in which patterns of valid inference are characterized without regard to their content. They are accordingly concerned with such rules of inference as the following one (known as *modus ponens*):

If p then q

p

_____

∴ q

that yield valid deductions regardless of what actual propositions are substituted for *p* and *q*. There are three main branches of logic: *propositional* logic, *relational* logic, and *quantificational* logic. Propositional logic is concerned with inferences that depend on the interconnections between propositions. It includes such rules of inference as *modus ponens*. Quantificational logic embraces propositional logic but is a more powerful system since it is also concerned with the internal structure of propositions and in particular with deductions based on quantifiers (*all, some, none*, etc.). The simplest sort of quantified inferences are the so-called *syllogisms* such as:

All B are A

Some C and B

_____

∴ Some C are A

which were studied by Aristotle. Relational logic is perhaps the simplest system of the three (it, too, is often incorporated within the quantificational calculus), although its study is a relatively recent phenomenon. It concerns the validity of inferences that hinge on the relational terms within assertions. Thus, a transitive relational term, R, such as *taller than* yields the valid inference schema:

$$xRy$$
$$yRz$$
___
$$\therefore \quad xRz$$

regardless of what x, y, and z denote. As a result of the great growth of logical expertise during the last eighty years, many other systems of symbolic logic have been designed, including an infinite number of modal logics for the notion of *possibility* (see Hughes and Cresswell, 1968), but quantificational logic in its most general form is powerful enough for proving most theorems.

What use is logic in discovering new knowledge? Russell (1927) provides an amusing answer about syllogisms:

> This form of inference does actually occur, though very rarely. The only instance I have ever heard of was supplied by Dr. F. C. S. Schiller. He once produced a comic number of the philosophical periodical *Mind*, and sent copies to various philosophers, among them to a certain German, who was much puzzled by the advertisements. But at last he argued: 'Everything in this book is a joke, therefore the advertisements are jokes.' I have never come across any other case of new knowledge obtained by means of a syllogism. It must be admitted that, for a method which dominated logic for two thousand years, this contribution to the world's stock of information cannot be considered very weighty.

In fact, however, *no* branch of logic is a particularly valuable method of discovery, for a very simple reason: logic does not specify what conclusions, if any, should be drawn from a given set of premises. There are many conclusions that could be validly drawn from even a simple set of premises, but most of them will be extremely trivial, as the following set of conclusions illustrates:

If p then q

p
___

$\therefore$ p & (if p then q)
$\therefore$ p & (p & (if p then q))
$\therefore$ p & (p & (p & (if p then q)))

. . .

etc., *ad infinitum*

The function of logic is to prove that one proposition does indeed follow from others, and the certainty that it provides can make a major contribution to knowledge. Some conclusions are, of course, surprising consequences of the premises from which they follow: particular ingenuity will have to be exercised in order to consider it worthwhile to try to prove them and, perhaps, in constructing the proof itself.

Psychologists have, of course, been interested in their subjects' deductive ability for some considerable time. An investigation of syllogistic inference, for instance, was carried out by Störring as early as 1908. However, as we shall see, there is not much of a consensus about the psychological mechanism underlying deduction or even about so fundamental a matter as whether or not human beings are basically capable of rational inference. Let us review the evidence, beginning with simplest deductions and then moving on to more complex ones.

Perhaps the simplest possible deduction is negation: if the negation of a proposition is true, then that proposition is false. Many of the studies of concept attainment (see Part III) have concerned the role of negative information, and have inspired the investigation of negative inferences. For instance, Margaret Donaldson (1959) showed that in problem-solving negative information is distrusted as 'good currency', and that there is a particular reluctance to derive positive information from it. Similarly, Wason (1959) devised a chronometric technique, the 'verification task', which has been subsequently used in a large number of studies to determine the variables which may make a negative sentence harder to grasp than an affirmative sentence. One problem with the laboratory investigation of negation is that the negative sentences appear out of context – their spontaneous use in this way was taken by Freud (1925) as evidence of a neurotic symptom. When pains are taken in a laboratory setting to use them more appropriately, as correctives to potential misconceptions, their difficulty is much reduced (Wason, 1965). It may often disappear altogether in everyday life. Current models of verification tend to ignore appropriateness (cf. Trabasso, Rollins, and Shaughnessy, 1971; H. H. Clark, 1974; Carpenter and Just, 1975): they might be deemed models of how subjects verify a neurotic's descriptions.

After negation, the next simplest inferences are probably those that hinge on a transitive relation, such as:

> John is shorter than Fred
> John is taller than Charles
> _____
> ∴   Charles is shorter than Fred

Such inferences are known as a 'three-term series problem', or 'linear syllogism'. They have been exploited in intelligence tests, and have recently become the focus of the three main sorts of psychological approach to inference:

1. *Mental operations.* According to this theory reasoning involves some sort of abstract mental operations. Such a view was taken by William James (1890), and received its clearest expression with respect to three-term series problems in Hunter (1957). Hunter argued that the problem above involved two separate operations: first, the second premise must be converted to *Charles is shorter than John,* and second, the two premises must be mentally reordered to yield:

> Charles is shorter than John
> John is shorter than Fred

Like William James, he took the view that once such a canonical set of premises had been constructed, the transitive deduction could easily be made:

> ∴   Charles is shorter than Fred

Hunter's work was ahead of its time, for the three-term series problem was then neglected for a number of years.

2. *Visual imagery.* In 1965, a seminal paper was published by De Soto, London, and Handel. These investigators suggested that individuals solve three-term series problems by combining the premises into a unitary representation which takes the form of a visual image – a plausible supposition. A fundamental point

in their theory is that a premise is easier to represent in the imaginary visual array if its first item occurs as an 'end-anchor', i.e. an item at one end of the visual array rather than in its middle position. Thus, the problem above is difficult because neither premise contains an end-anchor as its first item, unlike the relatively easy problem:

> Arthur is taller than Bill
> Tom is shorter than Bill
>
> ∴ Arthur is taller than Tom

They noted that the terms of some problems tended to be represented vertically such as those using the 'taller–shorter' relation or the evaluative 'better–worse' relation; while others, such as those using the 'lighter–darker' relation, tended to be represented horizontally, However, it has been shown by Sheila Jones (1970) that such preferences are more arbitrary than had originally been supposed. Indeed, individuals tend to work downwards rather than upwards, and from left to right rather than from right to left, but these preferences probably reflect nothing more interesting than occidental reading habits.

3. *Linguistic comprehension.* The third approach to inference has been promulgated most notably by H. H. Clark. He has argued that the relative difficulty of the three-term series problems is due principally to linguistic factors affecting the comprehension of the premises and conclusions, and the semantic congruity between them. This hypothesis led Clark to broaden the range of problems he studied to include those with 'negative equative' premises such as 'Arthur isn't as tall as Bill', and to vary systematically the nature of the putative conclusions to problems.

The three approaches to inference – mental operations, integrated visual images, and linguistic comprehension – are by no means incompatible in principle. However, we have tried to choose 'pure' examples of them in order to bring out their fundamental assumptions with the greatest clarity. The paper we have selected by Huttenlocher presents a rigorous formulation of the 'visual image' theory of three-term series problems. With an ingenious technique she was able to externalize the thought processes assumed to be operative in the solution of such problems. In sharp contrast, the paper by Clark, which follows it, attempts to explain all the phenomena in terms of three linguistic principles. In its ability to explain performance with negative equative sentences, Clark's theory seemed more accurate than Huttenlocher's. However, as Johnson-Laird (1972) pointed out, it is a simple matter to reformulate Huttenlocher's theory by assuming that such negative forms are mentally 'converted' into affirmative expressions. The re-introduction of mental operations seemingly renders the two theories compatible with each other. However, some recent evidence has tended to favour Huttenlocher. For instance, Potts and Scholz (1975) in a series of ingenious experiments, using a technique similar to one developed by Wood and Shotter (1973), withheld the question about the conclusion until subjects had signified they understood the problem. It was found that the time taken to answer an unexpected question suggested that both 'marked' and 'unmarked' adjectives were stored in the same representation – a finding which contradicts the effects of one of Clark's linguistic principles. In a third experiment the time taken to read each premise was recorded, and the results suggested that a critical factor is the congruence between the adjectives used to describe a term, and the appropriate placement of that term in the series. This finding, too, supports the postulation of an integrated mental array in which the terms are ordered. However, Shaver, Pierson, and Lang (1974/5) report wide individual differences in the employment of imagery, and even differences within the same individual at different stages of the task. They suggest that imagery plays a functional (supportive), but not a necessary, role in the solution.

It would seem (with the advantage of hindsight) that the fundamental issue between the theories is not really about differences in the use of mental operations or visual imagery, nor about the relevance of linguistic explanations. It is about whether the two premises of the problem are stored separately, or combined into a unified representation. The critical issue is the integration (or lack of integration) of the terms, and thus the specific way in which knowledge is stored, represented, and accessed in this particular type of problem.

In order to increase the complexity of deductions still further, we must turn to the relations between propositions. The logic of inferences that hinge on such relations is analysed by logicians in the propositional calculus. This is a calculus that treats such relations as *and*, *or*, and *if . . . then*, which are also familiar to computer programmers as Boolean operations.

Piaget and his colleagues have long argued that the attainment of logical maturity in early adolescence, the stage of 'formal operations', corresponds to acquiring a grasp of the propositional calculus (see, for example, Inhelder and Piaget, 1958; Beth and Piaget, 1966). The calculus was first used in investigations of problem solving by Moore and Anderson (1954), and the proofs of theorems within it have been simulated by computer in programs devised by Newell and Simon and their collaborators at Carnegie–Mellon University (see Part i). The ability of logically naive but intelligent adults to make propositional deductions has been much studied, but, before we deal with this work, a word about the calculus itself is in order.

Within the propositional calculus, a proposition has only two possible truth values: it is true, or else it is false. Negation simply changes the truth value of a proposition; and all connectives are defined as functions of the truth values of the propositions they interrelate. Thus, for example, conjunction, &, can be defined by saying that p & q is true if and only if p is true and q is true. These two assumptions drive a wedge between the calculus and ordinary language. If John has no children, one is inclined to say that a statement such as 'All of John's children are asleep' is neither true nor false, but void or irrelevant. Likewise, there is a marked difference between the conjunction:

> She inherited a fortune and he married her.

and its converse:

> He married her and she inherited a fortune.

They are, of course, identical within the propositional calculus which cannot accommodate temporal or causal relations. Connectives are defined solely as a function of the truth values of the constituent propositions they connect. Such 'truth-functional' definitions become most problematic in the case of the calculus's analogue to the conditional (*if—then*) statements of ordinary language. The best translation of a conditional is into a *material implication*, which we shall symbolize ' ⊃'. An assertion of the form $p \supset q$ (roughly speaking, *if p then q*) is defined to be true whenever p is true and q is true. It is defined to be false whenever p is true and q is false. So far, then, it accords with the ordinary interpretation of *if p then q*. But what if p is false? How would you evaluate the following assertion if John has no children?

If John has children, then they are at home.

Once again, such sentences may well be treated as void (see Johnson-Laird and Tagart, 1969; Evans, 1972c); but the propositional calculus allows only two truth values, true or false. A material implication is taken to be true when its antecedent is false.

The propositional calculus can be formalized in a variety of ways, but in most formalizations the fundamental rule of inference is *modus ponens*:

If p then q

p
_____

∴ q

which allows by substitution, for example, the following deduction:

If John is tall, then Charles is short
John is tall
_____

∴ Charles is short

Another rule of inference, *modus tollens*, is often postulated:

If p then q	(If John is tall, then Charles is short)
not-q	(Charles is not short)
_____	_____
∴ not-p	(∴ John is not tall)

although, as we shall see, this rule can be derived from *modus ponens*. There are two fallacies related to the valid patterns of inference. The first fallacy is based on *affirming the consequent* of the conditional:

If p then q

q
_____

∴ p

The second fallacy is based on *denying the antecedent* of the conditional:

If p then q
not-p
_____

∴ not-q

The abilities of adults and children to make the valid deductions and to refrain from committing the fallacies has been much studied (see, e.g. Hill, in Suppes,

1965; Wason and Johnson-Laird, 1972; Staudenmeyer, 1975). The picture that has emerged is not clear-cut: performance is affected by a number of factors including the content of the problems. We have accordingly included the third reading in this section, a specially written paper by Wason, on the somewhat clearer role of self-contradiction in propositional reasoning. Wason shows, for example, that subjects learn to refrain from committing the fallacies if their conclusions lead to a contradiction. He is also concerned with another pattern of inference called *reductio ad absurdum*. This inference is based on assuming some proposition for the sake of argument and deducing a contradiction from it. You are then entitled to infer the negation of what you assumed. We can illustrate a *reductio* by showing how it might be used in order to make the *modus tollens* deduction. Suppose you are given as premises:

1. If the room is occupied then the light is on.
2. The light is not on.

the *reductio* proceeds as follows:

3. Assume: The room is occupied.
4. ∴ The light is on. (by *modus ponens*)
5. ∴ The light is on and the light is *not* on. (this contradiction follows from lines 2 and 4)
6. ∴ The room is not occupied. (by the *reductio* rule)

The *reductio* is, of course, usually employed to prove an hypothesis by assuming its contradictory, and then reducing it to an absurdity. As an illustration, consider Eleanor Rosch's argument in her paper on linguistic relativity in Part VI based on the assumption that word order in a language is a reflection of its underlying metaphysics.

The final step in logical complexity is, for our purposes, the introduction of quantifiers. The quantificational calculus can be formalized in a variety of ways, and it may be instructive to consider for a moment the question of alternative formulations of logic. Logicians distinguish between axioms and rules of inference: the proof of a theorem consists in deriving it from the axioms by using rules of inference. A system may accordingly be formalized with a large number of axioms and a small number of rules of inference, or alternatively, a small number of axioms and a large number of rules of inference. There is a 'trade-off' between the two; and in fact systems of logic have been devised at both extremes. Since human deduction is likely to lie somewhere between the bounds, it will be useful to consider them. An example of a deductive system that contains a great many rules of inference is PLANNER (see Winograd's paper in Part I): any generalization is represented within it, not as an assertion, but as a rule of inference. In other words, general facts are represented as procedures that can be used to make deductions. At the other extreme, there are unified theorem provers which have been developed by workers in Artificial Intelligence. Here, the idea is to develop a standard procedure that can be used to prove any theorem, and to derive any conclusion, in a uniform way. The procedure is typically based on a single rule of inference, the 'resolution' rule (see, e.g. Robinson, 1965). We can best illustrate the way in which a uniform proof procedure works by considering a simple deduction:

1. Percy is a psychopath
2. All psychopaths are neurotic

3. ∴ Percy is a neurotic

The uniform proof procedure has the overall pattern of a *reductio ad absurdum*, but in order to apply the single rule of inference it is necessary to translate the sentences of the putative theorem into a special notation. The first move is to get rid of the quantifiers. Special steps have to be taken in order to eliminate the quantifier *some*, but fortunately this problem does not arise in our example. We simply have to put its assertions into a form in which the predicates precede the terms they modify, and in which the work of *all* is done by variables. The premises are accordingly rewritten as:

1. Psychopath (Percy)
2. If Psychopath (x) then Neurotic (x)

and to them is added the negation of the original conclusion in accordance with the *reductio* plan:

3. Not (Neurotic (Percy))

The second step is to translate all connectives into disjunctions – a method that is feasible within the calculus because its connectives are 'truth-functional' in the sense we defined earlier. Material implications, $p \supset q$, which represents the conditional, is accordingly logically equivalent to the inclusive disjunction, *not-p or q*, and so premise (2) can be rewritten in this form. The standardized notation of the problem is therefore:

1. Psychopath (Percy)
2. Not (Psychopath (x)) or Neurotic (x)
3. Not (Neurotic (Percy))

The final step is to put to work the single rule of inference as often as need be. The 'resolution' rule of inference has the following general form:

A or B
not-A or C

∴ B or C

In other words, whenever a proposition and its negation are found among the statements in a problem, they can be deleted to leave a disjunction of whatever is left. (Obviously, this rule is only valid if all quantifiers have been eliminated, and the only connectives in a problem are disjunctions.) The one complication about applying this rule is that the relevant pair of propositions do not have to consist of one proposition and its literal negation. For example, *Neurotic (x)* and *Not (Neurotic (Percy))* will do – it may help the reader to bear in mind that the variable, *x*, might well take a value equal to Percy, in which case there would be a literal negation. Granted this subtlety, it is clear that *Neurotic (x)* and *Not (Neurotic (Percy))* can be eliminated from the problem by the resolution rule.

This step leaves only:
1. Psychopath (Percy)
2. Not (Psychopath (x))

Once again, these two statements fall within the purview of the resolution rule, and so they too can be eliminated. When everything has been eliminated in this way, the proof is complete – the absurdity of assuming the *negation* of the conclusion-to-be-proved is established. It follows that the original conclusion that Percy is a neurotic is valid.

Resolution theorem provers will always eventually find a proof for any valid deduction. However, there is and can be no general algorithm for establishing that a quantified deduction is invalid. An attempt to prove a theorem may go on for a very long time and there is no way of knowing whether it will ever stop. Only if the theorem is valid, will it ultimately yield a proof. It is therefore important to cut down the time to prove valid theorems, and the problem is to find the best way of eliminating propositions and their negations; a number of heuristics have been devised to help to speed up the search (see Meltzer, 1973).

Human beings are most unlikely to make deductions by way of a uniform proof procedure, yet they are not totally dependent on content to make deductions. Hence, it would seem that they possess certain rules of inference applicable to any sort of materials. The fact that adults perform competently with *modus ponens*, but rather less well with *modus tollens*, suggests that for many people the latter is not a well-entrenched pattern of inference – it may well, as we have suggested, be based on a *reductio*. However, such evidence is only suggestive and there is no definitive technique for establishing the *rules* of inference that an individual possesses.

The introduction of quantifiers leads to a logic of great power and for which there can be no algorithmic procedure for evaluating theorems as valid or invalid. However, the complexities of the quantificational calculus are seldom matched by inferences in everyday life. The lowly syllogism, for which there is an algorithmic decision procedure, is a more likely mirror of mundane deduction:

> All trains from this platform go to Uxbridge.
> All trains that go to Uxbridge stop at Ickenham
> _____
> ∴ All trains from this platform stop at Ickenham

It is sometimes claimed that syllogisms are highly artificial deductions, and that psychologists should study real-life inferences rather than artificial ones; hence psychologists should not study syllogisms. This argument is self-refuting . . . it is itself a syllogism. It is the regulated language and formal way in which the syllogisms are laid out which tends to persuade psychologists that they are artificial. Notwithstanding Russell's joke, their occurrence is common enough in ordinary discourse if you look beneath its surface. Indeed, whenever an appeal is made to a general principle in order to evaluate a particular instance, the argument has the underlying form of a syllogism (e.g. All American electrical appliances run on 110 volts; This is an American electrical appliance; ∴ It runs on 110 volts).

Psychologists have known for a long time that ordinary individuals are prone to err in evaluating putative conclusions to syllogisms. There is a division of opinion about the cause. Some psychologists have argued that the phenomenon is a reflection of a temporary lapse, distraction, or seduction by the content (or lack of it) in the deduction, and that man is fundamentally capable of rational thought (see, e.g. Henle, 1962). Other theorists have – at least implicitly – taken a bleaker view of the layman's logical competence, and, once again, different theories tend to stress the importance of mental operations, linguistic factors, or integrated internal representations.

An early explanation of performance in evaluating syllogisms stressed the importance of their linguistic character. Woodworth and Sells (1935) argued that the global impression of the form of the premises created an 'atmosphere effect' that predisposed subjects to accept conclusions congruent with the global impression. Thus, the premises:

> Some Greeks are men
> Some Greeks are clever

may lead to the invalid deduction:

> Some men are clever.

This conclusion is true, no doubt; the point is that it does not follow logically from the premises. The principles of the 'atmosphere effect' have been formulated succinctly (Begg and Denny, 1969):

(1) Whenever at least one premise is negative, the most frequently accepted conclusion will be negative.
(2) Whenever at least one premise contains the quantifier, *some,* the most frequently accepted conclusion will contain it, too.

When neither principle applies, the most frequently accepted conclusion will accordingly be affirmative and contain the quantifier *all*. Clearly, such a theory either presupposes some underlying deductive ability or else assumes that human beings make superficial linguistic matches between premises and conclusions rather than real deductions. The evidence in favour of the theory is by no means secure: some studies have failed to support it (Ceraso and Provitera, 1971; Mazzocco, Legrenzi, and Roncato, 1974).

An alternative approach to the explanation of errors in syllogistic inference relies on the idea of mental operations analogous to those postulated by Hunter (1957) for the three-term series problem. Chapman and Chapman (1959) have argued that there is a tendency to *convert* premises. This operation sometimes results in a valid, and sometimes an invalid, inference: 'All A are B' does not mean the same thing as 'All B are A', but 'No A are B' does mean the same thing as 'No B are A.' The Chapmans also postulated a further source of error: there is a tendency to accept that entities with a predicate in common are *probably* the same sort of thing. In the past, both invalid conversion and this common-predicate fallacy have been treated as typical 'thought disorders' of schizophrenics (see, for example, von Domarus, 1944; Matte-Boanco, 1965). Thus, a patient is said to argue:

Nuns dress alike
Those twins dress alike

∴ Those twins are nuns

because of the predicate common to nuns and twins. It is ironic that such features of thought are postulated to explain errors of reasoning made by ordinary subjects in the laboratory.

Although Revlis (1975) has recently developed explicit models of both the 'atmosphere' theory and the 'conversion' theory, the first model to embody the notion of an integrated representation of the premises was proposed by Erickson (1973). His model postulates three main stages in making an inference. In the first stage, the premises are given a mental representation isomorphic to so-called 'Euler' circles. Thus, for example, a premise of the form, 'No A are B', would be represented by two non-overlapping circles, one denoting the set A, and the other denoting the set B. A premise of the form, 'All A are B', necessitates two alternative representations: it can mean that set A is included with set B (one circle included within the other), or it can mean that set A is co-extensive with set B (one circle coincident with the other). A premise of the form, 'Some A are B', requires four separate representations! In fact, Erickson assumes that subjects usually fail to consider all the possible representations of a premise. They often, for example, treat 'All A are B' as meaning simply that set A is coextensive with set B, a failing that gives rise to exactly the same errors as an illicit conversion. Erickson makes the further simplifying assumption that in combining the representations of the premises, stage 2 of the process, subjects fail to consider all the combinatorial possibilities and, indeed, consider only one such combination. Finally, in stage 3, they select an answer that is compatible with the combined representation *and* the 'atmosphere' hypothesis.

Before we consider one further approach to syllogisms, let us briefly recapitulate their orthodox logical description. The premises and conclusion of any syllogism must be expressed in one of the following *moods*:

All A are B
Some A are B
No A are B
Some A are not B

Consider the simplest type of syllogism:

All men (B) are mortal (A)
All Greeks (C) are men (B)

∴ All Greeks (C) are mortal (A)

It is a necessary condition that the two terms in the conclusion (C are A) be related through the middle term (B) which occurs in both premises. There are four orthodox *figures* in which such a relation can be achieved.

B – A	A – B	B – A	A – B
C – B	C – B	B – C	B – C
∴ C – A	∴ C – A	∴ C – A	∴ C – A

Since there are 64 (4 × 4 × 4) possible moods and four figures it is supposed in logic that there are 256 (4 × 64) possible syllogisms. However, as Johnson-Laird points out in Reading 8, there are really twice that number because the order of the premises can be reversed. Indeed, this variable turned out to have an important effect on performance.

The model proposed by Johnson-Laird combines aspects of all three of the approaches to reasoning. Its distinctive features, however, are that the information in a premise is assumed to be represented in terms of arbitrary numbers of members of the relevant classes, and that it contains a heuristic for forming putative conclusions from the combination of such representations. Such a heuristic goes beyond mere logic, which never determines which particular conclusion should be drawn, but a logical component is incorporated in the form of a number of falsifying tests of putative conclusions. According to the model, rational performance depends on carrying out all the falsifying checks and hence it is assumed to be within the competence of the intelligent layman.

We have so far considered the ability to evaluate and to make deductions. An important higher-order skill is the deductive testing of hypotheses, rules, or generalizations. We shall have more to say about hypotheses in Part IV. Here, we want to discuss how they are evaluated. This has been investigated using a deceptively simple 'selection task' devised by Wason. In essence, it presents subjects with the problem of determining what potential evidence would be relevant to establishing the truth or falsity of a hypothesis. Reading 9 in this Part presents a summary of some of the initial findings from experiments using this task, and attempts to account for them in terms of a bias towards considering only items explicitly mentioned in the hypothesis, and a bias towards verifying it rather than falsifying it. Such biases can be very strong and, as Wason shows in the reading on self-contradiction, subjects in the selection task sometimes evade the force of contradictions that they have been led into by an erroneous performance. Reading 9 concludes with a brief postscript about alternative explanations of the findings, and the very striking improvement in performance when the hypothesis-to-be-tested has an everyday or realistic content. In a pioneering study of syllogisms, Wilkins (1928) found that presentation with a sensible content generally diminished their difficulty. It is worth remarking that when we reanalysed Wilkin's data, we found instances where the realistic content had also led subjects into error. The interaction of content and form is a major theme of Wason and Johnson-Laird (1972).

The investigations of the 'selection task' have revealed phenomena that appear to be incompatible with Piaget's theory of the growth of intelligence: the young adolescent is supposed to have a logical competence that can be modelled by the propositional calculus. Performance should accordingly be unaffected by the content of problems, and reflect only their logical structure. As we understand the theory of 'genetic epistemology', Piaget conceives of thought as essentially internalized action, and the development of intelligence occurs through a number of well-defined, invariant stages. For example, one important transition is between the 'pre-operational period' and the 'concrete operational period'. In the pre-operational period thinking is *syncretic* – unrelated events or items are grouped into a confused whole; it is *centred* – the child focuses on one particular item or dimension of a stimulus array at a time; it is *irreversible* – there is an inability to consider a series of reverse operations that will restore an original situation. In the period of concrete operations, however, all these operations become available. He can now seriate a number of items in terms of a dimension, and he can demonstrate that he understands the meaning of relational terms like 'longer' or 'darker'. What he still cannot do, however, is to carry out operations upon operations. He is still tied to the concrete; he cannot reason in a hypothetico-deductive way. During the final state of 'formal operations' the adolescent is capable of solving a problem by using a combinatorial analysis of its variables within a framework corresponding to the propositional calculus, i.e. he can consider combinations of the variables systematically in order to see their effects so that the 'real' is just one among many possibilities. And this is not done in a trial-and-error way but in accordance with a principle. In fact, Inhelder and Piaget (1958) show how the adolescent can solve a number of miniature scientific problems in a strikingly mature way. In *The Principles of Genetic Epistemology* (1972, p. 46), Piaget summarizes the stages of formal operations: 'Here knowledge transcends reality itself, relating it within the possible and the necessary; thus dispensing with the concrete as intermediary.' His view has been repeated in a number of educational textbooks devoted to Piaget: 'Finally, to say that cognition is relatively independent of concrete reality is to say that the *content* of a problem has at last been subordinated to the *form* of relations within it' (Phillips, 1969).

Piaget's empirical discoveries are often striking. His theories have often exerted a strong aesthetic appeal. But he is not without his critics. Some of his findings have been revised in the light of better controlled experiments. The theory of 'genetic epistemology' has been criticized on the grounds of obscurity and incoherence. Most recently, Fodor (1976) has argued that it is difficult to see how sheer experience can lead to a growth in the *logical* power of the intellect. Despite all these criticisms – including our own – it is important for the psychologist to become acquainted with Piaget's ideas. As our final reading in this Part, we have selected a recent and little-known paper in which Piaget himself presents a radical dilution of the original theory; the idea of formal operations is now assumed to be operative within particular thematic contents appropriate to the individual. The abstract (deleted from the reading) shows just how far the theory has been modified: 'it is best to test the young person in a field which is relevant to his career and interests'. The date of this paper, 1972, coincides with that of the criticism of formal operations which was forced upon us by our own experiments (Wason and Johnson-Laird, 1972). Instead of being read as criticism our research can now be read as empirical corroboration of Piaget's somewhat discrepant insight.

5. Constructing spatial images: a strategy in reasoning[1]

Janellen Huttenlocher

When someone is asked for the tallest of three men *John, Sam,* and *Tom,* given that *Tom is taller than Sam* and *John is shorter than Sam,* he will pause and the probably choose Tom. There are eight alternative ways to present the same information about the order of the three men; for example, one might have said that *Sam is taller than John* and *Sam is shorter than Tom.* The time required to answer questions about the order of the three items and the probability of error depend on the form of presentation. The order of difficulty of the alternative forms is the same for most people.

This paper presents an explanation of how people solve such problems (commonly called three-term series problems). We will consider both the form people use to represent to themselves the order of the three items and the intellectual operations they carry out to achieve this representation from the two premises they are given.

. . . The Ss (subjects) describe their strategy as follows: First, they say, they arrange the two items given them in the first premise. Sometimes Ss describe this array as horizontal and sometimes as vertical. For vertical arrays, Ss claim that they start 'building' at the top and work towards the bottom. For horizontal arrays they claim to start at the left and work towards the right. Sometimes Ss report that they place the item mentioned first, the grammatical subject of the premise, to the top or to the left, and then label the axis correspondingly; for example, for 'Sue is less pretty than Ann', S might place Sue first, and thus prettier would proceed towards the bottom or the right. Sometimes, however, Ss report that the poles of the axis are definitely fixed in their minds: for example, taller to the top. When the poles are fixed and the premise describes the bottom or right end of the axis, as in 'John is shorter than Sam', Ss report that they first place the item mentioned last (Sam) at the left or top. After creating such a spatial array from the first premise, Ss consider the second premise. Even though the premise is a relational statement like the first, Ss do not report making a spatially ordered pair from its items. Rather, the analysis of the second

[1] Excerpts from the paper in *Psychological Review*, **75** (1968), 550–60.

premise is contingent on the analysis of the first; the goals are to identify the third item and to determine its position with respect to the other two items.

The Ss' introspections about their strategy guide the present attempt to describe how people actually solve these problems. . .

Arranging real objects to correspond to verbal descriptions

Consider the following study where children had to place differently coloured blocks in a five-shelf ladder to correspond to descriptions like 'The red block is on top of the green block' (Huttenlocher and Strauss, 1968). The procedure was as follows: Two differently coloured blocks (A_1 and A_2 for the top and bottom blocks respectively) were placed in the two centre shelves of the ladder. A third block (B) was placed alongside the ladder, and S was asked to put it in the ladder so that it corresponded to a relational statement which indicated whether B should be above or below the two fixed blocks. There were two alternative ways of describing B's relation to A_1 and A_2 in each case; (1) if B went on top, either (a) 'B is on top of A_1', or (b) 'A_1 is under B'; (2) if B went underneath, either (a) 'B is under A_2', or (b) 'A^2 is on top of B.'

This task may be regarded as a concrete form of the three-term series problem. Instead of starting with a first premise describing the relation between A_1 and A_2, however, the experimenter (E) placed the first two blocks himself, in order to evaluate separately the relative difficulty of the four alternative possible second premises, 1a, 1b, 2a, and 2b. Given that the first premise could have described the relation between A_1 and A_2 in two alternative ways (either 'A_1 is on top of A_2' or 'A_2 is under A_1'), this would make eight possible combinations of premises which correspond to the eight sequences in table 1. The E's statement described B either as grammatical subject (as in 1a and 2a) or as grammatical object (as in 1b and 2b). B's grammatical status markedly affected the difficulty of completing the pile of blocks; when B was described as grammatical object, there were many more errors, and correct placements took longer.

Table 1. Eight alternative ways to order three items (x, y, and z) using two relational statements

1A $x > y$, $y > z$	1B $z < y$, $y < x$
2A $x > y$, $z < y$	2B $z < y$, $x > y$
3A $y > z$, $x > y$	3B $y < x$, $z < y$
4A $y > z$, $y < x$	4B $y < x$, $y > z$

Note. The symbols $>$ and $<$ apply to any pair of relational terms indicating direction along some dimension; e.g. 'taller–shorter'; 'better–worse.'

B's grammatical status had similar effects with only one fixed block. The next experiment (also reported in Huttenlocher and Strauss, 1968) was identical to the first, except that only one block was fixed in the ladder. There were four alternative ways to describe the relation between the mobile block (B) and the fixed block (A) corresponding to the four types of statement above (read A where either A_1 or A_2 appear). Again, there were significantly more errors and longer latencies when the mobile block was described as grammatical object. We proposed the following explanation for this phenomenon: Comprehension requires a correspondence between the form of a linguistic expression and the situation it describes. In particular, the active element (here, the mobile block) is naturally described as the grammatical subject of a simple statement. It was harder to place the mobile block when it was described as grammatical object because S had to carry out mental operations to create a correspondence between the mobile block and the grammatical subject; namely, to transform E's statement by exchanging subject and object and reversing the relational term. Evidence for this proposal was found in Ss' spontaneous comments; e.g. given a mobile green block and the statement 'The red block is on top of the green block', S might say, 'Oh, you mean the green block goes under the red one.'

Given only these experiments, the proposed explanation is speculative. In an active statement, the grammatical subject ordinarily describes an actor; e.g. 'The dog chased the cat', 'The boy hit the ball.' Such statements also have a passive form where the described recipient of the action (logical object) is the grammatical subject, and the described actor (logical subject) is the grammatical object; e.g. 'The cat was chased by the dog', 'The ball was hit by the boy.' A relational statement, however, has no described actor in the usual sense; it merely indicates the relative positions of two items along some dimension. Such statements have no passive form: either term can serve equally well as grammatical subject if the relational term is adjusted appropriately. Our proposal is that S assigns the role of actor to the grammatical subject of these relational statements, and that comprehension requires that this described actor correspond to the perceived actor. The argument would be strengthened if the comprehension of ordinary active statements, where the grammatical subject does describe an actor, also proves easier when there is a correspondence between the grammatical subject and the perceived actor. In addition, the passive form of such statements could be used to test whether comprehension is easier when perceived actor and described actor correspond, even when the temporal position of the described actor in the statement is varied.

In the next experiment (Huttenlocher, Eisenberg, and Strauss, 1968) one truck could 'push' or 'pull' another by being placed, respectively, behind or in front of it. One truck (A) was fixed in the centre of a three-part board, and S had to place the other (B) with respect to it so as to correspond to one of the following descriptions: (1) 'B is pushing (pulling) A', (2) 'A is pushing (pulling) B', (3) 'B is pushed by (pulled by) A', (4) 'A is pushed by (pulled by) B.' The results supported our interpretation. For active statements, (1) and (2), as for relational statements, it was easier to place the mobile truck when it was described as logical-grammatical subject (1). For passive statements, (3) and (4), it was easier to place the mobile truck when it was logical subject-grammatical object (4).

Thus, it is easier to place an item with respect to one or more fixed items according to a verbal description when the described actor corresponds to the perceived actor. For relational statements, Ss apparently assign the role of actor to the grammatical subject, even though this term does not describe an actor in the usual sense. When correspondence between perceived and described actor is lacking, we have proposed, Ss must carry out mental operations to achieve such a correspondence in order to understand the statement. We have suggested (see Huttenlocher, Eisenberg, and Strauss, 1968), however, that these mental operations differ for relational statements and for statements which describe one item acting on another.

Implications for three-term series problems

When Ss introspect about their strategy, they claim that they first imagine arranging the two items from the first premise, and next imagine placing the third item with respect to these 'fixed' items, according to the description in the second premise. If the construction of these imagined arrays parallels the construction of actual arrays, the difficulty of the second premise should depend on the grammatical status of the third item; that is, if determining the position of the third item relative to the other two in these problems is like placing a real mobile item relative to fixed items, the third item would best be described as the subject of the relational term.

The principle of end-anchoring in reasoning states that it is easier to understand a premise that 'proceeds from an end toward the middle rather than from the middle toward an end'. An alternative formulation is that it is easier to understand a premise that describes an end item as grammatical subject rather than grammatical object. The equivalence of these two formulations can be seen by examining those sequences of premises which completely define the order of the three items (there are sequences which do not completely define an ordering; e.g. x > y, y < z). In a determinate sequence, each premise compares one end item to the middle item; the middle item thus appears in both premises (in table 1, y is always the middle item). The third item is that end item which is compared to the middle item in the second premise; when it is described as grammatical subject, the second premise 'proceeds from an end'. Thus, if Ss' introspections about constructing imaginary spatial arrays are accurate, an end-anchoring effect would occur in the second premise. This interpretation of end-anchoring thus explains the differential difficulty of alternative forms of the problem as a direct result of Ss' strategy of constructing imaginary spatial arrays.

The two experiments below provide additional evidence that Ss' mental operations in determining the position of the third item in these reasoning problems does indeed parallel their mental operations in determining the place of a real item in a spatial array from a verbal description.

Experiment I

Method

The Ss forty-eight Harvard and Radcliffe undergraduates were given three-term series problems which compared people by height. The form of presentation was modified so the difficulty of the second premise could be evaluated separately from that of the first. Ordinarily, the entire problem is either read by E or printed out for S to read. Here, presentation of the two premises was broken up by testing S following the first premise to make sure he understood it before the second premise was presented.

Design and procedure. Let us call the three people in each problem A_1 and A_2 (for the taller and shorter people described in the first premise, respectively) and B (for the third person, who is described in the second premise). The relation between A_1 and A_2 was described in one of two ways: either (1) "A_1 is taller than A_2', or (2) 'A_2 is shorter than A_1.' After the first premise, S was asked either 'Who is taller?' or 'Who is shorter?' After answering one of these questions, he was asked the other. The second premise described the relation between B and either A_1 or A_2 in one of four ways: In two, B was grammatical subject, (1) 'B is taller than A_1', or (2) 'B is shorter than A_2'; in the other two, B was grammatical object, either (3) 'A_1 is shorter than B', or (4) 'A_2 is taller than B.' After the second premise, S was asked either 'Who is tallest?' or 'Who is shortest?' Latencies were recorded from the end of the second premise until S responded. The two possible ways of stating the first premise, taken together with the four possible ways of stating the second, make eight premise combinations, corresponding to those in table 1.

Table 2. Percentage of errors and mean reaction time in experiment I when third item (B) was subject versus object of the relational term in the second premise

Item	Percentage of errors	Mean reaction time (for correct responses in centiseconds)
B as subject		
(2A) A_1 taller A_2, B shorter A_2	10	141
(2B) A_2 shorter A_1, B taller A_1	9	142
(3A) A_1 taller A_2, B taller A_1	11	135
(3B) A_2 shorter A_1, B shorter A_2	8	142
Overall mean with B as subject	10	140
B as object		
(1A) A_1 taller A_2, A_2 taller B	17	155
(1B) A_2 shorter A_1, A_1 shorter B	14	161
(4A) A_1 taller A_2, A_1 shorter B	19	157
(4B) A_2 shorter A_1, A_2 taller B	18	157
Overall mean with B as object	17	158

Note. The problem type from table 1 is indicated in parentheses before each premise combination below; taller $=>$ shorter $=<$.

Results

The results are shown in table 2. There were fewer errors for all premise combinations with B as grammatical subject (10 per cent overall) than grammatical object (17 per cent overall) of the second premise ($p < 0.01$ using a Wilcoxon signed-ranks test). Similarly, latencies of correct responses were shorter for all premise combinations with B as grammatical subject (140 centiseconds overall) than as grammatical object (158 centiseconds overall) of the second premise ($p < 0.01$ using a Wilcoxon signed-ranks test). The results were entirely comparable to those in the block experiments where S placed a mobile block with respect to fixed blocks according to E's relational statement, thus supporting S's claims about constructing spatial images.

Experiment II

  Method

For real spatial arrays, we investigated how comprehension of passive statements was affected by the grammatical status of the mobile item in E's description; comprehension was easiest when the perceived actor corresponded to the described actor (logical subject), even if the described actor was the grammatical object. If S treats the items in the three-term series problems as real objects, then, analogous to the truck experiment, a passive second premise should be easier when the third item (described actor) is grammatical object rather than grammatical subject. This issue cannot be investigated with ordinary three-term series problems because relational statements have no passive form. However, some verbs with a passive form do describe a transitive ordering; e.g. consider a race where one runner may 'lead' or 'be led by' another, or may 'trail' or 'be trailed by' another. The present experiment involved problems describing such races with three runners. The form of presentation was modified as in experiment I, so the difficulty of the second premise could be evaluated separately from that of the first.

  Subjects. The Ss were fifty-six students at Teachers College, Columbia University; they ranged in age from approximately 22 to 45 years.

  Design and procedure. The design and procedure were like those in experiment 1, except that there were four instead of two alternative forms for the first premise, and eight instead of four alternative forms for the second premise, because each premise had a synonymous passive form. As above the two people described in the first premise are called A_1 and A_2 (for the one who is ahead and the one who is behind, respectively) and the third person, described in the second premise, B. After the first premise, S was asked 'Who is ahead?' or 'Who is behind?' Of the eight possible second premises, four were active; in two, B was grammatical and logical subject: (1) 'B is leading A_1', and (2) 'B is trailing A_2'; in two, B was grammatical and logical object: (3) 'A_2 is leading B', and (4) 'A_1 is trailing B.' The remaining four were passive; in two, B was grammatical subject and logical object: (5) 'B is led by A_2', and (6) 'B is trailed by A_1'; and in two, B was grammatical object and logical subject: (7) 'A_1 is led by B', and (8) 'A_2 is trailed by B.' After the second premise S was asked either 'Who is first?' or 'Who is last?' Latencies were recorded from the end of the question until S responded. The Ss were given thirty-two problems, one of each of the thirty-two types. All problems used boys' names.

  Results

The results are shown in table 3. . . . Differences in errors for the four different types of problems were significant using a Friedman two-way analysis of variance ($p < 0.01$). Differences in latencies for the four different types of problems were also significant using a Friedman two-way analysis of variance ($p < 0.01$).

Table 3. Percentage of errors and mean reaction time in experiment II when third item (B) was logical subject versus logical object in active and passive second premises

Item	Percentage of errors	Mean reaction time
B as grammatical-logical subject		
B leading (trailing) A	5	139
B as grammatical-logical object		
A $(1, 2)$ leading (trailing) B	10	138
B as grammatical object-logical subject		
A $(1, 2)$ led by (trailed by) B	8	144
B as grammatical subject-logical object		
B led by (trailed by) A $(1, 2)$	18	214

Problem difficulty, as indexed by errors, depended on both (a) the grammatical status of the mobile item, B, in the premise, and (b) the grammatical form of the premise. Active premises were easier when B was described as subject than object. Passive premises were easier when B was described as the logical subject even though in this case it was the grammatical object. Passive premises were harder than corresponding active ones (probably reflecting the greater difficulty of identifying the logical subject from the grammatically more complex passive premises).

Problem difficulty, as indexed by latencies of correct responses, was greatest when B was grammatical subject-logical object of a passive premise, and virtually identical under the other three conditions. Latencies in the truck experiment, where errors were rare, paralleled errors in the present experiment.

As predicted then, both errors and latencies were greater for passive premises when B was logical object-grammatical subject than *vice-versa*, suggesting that S does indeed imagine A_1, A_2, and B as real objects to be arranged in space. As in the truck experiment, this difference is taken as evidence that S must create a correspondence between perceived actor and logical subject in order to understand where B goes.

Discussion

The evidence clearly supports Ss' claims that they construct imaginary arrays to solve three-term series problems. Let us review the mental operations involved. First, S arranges the items described in the first premise, starting at the top or left of his imaginary space. If the relational term describes a dimension to which he assigns a particular orientation, this determines which item he places first. For other dimensions, S starts with the item mentioned first, the grammatical subject. Where the orientation of the axis is fixed, S places the top or leftmost item first even if it is not mentioned first; this makes placement harder, Ss claim and De Soto, London, and Handel's (1965) evidence agrees. The reason may be that S transforms the premise so as to place the subject term first, but the matter requires further study. After constructing an array from the first premise, S uses the second premise to add the third item to his construction. The situation, as S imagines it, is like that in the first block experiment; two items are fixed, and one mobile item must be placed according to a verbal description (here, the second premise). When the mobile item is the grammatical object, S transforms the relational statement, exchanging subject and object, and reversing the relational term, so the mobile item becomes the grammatical subject. The mental work required to bring about this correspondence is reflected in an end-anchoring effect in the second premise.

Thus far, the end-anchoring effect in the first premise has not been examined. This effect is consistent with the proposed strategy, although no such striking explanation can be given as for the second premise effect. The first premise is end-anchored if its subject describes an end item in the total set of three items; this depends on the second premise, which indicates the position of the third item (B). B goes either to (1) the bottom or right or (2) the top or left, of the first pair. One would expect (1) to be easier than (2) if one assumes that S works downward or to the right on the first pair because this direction is easiest for him.

Consider how B's position affects the first pair, in particular, the top or left member of that first pair (which we will call TL). When B goes to the bottom or right, TL is an end item; when B goes to the top or left, TL is the middle item. Given that TL is an end item when B goes to the bottom or right, and that it is easiest to put B at the bottom or right, a problem should be easier when TL is an end rather than a middle item. TL is usually described as grammatical subject, and therefore one would obtain a first premise end-anchoring effect. TL is only described as grammatical object when the first premise proceeds from the wrong end of a fixed axis (e.g. for 'better-worse', S starts with 'better' at the top: thus for 'x is worse than y', TL is y, the object). Such problems should be harder, rather than easier, when the first premise is end-anchored. For problems with axes which some Ss fix one way and some the opposite way, there should be no first premise end-anchoring effect. Problems in experiment I ordered people by height; most people lay out this dimension horizontally, but they vary as to which pole (taller or shorter) goes to the left and which to the right. There was no first premise end-anchoring effect in experiment I; problem difficulty depended only on the end-anchoring of the second premise. The results thus support the proposed explanation; however, the procedural variation introduced in this experiment, breaking up the two premises, may have been the critical factor instead.

The Ss are satisfied that they understand the meaning of these sequences of premises when they have created from them a spatial array of items along a directionally marked axis. They attribute their mistakes to difficulties in constructing accurate arrays, not to difficulties in obtaining answers from them. Such spatial arrays do provide a satisfactory form of representation, since they preserve the information given in the premises.

. . . Rather than making spatial arrays from these imaginary objects, S could have indicated their order by marking each item, for example, by varying the height of items in taller–shorter problems. Some Ss did this, but only on the very first problems, and even then, in conjunction with spatial ordering. The construction of spatial images in these problems parallels the procedure of arranging real objects spatially according to some dimension which will enable S to retrieve the objects; for example, clothing shops arrange dresses by size, books are alphabetized, etc. Such rules of correspondence between spatial and nonspatial dimensions enable one to find particular items without hunting through an entire collection, and preserve order without requiring that items be individually marked. It is therefore not suprising that Ss use spatial arrays to represent order, and that randomly arranged collections are not ordinarily regarded as ordered, even if individual items are marked.

The Ss easily assign spatial axes to nonspatial dimensions in these reasoning problems just as they easily arrange real objects along various nonspatial dimensions. The Ss report that they need not give themselves explicit instructions about the spatial positions of the items, but rather have an implicit sense of the spatial orientation of the dimension, just as when they arrange real objects. These introspections are probably accurate, since problems which are laid out left to right are frequently easier than those using the terms 'left' and 'right' (see De Soto, London, and Handel, 1965).

The S's strategy for constructing these arrays is not simply an internalization of a single type of activity; it blends imaginary use of written symbols with imaginary manipulation of objects. The Ss represent items as words (or abbreviations) rather than pictures, but they do not imagine having to write out these words. Instead, each word 'appears' as E reads it, and S then treats it as a material object which can be picked up and moved. The S constructs arrays in the direction in which he reads and writes, downward and to the right, not in the direction in which he builds with real objects, from the bottom up.

This strategy is most economical, requiring no new procedures beyond S's ability to carry out already familiar activities in his imagination, and to use spatial images rather than real arrays to answer questions about order. By representing individual items as words, S can apply this strategy with equal ease to any ordering problems regardless of how abstract the categories being compared. Ironically, however, Ss are ashamed of this strategy; with what seems more than ordinary human perversity, they regard their spatial imagery as an intellectual crutch, unseemly for the solution of formal reasoning problems.

6. Linguistic processes in deductive reasoning[1]

H. H. Clark

Deductive reasoning has often been studied in particular types of reasoning problems. The strategies suggested for their solution have therefore often been of limited generality: they apply in one kind of problem and that kind alone. The present paper proposes, instead, that reasoning is accomplished mainly through certain very general linguistic processes, the same mental operations that are used regularly in understanding language. Furthermore, the present paper demonstrates in several experiments that these processes, rather than the strategies proposed in the past, correctly account for the difficulties in a variety of reasoning problems.

When a person has comprehended a sentence, he is said to 'know what it means'. It is this knowledge that is at the heart of the theory developed here. The theory specifies in part both the form this knowledge takes in memory and the process by which it is later retrieved for other purposes. Knowledge of this kind is presumed to be quite abstract. Thus, to answer a question about the content of a sentence, one must know more than the phonological shape of the sentence: one must have come to an interpretation of it. The distinction here is the same as that in the linguistic concepts of 'surface' and 'deep' structure (Chomsky, 1965; Postal, 1964). The surface structure of a sentence is the structure which allows it to take on phonological shape; but it is the more abstract deep structure which is necessary for its interpretation. The abstract entities one is presumed to know after interpreting a sentence, then, are closely related to certain linguistic facts about deep structure and the lexicon. And it is at this abstract level that a search for previous information is carried out.

For their study of reasoning, many investigators (Burt, 1919; De Soto, London, and Handel, 1965; Donaldson, 1963; Handel, De Soto, and London, 1968; Hunter, 1957; Huttenlocher, Reading 5) have chosen the so-called three-term series problem, which consists of two propositions and a question, e.g. *If John is better than Dick, and Pete is worse than Dick, then who is best?* The wording of these problems is critical. In all past studies, for example, the above problem has

[1] Excerpts from the paper in *Psychological Review*, **76** (1969), 387–404.

been easier than the following one: *If Dick is worse than John, and Dick is better than Pete, then who is best?* The difference occurs even though both problems present exactly the same information, at least superficially. Despite the importance of wording in these problems, however, past accounts of reasoning have neglected to deal directly with the logically prior process of how the language of the problems is itself understood. In one way or another, the past accounts all have the subjects (Ss) solving the problems with something less than an abstract interpretation of the propositions. The experiments to be reported here, then, besides lending support to the present theory, also appear to disconfirm the earlier explanations. The contradictory evidence comes mainly from a previously untouched set of three-term series problems in which the customary propositions, like *John is better than Pete,* are replaced by new ones, like *John isn't as bad as Pete.* Although these two propositions have a superficially similar appearance and seem almost synonymous, they have radically different abstract interpretations. Because of this property, they allow strong tests of the previous theories as well as of the present one.

The present theory will be formulated as three principles: two specify what it is that the listener knows of a sentence he has heard and a third specifies how he searches his memory for the wanted knowledge. These three principles will then be used as a basis for predicting the relative times it takes Ss to solve two-term series problems (e.g. *If John is better than Pete, then who is worse?*) and three-term series problems. Finally, the theory will be applied to previous data on three-term series problems as well as to other, less directly related phenomena in deductive reasoning.

The three principles

Principle of the primacy of functional relations

Functional relations are the primitive conceptual relations out of which sentences are constructed. Chomsky (1965) lists four such relations which he claims are universal: Subject-of, Predicate-of, Direct-object-of, and Main-verb-of. For example, in both *John watched the monkey* and *The monkey was watched by John,* a listener knows that *John, watch,* and *monkey* are in the relation subject, verb, and direct object: it was John who watched, what John did was watch, and it was the monkey which was watched. But the listener also knows that the theme of the first sentence – what the sentence is about (Halliday, 1967) – is John, whereas the theme of the second is the monkey; this information, of a quite different sort, is not to be found in the functional relations that underlie a sentence. The principle of the primacy of functional relations asserts simply that functional relations, like those of subject, verb, and direct object, are stored, immediately after comprehension, in a more readily available form than other kinds of information, like that of theme. . .

Principle of lexical marking

According to the principle of lexical marking, the sense of certain 'positive' adjectives, like *good* and *long*, are stored in memory in a less complex form than the senses of their opposites. This principle is derived from certain linguistic facts relevant to the lexical component of English, that part of the grammar which defines the senses of words; these words, when inserted in the base component, give phonological shape to the abstract characterizations of the base. It is the lexicon that specifies that *bird* is superordinate to *oriole*, that *man* is animate, that *good* and *bad* are antonymous, and so on.

Antonymous adjectives, like *good* and *bad*, and *long* and *short*, are often found, on close scrutiny, to be asymmetric (Bierwisch, 1967; Greenberg, 1966; Lyons, 1963, 1968; Sapir, 1944; Vendler, 1968). The first piece of evidence for this is that the 'positive' member of many such pairs can be neutralized in certain contexts. A speaker asking 'how good is the food?' can merely be asking for an evaluation of the food. He will be satisfied whether he is told the food is good *or* bad. But the speaker asking 'How bad is the food?' is implying something more: rightly or wrongly, he is pronouncing the food to be bad and is asking about the extent of its badness. Since *good* can be neutralized and *bad* cannot, *good* is said to be 'unmarked' and *bad* 'marked'. Other unmarked–marked pairs by the same criterion are *long–short*, *wide–narrow*, and *interesting–uninteresting*; in the last pair, the marking is made explicit morphologically.

The second piece of evidence, obviously related to the first, is that the unmarked member of each pair also serves as the name of the full scale. The names of the *good–bad* and *long–short* scales are *goodness* and *length; badness* and *shortness* name only half of their respective scales. Also, in sentences like *The board is six feet long, long* names the dimension to be measured and nothing more; *six feet long* is exactly paraphrased by *six feet in length*. The *long* in *six feet long* obviously is in the same class with other dimensional names, like *wide, deep, thick,* and *high* – other unmarked adjectives – and not with its opposite *short:* the sentence *the board is six feet short* is unacceptable to English speakers. . .

Principle of congruence

Answering a question requires more of a listener than a mere understanding of the question itself. He must 'search' his memory for the wanted information and formulate that information in an answer. It is proposed here that his search is guided by the principle of congruence. What he seeks from his previous knowledge is information congruent, at the level of functional relations, with the information asked for in the question. He cannot answer the question until he finds congruent information, or until he reformulates the question so that he is able to do so.

Application of the principles to comparative sentences

The role these three principles play in two- and three-term series problems depends first on the role they play in the sentences that make up these problems. The sentences of interest are comparative constructions, such as *John is better than Pete,* negative equative constructions, such as *John isn't as bad as Pete,* and questions such as *Who is best?* The three principles will be examined in turn for their application to these types of sentences.

Principle of the primacy of functional relations. By this principle, the information most readily available from an interpretation of a sentence is its underlying functional relations. But what are the functional relations in comparative and negative equative constructions? Lees (1961), Smith (1961), and Huddleston (1967) argue that both types of constructions are generated linguistically from two primitive base strings. Underlying *John is better than Dick* are the base strings, *John is good* and *Dick is good.* It is here in the base strings that the subject–predicate relations of *John* and *good* and of *Dick* and *good* are found. The two strings are also designated in the base component as parts of a comparative construction. After the first transformations, there is a result that reads, roughly, *John is more good than Dick is good.* By a further transformation the last redundant *good* is dropped; and finally, *more good* is changed to *better* to form *John is better than Dick is* or, simpler still, *John is better than Dick.* Had the two base strings been *the door is wide* and *the desk is long,* the resulting sentence would have been *The door is wider than the desk is long*; in this case, the second adjective could not be deleted, since it was not identical to the first. The positive equative construction *John is as good as Dick,* as well as the negative *John isn't as good as Dick,* are derived analogously, with *as–as* in place of *more–than.*

Comparative sentences then contain, roughly, two kinds of information: (*a*) the functional relations, as in *John is bad,* and (*b*) the comparison *more than.* Applied to the comparative, the principle of the primacy of functional relations asserts that *a* is more available than *b.* In *John is worse than Pete,* the listener realizes that John and Pete are bad more readily than that John is more extreme that Pete in badness. To emphasize the functional relations in a convenient notation, the present paper will represent *John is worse than Pete* as (*John is bad* + ; *Pete is bad*), *John isn't as bad as Pete* as (*John is bad; Pete is bad* +), and *Who is worst?* as (*X is bad* + +). One + is one degree more extreme than none, and two +'s indicate the most extreme. . .

Principle of lexical marking. This principle asserts that the nominal sense of *good* – the sense found in noncommittal *How good?* questions – is stored in a less complex and more available form than the contrastive sense of *good* and *bad.* . . . It has direct application to sentences that contain *better, worse, isn't as good as,* or *isn't as bad as.* The *good* underlying *John is better than Pete* can be interpreted either nominally or contrastively. From the principle of lexical marking, however, it follows that since the contrastive sense takes longer to store and retrieve, this *good* will usually be interpreted in its simpler nominal sense. The *bad* underlying *Dick is worse than Jack,* of course, can only be interpreted contrastively. This agrees with intuition, leaving *John is better than Pete* normally noncommittal in tone, but *Dick is worse than Jack* clearly negative in tone. The principle predicts that *better* and *isn't as good as* propositions will be more quickly registered and retrieved than *worse* and *isn't as bad as* propositions.

Principle of congruence. By this principle, information cannot be retrieved from a sentence unless it is congruent in its functional relations with the information that is being sought. This can be illustrated in the following two-term series problem: *If John is better than Pete, then who is best?* (Although this question is 'bad English' by grammar school standards, it was used in the experiments that follow because *good, better,* and *best,* and *bad, worse,* and *worst,* all have different phonological forms and because the three-term series problem uses the same form of questions; as expected, no *S* objected to it.) The proposition provides the information, *(John is good +; Pete is good)*. The question requests an *X* so that (*X is good + +*); that is, it requires a search for the term with the most-plussed *good.* The underlying form of the question is congruent with that of the proposition, so the solution is immediately forthcoming – 'John is best' or just 'John.' But when *who is best?* is replaced with *who is worst?*, a question requesting information not congruent with the proposition's information, then the problem solver will search for the most-plussed bad term and, finding none, implicitly reformulate the question to read *who is least good?* So (*X is bad + +*)becomes (*X is good − −*), in which the minuses direct the search for the term with least-plussed *good.* In this search, the *S* will find congruent information and will formulate the solution 'Pete is worst' or 'Pete.' The principle of congruence implies, then, that retrieving an answer should take less time when propositions and questions are congruent in their base strings than when they are incongruent.

Two- and Three-Term Series Problems

Implicit in the previous three principles is a process by which people solve problems in deductive reasoning. Its identifiable stages are (a) comprehension of the propositions; (b) comprehension of the question; (c) search for information asked for in the question; and (d) construction of an answer. The three principles affect the outcome of this process at one or more of its stages. It is convenient, then, to examine the application of the principles to the process as it is supposed to occur in two-term series problems. These problems consist of eight types, the ones formed when one of four simple propositions (*A is better than B, B is worse than A, A isn't as bad as B,* and *B isn't as good as A*) is each followed by one of two questions (*Who is best?* and *Who is worst?*).

The first two stages – comprehending the proposition and question – entail setting up a representation like (*A is good +; B is good*) and (*X is good + +*), by the principle of the primacy of functional relations. At these stages and later on, the principle of lexical marking predicts that the base-string pair (*A is good* +; *B is good*) should be more quickly registered and retrieved than (*B is bad* +; *A is bad*), since the memory coding for *bad* is more complex than that for *good*. At the third stage, that of searching for information asked for in the question, *S* carries out the instructions implicit in the question. It is at this stage that the principle of congruence comes into play. Whenever the question is congruent with the proposition, *S* should take little time; if he needs to reinterpret the question to make it congruent, he will take more time.

Experiment I: The two-term series problem

The four propositions of the two-term series problems, shown in table I, can be matched on superficial or deep structure. Proposition I, *A is better than B*, has the same order of terms in surface structure as I′, *A isn't as bad as B*. In both propositions, *A* is the subject, *B* is the term in the predicate, and the relation between the terms means 'strictly greater in goodness than'. But proposition I does not have the same deep structure as I′. Proposition I is generated from base strings containing *good*, as indicated in the 'Analysis' column, whereas I′ is generated from base strings containing *bad*. In deep structure, proposition I is like II, *B isn't as good as A*. The four propositions, then, allow an orthogonal comparison of order in surface structure and of deep structure: pairs I and I′, and II and II′, have the same order in surface structure; pairs I and II′, and II and I′, are similar in deep structure. By the three principles, it is claimed that the solution times of the eight problem types should be affected mainly by the proposition's – and the question's – deep structure.

Table 1. Mean time to solve two-term series problems

Form of problem	Analysis	Form of question		Mean time (in seconds)
		Best?	Worst?	
I A better than B	A is good B is good	0·61	0·68	0·64
II B worse than A	A is bad B is bad	1·00	0·62	0·81
I′ A not as bad as B	A is bad B is bad	1·73	1·58	1·66
II′ B not as good as A	A is good B is good	1·17	1·47	1·32

Method

Four examples of each of the eight problem types were constructed using as terms common English four-letter men's names, no pair of which occurred together in more than one problem. Each of the thirty-two problems was typed in one continuous line on the middle of a blank IBM card in the following form: If Pete isn't as bad as John, then who is best? The problems were arranged in four blocks of eight, each block containing one problem of each type. The order within each block was random and different for each S. The first block was considered practice and was later discarded.

The S, at a signal, turned over a card, read the problem aloud, and gave an answer as quickly as he could consistent with high accuracy. He was timed from the first signal to his answer in hundredths of a second. After attempting all thirty-two problems in this manner, he repeated the procedure, omitting the answer. The time duration on the first go-round, minus the time duration on the second, was taken as the solution time for each of the thirty-two problems; this procedure was meant to correct for possible differences in the reading times of the problems. . .

Results

The mean solution times for the two-term series problems are shown in table 1; arithmetic means were used in place of the more generally used geometric means, because it was possible here to have null or negative solution times. The predictions made by the foregoing theory are clearly confirmed by these solution times.

First, the principle of the primacy of functional relations predicts that solution times will correlate with underlying, rather than superficial, structure. It was found that problem type I took less time than II. If this difference had been the result of the superficial order and meaning of the terms, then I′ should take less time than II′; but if it had been the result of their different underlying base strings, then II′ should take less time than I′. The data clearly support the second interpretation: I and II′ had significantly shorter solution times than II and I′, $F = 8.79$, $df = 1/19$, $p < 0.01$, and there was no significant interaction.

The principle of lexical marking predicts that problems with underlying *good* will take less time than those with underlying *bad*. This is confirmed by the same evidence as above. First, note that the principle of primacy of functional relations would also have been supported if I and II′ had had *longer* solution times than II and I′, respectively; support for this principle requires only that the two problems with similar deep structure be consistently different in the same direction from the other two problems. But the results are quite specific: overall, the *good* problems, I and II′, took significantly less time than the *bad* ones, II and I′. This supports lexical marking.

Finally, the principle of congruence predicts that questions congruent with a proposition in their underlying base strings will be answered more quickly than incongruent questions. This was supported, $F = 11.32$, $df = 1/19$, $p < 0.005$, with no other significant interactions. The question *Who is best?*, rather than *Who is worst?*, had the shorter solution times for problem types I and II′, built on an underlying *good*, but the longer solution times for problem types II and I', built on an underlying *bad*.

Deep structure was clearly dominant over the order of terms in surface structure. In types I and II, the subject term of the proposition was more quickly retrieved than the term in the predicate. But this was not true for types I' and II'. For them, the terms in the predicate were more quickly retrieved. Order in surface structure, therefore, is of no detectable importance in these problems.

A final result is that the problems with comparative propositions were more quickly solved than those with negative equative propositions, $F = 18.65$, $df = 1/19$, $p < 0.001$, with no other significant interactions. There is little doubt that the negative equative is syntactically more complex than the comparative; in current versions of transformational theory, there is at least one more transformation – the negative – needed in generating the negative equative construction. Conceptually, *B isn't as good as A* is the denial of *B is as good as A*, a construction of the same level of complexity as *B is better than A*. As one more piece of semantic information, denial itself takes time to process (Gough, 1965, 1966; Wason, 1961).

Experiment II: the three-term series problem

Two-term series problems are, for the most part, trivial to solve. But, as it will be seen, the principles which explain the difficulties of these problems also explain most difficulties of the three-term series problems. There is one additional assumption needed to account for the further difficulties of storing the information in three-term series problems.

Three-term series problems consist of two propositions and a question, as in *If John is better than Pete, and John is worse than Dick, then who is worst?* The three terms (*John, Pete,* and *Dick*) can be placed in the same evaluative order in 16 different problem types which use *better, worse, best,* and *worst*. As shown in table 2, there are four basic pairs of propositions, labelled I–IV. Completing the sixteen types, the two propositions of each pair can occur in either order, and the question can be either *Who is best?* or *Who is worst?* In addition, sixteen more problem types are possible when *isn't as bad as* is substituted for *is better than*, and *isn't as good as* for *is worse than*. These are the four pairs of propositions labelled I'–IV' listed on the right of table 2. Although problem types I–IV have been studied before, I'–IV' have not. For ease of comprehension the convention is used that the A term is best, the C term worst, and the B term in the middle.

Like the problems in table 1, those in table 2 can be paired for the similarity of either superficial order or deep structure. The Roman numerals match the problem types for superficial similarity. Types I and I', for example, are identical except for the relational terms, and in both cases the relation term (*is better than* and *isn't as bad as,* respectively) means 'strictly greater than'. The deep structure of each pair, however, is different. Underlying problem type I is the adjective *good*, and underlying I' is *bad*. In their underlying base strings (shown in the 'Analysis' column), I and II' are alike, as are II and I', III and IV', and IV and III'.

The three principles afford a number of predictions about the problems with homogenous propositions (types I, II, I′, and II′). The problems with *good* relational terms (I and II′) should, as in the two-term series problems, be easier than those with *bad* (II and I′). Also, a question which is congruent with the information in the propositions should be easier than an incongruent question: *Who is best?* should be the easier question for types I and II′, and *who is worst?*, for types II and I′.

Table 2. Types of three-term series problems

	Form of problem	Analysis		Form of Problem	Analysis
I	A better than B B better than C	A is good B is good C is good	I′	A not as bad as B B not as bad as C	A is bad B is bad C is bad
II	C worse than B B worse than A	A is bad B is bad C is bad	II′	C not as good as B B not as good as A	A is good B is good C is good
III	A better than B C worse than B	A is good B is good, bad C is bad	III′	A not as bad as B C not as good as B	A is bad B is bad, good C is good
IV	B worse than A B better than C	A is bad B is bad, good C is good	IV′	B not as good as A B not as bad as C	A is bad B is good, bad C is bad

The predictions for problem types III, IV, III′, and IV′ – those with heterogeneous propositions – are slightly more involved. Consider type III problems, which contain the underlying base strings *A is good, B is good, B is bad,* and *C is bad.* The answer to *Who is best?* is *A*, a term which belongs to a base string congruent with that of the question (*X is good* + +). The answer to *Who is worst?* is *C*, which also fulfils the congruence conditions. Type IV problems, on the other hand, show complete incongruence of the propositions and questions. *A*, the answer to *Who is best?*, is part of the base string *A is bad*, and *C*, the answer to *Who is worst?*, is part of *C is good*. Because of this internal disagreement, type IV problems should be harder than type III problems. In their deep structure, III′ is like IV, and IV′ is like III, so, for the same reasons, the internally incongruent type III′ problems should be harder than the internally congruent type IV′ problems.

Method

Three problems were constructed for each of the thirty-two problem types indicated in table 3. Common four-letter English men's names were used, such that no pair of them would occur together in more than one problem. Each problem was typed on a blank IBM card in the following form:

If John isn't as good as Pete,

And John isn't as bad as Dick,
Then who is best?
Dick   Pete   John

In addition, there were eight practice problems each containing one comparative and one negative equative proposition. The problems were arranged in four blocks: the practice problems and then three blocks of thirty-two, each latter block consisting of one of each problem type. Within blocks, the problems were random and different for each S. The order of the names following the question was counterbalanced across the last three blocks and across problem types.

On a signal, S turned a problem card face up, read the problem silently to himself, and produced an answer as quickly as he could without sacrificing accuracy. He was timed from the initial signal to the answer in hundredths of a second. He solved the 104 problems with short breaks between each. Unlike experiment I, the solution time was taken as the time duration from the signal to the answer; Ss found that reading aloud was very disruptive on this complex a problem. In the following results, then, reading time is confounded with solution time. If anything, this would militate against the predicted results in one case, for *better* is one syllable longer than *worse*. Again, the longest solution time was discarded for each problem type for each S, and so were the errors (7 per cent of the answers). The Ss were thirteen students fulfilling a course requirement for introductory psychology.

Results

The geometric mean solution times in table 3 confirm each of the predictions of the present theory. . .

The principles of the primacy of functional relations and of lexical marking predict that problem types I and II′ will be solved more quickly, overall, than II and I′, respectively. The solution times in table 3 confirm this prediction, $F = 5.38$, $df = 1/12$, $p < 0.05$, with no significant interaction. The principles of the primacy of functional relations and of congruence predict that III and IV′ will be solved more quickly, overall, than IV and III′, respectively. The prediction was confirmed here too, $F = 4.92$, $df = 1/12$, $p < 0.05$, with no significant interaction. These two principles also predict that solutions will be faster for problem types I and II′ when the question is *Who is best?* and for problem types II and I′ when the question is *Who is worst?* The results support this prediction, $F = 9.73$, $df = 1/52$, $p < 0.005$, with no other significant interactions. Comparative problems (I–IV) had shorter solution times than negative equative problems (I′–IV′), $F = 25.06$, $df = 1/12$, $p < 0.001$. Again, all results show the relative importance of deep structure over the order of terms in surface structure. . .

Solution of three-term series problems by children

Previous investigators interested in the development of reasoning have studied the solution of three-term series problems by children. Their careful observations, though usually more informal in nature, lend considerable support to the present theory.

Burt (1919) originally, and later Piaget (1921, 1928), Hunter (1957),

Donaldson (1963), and Luria (1966) have all noticed what Piaget (1921) called 'judgment of membership' in the child's interpretation of comparative sentences. Piaget (1921), for example, reports that nine- and ten-year-olds were unsuccessful in solving the following type IV problem (from Burt, 1919): 'Edith is fairer than Suzanne; Edith is darker than Lili. Which of the three has the darkest hair?' To quote Piaget (1928, p. 87),

It is as though [the child] reasoned as follows: Edith is fairer than Suzanne so they are both fair, and Edith is darker than Lili so they are both dark. Therefore Lili is dark, Suzanne is fair, and Edith is between the two. In other words, owing to the interplay of the relations included in the test, the child, by substituting the judgment of membership (Edith and Suzanne are 'fair', etc.) for the judgment of relation (Edith is 'fairer than' Suzanne), comes to a conclusion which is exactly opposite of ours.

This is to say, the children have understood the functional relations – the base strings – underlying the propositions, but have not grasped the comparative

Table 3. Geometric mean times in solving three-term series problems

Form of problem	Form of question Best?	Worst?	Mean time (in seconds)	Overall mean time (in seconds)
I (a) A better than B; B better than C	5·42	6·10	5·57	
(b) B better than C; A better than B	4·98	5·52	5·25	5·49
II (a) C worse than B; B worse than A	6·27	6·53	6·40	
(b) B worse than A; C worse than B	5·93	5·04	5·47	5·91
III (a) A better than B; C worse than B	5·35	5·34	5·34	
(b) C worse than B; A better than B	4·84	5·84	5·32	5·33
IV (a) B worse than A; B better than C	5·00	6·02	5·49	
(b) B better than C; B worse than A	6·12	5·45	5·77	5·63
I′ (a) A not as bad as B; B not as bad as C	6·77	5·95	6·34	
(b) B not as bad as C; A not as bad as B	7·16	6·56	6·85	6·59
II′ (a) C not as good as B; B not as good as A	5·58	6·63	6·08	
(b) B not as good as A; C not as good as B	6·11	6·60	6·35	6·22
III′ (a) A not as bad as B; C not as good as B	6·34	6·66	6·50	
(b) C not as good as B; A not as bad as B	6·73	6·34	6·53	6·52 ·
IV′ (a) B not as good as A; B not as bad as C	6·10	6·18	6·14	
(b) B not as bad as C; B not as good as A	5·48	7·12	6·25	6·19

information. Developmentally, the ability to judge membership in comparative statements arrives earlier than the ability to judge relations, and this fact is closely akin to the principle of the primacy of functional relations.

In solving problems out loud, many children verbalize the underlying base strings of comparative statements directly. For example, Donaldson (1963) quotes one child as saying, 'It says that Dick is shorter than Tom, so Dick is short and Tom is short too.' But in the next breath the child said, 'And Dick is taller than John so Dick is tall and John is short' (p. 131). The child appears to be vascillating between an interpretation of the base strings alone and an interpretation of the comparative information. The child, in the second instance, is stating the comparative relation in the only terms she knows how – as the positive adjectives *tall* and *short*.

The children in Donaldson's (1963) studies often made other errors as a result of their comprehension of propositions as base strings. For example, children were given the following type IV problem: 'Dick is shorter than Tom. Dick is taller than John. Which of these three boys is tallest?' Even though the problem explicitly states that there are three boys, many children assumed there were four. They said there were two Dicks – a tall one and a short one – following the analysis of the base strings. One girl's solution to the above problem was, 'This Dick [second premise] is tallest, John is next tallest, Tom is third and then it's Dick [first premise]' (p. 131). Although Donaldson's Ss made the two-Dick error on problem types I and II, they did so more often on types III and IV, problems which, because they describe Dick as both tall and short, encourage this kind of error. In all, fully 70 per cent of the errors Donaldson observed in children on problem types I–IV can be traced to the children's selective interpretation of the base strings alone.

Although the principle of congruence is implicit in some of the above examples of children's reasoning, children often made it explicit. Given the problem, 'Tom is taller than Dick, Dick is taller than John. Which of these three boys is shortest?' one boy explained, 'This means Dick is shorter than Tom, John is shorter than Dick. So that gives the answer – it's John' (Donaldson, 1963, p. 121). When asked why he changed the lines around, he said, 'I thought it would help.' He, as well as other children Donaldson reports, apparently changed the lines around to make them congruent with the question. In the present study, it has been assumed instead that it is the question that is reformulated and that it is done so implicitly. This assumption was made because the present Ss seemed to process the question after the propositions had been comprehended and stored. The assumption could be reversed, but evidence internal to experiment II seemed to favour it as it stands.

Finally, there is evidence for the principle of lexical marking in Donaldson's and in Duthie's (1963) protocols. Both experimenters found that children sometimes misinterpreted a sentence like 'Betty is older than May' to mean 'May is older than Betty.' For adults this is a contradiction, but for these children, it is not. The first sentence meant only that Betty is different in age from May and, as a symmetrical relation, it was synonymous with the second sentence. But 'Betty is older than May' was also taken to mean 'Betty is younger than May.' Apparently, both *young* and *old* are interpreted in a nominal sense, so that both sentences can mean, 'Betty is different in age from May.' Duthie (1963) found children who made this quite explicit in quantified comparative sentences. When one child was asked in the middle of a problem how he knew that Tom was four, he replied, 'Because it says that Tom is four years younger than Dick' (p. 237). Children also made this mistake in 'five years older'. Both Donaldson and Duthie argue convincingly that these errors result, not from misreadings, but from misinterpretations of the sentences in question. This evidence is related to some further observations on comparatives by Donaldson and Wales (1970). They found that young Scottish children could use the comparatives of unmarked adjectives, like *more, bigger, longer, thicker, higher,* and *taller,* earlier and more correctly than their marked counterparts, *less, wee-er, shorter, thinner, lower,* and *shorter.* On this and other evidence, it has been argued (Clark, 1969a) that children develop the semantically prior nominal sense of adjectives in comparisons before they do the contrastive senses. Thus, children appear to acquire the more primitive underlying entities of a comparative before they do the more complex ones: just as they understand functional relations before they do comparisons, they understand nominal senses before they do contrastive senses.

An alternative theory for three-term series problems

. . . The *theory of constructing spatial images* (Huttenlocher, Reading 5) posits that Ss arrange mental objects in imaginary spatial arrays to enable them to solve three-term series problems. The main proposal rests on the presupposition that arranging things mentally should show the same difficulties as arranging things physically.

In physical situations, Ss have difficulties under certain instructions in placing a movable object, like a block, in relation to a fixed one (Huttenlocher, Eisenberg, and Strauss, 1968; Huttenlocher and Strauss, 1968). Given the instruction, 'Make it so that the red block is under the blue block', children find it easy if the red block is in hand and the blue block is fixed, but difficult if the blue block is in hand and the red block is fixed. To summarize their results, arranging objects from an instruction is easy only when the movable object is the logical subject of a transitive verb or the grammatical subject of a 'relational' sentence.

The imagerial counterparts of these manipulations, the theory states, should show the same difficulties. Consider a type *1b* problem, *B is better than C, and A is better than B.* The first proposition fixes the terms B and C in mind, B above C. The third term of this array, A, is now the 'movable' term to be placed in relation to B and C. Since A is the subject of the second proposition, a 'relational' sentence, the task is easy and *1b* is quickly solved. It is not so easy to solve a type *1a* problem, *A is better than B, and B is better than C.* Here A and B are first fixed in mind with A above B, then the third term, C, is placed in relation to A and B. In this case, the 'movable' term C is not the subject of the second proposition, so it is hard to place C in order to solve the problem. Just as ɪ*b* should be easier than ɪ*a*, ɪɪ*b* should be easier than ɪɪ*a*, ɪɪɪ*a* than ɪv*b*, and ɪɪɪ*b* than ɪv*a*. The data in Huttenlocher (Reading 5), the present experiment ɪɪ, and Clark (1969b) all confirm these predictions.

The critical comparison of Huttenlocher's spatial image theory (Reading 5) and the present one, however, is found in the problems containing *isn't as good as* and *isn't as bad as*. By the former theory, a type ɪ'*b* problem, *B isn't as bad as C, and A isn't as bad as B,* like a type ɪ*b* problem, should be easy. In ɪ'*b*, the third term, A to be placed relative to the two fixed terms B and C, is the subject of the second proposition, hence its placement is easy. But in ɪ'*a, A isn't as bad as B, and B isn't as bad as C,* as in ɪ*a*, the third term C is difficult to place; it is the predicate of the second proposition. By the same analysis, ɪɪ'*b should be easier than* ɪɪ'*a*, ɪɪɪ'*a* than ɪv'*b*, and ɪɪɪ'*b* than ɪv'*a*. The present theory and analysis predict exactly the opposite. Compressing information from the first proposition for use in the second, as discussed above, should make ɪ'*a* easier than ɪ'*b*, and ɪɪ'*a* easier than ɪɪ'*b*. Also, by the principle of congruence, ɪv' should be easier than ɪɪɪ', overall, rather than the reverse. Each of the four possible comparisons in the results of experiment ɪɪ and Clark (1969b) support the present theory and run counter to the theory of constructing spatial images; the appropriate significance tests have been presented previously. Thus the latter theory is disconfirmed as a general explanation of reasoning in three-term series problems.

It does not follow from the disconfirmation of these two theories of spatial imagery, of course, that imagery does not occur in solving three-term series problems. It certainly does occur, although only 49 per cent of the Ss in Clark (1969b) claimed that they used spatial imagery. The only firm conclusion we can draw at this time is that it has not been demonstrated that the use of spatial imagery differentially affects the solution of three-term series problems.

Other kinds of reasoning

To be of use, the present explanation for certain processes in deductive reasoning must have generality. It should not be restricted to three-term series problems alone or to problems containing comparative propositions. Several examples of another kind of reasoning problem will serve to illustrate the wider applicability of the theory proposed here.

The reasoning problem to be examined requires Ss to judge the truth or falsity of positive or negative statements. In Wason and Jones (1963), Ss were presented sentences like *29 is not an even number* and were required to reply 'true' or 'false' while they were timed. In Gough (1965, 1966), Ss listened to sentences like *The boy didn't hit the girl*, examined a picture of either a boy hitting a girl or a girl hitting a boy, then pressed a 'true' or 'false' button while they were timed. The main result of interest is the interaction between the truth and positivity of the sentence: true positive and false negative sentences took less time, respectively, than false positive and true negative sentences.

When these tasks are viewed as reasoning problems, the present theory provides at least a partial explanation for the results. Wason and Jones's task can be thought of as consisting of a proposition and a question. The proposition is some previously known fact – for example, *29 is an odd number* – and the question is implicit in the presented sentence, *Is it true that 29 is not an odd number?* The underlying structure of the proposition is simply (*29 is odd*), whereas that of the question is something like (*is it true that (it is false that (29 is odd))*). The four truth and positivity questions, then, can be represented as: (*a*) true positive (*is it true that (29 is odd)*); (*b*) false positive (*is it true that (29 is even)*); (*c*) true negative (*is it true that (it is false that (29 is even))*); and (*d*) false negative (*is it true that (it is false that (29 is odd))*). By the principle of congruence, *S*s will answer more quickly when the functional relations underlying these questions are congruent with (*29 is odd*), the functional relations of the proposition. Congruence is found for *a*, but not *b*, so true positives should take less time than false positives. This agrees with the results. Congruence is also found for *d*, but not *c*, so false negatives should take less time than true negatives. This is also supported by the results. In Wason and Jones's study, *S*s also made more errors on true negatives (*c*) than on anything else; they gave 'false' so often presumably because a preliminary comparison showed that the functional relations of the proposition and question were different. Gough's (1965, 1966) tasks, analysed in a similar way, further confirm these predictions; the present explanation, in fact, is essentially the same as one of the alternatives he offered for his results.

The principle of lexical marking, however, accounts for yet another part of Wason and Jones's (1963) and Gough's (1965, 1966) results. The question in the above analysis was always formulated as (*is it true that (such and such is so)*). It contained *true*, not *false*. The reason, of course, is that *true* is unmarked and *false* marked: *Is it true?* implies no presuppositions about the answer – it could be either 'true' or 'false' – but *Is it false?* implies that the answer is expected to be 'false' (cf. also Fillenbaum, 1968). Thus, to answer false questions, *S* must reformulate his representation in memory to read (*it is false that (such and such is so)*), before he can give the answer, elliptically as 'false'; true questions are already in the correct form. This reformulation should take time, causing false questions to take more time overall than true questions. This prediction is confirmed in Wason (1961), Wason and Jones (1963), and Gough (1965, 1966).

Conclusion

In the past, deductive reasoning has often been studied as if it were an isolated process – even as if it were specific to a certain kind of task, such as the solution of three-term series problems. The processes described in the present paper, on the other hand, are quite general. They are not meant to explain the solution of two- and three-term series problems alone, but to account for certain linguistic processes in understanding statements and answering questions wherever they occur. The most important demonstration here has been that the principal difficulties inherent in many reasoning problems are not due to cognitive processes specific to these problems, but to the very language in which the problems are stated. Linguistic processes like these arise in every situation in which a problem is stated in linguistic terms.

7. Self-contradictions[1]

P. C. Wason

The aim of this article is to say something about the conditions under which self-contradiction acts to correct faulty reasoning, and the conditions under which it fails to act in this way. Obviously, to contradict oneself is to say nothing at all; for when a person does this it could be claimed that he must know that a mistake in reasoning had been made unless the contradiction is due merely to a change of mind. But self-contradiction does not imply that a person knows he has contradicted himself. The first assertion may have been so vaguely expressed that he is not at all sure about the contradiction, or he may feel so sure about the grounds of the assertion, even if he cannot spell them out, that he disbelieves (or evades) the force of the contradictory assertion. In cases of this kind 'conceptual conflict' is involved. I shall consider experimental studies of these sorts of self-contradiction, ranging from the fundamental process of denial in reasoning, to contradictions occurring in much more complex situations.

The process of denial

The *reductio ad absurdum* (RAA) inference provides a picture of the basic procedures of denial in reasoning. According to Quine (1952) it 'consists in assuming the contradictory of what is to be proved and then looking for trouble'. In a formal sense, it is closely related to the *modus tollens* (MT) inference in the propositional calculus (see Introduction to Part II). The main difference is that in RAA the fundamental problem is 'to select a fruitful proposition to put forward as a hypothesis in order to get the deduction in motion' (Wason and Johnson-Laird, 1972, p. 49). But Johnson-Laird and Shapiro (cited in Wason and Johnson-Laird, 1972) have demonstrated that detecting such a proposition leads to no extra difficulty. Hence we shall assume that the psychological processes involved in both RAA and MT are similar. As pointed out in the Introduction to Part II, the present formulation of RAA differs from that strictly employed in logic. In the experiment to be discussed the subjects are not required to assume

[1] This paper has been specially written for this volume.

'the contradictory of what is to be proved', but merely required to try to solve the problem. The remaining steps of the RAA inference, however, are open to the subject.

In a pioneering experiment, Jonathan Evans (1972a) postulated that the difficult stage in the RAA inference lies, neither in making an assumption, nor in deriving a contradiction from it, but in deducing a conclusion from the denial of the assumption. If this hypothesis is correct, then the process of denial would be critically affected by whether the assumption is expressed affirmatively or negatively. This follows from the theory that the 'natural semantic function' of negatives is to make denials of preconceptions which are generally (and implicitly) given affirmative expression (Wason, 1965; Greene, 1970). Evans predicted that a 'natural problem', in which a negative contradicted an affirmative assumption, would be easier to solve than an 'unnatural problem', in which an affirmative contradicted a negative assumption. Both types of problem were presented in the guise of stories which posed a dilemma about the reconciliation of two statements.

The 'natural problem' can be reduced to the following two statements:

(Father's statement) You must either go to the pictures tonight or not go for a walk tomorrow, but not both.

(Mother's statement) If you go to the pictures tonight, then you must not go for a walk tomorrow.

The RAA solution is (1) to assume the truth of the antecedent of the mother's statement: 'suppose I do go to the pictures tonight'. Then it follows (2) from the mother's statement that 'I must not go for a walk tomorrow.' But it follows from the father's statement that 'I cannot not [i.e. I must] walk tomorrow.' This is a contradiction (3). Hence it follows from RAA that the hypothesis (1) is false, and it can be concluded (4), 'I cannot go to the pictures tonight.'

The 'unnatural problem' can be reduced to the following two statements:

(Father's statement) You must either not go to the pictures tonight, or go for a walk tomorrow, but not both.

(Mother's statement) If you don't go to the pictures tonight, then you must go for a walk tomorrow.

The RAA solution involves assuming the truth of the negative premise, 'suppose I don't go to the pictures tonight', deriving a contradiction as in the 'natural problem', and concluding that the assumption is false, and that it follows that, 'I must go to the pictures tonight.'

Qualitative observation of the protocols, however, revealed two other strategies which can be used to reach correct conclusions. One is called by Evans 'conversion'. Some subjects reasoned that the Father's statement (in both problems) is compatible with either (1) 'You must go to the pictures tonight and go for a walk tomorrow', or (2) 'You must neither go to the pictures tonight, nor go for a walk tomorrow.' In the 'natural problem' the Mother's statement is incompatible with (1), and hence (2) must be true. Similarly, in the 'unnatural problem' the Mother's statement is incompatible with (2), and hence (1) must be true.

The other strategy is called by Evans 'truth table analysis'. For example, one subject simply constructed all the possible cases of the 'natural problem':

1. Pictures – no walk. Impossible – father.
2. Pictures – walk. Possible, father – impossible, mother
3. No pictures – no walk. O.K.
4. No pictures – walk. Impossible – father.

Only one case, 'no pictures and no walk', is compatible with the premises, and hence it must contain the conclusion. As Evans (1972a) points out: 'The subject uses a self-terminating serial process, checking each combination first against the father's statement, and then against the mother's statement if the first check had failed to eliminate a combination.'

Table 1 gives the number of correct and incorrect solutions as a function of the different strategies used. The criteria for correctness were that the subject (1) gave the correct solution, and (2) indicated in what he wrote that the conclusion was based on a sound strategy.

Table 1. Number of solutions to both 'natural' and 'unnatural' problems (Evans, 1972a)

	Natural problem	Unnatural problem
Correct		
RAA	10	2
Conversion	3	2
Truth table	3	1
Other	1	1
Incorrect	7	18

It will be noted that, among the strategies, RAA was most frequent, and that the prediction that the 'natural problem' would be easier, is confirmed. It is evident that in RAA the difficulty occurs in denying a negative assumption. However, from this result alone it may be that the disjunction containing the negative in its first component, which occurs in the 'unnatural problem', is simply harder to understand (see Roberge, 1976). (One improvement might have been to have involved the RAA in its standard logical form by stipulating the conclusion which is to be proved. The counter-intuitive step of postulating a contradictory could then have been examined with more rigour.)

Further light was thrown on the main result by an experiment (Evans, 1972b) in which the *modus tollens* (MT) inference was substituted for RAA. The material was abstract, and the negative was systematically permuted in the antecedent and consequent of the conditional premise. The prediction that the inference would be less frequently made when the antecedent was negated was confirmed, e.g. (1) if the letter is not G, then the number is 9; (2) the number is not 9;

therefore the letter is G. However, a second prediction that it would be less frequently made when the consequent was negated was not confirmed, e.g. (1) if the letter is E, then the number is not 3; (2) the number is 3; therefore the letter is not E. Both predictions were based on the 'natural semantic function' of negation theory, but it is evident that the operation of denial is sensitive to a negated assumption, but the perception of a contradiction is insensitive to a negated consequent. This result delineates the precise difficulty noted in RAA (Evans, 1972a). It has been corroborated by Johnson-Laird and Tridgell (1972) and by Roberge (1976), when a disjunctive statement replaced the conditional premise.

The precise nature of the difficulty may be simply due to 'double negation' – the denial of a negative increases the number of information-processing steps which have to be performed. On the other hand, it also follows from the 'natural semantic function' theory. The negative in the antecedent does not occur in a plausible context. In everyday life negatives do generally occur in such a context, and they may be easier to understand in such contexts because one has already processed the misconception which they deny (Wason and Johnson-Laird, 1972, p. 39).

In the RAA and MT inferences it has been convincingly demonstrated that success in deduction is crucially dependent on the way in which the assumption is expressed. But it is only an assumption made by the individual which is denied, and this leads to no abandonment of an assertion, or commitment. In a much earlier experiment (Wason, 1964) I tried to investigate the effects of self-contradiction caused by inconsistency between two inferences made by the same individual.

Self-contradiction (1)

In the experiment inconsistency was induced by exploiting the distinction between valid and fallacious inferences. The task simulated a realistic situation in which the subject had to discover an unknown principle by making a series of deductive inferences from information presented at each of ten trials. This information allowed valid inferences on the odd numbered trials and fallacious inferences on the even numbered trials. The material consisted of an incomplete conditional rule relating ages and salaries of employees in a hypothetical firm, each trial consisting of an employee's actual age and salary. The task was to derive the omitted age (or salary) in the rule. In the 'antecedent task' the rule was: 'Any employee aged 34 years, or more, will receive a salary of at least £.......... a year.' Valid inferences could be made, from employees aged at least 34, about the upper limit of the unknown salary, and fallacious inferences about its lower limit, from employees aged less than 34. However, since only ten out of thirty subjects (students) were susceptible to this fallacy in the first place, this particular task will not be explained further.

In the 'consequent task' the rule was: 'Any employee aged – years, or more, will receive a salary of at least £1,900 a year.' In this task valid inferences could be made, from employees earning less than £1,900, about the lower limits of the unknown age, and fallacious inferences, from employees earning at least £1,900 about its upper limits. For example, from an employee aged 37 earning £1,700, it would be valid to infer that the unknown age must be more than 37; but from an employee aged 41 earning £2,500, it would be fallacious to infer that the unknown age could not be more than 41. Twenty out of thirty subjects were initially susceptible to the fallacy.

At each trial the subject made a written estimate of the unknown age which provided a cumulative record: no memory was involved. A written question was also posed, the answer to which signified whether an inference had been made, or withheld. Both tasks had an experimental and a control group, the functions of which will emerge. Table 2 shows the information presented, and the inferences which could be made at each trial. Over the first four trials these are the same for both groups, but thereafter they differ. In the experimental group inconsistency is first introduced on trial 5, and is maintained between successive fallacious and valid inferences on each subsequent odd numbered trial. For example, on trial 5 it would be valid so infer that the unknown age is more than 37 because this employee earns less than £1,900. But this would contradict a fallacious inference on trial 4 that the unknown age could not be more than 35. However, a potential fallacious inference on trial 6, that the unknown age could not be more than 38, is consistent with a valid inference on trial 5. The contradiction between (say) trials 4 and 5 would be brought home to the subject, not simply from his answers to the questions, but from his concrete estimates of the unknown age at each trial. At trial 4 he might have estimated, 'less than 35', but at trial 5 a valid inference would compel the estimate, 'more than 37'. But there is no direct impediment to recording a subsequent inference, 'less than 38' at trial 6.

Table 2. Inferences in the 'consequent task' about the unknown age

Trials	Salary £	Experimental group Age and inference	Control group Age and inference
1.	1,300	>26(V)	>26(V)
2.	2,400	≯36(F)	≯36(F)
3.	1,400	>27(V)	>27(V)
4.	2,300	≯35(F)	≯35(F)
5.	1,500	>37(V)	>28(V)
6.	2,200	≯38(F)	≯34(F)
7.	1,600	>40(V)	>29(V)
8.	2,100	≯41(F)	≯33(F)
9.	1,700	>43(V)	>30(V)
10.	2,000	≯45(F)	≯32(F)

Column (1) shows the salary earned by an employee at each trial. Columns (2) and (3) show the age of the employee, combined with the inference about the unknown age.

(V) = valid   (F) = fallacious   > = more than   ≯ = not more than

In the control group, on the other hand, no contradiction between inferences is ever introduced. Potential fallacious and valid inferences form a converging series with respect to the unknown age. It was predicted that fewer fallacious inferences would be made on the critical trials (6, 8 and 10) in the experimental group compared with the control group.

The prediction was confirmed. The results (combined over both tasks) showed that nine out of fourteen, initially susceptible to a fallacious inference, permanently withheld them after inconsistency had been induced on trial 5 in the experimental groups. On the other hand, only four out of fourteen withheld them in the control groups. This suggests that inferences were withheld because previous inferences of the same type had been recognized as inadmissible in relation to the logic of the rule. Knowledge of fallaciousness lies within the individual's logical competence, and the function of contradiction is merely to act as a prompt or cue.

The experiment is open to criticism. It required a large number of subjects (sixty) to demonstrate a simple result, and the 'antecedent task' should not have been used at all. Above all, the experiment yielded no qualitative data about the effects of self-contradiction. One subject (P.N.J.-L.) vividly recalled treating the rule as an equivalence (i.e. a conditional in which the converse is true) until this led him into a contradiction, at which point he realized that the rule was thereby clearly intended to be a one-way implication.

The next problem (Wason, 1966) was conceived before the present experiment had been conducted. The first experiment on it (Wason, 1968) suggested it had more potential for revealing the effects of conceptual conflict.

Self-contradiction (2)

Consider the state of puzzlement induced when an individual knows that the solution to a problem is wrong, but is unable to realize what is wrong about it. Such a state was fortuitously achieved by the 'selection task' (Wason, 1966, 1968). A seemingly certain, 'obvious', solution is contradicted by the subject's own subsequent evaluation of the problem material, or by the presentation of information inconsistent with the solution.

Basically, the problem consists in establishing the conditions which allow the truth value of a conditional sentence to be ascertained. It is thus really a 'meta-inference' problem – it requires a deductive inference about the conditions from which a valid inference could be made. Since many people fail to understand the solution it may help the reader to introduce the problem in two forms. Its most recent version, devised specially for the 1977 Science Museum Psychology Exhibition under the title, 'How Rational are Humans?', aimed to eliminate some confusing features in the original version of the problem.

You are shown a panel of four cards (a), (b), (c), (d) (see figure 1) together with the following instructions:

Which of the hidden parts of these cards do you need to see in order to answer the following question decisively?

FOR THESE CARDS IS IT TRUE THAT IF THERE IS A CIRCLE ON THE LEFT THERE IS A CIRCLE ON THE RIGHT?

You have only one opportunity to make this decision; you must not assume that you can inspect cards one at a time. Name those cards which it is absolutely necessary to see.

The solution is cards (a) and (d) because only a circle on the left without a circle on the right allows a negative answer to the question. (c) is superfluous because although it could allow an affirmative answer it could not allow a negative answer; hence it is useless.

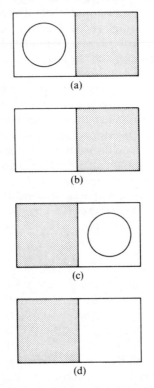

Figure 1. The selection task (Psychology Exhibition, Science Museum, 1977)

Its first published form (Wason, 1966) was as follows. There are four cards in front of you showing (respectively) a vowel, a consonant, an even number, and an odd number, e.g. E, F, 4, 7. You know that each card has a letter on one side and a number on the other side. You are then presented with the following test sentence: 'If a card has a vowel on one side, then it has an even number on the other side.' Your task is to name those cards which need to be turned over to find out whether the test sentence is true or false.

The solution is, of course, the vowel and the odd number because only instances of these two values on the same card would falsify the test sentence.

Reading 9 in this volume summarizes a large number of studies which show that, with abstract material, the vast majority of student subjects wrongly select the equivalents of the vowel and the even number, or just the vowel. It presents an information-processing model of performance in terms of verifying and falsifying thought processes, and an alternative conception in terms of a tendency to select cards as a function of a 'matching response bias' (Wason and Evans, 1974/5). My concern in this article is not with such issues, but with qualitative data related to the effects of contradiction on erroneous attempted solutions. Johnson-Laird and Wason (Reading 9) have pointed out that the response to such contradictions is not uniform. Over the samples as a whole they do appear (statistically) to modify an initial incorrect solution, but it is also evident that many individuals need considerable experience of self-contradiction before they modify their initial conclusion even at the verbal level, and some never relinquish their initial conclusion. Furthermore, it is often the failure of an individual to respond to contradiction which is more illuminating than a verbal correction. And in these cases the ways in which contradictions seem to be 'evaded' are highly distinctive. Two kinds of 'evasion' were found to occur in four published studies. They can be described briefly by reference to the very first experiment (Wason, 1968). First, a subject might agree that an odd number on the other side of the vowel would falsify the test sentence, but then claim that no symbol on the other side of the odd number would do so. Similarly, they might agree that a consonant on the other side of the even number would falsify, but then claim that no symbol on the other side of the consonant would do so. The crucial factor which accounts for these inconsistencies is that both the vowel and the even number had been selected in the initial attempted solution, but neither the odd number, nor the consonant had been selected. This kind of 'evasion' is called 'irreversibility': an inference is made from a selected card, but withheld from a potentially identical unselected card when it is upside down. Selection confers meaning on only the selected cards. Second, after questioning, a subject would agree that an unselected card could falsify the test sentence (e.g. an odd number, if it were to have a vowel on the back), but then refuse to modify his attempted solution by including that card. This kind of 'evasion' is called 'denial'.

It might seem that, in the original experiment, these strategies were merely due to lapses of attention or memory, but subsequent studies showed that they were pervasive and enduring. They were revealed in stark form in an experiment (Wason, 1969) in which degrees of contradiction, ranging from hypothetical to actual, were systematically increased in a kind of cognitive 'therapy'. But it was argued that such procedures resembled an 'interrogation' rather than a 'therapy'. Accordingly, in the next experiment to be discussed (Wason and Johnson-Laird, 1970) a clinical interview was substituted for a standardized procedure after the subjects' attempted solutions had been immediately contradicted by facts. An explanation of the effects of this contradiction will be given after the results and the illustrative protocols have been cited.

The rule (test sentence) was: 'Every card which has a circle on it has a border round it.' The four cards (see figure 2) consisted of (a) a 'circle' with a mask round the edge where a curly border might be present or absent; (b) 'no circle' with a similar mask round the edge; (c) a curly 'border' round the edge of the card with a mask over the centre where a circle might be present or absent; (d) 'no border' with a similar mask over the centre. The solution, to determine whether the rule is true or false, is to see fully cards (a) and (d), i.e. 'circle' and 'no border'.

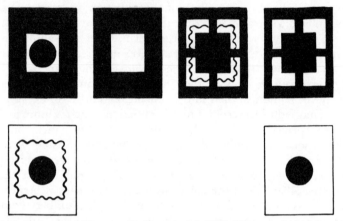

Figure 2. The 'selection task' (Wason and Johnson-Laird, 1970). 'Every card which has a circle on it has a border round it.' The top row shows the masked cards, and the bottom row shows the two which are fully revealed

When the subject had proposed his solution, he was immediately confronted with a real contradiction if he had failed to include the 'no border' card. The two correct cards ('circle' and 'no border') were simultaneously fully revealed by the experimenter (Diana Shapiro) to show (a) 'border with circle', verifying the rule, and (d) 'no border with circle', falsifying it (see figure 1). Since the subjects had nearly always selected (a), but not (d), they were shown that their solution made the rule *true*, and that information neglected by them made it indisputably *false*. The subjects were asked about the consequences of these two exposed cards, and invited to modify their initial attempted solutions. An unstructured interview followed about the potential consequences of the other two cards, if they were to be fully revealed. It was terminated at the discretion of the experimenter when, in her judgment, there would be no point in further talk.

Table 3 presents the quantitative results with respect to giving a verbal modification of an initially attempted solution as a function of the treatment involved.

The criterion for 'correctness' was very conservative: a verbal acknowledgment of the correct solution. A stringent test would require any supposed gain of insight to be transferred to different stimulus materials. What is remarkable about the results, even with a lax criterion of insight, is not that 62 per cent (twenty-one out of thirty-four) of the subjects eventually satisfied the

Table 3. Correct and incorrect solutions proposed at different stages of the task

Correct initially	2
Correct only after exposure of cards	9
Correct only after interview	12
Incorrect throughout	13
	N = 36

criterion of enlightenment. After all, the interview was designed to be helpful. What is remarkable is that 74 per cent (twenty-five out of thirty-four) failed to correct their solution after the relevant information had been revealed and evaluated, and that only 48 per cent of them (twelve out of twenty-five) succeeded at the end of the interview. Three (hitherto unpublished) protocols have been annotated to illustrate the response to contradiction and the mechanisms of 'irreversibility' and 'denial'.

S.16 female undergraduate: 'A' levels in pure and applied mathematics. Attempted solution: 'circle' and 'border'. [Correct cards fully revealed.]

Experimenter: Are you still happy about the choice of cards you needed to see?
 Subject: Yes.
  E: Can you say anything about the truth or falsity of the rule from this card? [Circle with border.]
  S: It tells me the sentence is true.
  E: Can you say anything about the truth or falsity of the rule from this card? [No border with circle.]
  S: It tells me it's false.
  E: Are you still happy about the choice of cards you needed to see?
  S: Yes. [The exposed cards have been evaluated, and the subject exhibits 'denial': the falsifying card is not considered admissible.]
  E: Well, you've just said this one makes it false.
  S: Well, it hasn't got a squiggly border on it, so it doesn't matter. ['denial' again.]
  E: Can you say anything about the truth or falsity of the rule from this card? [No circle.]
  S: It's got nothing to do with it because there's no circle.
  E: Can you say anything about the truth or falsity of the rule from this card? [border – selected.]
  S: There has to be a circle under it for the sentence to be true.
  E: What if there is no circle?
  S: Then the sentence would be false. ['Irreversibility': an inference made from a selected card is withheld from a potentially identical unselected card.] Interview terminated.

S. 34 female undergraduate: 'A' levels in physics, chemistry and zoology. Attempted solution: 'border' [an idiosyncratic choice based on a superficial error]. [Correct cards fully revealed.]

  E: Are you still happy about the choice of cards you needed to see?
  E: No – I would need to see the one with the circle and the one with the border. [Superficial error remedied.]
  E: Can you say anything about the truth or falsity of the rule from this card? [Circle with border.]

E: That one proves it.

E: Can you say anything about the truth or falsity of the rule from this card? [No border with circle]

S: That one disproves it.

E: Are you still happy about the choice of cards you needed to see?

S: Yes, I would need to see the one with the circle and the one with the border. ['Denial' of the falsifying card.]

E: Can you say anything about the truth or falsity of the rule from this card? [Border.]

S: I'd expect to find a circle. The only way you can verify the sentence is to look at the circle and the border. This card [no border with circle] is totally useless as it doesn't have a border on it, so it doesn't matter. ['Methinks the lady doth protest too much.']

E: You have seen this card [no border with circle] and that it has got a circle on it. Do you still think it doesn't matter?

S: Yes, I do.

E: Are you still happy about the choice of cards you needed to see?

S: No. I would now choose the circle only. [It should be noticed that the falsifying card is not dismissed because it falsifies. More interestingly the subject says: 'it is totally useless' and 'it doesn't matter'.] Interview terminated.

S.12 male undergraduate: 'A' levels in physics, biology and chemistry. [This subject worked under another condition in which the symbols were positioned on both sides of the cards. The rule was: 'Every card which has a circle on one side has two borders on the other side.' The cards displayed: circle, triangle, two borders and one border.] Attempted solution: circle. [Correct cards fully revealed: circle with two borders (verifying) and one border with circle (falsifying).]

E: Are you still happy about the choice of cards you needed to see?

S: No. It would also be necessary to turn over the one with two borders on it. [The redundant verifying card is included.]

E: Can you say anything about the truth or falsity of the rule from this card? [Circle with two borders.]

S: It's true.

E: Can you say anything about the truth or falsity of the rule from this card? [One border with circle.]

S: That card contradicts the statement.

E: Are you still happy about the choice of cards you needed to see?

S: No. I would turn them all over except the triangle. [He does not succumb to 'denial'.]

E: Yes, O.K. Why would you leave the triangle out?

S: Because the sentence is concerned with circles.

E: Yes, fine. Now what would you expect to find on the back of this card? [Two borders.]

S: [Long pause] It wouldn't tell you anything about the statement. ['Irreversibility' seems to be avoided at the verbal level, but two borders is still included in his choice.]

E: Are you still happy about the choice of cards you needed to see? [Which will win: words or choice?]

S: It's still necessary to turn it over! I stick to my earlier choice of circle, two borders and one border. [Choice wins. 'Irreversibility' is not apparent at the conscious level but it remains implicit in the choice. This is strong evidence for information-processing at two levels.] Interview terminated.

This subject's 'irreversibility' was unacknowledged; it was succinctly expressed by another subject (S.30). '*E*: Can we consider triangle and two borders? *S*: Triangles aren't mentioned, so I left that one out. *E*: What do you expect to find on the back of two borders? *S*: Well, if it's a triangle the sentence is false.'

Similar phenomena occurred in a further experiment (Wason and Golding, 1974), in which the test sentence was expressed as a declarative: 'A letter is above each number.' The subjects were eventually shown two identical, fully revealed cards which falsified the test sentence: a blank above a number. They had initially selected the one in which only the number had been visible, and ignored the other in which only the blank had been visible. When asked why they had selected one and not the other, a typical response was: 'I saw a number on the bottom, and therefore that card could be true or false. On the other card I saw there was a blank on the top, which meant there was no letter, so it had to be untrue.' When asked whether the two cards were identical, 32 per cent (seven out of twenty-two qualified their answer, e.g. 'As they are at the moment but before they were completely different.'

The rather odd impression created by the utterances in both these experiments may seem less surprising to the readers than they did to the experimenters. Superficially, it might seem that the subjects are 'confused', 'obstinate', or have difficulty in 'changing their minds'. However, the interest lies, not in such phenomenal descriptions, but in the causes of such states of mind which make the subjects deny the relevance of facts in front of them, or contradict themselves.

More strongly, it might be claimed that the protocols imply that the instruction, '. . . to find out whether the rule is true or false' had been misinterpreted (or transformed) into, '. . . to find out whether the rule is *true*'. Such a reinterpretation would logically still entail the same solution but it might (subjectively) have accentuated verification at the expense of falsification. In the Wason and Golding (1974) experiment the subjects were asked to recall the instructions at different stages of the task. Twenty-seven per cent (twelve out of forty-five) of the subjects did indeed recall the instructions, on at least one occasion, as finding out whether its rule was true, or even as proving it true. The remaining 73 per cent never made such an error. But there was no association between successful performance and successful recall. It does not follow that verbatim recall necessarily mirrors the subjects' intentions, but it does suggest that a conscious transformation of the instructions had not occurred in the direction of verification for the majority of subjects.

To the behaviouristically inclined psychologist the protocols might be dismissed as mere unreliable rationalizations. The cognitive psychologist might construe them as veridical statements about how the problem is perceived at different stages. My own explanation is a compromise between these extreme views. Why did the majority of subjects in Wason and Johnson-Laird (1970) fail to exploit such a blatant contradiction, when 64 per cent (nine out of fourteen) did so when a valid inference contradicted a fallacious one in the previously discussed study (Wason, 1964)? In the 'selection task' problem we have postulated a distinction between a 'selection process', governing the initial attempted solutions, and an 'evaluation process', referring to the subsequent discussion of individual cards in relation to the test sentence. In cases of a wrong attempted solution the 'selection process' is assumed to dominate the 'evaluation process' just because it appears to be intuitive and inchoate, rather than based on combinatorial analysis of the problem. When a subject is forced to acknowledge that an unselected card falsifies the test sentence, he tends to be unable to assimiliate this evaluative knowledge to modify his attempted solution. The grounds for the initial solution have been dominated by the 'selection process'; they have not been articulated so that they can be seen as incompatible with the truth. The resulting conceptual conflict is analogous to the contradiction in what Kuhn calls a 'thought experiment' (see Reading 17). There are inconsistencies between 'instantaneous velocity' and 'average speed' in both Aristotle's theory of physics and in Piaget's developmental observations. Piaget observed that the child's concept of 'instantaneous velocity' is based on a direct perception of speed ('I watched it ') which Kuhn calls 'perceptual blurriness'. It is plausible to suppose that in our results the selection process is based on an analogous 'conceptual blurriness' – a spurious sense of correctness, whether it be called 'verification' (Johnson-Laird and Wason), 'matching response' (Evans), or 'focus of attention' (Brée). The selection process is like an impression which may be irreducible to further analysis, and not an inference based on logical appreciation. Hence when it has to compete against a rational evaluation process it is as if the individual judgment is confronted by the possibility of two incompatible solutions.

Self-contradiction (3)

In 1976 I formulated a new problem for investigating the effects of self-contradiction; the selection task was becoming too well known to potential subjects. The problem (THOG) seems particularly pertinent for this requirement because there is an element of contradiction in its structure.

In front of you are four designs: a black diamond, a white diamond a black circle, and a white circle (see figure 3). You are given a rule which allows an arbitrary name to be applied to the designs.

Figure 3. The THOG problem

Rule: In the above designs there is a particular shape and a particular colour, such that any of the four designs which has one, and only one, of these features is called a THOG.

The black diamond is called a THOG. What can you say, if anything, about whether each of the three remaining designs is a THOG?

This problem has the interesting property that the most frequent wrong solution, revealed by a number of informal tests, is the mirror image of the correct solution: the individual is likely to go wrong about each of the three remaining designs. He is likely to claim that the white circle can't be a THOG, and that the white diamond and black circle either could be (or must be) THOGS. An exploratory experiment, conducted on medical students, showed that 65 per cent (seventeen out of twenty-six) of wrong solutions were of one of these kinds although the chance probability of each is one in twenty-seven. The correct solution is that the white circle is a THOG and that neither the white diamond, nor the black circle, are THOGS.

The contradictory element within the problem, responsible for wrong solutions, is due to the logical relation (exclusive disjunction) involved in it. Table 4 shows the relation between each design and the corresponding particular shapes and colours ('particular features') which underlie the rule. If any design is a THOG, then its corresponding shape and colour could not be among the particular features responsible for its being a THOG. Conversely, if any design is not a THOG, then its corresponding shape and colour must be among the particular features responsible for it not being a THOG.

Table 4. Relation between the designs and particular features which underlie the THOG rule

Designs		Particular features	
Black diamond	√	Black and diamond	×
Black circle	×	Black and circle	√
White diamond	×	White and diamond	√
White circle	√	White and circle	×

Note. The outcomes have been made consistent with the terms of the problem, i.e. the Black diamond is given as a THOG.

It is apparent from an inspection of the table that the only tenable features, consistent with the black diamond being a THOG, are 'black and circle' and 'white and diamond'. But the designs corresponding to these features cannot be THOGS because each would either possess both the particular shape and the particular colour, or neither of them. On the other hand, the white circle must be a THOG because it is compatible with both sets of features by virtue of either its shape or its colour.

Research is in progress, in collaboration with Lunzer and his associates, to determine the extent to which the problem is a fair test of Piaget's (original) theory of formal operations in adolescents. The problem seems easier than the selection task, but it would be premature to report definitive results other than to say that presenting the problem in a realistic guise has a detrimental rather than a beneficial effect on performance. The logic of exclusive disjunction, pertinent to this problem, cannot readily be mapped on to everyday life situations. For example, it is implausible to suppose that a positive instance is a person who is either female, or under thirty-five, but not both. In this respect the problem is unlike the selection task in which a realistic guise facilitates performance.

An experiment is planned in which self-contradiction will be induced as a potential therapy after an individual has reached an incorrect solution. If he declares that the white circle is definitely not a THOG, he will be asked to state which particular features are consistent with the black diamond being a THOG. A self-contradiction will be elicited if he declares (correctly) that 'black and circle' and 'white and diamond' are possible candidates, but still insists (wrongly) that the white circle can't be a THOG. This method can similarly be used to try to correct a wrong classification of the black circle and the white diamond. Thus a clinical procedure is envisioned in which the individual (whether child or adult) is exposed to contradictions between the designs and the particular features. The main interest is to establish whether the perceptual characteristics of the designs dominate (or even block) a consideration of the features subserving them in this looking-glass world.

Conclusions

I have tried to show that in simple situations individuals can make deductions from contradictions in order to deny an assumption although, if the assumption is expressed negatively, the deduction is about twice as difficult. Similarly, individuals can recognize, and abstain from, fallacious inferences when they have been contradicted by valid inferences. However, in more complex situations, in which the premises are misconstrued, the effect of contradictions seems to be evaded in systematic ways. The consequences of conceptual conflict in real life cannot readily be made manifest, but the use of artificial problems to elicit the operation of thought processes at different levels, enables them to be delineated.

8. Reasoning with quantifiers[1]

P. N. Johnson-Laird

A set of principles is required for inference with quantifiers. These terms include the familiar items 'all', 'some', 'none', 'many', 'few', etc., and a wide range of implicit quantifiers, e.g. 'usually', 'often', 'certain', 'possible', and 'permissible'. Logically speaking, it is possible to develop the usual apparatus of axioms and rules of inference for quantifiers and to raise the customary question of completeness with respect to an appropriate semantical model. Psychologically speaking, however, matters are less clear-cut. Despite the many experimental studies of the syllogism, going back at least seventy years (see the work of Störring, cited in Woodworth, 1938), it is only very recently that actual models of syllogistic inference have been proposed (Erickson, 1973: Revlis, 1975). The majority of theories are about factors that create difficulty in dealing with syllogisms (e.g. Woodworth and Sells, 1935; Chapman and Chapman, 1959; Ceraso and Provitera, 1971). Indeed, the concentration of interest on the syllogism, that traditional but minor province of quantified inference, is symptomatic of the backward state of knowledge in this area.

The model of propositional inference incorporated the mechanism for lexical inference, and they must both in turn be contained within any model of quantified inference. Inferences based on synonymity are a very salient feature because the diposition of quantifiers allows the same basic fact to be expressed in a variety of ways, e.g.

> Not all the critics admired all of his films.
> Some of the critics did not admire all of his films.
> Some of the critics did not admire some of his films.
> All the critics did not like all his films

A similar flexibility extends to terms that are implicit quantifiers, e.g.

> You are not compelled to vote.

[1] Excerpts from the paper 'Models of deduction'. Reprinted with permission of the author and publishers from R. C. Falmagne (ed.) *Reasoning: representation and process* (Hillsdale, N. J.: Lawrence Erlbaum Associates, 1975).

You are allowed not to vote.
It is not necessary for you to vote.
It is possible for you not to vote.

There are at least two alternative ways in which these sorts of semantic relations may be handled. The first alternative is parasitic on a speaker's knowledge of how to give a surface form to an underlying semantic content. I have elsewhere specified a set of grammatical transformations that derive such synonymous sentences from a common underlying form (Johnson-Laird, 1970); and a number of other linguistic accounts of the synonymities involving quantifiers have been proposed (Leech, 1969; Seuren; 1969; Lakoff, 1970; Jackendoff, 1972). Here is not the place to try to weigh up the respective merits of these accounts; what they appear to have in common is the realization that the behaviour of quantifiers with negation conforms only in a covert and complicated way to the behaviour of these items in a logical calculus. As in logic, one quantifier within the scope of a negation, e.g. 'Not all of his films were admired', is equivalent to the alternative quantifier outside the scope of the negation, e.g. 'Some of his films were not admired.' The complexities arise because of the lack of clear devices in natural language for marking the scope of operators. Sometimes, for example, the scope of negation is indicated by the choice of quantifier, as in the contrast between the following sentences:

I did not like any of his films.
I did not like some of his films.

And sometimes scope is indicated by word order – although rarely definitively, because in a sentence such as 'None of the critics like some of his films' the first quantifier is within the scope of the second.

The second approach to the problem of synonymity is to provide a direct semantic representation or model for each sentence. The equivalence between sentences is then established by noting that they give rise to the same representation rather than by first reducing the sentences to a common underlying linguistic structure, and then providing a semantic interpretation for it. The direct approach is relatively unexplored for natural language, although Julian Davies at Edinburgh (personal communication) has written a computer program with this sort of facility for quantifiers. The contrast between the two alternative approaches resembles, in many ways, the contrast between an intensional and an extensional semantics. For example, the linguistic approach is well suited to accounting for relations between sentences, whereas the direct approach is well suited to accounting for the relations between sentences and what they describe in the real world. It is too soon either to determine which approach makes the better psychological sense or to grasp the extent to which they are empirically distinguishable.

A more important question is whether it is possible to devise a general model of inference with quantifiers. There is virtually no empirical data apart from the results of experiments on syllogisms, hence the main aim is to develop a model of how people cope with such syllogisms as the following typical example (from Lewis Carroll):

> All prudent men shun hyenas
> All bankers are prudent men
> _____
> ∴ All bankers shun hyenas

Psychological studies of the syllogism have been dogged by the baleful tradition of scholastic logic. Not that this logic is necessarily bad – it has simply been bad for psychologists, blinding them to some rather obvious points. Most introductory texts give a standard account of the syllogism, describing its four figures and its sixty-four moods, and concluding that there are 256 syllogisms. A psychologist, however, should recognize that there are exactly twice this number, because there is nothing God-given about the assumption, underlying the four traditional figures, that the predicate of the conclusion occurs in the first premise. A psychologist might be interested, for example, in the evaluation of a syllogism of the form

> All bankers are prudent men
> All prudent men shun hyenas
> _____
> ∴ All bankers shun hyenas

This syllogism, of course, is in a figure that does not correspond to any of the traditional four.

The early experimenters (e.g. Wilkins, 1928; Woodworth and Sells, 1935; Sells, 1936) relied on tasks that required given syllogisms to be evaluated rather than on tasks that ensured a syllogistic inference was made. They selected the syllogisms from what they thought was a population of 256 in an arbitrary way. (More recent studies have sometimes added the further vice of presenting pooled data from syllogisms of the same mood but different figures, a habit that unfortunately has made it difficult to use the results in constructing a model of inference.) Nevertheless, the pioneering studies led to the important idea of an 'atmosphere' effect in which negatives and the quantifier 'some' exert a potent bias on the form of an acceptable conclusion to a syllogism – or so, at least, the protagonists of the theory believed.

In order to test the theory and, more importantly, to develop a theory of syllogistic reasoning a systematic study of syllogisms is required. There are 512 possible syllogisms but there are only sixty-four different combinations of premises (of which twenty-seven yield valid inferences). If experimental subjects are asked to state what follows from each different premise combination, there is a strong presumption that they will be forced to make an inference; and, of course, the population of premise combinations is of a manageable size. Two recent studies, one of which is reported here have tested the ability of intelligent subjects to perform this task. The first study investigated only the twenty-seven valid premise combinations. The second study, carried out in collaboration with Huttenlocher, investigated all sixty-four pairs of premises. In both these studies, the syllogisms were presented with a sensible everyday content, but a content that lacked any perceptible bias toward particular forms of conclusion, e.g.

> Some of the parents are scientists.
> None of the drivers are parents.

The patterns of inference that were made in both experiments were very similar, even though the experiments were carried out with different materials on opposite sides of the Atlantic. This discussion will therefore concentrate on the second and more comprehensive study.

The most salient feature of the results is that there is a very wide divergence in the relative difficulty of syllogisms. To take two extreme examples, all twenty subjects presented with premises of the form

> Some B are A
> All B are C

correctly deduced a conclusion of the form *Some A are C* or its equivalent *Some C are A*. However, when these same subjects were presented with premises of the form

> All B are A
> No C are B

none of them gave the correct response. *Some A are not C.* Perhaps part of the fascination of syllogisms to psychologists is that the manipulation of a handful of variables can yield such very large differences in performance.

The results also demonstrated the inadequacy of the atmosphere hypothesis as a complete account of what goes on in syllogistic reasoning. As there is no point in belabouring this point, amply confirmed in another recent study (Mazzocco, Legrenzi, and Roncato, 1974), it can simply be stated that 40 per cent of the conclusions drawn by the subjects are in accordance with the hypothesis, 8 per cent of their conclusions are incompatible with the hypothesis, and the remaining 52 per cent of their responses are neither compatible nor incompatible with the hypothesis because they consisted almost entirely of the response that no conclusion could be drawn from the premises. It may be objected that the atmosphere hypothesis, in fact, accounts for most of the results if one ignores those syllogisms for which no conclusion was drawn from the premises. However, this objection merely begs the question: How is it that subjects realize that no conclusion follows? The atmosphere hypothesis cannot explain this phenomenon.

There was one striking and unexpected aspect of the results. Certain figures of the syllogism exerted a strong influence on the form of the conclusion that subjects inferred, and this influence did not depend on the logic of particular syllogisms. Where the premises were of the form below (where A–B designates the order in which terms A and B were mentioned, regardless of the quantifiers used)

A–B
B–C

85 per cent of the conclusions that were drawn had the form A–C. Where the premises were of the form

B–A
C–B

86 per cent of the conclusions that were drawn had the form C–A. In the case of the other two sorts of syllogisms, however, there were only slight biases, as the following percentages show:

B–A	A–B
B–C	C–B
—	—
A–C (54%)	C–A (67%)

Although the 'figural' effect provides an important clue to how people make syllogistic inferences, it is not the whole story. There is an interaction between the figure and the mood of the premises; and the main goal of a model of syllogistic inference must be to account for the interaction.

Why has this figural effect never been noticed before? The answer is simply because of the neglect of half the possible syllogisms, a neglect fostered by relying on a traditional account of the logic of syllogisms. Indeed, it is a pity that psychologists have not gone back to Aristotle, because the first of his figures has the form

All A are B
All B are C
————————
∴ All A are C

This form of syllogism is the only one that Aristotle considered to be perfect, perhaps because the transitivity of the connection between its terms is obvious at a glance (see Kneale and Kneale, 1962, p. 73).

Aristotle's method of validating syllogisms involved their 'reduction', by way of a variety of transformations, to the pattern of his perfect syllogism. Subsequent recipes for syllogistic inference have tended to be more mysterious. They are mechanical procedures that work, but their workings are in no way intuitive. It is natural to wonder how such procedures have been established as infallible. One possibility is that they have been tested by exhaustive searches for counter-examples. Another possibility, however, is simply that people, even logically naïve people, are capable of syllogistic inference and, with sufficient care, can elucidate a syllogism of any form. This possibility obviously demands that a model of syllogistic inference be able to account for valid and invalid deductions.

The essence of the model to be developed here is that an initial representation of the premises is set up, from which a conclusion may be read off. This initial representation, however, may be subjected to a series of tests. Where it is submitted to all of these tests, any ultimate conclusion corresponds in all cases to a valid inference. Where some of the tests are omitted, the conclusion may or may not be valid. The syllogisms that are easy to solve turn out either not to permit tests of the initial representation or else not to require their initial conclusions to be modified. The syllogisms that are difficult to solve do permit tests of the initial representation and invariably these tests call for a modified conclusion.

It is impossible from mere introspection to determine how the different sorts of syllogistic premises are mentally represented. They may be represented in a format resembling Euler's diagrams (see Erickson, 1973; Revlis, 1975; Neimark and Chapman, 1975). However, one difficulty with this representation is that it cannot account for the 'figural' effect because, for example, the representation of *Some A are B* is identical to the representation of *Some B are A*. It is unfortunate that, in developing his interesting set-theoretic model of syllogistic inference, Erickson (1973) has overlooked the possibility of a 'figural' effect by neglecting half the possible syllogisms. The fact that human reasoners often show a pronounced 'figural' bias in stating their conclusions, even where such a bias is logically unwarranted, demonstrates the need to modify any simpler representation of premises in the form of Euler's circles. However, instead of attempting such a modification, an entirely different format has been chosen for the present model. The model assumes that human reasoners represent a class by imagining an arbitrary number of its members. For example, a class of artists is represented by a set of elements that are tagged in some way as artists. The nature of the elements and their tags is immaterial – they may be vivid visual images or ghostlike verbal tags. The crucial point is simply that they are discrete elements. A statement such as 'All the artists are beekeepers' relates two separate classes and it is represented in the following way:

$$\begin{array}{cc} \text{artist} & \text{artist} \\ \downarrow & \downarrow \\ \text{beekeeper} & \text{beekeeper (beekeeper)} \end{array}$$

where representatives of one class are mapped on to representatives of the other class, and the parenthetical item indicates that there may be beekeepers who are not artists. This representation is similar, but not isomorphic, to an Euler diagram. The discrepancy arises from the function of the arrows, which may be interpreted as pointers within a list-processing language. In other words, although the mapping represented by a single arrow is logically symmetrical, i.e. $a \rightarrow b$ is equivalent to $a \leftarrow b$, the two expressions are not psychologically equivalent. Intuitively, the item at the tail of the arrow can be thought of as having stored with it the address in memory of the item at the head of the arrow. Therefore, a fundamental assumption of the model is that it is easier to read off information from such representations proceeding in the direction of the arrows. It is possible to proceed in the opposite direction, but it is harder because it will be necessary to search memory for the item at the tail of the arrow. The model is accordingly very far from making the assumption that subjects tend readily to convert statements (*pace*, Chapman & Chapman, 1959). It does not even assume that they make valid conversions spontaneously during syllogistic reasoning, e.g. from 'Some artists are bricklayers' to 'Some bricklayers are artists.' There is good reason to suppose that such pairs of statements are not always equivalent in ordinary discourse. The former statement, as Hintikka (1973, p. 69) has emphasized, presupposes that the field of search includes all artists, whereas the latter statement presupposes that the field of search includes all bricklayers. This divergence may even lead to a rather special interpretation of the predicate term, suggesting in the second example above, for instance, that some bricklayers are artists in their manner of laying bricks.

In general, a universal statement, *All A are B*, is represented in the following way:

$$\begin{matrix} a & a \\ \downarrow & \downarrow \\ b & b & (b) \end{matrix}$$

where the parenthetical item (*b*) indicates that there may be a *b* that is not *a*. The number of *a*'s and *b*'s in the representation is, of course, entirely arbitrary – we may just as well have linked fifteen *a*'s to fifteen *b*'s and included thirty parenthetical *b*'s; for convenience, we have chosen two *a*'s in representing each of the different sorts of premise. A particular affirmative statement, *Some A are B*, is represented in the following way:

$$\begin{matrix} a & (a) \\ \downarrow & \\ b & (b) \end{matrix}$$

where (*a*) indicates that there may be an *a* that is not *b*, and (*b*) indicates that there may be a *b* that is not *a*.

The representation of a negative statement involves a negative link: there is no mapping of the sort defined above and, moreover, none can be established by any subsequent manipulations of the representation. The representation of a universal negative statement *No A are B* requires an arbitrary number of negative mappings, which are here indicated by stopped arrows:

$$\begin{matrix} a & a \\ \downarrow\!\!\!/ & \downarrow\!\!\!/ \\ b & b \end{matrix}$$

If there is a negative link between *a* and *b*, neither of them may be involved in any positive links from *a* to *b*, or from *b* to *a*. A particular negative statement, *Some A are not B*, is represented by

$$\begin{matrix} a & (a) \\ \downarrow\!\!\!/ & \downarrow \\ b & b \end{matrix}$$

where the positive mapping, (*a*) → *b*, indicates that some *a* may be *b*. . .

It is a simple matter to write a program that sets up a representation for the first premise of a syllogism. The representation of the second premise is a more complicated matter because one term – the middle term of the syllogism – will have already been represented. The logical work, in fact, commences with the representation of the second premise because it is grafted on to the representation of the first premise. The process is perhaps best described by way of an example.

Suppose that the first premise of a syllogism is of the form *Some A are B*, and can accordingly be represented as

A crucial distinction is whether or not the middle term is the quantified item in the second premise. The representation of the premise *All B are C* simply involves mapping the existing members of *B* on to representative elements of *C*:

The valid conclusion *Some A are C* may be read off from this representation, proceeding in the direction of the arrows. However, if the second premise is *All C are B* then it is necessary to set up some representative elements of *C* and to map them on to *B*. It is also necessary to allow that there may be other *b*'s that are not *c*'s; therefore, an initial representation of this syllogism is

a   (a)
↓
b   (b)   (b)
↑   ↑
c   c

Because the mappings do not proceed in a uniform direction, there is no firm anchor on which to base the inference; and the model predicts that subjects will tend to be divided between concluding (invalidly) *Some A are C* and concluding (invalidly) *Some C are A*.

Both the representations that have been described reflect an initial bias of the model toward establishing transitive mappings. This feature has been introduced in order to account for the subjects' bias toward drawing conclusions where, in fact, none are warranted. Because many subjects are capable of a more sophisticated syllogistic performance, the model assumes that once an initial representation of the premises has been created, it may be submitted to tests before any attempt is made to read off a conclusion. These tests can be characterized as efforts to test to destruction any initial transitive mappings. The initial phase is analogous to a process of verification; the testing phase is analogous to a process of falsification and, as with falsification, it is often overlooked by subjects (see Johnson-Laird and Wason, Reading 9).

The procedure for falsifying a mapping involves trying to modify the representation of the second premise so that it is no longer connected to items that are themselves involved in a mapping relation. The procedure has no effect on the first illustrative syllogism but it is possible to modify the intial representation of the second illustrative syllogism from

$$
\begin{array}{ccc}
a & (a) & \\
\downarrow & & \\
b & (b) & (b) \\
\uparrow & \uparrow & \\
c & c &
\end{array}
$$

to

$$
\begin{array}{ccc}
a & (a) & \\
\downarrow & & \\
b & (b) & (b) \\
& \uparrow & \uparrow \\
& c & c
\end{array}
$$

The critical link has been broken; and because both its presence and its absence are consistent with the interpretation of the premises, it follows that no valid conclusion can be deduced from them.

The predictions of the model for the two illustrative syllogisms are summarized below, together with the numbers of experimental subjects (out of 20) deducing the predicted conclusions:

Some A are B		Some A are B	
All B are C		All C are B	
∴ Some A are C: 16		∴ Some A are C:	5
		∴ Some C are A:	5
		No conclusion follows:	9

A simple set-theoretic model does not account for the results with the first of these syllogisms because it predicts a response of *Some A are C* as often as a response of *Some C are A*.

Certain features of the present model can only be illustrated by considering the representation and testing of negative premises. Consider premises of the form

$$
\begin{array}{l}
\text{No B are A} \\
\text{All C are B}
\end{array}
$$

The first premise is represented as

$$
\begin{array}{cc}
a & a \\
\uparrow & \uparrow \\
b & b
\end{array}
$$

The second premise, of course, requires an additional *b* to be introduced and, when such an introduction occurs, the model bears in mind the universal nature of the first premise:

It is a straightforward matter to read off the conclusion, *No C are A*, but a more difficult matter to read off the conclusion *No A are C*.

The initial representation of the premises

No B are A
All B are C

is set up in a similar way:

$$\begin{array}{ccc}
a & a & \\
\uparrow & \uparrow & \\
b & b & \\
\downarrow & \downarrow & \\
c & c & \text{(c)}
\end{array}$$

However, the mappings do not proceed in a uniform direction and the model predicts that subjects will be divided between the (invalid) conclusions *No A are C* and *No C are A*.

The falsification tests of a negative mapping consist in trying to establish that a transitive link can be set up between the elements in the representation. The only constraint on this manoeuvre is that elements cannot be linked in inconsistent ways such as these in the following example:

because these links imply inconsistencies, such as that *c* both is and is not an *a*. The first syllogism survives the falsification tests unmodified. The second syllogism does not. Its initial representation

$$\begin{array}{ccc}
a & a & \\
\uparrow & \uparrow & \\
b & b & \\
\downarrow & \downarrow & \\
c & c & \text{(c)}
\end{array}$$

allows the following links to be established:

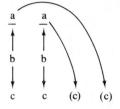

It is always possible to add new parenthetical items provided there are existing ones; it is never possible to add any items to a set that contains no parenthetical items. The distinction, in fact, corresponds to the traditional notion of a distributed term (no parenthetical items) and an undistributed term (parenthetical items). The new links in the representation are, of course, consistent. Yet subjects initially predisposed to conclude *No A are C* may find this second representation, which suggests *All A are C*, such a contrast that they may judge that no conclusion follows from the premises. More astute subjects, however, can appreciate that it is impossible to add further *a*'s to the representation and therefore that *Some C are not A*.

The predictions of the model for the two negative syllogisms are summarized below, together with the number of experimental subjects (out of 20) deducing the predicted conclusions:

No B are A	No B are A	
All C are B	All B are C	
∴ No C are A: 13	∴ No C are A:	4
∴ No A are C: 3	∴ No A are C:	3
	No conclusion follows:	4
	∴ Some C are not A:	7

The main features of the model of syllogistic inference have now been illustrated, and it should be obvious that it has the sort of flexibility needed to match the diversity of subjects' deductions. To generate quantitative predictions, however, would require the specification of various parameters and the estimation of their values from the experimental results. The exercise would not be very rewarding. A more appealing possibility is to try to derive assumptions about the relative value of these parameters from the processing properties of the model itself. The point can be illustrated by considering the figural effect in terms of the processing of lists. When the arrows in a representation lie in a uniform direction, they largely determine the direction in which conclusions are read off from it. It is possible to proceed in the opposite direction but at the cost of having to search memory for the items that are the tails of arrows. This asymmetry, which is reflected in human performance, is a simple consequence of the structure of lists. At a later stage of development of the model, it may be possible to derive some of fine-grain aspects of performance from similar sorts of information-processing considerations.

The reader familiar with the problems of manipulating Euler's circles can appreciate the computational advantage of the present style of representation. An Eulerian representation of, for example, *Some A are B* requires four separate diagrams to be created. When such representations are combined, the combinatorial consequences can become psychologically embarrassing, particularly where several premises are involved, e.g.

> Some A are B
> All B are C
> All C are D

An Eulerian deduction from these premises involves considering at least $4 \times 2 \times 2 = 16$ different combinations of diagram, whereas the list representation is simply

$$
\begin{array}{cccc}
a & \text{(a)} & & \\
\downarrow & & & \\
b & \text{(b)} & & \\
\downarrow & \downarrow & & \\
c & c & \text{(c)} & \\
\downarrow & \downarrow & \downarrow & \\
d & d & d & \text{(d)}
\end{array}
$$

from which it is easy to infer *Some A are D*. It may be that in making such inferences human reasoners break the problem down into a series of syllogisms; but it is also feasible that they set up a complete representation of several premises in this way.

There are, of course, alternative models of syllogistic inference that can be couched in the list format. Mark Steedman (personal communication) has devised a model, involving a more elegant representation, in which invalid inferences arise not from a failure to test initial and improper representations of the combined premises but from actual errors in the representations of single premises. In particular, the model assumes that parenthetical items are often neglected so that universal premises come to be interpreted as *All and only A are B*. The list representations may also be extended in order to deal with quasi-numerical quantifiers (e.g. 'many', 'most', 'few') and with statements involving several quantifiers. A statement such as 'Some of the tenants will not vote for all the representatives' may be represented in the following way:

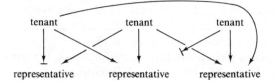

where the mapping represents the relation *votes for*. The combination of these diagrams is a complicated affair, but from the few studies of inference with such statements (Johnson-Laird, 1969) it seems that untrained human reasoners have fairly restricted powers with them, too. It is likely that the list representation is sufficiently flexible to form part of a general model of quantified inference. . .

Conclusions

When information is combined the process often seems to involve the creation of an internal 'model' of the world. This procedure seems to be necessary for syllogistic inference; and it has the great advantage that the transitivity of relational terms can be made a direct consequence of their representation rather than an indirect consequence of an additional rule of inference. Indeed, it is seldom that it can be conclusively demonstrated that the transformation of information does not proceed by the construction of internal models.

What of the role of content? Do different contents introduce perhaps different principles of inference? It is certainly noticeable that a listener is able to draw on general knowledge to allow a speaker to leave many things unsaid. The sorts of inference that a listener can make are illustrated in the following examples culled from current work in a variety of diciplines:

He went to three drugstores.
Therefore, the first two drugstores didn't have what he wanted.
(Abelson & Reich, 1969)

The mirror shatttered because the child grabbed the broom.
Therefore, the child hit the mirror with the broom and broke it.
(Bransford and McCarrell, 1972)

The policeman held up his hand and the cars stopped.
Therefore, the policeman was directing the traffic.
(Collins and Quillian, 1972)

Harry is enjoying his new job at the bank, and he hasn't been to prison yet.
Therefore, Harry may be tempted to steal some of the money in the bank.
(Wilson, 1972)

John gave Mary a beating with a stick.
Therefore, John wanted to hurt Mary.
(Schank, Goldman, Rieger, and Riesbeck, 1973)

Janet needed some money. She got her piggybank and started to shake it.
Therefore, Janet got her piggybank and shook it in order to get some money from it.
(Charniak, 1973)

Of course, the man may have visited three drugstores in order to enforce a protection racket; and the mirror may have shattered because it was balanced on top of the broom; and so on. The inferences are therefore plausible rather than valid. What appears to happen, however, is that people exploit a communal base of knowledge that includes such assumptions as:

> Drugstores are shops that have certain sorts of goods.
> People visit shops in order to buy goods.
> If one shop does not have an item that it normally stocks, then another shop of the same sort may have it.

This knowledge will be automatically elicited by any utterance with a relevant topic, and it can be used by the inferential machinery in order to make good any gaps in the explicit discourse. The procedure relies on a convention that a speaker will draw attention to any special circumstances that render communal assumptions inappropriate. . .

9. A theoretical analysis of insight into a reasoning task[1]

P. N. Johnson-Laird and P. C. Wason

Previous research on deductive reasoning has usually involved the evaluation of given inferences as valid or invalid, or the making of inferences from given premises. These techniques have been a characteristic feature in studies of syllogistic reasoning, in studies of the effect of personality variables upon the deductive process, and in miscellaneous investigations of logical competence. Such research has increased our knowledge about the interactions between cognitive and affective processes and about the layman's general logical ability, but it has perhaps been less revealing about the process of reasoning itself. A notable exception is, of course, provided by research on the computer simulation of thinking (e.g. Newell, Shaw, and Simon, 1958b; Reitman, 1965.) In the tasks which we shall consider the Ss (subjects) have neither to make inferences in a direct fashion from premises presented to them, nor to evaluate given conclusions as valid or invalid. They have to choose the conditions which would allow a valid inference to be made. These tasks are structurally simple but deceptively difficult, and the present paper offers a theoretical analysis of the attempts to solve them.

The problem

This is one example of the problem (Wason, 1966). You are presented with four cards showing, respectively, 'A', 'D', '4', '7', and you know from previous experience that every card, of which these are a subset, has a letter on one side and a number on the other side. You are then given this rule about the four cards in front of you: 'If a card has a vowel on one side, then it has an even number on the other side.'

Next you are told: 'Your task is to say which of the cards you need to turn over in order to find out whether the rule is true or false.'

The most frequent answers are 'A and 4' and 'only A'. They are both wrong.

[1] Excerpts from the paper in *Cognitive Psychology*, **1** (1970), 134–48. A postscript (1977) has been added, written specially for this volume.

The right answer is 'A and 7' because if these two stimuli were to occur on the same card, then the rule would be false but otherwise it would be true. Very few highly intelligent S's get the answer right spontaneously; some take a considerable time to grasp it; a small minority even dispute its correctness, or at least remain puzzled by it. . .

The extreme difficulty of this task would seem to be of theoretical importance. In addition, the thought processes engaged in it are not as entirely removed from reality as they might seem: they are analogous to the crucial role which disconfirmation plays in hypothetico–deductive systems (e.g. Popper, 1959.)

Notation

The theoretical analysis is based on the combined results of four experiments. But before presenting their results, the notation used for referring to the problems will be described.

The rule, or test sentence, always had the same underlying logical form of a conditional sentence: 'if p then q.' In logic the variables p and q refer to atomic propositions. The convention will be adopted, however, that these variables refer, not to propositions, but to the stimuli designated by them. Hence, in the present example, p refers to a vowel, $\bar{p}$ (not-p) to a consonant, q to an even number, and $\bar{q}$ (not-q) to an odd number.

The selection of the cards will be referred to by citing the appropriate letters, e.g. 'p and q', 'p, q, and $\bar{q}$'. Since the constraint is always imposed that there is a value of p (or $\bar{p}$) on one side of a card and a value of q (or $\bar{q}$) on the other side, the correct solution is the selection of p and $\bar{q}$.

When reference is made to a card, irrespective of the value on its other side, the appropriate letter will simply be cited. When the values on both sides are relevant, but the S has not seen the value which is face downwards, the latter value is mentioned second and placed in parentheses, e.g. $q(p)$. When both sides of a card have been seen, the parentheses will be omitted and the value which was originally face upwards cited first.

Experimental results

Table 1 shows the frequency with which cards were initially selected in four experiments in which all the Ss were university students (Wason, 1968; Wason, 1969; Wason and Johnson-Laird, 1970).

It will be noted that two errors frequently occur: the selections are not random. $\bar{q}$ is omitted and q is selected, but the former error is much more pervasive. The thirteen errors classified under 'Others' consisted in ten cases of the inclusion of $\bar{p}$, or the omission of p, and in three cases of the selection of all four cards. The latter selection was difficult to interpret. It is the correct response if the rule is construed as equivalence, i.e. 'if, and only if, p then q'. But there was considerable introspective evidence that the Ss were selecting all four cards in order to avoid any possible error of omission. Indeed, when the Ss claimed to be construing the rule as an equivalence (e.g. 'I assume the converse holds'), they nearly always selected just p and q.

In the pilot study (Wason, 1966) the task was binary in the sense that values of both p and q were dichotomized: a letter which is not a vowel is a consonant, and a whole number which is not even is odd. But the actual stimuli on the cards were not binary; they were letters and numbers falling under these classes. The initial selections, however, were similar under all the following experimental modifications.

1. The task was strictly binary. The Ss knew that only two possible stimuli could occur on the other side of each card, e.g. a red triangle had only a red or a blue circle on the other side (Wason, 1969). It was argued by others that under this tightly controlled situation error would be significantly reduced.

2. In another condition, $\bar{p}$ could be satisfied by any geometric figure other than a square and $\bar{q}$ by any coloured scribble other than a red one (Wason, 1968.) It was argued by others that $\bar{q}$ would be more likely to be recognized as such, and hence selected, when it could not be named *a priori*.

Table 1. Frequency of initial selection of cards in four experiments

p and q	59
p	42
p, q, and $\bar{q}$	9
p and $\bar{q}$	5
Others	13
	N = 128

3. All the information was potentially visible on the same side of the cards but partially masked (Wason and Johnson-Laird, 1970). It was argued by others that Ss tended to interpret the 'other side' of a card as being the side which is face downwards.

4. The values of $\bar{p}$ and $\bar{q}$ consisted in the absence of any stimulus at all (Wason and Johnson-Laird, 1970). It was argued by us that $\bar{q}$ would be appreciated as such more readily if it were to consist in the absence of q rather than being satisfied by some stimulus other than q.

5. The rule was expressed as a quantified sentence rather than a strict conditional, e.g. 'every card which has a red triangle on one side has a blue circle on the other side' (Wason, 1969). It was argued (H. H. Clark, personal communication) that a sentence in the form, 'if p then q', has the undersirable connotation of a temporal, or even causal, relation between p and q.

6. Detailed instruction was given that the converse of the rule could not be assumed (Wason, 1968.)

An algorithm for testing the rule

Before presenting the model of human performance it will be useful to consider one simple way that a computer might be programmed to solve the problem. The algorithm provides a base line that contrasts sharply with human performance.

The first step for the computer would be to retrieve the truth table appropriate to the rule, in the present case, 'if p then q'. In the propositional calculus a rule in this form is known as material implication. It is true under the following combinations of values: (p and q), ($\bar{p}$ and q), and ($\bar{p}$ and $\bar{q}$), and false in only one instance (p and $\bar{q}$). However, it is unreasonable to assume that Ss construe a conditional as true when its antecedent is false. And it has been demonstrated (Johnson-Laird and Tagart, 1969) that most Ss (79 per cent) evaluate ($\bar{p}$ and q) and ($\bar{p}$ and $\bar{q}$) as irrelevant to the truth or falsity of the rule. In fact, only 4 per cent construed the rule as material implication. But in the present context, the important point is that both the truth table for material implication and the 'defective' truth table in which the two $\bar{p}$ cases are irrelevant rather than true, and which most Ss evidently use, give identical results in relation to the values which have to be selected in order to determine the truth of the rule.

Having retrieved either truth table the computer would scan each card in turn with reference to all four combinations in the truth table. Its algorithm is then governed by the following simple principle: a card is selected as potentially informative if, and only if, a value on it can make the rule false when it is associated with another value. Thus p would be selected because it would falsify the rule if it were associated with $\bar{q}$; and for the same reason $\bar{q}$ would be selected. But neither q nor $\bar{p}$ can falsify under any circumstances, and hence they would not be selected.

It is quite evident from the experimental results not only that human Ss fail to perform in accordance with this algorithm, but that they do not even perform in accordance with their own truth table for the rule. The source of error in the problem would seem to be connected with the failure to appreciate the crucial importance of falsification as opposed to verification.

Remedial procedures [see Wason, Reading 7]

Simply asking the Ss to think again about their selections or getting them to imagine falsifying values on the back of the cards (Wason, 1968) does not make the Ss change their selection. Similarly, treating the problem as a learning task (Hughes, 1966) is unenlightening. A drastic simplification in the structure of the task, i.e. a choice between only values of q and $\bar{q}$, does however enable all the Ss to gain insight eventually (Johnson-Laird and Wason, 1970).

When the material consists of all four values the introduction of certain remedial procedures by E (experimenter), after the Ss had made their initial selections, does also enable the majority to achieve the correct solution eventually. The rationale of these procedures was to create a conflict, or contradiction, between the Ss initial *selection* of cards and a subsequent *evaluation* of the cards with respect to the truth or falsity of the rule. Such evaluations were either hypothetical when the S considered the effect of a possible value on the other side of a card, or actual when he saw the values on both sides of a card.

These procedures were used in two experiments (Wason, 1969; Wason and Johnson-Laird, 1970). There appeared to be four qualitatively distinct stages with respect to the interaction between the selection and evaluation processes. They may seen incredible to anyone who has not experienced them directly.

1. In the first stage it is assumed that the S merely evaluates the cards by reference to what was, or was not, initially selected. In this way the selection process totally dominates the evaluation process. For example, suppose p were initially selected and $\bar{q}$ not selected, then p ($\bar{q}$) would be evaluated as falsifying, but $\bar{q}$ (p) denied such a status. Similarly, if q were selected and $\bar{p}$ not selected, then q ($\bar{p}$) would be evaluated as falsifying, but $\bar{p}$ (q) dismissed as irrelevant. These bizarre phenomena occurred quite frequently in the earlier experiments but less frequently in the later ones: they clearly suggest that the reversibility of the cards is not always recognized.

2. In the second stage it is assumed that the S does appreciate the reversibility of the cards. Hence he is consistent in his evaluations, regardless of which cards had been selected and which side had been face upwards. But surprisingly this does not necessarily lead to any gain of insight. The $\bar{q}$ (p) card may be evaluated as falsifying, but $\bar{q}$ may not be selected after this correct evaluation, even when both sides of the card have been exposed. Similarly, the q ($\bar{p}$) card may be evaluated correctly as irrelevant, but q may still be selected. Responses of this kind pervaded the protocols of the Ss amd were the most characteristic feature of performance in the tasks. Clearly, the insight that a card should be selected if it falsifies, or rejected if it is irrelevant, does not follow merely from the correct evaluation of the cards.

3. In the third stage it is assumed that the S appreciates, for the first time, the crucial importance of cards which could falsify the rule; and that this comes about from a consideration of the effects of two cards: p (q) and $\bar{q}$ (p). The former indicates that the rule is true; the latter indicates that it is false. Quite a large proportion of the Ss are unable to resolve this conflict, even when both sides of the cards are revealed, and dismiss $\bar{q}$ p with rationalizing remarks. Others do gain the necessary insight and accordingly select $\bar{q}$.

4. In the final stage it is assumed that the S appreciates that only cards which could falisify should be selected, and this would seem to involve the evaluation of the rule with reference to q (p) and $\bar{p}$ (q). The former verifies; the latter is irrelevant. It seems likely that two factors make this insight particularly difficult. First, a conflict between a card which verifies and one which is merely irrelevant is unlikely to be so intense as a conflict between a card which verifies and one which falsifies. Second, q is likely to have been selected at some point, and hence the S may be reluctant to reconsider it. . .

The model

Figure 1 shows the flow diagram of the model of the selection process, which attempts to take account of the initial selection of the cards, the order in which they are selected, and changes in selection due to remedial procedures. It is thus a model which allows both for differences between Ss and for changes within an individual S's performance.

The model assumes that the S without insight will focus on cards mentioned in the rule. If he assumes that the rule implies its converse, then both p and q will be selected. If the converse is not assumed, then only p will be selected. This provides a plausible reason of why so many Ss chose only p initially, and it is more consistent with their introspective reports.

'Partial insight' consists in realizing that cards which could falsify should be selected. 'Complete insight' consists in realizing that only cards which could falsify should be selected. (It will be noted that this insight corresponds to the central principle of the algorithm considered earlier.) Hence complete insight entails partial insight: the former cannot be gained without gaining the latter. There is empirical support for this proposal. Many Ss maintain a final selection of p, q, and $\bar{q}$ (partial insight), but hardly any maintain a final selection of only p.

All Ss will begin by placing either p and q (0, 1, 2) or only p (0, 1,3) on their list of items to be tested. There are then three possible levels of insight.

No insight. Ss without any insight will select only these values because they alone could verify the rule (4, 5, 6, 7, 10). They will test no further cards (4, 13, 14, 16).

Partial insight. Ss with partial insight will go on to place the remaining cards on the list of items to be tested (4, 13, 14, 15). Regardless of the initial selection, $\bar{p}$ will be considered irrelevant because it could neither verify nor falsify (4, 5, 6, 8, 12), and $\bar{q}$ will be selected because it could falsify (4, 5, 6, 7, 8, 9, 10). An S, who did not initially place q on the list, will do so now and select it because it could verify. Thus an S with partial insight will ultimately select p, q and $\bar{q}$.

Complete insight. Ss with complete insight will select p and $\bar{q}$ and reject q because it could not falsify (4, 5, 6, 7, 8, 12). Since the question of complete insight arises when S encounters a card which could verify the rule, it can occur in two main ways. It may be gained during the initial tests. But if S initially rejected the converse, it may be gained after partial insight when S is testing q for the very first time. However, an S who initially accepts the converse and selects both p and q should be much less likely to gain complete insight after gaining partial insight. He would have no occasion to retest q and hence could not take the appropriate path in the flow diagram (from 6 to 7).

There is some empirical support for this aspect of the model. Many more of the Ss who initially selected only p gain complete insight than do Ss who initially selected both p and q. It is also particularly rare for the latter group of Ss to pass from partial insight to complete insight.

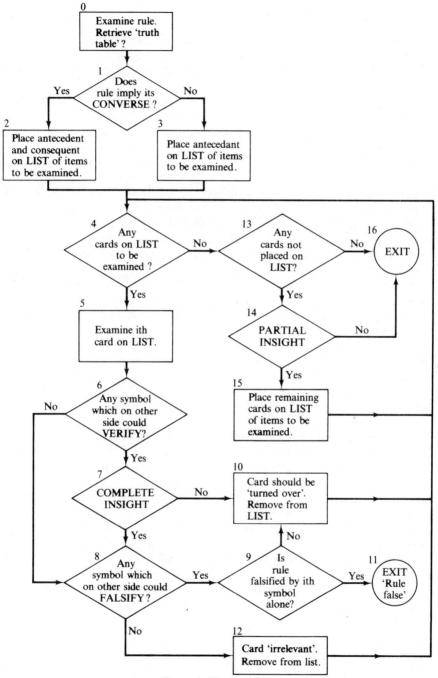

Figure 1. The model

The conceptual status of the model

The model provides a precise statement, in information–processing terms, of the extremely complex behaviour exhibited by highly intelligent Ss performing the selection task. Such an analysis brings out clearly the differences in the way in which a machine and a human being attempt to solve the problem. But what sort of evidence would refute the model and show it to be inadequate as an explanation of performance? There are several possibilities.

It will be noted that the greater the insight of an S, the greater the number of routines in the model through which he passes. Hence it is possible to derive predictions about reaction times. One might consider an experiment in which a decision has to be reached about the cards presentéd individually. The model would predict that, when p is presented, all the Ss would select it, and the reaction time would be relatively rapid. But the selection of $\bar{q}$, which depends upon an additional falsification routine, should take a relatively longer time. Such an experiment would obviously allow a more sensitive degree of measurement than the merely nominal classification used in the experiments under consideration.

Second, other logical connectives could be used to test the model. For instance, with the disjunctive rule, 'p or q,' the correct selection is $\bar{p}$ and $\bar{q}$. But a partial insight would lead to the selection of all four cards – a result which hardly ever occurs with a conditional rule. Hence, if a considerable number of Ss went through the following stages: (1) p and q, (2) p, $\bar{p}$, q, and $\bar{q}$, (3) $\bar{p}$ and $\bar{q}$, then the validity of the model would be corroborated. If other responses, or sequences of responses occurred, then doubt would be cast on its general validity. Some promising results have been obtained (Wason and Johnson-Laird, 1969), but unfortunately Ss were constrained by having to select a limited number of cards in the experiment.

An experiment by Legrenzi (1970) is also relevant. The rule was, 'It is not possible for there to be a vowel on one side of a card and an odd number on the other side.' In an independent evaluation study Legrenzi found that only the contingency 'A and 3' was considered to falsify the rule. Hence, on the assumption that the rule is construed as symmetric, the model generates the following predictions. An S without insight will make the correct selection, 'A and 3', since both A and 3 could verify the rule. However, an S with partial insight will consider them all. Finally, an S with complete insight will also make the correct selection since only 'A and 3' could falsify the rule. In fact, Legrenzi found that 77 per cent of the Ss made the correct selection, and 17 per cent selected all four cards. Moreover, he had the impression that many of the Ss who made the correct selection had little insight into the task. . .

Conclusions

The selection task, using a conditional rule, is an extremely difficult problem although, unlike the classic Gestalt problems, the Ss initially experience no sense of difficulty. They are nearly always content to verify the rule by attending to the values explicitly mentioned in it. It is as if the values unmentioned in the rule play no part in the problem, a supposition very frequently corroborated by introspective reports. This results in error and may well lead to striking inconsistencies between previous selection and current evaluation of the material – inconsistencies which may, or may not, be recognized, tolerated, and resolved. When they are not recognized or resolved, an individual S begins to sound almost as if he were really two different people talking.

Gain of insight seems to depend upon three factors. First, the S must appreciate that the cards are reversible. He then has information which, in principle, can provide an escape from the effects of his own initial selection and enable him to evaluate the cards correctly. Second, he must be able to resolve the apparent conflict between his correct evaluation of p (q) and $\bar{q}$ (p). This leads to the partial insight that cards which could falsify should be selected. Finally, he must resolve the conflict between his correct evaluations of q (p) amd $\bar{p}$ (q) in order to gain the complete insight that only cards which could falsify should be selected.

This analysis of the development of insight is considerably more tentative than that of the information–processing model itself. While it may be necessary to modify the detail of this model, its general explanatory principle, involving the distinction between verification and falsification, seems to provide a satisfactory account of performance.

Postscript, 1977

Performance on the selection task up to 1970 was conducted on the abstract version of the problem, and the main interest was to account for the initial selection and the effects of remedial procedures (see Wason, Reading 7). Two main developments occurred subsequently. They concern (1) the effects of presenting the task in a 'realistic guise', and (2) alternative theories about the initial selections.

We argued on the basis of the initial results that performance is incompatible with Piaget's theory of 'formal operations', as it had been formulated up to 1972 (Beth and Piaget, 1966; Inhelder and Piaget, 1958; Piaget, 1972; Wason and Johnson-Laird, 1972; Wason, 1977; but see Piaget, Reading 10 for a radical reformulation). The traditional theory assumes that in the highest stage in the development of intelligence, form and content become dissociated in thinking about a formal problem. Piaget (Beth and Piaget, 1966, p. 181) claimed that the adolescent, confronted by a complex causal situation, will ask himself whether fact x implies fact y, and frequently do this by formulating a proposition in the form, 'if p then q'. In order to test this proposition, he will search for the counter-example, x and non-y, i.e. p and $\bar{q}$. Such a description reads like an accurate account of what our highly intelligent subjects conspicuously fail to do.

We discovered, however, that by attempting to relate the selection task more closely to the subjects' experience, performance was dramatically improved. Such an improvement strengthens our criticism of the traditional theory of formal operations: difficulty is not so much intrinsic to the logical structure of the task, but to its content or mode of presentation. Improvement due to a realistic guise was first shown by Wason and Shapiro (1971). The conditional rule: 'Every time I go to Manchester I travel by train.' The four cards showed (respectively) 'Manchester' (p), 'Leeds' (p̄), Train (q) and Car (q̄). The task was to imagine that each card represented a journey (with destination on one side of a card and mode of transport on the other side) made by the experimenter, and that the rule represented a claim about these journeys. Ten out of sixteen subjects were correct, compared with two out of sixteen in a control group which utilized abstract material. This result was independently corroborated by Lunzer, Harrison, and Davey (1972) with pictorial material. A more remarkable demonstration was achieved by Johnson-Laird, Legrenzi, and Sonino Legrenzi (1972). The subjects were instructed to imagine that they were postal workers engaged in sorting letters on a conveying belt; their task was to determine whether the following rule had been violated: 'If a letter is sealed, then it has a 5d stamp on it.' The material consisted of four envelopes arranged as follows: the back of a sealed envelope (p); the back of an unsealed envelope (p̄); the front of an envelope with a 5d stamp on it (q); the front of an envelope with a 4d stamp on it (q̄). The instructions were to select only those envelopes which definitely needed to be turned over to find out whether, or not, they violated the rule (see figure 2). There were twenty-four subjects, and they performed the task under both this 'concrete' condition, and under an 'abstract' control condition in which arbitrary symbols were associated in the usual way. Under the 'concrete' condition twenty-two subjects were correct, and under the control, 'abstract' condition seven subjects were correct. There was obviously no transfer between the two forms of the task, and only two subjects subsequently acknowledged any logical relation between them.

'Concrete condition'

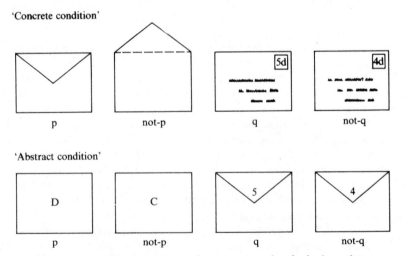

'Abstract condition'

Figure 2. Material used in the 'envelope experiment' under both conditions

Subsequent research attempted to determine whether the concrete terms, or the realistic relation between the terms, facilitated performance. Bracewell and Hidi (1974) found that only the relation between the terms tended to elicit insight; Gilhooly and Falconer (1974) found the opposite: the realistic nature of the terms proved a more potent factor than the relation between them. Van Duyne (1974, 1976) partially resolved the issue by showing it was much more complex: 'degrees' of realism affected performance in a continuous, linear way. Furthermore, contingent sentences, e.g. 'All soldiers have guns' were found to be significantly easier to process than necessary sentences, e.g. 'All glucose is sweet.' The results of all these studies reinforce our criticism of the traditional theory of formal operations, and corroborate Piaget's (Reading 10) revised formulations. The subjects' ordinary experience is relevant to problem solving performance, and our use of 'realistic guise' touches this experience.

The present information-processing model has been corroborated by Goodwin and Wason (1972) who showed that the subjects' degree of insight, postulated by the model, correlated with their verbal protocols. But at least three other explanations of the intial choice of cards have been proposed. Brée and Coppens (1976) have proposed an alternative model which assumes that subjects neither retrieve a truth table, nor seek to verify the test sentence. Their model assumes simply that subjects generally fail to make hypotheses about the hidden symbols on the other side of the cards. Such an idea appears to be only slightly different from the present model in its empirical consequence. Bracewell (1974) and Smalley (1974) have been more concerned about possible 'ambiguities' in the standard selection task. For example, Bracewell (1974) detects ambiguity in the phrase, 'one side of the card'. He suggests it is ambiguous precisely because it could mean either, 'the showing side', or 'the showing side and the hidden side'. Improved performance resulted when the rule was rephrased: 'If J is on either the showing face or the underside face of the card, then 2 is on the remaining side.' It would seem (incidentally) that such a reformulation could be relevant only to those versions of the selection task when the symbols are positioned on both sides of the cards, and could not be relevant to more recent versions (e.g. Wason and Johnson-Laird, 1970) in which all the information is potentially visible on the same side of the card. But, more important, it could be argued that Bracewell's reformulation of the rule constitutes a different problem. It does not so much disambiguate the test sentence; it makes explicit the assumptions which subjects fail to take into account. It is not too much of a *reductio ad absurdum* to claim that any deductive problem can be made easier by widening the individual's horizon of assumptions. In the well known 'nine dot problem' the individual has to join up nine dots (arranged in a 3 × 3 matrix) by four continuous straight lines. This is difficult because the individual unconsciously assumes that the lines must not extend beyond the boundary of the matrix. This assumption, however, could be made explicit by instructing the individual to join the dots by four continuous straight lines which may (or may not) extend beyond the area bounded by the dots. This extra hint spoils the problem. It is analogous to Bracewell's reformulation of the

selection task rule. However, it could be argued that such systematic refor-
mulations do enable the investigator to identify which assumptions limit a
subject's interpretation.

Finally, Wason and Evans (1974/5) have presented a radically different conception of the selection task. Evans and Lynch (1973) and Evans (1972c)
obtained evidence to suggest that performance in the selection task, and in a task
designed to elucidate the truth table underlying the conditional, is more primitive than had been supposed. It appeared to be relatively indifferent to the
presence of a negative in the conditional rule, especially when the consequent is
negated. For example, given the sentence: 'If there is a B on one side of a card,
then there will not be a 3 on the other side', there is a strong tendency for subjects
to select the B and the 3, and to be correct in so doing. But Evans argued that this
was not due to any logical acumen, but to a 'matching response bias': a simple
tendency to match the symbols mentioned in the test sentence with their
corresponding cards. ('The idea that a one-to-one relation is easy is so fundamental that one can hardly ask for a psychological justification for it.' Wason
and Johnson-Laird, 1972, p. 241.) Such an account is consistent with the present
information-processing model which assumes that 'the S without insight will
focus on the cards mentioned in the rule'. But it is inconsistent with the model's
assumption that, without insight, the subject will seek to verify the rule. If they
were seeking to verify, they would not choose the 3 but a number other than 3.
However, if it were merely the case that 'matching response bias' is a statistical
regularity, based on ignoring negatives, the finding of 'fortuitous correctness'
would not be particularly interesting. It would suggest that intelligent subjects
simply fail to reason in a complex task. This seems an over-simplification. In the
much easier disjunctive task, Wason and Johnson-Laird (1969) found that
'matching response bias' was conspicuously absent. Given an instruction to
prove the truth (or falsity) of a sentence like, 'Every card has a square which is
black on one side, or a line which is crooked on the other side', the dominant
tendency was one of double 'mismatching'. The subjects (correctly) tended to
select a 'white square' and a 'straight line'. In fact, 'double mismatching'
occurred 75 per cent of the time, and 'double matching' 19 per cent of the time. A
disjunctive relation seems undoubtedly easier than a conditional relation, and it
may simply be this difference in difficulty which tends to make subjects 'match'
on the conditional rule. Matching may be a response peculiar to extreme
bafflement, or lack of appreciation of logical structure.

It consequently seemed of considerable interest to relate 'matching bias' under
the (conditional) selection task to the subjects' own accounts of their behaviour.
Accordingly, Wason and Evans (1974/5) tested the same subjects under two
versions of the rule, one in which the consequent of the conditional was negated
(e.g. 'If there is a D on one side of the card, then there will not be a 5 on the other
side'), and one in which it was unnegated (e.g. 'If there is an F on one side of a
card, then there will be a 6 on the other side'). The innovation consisted in
collecting written protocols in the form of reasons for selecting (or not selecting)
each of the four cards under both presentations of the task. Out of the twenty-

four subjects, fifteen were 'correct' on the 'negative task' (consequent negated), and none 'correct' on the 'affirmative task' (consequent unnegated). This confirmation of the prediction was not at all surprising. More surprising was that, under the affirmative task four of the twenty-four protocols were classified as betraying thought processes in terms of falsification, but under the negative task eleven of the twenty-four protocols reflected such processes. Some typical examples were: 'If there is a B on the other side, then the statement is false'; 'To see if there is a Y on the other side to disprove the statement'; 'If this card is overturned and there is an F the statement is false,' etc. Table 2 shows the protocols for three subjects under both presentations of the task. (For purposes of exposition the symbols have been held constant; in the experiment they were, of course varied.)

Just like the present information-processing model, Wason and Evans postulated two kinds of thought process to account for the results. However, unlike the initial 'selection process' and subsequent 'evaluation process', postulated to account for the response to remedial procedures, Wason and Evans assume that even the initial 'reasons for choice' represent a tendency for the individual to construct a justification (or rationalization) of his 'matching bias choice', consistent with his knowledge of the situation. Hence, under the negative task, the test sentence would tend to elicit thought processes in terms of falsification, or denial. It follows that the protocols collected by Goodwin and Wason (1972) are not construed as independent evidence for the stages postulated in the Johnson-Laird and Wason (1970) model, but as justifications for the choices which define the stages.

The proclivity for finding explanations for data is further illustrated by Evans and Wason (1976). Both correct and incorrect solutions to the selection task were presented to independent groups of subjects, but all these solutions purported to be correct. The subjects' task was simply to supply reasons for selecting, or rejecting, each card, and to rate their confidence in the correctness of their reasons on a four-point scale. As expected, the 'reasons' tended to fit the solutions (whether correct or incorrect). This could be construed as a form of 'social compliance'. What was rather more interesting was that the vast majority of 'reasons' were assigned a high level of confidence, and this is not entailed by social compliance. It suggests that the subjects really believed in the appropriateness of their justifications.

In its strong form the Wason and Evans 'dual process' hypothesis postulates that response determines conscious thought, in the same way that the James-Lange theory of emotion assumes that a physiological response determines emotion. This may be an over-simplification. In a weak form, suggested originally by Smalley (1974), there may be a process of rapid, continuous feedback between tendencies to respond and conscious thought, rather than two distinct temporal phases. The 'dual process' hypothesis is merely critical of the assumption that a reason, elicited from an individual, necessarily reflects the causal antecedents of his overt subsequent response. Cases in which the two are concurrent, or in which the response determines the reason, may (speculatively) be those situations which possess a deceptive simplicity and a complex structure. Methods for tracking eye movements may elucidate the issue.

It should be noted that predictions of the Johnson–Laird and Wason (1970) model, and the Wason and Evans (1974/5) 'dual process' hypothesis, diverge only when the solution is wrong. When the subject gains insight (typically shown in those experiments which utilize realistic material) there is no divergence although the 'dual process' hypothesis would still maintain that reasons given for the solution are (correct) rationalizations of an 'intuitive' response. In this respect, the hypothesis is consistent with some accounts given by mathematicians (e.g. Poincaré) about their discoveries; typically, they say that the solutions to their problems occur 'in a flash', and that the construction of the proof is worked out afterwards.

Table 2. Protocols of three subjects (Wason and Evans, 1974/5)

	Cards and responses		Negative task	Affirmative task
			If there is a B . . . then there will not be a 3.	*If there is a B . . . then there will be a 3.*
			Reasons	Reasons
(1)	B	yes	'If the rule was false, there would be a 3 on the other side. If true there would not be a 3. B and 3 should be taken as part of the same assumption'.	'The rule only says that B is related to 3. It does not say anything about there being a logical sequence of letters to numbers, so no assumptions about letters and numbers other than B and 3 can be made.'
	3	yes	'If the rule was false, there would be a B on the other side.'	'As above.'
	U	no	'The rule only states that there is no relation between 3 and B. It does not state whether there is a relation between other numbers and letters.'	'Logical extension of argument above.'
	6	no	'As above.'	'As above.'
(2)	B	yes	'To see that it is not a 3.'	'To ensure that the reverse is 3.'
	3	yes	'To ensure that it is not a B.'	'To ensure that the reverse is B.'

	U	no	'It need not prove anything.'	'The result might be inconclusive.'
	6	no	'It need not prove anything.'	'The result might be inconclusive.'
(3)	B	yes	'If there is a 3 on the other side, then the statement is false.'	'If there is a 3 on the other side then the statement is true.'
	3	yes	'If there is a B on the other side then the statement is false.'	If there is a B on the other side, then the statement is true: otherwise it is false.'
	U	no	'Whatever number is on the other side will not show if the statement is true or false.'	'Any number may be on the other side.'
	6	no	'Any letter may be on the other side, therefore no way of knowing if statement is true.'	'If numbers are fairly random, then there may be any letter on the other side, thereby giving no indication unless the letter is B.'

It is a healthy sign that there should be disagreement about the theoretical status of the selection task. There is still much that remains unclear about it. What is more difficult is to devise tests of the competing hypotheses. It would be a parochial and positivist view to suggest that an hypothesis should never be postulated without a statement of how it could be tested. After all, somebody may devise such a test in the future.

10. Intellectual evolution from adolescence to adulthood[1]

J. Piaget

We are relatively well informed about the important changes that take place in cognitive function and structure at adolescence. Such changes show how much this essential phase in ontogenic development concerns all aspects of mental and psychophysiological evolution and not only the more 'instinctive', emotional or social aspects to which one often limits one's consideration. In contrast, however, we know as yet very little about the period which separates adolescence from adulthood.

In this paper we would first like to recall the principal characteristics of the intellectual changes that occur during the period from 12–15 years of age. These characteristics are too frequently forgotten as one tends to reduce the psychology of adolescence to the psychology of puberty. We shall then refer to the chief problems that arise in connection with the next period (15–20 years); firstly, the diversification of aptitudes, and secondly, the degree of generality of cognitive structures acquired between 12 and 15 years and their further development.

The structures of formal thought

Intellectual structures between birth and the period of 12–15 years grow slowly, but according to stages in development. The order of succession of these stages has been shown to be extremely regular and comparable to the stages of an embryogenesis. The speed of development, however, can vary from one individual to another and also from one social environment to another; consequently, we may find some children who advance quickly or others who are backward, but this does not change the order of succession of the stages through which they pass.

. . . From 11–12 years to 14–15 years a whole series of novelties highlights the arrival of a logic that will attain a state of equilibrium once the child reaches adolescence at about 14–15 years. We must, therefore, analyse this new logic in

[1] Excerpts from the paper in *Human Development*, **15** (1972), 1–12.

order to understand what might happen between adolescence and full adulthood.

The principal novelty of this period is the capacity to reason in terms of verbally stated hypotheses and no longer merely in terms of concrete objects and their manipulation. This is a decisive turning point, because to reason hypothetically and to deduce the consequences that the hypotheses necessarily imply (independent of the intrinsic truth or falseness of the premises) is a formal reasoning process. Consequently the child can attribute a decisive value to the logical form of the deductions that was not the case in the previous stages. From 7–8 years, the child is capable of certain logical reasoning processes but only to the extent of applying particular operations to concrete objects or events in the immediate present: in other words, the operatory form of the reasoning process, at this level, is still subordinated to the concrete content that makes up the real world. In contrast, hypothetical reasoning implies the subordination of the real to the realm of the possible, and consequently the linking of all possibilities to one another by necessary implications that encompass the real, but at the same time go beyond it.

From the social point of view, there is also an important conquest. Firstly, hypothetical reasoning changes the nature of discussions: a fruitful and constructive discussion means that by using hypotheses we can adopt the point of view of the adversary (although not necessarily believing it) and draw the logical consequences it implies. In this way, we can judge its value after having verified the consequences. Secondly, the individual who becomes capable of hypothetical reasoning, by this very fact will interest himself in problems that go beyond his immediate field of experience. Hence, the adolescent's capacity to understand and even construct theories and to participate in society and the ideologies of adults; this is often, of course, accompanied by a desire to change society and even, if necessary, destroy it (in his imagination) in order to elaborate a better one.

In the field of physics and particularly in the induction of certain elementary laws, the difference in attitude between children of 12–15 years, already capable of formal reasoning, and children of 7–10 years, still at the concrete level, is very noticeable. The 7- to 10-year-old children when placed in an experimental situation (such as what laws concern the swing of a pendulum, factors involved in the flexibility of certain materials, problems of increasing acceleration on an inclined plane) act directly upon the material placed in front of them by trial and error, without dissociating the factors involved. They simply try to classify or order what happened by looking at the results of the covariations. The formal level children, after a few similar trials stop experimenting with the material and begin to list all the possible hypotheses. It is only after having done this that they start to test them, trying progressively to dissociate the factors involved and study the effects of each one in turn – 'all other factors remaining constant'.

This type of experimental behaviour, directed by hypotheses which are based on more or less refined causal models, implies the elaboration of two new structures that we find constantly in formal reasoning.

The first of these structures is a combinatorial system, an example of which is clearly seen in 'the set of all subsets'. . . This generalized combinatorial ability (1 to 1, 2 to 2, 3 to 3, etc.) becomes effective when the subject can reason in a hypothetical manner. In fact, psychological research shows that between 12 and 15 years the pre-adolescent and adolescent start to carry out operations involving combinatorial analysis, permutation systems, etc. (independent of all school training). They cannot, of course, figure out mathematical formulae, but they can discover experimentally exhaustive methods that work for them. When a child is placed in an experimental situation where it is necessary to use combinatorial methods (for example, given five bottles of colourless, odourless liquid, three of which combine to make a coloured liquid, the fourth is a reducing agent and the fifth is water), the child easily discovers the law after having worked out all the possible ways of combining the liquids in this particular case.

This combinatorial system constitutes an essential structure from the logical point of view. The elementary systems of classification and order observed between 7 and 10 years, do not yet constitute a combinatorial system. Propositional logic, however, for two propositions p and q and their negation, implies that we not only consider the four-base associations (p and q, p and not-q, not-p and q, not-p and not-q) but also the sixteen combinations that can be obtained by linking these base associations 1 to 1, 2 to 2, 3 to 3 (with the addition of all four-base associations and the empty set). In this way it can be seen that implication, inclusive disjunction, and incompatibility are fundamental propositional operations that result from the combination of three of these base associations.

At the level of formal operations it is extremely interesting to see that this combinatorial system of thinking is not only available and effective in all experimental fields, but that the subject also becomes capable of combining propositions: therefore, propositional logic appears to be one of the essential conquests of formal thought. When, in fact, the reasoning processes of children between 11–12 and 14–15 years are analysed in detail it is easy to find the sixteen operations or binary functions of a bivalent logic of propositions.

However, there is still more to formal thought: when we examine the way in which subjects use these sixteen operations we can recognize numerous cases of the four-group which are isomorphic to the Klein group and which reveal themselves in the following manner. Let us take, for example, the implication $p > q$, if this stays unchanged we can say it characterized the identity transformation I. If this proposition is changed into its negation N (reversibility by negation or inversion) we obtain $N = p$ and not-q. The subject can change this same proposition into its reciprocal (reversibility by reciprocity) that is $R = q > p$; and it is also possible to change the statement into its correlative (or dual), namely $C =$ not-p and q. Thus, we obtain a commutative four-group such that $CR = N$, $CN = R$, $RN = C$ and $CRN = I$. This group allows the subject to combine in one operation the negation and the reciprocal which was not possible at the level of concrete operations. An example of these transformations that occurs frequently is the comprehension of the relationship between action (I and N) and reaction (R and C) in physics experiments; or again, the understanding of the relationship between two reference systems, for example: a moving object can go forwards or backwards (I and N) on a board which itself can go forwards or backwards (R and C) in relation to an exterior reference system. Generally speaking the group structure intervenes when the subject understands the difference between the cancelling or undoing of an effect (N in relation to I) and the compensation of this effect by another variable (R and its negation C) which does not eliminate but neutralizes the effect.

In concluding this first part we can see that the adolescent's logic is a complex but coherent system that is relatively different from the logic of the child, and constitutes the essence of the logic of cultured adults and even provides the basis for elementary forms of scientific thought.

The problems of the passage from adolescent to adult thought

The experiments on which the above-mentioned results are based were carried out with secondary school children, 11–15 years, taken from the better schools in Geneva. However, recent research has shown that subjects from other types of schools or different social environments sometimes give results differing more or less from the norms indicated; for the same experiments it is as though these subjects had stayed at the concrete operatory level of thinking.

Other information gathered about adults in Nancy, France, and adolescents of different levels in New York has also shown that we cannot generalize in all subjects the conclusion of our research which was, perhaps, based on a somewhat privileged population. This does not mean that our observations have not been confirmed in many cases: they seem to be true for certain populations, but the main problem is to understand why there are exceptions and also whether these are real or apparent.

A first problem is the speed of development, that is to say, the differences that can be observed in the rapidity of the temporal succession of the stages. We have distinguished four periods in the development of cognitive functions: the sensory-motor period before the appearance of language; the pre-operatory period which, in Geneva, seems on the average to extend from about $1\frac{1}{2}$–2 to 6–7 years; the period of concrete operations from 7–8 to 11–12 years (according to research with children in Geneva and Paris) and the formal operations period from 11–12 to 14–15 years as observed in the schools studied in Geneva. However, if the order of succession has shown itself to be constant – each stage is necessary to the construction of the following one – the average age at which children go through each stage can vary considerably from one social environment to another, or from one country or even region within a country to another. In this way Canadian psychologists in Martinique have observed a systematic slowness in development; in Iran notable differences were found between children of the city of Teheran and young illiterate children of the villages. In Italy, N. Peluffo has shown that there is a significant gap between children from regions of southern Italy and those from the north; he has carried out some particularly interesting studies indicating how, in children from southern families migrating north, these differences progressively disappear. Similar comparative research is at present taking place in Indian reservations in North America, etc.

In general, a first possibility is to envisage a difference in speed of development without any modification of the order of succession of the stages. These different speeds would be due to the quality and frequency of intellectual stimulation received from adults or obtained from the possibilities available to children for spontaneous activity in their environment. In the case of poor stimulation and activity, it goes without saying that the development of the first three of the four periods mentioned above will be slowed down. When it comes to formal thought, we could propose that there will be an even greater retardation in its formation (for example, between 15 and 20 years and not 11 and 15 years); or that perhaps in extremely disadvantageous conditions, such a type of thought will never really take shape or will only develop in those individuals who change their environment while development is still possible.

This does not mean that formal structures are exclusively the result of a process of social transmission. We still have to consider the spontaneous and endogenous factors of construction proper to each normal subject. However, the formation and completion of cognitive structures imply a whole series of exchanges and a stimulating environment; the formation of operations always requires a favourable environment for 'cooperation', that is to say, operations carried out in common (e.g. the role of discussion, mutual criticism or support, problems raised as the result of exchanges of information, heightened curiosity due to the cultural influence of a social group, etc.). Briefly, our first interpretation would mean that in principle all normal individuals are capable of reaching the level of formal structures on the condition that the social environment and acquired experience provide the subject with the cognitive nourishment and intellectual stimulation necessary for such a construction.

However, a second interpretation is possible which would take into account the diversification of aptitudes with age, but this would mean excluding certain categories of normal individuals, even in favourable environments, from the possibility of attaining a formal level of thinking. It is a well-known fact that the aptitudes of individuals differentiate progressively with age. Such a model of intellectual growth would be comparable to a fully expanded hand fan, the concentric layers of which would represent the successive stages in development whereas the sectors, opening wider towards the periphery, correspond to the growing differences in aptitude.

We would go so far as to say that certain behaviour patterns characteristically form stages with very general properties: this occurs until a certain level in development is reached; from this point onwards, however, individual aptitudes become more important than these general characteristics and create greater and greater differences between subjects. A good example of this type of development is the evolution of drawing. Until the stage at which the child can represent perspectives graphically, we observe a very general progress to the extent that the 'draw a man' test, to cite a particular case as an example, can be used as a general test of mental development. However, surprisingly large individual differences are observed in the drawings of 13- to 14-year-old children, and even greater differences with 19–20-year-olds (e.g. army recruits): the quality of the drawing no longer has anything to do with the level of intelligence. In this instance we have a good example of a behaviour pattern which is, at first, subordinate to a general evolution in stages (cf. those described by Luquet and other authors for children from 2–3 until about 8–9 years) and which, afterwards, gradually becomes diversified according to criteria of individual aptitudes rather than the general development common to all individuals.

This same type of pattern occurs in several fields including those which appear to be more cognitive in nature. One example is provided by the representations of space which first depends on operatory factors with the usual four intellectual stages – sensory-motor (cf. the practical group of displacements), preoperatory, concrete operations (measure, perspective, etc.) and formal operations. However, the construction of space also depends on figurative factors (perception and mental imagery) which are partially subordinated to operatory factors and which then become more and more differentiated as symbolical and representative mechanisms. The final result is that for space in general, as for drawing, we can distinguish a primary evolution characterized by the stages in the ordinary sense of the term, and then a growing diversification with age due to gradually differentiating aptitudes with regard to imaged representation and figurative instruments. We know, for example, that there exist big differences between mathematicians in the way in which they define 'geometrical intuition': Poincaré distinguishes two types of mathematicians the 'geometricians', who think more concretely and the 'algebrists', or 'analysts', who think more abstractly.

There are many other fields in which we could also think along similar lines. It becomes possible at a certain moment, for example, to distinguish between adolescents who, on the one hand, are more talented for physics or problems dealing with causality than for logic or mathematics and those who, on the other hand, show the opposite aptitude. We can see the same tendencies in questions concerning linguistics, literature, etc.

We could, therefore, formulate the following hypothesis: if the formal structures described in Part I do not appear in all children of 14–15 years and demonstrate a less general distribution than the concrete structures of children from 7–10 years old, this could be due to the diversification of aptitudes with age. According to this interpretation, however, we would have to admit that only individuals talented from the point of view of logic, mathematics and physics would manage to construct such formal structures whereas literary, artistic and practical individuals would be incapable of doing so. In this case it would not be a problem of underdevelopment compared to normal development but more simply a growing diversification in individuals, the span of aptitudes being greater at the level of 12–15 years, and above all between 15 and 20 years, than at 7–10 years. In other words, our fourth period can no longer be characterized as a proper stage, but would already seem to be a structural advancement in the direction of specialization.

But there is the possibility of a third hypothesis and, in the present state of knowledge, this last interpretation seems the most probable. It allows us to reconcile the concept of stages with the idea of progressively differentiating aptitudes. In brief, our third hypothesis would state that all normal subjects attain the stage of formal operations or structuring if not between 11–12 to 14–15 years, in any case between 15 and 20 years. However, they reach this stage in different areas according to their aptitudes and the professional specializations (advanced studies or different types of apprenticeship for the various trades): the way in which these formal structures are used, however, is not necessarily the same in all cases.

In our investigation of formal structures we used rather specific types of experimental situations which were of a physical and logical-mathematical nature because these seemed to be understood by the school children we sampled. However, it is possible to question whether these situations are, fundamentally, very general and therefore applicable to any school or professional environment. Let us consider the example of apprentices to carpenters, locksmiths, or mechanics who have shown sufficient aptitudes for successful training in the trades they have chosen but whose general education is limited. It is highly likely that they will know how to reason in a hypothetical manner in their speciality, that is to say, dissociating the variables involved, relating terms in a combinatorial manner and reasoning with propositions involving negations and reciprocities. They would, therefore, be capable of thinking formally in their particular field, whereas faced with our experimental situations, their lack of knowledge or the fact they have forgotten certain ideas that are particularly familiar to children still in school or college, would hinder them from reasoning in a formal way, and they would give the appearance of being at the concrete level. Let us also consider the example of young people studying law – in the field of juridical concepts and verbal discourse their logic would be far superior to any form of logic they might use when faced with certain problems in the field of physics that involve notions they certainly once knew but have long since forgotten.

It is quite true that one of the essential characteristics of formal thought appears to us to be the independence of its form from its reality content. At the concrete operatory level a structure cannot be generalized to different heterogeneous contents but remains attached to a system of objects or to the properties of these objects (thus the concept of weight only becomes logically structured after the development of the concept of matter, and the concept of physical volume after weight): a formal structure seems, in contrast, generalizable as it deals with hypotheses. However, it is one thing to dissociate the form from the content in a field which is of interest to the subject and within which he can apply his curiosity and initiative, and it is another to be able to generalize this same spontaneity of research and comprehension to a field foreign to the subject's career and interests. To ask a future lawyer to reason on the theory of relativity or to ask a student in physics to reason on the code of civil rights is quite different from asking a child to generalize what he has discovered in the conservation of matter to a problem on the conservation of weight. In the latter instance it is the passage from one content to a different but comparable content, whereas in the former it is to go out of the subject's field of vital activities and enter a totally new field, completely foreign to his interests and projects. Briefly, we can retain the idea that formal operations are free from their concrete content, but we must add that this is true only on the condition that for the subjects the situations involve equal aptitudes or comparable vital interests.

Conclusion

If we wish to draw a general conclusion from these reflections we must first say that, from a cognitive point of view, the passage from adolescence to adulthood raises a number of unresolved questions that need to be studied in greater detail.

The period from 15 to 20 years marks the beginning of professional specialization and consequently also the construction of a life programme corresponding to the aptitudes of the individual. We now ask the following critical question: Can one demonstrate, at this level of development as at previous levels, cognitive structures common to all individuals which will, however, be applied or used differently by each person according to his particular activities?

The reply will probably be positive but this must be established by the experimental methods used in psychology and sociology. Beyond that, the next essential step is to analyse the probable processes of differentiation: that is to say, whether the same structures are sufficient for the organization of many varying fields of activity but with differences in the way they are applied, or whether there will appear new and special structures that still remain to be discovered and studied.

. . . Unfortunately the study of young adults is much more difficult than the study of the young child as they are less creative, and already part of an organized society that not only limits them and slows them down but sometimes even rouses them to revolt. We know, however, that the study of the child and the adolescent can help us understand the further development of the individual as an adult and that, in turn, the new research on young adults will retroactively throw light on what we already think we know about earlier stages.

Part III

Conceptual Thinking

Introduction to conceptual thinking

Consider for example the proceedings we call 'games'. I mean board-games, card-games, ball-games, Olympic games, and so on. What is common to them all? – Don't say: 'There *must* be something common, or they would not be called "games" ' – but *look and see* whether there is anything common to all. – For if you look at them you will not see something that is common to *all*, but similarities, relationships, and a whole series of them at that. To repeat: don't think but look! – Look for example at board-games, with their multifarious relationships. Now pass to card-games; here you find many correspondences with the first group, but many common features drop out, and others appear . . .

And the result of this examination is: we see a complicated network of similarities of detail.

I can think of no better expression to characterize these similarities than 'family resemblances' . . .

Wittgenstein (1958)

Concepts are the coinage of thought. Without a conceptual system thinking would be impossible because each event or entity would be unique. Thought processes necessitate treating different things as the same for some purposes, and concepts provide the necessary classificatory system for relating events and entities to classes of similar kinds. Conceptual classification, like many other cognitive functions, seems to exist at two distinct levels: one level consists of the intuitive and implicit categories of daily life, many of which are reflected in ordinary language, and the other level consists of the more self-conscious and cold-blooded categories of an explicit classification system such as one finds in a science. There are, of course, some interesting parallels between the two domains, and our first reading in this Part is a useful survey of the scientific theory of classification, and its relation to psychology, by one of the founders of contemporary taxonomic theory, Robert R. Sokal. We have retained the last two sections of the paper even though they introduce some of the technicalities of cluster analysis and multi-dimensional scaling, because these techniques are increasingly used by psychologists (e.g. Miller, 1969; Shepard, Romney, and Nerlove, 1972).

Any psychologist interested in thinking has to confront the question of what a concept is, and to consider how a concept is acquired. Indeed, for a very long time there was a tendency in psychology to approach concepts solely through the business of their explicit acquisition. Thus, in an early study, Hull (1920) argued that a concept is the same response to different entities that is acquired in virtue of some element common to all of them. He thus took the view, in the terminology of taxonomic theory, that concepts are monothetic. He investigated this hypothesis in a form of discrimination learning in which the task was to learn a separate nonsense name for each of twelve Chinese ideographs. When the subjects had learned the names of one such set, they had to start all over again with a new set. However, the same names were used and, in fact, each name was correlated with a particular figure hidden within the ideographs as shown in figure 1. The task was repeated for six such lists altogether. Hull observed that the percentage of correct responses on the first trial with each new pack went up markedly during the course of the experiment: the subjects' responses were progressively attached to the common elements running through all the packs. At the end of the experiment a subject was often able to name characters correctly without being able to say what the common element was or to draw it.

Figure 1. Six of the hidden figures, their nonsense names, and characters containing them from Hull's (1920) experiment

Hull extended his ideas to the acquisition of concepts in real life. He argued, much in the spirit of the Empiricist philosopher, John Locke, that the meaning of a word such as 'dog' is 'a characteristic more or less common to all dogs and not common to cats, dolls, and teddy-bears'. A child by dint of experience of different pairings of the word and the entity acquires the common element. 'But to the child the process of arriving at this meaning or concept has been largely unconscious' (Hull, 1920, pp. 5–6).

The 'common element' or monothetic view of concepts is also apparent in the work of another pioneer, the Russian psychologist, L. S. Vygotsky, whose book *Thought and Language* was originally published in 1934. Vygotsky devised a sorting task with some resemblances to Hull's technique. Twenty-two blocks of various shapes, dimensions, and colours, are randomly arranged on a table in front of the subject. The experimenter explains that there are four sorts of block, each of which has its own nonsense name (written on the bottom of the blocks). The experimenter turns over one of the blocks displaying its name, and then asks the subject to pick out blocks of the same sort. The task proceeds in this way, with the experimenter correcting erroneous groupings by revealing the hidden nonsense names until the subject is able to sort the blocks correctly. The four categories are: large thick blocks, large thin blocks, small thick blocks, and small thin blocks; hence the shapes and colours of the blocks are irrelevant to the categories. In this task, children often fail to group the blocks into coherent classes (see Reading 15 for an account of what they do). Vygotsky argued that children are not capable of the abstract thought required in order to isolate the relevant attributes from the irrelevant ones. He drew similar conclusions about the performance of schizophrenics. There are, as we shall see, grounds for scepticism about such conclusions, although the 'Vygotsky' test and others like it have often been used in assessing intellectual impairment.

The standard experimental techniques for investigating conceptual thinking – sorting tasks, matching tasks, and concept attainment tasks (see Campbell, Donaldson, and Young, 1976) – all have their origins in such pioneering studies. The techniques are remarkable for embodying one crucial assumption: they take for granted that the processes by which subjects deliberately seek to acquire explicit concepts are similar to those that occur in the more implicit acquisition of everyday concepts. The results of more recent work cast considerable doubt upon such an assumption. However, in order to establish this point, it is necessary to consider the historical development of the experimental paradigms.

The early studies gave rise to a considerable pressure for adopting a sounder methodology in the study of concept attainment. The issues can be illustrated by considering a phenomenon that is easy to demonstrate in the laboratory: the experimenter points to some particular stimulus such as a large red triangle and announces, 'I have a particular concept in mind and that is *not* an exemplar of it.' Such information appears to be virtually useless. However, according to Hovland and Weiss (1953), for a genuine comparison of positive and negative instances, the relevant attributes of the stimuli must be clear to the subjects, and the amount of information (in the statistical sense of communication theory) conveyed by positive and negative instances must be equal. Hovland and Weiss carried out a study satisfying these methodological points. Nevertheless, they found that a series of wholly positive instances yielded a better performance than a series of wholly negative instances, and a mixed series of positive and negative instances yielded an intermediate performance.

A similar failure to assimilate negative information was established in an experiment carried out by Whitfield (1951). The subjects had to discover the correct arrangement of a number of objects in a number of locations. (One variant of this task is a recently available game known as 'Mastermind'.) Thus, for example, a subject might be asked to discover the correct arrangement of eight common objects (a block of wood, a match box, a bolt, etc.) in two possible locations (the left-hand and right-hand side of a sheet of paper). Whitfield suggests that negative information can be difficult to assimilate in coping with this task. Suppose you were a subject and had offered the following arrangement of the objects:

a z d x | y b w c

and the experimenter indicates that *none* of the objects is in its correct location. What should you do? The solution is, in fact, simply to swap round the two sets of items, moving those on the left to the right and *vice versa*. Three of Whitfield's subjects reached such a position; only one of them after considerable thought appreciated what had to be done.

Both the Hovland and Weiss and the Whitfield studies have a sound methodology. Yet the clear identification of attributes, the balancing of information, the unequivocal nature of the feedback, and other kindred aspects of their procedures, render the subjects' task a completely 'cut-and-dried' affair, far removed from the messy business of the formation of concepts in everyday life. Another feature of Whitfield's study led unwittingly to a further divorce from reality. By observing the sequences of his subjects' responses, he was able to determine certain aspects of the *strategies* they had adopted in order to solve the problem. This quest for delineating strategies was taken up by Bruner, Goodnow, and Austin (1956), who introduced an extremely influential technique.

Suppose you have in front of you a set of cards such as those depicted in figure 2, your task is to discover a particular concept that the experimenter has in mind, and he has told you that the stimulus consisting of *one green square* is a positive instance of this concept. How would you go about choosing cards in the array in order to discover the concept, given that after each choice you will be told whether or not it is an instance of the concept?

Bruner and his colleagues distinguished a number of idealized strategies in such a task. You can try to keep track of all currently relevant hypotheses and select instances with the aim of eliminating as many as possible of them (*Simultaneous scanning*). A more practical strategy is to consider a single hypothesis and test it by selecting exemplars of it; if and when your hypothesis is disconfirmed, then you select a new one (*Successive scanning*). An alternative approach is to focus on an initial positive instance and to select stimuli that differ from it either on a single attribute (*Conservative focusing*) or on a number of attributes (*Focus gambling*). If the new stimulus is also a positive instance of the concept, then the attribute(s) on which it differs from the focus are plainly irrelevant. On the other hand, if the new stimulus is a negative instance of the concept, then the difference is critical. Where only a single attribute differs, the concept involves the value possessed by the focus. Where you have gambled and a number of attributes differ, it may be impossible to determine which one is crucial. Bruner and his colleagues were able to establish the sorts of strategies their subjects used, and to manipulate them experimentally, e.g. with an orderly array of stimuli subjects are more likely to adopt a focusing strategy, and with only a few selections permitted subjects are more likely to gamble.

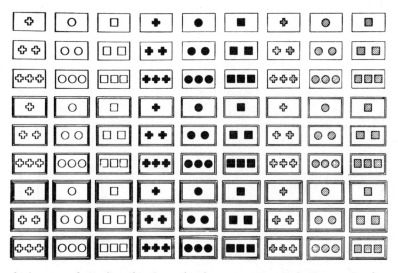

Figure 2. An array of stimuli used in the study of concept attainment by Bruner, Goodnow, and Austin (1956). There are four attributes, each with three values. Plain figures are in green, striped figures in red, and solid figures in black

The experimenters also attempted to introduce some realism into their studies, not by changing the task, but by using thematic materials, examples of which are depicted in figure 3. It turned out to be harder to attain a concept such as *smiling man* than a concept such as *black triangles*. What seemed to happen was that subjects developed plausible 'scenarios' about the events depicted in the picture, and they adopted the successive scanning strategy, developing one such hypothesis after another without taking into account information from past instances.

Another study conducted by R. E. Goodnow examined the effect of probabilistic cues. The subjects had to attain the concept of a Type-X aircraft, as shown in figure 4, on the basis of cues provided by wing, air scoop, and tail. In fact, only one cue was completely valid, the other two were associated with the Type-X plane only two-thirds of the time. However, in presenting the stimuli for identification, the experimenter showed only either one cue or two cues, never all three (see figure 4). In essence, there was an adaptation level effect: in the one–cue instances, subjects treated the valid cue with less than complete certainty and overestimated the validity of the other cues. There was also a predilection for working with one cue at a time, accepting a two–thirds valid cue as completely valid for a while (cf. Karmiloff-Smith and Inhelder's paper on how children develop theories, Reading 18). Of course, the cues differ in their salience, and this too biased performance.

Figure 3. Four instances of thematic material used by Bruner, Goodnow, and Austin (1956)

These attempts to inject some realism into the study of conceptual thinking failed to divert the main impetus of experimental studies from other matters. There was a considerable preoccupation with whether the common element defining a concept is merely stamped in by a passive process of association or sought out by an active process of hypothesis testing; mathematical models of both sorts of theory were proposed (see Bourne and Restle, 1959; Restle, 1962; Bower and Trabasso, 1964; and for more general reviews, Bourne, 1966; Levine, 1975). There were also proposals to supplement simple associations between stimuli and responses by an intervening verbal mediation (Kendler and Kendler, 1962). With hindsight it does not seem that these exercises in neo–behaviourism contributed very much to an understanding of conceptual thinking; unfortunately, the alternative information-processing approach following in the wake of Bruner was about to embark on a journey that finally severed all but the slenderest connection with everyday concepts.

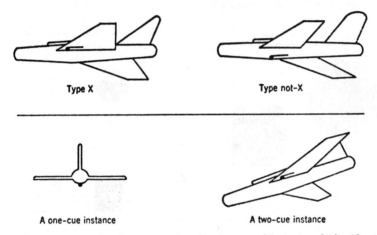

Figure 4. The type-X aircraft and two examples of instances used in an aircraft identification task (from Bruner *et al.* 1956)

The decisive step was the introduction of disjunctive concepts into the laboratory. It turned out that a concept such as *black or circle* was extremely difficult to attain: subjects did indeed tend to perform according to Hull's 'common element' theory, relying excessively on positive instances of the concept and seeking to amalgamate all the attributes they had in common (see, e.g. Bruner *et al.* 1956). Thus, shown a black square and a white circle as positive instances of a concept, a subject is much more likely to suggest that the concept is *black square or white circle* than that it is *black or circle*.

Negation, conjunction, and inclusive disjunction (i.e. A or B, or both) constitute a very simple logic of attributes known after its founder as a Boolean algebra. Neisser and Weene (1962) took these three notions as psychologically primitive, and argued that the simplest concepts are defined by a single attribute (or its negation), concepts of an intermediary difficulty are defined by con-

junction or disjunction (of attributes or their negations), and the hardest concepts are those defined by a disjunction *of* conjunctions, e.g. *black and circle or
not-black and not-circle*. Haygood and Bourne (1965) distinguished between
identifying the attributes relevant to a concept and learning the actual Boolean
rule that relates them. They obtained consistent differences within the intermediary category, and this result suggested that Neisser and Weene's theory is
too crude.

Perhaps the most parsimonious explanation of the psychological hierarchy of
Boolean concepts is a theory based on a form of the focusing strategy and
implemented in a computer program by Hunt and his colleagues (see Hovland
and Hunt, 1960; Hunt, 1962; Hunt, Marin, and Stone, 1966). It assumes that
subjects focus on positive instances regardless of the logical form of the concept,
and that they build up a 'decision tree' in order to categorize instances. We can
briefly illustrate the operation of the program by considering its performance
with the stimuli shown in figure 5.

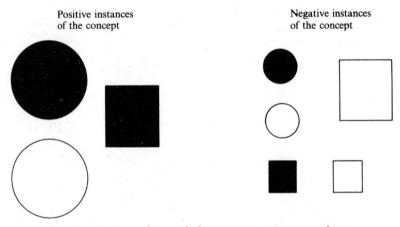

Positive instances
of the concept

Negative instances
of the concept

Figure 5. A set of materials for a concept attainment study

The program checks that there are no irrelevant characteristics common to all
the stimuli. It then looks for a characteristic that distinguishes the positive set
from the negative set. In the present case, there is no such characteristic. Hence,
it looks for a frequent characteristic of the positive stimuli (e.g. largeness) and
makes this the first test in the decision tree (see figure 6). The set of instances that
pass the test are now treated as a subproblem *in exactly the same way* – a process
which in turn creates further subproblems. Once they have all been solved, the
program returns to the fate of the items that failed the first test: it is unnecessary
to analyse them any further since none of them is an instance of the concept.
Armed with the resulting decision tree (see figure 6), the program can now
perform perfectly in a test of its attainment of the concept.

Hunt used his model in conjunction with an analysis of the content of suicide
notes, both genuine and simulated (see Shneidman and Farberow, 1957). The

decision tree that emerged is shown in figure 7. Plainly, given a plausible analysis of the contents of the notes, the program is successful at discriminating between real and simulated notes. For more recent developments, the reader is referred to Egan and Greeno (1974), who extend the theory still further in order to deal with serial pattern learning.

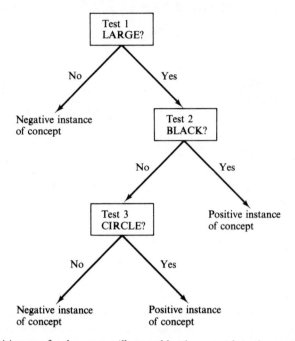

Figure 6. A decision tree for the concept illustrated by the materials in the previous figure (after Hunt, 1962)

Our own view is that the experimental investigation of concept attainment – even when it has been prompted by theories of hypothesis testing – has been for the most part systematically misleading and that it has failed to elucidate the ways in which human beings actually acquire new concepts. This is a sweeping claim, and we must now attempt to justify it and to justify the remaining readings in this Part.

The essence of our case against conventional studies of concept attainment is that they are not representative of what happens in real life because they use the wrong sorts of concept and the wrong sorts of experimental procedure.

Consider first the sorts of concepts that occur in everyday life. The concept of a *table* presumably involves a common function, but it is not represented by instances that possess any perceptual attributes in common. Hence, the first failing of the conventional studies is that they do not distinguish between a concept and the perceptual characteristics of its exemplars: they define concepts in terms of their appearance. Thus, Anisfeld (1968) has argued that it is a mistake to assume that a concept is disjunctive simply because the perceptual cues to it are disjunctive. However, as the quotation from Wittgenstein at the head of this Part rightly emphasizes, many everyday concepts do not even involve a common function. It is difficult to see how one could frame a single conjunctive

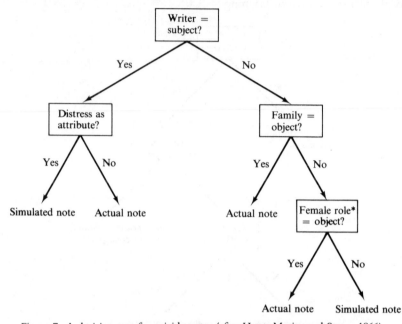

Figure 7. A decision tree for suicide notes (after Hunt, Marin, and Stone, 1966)
* Examples of the relevant sort of role include mother, wife, and housekeeper.

definition of *games, furniture,* or *tools,* that would capture their necessary and sufficient conditions. If you are sceptical of this claim, consider whether television sets, telephones, and typewriters, should ever be treated as items of furniture. Natural concepts are indeed often polythetic. It might be argued that they are defined by a disjunction of attributes, but real-life concepts are seldom composed of Boolean combinations of otherwise independent attributes (see Fodor, 1972, for a criticism of Vygotsky's work from this point of view). On the contrary, they have an internal relational structure – a logic that cannot be captured by Boolean algebra. Thus, a table is not just a conjunction of a top and some legs: the legs *support* the top. When concepts with a relational structure are introduced into the laboratory they give rise to a pattern of performance that is significantly different to performance with Boolean concepts. Let us consider two such examples.

1. It is well known from the work of Piaget (1950) that children find it difficult to keep a whole class in mind while attending to one of its subclasses. Piaget writes (1950, p. 133):

To study the formation of classes, we place about twenty beads in a box, the subject acknowledging that they are 'all made of wood', so that they constitute a whole, B. Most of these beads are brown and constitute part A, and some are white, forming the complementary part A'. In order to determine whether the child is capable of understanding the [Boolean] operation $A + A' = B$, i.e. the uniting of parts in a whole, we may put the following simple question: In this box (all the beads still being visible) which are there more of – wooden beads or brown beads, i.e. is $A < B$?

Now, up to about the age of 7 years, the child almost always replies that there are more brown beads 'because there are only two or three white ones.'

Such children in Piaget's terms have yet to attain the level of 'concrete operations'. There is a considerable variation in the likelihood of error in this problem as a function of its actual content (see Klahr and Wallace, 1972; Wilkinson, 1976), but nevertheless the phenomenon is well established. Markman and Seibert (1976) showed some kindergarten children some toy frogs – two big frogs and four baby frogs. They asked: 'Are there more frogs or more baby frogs?' The 'pre-operational' children made the usual error and responded: 'more baby frogs'. In another condition, however, the children were told that there was a *family* of frogs, and this introduction of a relational concept led to a dramatic improvement of performance in the comparison of the baby frogs to the family of frogs. The same effect was apparent in other structured classes of entities such as bunches of grapes, and piles of bricks. The experimenters suggest that such organized collections have a psychological integrity comparable to a single physical object. Such findings, of course, throw considerable doubt on the general notion of cognitive development that one finds in thinkers as diverse as Piaget and Vygotsky. It is not that a child's thinking develops in logical power – it is hard to see how such developments could occur – but that there is a progressive extension of the sorts of content to which specific computational processes can be applied (see Fodor, 1972, 1976).

2. Modigliani and Rizza (1971) carried out a study of concepts using stimuli involving seven binary features of houses, straight vs. curved walls, plain vs. paved path, and so on. The stimuli consisted either in coherent arrangements that maintained the usual structural relations to be found in a house (the 'bounded' stimuli) or else in a disconnected and arbitrary arrangement of the different features (the 'unbounded' stimuli) as is shown in figure 8. The subjects learned a concept defined by a single feature and then they were given a test of transfer. The test stimuli had either 2, 4, or 6, of the irrelevant attributes deleted (see figure 8). With the arbitrarily arranged stimuli, the subjects tended to maintain the same classificatory rule that they had acquired in the original training; whereas with integrated stimuli they often changed their classificatory rule. It was as though the effect of deleting 'irrelevant' features seriously disturbed the structure of the integrated stimuli (see Garner, 1976).

Turning to the question of experimental procedure, if you were required in real life to acquire a concept such as *black circles*, then it is most unlikely that you would have to learn it according to the procedure of conventional concept attainment studies. You would simply be told the definition. The London Building Acts of 1930, for example, introduce a number of complex Boolean definitions such as: 'Members of the warehouse class of building include warehouse, manufactory, brewery, distillery, and any other building exceeding 150 thousand foot cube which is neither a public nor a domestic building.' But, of course, the main discrepancy arises from the simple fact that the acquisition of most other concepts occurs in an implicit or – to use Hull's description – unconscious manner. Concepts tend either to be picked up willy-nilly without conscious effort or else to be acquired more deliberately by word of mouth. Neither of these processes is mirrored in conventional studies of concept attainment: no wonder the introduction of 'realistic' materials into them tends to make the task still harder.

Many of these criticisms were anticipated by workers in the Gestalt tradition. The 'common element' concept of a concept was, of course, anathema to them.

Training stimuli

Test stimuli

Figure 8. Examples of the training and test stimuli used by Modigliani and Rizza (1971). In the top figure the training stimuli have opposite values for each dimension. In the bottom figure, the roof is the relevant attribute and the stimuli have 2 (upper cells), 4 (middle cells), and 6 (bottom cells) irrelevant attributes omitted.

As Smoke (1932, p. 5) pointed out: 'As one learns more and more about dogs, his concept of "dog" becomes increasingly rich, not a closer approximation to some bare "element". . . . No learner of "dog" ever found a "common element" running through the stimulus patterns through which he learned.' Smoke's own prescient view was that it was the total pattern that constituted the concept: one has to learn to respond to the relations embodied in it. Unfortunately, at that time there was no way to make explicit what was meant by such a phrase as 'the total pattern'. Smoke studied the acquisition of concepts involving geometrical relations, e.g. a circle with one dot inside it and another dot outside it. The paper by Winston, which is the second reading in this Part, shows how such structural concepts can be made explicit within a theory embodied in a computer program. Winston also proposes a theory of learning that depends on presenting both examples of what is, and what is not, an instance of the concept; the negative instances have to be judiciously chosen cases of 'near misses' of the concept. It is perhaps symptomatic of the present gulf between Artificial Intelligence and Psychology that Winston is unaware that this idea was anticipated by Smoke more than forty years before. It is certainly symptomatic of the methodological obsessions of Experimental Psychology that one of Smoke's key findings has failed to get into the textbooks. In his first study, Smoke (1932) used a technique rather like Hull's in order to examine the effects of negative instances on concept learning. Rather to his surprise he found no facilitatory effects in a whole series of experiments; however, he examined how long his subjects spent studying the instances of concepts rather than how adequately they mastered them (even though he had obtained such measures). In a subsequent study, however, Smoke (1933) observed that negative instances did indeed discourage 'snap' judgments. He reports that his subjects 'tended to come to an initial wrong conclusion less readily and to subsequent wrong conclusions less frequently, than when they were learning from positive instances alone'. In other words, negatives are easier to assimilate when they correct misconceptions (cf. Reading 7 on self-contradiction in Part II). However, Smoke's finding seems to have been lost in all the methodological demands for negative instances to convey the same amount of information as positive ones, and for materials to have clearly defined attributes. Such correctives led to the artificiality of much subsequent work.

What form do real concepts take? Since they are used to classify the events and entities of the world, they reflect the fact that the world is not entirely arbitrary: not all possible combinations of values of attributes occur, many combinations that do occur are not deemed to be significantly different from one another, and significance is largely a function of the structural relations embodied in events and entities. Reading 13, a paper by Eleanor Rosch, proposes that the fundamental conceptualization of the world is in terms of discrete *prototypes*. A crucial piece of evidence compatible with such a theory is that not all instances of a concept are deemed equally representative – a robin is a prototypical bird, a chicken is not. Judgments of membership seem to depend on distance from the prototype. Rosch also argues that in any classificatory hierarchy, e.g. *furniture – chair – kitchen chair*, there is one level that is basic, that is to say, a level at which the classification yields entities tending to have attributes and functions in common. It is this level at which the prototypes are represented, perhaps in the form of concrete images.

The notion of conceptual prototypes is undoubtedly a seminal idea. Bruner *et al.* (1956, p. 64) talked of a 'typical instance', and reported that subjects had less difficulty in setting a colour wheel to the typical colour of an eating orange than to the acceptable boundaries of its colour. And in one of the very first studies of concept attainment, Fisher (1916) reported the development of schematized and conventional images corresponding to an idealized picture of the conceptualized object. Nevertheless, the theory is not without its difficulties. The major problem is to make explicit the nature of a prototype and the process of estimating the difference from it of various exemplars. As Miller and Johnson-Laird (1976) have pointed out in connection with some of Carelman's (1971) absurd tables, such as the ones depicted in figure 9, an object such as a packing case might resemble a prototypical table more than either of the absurd tables. Yet the latter are 'technically' tables, to use an appropriate hedge, whereas a packing case is not. It is difficult to explain this difference if the judged distance from a

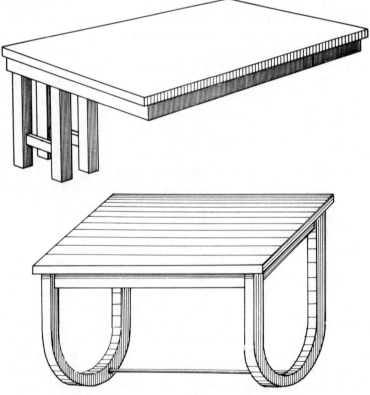

Figure 9. Two absurd tables from Carelman, 1971

prototype were the only mechanism available for categorization. The existence of such hedges as 'technically', 'strictly speaking', etc., does indeed suggest that some attributes are criterial, and others are optional – a point that emerges from Winston's analysis (see also Lakoff, 1972; Labov, 1973).

In discussing concepts that correspond to lexical items, Miller and Johnson-Laird have argued for a slightly different system summarized in figure 10. Concepts are organized into semantic fields that have a *conceptual core*. A conceptual core is an abstract entity that in reflecting a deeper conceptualization of the world integrates the different concepts within the semantic field. It underlies the paramount fact that concepts do not come in isolation, but are organized in a taxonomy that enables entities within the field to be correctly categorized.

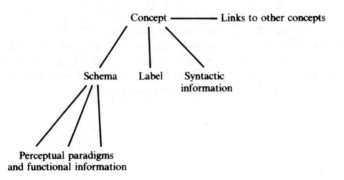

Figure 10. The relations between words, concepts, and schemata as envisaged by Miller and Johnson-Laird (1976)

A lexical concept interrelates a word ('table'), rules for its syntactic behaviour, and a schema. The schema is made up of both functional and perceptual information, and may also include information that has no direct perceptual consequences (see Miller, Reading 24). It seems plausible to suppose that prototypical schemata define the segments into which a taxonomy divides the universe by taking up central positions within them – birds fly, fishes swim, animals walk on the surface of the earth, etc. – and that boundary disputes are often resolved by more technical criteria.

Lexical concepts are acquired as part of the process of learning a native tongue. Yet, paradoxically, investigators such as Vygotsky and Piaget have always stressed the poor classificatory behaviour of young children. Once again, however, their evidence is largely culled from performance in overt tasks – what could be a better demonstration of a superb classificatory skill than the rapid mastery of the syntactic and semantic basis of a natural language? The fourth reading in this section is a paper by Katherine Nelson in which she describes some ingenious studies of the ability of very young children to categorize objects before they are able to name them. She interprets her evidence to show that the basis of such classifications is often the function of an object. This claim is controversial and runs directly counter to a theory proposed by Eve Clark

(1973) in which perceptual similarity is of fundamental importance. Since some of the currently most exciting work in the psychology of categorization revolves around this issue we have selected a further paper on the topic as the final reading in this Part: Melissa Bowerman takes her data on the spontaneous errors in children's usage of words to support the importance of perceptual rather than functional characteristics in early concepts. However, she stresses the importance of all sorts of information at this stage. She also advocates a compromise between the theory of 'prototype' and the theory of Boolean features: a prototype is a privileged set of features. The notion that different features are weighted differently in the composition of concepts is an attractive one, but what it leaves to be explained is the origin of such a system; it is descriptively adequate but has little explanatory value. Perhaps a more important idea implicit in this paper is that concepts may themselves differ one from another. In some cases perceptual cues may be used only as a basis for identification – compare, for example, the concept of a table with the sorts of cues used to identify one; in other cases the perceptual cues may constitute the concept as in the case of colours; in still other cases perception has no role whatsoever to play, as in the case of kinship, and numerous abstract concepts.

11. Classification: purposes, principles, progress, prospects[1]

Robert R. Sokal

The origin of the science of classification goes back to the writings of the ancient Greeks. However, the process of classification, the recognition of similarities, and the grouping of organisms and objects based thereon dates back to primitive man (Mayr, 1963; Berlin, Breedlove, and Raven, 1966, 1974; Raven, Berlin, and Breedlove, 1971). Even before the advent of man, classificatory ability must have been a component of fitness in biological evolution. Regardless of whether behaviour is learned or instinctive, organisms must be able to perceive similarities in stimuli for survival (Ricklefs, 1973). Thus the recognition of similarities in patterns of sensory input is probably as old as the earliest forms of sense perception in living organisms.

The study of classification has always had two major interrelated components: How do we classify? and How should we classify? If we restrict the discussion to classification by man of the world around him, the first component falls into the domain of the psychology and philosophy of sense perception: What is similarity? How do human beings recognize similarity? What are the criteria, conscious and unconscious, by which man groups objects and events into some system? What are the relationships between the names man gives to classes of entities and their objective definition? Are there individual differences in the perception of similarity and in the ability to group objects, and how do these affect everyday and scientific communication? The second component is the subject matter of taxonomy , the science of classification. It arises from the conceptualization of the questions raised earlier. Knowing how man classifies, can one derive general principles of classification from this knowledge and, if so, are these principles the best conceivable ones, given that choices between different classificatory principles and procedures are permitted? This paper will

[1] An edited extract from the paper in *Science*, **185** (1974), 115–23. © 1974 the American Association for the Advancement of Science. (The reader is referred to the original for many of the more technical details of computer algorithms, etc., and for references to more specialized scientific applications.)

mainly concern itself with the second aspect of classification, the principles and procedures.

Classification is an important aspect of most sciences, and similar principles and procedures have been developed independently in various fields. Fortunately, substantial interdisciplinary communication has accompanied recent progress (Jardine and Sibson, 1971; Lerman, 1970; Sneath and Sokal, 1973), and a body of general classificatory theory and methodology is rapidly being developed, a task that is attracting the interest of statisticians and mathematicians. In classification, theory has frequently followed methodology and has been an attempt to formalize and justify the classificatory activity of workers in various sciences. In other instances, classificatory systems have been set up on *a priori* logical or philosophical grounds and the methodology tailored subsequently to fit the principles. Both approaches have their advantages and drawbacks; modern work tends to reflect an interactive phase in which first one and then the other approach is used, but in which neither principles nor methodology necessarily dominate.

Computers and classification

Even though the principles and many of the mathematical ideas underlying modern classificatory methods antedate the appearance of the electronic computer, the recent great increase in classificatory work is intimately related to the development of this new tool. It is difficult to assess the degree to which the acceleration of work in classification is due to the almost simultaneous, rapid increase in the availability and capability of computers. It might be argued that other developments in modern science could have renewed the interest in classification. An unprecedented number of scientists is at work and new, automated methodologies are yielding information on many properties of numerous objects. This process alone could easily have forced the development of new classificatory techniques to cope with the flood of information. Yet without computers it is inconceivable how such developments could have been implemented.

Computers play a central role in modern classification for four reasons. First, they have helped to find solutions to problems that were analytically intractable (or at least seemed so to the scientists involved). Second, computers are able to carry out computations whose numerical solutions were known but exceedingly tedious, for example, the computation of eigen-values of large matrices. Also, computers have been able to classify simultaneously far larger numbers of objects, using many more features of these objects, than any human taxonomist. A third and most important by-product of the application of computers has been the necessary development of algorithms for classification, which in turn has led to attempts to objectivize and optimize the classificatory process. This is a clear example of the influence of methodological development on theory. Finally, because of the general development of pattern recognition and perceptron technology, the availability of computers has given rise to fundamental

investigations into how human beings and other organisms perceive the world around them. One hopes, in these studies, to have the computer imitate man or other organisms in their perceptive and classificatory abilities. Such work relates largely to the first of the questions raised earlier (How do we classify?), but it has also brought in its wake debate on whether the classificatory systems to be established in various sciences should conform to man's intuitive 'natural' classificatory ability or whether other criteria of goodness of a classificatory system are preferable. . .

Definition of terms

Before we proceed we must guard against possible confusion: several important terms are employed with varying meanings in different sciences.

Classification will here be defined as the ordering or arrangement of objects into groups or sets on the basis of their relationships. These relationships can be based on observable or inferred properties. Some philosophers, mathematicians, and statisticians also employ the term 'classification' for what is here called 'identification', the term being defined as the allocation or assignment of additional unidentified objects to the correct class, once such classes have been established by prior classification. Thus we 'identify' an object as being a chair, or a plant as being a buttercup.

In addition to indicating a process, the term classification is frequently employed to denote the end-product of this process. Thus the result of classification is a classification. It seems better to term such an end result a 'classificatory system' (Jardine and Sibson, 1971).

The term 'taxonomy' is used here to mean the theoretical study of classification including its bases, principles, procedures, and rules (Simpson, 1961). This would include classification as well as identification. It is the science of how to classify and identify.

The term 'taxon' (plural: 'taxa') is useful to designate a set of objects of any rank recognized as a group in a classificatory system. A taxon has therefore been arrived at by some classificatory procedure, but not necessarily as the result of an explicit methodology; for example, one can have taxa in a folk taxonomy.

Purposes of classification

Much classificatory work in various sciences aims to describe what is known as the 'natural system'. This is a difficult concept and differs in meaning across disciplines and even among workers in any one field. Natural systems are believed to be in accord with nature. If it is the purpose of science to discover the true nature of things then it is the purpose of a correct classification to describe objects in such a way that their 'true' relationships are displayed. In many sciences this has led to essentialist systems whose philosophical origins go back to Aristotle. The difficulty with essentialism is that it is based on Aristotelian logic expressed in axioms that give rise to properties that are inevitable consequences of these axioms. Such conditions apply to classifications of some entities, such as colours or geometrical figures, but not to others.

One view of natural classifications is that they reflect the natural processes that have led to the observed arrangement of the objects. One hopes from such an ordering to learn about the laws governing the behaviour of these objects. In biology there supposedly is such a natural system, reflecting the end-products of the evolutionary process. Yet natural systems are not necessarily isomorphic with the common, mutually exclusive classificatory arrangements employed by taxonomists in various fields. The process giving rise to the differentiated objects may be such as to create overlapping classes or fuzzy boundaries. The borrowing of stylistic features in human artifacts is an example in point. Others would be textual materials, hybrid languages, social systems, or organisms.

All classifications aim to achieve economy of memory. The world is full of single cases: single individuals of animal or plant species, single case histories of disease, single books, rocks, or industrial concerns. By grouping numerous individual objects into a taxon the description of the taxon subsumes the individual descriptions of the objects contained within it. By saying that Jean Duval speaks French, we imply that his linguistic inventory resembles that of millions of other persons in the taxon 'French-speaking persons', and we save ourselves a whole catalogue of statements about the particular word lists and sentence structures familiar to Duval. Unless we qualify our statement further we are lumping together varieties of thought, speech, and writing patterns collectively known as the French language, and without a clearer definition of boundaries we cannot be certain whether local dialects such as Parisian argot or Provençal are included, or which variety it is that Duval speaks. Yet without the ability to summarize information and attach a convenient label to it we would be unable to communicate.

Yet another purpose of classification is ease of manipulation. The objects are arranged in systems (that may or may not be hierarchic) in which the several taxa can be easily named and related to one another. If the relationships are very complex, as are functional roles of individuals in certain societies, for example, no easy labelling or handling of the taxa will be possible. Ease of retrieval of information from a classificatory system is also a criterion frequently considered desirable.

The paramount purpose of a classification is to describe the structure and relationship of the constituent objects to one another and to similar objects, and to simplify these relationships in such a way that general statements can be made about classes of objects. The definition, description, and simplification of taxonomic structure is a challenging task. It is easy to perceive structure when it is obvious and discontinuous. Disjoint clusters separated by large empty regions are unambiguous. Thus horseshoe crabs or ginkgo trees are unique species quite different from their nearest relatives. A language such as Basque is in a similar position. But this situation is not typical. Much of what we observe in nature changes continuously in one or another characteristic, but not necessarily with equally steep gradients for each characteristic. Where should boundaries be

drawn in such cases? Must classification be a drawing of boundaries? Would an adequate description and summarization of the continuity of the objects be preferable to artificially erected boundaries? Uniform continuous change is, of course, not very frequent in nature. Centripetal forces frequently hold together a certain structure over a given domain and loosen their control only at zones of rapid intergradation. In biology, stabilizing selection within a gene pool would be a case in point. Another example of such a normative force is the effect on regional languages or dialects of the publication of newspapers and the broadcasting of radio and television programmes. Thus the boundary between Catalan and Castilian in Spain is undoubtedly reinforced by the existence of media and centres for diffusion of the respective languages and cultures. Often the clusters will obey gravitation-like laws with boundaries definable as equilibrium points, while in other cases diffusion or stepping-stone models best describe the transition between clusters. Taxonomists must decide the relative importance of diameters and densities of clusters, the number of objects, and the gaps between the clusters.

Classifications that describe relationships among objects in nature should generate hypotheses. In fact the principal scientific justification for establishing classifications is that they are heuristic (in the traditional meaning of this term as 'stimulating interest as a means of furthering investigation') and that they lead to the stating of a hypothesis which can then be tested. A classification raises the question of how the perceived order has arisen, and in a system in which forces and relationships are transitory one may conjecture about the maintenance of the structure. Examples are inferences about evolutionary lineages obtained from biological classifications based on morphological or biochemical characters, inferences about population structure in biology and anthropology resulting from patterns of geographic variation, and inferences about acculturation which certain models of linguistic and artifactual evolution engender in anthropology.

The search for immanent structure in nature is far from the only purpose of classification. Especially in applied, practical fields the question is often asked: What is the best classification of the objects at hand into two or three or k classes? In regionalization studies a given political area is to be divided into a fixed number of districts given some criterion of optimality. What is the best way to subdivide a county into five voting districts to achieve maximal – or in some recent redistricting problems minimal – intra-class homogeneity? Many routing problems can be considered classification problems in this sense. If a bakery possesses four trucks how can it best route these through the city to cover the set of n grocery stores in the city at minimal cost or in minimal time?

The two kinds of approaches, the search for natural structure and the imposition of an external constraint by fitting the data to a fixed number of classes, are not necessarily categorically distinct. I suspect that many biological taxonomists, without explicitly saying so, assume that they already know the major subdivisions of the organisms they study and only need to allocate properly the finer taxonomic units to these major subdivisions. In biological and some other classifications it is sometimes stated that the number of major subdivisions should be partly a function of the number of included taxonomic units. Such a scheme clearly is not based on fundamental scientific principles but largely on considerations of practicality. They may also be related to the number of names human beings are able to recall from a data base (Berlin, Breedlove, and Raven, 1966).

Principles of classification

Of the various principles applied in recent classificatory theory, the distinction between monothetic and polythetic classification, first clearly enunciated by Beckner (1959), is probably of greatest importance. Monothetic classifications are those in which the classes established differ by at least one property which is uniform among the members of each class. Such classifications are especially useful in setting up taxonomic keys and certain types of reference and filing systems. From the practical point of view of information retrieval it is obviously desirable that certain properties of taxa be invariant (Sneath and Sokal, 1973, ch. 8).

In polythetic classifications, taxa are groups of individuals or objects that share a large proportion of their properties but do not necessarily agree in any one property. Adoption of polythetic principles of classification negates the concept of an essence or type of any taxon. No single uniform property is required for the definition of a given group nor will any combination of characteristics necessarily define it. This somewhat disturbing concept is readily apparent when almost any class of objects is examined. Thus it is extremely difficult to define class attributes for such taxa as cows or chairs. Although cows can be described as animals with four legs that give milk, a cow that only has three legs and does not give milk will still be recognized as a cow. Conversely there are other animals with four legs that give milk that are not cows (see the account of a lecture by John Wisdom in Good, 1962). It is similarly difficult to find necessary properties of the class 'chairs'. Properties that might commonly be found in any chair may be missing in any given piece of furniture that would clearly be recognized as a chair. These somewhat contrived examples can be bolstered by numerous instances of classification ranging from archaeology to zoology (e.g. Ruud, 1954; Doran and Hodson, 1966). When viewed from a historical perspective we find remarkable parallels in the gradual rejection of the type concept and the adoption of polythetic criteria in these various disciplines.

A corollary of polythetic classification is the requirement that many properties (characters) be used to classify objects. This is true of almost any type of object being classified. Biological organisms, with their complex sequences of nucleotides and great diversity of structure and function, are rich in variability and yield numerous characters; but artifacts or art objects, languages, industries, or case histories of physical or mental disease yield many characters as well. Some may argue that a few attributes are sufficient to characterize taxa in these fields. Most instances quoted to support this point of view are cases of iden-

tification. Once a classification has been established, few characters are generally necessary to allocate objects to the proper taxa. But it is unlikely that few characters will suffice to establish the taxa in the first place. Initial classifications based on few characters usually have had to be modified once information on additional characteristics was acquired. Diseases not differentiated in earlier times now represent separate clinical entities with the accumulation of new knowledge; Linnaeus's *Vermes* has become numerous animal phyla.

Classifications based on many properties will be general; they are unlikely to be optimal for any single purpose, but might be useful for a great variety of purposes. By contrast, a classification based on few properties might be optimal with respect to these characters, but would be unlikely to be of general use (e.g. Gilmour, 1951). Thus an alphabetical ordering of books by author in a library will be the ideal classification for an alphabetical author catalogue but will not contribute to a meaningful classification by subject matter. A classification of plants by growth form will not reflect the natural taxa, although it might be useful from an ecological or landscaping point of view. For many practical purposes special classifications based on few characters are desirable.

Weighting

The problem of weighting characters has troubled taxonomists in all disciplines. Should certain characters be weighted more heavily than others? Many biologists maintain that traits indicating common evolutionary descent be weighted more heavily than others, and they weight the discordant characters less than others when constructing a classification. Established differentiae between diseases, languages, or cultures might be similarly emphasized. The difficulty with such weighting is that one needs initial classifications to provide weights for the characters. But once classifications are correct there is little value in computing weights for the characters that established them, except for future identification of unknown objects. Many modern taxonomists have therefore adopted the doctrine of equal weighting of characters for classification. Those that do not advocate equal weighting have been forced to state a basis upon which they propose to weight characters – and many such proposals are found wanting (see Sneath and Sokal, 1973, p. 109).

Once a taxonomist becomes convinced that a particular trait is of great importance in dividing up his material he subsequently, almost inevitably, becomes quite selective about the other evidence he collects. He will more readily use characters that support his earlier views and weight fewer characters that are discordant. Such tendencies are found in every field of classification. For example, having decided that locusts are divisible into migratory and solitary phases on the basis of body proportion, entomologists attempted to fit discoveries of other differences in pigmentation and behaviour into the framework set up by the original classification into phases. It took considerable conceptual liberation from the earlier system to arrive at the more complicated, essentially polythetic view of phase formation in locusts. . .

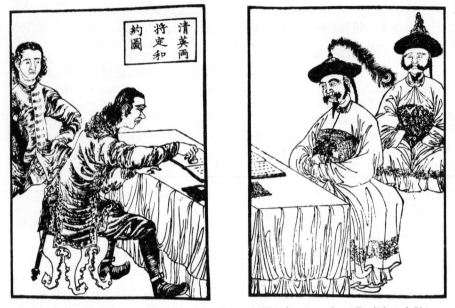

清英兩
將定和
約圖

Figure 1. Cultural biases in depicting racial differences. The drawings show English and Chinese representatives during the Opium War signing a treaty. The contemporary Chinese artist (Mineta, 1849) emphasized the prominent noses of the Westerners by receding the upper lip. The curly hair of the 'Western barbarians' was equally stressed. These are not wigs, since other illustrations in the same source show every Englishman, including fighting and looting British Army privates, with similar exaggerated curly hair. Curiously, the hairiness of the Westerners or their tallness are not stressed in this or other illustrations of the Opium War, although most present-day Chinese when queried will stress these features of Europeans as important differentiae. It is interesting that the acculturation is evident in modern Chinese cartoons where characters intended to be Chinese frequently appear undistinguishable from Europeans, at least to the Western observer.

The selection and recognition of characters is but an extreme example of weighting. Traits that are not employed are given a weight of zero. Cultural and personal biases affect character selection in virtually every field of classification. To take an example from physical anthropology, let us compare two human populations belonging to different races. Samples of natives from, say, England and China, would differ in numerous traits. It is possibly a truism that each and every member from a sample of one group could, with statistical assurance, be distinguished from every member in a sample of the other group, if characters were selected in an unbiased fashion. These characters would undoubtedly cover aspects of external appearance, musculature, skin colour, pubescence, and bone measurements, for example. Yet if members of these two groups were asked to describe each other, the differential characters noted by them would be quite different. Thus, when a typical European or American is asked to list the salient distinguishing traits of the Chinese he will most frequently mention the 'slanted eyes' and secondly the yellow skin colour. Prominent cheekbones and straight black hair would be mentioned frequently as well. Possibly because eye

Figure 2. This illustration, drawn by a well-known German cartoonist (Heine, 1925; also in
    Schütze, 1963), stresses the prominent cheekbones and slanted eyes of the Chinese

shape and the presence of the epicanthic fold are quite variable among the
Chinese, they do not describe Europeans by such characters. The descriptors
that readily come to the minds of the Chinese are the tallness of the Westerners,
their blond or brown curly hair that is quite absent in China, their hairiness, as
well as their prominent noses. These culturally conditioned differentiae not only
lead to epithets for the other race in both cultures but some are also seen in
drawings by Chinese and European artists (see figures 1 and 2). The two
populations can be compared on either the European or the Chinese set of
characters but they clearly differ on both of these and in other properties as well.
Although popular descriptive terms may not affect the more objective judgment of physical anthropologists, differences of this sort may still guide classi-

ficatory behaviour in various covert ways. A well-known analogous case is the great diversity of the negroid populations of Africa which, to the casual observer, is hidden by the blackness of the skin.

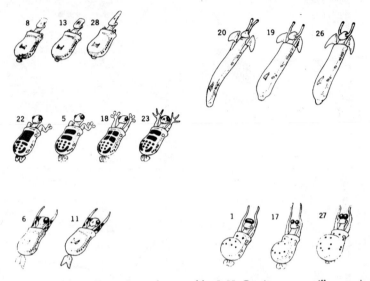

Figure 3. Caminalcules, imaginary animals created by J. H. Camin, serve to illustrate individual differences in taxonomic judgment.

Twenty-nine different organisms were presented to a large number of persons ranging from professional taxonomists to children. The data presented here are a small sampling from a study in progress. Three taxonomists, A (a distinguished systematic entomologist), B (an invertebrate palaeontologist), and C (a graduate student in palaeontology), were asked to group the organisms by their similarities. From the classifications established by the three persons, the following relationships illustrated by groups of Caminalcules in the figure can be extracted. Taxonomists A and C thought 13 was more similar to 8, but B placed it closer to 28. All three taxonomists thought 6 was most similar to 11. While taxonomist C placed 5 and 18 together, taxonomist A grouped 5 with 22, and 18 with 23, and B did not form a close group with any of these Caminalcules. Taxonomist A thought 17 was most similar to 1, C held it most similar to 27, and B described the three organisms as equally similar. Taxonomists A and C recorded 19 most similar to 26, but B considered it closer to 20. By multiple regression of the similarities implied by the taxonomists on 112 objectively defined criteria differentiating the 29 animals (these criteria were not furnished to the experimental subjects), the relative importance of various criteria in judging taxonomic similarity can be inferred. The judgments by persons A and C were more similar to each other than either was to B; most dissimilar were B and C. Table 1 shows which features of the organisms appeared important to each of the three taxonomists. A plus sign indicates a feature important to the stated taxonomist. No one feature was important to all three persons, and quite different aspects of the creatures were stressed by the subjects.

Not only the culturally conditioned biases of entire populations need to be corrected by objective classificatory systems, but individual variability in the perception of similarity and shape must be allowed for. It is now well established that individual differences in recognition of form and shape are in part due to individual differences in eye scan patterns (Noton and Stark, 1971a, b). Attempts are being made to show individual components to taxonomic judgment (see, e.g. Shepard, Romney, and Nerlove, 1972). While there is considerable commonality in judgment of similarities, individual observers do differ in the importance which they intuitively assign to different aspects of shape, form, or colour, for example (see figure 3).

Progress in classification

A convenient way of developing classifications is to compute functions that yield similarities or dissimilarities (distances) between all objects taken a pair at a time. A symmetric matrix of such similarity or dissimilarity coefficients is then analysed to represent their relationships as clusters or in various other ways. The type of pair function will depend on the data to be analysed. Binary data usually lead to association coefficients (section 4.4. in Sneath and Sokal, 1973), continuous variables to some type of distance or correlation coefficient.

Much recent progress in classification has consisted of devising methods of clustering. This would suggest that the concept of a cluster is clearly understood by those who do the clustering. Regrettably this is not always so. The various algorithms developed for clustering impose a structure on the objects to be clustered (generally known as OTUs, operational taxonomic units) which are represented as vectors of descriptors (character states). An attempt at clustering the OTUs implies a belief that they exhibit some structure and are not randomly or uniformly distributed through the hyperspace defined by the descriptors. Definitions of clusters are hard to come by. One book on cluster analysis does not define clusters at all (Tryon and Bailey, 1970), another (Sneath and Sokal, 1973) deliberately defines it loosely as 'sets of OTUs in hyperspace that exhibit neither random nor regular distribution patterns and that meet one or more of various criteria imposed by a particular cluster definition'. A more intuitively appealing but at the same time more restrictive definition is 'a set of objects characterized by the properties of isolation and coherence' (Jardine and Sibson, 1971). Clusters can be described by the different densities encountered on sweeping out the hyperspace. Properties of clusters include their location in space (some measure of central tendency), their dispersion, their shapes (for example, hyperspheres or hyperellipsoids), their connectivity (a measure of how many of the pairs of OTUs within a cluster are more similar to each other than a certain arbitrary criterion), and the magnitude of gaps between clusters.

Clustering algorithms can be agglomerative or divisive. In agglomeration the OTUs can be considered as the disjoint partition of the whole set and can be aggregated to form ever larger clusters until the conjoint partition, an entire set consisting of all the OTUs, is reached. The converse, divisive approach is to break down the conjoint partition into subsets until the disjoint partition is reached where each subset is a single OTU. In most clustering techniques, especially in polythetic methods, the agglomerative approach is preferred for practical reasons in devising a workable computer algorithm (see figure 4). . .

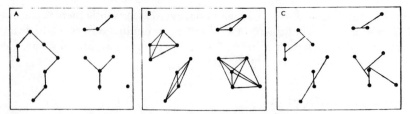

Figure 4. The effect of different agglomerative clustering methods.

Sixteen arbitrary points plotted in a two-dimensional space are clustered by: (A) single linkage clustering [in which candidates for membership join a cluster if they are connected to any member of the cluster at or above the accepted criterion of similarity], (B) complete linkage clustering [in which a candidate must connect to all members of the current cluster by the accepted criterion], and (C) an average linkage clustering method [in which a candidate joins a cluster on the basis of some average of its similarity to all the members]. Approximately corresponding stages in the clustering process are shown for the three methods yielding four open, loose clusters in single linkage (one cluster has a single member), four tight and discrete clusters in complete linkage, and an intermediate solution by an average linkage method. Continuation of the clustering process in all three cases would yield the conjoint partition in which all sixteen points would form a single cluster (after Sneath and Sokal, 1973).

The results of cluster analysis are often represented by dendrograms which are hierarchic representations of the similarity relations among the OTUs. An example is shown in figure 5. One axis is graduated in the similarity or dissimilarity scale and the branching points along the scale indicate the resemblance between the stems being joined.

Table 1. Features of Caminalcules that appeared important to three taxonomists

Feature of Caminalcules	Taxonomists		
	A	B	C
Horns on head		+	
Stalked eyes	+		+
Groove in neck		+	
Anterior appendage			
length	+		+
flexion		+	
subdivision	+		
bulb		+	
Posterior appendage			
disklike	+		+
platelike	+		
Anterior abdomen spots			+
Posterior abdomen bars	+	+	
Abdomen			
width	+		
large pores	+		+
small pores		+	

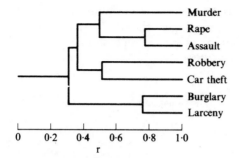

Figure 5. Results of a cluster analysis of seven crimes based on their incidence in sixteen US cities. Relationships are represented by means of a dendrogram (phenogram) in which the implied similarity between any two crimes can be read off the horizontal axis graduated in correlation coefficient scale (r). Thus burglary and larceny resemble each other at a level of 0·76 while the implied correlation between murder and larceny is only 0·31. The phenogram shows a clear separation between crimes of property and the more serious crimes, and distinguishes a cluster of crimes of violence (based on data compiled by J. A. Hartigan, Yale University).

Classifications need not be hierarchic and the clusters may overlap (intersect). The whole idea of hierarchic, nonoverlapping (mutually exclusive) classifications which is so attractive to the human mind is currently undergoing re-examination. From studies in a variety of fields the representation of taxonomic structure as overlapping clusters or as ordinations appears far preferable. By ordination we mean projection of the OTUs in a space of fewer dimensions than the original number of descriptors. When tested by any of several measures of distortion, ordinations in as few as two or three dimensions will frequently represent the original similarity matrices considerably more faithfully than dendrograms. A common means of ordination is by principal components analysis (Harman, 1967) or any of its variants . . . (see figure 6). An elegant method popular in recent years is nonmetric multidimensional scaling (Kruskal, 1964) which ordinates the OTUs into a space of predetermined dimensionality on a criterion of best fit to a monotonic function of the original similarity matrix. Since only rank order and monotonicity of the similarity coefficients is assumed, this method is particularly robust and gives unusually good results in a great variety of fields. . .

Prospects for classification

The generality of the applications discussed above rests on the near universal desire in many fields of science to classify OTUs into taxa and on the wide availability of multiple descriptors for these OTUs. This almost necessitates computer handling in a multivariate manner as I have described. The problem of correct classification of phenomena is one that constantly crops up in scientific work, and many controversies could be avoided, or at least the area of disagreement narrowed and the point under contention refined, if proper principles of classification were adhered to. An example in point is the recent controversy regarding the classification of psychotic symptoms (see Rosenhan, 1973, and subsequent letters commenting on the article). The areas of disagreement could have been narrowed if the existence and desirability of polythetic taxa had been made explicit by the writers.

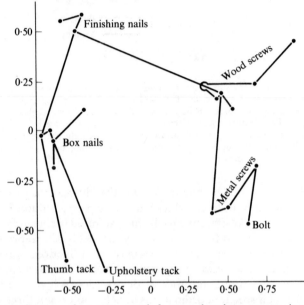

Figure 6. An ordination of nineteen metal fasteners based on twenty-three characteristics. The graph shows the first two principal axes, which are linear combinations of the twenty-three descriptive characters. The first axis (abscissa) separates objects that are turned (screws and bolts) from objects that pierce the substrate (nails and tacks), and reflects also differences in the surfaces of the heads and in the points of the shafts. The second axis (ordinate) is affected by the relative magnitude of head versus stem and by the angle of head to the shaft. The lines connecting the points give the minimum spanning tree for the nineteen objects in a full-dimensional space and serve as an indicator of possible distortion. Objects close to each other in the two-dimensional space but not directly connected are likely to be differentiated in a dimension not shown here. An example is the apparent difference between the thumbtack and the upholstery tack, which in the full-dimensional space resemble separate box nails more than they do each other. The overall classification achieved by this method is quite satisfactory, although the correspondence between the similarities ordinated in the three-dimensional space and the original similarity matrix is not as great as in other studies.

The extent of the application of these methods has been far-ranging. . . Among the major unsolved problems in computer classification are (i) the appropriate coding of characters so as to give unbiased measures of similarity among objects to be clustered; (ii) the best criteria of optimality for clustering or ordination to represent the similarity among objects with a minimum of distortion; and (iii) tests of significance of taxonomic structure found in nature. . .

12. Learning to identify toy block structures[1]

Patrick Winston

Learning

This paper describes a working computer program which embodies a new theory of learning. I believe it is unlike anything previously known in the literature because its basic idea is to understand how concepts can be learned from a few judiciously selected examples. The sequence in figure 1, for example, generates in the machine an idea of an arch sufficient to handle correctly all the configurations in figure 2 in spite of severe rotations, size changes, proportion changes, and changes in viewing angle.

Although no previous theory in the Artificial Intelligence, Psychology, or other literatures can completely account for anything like this competence, the basic ideas are quite simple:

1. If you want to teach a concept, you must first be sure your student, man or machine, can build descriptions adequate to represent that concept.

2. If you want to teach a concept, you should use samples which are a kind of nonexample.

The first point on description should be clear. At some level we must have an adequate set of primitive concepts and relations out of which we can assemble interesting concepts at the next higher level, which in turn become the primitives for concepts at a still higher level. But what is meant by the second claim that one must show the machine not just examples of concepts, but something else? First of all, something else means something which is close to being an example, but fails to be admissible by way of one or a few crucial deficiencies. I call these samples *near misses*. My view is that they are more important to learning than examples, and they provide just the right information to teach the machine directly, via a few samples, rather than laboriously and uncertainly through many samples in some kind of reinforcement mode.

[1] This paper was originally published in R. L. Solso (ed.) *Contemporary Issues in Cognitive Psychology: The Loyola Symposium* (Washington, D. C.: Winston, 1973), pp. 3–16. Reprinted with the permission of the author and Hemisphere Publishing Corp.

199

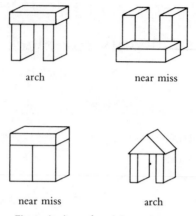

arch　　　　　　　　near miss

near miss　　　　　　arch

Figure 1. An arch training sequence

Now, the purpose of this learning process is to create in the machine whatever is needed to identify instances of learned concepts. This leads directly to the notion of a model. To be precise, we define the term as follows:

A model is a proper description augmented by information about which elements of the description are essential and by information about what, if anything, must not be present in examples of the concept.

The description must be a proper description, because the descriptive language – the possible relations – must naturally be appropriate to the definitions expected. For this reason one cannot build a model on top of a data base that describes the scene in terms of only vertex coordinates, for such a description is on too low a level. Nor can we build a model on top of a higher level description that contains only colour information, for example, because that information is irrelevant to the concept in question.

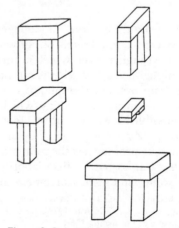

Figure 2. Structures recognized as arches

The key part of our definition of a model is the idea that some elements of the description must be underlined as particularly important. Let us see how this can be done. Figure 3 shows a training sequence that conveys the idea of a pedestal. The first step is to show the machine a sample of the concept to be learned. From a line drawing, some powerful scene analysis routines, which have been developed over the last few years, produce a hierarchical symbolic description which carries the same sort of information about a scene that a human uses and understands. Blocks are described as bricks or wedges, as standing or lying, and as related to others by being *in front of* or *supporting* them, and so on.

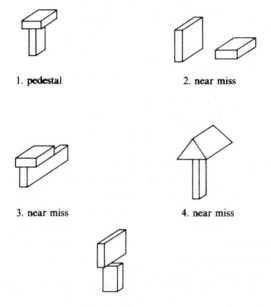

1. **pedestal**   2. near miss

3. near miss   4. near miss

5. near miss

Figure 3. A pedestal training sequence

In this paper I will present a description as a network of nodes and pointers, the nodes representing objects, and the pointers representing relations between them. See figure 4 where a pedestal network is shown. In this case, there are relatively few things in the net: just a node representing the scene as a whole, and two more for the objects. These are related to each other by the supported-by pointer, and to the general knowledge of the net via pointers like *is-a*, denoting set membership, and *has-posture*, which leads in one case to standing and in the other to lying. [In other words, a pedestal has two *parts* : one *is-a* board, and the other *is-a* brick. The board is *supported by* the brick; the board *has* a lying *posture*, and the brick *has a* standing posture.]

Now in the pedestal, the support relation is essential – there is no pedestal without it. Similarly the posture and identity of the board and brick must be correct. Therefore, the objective in a teaching sequence is to somehow convey to the machine the essential, emphatic quality of those features. (Later on we will see further examples where some relations become less essential and others are forbidden.)

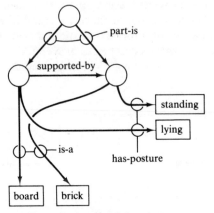

Figure 4. A pedestal description

Returning to figure 3, note that the second sample is a near miss in which nothing has changed except that the board no longer rests on the standing brick. This is reflected in the description by the absence of a supported-by pointer. It is a simple matter for a description–comparison program to detect this missing relation as the only difference between this description and the original one admissible as an instance. The machine can only conclude, as we would, that the loss of this relation explains why the near miss fails to qualify as a pedestal. This being the case, the proper action is clear. The machine makes a note that this supported-by relation is essential, replacing the original pointer with must-be-supported-by. Again note that this point is conveyed directly by a single drawing, not by a statistical inference from a boring sequence of trials. Note further that this information is quite high level. It will be discerned in scenes as long as the descriptive routines have the power to analyse that scene. Thus we need not be as concerned about the simple changes that hurt older, lower level learning ideas. Rotations, size dilations, and the like are easily handled, given the descriptive power we have in operating programs.

Continuing now with our example, the teacher proceeds to strengthen the other relations according to whatever prejudices he has. In this sequence the teacher has chosen to reinforce the pointers which determine that the support is standing and the pointers which similarly determine that the supported object is a lying board. Figure 5 shows the resulting model.

Now that the basic idea is clear, the slightly more complex arch sequence will bring out some further points. The first sample, shown in figure 1, is, as always, an example. From it we generate an initial description as before. The next step is similar to the one taken with the pedestal in that the teacher presents a near miss with the supported object now removed and resting on the table. But this time not one, but two differences are noticed in the corresponding description networks, as now there are two missing supported-by pointers. This opens up the question of what is to be done when more than one relationship can explain why the near miss misses. What is needed, of course, is a theory of how to sort out observed differences so that the most important and most likely to be responsible difference can be hypothesized and reacted to. The theory itself is somewhat detailed, but it is the exploration of this detail through writing and experimenting with programs that gives the overall theory substance. Repeated cycles of refinement and testing of a theory, as embodied in a program, are an important part of an emerging artificial intelligence methodology.

The results of this approach include the following points:

First, if two differences are observed which are of the same nature and description, then they are assumed to contribute jointly to the failure of the near miss, and both are acted on. This handles the arch case where two support relations were observed to be absent in the near miss. Since the differences are both of the missing-pointer type, and since both involve the same supported-by relation, it is deemed heuristically sound to handle them both together as a unit.

Second, differences are ranked in order of their distance from the origin of the net. Thus a difference observed in the relationship of two objects is considered more important than a change in the shape of an object's face, which in turn is interpreted as more important than an obscured vertex.

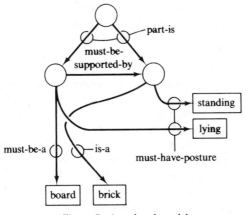

Figure 5. A pedestal model

Third, differences at the same level are ranked according to type. In the current implementation, differences of the missing-pointer type are ranked ahead of those where a pointer is added in the near miss. This is reasonable since dropping a pointer to make a near miss may well force the introduction of a new pointer. Indeed we have ignored the introduction of a support pointer between the lying brick and the table because the difference resulting from this new pointer is inferior to the difference resulting from the missing pointer. Finally, if two differences are found of the same type on the same level, then some secondary heuristics are used to try to sort them out. Support relations, for example, make more important differences than one expects from touch or left–right pointers.

These factors constitute only a theory of hypothesis formation. The theory does make mistakes, especially if the teacher is poor. We will return to this problem after completing the tour through the arch example. Recall that we diverted our attention just when the machine learned the importance of the support relations. In the next step it learns, somewhat indirectly, about the hole. This is conveyed through the near miss with the two side supports touching (see figure 1). Now the theory of most important differences reports that two new touch pointers are present in the near miss, symmetrically indicating that the side supports have moved together. Here surely the reasonable conclusion is that the new pointers have violated the concept. The model is therefore refined to have must-not-touch pointers between the nodes of the side supports. This dissuades identification programs, described later, from ever reporting an arch if such a forbidden relation is in fact present. We now see how information of a negative sort is introduced into models. They can obtain not only information about what is essential, but also information about what sorts of characteristics prevent a sample from being associated with the modelled concept.

So far we have seen examples of emphatic relations, both of the must-be and must-not-be type as introduced by near miss samples. Next in figure 1 we have an example of the inductive generalization introduced by the sample with the lying brick replaced by a wedge. Whether to call this a kind of arch or to report it as a near miss depends on the taste of the machine's instructor, of course. We want to explore the consequence of introducing it as an example, rather than as a near miss. In terms of the description–network comparison, the machine finds an is–a pointer moved over from brick to wedge. There are, given this observation, a variety of things to do. The simplest is to take the most conservative stance and form a new class, that of the brick or wedge, a kind of superset. To see what other options are available, we must take a look at the descriptions of brick and wedge and the portion of the general knowledge net that relates them together (see figure 6). There we see various sets linked together by the a-kind-of relationship. From the diagram we see that our first choice was a conservative point on a spectrum whose other end suggests that we move the is–a pointer over to object, object being the most distant intersection of a-kind-of relations. We choose a conservative position and fix the is–a pointer to the closest observed intersection, in this case right prism. We see again that a hypothesis has to be made, and the hypothesis may well be wrong. In this case it is a question of interpreting a difference rather than the question of sorting out the correct difference from many, but the effect is the same. We simply must provide mechanisms for detecting errors and correcting them.

Errors are detected when an example refutes a previously made assumption. If the first scene of figure 7 is reported as an example of concept X while the second is given as a near miss, the natural interpretation is that an X must be standing. But an alternate interpretation, considered secondary by the ranking program, is that an X must not be lying. If a shrewd teacher wishes to force the secondary interpretation, he need only give the tilted brick as an example, for it has no standing pointer and thus is a contradiction to the primary hypothesis. Under these conditions, the system is prepared to try an alternative. As the alternative may also lead to trouble, the process may iterate. . . Someone could do better by devising a little theory that would discover more intelligently the decision most likely to have caused the error. . .

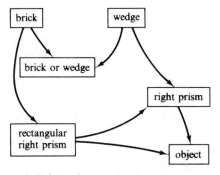

Figure 6. Relation between brick, wedge, and object

We mentioned just now the role of a shrewd teacher. I regard the dependence on a teacher as a feature of this theory. Too often in the past history of machine learning theory the use of a teacher was considered cheating, and mechanisms were instead expected to self-organize their way to understanding by way of evolutionary trial and error, or reinforcement, or whatever. This ignores the very real fact that humans as well as machines learn very little without good teaching. An inspirational leap is a rare phenomenon, and before we can hope to understand it or expose it to be an illusion, we must surely first attempt to understand the kind of learning that is at once the most common and the most useful.

1. an X   2. near miss   3. an X

Figure 7. A training sequence that leads to backups

There is an opposite form of extremism where learning really disappears and the machine only assimilates new facts more or less by rote from direct teacher entry. I have avoided this as well. It is clear that the system assimilates new models from the teacher and that it is in fact dependent on good teaching, but it depends fundamentally on its own good judgment and previously learned ideas to understand and disentangle what the teacher has in mind. It must itself deduce what are the salient ideas in the training sequence, and it must itself decide on an augmentation of the model which captures those ideas. By carefully limiting the teacher to the presentation of a sequence of samples, low-level rote-learning questions are avoided while allowing study of the issues which underly all sorts of meaningful learning, including interesting forms of direct telling.

I am therefore encouraged by the fact that our system responds to good and bad teaching as any reasonable student would. If the teacher is sloppy and tries to go too fast, or if he gives a sample differing wildly from what the machine has so far assimilated, then it is swamped with observed differences and has a reduced chance of sifting out the real message. It will be frustrated by repeated dead ends of contradiction, and the ensuing tree search for an uncontradictory path will involve a great deal more effort.

Identification

Once there are programs that describe scenes, compare description networks, and build models, one may go on to using these programs as elements in a variety of other goal-oriented programs. The problem solving programs described here have the following responsibilities:

1. To compare some scene with a list of models and report one as an acceptable or the most acceptable match. This is the identification problem in its simplest form.

2. To identify some particular object in a scene. This is not the same as identifying an entire scene, because important properties may be hidden and because context may make some identifications more probable than others.

3. To find instances of some particular model in a scene. It is frequently the case that the presence of some configuration can be confirmed even though it would not be found in the ordinary course of scene description. This requires the ability to discern groups with the required properties in spite of a shroud of irrelevant and distracting information.

Let us first explore the problem of elementary identification. The obvious procedure is to match an unknown description against those for each of the possible models and then to determine which of the resulting difference descriptions implies the best match. Recall that models generally contain must-be and must-not-be pointers, while ordinary descriptions do not. These pointers tend to be decisive in the identification process. Consider the case where some pointer in a scene's description corresponds to its must-not-be satellite in the model. This clearly means a relation is present that the model specifically forbids. This result is such a serious association impediment that identification of the unknown with the model is rejected outright, without further consideration. Therefore the near-arch in figure 8(a) cannot be identified as an arch because the network describing the near-arch has touch pointers between the two supports, while the model has must–not–touch pointers in the same place. The combination positively prevents matching. Identification with a particular model is also rejected when essential relations or properties are missing in the unknown. Thus the two bricks in figure 8(b) do not form a pedestal because the model for the pedestal has a must–be–supported–by pointer where the unknown in question has nothing.

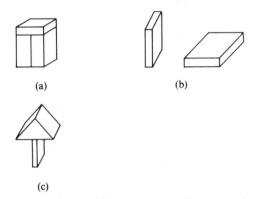

(a)   (b)

(c)

Figure 8. Configurations leading to failure when matched against arch and pedestal

Occasionally two nodes share properties that are not identical, but which fall into the same general class. Consider the situation in which the two nodes exhibit the same pointers to two other nodes from which paths of a–kind–of pointers lead to a common intersection node. Figure 8(c) shows such a situation. In this case the supported object in the unknown configuration is a kind of wedge, while the corresponding object in the model must be a kind of board. Both wedge and board are kinds of objects. But the fact that the unknown has a property in the same class as a property required by the model is insufficient. To ensure rejection of such matches, the rule is that identification is refused if the model's pointer is a must–be form.

Matches of the house in figure 9 against the pedestal, the tent, and the arch all lead to difference descriptions that positively forbid identification. The pedestal fails because the required a–kind–of relation between the top object and brick is missing. The tent similarly fails because both of its objects must be wedges. The arch fails because the model has a must–be–supported–by pointer to an object missing in the unknown. Indeed similar arguments make it clear that any pair of structures in figure 9 will fail to match if one is taken as an unknown and the other as indicating a model.

While many possible identifications are rejected outright by inspection of the emphatic relations, what if some unknown matches acceptably more than one model in the trial list? Given several possible identifications, there should be some way of ordering them so that one could be reported to be best in some sense. To do this we associate each kind of difference with a number and combine the results by forming a weighted sum for each comparison. This seems to work well enough for the moment, but we do not think it would pay to put much effort into tuning such a formula. Instead more knowledge about the priorities of differences should lead to far better programs that do not use a primitive scoring mechanism.

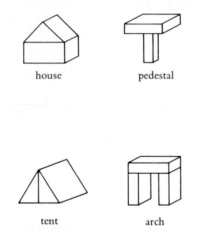

house   pedestal

tent   arch

Figure 9. Some simple concepts

A more interesting generalization is required by attempts to do identification in context. Notice in figure 10 that object B seems to be a brick, while object D seems to be a wedge. This is curious because B and D show exactly the same arrangement of lines and faces. The result also seems at odds with the machine's identification process as described, because so far anything identified as a wedge must have a triangular face. Of course, the context has made the difference. Different rules must be used when programs try to identify objects or groups of objects that are only parts of scenes. In the case where the question is whether or not the whole scene can be identified as a particular model, it is reasonable to insist that all relations deemed essential by the model be present, while all those forbidden, be absent. But when the question is whether or not a few parts of a scene can be identified as a particular model, then there is the possibility that some important part may be obscured by other objects. In these situations, our identification program uses two special heuristics. First, the coincidence of objects lying in a line seems to suggest that each object is the same type as the one obscuring it unless there is good reason to reject this hypothesis. This is what suggests that object D is a wedge in figure 10. Second, essential properties in the model may be absent in the unknown because the parts involved are hidden. This is why identification of object D as a wedge works, even though D lacks the otherwise essential triangular face. The requirement that forbidden properties do not occur remains in force, however.

Elaborate work can be done on the problem of deciding if the omission of a particular feature on some model is admissible in any particular situation. Our program takes a singularly crude view and ignores all omissions. Rejection of the hypothesis that the obscured object is like the object hiding it, happens only if the machine notices details specifically forbidden by relations in the model.

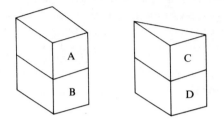

Figure 10. Context creates the impression that B is a brick but D is a wedge

Thus the effort is not to select the best matching model, but only to verify that a particular identification is not obviously contradictory. This means that object B in figure 11 is confirmed to be bricklike. Object C is not, because of its triangular side face. Of course, if the propagation of a property like brickness or wedgeness down a series of objects is interrupted, then the unknown must be compared with a battery of models, with the program still forgiving omissions but now searching for the best of many possible identifications using the scoring scheme for observed differences previously described.

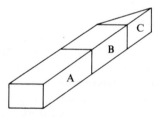

Figure 11. The brick identification propagates to B but not to C

Still another kind of generalization is required if a program is actively to look for something, rather than simply roam over a scene. The scene of figure 12, for example, is curious in that one can find an arch, a pedestal, a house, and a tent in it if one is looking for them. But if they are not specifically searched for, mention of these particular models is unlikely to appear in a description of the scene. Although the configurations are present, they are hidden by extraneous objects so well that general grouping programs are unlikely to sort them out. Yet the question, 'Does a certain model appear in the scene?' is certainly a reasonable one. One way to attack it divides nicely into three parts:

1. Find those objects in the scene that have the best chance of being identified with the model. If the model has unusual pointers or references unusual con-

cepts, the program pays particular attention to them. Similarly, extra attention is paid to the emphasized parts of the model, for if mates cannot be established for them, an identification cannot be affirmed. The result is a set of links between the objects of the model and their nearest analogues in the scene.

2. Once a good group of objects is picked, then the pointers relating these objects to the other objects in the scene are temporarily forgotten. In human terms, this is like painting the subgroup a special colour.

3. Finally, with the best group of objects set into relief by the previous excision, the ordinary identification routines are applied with the expectation of reasonable performance.

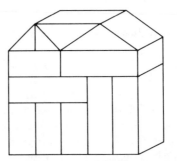

Figure 12. A situation where several instances of familiar structures are camouflaged by their context

The problem with a direct application of the identification programs lies in the myriad irrelevant differences that the extra objects in the scene would cause. Clutter leaves the machine as bewildered as it does humans.

Consider now the different question of learning something useful from attempts to match which unfortunately fail. Suppose the program attempts to identify a house as a pedestal. Identification fails because the resulting type of comparison cannot be tolerated. Still it would be a pity to throw away the information about why the match failed. Instead the otherwise wasted matching effort can be used to suggest new identification candidates. The way this works is quite simple. The machine spends idle time comparing the various models in its armamentarium with one another. Whenever the number of differences observed are few, a simplified description of those differences is stored. Thus the machine knows that a house is similar to a pedestal, from which it differs only in the nature of the top object. These descriptions link the known models together in a sort of similarity network. This network and the difference descriptions noted in the course of identification failure help to decide what model should be tried next. The description stating the differences between an unknown and a particular model is compared with the descriptions of the similarity net which link the model to similar models. If the differences between the unknown and a particular model match the difference between that model and some other model, then identification with that other model is likely. For example, our unknown (which of course is a house) relates to the model of a pedestal in roughly the same way that the model of a house relates to the model of a pedestal. House is consequently elevated to the top of the list of trial models.

New directions

This theory of learning and identification is oriented toward the structures one can imagine as reasonable in the world of children's blocks. The next step will be to generalize it to more complicated and more realistic universes. This, I believe, will perhaps involve some expansion of the learning theory together with massive improvement in our understanding of how to describe objects and concepts in whatever new universe we choose. Beyond this, the next great advance will be a theory of learning oriented toward procedures. This will be a theory capable of supporting programs which learn new programs from examples of processes, just as our theory learns physical concepts from examples of structures. This has been a dream of Artificial Intelligence for many years. . .

13. Classification of real-world objects: Origins and representations in cognition[1]

Eleanor Rosch

The world consists of a virtually infinite number of discriminably different stimuli. One of the most basic functions of all organisms is the cutting up of the environment into classifications by which nonidentical stimuli can be treated as equivalent. Yet there has been little explicit attempt to determine the principles by which humans divide up the world in the way that they do. On the contrary, it has been the tendency both in psychology and anthropology to treat the segmentation of the world as originally arbitrary. A typical statement of such a position is: 'the physical and social environment of a young child is perceived as a continuum. It does not contain any intrinsically separate "things". The child, in due course, is taught to impose upon this environment, a kind of discriminating grid which serves to distinguish the world as being composed of a large number of separate things, each labelled with a name' (Leach, 1964).

Such a position has been implicit in virtually all work in semantic memory. The categories and relations of a language are taken as unanalysed givens, and the worker then proceeds either to attempt to build a model which will encompass all of memory organization or to concentrate on specific problems of storage, coding, forgetting, or retrieval of information in memory (see Tulving and Donaldson, 1972, for papers representing both approaches). Contrary to such approaches, the work to be summarized in this paper has focused on that issue normally ignored in memory research, the nature, rationale and possible origins of the categories which are put into memory in the first place.

A basic argument of the present paper is that a view of categories as initially arbitrary would be reasonable only if the world were entirely unstructured: that is, using Garner's (1974) definition of *structure*, if the world formed a set of stimuli in which all possible stimulus attributes occurred with equal probability combined with all other possible attributes. Thus, if the attributes were size (large, small), colour (red, green), and form (square, circle), the set would consist of a small red square, a small red circle, a small green square, a small

[1] This paper first appeared in S. Ehrlich and E. Tulving (eds.), *La memoire semantique* (Paris: *Bulletin de psychologie*, 1976).

green circle, a large red square, etc. (In this example, to make the stimuli more of a continuum, we need only increase indefinitely the number of values for each attribute with a subsequent increase in possible combinations.) While such stimulus arrays have been typically used in concept identification research (see Bourne, 1966) and in many studies of free sorting behaviour (Shepard, Hovland, and Jenkins, 1961; Wing and Bevan, 1969), they may not adequately represent the structure of stimuli in the real world.

The aim of the research to be summarized was to show that the world does, in a sense, contain 'intrinsically separate things'. I and my co-workers believe that the world is so structured because of three principles. In the first place, real-world attributes, unlike the sets often presented laboratory subjects, do not occur independently of one another. Creatures with feathers are more likely also to have wings than creatures with fur, and objects with the visual appearance of chairs are more likely to have functional sit-on-able-ness than objects with the appearance of cats.

In the second place, the objects of the world are determinately structured because levels of abstraction in class-inclusion hierarchies are themselves not random but are highly structured. One of the basic claims of the present research is that, of the many levels of abstraction at which any given thing can be classified, there is one basic level of abstraction at which the organism can obtain the most information with the least cognitive effort. That is, in so far as categorization occurs to reduce the infinite differences between stimuli to behaviourally and cognitively usable proportions, two opposing principles of categorization are operative: (a) On the one hand, it is to the organism's advantage to have each classification as rich in information as possible. This means having as many properties as possible predictable from knowing any one property (which, for humans, includes the important property of the category name), a principle which would lead to formation of large numbers of categories with the finest possible discriminations between categories. (b) On the other hand, for the sake of reducing cognitive load, it is to the organism's advantage to have as few classifications as possible, a principle which would lead to the smallest number of and most abstract categories possible. We believe that the basic level of classification, the primary level at which 'cuts' are made in the environment, is a compromise between these two levels; it is the most general and inclusive level at which categories are still able to delineate real-world correlational structures.

In the third place, categories become definitively structured because, even when correlational structure in the world is only partial or when attributes are continuous, thus, producing categories which might tend to blend with other categories at the same level of abstraction, categories are maintained as discrete by being coded in cognition in terms of *prototypes* of the most characteristic members of the category. That is, many experiments have shown that categories are coded in the mind neither by means of lists of each individual member of the category nor by means of a list of formal criteria necessary and sufficient for category membership but, rather, in terms of a prototype of a typical category member. The most cognitively economical code for a category is, in fact, a concrete image of an average category member.

The first part of the present paper will summarize some evidence that there are basic objects (categories at basic levels of abstraction) in the world determined by real-world correlational structure. The second part will summarize evidence that categories can be coded in terms of prototypes and distance from the prototypes, and will show how such a manner of coding is integrated with basic levels of abstraction. Some implications for developmental psychology and psycholinguistics which have already been tested will be presented. Finally, the issue of the universality of these theories will be discussed.

Basic objects in natural categories

Real-world correlational structure of concrete objects itself consists of a number of inseparable aspects, any one of which could serve as the point of departure for the present analysis. The four aspects for which experimental evidence will be given below are: (1) attributes in common, (2) motor movements in common, (3) objective similarity in shape, and (4) identifiability of averaged shapes.

Common attributes

Basic level objects should be the most inclusive level of classification at which objects have numbers of attributes in common. This hypothesis was tested (see Rosch, Mervis, Gray, Johnson, and Boyes-Braem, 1976) for categories at three levels of abstraction in the nine systematically chosen taxonomies shown in table 1. Criteria for choice of these specific items were that the taxonomies contain the most common (defined by word frequency) categories of concrete nouns in English, that the levels of abstraction bear simple class inclusion relations to each other, and that those class inclusion relations be generally known to our subjects (be agreed upon by a sample of native English speakers). The middle level of abstraction was the hypothesized basic level: for non-biological taxonomies this corresponded to the intuition of the experimenters; for biological taxonomies it corresponded to the level of the species hypothesized as basic by previous anthropological and historical linguistic treatments of biological categories (see Berlin, 1971).

The nine taxonomies shown in table 1 were divided into sets of nine words, all of which were at the same level of abstraction, and each of which belonged to a different superordinate category (or were the superordinate term itself). Twenty subjects received each set of words; the subject's task was to list all of the attributes he could think of which were true of the items included in the class of things designated by each object name. Subjects were given one and a half minutes per object. These attribute lists were tallied; a cut-off point of six or more listings of an attribute was adopted as the criterion for inclusion of the attribute in the final tally. The veracity of attributes was rated by seven additional judges and a second tally, slightly amended by the judgments, was also computed.

Results showed that for both the raw and the judge-amended tallies, very few attributes were listed for the superordinate categories, and a significantly greater number of attributes were listed for the supposed basic level objects. Subordinate level objects did not receive significantly more attributes listed than basic level objects. The few additional attributes listed for subordinate object names tended to be adjective rather than noun or functional attributes. A check on the likeness of attributes listed for object names and for visually present objects, using one basic level object category from each of the nine taxonomies, showed that a single subject listing all attributes observable in one and a half

Table 1. The nine taxonomies used as stimuli

Superordinate	Basic level	Subordinates	
		Non-biological taxonomies	
Musical instrument	Guitar	Folk guitar	Classical guitar
	Piano	Grand piano	Upright piano
	Drum	Kettle drum	Bass drum
Fruit*	Apple	Delicious apple	Mackintosh apple
	Peach	Freestone peach	Cling peach
	Grapes	Concord grapes	Green seedless grapes
Tool	Hammer	Ball-peen hammer	Claw hammer
	Saw	Hack hand saw	Cross-cutting hand saw
	Screwdriver	Phillips screwdriver	Regular screwdriver
Clothing	Pants	Levis	Double knit pants
	Socks	Knee socks	Ankle socks
	Shirt	Dress shirt	Knit shirt
Furniture	Table	Kitchen table	Dining room table
	Lamp	Floor lamp	Desk lamp
	Chair	Kitchen chair	Living room chair
Vehicle	Car	Sports car	Four-door sedan car
	Bus	City bus	Cross country bus
	Truck	Pick-up truck	Tractor-trailer truck
		Biological taxonomies	
Tree	Maple	Silver maple	Sugar maple
	Birch	River birch	White birch
	Oak	White oak	Red oak
Fish	Bass	Sea bass	Striped bass
	Trout	Rainbow trout	Steelhead trout
	Salmon	Blueback salmon	Chinook salmon
Bird	Cardinal	Easter cardinal	Grey tailed cardinal
	Eagle	Bald eagle	Golden eagle
	Sparrow	Song sparrow	Field sparrow

* Fruit is not considered a biological taxonomy by the criteria in Berlin (1971).

minutes per item for twenty different actual objects of the category produced essentially identical attribute tallies to those produced by twenty subjects for a single object name. The single unpredicted result was that for the three biological taxonomies shown in table 1, the basic level, as defined by numbers of attributes in common, appeared to be the level we had originally expected to be superordinate, that is, one level higher in abstraction in the taxonomy than predicted by Berlin (1971). These results will be discussed further below.

Motor movements

Inseparable from the attributes of objects are the ways in which humans habitually use or interact with those objects. For example, when performing the action of sitting down on a chair, a sequence of body and muscle movements are typically made which are inseparable from the nature of the attributes of chairs – legs, seat, back, etc. It is outside the scope of the present research to consider whether attributes or action sequences are more fundamental; the import of our argument is simply the claim that humans have consistent motor programs with which virtually all humans interact with virtually all objects of a certain class. Little attention has been previously paid to this motoric aspect of concepts except in Piaget's notion of sensory-motor schemata (Piaget, 1952) and in developmental theories which attempt to include Piaget's concept of sensory-motor schemata (Bruner, Olver, and Greenfield, 1966; Nelson, 1974). The purpose of the methodological part of our present research was to develop systematic techniques which could operationalize and specify in some detail the actual motor programs which adults employ when using or interacting with the most common objects in our environment. Our hypothesis was that, when motor programs could be measured, basic level objects, the most inclusive classes at which common attributes co-occurred in the previous experiment, would, likewise, be the most inclusive classes at which consistent motor programs were employed for all objects of a category.

Each of the nine word sets that had been used in the previous experiment was administered to twenty subjects. Instructions were for the subject to describe, in as much finely analysed detail as possible, the sequences of muscle movements he made when using or interacting with the object. Subjects were given three minutes per object. Subjects' protocols were analysed as follows: the description was first divided into the major activities which appeared to be described (such as sitting down on a chair or watching a bird). Each major activity was then divided into the part of the body used in each part of the sequence, and each body part for each part of the sequence was divided into the specific movement(s) made by that body part at that point. Tallies of four or more listings of these same movements of the same body part in the same part of the movement sequence formed the basic unit of analysis; these repeated movements were tallied and analysed as the attributes had been in the previous experiment.

Results were identical to those of the attribute listings: virtually no motor movements occurred in common for the supposed superordinates (supposed superordinates displaced upwards one level of abstraction for the three biological taxonomies); a large number of movements were made in common to basic level objects; and no more movements were made in common to subordinate than to basic level objects. For example, there are few motor programs we carry out to items of furniture in general, several specific motor programs carried out in regard to sitting down on chairs, but we sit on kitchen and living room chairs using essentially the same motor programs. As with the attributes, the results obtained from subjects' protocols based on introspection of motor movements were checked against subjects' descriptions of naïve models performing the dominant activity for four objects (sitting on a chair, eating grapes, putting on a sock, hammering in a nail). Essentially identical results were obtained from the introspective and live protocols. (For details of the method and results of this experiment, see Rosch *et al.* 1976.)

Similarity in shapes

Another aspect of the meaning of a class of objects is the way the objects of the class look. In order to be able to analyse real-world correlational structures by different but converging methods, we wished to find a method for analysing similarity in the visual aspects of objects which was not dependent upon subjects' descriptions (as the previous experiments had been), which was free from effects of the object's name (which would not have been the case for subjects' ratings of similarity), and which went beyond similarity of analysable, listable attributes which had already been used in the first experiment described. For this purpose, we chose outlines of the shape of two-dimensional representations of objects, an integral aspect of natural forms. Pilot studies showed that a set of objects were as recognizable from outline tracings of this type as they were from lists of attributes or from full colour photographic views of half of the object, thus confirming the idea that shape was a reasonable, identifiable aspect of the overall look of an object which could be used to represent an object's 'look'.

The basic hypothesis of this experiment was that shapes of objects would show the same correlational structure as had attributes and motor movements in the previous experiments; specifically, that the same basic objects would prove the most inclusive categories in which the shapes of objects showed a great gain in objective similarity over the next higher level of abstraction. Four superordinate categories were chosen for which it was possible to obtain a very large sample of pictures from books and/or from objects available in the immediate environment (furniture, clothing, vehicles, animals). Out of a possible 125–200 pictures, four pictures of four basic level objects in each category were chosen by essentially random decision methods and were normalized for size and orientation photographically. These pictures served as subjects for this experiment. Similarity in shape was measured by the amount of overlap of the two outlines when the normalized outlines were juxtaposed.

Results showed that the ratio of overlapped to nonoverlapped area when two objects from the same basic level category (e.g. two chairs) were overlapped was far greater than when two objects from the same superordinate category were overlapped (e.g. a chair and a bed – recall that the pictures were normalized for size). While some gain in ratio of overlap to nonoverlap also occurred for subordinate category objects (e.g. two kitchen chairs), it was significantly less than the gain between the superordinate and basic level objects (a more detailed account of this experiment is in Rosch *et al.* 1976).

Identifiability of averaged shapes

If the basic level is the most inclusive level at which shapes of objects of a class are similar, a possible result of such similarity may be that the basic level is also the most inclusive level at which an average shape of an object can be recognized. Such a result would be particularly important because, if that is the case, the basic level may be the most inclusive level at which it is possible to form a mental image which is isomorphic to an average member of the class and, thus, the most abstract level at which it is possible to have a relatively concrete image.

To test this hypothesis, the same normalized overlaps of shapes used in the previous experiments were used to draw an average outline of the overlapped figures – that is, the central point of all nonadjacent points was taken and connected with lines. Subjects were then asked to identify both the super-ordinate category and the specific object depicted. Results showed that basic level objects were the most general and inclusive level at which the objects depicted could be identified. Furthermore, overlaps of subordinate objects were no more identifiable than objects at the basic level.

In summary: converging experiments have shown a basic level of abstraction in human classification of concrete objects. Basic objects were found to be the most inclusive categories whose members consisted of clusters of correlated attributes, were used by means of the same motor movements, had objectively similar shapes, and for which an averaged shape of members of the class was recognizable. It is the last finding which makes it possible to articulate this research with previous findings in regard to coding categories by means of prototypes.

The coding of natural categories by means of prototypes

Rosch (1973b, 1975a) has previously argued that categories are not – as many traditions of thought in philosophy, psychology, linguistics, and anthropology imply – logical, bounded entities, membership in which is defined by an item's possession of a simple set of criterial features, in which all instances possessing the criterial attribute have a full and equal degree of membership. Rather, many natural categories are internally structured into a prototype (clearest cases, best examples) of the category with nonprototype members tending toward an order from better to poorer examples. The domain which has most readily lent itself to the demonstration of a prototype and surround structure is that of colour [see Rosch, Reading 30; and Rosch, 1975c; Mervis, Catlin, and Rosch, 1975]. . .

That semantic categories can also be coded in terms of prototypes and distance from the prototype has been demonstrated by several experiments. In the first place, subjects can reliably rate the extent to which a member of a category fits their idea or image of the meaning of the category name (Rosch, 1973b, 1975b). Such ratings predict verification times for statements of the form 'A (member) is a (category)' (Rips, Shoben, and Smith, 1973; Rosch, 1973b), a fact which has been used as the basis of a general model of retrieval from semantic memory (Smith, Shoben, and Rips, 1974). The priming technique (see below) has shown that the representation generated by the category name for superordinate categories, though not as concrete a visual image as was the code for colours, is more like members rated as good examples than those rated as poor examples of the category (Rosch, 1975b).

In the first part of the present paper, the argument was made that division of the world into basic level objects was not arbitrary. A similar argument can be made in regard to the development of the internal structure of categories (e.g. the formation of category prototypes and of gradients of category membership). For some categories which probably have a physiological basis such as colours, forms, and facial expressions of basic human emotions (Ekman, 1972; McDaniel, 1972; Rosch, 1975a, Reading 30), prototypes may be stimuli which are salient prior to formation of the category, and whose salience initially determines the categorical structuring of those domains. For most domains, however, categories probably form in accordance with the perceived correlational structure of the environment, prototypes developing at the same time as categories through principles similar to those governing the formation of the categories. Rosch and Mervis (1975) found from subjects' listings of attributes that, although superordinate categories had few, if any, attributes common to all members, the higher a member was rated a good example of the category, the more of a family resemblance (Wittgenstein, 1958) it bore to other members of the category – that is, the more attributes it had which other members of the category also had.

Basic level categories have variation among members (though, perhaps, less of it) and unclear boundaries, just as do other types of categories. Thus, it is most reasonable that prototypes of basic level categories should be those members that have the most attributes in common with other members of the category (even when not in common to all members), the most motor movements in common, and the greatest general similarity in shape.

It is at this point that an articulation can be seen between prototype research and the research reported in the first part of the paper. Basic level names were the most general and inclusive categories at which the physical features of an averaged shape of an item could be recognized. If this means that it is possible to form an image of an average member of a basic level category, advance information concerning the category name should facilitate responses even in a task requiring a quite concrete visual code. To test this hypothesis, the priming technique (which had shown cognitive representations generated by basic colour names to be concrete visual images but the representations of superordinate semantic category names to be more abstract) was applied to basic level categories. [The technique involves presenting the name of some entity prior to a perceptual task involving a picture of the object, see Rosch *et al.* 1976] Results showed, as predicted, that the basic level name was the most abstract name from which a concrete image could be generated.

The preceding discussion of coding categories as prototypes has contributed two major factors to our understanding of the formation of the basic category cuts in the world. In the first place, the same nonarbitrary principles which determine categorization appear to iterate to determine the internal structure of categories; the prototypes of categories appear to be simply those members of the category which most reflect the correlational structure of the category as a whole. In the second place, it may be through prototypes that the efficiency of basic level categories in providing the most information for the least cognitive effort can be translated into an actual cognitive code; coding of basic level categories by means of the prototype would seem to be the form of cognitive representation which can provide the most information about the category obtainable in a single, concrete image.

Implications for other fields

The theory of categorization outlined above has several implications which have already been tested for developmental psychology. Basic level objects should be those first learned by means of visual perception and sensory motor interaction with the object and, thus, should be the first divisions of the world at which it might make sense to a child to put things together because they are the same type of thing. There is a long tradition of sorting research in the developmental literature which indicates that children, unlike adults, do not put things together because they are the same sort of thing, but, rather, because of associations, stories, chains, and other nontaxonomic criteria (Bruner *et al.* 1966). However, in *all* previous studies, the possible taxonomic categories were invariably at the superordinate level, e.g. the child would have to put a cat and a horse together as animals rather than two cats as cats. We performed a study in which subjects, with ages from 3 years to adult, were divided into two groups, one of which was given an opportunity to sort sets of colour pictures of common objects into groups of basic level objects, another of which was given the same pictures but in sets cross-cutting the basic level so that taxonomic sorting would necessarily be at the usual superordinate level. At all age levels (in which a ceiling had not been reached), taxonomic grouping of basic level objects occurred far more frequently than of superordinate objects, an effect which we could show was independent of language (Rosch *et al.* 1976). Thus, what may look like a difference in the structure of thought was shown to be partly due to an artifact of the content of the usual tasks provided, an artifact which was caused by an exclusive focus on cognitive developmental factors internal to the child and a lack of understanding of actual real-world structures and their reflection in psychological categories.

Other developmental implications concern the acquisition of language. Basic level objects should be those first named by the child. Furthermore, category membership of prototypical examples of objects should be learned before that of less good examples. Thus, basic level objects which are good representatives of their basic level category should be learned before any other concrete nouns. Using the protocols from Roger Brown's Sarah (Brown, 1973), we found that, for the nine taxonomies in table 1, in all cases, the basic level names were learned and used before either superordinate or subordinate names (Rosch et al. 1976). Furthermore, using a mixture of category types, Anglin (1976) has shown that good examples of categories are learned before poor examples.

The second field to which this theory has direct implication is that of language use and language evolution. From all that has been said, we would expect the most useful and, thus, most used name for an item to be the basic level name. In fact, we found that adults almost invariably named pictures of the subordinate items of the taxonomies in table 1 at the basic level, though, when asked, they agreed that the superordinate and subordinate terms were also names for the objects (Rosch et al. 1976).

On a more speculative level, in the evolution of languages, one would expect names to evolve first for basic level objects, spreading both upwards and downwards as taxonomies increased in depth. Berlin (1971) claims such a pattern for the evolution of plant names, although that work is rendered equivocal by the difficulties in location of the basic level which we found for biological taxonomies. Of great relevance to this speculative evolutionary hypothesis is our finding that for the American sign language of the deaf, single signs existed most often for the basic level terms of the nine taxonomies of table 1. Super- and subordinate items, when indicated at all in sign, were designated by explanatory phrases (Rosch et al. 1976). A historical linguistic study of this hypothesis for domains other than botanical nomenclature is very much needed.

Discussion

From the beginning of this paper, it has been implied that we were discussing universal principles of categorization of the concrete perceptual stimuli of the world. But what aspects of the theory are intended to be universals? The content of categories should not be; our argument is that categories reflect real-world correlational structures. Since the structure of the environment, both the man-made objects and the flora and fauna of a region, should differ radically in different parts of the world, we would expect the categories of different cultures to differ.

At this point, it is necessary to clarify what is meant by categories reflecting real-world correlational structures. In the first place, we are not discussing the philosophical issue of a metaphysical real world which may exist apart from perceivers. We mean simply that, given an organism which can perceive attributes such as *feathers, fur,* and *wings,* it is an empirical fact 'out there' that wings co-occur with feathers more than with fur. It is obvious that all cognitive categories are interactions between the correlational structures that exist in the world and the state of knowledge of the perceivers. However, the structures in the world place limitations on human knowledge; humans cannot perceive correlational structures where there are none; they can only be ignorant of structures which exist. It is such ignorance which may account for the fact that for our subjects, basic level objects for the three biological taxonomies were consistently at one level of abstraction higher than that predicted by anthropological and linguistic data (Berlin, 1971). Biological taxonomies may contain correlational structures at two levels of abstraction which are potential basic level objects; our subjects, who were both city dwellers and nonexperts in botany or zoology, may not have known of the attributes in common, potential movements to be made in interaction with the objects, and the similarities in shape which might be characteristic of the species level categories provided them. Thus, in different cultures, not only available real-world structures may differ, but interest in attributes and their correlation for specific domains may differ – thereby, contributing to differences in the content of categories.

What is claimed to be universal in the present research are the principles of category formation once correlational structures exist in the environment and are known and attended to by a culture. Our claim is that, given those conditions, both the basic category cuts in the environment and the cognitive prototypes of those basic categories are determined. Basic object categories will be the most inclusive categories which have many perceived attributes in common, very similar motor movement sequences made to objects of the category, and which are similar in their overall look. The same principles determine which members of the category will be perceived as most prototypical; they will be those that have the most attributes and motor movements in common with the most members of the category, thus also being the items most typical of the category in overall look. . .

14. Some evidence for the cognitive primacy of categorization and its functional basis[1]

Katherine Nelson

Categorization of sound patterns and of objects and events in the real world is basic to learning a language. This thesis was developed by Brown (1956) who termed first language learning 'a process of cognitive socialization' involving 'the coordination of speech categories with categories of the nonlinguistic world' (p. 247). More recently, Lenneberg (1967) has argued that categorization must be the basic cognitive process: 'Thus categorization by a principle, or the formation of an (abstract) concept is apparently prior to and more primitive than the association of a sound pattern with a specific sensory experience.' And, 'the abstractness underlying meanings in general . . . may best be understood by considering concept-formation the primary cognitive process, and naming (as well as acquiring a name) the secondary cognitive process. Concepts . . . are not so much the *product* of man's cognition, but conceptualization is the *cognitive process itself*' (pp. 332–3, italics in the original). In this view, both differentiation and 'interrelating of categories or the perception of and tolerance for *transformations*' derive from the basic mode of organization which is categorization. Thus, for Lenneberg, words tag cognitive processes and it is words that make these processes seem more static than they actually are.

The difference between Brown's (1956) view and Lenneberg's lies in the distinction between categories that exist ready-made in the world outside the child (linguistic and nonlinguistic) and categories generated by the child himself. Essentially this is the distinction between linguistic and cognitive determinism. In turn this implies a difference in the language learning *process*, particularly in the acquisition of a lexicon; namely, the difference between learning the categories of the real world through identifying the referents of target names (a concept identification paradigm) and learning the appropriate names for cognitive distinctions already made (a concept matching paradigm).

The question to be explored here is not the referent of the word, which is assumed to be the child's concept (cf. Furth, Youniss, and Ross, 1970; Olson,

[1] This paper was originally published in *Merrill-Palmer Quarterly of Behaviour and Development*, **19** (1973), 21–39.

1970), but whether concept formation precedes word learning or is determined by it. Is there empirical evidence that children engage in categorizing behaviour prior to the acquisition of language? If so, what are the bases of their categories? Inhelder and Piaget (1964) and Vygotsky (1962), based on studies with pre-school children, both stress the relative deficiency of young children in classification behaviour. Bruner, Olver, and Greenfield (1966) and Kagan, Moss and Sigel (1963) among others have studied categorization in school children and found a progression from perceptual to functional bases of categorization and from nonanalytical to more analytical bases, respectively. Flavell (1970) in a recent summary stated 'there appears to be an ontogenetic shift . . . from equivalences based on the more concrete and immediately given perceptual, situational, and functional attributes to equivalences of a more abstract, verbal-conceptual sort' (p. 996). Thus, the total picture of classification behaviour in pre-linguistic children that one might expect to find (if indeed one could expect to find any at all) is one of the formation of concrete, perceptual, global, logically incomplete groups.

If one asks what we know independently about the cognitive status of the pre-linguistic one-year-old child, one finds that, according to Piaget (1952, 1954) and those who have verified and standardized his findings, the child at this age, far from forming categories of objects, is still forming notions of the permanent object and of causality. Inhelder and Piaget (1958), however, do state that the infant's activity is *analogous* to classification in its assimilation of objects to sensory-motor schemata. Can the child categorize objects before he believes in their permanent identity? What is the relation of word, object, and category in the development of language and thought?

Three aspects of these questions are considered here, together with the results of three exploratory studies carried out in the course of a longitudinal study of early language development. The hypotheses upon which these studies were based are as follows:

1. An infant engages in sorting and grouping (i.e. categorizing) objects in a consistent way before he or she has acquired a language. This behaviour reflects a primitive but rule-based cognitive organization.

2. The rules by which such categories are generated are predominantly functional in nature. That is, they are based on characteristic actions on or by the objects categorized. (Object in this case is to be understood to imply people, animals, and events as well as things.)

3. The generalization of a category to new members takes place on the basis of recognizing the typical form exhibited by the instances generating the rule. . .

Subjects and Setting

The studies in this report were carried out in the course of a longitudinal language research project in which each child was visited at home at approximately monthly intervals between the ages of 12 and 24 months. Eighteen children (seven boys, eleven girls) from middle-income homes participated, although every child was not used in each of the substudies.

1. Grouping

Several attempts were made in the course of this research to elicit categorization behaviour. What seemed to be functionally based comparative grouping or pairing behaviour was observed frequently in the course of the child's play with selected objects that were novel to him. The standardization of these observations was more difficult. Free classification situations similar to Inhelder and Piaget's (1958) using a large number (twelve or more) of objects that could be classified along a wide variety of dimensions produced behaviour much like that which Piaget has reported in young children: heaps and graphic collections with frequent shifts in the basis of classification. On these grounds one might conclude, as does Piaget, that such children are incapable of even the most rudimentary classifying behaviour.

Ricciuti (1965), however, in a pioneering study presented evidence that infants of 12 to 24 months of age spontaneously exhibit sequential and spatial grouping behaviour when they are confronted with objects differing along one or more dimensions. His situation differed from the usual free classification experiment in important ways: it used a small number of objects classifiable into two mutually exclusive subsets on the basis of a single principle. Ricciutti presented each child with four tasks. In each task the child was given eight objects belonging to two contrasting subsets of four objects each. The subsets contrasted size (used in two tasks), form, and a redundant multiple-contrast of colour, form, and texture. The subjects in this experiment were required to arrange the objects. They showed more sequential ordering or temporal grouping than spatial grouping and more formations of one group than of two groups (complete classification).

The latter finding is consistent with the expectation that younger children can attend to only one thing (or class) at a time (Inhelder and Piaget, 1964). They are in effect separating A from not-A (a task that requires only that the child focus on A) rather than A from B (which requires attending to the class basis of both categories and acting upon both categories). The sequential ordering found by Ricciuti implies a temporal – rather than or in addition to – a spatial basis for categorization.

Ricciuti's tasks did not produce equal amounts of grouping behaviour: the multi-contrast set elicited most, followed by both size contrasts, with the form contrast eliciting very little. He also found an increase in grouping behaviour with increasing age over the range from 12 to 24 months, although some grouping was evident at the earliest age.

Although Ricciuti's study demonstrated the tendency of very young children to engage in grouping or categorizing behaviours, it tapped only a limited number of perceptual bases for such behaviours. It is hypothesized here that the *function* of objects – their use or action – serves as the most primitive dimension along which the child will group objects, rather than such invariant visual attributes as size, colour, or form. Indeed, the argument can be made that size and colour are largely irrelevant to basic categorization behaviour. Also, Ricciuti's study used abstract nonmeaningful forms, thus requiring that bases for categorization be discovered in the course of experimental manipulation. A grouping situation is needed that also includes realistic objects (in order to tap already formed categories) that can be grouped along one or two contrasting dimensions, including that of function. Such a situation was therefore presented to the children in this study and was found to succeed where the free classification methods had failed.

Method and Procedure

Only seven of the eighteen subjects were available for this experiment when they were between the ages of 19 and 22 months; thus, it is little more than a pilot for the necessary exploration of dimensions and stimulus sets possible in this situation. At the time of testing the active vocabularies of these children ranged from 15 to over 300 words. Five of the seven children had vocabularies of less than 50 words. Of the possibly relevant labels, all of the children knew the word 'car'. Four knew the word 'dog' or its equivalent and three knew 'block'. Only one child had learned any size or colour words. It is recognized that word usage may not be a true indication of word knowledge at this point in development (cf. Study 3 below). Nevertheless, the two can be assumed to be closely related (Nelson, 1974), and therefore word usage is taken as the best available indicator of word knowledge.

The procedure was similar to Ricciuti's. The child was seated in his high chair. E (experimenter) presented four to six sets of eight objects each, one set at a time, laid out in haphazard order on the high chair tray. E's instructions were: 'Here, you fix them up, put them the way they ought to go.' These 'instructions' were more for E's benefit (and the mother's) than for the child, since the majority of the children did not have the verbal capacity to understand this sentence. They did, however, invariably proceed to act upon the objects. S (subject) was given two to two and a half minutes to play freely with the objects. If not groups were formed spontaneously, E divided the objects into two groups for S, then mixed them up again and asked S if he could fix them. Few modelled groups were produced; they are not included in the analysis below.

The order of presentation (shown in table 1) was the same for each child, with minor exceptions and omissions due to shifts of the child's interest. Not all children were tested on all concepts due to differences in length of attention span. A sixth set based on size and form (and function) was given to too few children to be included here. The function of an object is defined as the use or action associated with the object. In this situation whenever form varies some aspect of function varies with it, since the child can act on and explore the objects. When such action is not possible the two are separable concepts (see Study 3 below).

Table 1. Groups and classification basis in order of presentation

Group		Classification basis
1. 4 Large blue plastic planes 4 Small blue plastic planes		Size
2. 4 Small green plastic animals (varied) 4 Small yellow plastic animals (varied) or 4 Blue cars (varied) 4 Yellow cars (varied)		Colour
3. 2 Blue cylinders 2 Yellow cylinders	2 Blue blocks 2 Yellow blocks	Colour *or* Form (and function)
4. 4 Small plastic green animals (varied) 4 Small plastic green eating utensils (varied)		Function
5. 4 Small yellow plastic cars (varied) 4 Small blue plastic planes (varied)		Colour *and* form (and function)

A checklist was used to record S's actions upon each object in sequence. Any spatial groups formed were reproduced graphically.

Results

In the present study the child's sequential choice behaviour within each set was compared with that expected by chance. Given that he has acted upon subset A, will he shift to subset B, or act upon another member of A? For each set, the actual proportion of sequential and alternate choices was compared to the probability for random choices. Table 2 shows the number of cases for each set in which the number of sequential choices exceed those expected by chance.[2]

It is clear that overall sequences were significantly more frequent than would be expected by a random choice model. However, since this result might be obtained if one set of objects were acted upon to the exclusion of the other (that is, if the child's preference for one subset was so great that he did not attend to objects in the other), all sets in which the child chose one subset 75 per cent or more of the time were eliminated, yielding the revised figures in table 2, in which sequences were still found to be significantly greater than alternations. It is also clear from this table, however, that the groups were not equally powerful in producing sequential choices. Size and colour produced as much alternating

[2] Group 3, based on nonredundant form and colour is not included in this tabulation, although sequential choices (for either colour or form) were greater than expected by chance. However, in this situation it is not certain whether from the child's point of view these choices should be classified as sequential or alternate.

as sequential behaviour, while sequential behaviour predominated with the function groups, whether alone or combined with form and colour.

Table 2. Number of subjects making sequential choices greater than expected by chance

Basis for grouping	N	Number making sequential choices			Number making sequential choices, high preference eliminated		
		>E	<E	p^*	>E	<E	p^*
Size	6	3	3	ns.	2	3	ns.
Colour	6	3	3	ns.	3	3	ns.
Function	7	7	0	<0·001	5	0	<0·01
Function, form, and colour	5	5	0	<0·01	4	0	<0·05
Totals		18	6	<0·001	14	6	<0·01

* Chi-square analysis of the number of the sequential choices made by each child.

Ricciuti defined spatial groups by the following criteria:

Two groups: A_1. Four objects of each kind are displaced from original location and constituted as spatially separated groups.

A_2. Incomplete or partially correct groups are constituted and spatially separated (at least three of a kind in each group).

Single group: B_1. All four objects of one kind are constituted as a group and spatially separated from other objects.

B_2. An incomplete or partially correct group is constituted and separated from the others (three of one kind, or four of one kind plus one of other).

All children in this study produced at least one group by these criteria. Table 3 shows the number of children forming spontaneous groups of each type, the number of children forming any group for each set, and the proportion of sets eliciting sequential behaviour for each type of classification situation. A given type of spatial group was tabulated only once for each child for any one set.

Again it can be seen that there is a difference in the extent to which these sets are effective in eliciting groups, although with these somewhat fragmentary data the difference is not significant ($p \leqslant 0.20$). However, when function or form was a possible basis for grouping, 70 per cent or more of the children formed groups; while with size as the basis, no children formed groups. These data differ from the order found by Ricciuti, where more groups were produced for his size contrast set than for his form contrast. Obviously, a great deal more exploration of these varying dimensions is needed both with realistic and abstract forms.

It is clear that varying stimulus properties elicit varying degrees of spontaneous categorizing behaviour at this age but the relevant properties are not yet delineated. This study has, however, indicated that the function or use of objects is a salient principle of categorizing behaviour with children less than two years of age. Most important, when conditions are appropriate, young children will sort or group objects according to a consistent principle before they have adequate language to name the groups formed, to identify their basis of classification, or to understand classifying instructions. This strongly indicates that categorizing is a very basic cognitive process, supporting the first hypothesis above.

Table 3. Summary of grouping performance by classification basis and type of group

	Subjects exceeding expected sequential choices		Number of different spatial groups formed by type of groups					Subjects forming spatial groups	
	N	%	A_1	A_2	B_1	B_2	Total	No	%
Size	6	50	0	0	0	0	0	0	0
Colour	6	50	0	2	1	1	4	3	50
Function	7	100	1	0	4	2	7	5	71
Form and colour	7								
Colour		57	0	0	0	1	1	1	14
Form		71	1	0	2	4	7	5	71
Function, form and colour	5	100	1	0	2	2	5	5	100
Totals			3	2	9	10	24		

2. Identifying categorization criteria

Every category has a principle or rule that relates its members to each other. Such rules reflect the criterial attributes of the members of the set. These attributes may be perceptual (e.g. size, colour, contours, features) or functional (e.g. vehicle, food, plaything). They may be concrete or abstract, apparent or potential. Objects in the world exhibit a large number of attributes which enable them to be classified in many different ways. In the concept identification paradigm, if the child is attempting to identify a certain category (learn the referents for *chair*, for example), some attributes exhibited by the members of the class will be irrelevant (size, colour, pattern, material) while others define the class (are criterial) and he must identify which is which on the basis of association of cues. However, on the assumption that the child is forming categories independently of learning their class labels, he must determine for himself which attributes are relevant or criterial. To avoid cognitive overload he must operate with some consistent principles of dimensionalizing the world in order to form appropriate and useful categories. The principle, rule, or dimension must come first and the categories emerge from it, rather than the rule being discovered or emerging from the identification of the category or its members. Thus, if categorizing behaviour is prior to language, it should be possible to find a small group of basic principles used by pre-linguistic children for classifying the environment. Some possible principles (form and function) were discussed in Study 1 above.

Palmer and Rees (1969) devised a test used with two- and three-year-olds that is relevant to this quest. Their test is called the Concept Familiarity Index (CFI), but it is actually a measure of the child's familiarity with terms that describe attributes, qualities, states, and relationships: terms that refer to the criteria by which objects and events may be classified. These terms can be divided into the following types:

1. Perceptual: permanent apparent quality of the object such as colour, form, texture.

2. Functional: temporary or potential state of the object.

3. Perceptual–relational: permanent apparent qualities judged in relation to other objects such as size.

4. Functional–relational: temporary state dependent on the relation between two objects.

The items in the CFI are built around more than forty such concepts. In Palmer's test each concept was tested twice with each child in a different form. Most items require the child to choose between two objects (e.g. which is the big horse?) but the items are carefully counter-balanced to eliminate position effects. Palmer used this test as one assessment instrument in a large-scale study of concept development in lower- and middle-class ghetto children. The data he provides for the percentage of items passed at ages two and three by the children in his sample reveal striking relationships when they are classified according to the scheme above.

1. Functional attributes and relations appear to be learned earlier than perceptual ones. What are called functional here may be equally well termed states or temporary aspects of the object. They involve change or potential, while the perceptual attributes describe permanent, immediately apparent qualities of the object.

2. Relations are no more difficult than simple concepts according to this test. (For a related discussion see Donaldson and Wales, 1970, who term the relations in question two-state comparisons.)

These findings suggest that the two-year-old child is sensitive to within-things variability (temporary states) but is relatively insensitive to between-things variability (colour, size; see Elkind, 1969). This is consistent with the model of a child who focuses on defining the relevant attributes of a single object and then generalizes his concept definition to other similar objects. In contrast is the model of a child who compares instances of a concept, extracts relevant cues (the invariant attributes), and uses these to identify other instances. The difference just described is that between a *concept-former* and a *concept-learner*.

A short version of Palmer's CFI was devised and administered to all of the subjects in this study (N = 18) when they were 24–25 months of age. This form included 10 perceptual, 8 functional, 10 perceptual–relational, and 11 functional–relational items. The order of difficulty of items in this form was compared by the Spearman rank correlation with the order of difficulty for the same items reported for Palmer's subjects at the two- and three-year-old levels. For the comparison with the two-year-olds in the original sample *rho* equalled 0·59 and for the comparison with the three-year-old sample it was 0·54 (both significant at $p < 0.001$). These figures compare with *rho*'s reported by Palmer of the stability of item difficulty from age two to three in his sample ranging from 0·72 to 0·82. The present level thus seems satisfactory as a replication despite the difference in sample composition, sample size, and conditions of administration.

Results and discussion

The items used and the proportion of subjects answering each item correctly are given in table 4. An analysis of variance using an arcsin transformation of scores based on the proportion of items correct within each type was performed with Concept Criteria (perceptual-functional) and Complexity (simple-relational) as factors. This analysis showed a main effect of Concept Criteria ($F_{1, 17} = 5·00$, $p < 0.05$; Functional terms higher than Perceptual) but no significant effect for Complexity ($F_{1, 17} = 2·54$) and no interaction term. This confirms the conclusion drawn from Palmer's data on the relative difficulty of these items. As is evident in table 4 the order of difficulty by group is not invariant. Some items within each group are easier, some are more difficult than items in other groups. Some of the reasons for this are discussed below. In addition, it should be noted that the partition of these items leaves uncontrolled variance of undetermined origin. It is not known, for example, whether the functional items may simply be more familiar to the children than those termed perceptual. For this reason conclusions based on this partitioning can be only tentative.

In this test, as in many other situations, opposites are frequently not discriminated. Thus, a child may put the doll's hands up when asked to put them down, as well as when asked to put them up. This tendency has been often noted in young children and seems to designate a stage where the domain of the concept has been identified but it has not yet been differentiated. In scoring the items a response indicating the opposite of the concept in question was of course scored as an error.

Relationships on this form of the test produced lower scores relative to simple concepts than was true for Palmer's sample, although the scores overall were higher than for his two-year-olds. This may be partially explained by one or two items that artificially depressed these scores. In particular, only 12 per cent of the subjects passed the item asking them to 'make the dog jump over the wood'. The almost universal response was to make the dog jump on top of the wood (a $1\frac{1}{4} \times 5\frac{1}{2}$ inch wooden block). This was puzzling to E until one mother pointed out that the child knew 'over' as the term for going 'over the bridge', a use in which it appropriately indicates 'on top of'. This instance is similar to Donaldson and Wales's (1970) finding that less equals more for young children, perhaps because more is learned by the child in its additive sense – when one needs more one has less. Such concepts obviously do not have simple referents and it is striking that they are learned as well as they are by this age.

Table 4. Proportion correct answers for each concept item

(N = 18. Age 2–0)

Perceptual	
Smooth	0·37
Many	0·44
Rough	0·44
Square	0·46
Black	0·50
White	0·50
Soft	0·53
One	0·53
Hard	0·65
Circle	0·88
Mean perceptual	0·54
Perceptual–relational	
Biggest	0·17
Long	0·18
Heavy	0·28
Light	0·43
Short	0·47
Skinny	0·47
Fat	0·47
Littlest	0·50
Little	0·72
Big	0·83
Mean perceptual–relational	0·43
Functional	
Dry	0·18
Empty	0·47
Full	0·50
Wet	0·71
Dirty	0·71
Open	0·78
Clean	0·82
Closed	0·89
Mean functional	0·63

Functional–relational

Over	0·12
Around	0·22
Up	0·29
Into	0·33
Under	0·42
Low	0·44
High	0·65
Down	0·65
Out of	0·76
Through	0·94
On top of	0·94
Mean functional–relational	0·57

Many (but not all) of the items in this test involve a choice between two alternatives and thus random choices would produce 50 per cent correct responses. It should be noted, however, that, unlike older children, two-year-olds are reluctant guessers; their most frequent responses when they do not know (or think they don't) the answer is to offer both items, to ignore the question, or refuse to answer, a figurative 'leaving the field'. Thus, it seems possible that the proportions of correct responses given here actually reveal a higher proportion of the child's concept knowledge than a random choice or guessing game model would indicate. It should also be noted that more of the functional items than the perceptual (11 vs. 2) required an action by the child rather than a simple choice. Thus, if scores on simple choice items are inflated by guessing responses, the superiority of performance on functional items may actually be understated.

Perhaps more notable still is the fact that the functional–relational items are for the most part prepositions while other items are adjectives – they are relating rather than contentive words. Yet contrary to the prediction of most linguistic and cognitive theories they are actually easier for the young child to comprehend.

It thus seems to be true that qualities and relationships that change with time are easier for the child to identify than qualities and relationships that are stable over time in support of the second hypothesis above. Obviously if a quality of an object changes it cannot be a criterial attribute of that object-concept. However, the potential for change may be: thus, a bottle may be a container that can be filled. Changes in state may be simply more salient to young children than stable qualities, but this very salience enables the child to categorize objects along this dimension.

3. Form vs. function

Suppose that a given category includes objects that differ in their formal properties although their functions are similar. Such categories are often considered to be abstract and beyond the capacity of young children (Bruner, Goodnow, and Austin, 1956). Yet they are in fact quite common among the early categories used by young children. *Chair* is such a category; so is *lamp*, *candy*, *hat*, and many others that are not superordinates or abstractions. To define such categories properly the child must rely on the functions of members; but to recognize new instances in the absence of experience with their function, he must also store information about *typical form*. Thus, the hypothesis is proposed that he forms categories on the basis of function and generalizes to new instances on the basis of form.

An experimental test of this proposition was undertaken in the course of this study when the subjects ranged in age from 15 to 20 months and in vocabulary level from three to over 150 words.

On the basis of the hypothesis above the predictions were made that:

1. When faced with forms that are similar and forms that are dissimilar to that of a developed concept the child will apply the concept name to the similar but not to the dissimilar forms.

2. To the extent that the objects are similar and dissimilar in function to the standard they will be reclassified as concept member (similar) and nonmember (dissimilar) after the child has had the chance to experiment with them.

The concept *ball* was familiar to all the subjects, although it was in the active vocabularies of only ten at the time of the experiment.

It is obvious from what has been said so far that the concepts form and function are far from uni-dimensional. In general, form refers to shape and function to action or temporal state but in the real world such dimensions are infinitely variable. A way of operationalizing these concepts with ecological validity was needed in order to form a contrast for the child. Therefore, an empirical rather than a logical method was used as follows: A collection of twenty-seven objects varying in shape (spherical, cubical, elliptical, etc.), colour, texture, weight, use, and noise was assembled and sixteen adult judges (graduate students, faculty, and staff of the Yale Psychology Department) ranked them independently along the dimensions of Form and Function. The instructions for ranking by Form were:

The purpose of this task is to get a rank ordering of the objects displayed reflecting how similar or dissimilar in physical form the objects are to the prototype of the child's ordinary rubber ball. Thus, rank 0 is the ball itself. Rank 1 is to be given to the object you judge to be the most like a ball in its visually apparent physical characteristics. Rank 27 is to be given to the object most different from it in these characteristics. Opposite each number below write the identifying letter of the object assigned to that rank.

Instructions for ranking by Function were similar except that the subject was asked to rank the items according to their functional characteristics and 'in this respect, consider all of the things that you can do with a rubber ball: bounce it, roll it, throw it, etc.'. The median rank for each object was plotted along a two-dimensional scale and three objects in each of three categories were chosen for the experiment proper:

1. The three most like the ball in function and unlike in form: (a) An oval-shaped block covered in soft plastic. (b) A small soft rubber (American) football. (c) A large hard plastic 'whiffle' (American) football with holes.

2. The three most like the ball in form and unlike in function: (a) A heavy black ball of hard plastic used for a fortune telling game – the '8-ball'. (b) A rotating cork sphere on a stand with holes for holding pencils – the 'bulletin ball'. (c) A spherical rattle orbiting within a round flat stand.

3. The three most unlike in both form and function: (a) A small frisbee. (b) A square block similar to (a). (c) A cylindrical shaped rattle.

A child's rubber ball was included in the set as a standard.

The child was seated in his high-chair or in some cases he was held on his mother's lap with the objects laid out in front of him on a low table. The objects were arranged semi-circularly in front of the child in a predetermined random order that was different for each presentation to each child. When the ten objects were thus arranged E asked S to give her the ball. The child's actions were recorded on a checklist and his object-choices were recorded in order. He was considered to make a choice if he picked up one of the objects, and after he did so, the object was removed from the group and the request was repeated, until five choices had been made.

The five chosen objects were returned to the group and the child was allowed ten minutes of free play with all the objects, thus providing an opportunity for him to explore their properties. A checklist record was made of the child's actions upon each object in order. If he did not voluntarily attend to an object E brought it to his attention. Despite the free form of this situation and the lack of instruction the children almost without exception acted purposefully, exploring objects, comparing one to another, throwing, bouncing, dropping, rolling in what often seemed to be a deliberate exercise of the 'ball schema' to check whether it fitted.

After ten minutes of free play the objects were again laid out in front of the child in a different predetermined random order, he was again asked to 'Give me the ball', and five choices were recorded as before.

Results

The principal result of interest to the hypothesis stated above is whether the objects alike in form were chosen most frequently on the first test and those alike in function most frequently on the second test. Table 5 shows the sums of weighted ranks for each item (from 5 for the first choice to 0 for not chosen) and the change in rank from test I to test II. It can be seen that on the initial test both Form and Function generated equal choices. On the second test, however, Function choices were significantly greater than Form choices. In order to determine whether this result was a function of simple preference rather than the match to a verbal concept, a tabulation was made of the number of times each object was acted upon during the ten minute inter-test period. The total of these scores was correlated with the choices on tests I and II by the Spearman rank correlation. Neither correlation was significant at the 0·05 level, that for test I being + 0·03 and for test II being + 0·425.

Table 5. Sum of weighted ranks for items of the Form–Function test (N = 18)

	1 Unlike Form Like Function			2 Like Form Unlike Function			3 Unlike Form and Function			4 Ball
Items:	a	b	c	a	b	c	a	b	c	
Test I	18	31	40	23	18	46	15	13	18	48
Group mean		29·67			29·00			15·33		48
Test II	25	54	37	37	12	21	3	10	20	51
Group mean		38·67*			23·33†			11·00		51
Mean change		+ 9·00			− 5·67			+ 4·33		+ 3

* Significantly different from test I at $p < 0.025$.
† Significantly different from test I at $p < 0.025$.

Although all of the children tested demonstrated understanding of the verbal concept ball, only ten of the eighteen used the word actively. To determine whether this factor influenced their definition of the concept a comparison of the choices made by those using the word and those who did not was made. The only significant difference in choices between these two groups was on the first test where the verbal group chose items alike in form significantly ($p < 0.02$) more frequently than the nonverbal group. No differences on test II nor in magnitude or direction of change were found.

Thus, part of the hypothesis was supported in this experiment. The support was equivocal for the proposal that similar forms will determine initial choice, but examination of the choices of individual items shows that item 1(c) (the large football) accounted for many of the choices on the first test. Two factors became apparent during the course of the experiment which accounted for this. First, the discrepancy in size made the large football the most salient item in both tests; second, many of the children had a ball concept which had already been generalized to footballs, an unanticipated complication. This factor can be seen also in the number of initial choices of the small football (item 1(b)). The other discrepancy in direction that can be seen in these figures is for the 8-ball 2(a) which was chosen as frequently as the large football on the second test. It is possible that this object was found by the child on examination to conform to his ball concept in its functional aspects to a greater extent than the adult's ranking predicted. Although weighty and nonresilient, it rolls in a manner similar to the child's ball. It bears, in fact, a strong resemblance to a bowling ball. Thus, it seems likely that there was less independence of dimensions in this experiment than was intended; the significant changes are, however, no less striking. Obviously, more systematic exploration of these global dimensions is needed in an effort to substantiate the hypothesis. This experiment has, however, indicated what some of the important components of these dimensions are and has demonstrated that very young children do utilize function as a basis for the inclusion of items in their verbal concepts. The results indicate that in this experiment at least function was as potent as form in identifying new concept members and it was more potent than form when the child was given the opportunity to manipulate the objects.

Discussion

Can the child categorize objects before naming them? The evidence from these studies indicates that he can and does. When we speak of cognitive categories, of course, we speak of unobservables. When we study pre-verbal subjects we cannot use verbal reports or responses to substitute for direct observation. Thus, we are dependent upon observing overt behaviours that may reflect cognitive structures and strategy. The fact that the child groups objects according to discernible principles indicates that these principles are somehow available to him and we assume that they are present in cognition as well as overt behaviour. This is not necessarily the case; cognition may follow from behaviour instead of the reverse. However, the kind of categorizing that children undertake is such that the conceptual principles are not perceptually present in the objects themselves, but are imposed on the objects on some other basis. Thus, we must speak of the child's possession of cognitive rules.

What are the criteria that he uses for forming these early concepts? The evidence strongly indicates that the function of objects is a primary basis for categorization. This idea is not novel: it accords with Piaget's sensory-motor basis of early cognition, since the actions that one can perform with objects are a primitive definition in terms of function. It is also in accord with the general finding of action as a basis for early word definitions (e.g. 'a hole is to dig').

Yet studies of older children generally show a progression from perceptual to functional concept bases (e.g. Bruner and Olver, 1963; Bruner, Olver, and Greenfield, 1966). Although this paradox cannot be reconciled directly with the present data a developmental progression is suggested of the following type.

The young child attends to both perceptual and functional dimensions of objects and events. Change is more salient than invariance; thus actions and changes in states form the basis for the earliest concepts. Functional definitions will be found to vary in their complexity and abstraction from the earliest simple definitions in terms of action to definition in terms of higher order properties of the most abstract type such as hormones or S–R connections. (See Bruner, Goodnow, and Austin, 1956, for a related discussion of formal, functional, and affective categories.)

Similarly, perceptual definitions will vary from more global to more analytic (e.g. Kagan, Moss, and Sigel, 1963) and thus the earliest concepts will be defined perceptually in terms of simple form (see Nelson, 1973) while later concepts will utilize more features and more complex perceptual information. Reliance on perceptual attributes may also vary according to colour and form (e.g. Kagan and Lemkin, 1961) although the course of this developmental progression is still unclear.

Thus, rather than being competing dimensions, functional and perceptual properties can be seen as complementary aspects of concept definition with the functional definition underlying the intension of many concepts at all stages and the perceptual defining the extension for concepts that can be represented perceptually.

This theoretical scheme describes a child who actively organizes and categorizes the world on the basis of its observable functional properties, and then compares the categories used by others (as reflected in the language) to his own on the basis of the matching of instances. The comparison process leads to concept differentiation but a defining principle will be sought for the new categories, not simply a knowledge of correct instances, and this defining principle again will most often be functional rather than perceptual.

The studies carried out thus far support these notions but more work is needed to explore the relevant dimensions in children of all ages.

15. The acquisition of word meaning: an investigation of some current concepts

Melissa Bowerman[1]

The last few years have seen a rising interest in the question of how children acquire the meanings of words. In recent literature on the subject, several areas of conflicting opinion have begun to come into focus. In this study, three such conflicts are investigated through the analysis of spontaneous speech data from two children.

Briefly, the issues to be discussed are as follows: (1) What kinds of cues do children use as a basis for extending words to novel referents early in development? (2) Do all the referents for which a child uses a particular word share one or more features or are words typically used 'complexively', such that no one feature is common to all referents? (3) How do children organize and store word meanings? Controversy has centred on whether word meaning is described most accurately as a set of semantic features or in terms of prototypical referents or 'best exemplars'.

The data referred to in the following analyses come from my two daughters, Christy and Eva. Christy is the older child by two and a half years. I kept detailed records on both children by taking extensive daily notes and by tape recording periodically from the start of the one-word stage. Fairly complete records are available on the way in which almost every word was used from its first appearance in the child's spontaneous speech to about 24 months. Data on word use continue beyond that point but are more selective.

Bases for extending words to novel referents

Words for objects

In her 'Semantic Feature' theory of the acquisition of word meaning, Clark (1973, 1974) has argued that children's extensions of words to novel objects are initially based primarily on *perceptual similarity*. That is, objects that are referred

[1] This paper is to appear in N. Waterson and C. Snow (eds.) *Development of Communication: social and pragmatic factors in language acquisition* (New York: Wiley, in press).

to by the same word are perceptually similar in some way, particularly with regard to shape, and, to a lesser extent, size, texture, movement, and sound.

Nelson (1974) has recently argued strongly against this view. Citing Piagetian theory in support, she contends that children do not analyse objects into perceptual components like 'round' or 'four-legged' and use these components in isolation as a basis for classification. Nelson argues instead that children at first experience objects an unanalysed wholes and classify them in terms of the actions associated with them and the relationships into which they enter. They regard objects as similar if they are *functionally* similar, e.g. if they are acted upon or act spontaneously in a similiar way.

Unlike Clark, Nelson views the perceptual characteristics of objects as playing a secondary rather than a primary role in the way children form concepts. Perception is secondary because it is used not as the *basis* for classification but simply to *identify* an object as a probable instance of a concept even when the object is experienced apart from the relationships and actions that are concept-defining.

The theories of Clark and Nelson make divergent predictions about how children initially use words for objects. Clark's theory predicts that a given word will be used for objects that are perceptually similar, regardless of function, while Nelson's predicts that the word will be used to refer to objects that either function in the same way, regardless of perceptual properties, or that the child *predicts* would function in the same way on the basis of similar perceptual properties. Both the perceptual and the functional accounts of categorization agree on the salience of *spontaneous motion* as a basis for classifying animate creatures, vehicles, etc. Thus, the conflict is primarily over the relative importance of static perceptual features like shape.

Nelson (Reading 14) has presented some experimental material in support of her claim that shared function rather than similar perceptual properties is the primary basis for children's early object concepts, but the data are limited (only one concept, 'ball', was investigated). Previously reported naturalistic data on children's spontaneous use of words for novel objects offer little support for Nelson's theory. For example, some of the overextensions reported in the diary studies that Clark (1973) drew from in formulating her perception-based theory are clearly incompatible with a theory that stresses the prepotence of shared function (Clark, 1975). ('Overextension' refers to the child's application of a word to a referent that an adult regards as lying outside the semantic category labelled by that word – e.g. 'doggie' for a horse.)

The spontaneous speech data from the two subjects of the present study provide further strong evidence against the theory that functional similarity predominates over perceptual similarity in the child's classification of the objects to which his early words refer. In all the data from both children, there is only a handful of examples of overextensions of words to new objects purely on the basis of similar function in the absence of shared perceptual features, and these occurred relatively late, after many object words were already known. In contrast, there are scores of examples of overextensions based on perceptual similarity – especially shape – in the absence of functional similarity, and many of these occurred during the early period of word acquisition.

These data would not be incompatible with Nelson's theory if the instances of overextension based on perceptual cues could be interpreted in accordance with Nelson's proposal that perceptual cues are used primarily to *predict* the function of an object so that the object can be identified as a member of a known function-based category. However, this interpretation is not possible in many instances. Rather, the children often disregarded functional differences – i.e. gross disparities in the way objects act or can be acted upon – that were well known to them in the interests of classifying purely on the basis of perceptual similarities. Some examples illustrating this phenomenon are presented in table 1. Eva, for example, used the word 'moon' for a ball of spinach she was about to eat, for hangnails she was pulling off, for a magnetic capital letter D she was about to put on the refrigerator, and so on. These objects all have shape in common with the various phases of the real moon, but the child's actions upon them were completely dissimilar. The other examples illustrate a similar disregard for known functional differences among the objects in question. Such examples of classification on the basis of perceptual cues counter to known functional differences weigh heavily against Nelson's proposal that perceptual cues play a secondary, purely predictive role in the child's classificatory operations.

Table 1. Overextensions based on perceptual similarities, counter to known functional differences

---

Age given in months; days

All examples in all tables are spontaneous; there was no prior modelling of the word in the immediate context

All utterances were single words unless otherwise marked

M = Mommy; D = Daddy

1. Eva, 'moon' (selected e.g.s). 15; 26 (first use); looking at the moon, 16; 2: looking at peel-side of half-grapefruit obliquely from below, 16; 19: playing with half-moon shaped lemon slice, 16; 23: touching circular chrome dial on dishwasher, 16; 24: playing with shiny rounded green leaf she had just picked; touching ball of spinach M offers her, 17; 2: holding crescent-shaped bit of paper she'd torn off yellow pad, 18; 16: looking up at inside of shade of lit floor lamp, 18; 21: looking up at pictures of yellow and green vegetables (squash, peas) on wall in grocery store, 18; 29: looking up at wall hanging with pink and purple circles, 19; 7: pointing at orange crescent-shaped blinker light on a car, 20; 4: looking up at curved steer horns mounted on wall, 20; 11: putting green magnetic capital letter D on refrigerator, 20; 11: picking up half a cheerio, then eating it, 20; 13: looking at black, irregular kidney-shaped piece of paper on a wall, 23; 20: 'my moon is off' after pulling off a hangnail (a routine usage).

2. Christy, 'snow'. 16; 10 (first use): as handles and eats snow outdoors, 16; 16: looking at white tail of her spring-horse; touching white part of a red, white, blue toy boat; looking at a white flannel bed pad, 16; 17 after drops bottle and it breaks, spreading white puddle of milk on floor.

3. Christy, 'money'. 15; 30 (first use): holding a handful of pennies, a button, and a bead taken from a bowl; she has often played with these, 16; 11: scratching at wax circles on a coffee table, 18; 7: putting finger through round, penny-sized hole in bottom of new plastic toy box, 19; 14: feeling circular flattened copper clapper inside her toy bell.

A second factor that counts against the function-based theory of how children form object concepts and attach words to them can be mentioned only briefly. Nelson (1974) proposes, as a logical corollary of her theory, that 'when instances of the child's first concepts come to be named, it would be expected that they would be named only in the context of one of the definitionally specified actions and relationships' (p. 280). In other words, 'the name of an object will not be used independently of these concept-defining relations at this point; early object word use would be expected to be restricted to a definable set of relations for each concept' (p. 280). According to Nelson, this hypothesis 'describes accurately what is usually termed the holophrastic stage' (p. 280).

The early object naming behaviour of Christy and Eva does not accord with this prediction. Most of their first object words (e.g. 'ball', 'bottle', 'dog', 'dolly', 'cookie') were initially uttered *not* when the children (or others) were acting upon the objects in question (or, for animate objects, watching them act) but when the objects were static, seen from a distance ranging from a few feet to across a room (see e.g. table 3, examples 1 and 2). Greenfield and Smith (1976), who also studied two children longitudinally, report in like fashion that their subjects first used particular object words to 'label objects in a nonaction context' (p. 213). The findings from these two studies suggest that the role of function ('actions' and 'relationships') in a child's early formulation and naming of concepts is less crucial than Nelson proposes.

It is possible that the age at which particular words for objects are first uttered is a critical factor with regard to this issue. That is, the earlier an object name is acquired, the more likely it is that it will be uttered in connection with concept-defining actions, etc. However, Christy's and Eva's first object words were learned at 14 and 13 months, respectively, which is toward the lower end of the typical 'holophrastic' stage to which Nelson suggests her hypothesis applies. This indicates that even if Nelson's function-based theory accurately describes the acquisition of object words that are learned unusually early, the theory specifies constraints on the child's methods of formulating concepts and/or identifying new instances of existing concepts that no longer necessarily operate during most or – depending on the child's age at the start of word production – all of the holophrastic period during which the early lexicon is established.

Words for nonobject concepts

Words that do not refer to objects often figure importantly in children's earliest lexicons (e.g. Bloom, 1973; Nelson, 1973). How are these words acquired and extended to novel referents? Something other than perceptual similarity is clearly involved in the acquisition of words like 'more', 'allgone', 'up', etc., since the objects or activities involved in the contexts in which children say these words are extremely varied. For many such words, the governing concept or cross-situational invariance involves a certain kind of relationship between two objects or events or between two states of the same object or event across time. Despite Nelson's (1974) emphasis on the importance of relational, functional concepts, her theory does not explain how words for actions and relationships are acquired. This is because in her theory, actions and relationships are the givens by which *objects* are classified; there is no account of how these concepts themselves are formed, nor is it explicitly recognized that they, no less than object concepts, in fact are categories summing across nonidentical situations (see Bowerman, 1976, p. 124).

Words that reflect the child's recognition of constancies across his own *subjective experiences* or *reactions* to diverse events are particularly resistant to interpretation in terms of similarities among perceptual attributes or functional relationships. Nelson (1973) has observed that many children acquire words of this type (a subgroup of 'personal-social' words, in her study) relatively early. Some examples from the Christy and Eva data of words that were extended to new situations on the basis of similarities in subjective experience are given in table 2. The recurrent element in the use of 'there!' seems to have been a sense of having completed a project, for 'aha!' it was an experience of surprise at some unexpected object or event, for 'too tight' it was a feeling of being physically restrained or harassed, for 'heavy' it was a sense of physical effort expended on an object.

Table 2. Words extended to novel situations on the basis of subjective experiences

---

1. Eva, 'there!' At 12½ months in connection with the experience of completion of a project: as M finishes dressing her; as she gets last peg into hole of pounding board; after she carefully climbs off a high bed, etc. Drops out until 17th month, then 16; 24: after getting a difficult box open (D has just shown her how), 16; 25: after sticking each of several vinyl fish on side of bathtub, 16; 26: after getting a rubber band onto handle of kiddicar, etc.

2. Christy, 'aha!' From 18; 10: in many different situations involving her experience of discovery and surprise. E.g., 18; 10: as opens book and sees new picture; after gets up during the night and finds bowl of peanuts on table; it was not there earlier, 18; 13: when M comes home with paper bag, 18; 14: when sees D taking out a cake, 18; 15: after sticks hand in cannister and finds rice in bottom; as finds piece of candy on M's dressing table, 18; 16: discovering and looking into box, 18; 17: coming upon M who is furtively eating a cookie; finding unexpected pile of tiles in a corner of house.

3. Eva, 'too tight'. From 23rd month, protest in situations involving physical restriction or interference. E.g. as M holds her chin to give her medicine; pulls down her sleeves, bends her legs up to change diapers as she lies on back, washes her ears, pulls on her hands to wash them over a sink.

4. Christy, Eva, 'heavy'. In situations involving experience of physical exertion (often unsuccessful) with an object, whether or not it is actually 'heavy'. E.g., Christy, from 21; 12: carrying books, etc., 21; 16: trying to lift a packet of oatmeal out of a box above her shoulder level; it is stuck; pushing on and squeezing a small plastic cup (which does not bend), 21; 21: trying to lift soap bubble bottle as D holds it down. Eva, 23; 30: 'too heavy', trying unsuccessfully to unhook gas pump line on toy gas station.

To conclude, the implications of the various arguments presented above on the nature of children's early bases for classifying are that an adequate theory of the acquisition of word meaning has to be flexible enough to account for a child's ability, even from a very early age, to classify experiences on the basis of many different *kinds* of similarities. Theories built around only one basic class of similarities, whether perceptual or functional, are too restricted to account for the rich diversity of ways in which children can recognize constancies from one situation to the next.

The structure of children's early word concepts

Recent theorizing about the acquisition of word meaning has been predicted in part on the assumption that children identify words with one or more stable elements of meaning. In other words, it is assumed that all the referents to which a child extends a particular word *share* attribute(s), whether these attributes are perceptual or functional, and that the meaning of the word can be described in terms of these attributes or features. For example, all referents for a child's word 'dog' might share the perceptual feature 'four-legged' (Clark, 1973), all referents for the word 'ball' might share the functional features 'can be rolled/bounced' (Nelson, 1974).

This recent emphasis on words for which all referents are characterized by one or more common features contrasts with earlier accounts of the acquisition of word meaning. Theorists like Werner (1948), Vygotsky (1962), and Brown (1965) emphasized that children do *not* consistently associate a word with a single contextual feature, or set of features; rather, they use words 'complexively', shifting from one feature to another in successive uses of the word. Bloom (1973) has suggested that both kinds of word usage may occur in early development, but not typically at the same time. She argues that the association of words (at least words for objects) with consistent feature(s) requires a firm grasp of the concept of object permanence. Complexive usage reflects lack of that concept, according to Bloom, and occurs early in the one-word stage, while consistent usage does not occur until the concept is fully established during the second half of the second year.

The data from Christy and Eva do not support Vygotsky's sweeping claim that 'complex formations make up the entire first chapter of the developmental history of children's words' (1962, p. 70), nor are they consonant with Bloom's more qualified stage hypothesis. Both children used some words for both object and nonobject referents in a consistent, noncomplexive way virtually from the start of the one-word stage. In addition, they used other words complexively, but this kind of usage was not confined to the earliest period. Rather, it tended to flower a few months *after* the production of single-word utterances had begun and continued on well into the third year and, for certain words, even beyond. Moreover, the children's complexive use of words was somewhat more common for words referring to actions than for those referring to objects, which does not accord well with Bloom's view that complexive usage results from lack of firm mental representations of objects. In short, the complexive and the noncomplexive uses of words were not temporally ordered stages; rather, the two types of word use were contemporaneous.

Noncomplexive words

Some examples of words used *consistently* for referents sharing one or more features from early in the one-word stage are given in table 3. Examples 1 and 2 are words for objects (cf. also table 1, examples 2 and 3), while examples 3 and 4 are words for actions. The latter two examples are particularly interesting because they demonstrate how two children can differ dramatically in the concepts they attach to the same word, despite what is probably fairly similar input (see Bowerman, 1976, p. 135, for discussion). Notice that Christy's word [a:] ('on' and 'off'; it was not clear if these were two words or one, as she did not pronounce final consonants at this time) was overextended to refer to virtually any act involving the separation or coming together of two objects or parts of an object. Adults would refer to many of these acts by the words 'open', 'take apart/out', 'unfold', or 'close', 'join', 'put together/in', 'fold'. Eva's word 'off', unlike Christy's, was initially used in a restricted range of contexts from the adult point of view. It referred only to the removal of clothes and other objects from the body and did not generalize beyond this domain for several months. During this time Eva simply didn't have a way of referring to other kinds of separation, although she engaged in activities involving separation and joining just as much as Christy had.

Table 3. Words used noncomplexively for referents with shared attributes

---

1. Eva, 'ball'. From 13; 5 for rounded objects of a size suitable for handling and throwing. E.g. 13; 5 (first use): as spies a large round ball in adjoining room; then goes to pick it up, 13; 7: as picks up rounded cork pincushion; then throws it, 13; 9: as looks at a round red balloon; later; also as handles it, 14; 4: whenever sees or plays with balls or balloons, 14; 7: as holds an Easter egg; then throws it, 14; 8: after picking up a small round stone; then throws it, 14; 10: as sees plastic egg-shaped toy, 14; 18: as holds a round cannister lid; then throws it; etc.

2. Eva, 'ice'. From 13; 9 for frozen substances. E.g. 13; 9 (first use): watching M open a package of frozen peas; she likes to eat them, 14; 29: reaching towards ice in a glass, 15; 2: rushing towards M as M takes frozen spinach from package, 15; 2: after M gives her her first taste of frozen orange juice concentrate; etc.

3. Christy, [a:] 'on–off' (not clear if two words or one). From 15; 12 in connection with situations involving separation or rejoining of parts. E.g. between 15; 12 and 16; 17 in

connection with getting socks on or off, getting on or off spring-horse, pulling pop-beads apart and putting them together, separating stacked dixie cups, unfolding a newspaper, pushing hair out of M's face, opening boxes (with separate or hinged lids as well as sliding drawers), putting lids on jars, cap on chapstick, phone on hook, doll into highchair, pieces back into puzzle, while M takes her diaper off, trying to join foil-wrapped torn-apart towelettes, etc.

4. Eva, 'off'. From 14; 18 in connection with separation of things *from the body* only (as request or comment). E.g. between 14; 18 and 16; 22: for sleepshades, shoes, car safety harness, glasses, pinned-on pacifier, diaper, bib. Starting at about 15; 23: 'open' begins to be used in other 'separation' situation, e.g. between 15; 23 and 17; 0: for opening doors, boxes, cans, toothpaste tubes; pulling pop-beads apart; taking books out of case, tip off door stop, wrapper off soap; cracking peanuts; peeling paper off book cover, etc. 'Off' still used for taking things off the body.

Complexes

Several different types of complexive thinking have been described in the literature on concept formation (e.g. Vygotsky, 1962; Olver and Hornsby, 1966). Discussions of children's early complexive use of words most frequently refer to the type Vygotsky called 'chain complexes'. In forming a chain complex, whether in a block sorting task or by the use of a word, a child proceeds from one item to the next on the basis of attributes shared by two or more consecutive items but not by all the items. . . Despite the frequency with which children have been described as typically forming chain complexes in their early use of words, few examples of the phenomenon have actually been presented in the literature.

Chain complex formation was negligible in Christy's and Eva's linguistic development. In all the data from both children there is only one rather limited example. Almost all their complexive uses of words were 'associative' – a pattern that Vygotsky describes in connection with children's block sorting behaviour. In an associative complex, successive instances of the concept do not necessarily share anything with each other but all share at least one feature with a central or 'nuclear' instance, e.g. the sample block given to the child. . .

In Christy's and Eva's complexive use of words, the central referent for a word (which will be called here the 'prototype' to link it with a literature to be discussed in the following section) was, with a few exceptions, the *first* referent for which the word was used. In addition, it was the referent in connection with which the word had been exclusively or most frequently modelled. (Sometimes there were several 'prototypical' referents for a word; these all shared the entire set of attributes that appear to have been associated with the word, as judged by the child's subsequent overextensions, and they all figured importantly in both the adult's modelling and the child's earliest uses of the word.) Other referents appear to have been regarded as similar to the prototype by virtue of having any one or some combination of the attributes that – in the child's eyes – characterized it.

Some examples of complexive word usage that can be characterized in terms of variations around a prototype are given in table 4. Consider example 1, Eva's use of 'kick'. Some of the referents for this word seem to share nothing with each other – e.g. a moth fluttering vs. bumping a ball with the wheel of a kiddicar. But all share something with the hypothesized prototypical 'kick' situation, in which a ball is struck by a foot and propelled forward. For instance, the moth is characterized by 'a waving limb', while the kiddicar referent is characterized by 'sudden sharp contact' plus 'an object (ball) propelled'. (In this example, prototypical 'kick' was not first referent for the word, as in most of the other examples. However, it seems to be implicit in the second referent (a cat with a ball near its paw) and it was almost certainly the most frequently modelled referent for 'kick'.) Example 2 in table 4 illustrates that, for Christy, 'night night' was associated with three primary features that were present one at a time in many of the situations in which she used the word: beds or cribs, blankets, and the 'nonnormative' horizontal position of an object that is usually oriented vertically. These three features are all present in prototypical 'night night' situations in which a normally vertical person is lying down in bed covered with a blanket. . . Examples 3–6 of table 4 present similar examples of complexive word usage revolving around prototypical referents.

Table 4. *Complexively used words with prototypical referents*

---

1. Eva, 'kick'.
    Prototype: kicking a ball with the foot so that it is propelled forward.
    Features: (a) a *waving limb*, (b) *sudden sharp contact* (especially between body part and another object), (c) an *object propelled*.
    Selected examples: 17; 14: as kicks a floor fan with her foot (features a, b), 17; 21: looking at picture of kitten with ball near its paw (*all* features, in anticipated event?), 17; 25: watching moth fluttering on a table (a), 17; 22: watching row of cartoon turtles on TV doing can-can (a), 18; 3 and 18;13: just before throwing something (a, c), 18; 20: 'kick bottle', after pushing bottle with her feet, making it roll (all features), 20; 6: as makes ball roll by bumping it with front wheel of kiddicar (b, c), 20; 7: pushing teddy bear's stomach against Christy's chest (b), 20; 19: pushing her stomach against a mirror (b), 20; 20: pushing her chest against a sink (b).

2. Christy, 'night night'.
    Prototype: person (or doll) lying down in bed or crib.
    Features: (a) crib, bed, (b) blanket, (c) nonnormative horizontal position of object (animate or inanimate).
    Selected examples: 15; 28 (first use): pushing a doll over in her crib; from this time on, frequent for putting dolls to bed, covering, and kissing them (features a, b, c), 16; 5: laying her bottle on its side (c), 17; 18: watching Christmas tree being pulled away on its side (c), 17; 26: after puts piano stool legs in box, one lying horizontally (c), 17; 27: after putting piece of cucumber flat in her dish and pushing it into a corner (c), 18; 3: as M flattens out cartons, laying them in pile on floor (c), from 18; 3: while looking at pictures of empty beds or cribs or wanting a toy bed given to her

(a, sometimes b), 18; 31: laying kiddicar on its side (c), 19; 11: 'awant night night', request for M to hand her blanket; she then drapes it over shoulders as rides on toy horse (b).

3. Eva, 'close'.
Prototype: closing drawers, doors, boxes, jars, etc.
Features: (a) bringing together two objects or parts of the same object until they are in close contact, (b) causing something to become concealed or inaccessible.
Selected examples: stating from 15; 23: for closing gates, doors, drawers (a, b). From 17; 0: for closing boxes and other containers (a, b), 18; 16: 'open, close', taking peg people out of their holes in bus built for them and putting them back in (a), from 21st month: while pushing handles of scissors, tongs, tweezers together and for getting people to put arms or legs together, e.g. 'close knees' (a), 20; 18: 'close it', as tries to push pieces of cut peach slice together (a); trying to fold up a towelette (a, (b?)), 20; 25: 'open, close', as unfolds and folds a dollar bill (a, (b?)), 21; 16: 'open, close', after M has spread a doll's arms out then folded them back over chest (a), 23; 8: 'Mommy, close me', 25; 9: 'I will close you, o.k.?'' both in connection with pushing chair into table (a), 23; 14: 'that one close', trying to fit piece into jigsaw puzzle (a, (b?)), 23; 30: 'I close it', as turns knob on TV set until picture completely darkens (b), etc.

4. Christy, Eva, 'open'.
Prototype: opening drawers, doors, boxes, jars, etc.
Features: (a) separation of parts which were in contact, (b) causing something to be revealed or become accessible.
Selected examples: Christy: from middle of 17th month, 'open' starts to take over the function of 'off' (see table 3, example 3) for 'separation' situations, both with and without 'revealing'. 16; 12 (first use): for cupboard door opening (a, b), 16; 19: pointing to spout in salt container that M had just opened (a, b), 16; 28: trying to separate two frisbees (a), 17; 1–7: for opening boxes, doors, tube of ointment, jars (a, b), 17; 26: trying to push legs of hand–operated can opener wider apart than they can go; spreading legs of nail scissors apart (both a), 18; 1: several times in connection with pictures in magazine; wants M to somehow get at the pictured objects for her (b), 18; 29: request for M to unscrew plastic stake from a block (a), 18; 31: request for M to take out metal brad that holds 3 flat pieces of plastic together (a), 19; 10: request for M to take stem off apple (a), 19; 17: 'awant mommy . . . open', request for M to pry pen out of piece of styrofoam (a), 19; 20: request for M to take pegs out of pounding bench (a), 19; 20: 'awant open hand', request for M to take leg off plastic doll (a), 19; 23: request for M to turn on electric typewriter (b), 19; 25: trying to pull pop beads apart (a), 20; 0: request for M to turn on water faucet [tap] (b), 20; 5: request for M to take pieces out of jigsaw puzzle, (a, (b?)), 20; 6: trying to get grandma's shoe off her foot (a), 20; 17: 'open light', after M has turned light off; request to have it turned on again (b), 21; 6: 'awant that open', trying to pull handle off of riding toy (a), etc.
    Eva (cf. table 3, example 4 for initial uses): later, 17; 20: request for M to take apart a broken toothbrush (a), for M to pull apart two popbeads (a), 17; 28: request for M to take pieces out of jigsaw puzzle (a, (b?)), 18; 0: pulling bathrobe off M's knee to inspect knee (a, b), 18; 9: request for M to turn TV on (b), 18; 18: 'open tape', request for M to pull strip off masking tape (a), 19; 10: 'open tangle', bringing M pile of tangled yarns to separate (a), 19; 14: taking stubby candle out of shallow glass cup (a), 20; 0: 'open mommy', trying to unbend a small flexible 'mommy' doll (a), 20; 11: unfolding a

towelette (a, b); 21; 16: 'open slide', request for M to set slide in yard upright (a, (b?)), 20; 19: request for M to put legs apart (a), 22: 20: 'I'm open it', after rips apart two tiny toy shoes that were stuck together (a), 24; 3: 'my knee open', as unbends her knee (a) 26; 1: 'I will open it for you', before taking napkin out of its ring for M, does not unfold it, then says 'I open it' as report on completed action (a), 31; 29: 'I'm gonna leave this chair open like this, I'm not gonna shut it', as leaves table with chair pulled out (a), etc.

5. Eva, [gi] (from 'giddiup').
   Prototype: bouncing on a spring-horse
   Features: (a) *horse* (later, other large animals and riding toys which one sits astraddle), (b) *bouncing motion*, (c) *sitting on* toy (especially astraddle).
   Selected examples: from 14; 9: while bouncing on spring-horse or as request to be lifted onto it (a, b, c), 14; 13: as picks up tiny plastic horse, then tries to straddle it (a, c), 14; 14: getting on toy tractor (c), 14; 15: looking at horses on TV (a), 14; 17: getting on trike (c), 14; 17: seeing picture of horse (a), 14; 20: bouncing on heels while crouching in tub (b), 14; 23: climbing into tiny plastic blow-up chair (c), 14; 24: looking at hobby horse (a), 14; 30: bouncing astraddle on M's legs (b, c). Later, continues to be used for pointing out horses, generalizes to other large animals like cows, and while pointing out or riding on trikes, tractors, kiddicars.

6. Eva, 'moon'.
   Prototype: the real moon
   Features: (a) *shape:* circular, crescent, half-moon. These shapes were distinct – i.e. a stretch of curved surface not enough to elicit 'moon', (b) *yellow* colour, (c) *shiny* surface, (d) *viewing position:* seen at an angle from below, (e) *flatness,* (f) *broad expanse* as background.
   Selected examples (see table 1, example 1 for details and dates): real moon (all features); half-grapefruit seen at an angle from below (a, b, d); lemon slice (a, b, e); dial on dishwasher (a, c, d, e, f); shiny leaf (a, c, e); ball of spinach (a – spheres were usually called 'ball'. There was perhaps a limited chaining effect here to the leaf, an e.g. earlier in the day, through shared greenness); crescent-shaped paper (a, b, e); inside of lamp shade (a, b, d); pictures of vegetables on wall (a, b, d, e, f); circles on wall hanging (a, d, e, f); crescent-shaped orange blinker light (a, (b?), c, e); steer horns on wall (a, d, f); letter D on refrigerator (a, d, e, f); half-cheerio (a, (b?)); kidney-shaped paper on wall (a, d, e, f); hangnails (a, e).

Instances of complexive word usage similar to those discussed here have been remarked on by a few other investigators. For example, Labov and Labov (1974) observed that their daughter apparently identified the word 'cat' – one of her first two words – with a set of features all of which characterize ordinary cats. She overextended the word to other animals that possess one or some of these features, but seemed more confident in using the word when many of the features were present. Clark (1975) notes that there are similar exemplars in the diary data from which she has drawn. She has modified her original (1973) theory of children's overextensions to account for this kind of usage by postulating that some overextensions are 'partial' rather than 'full' – i.e. they are based on only a subset of the features that the child associates with the word (Clark, 1975).
. . . The findings suggest that there is less discontinuity between child and

adult methods of classification than has often been supposed. First, the data from Christy and Eva provide evidence for an early ability to classify according to superordinate features (i.e. features characterizing all concept instances), a type of concept formation often thought to be beyond the capability even of children considerably older than they were at this time (e.g. Vygotsky, 1962). Second, the particular type of conceptual structure exhibited in their complexive use of words – a set of variations around one or more prototypical exemplars – does not reflect a 'primitive' mode of thought that later fades out. Rather, as recent research has demonstrated, a large number of *adult* semantic categories are characterized by this kind of structure. . .

The organization and storage of word meaning

A number of investigators . . . have recently focused attention on the role played by 'prototypes' or 'best exemplars' in the internal structure of natural categories (e.g. Rosch, 1973a, b, Reading 13; Smith, Shoben, and Rips 1974).

Some theorists have suggested that the representation of semantic categories (word meanings) in terms of prototypical exemplars should be regarded as an alternative to the more common practice of representing word meanings as sets of semantic features. For example, Fillmore (1975) argues that it may often be psychologically inaccurate to describe word meanings in terms of sets of features specifying conditions that must be satisfied before the word can be appropriately used. He proposes instead that 'the understanding of meaning requires, at least for a great many cases, an appeal to an exemplar or prototype – this prototype being . . . possibly something which, instead of being analyzed, needs to be presented or demonstrated or manipulated'. Anglin (1976), writing with specific reference to very young children, also suggests that word meanings are often stored in the form of prototypes or visual schemas that are not analysed into components. In making this proposal he draws upon Posner (1973), who has argued that being able to analyse a concept into a set of attributes or features is a relatively advanced skill, whereas the formation of prototypes is a more primitive process that does not require featural analysis.

The data presented in the last section indicate that accounting for referential prototypes does not have to be done at the expense of a featural analysis. Instead, both models can and should be combined, as Rosch and Mervis (1975) have also argued. The data indicate in addition that, contrary to Anglin's argument, even very young children are capable of performing a featural analysis upon a prototypical referent and extending a word to novel referents on the basis of this analysis.

. . . The data from Christy and Eva fit the 'family resemblances' model proposed by Rosch and Mervis (1975) very nicely. It will be recalled that for virtually all of Christy's and Eva's complexively used words, there was one referent (or, occasionally, a small group of referents) that had one or more features in common with every other referent. In other words, in one (or a few) referent(s), the various attributes associated with the word, as judged by the way in which the child extended the word to novel items, co-occurred or clustered to maximum degree possible.

How do categories structured around prototypical or 'best' exemplars arise? Rosch (1973b, Reading 30) has argued that the prototypes for certain categories, particularly physiologically determined ones, are salient prior to the categories and determine the nature of the categories. However, she doubts that all categories evolve in this manner. Some alternative sequences would be (a) prototypes are formed through principles of information processing subsequent to experience with a number of particular instances of their categories (Rosch, Reading 13), and (b) frequency of exposure to given instances 'may make some items salient in a not-yet-organized-domain and may influence how that domain comes to be divided' (Rosch, 1973b).

The complexive categories represented in the data from Christy and Eva appear to reflect the first- and/or last-mentioned sequence. That is, the pro-totypical referent was present from the beginning and constituted the core around which the subsequent category grew, rather than being an induction made later on the basis of diverse exemplars of the category. It is difficult to assess the relative importance of language-independent cognitive activity vs. linguistic input (e.g. frequency of exposure) in drawing a child's attention to particular objects or events such that they become the growing point or pro-totype for a category. For some of the examples in table 4, it seems most plausible that a particular referent for a word became more salient than other referents primarily because of the relatively greater frequency with which the word was paired with that referent in the input to the child (e.g. kicking a ball for Eva's 'kick'). For other examples, a referent may have been so salient for nonlinguistic reasons that the input did no more than supply the child with a word for an item that already had special status on nonlinguistic grounds and was 'ready', in a sense, to serve as a prototype (e.g. the moon, for Eva's 'moon').

The sequence in which complexive categories structured around a prototype appear to develop is as follows: The child hears a word modelled most fre-quently (often exclusively) in connection with one referent or a small group of highly similar referents: e.g. 'night night' as the child or a doll is put to bed, 'giddiup' as the child bounces on her horse, 'close' as someone closes doors, boxes, jars, 'moon' as the child looks at the real moon or at pictures of the moon. The child's first use of the word also occurs in connection with one of these referents. After a variable period of time (ranging from a few days to more than a month), the child begins to extend the word to referents that are similar to the original referent(s) in specifiable and consistent ways.

What has happened? A plausible inference is that the child has imposed a featural analysis on the original referent such that she is now capable of recog-nizing two or more of its attributes independently, i.e. in situations in which they do not co-occur blended into a single package but rather are recombined with entirely different contextual features. For example, the 'bringing together' of parts and the concealment of something, which are intimately connected in prototypical 'close' situations, can now be recognized independently of each other, each one being associated with the word 'close'.

The attributes that the child comes to recognize as components of a given prototypical referent may be quite varied in nature. Some that are represented in the Christy and Eva data as presented in table 4 include perceptual properties or configurations (e.g. flatness, yellowness for 'moon'; horse, or horselike animal for [gi]; associated actions (e.g. bouncing for [gi]; spatial relationships (e.g. horizontal positioning of normally vertical object for 'night night'; separation for 'open'); purpose or end state (e.g. concealment for 'close'); the child's viewing position (e.g. obliquely from below for 'moon'); and so on.

The account presented above of the development of categories revolving around prototypical exemplars is at odds with proposals made by Anglin (1976) and Fillmore (1975) in that it credits the very young child with the capacity to perform a featural analysis on a referent. As noted earlier, Anglin suggests that prototypes may be stored unanalysed as visual images. But if the prototype is unanalysed, how can we account for the child's ability to recognize attributes of an original referent when they are separated from each other and recombined in entirely new configurations? In particular, an appeal to a global notion of 'visual similarity' is inadequate to explain the child's extension of words to referents that are visually quite dissimilar to the prototype, such as 'open' for turning on a faucet[tap], light, or electric typewriter as well as for opening boxes and doors.

Another aspect of early word use that appears to require reference to the individual features of a prototype is the fact that some aspects of a prototypical exemplar may be more central or concept-defining for the child than others. The evidence for this is that the attributes of a prototype may turn up in new referents for the word with differing probabilities. Some may *always* be present, and hence appear to be criterial, while others are simply characteristic but not essential. For example, consider Eva's use of 'moon' as it is presented in table 4. *Shape* was obviously the most important determinant of whether or not a given item would be called 'moon': every referent for the word was either round, half-moon, or crescent shaped. But in addition to shape, almost every referent for 'moon' shared with the prototypical real moon one or a combination of several other less critical features: *flatness, yellowness, shininess*, having a *broad expanse as a background,* and being *seen at an angle from below.*

Variation in the centrality or importance of various attributes of a prototype cannot be accounted for when word meanings are represented as unanalysed wholes. In contrast, it can easily be handled by models that represent word meanings in terms of semantic features. For example, Smith *et al.* (1974) propose a model of word meaning that is similar to that suggested by Rosch and Mervis (1975) with the additional specification that semantic features should be differentially weighted according to their degree of 'definingness' for a category. Such a provision appears essential if we are to account for phenomena like Eva's use of 'moon'.

Conclusions

Three main arguments about the nature and development of children's early word meanings have been advanced in this paper. A common element linking all three has been an appeal for breadth and for the integration of theories that by themselves account for only a portion of the data. An adequate theory of the acquisition of word meaning must be sufficiently broad and flexible to handle many disparate phenomena with equal ease within a common framework. In particular, it must come to terms with the following findings: (1) Children need not adhere to a single classificational principle in the early stages of word acquisition (e.g. using only perceptual or only functional cues). Rather, they are capable of recognizing invariances of many different kinds, and consequently have a variety of methods of classification at their disposal. (2) The concepts governing children's early use of words are not necessarily either exclusively complexive, as earlier theorists maintained, or exclusively superordinate (i.e. with features held in common by all members of the category), as recent theorists have implicitly assumed. Nor do superordinate categories necessarily *replace* complexive ones over time. Rather, concepts of both types can exist contemporaneously, neither one being more 'primitive' than the other. Finally (3) the representation of children's word meanings in terms of feature sets or lists of conditions that must be satisfied is not incompatible with representation in terms of prototypes or 'best exemplars'. Rather, both can and should be incorporated within a single model, just as Rosch and Mervis (1975) have advocated in connection with adult semantic categories.

Part IV

Hypotheses

Introduction to hypotheses

Knowledge about the world is often derived from hypotheses. An hypothesis is like the premise of a deductive argument, and as soon as it has been explicitly formulated it can be elaborated into a theory and tested deductively. If the predicted consequences do not follow, the hypothesis can (in principle) be rejected as an explanation. This is the essence of the hypothetico–deductive method. But the crucial question we have to consider is this: where does the hypothesis come from in the first place?

The traditional answer, one which is opposed to the hypothetico–deductive method, is that they come from a quite different method: the method of induction. Inductive inferences are supposed to be based on observations, and they are more general than the observations on which they are based: 'red sky in the morning – shepherd's warning; red sky at night – shepherd's delight'. From having frequently observed the conjunction of two events – in this case the colour of sky and weather – we feel compelled to assert a connection between them. Indeed, it is often assumed that this is the way in which animals learn. A dog, which has always experienced food associated with a tone, will eventually salivate to the tone alone. The tone (a conditional stimulus) becomes associated with food (an unconditional stimulus) according to the principles of classical conditioning. The dog can be said to behave in an inductive way. But is such a simple kind of learning sufficient to secure the basis of an inductive method in science? As Hume first pointed out, there is nothing other than 'habit' or 'custom' to justify induction. It has no logical warrant.

But in the seventeenth and eighteenth centuries inductive inference was supposed to provide the method of the empirical sciences. Philosophers such as Bacon (1855) and J. S. Mill (1950) formulated a variety of methods to secure its validity. Bacon castigated 'induction by a simple enumeration' as 'childish and puerile'. This kind of induction draws conclusions by counting positive instances of the association between events. A contemporary example might be: 'All heavy cigarette smokers tend to develop lung cancer.' In order to make this statement of scientific value it is necessary to show that nonsmokers lack a

257

comparable tendency to develop lung cancer. In place of induction by simple enumeration, Bacon (1855) proposed 'eliminative induction': 'The induction which is to be available for the discovery and demonstration of sciences and arts, must analyse nature by proper rejections and exclusions; and then, after a sufficient number of negatives, come to a conclusion on the affirmative instances.'

This formulation looks like an obvious improvement. However, the reason that induction is regarded as controversial can be stated simply. Unlike the hypothetico–deductive method, it merges the distinction between acquiring an hypothesis and submitting it to a test. As Medawar (1969, p. 42) has put it: 'Inductive logic embodies both a rite of discovery and a ritual of proof.' In other words, the inductive method is itself supposed to be a way of both finding hypotheses and assessing their adequacy. Bacon argued that (in some way) hypotheses would emerge from the careful collection and classification of instances, with a concern for the various prejudices ('idols') which might bias observation. The hypothetico–deductive method, on the contrary, assumes a sharp distinction between the discovery of hypotheses (not derived from systematic observation) and their testing (based on deductive procedures).

The most influential critic of induction is Karl Popper who points out that the whole programme of induction is the wrong way round. Answers can be given only to questions; they do not emerge in some mysterious way from the assembly of data. According to Popper, whenever we collect data we do so with an explicit, or implicit, question in mind about it. Popper (1972) makes his point in an exercise for his class: 'My experiment consists in asking you to *observe*, here and now. I hope you are all co–operating and observing! However, I fear that at least some of you, instead of observing, will feel a strong urge to ask: 'WHAT do you want me to observe?' ' The point is taken: the task of the scientist is not to carry out a series of observations in order to get an idea. It is to propose bold conjectures, and then attempt to falsify them by deductive tests. The logic is simple: if a conjecture implies certain observable consequences, and if these consequences are falsified, then the conjecture can be eliminated. This is the basic theme of Popper's *Logic of Scientific Discovery* (1959), and the reading we have selected from his autobiography illustrates some of his thinking behind this theme. In this hypothetico–deductive view of science there is no place for inductive logic. The origin of conjectures is acknowledged to be of supreme importance, but it has nothing to do with methodology.

However, Popper's scorn of 'blind observation', in his attempt to demarcate conjectures from tests, is not universally shared. We may counter Popper's joke with a remark attributed to Bartlett. Valerie Stone (1977) reports: 'When he had a consignment of birds delivered to the Cambridge Laboratory in 1945, he instructed Margaret Vince to observe them for a certain number of hours each day and to keep her mind empty of hypotheses. "If one begins to form, try to empty your mind of it, as it will only start distorting your observations." ' This is exactly in accordance with Bacon's principles of induction: 'idols' must not be allowed to prejudice observations. But whatever Bartlett may have thought,[1] such a remark does not entail the necessity of an inductive method. It is a purely psychological point about the conditions of hypothesis formation. And it finds an echo in psychologists who have worked on the experimental study of concept formation (see Part III). Heidbreder (1924) noted that during the attempt to attain a concept in the laboratory, her subjects tended to engage in two kinds of behaviour. 'Participant behaviour' consisted in developing hypotheses, but 'spectator behaviour' consisted in letting the mind go blank in the expectation that an hypothesis would appear without conscious effort. Similarly, Shaffer (1961) in his study of concept formation (without feedback) states:

Subjects in the experiment discovered that regularity was a parameter ordering the sets of polygons in terms of area and were able to infer which was the largest polygon in the set. Some conjectured this property but were not prepared to use it since the evidence was not sufficient to validate the hypothesis; others used the property but seemed not to be aware that they had done so . . . a librarian classifying documents, or a child learning to balance on roller skates is not given a self-contained set of data and so must be prepared to make an iterative modification of his hypothesis, classification or skill as new data arrive.

'Spectator behaviour' is well known to research workers. It is like the stage of 'incubation' which Wallas (1926) recognized as important in his theoretical study of problem solving. During such a phase the mind is supposed to work unconsciously so that the problem spontaneously becomes articulated. The idea of 'unconscious work' in thinking has been studied by individuals interested in creativity (e.g. Rugg, 1963; Koestler, 1964). In Reading 16 Popper presents an original theory of creativity which involves the notion of the capacity to break through the 'assumed range of trials' in tackling a problem. This theory deliberately disregards the subjective experience supposed to be involved in creative achievement. Much has been made of sudden flashes of insight (e.g. Koestler, 1964), but Gruber (1974) in his study of Darwin stresses more the processes involved in the development of a new point of view: 'As in dream, thinking is not a straightforward advance . . . there are doubts, retreats, detours, and impasses; there are also impulsive moments of decision, leaps into the dark from points of no return.'

This brief digression on creativity is not intended as a support for an inductive method, but only as a reminder that Popper's emphasis on bold conjectures necessarily disregards the kinds of wayward thinking in which conjectures may have their origin. From a reading of Popper the psychologist might (unjustly) assume that everything important in science resides in its methodology. But, in fact, Popper claims nothing inconsistent with the accounts which have been given about creative experience.

Trial-and-error learning has often been construed as manifest induction. For example, Thorndike (1911) discussed such learning in terms of random behaviour, accidental discovery and the repetition of rewarded responses. But even at the level of the rat, such concepts have been disputed by psychologists. Lashley (1929) first suggested that 'position habits' during learning were not

[1] It seems that the anecdote is aprocryphal (see Vince, 1977).

random, but attempted solutions. And it was Tolman (1932) who coined the revolutionary slogan, 'Hypotheses in rats!' in an ethos dominated by Behaviourism. This insight was developed mainly by Krechevsky (e.g. 1932) who showed that even the responses made during the earliest part of learning were not haphazard. Rather, it appeared as if the rats were responding in a more orderly and systematic fashion from the start. This view forms the basis of Levine's (1975) mathematical 'hypothesis theory' which covers the learning of concepts. The basic assumption is that, in solving any problem, the subject samples hypotheses from a universe of hypotheses until the problem is solved. This theory, which has gained wide acceptance, undermines the inductive basis of learning. (For an alternative view, see Campbell, 1960.)

But would empirical findings of this kind affect the status of an inductive method in science? There is no clear-cut answer, and it is a fact that a variety of inductive logics do exist. Indeed, Meltzer (1973) claims that several inductive computer programs have been written. His argument for the mechanization of induction is as follows. In searching to explain an event (Y) we are searching for a sentence (X) which deductively implies it. However, (X) must be compatible with the existing body of knowledge relevant to the subject domain. It follows that the validity of an inductive inference from (X) to (Y) is relative to the existing body of knowledge at a given time. But this body of knowledge may alter through the discovery of new facts, and hence what was previously a valid inductive inference might now cease to be one. A new fact might then contradict some other deductive implication of (X). We cannot attempt to evaluate such an argument here. In the present context, what is more important than the philosophical justification of induction, is the usefulness of Popper's demarcation between conjectures and methods. It is not (incidentally) quite unique to Popper. Logical positivists, such as Reichenbach (1954) drew a similar distinction between 'the context of discovery' and 'the context of justification'.

The usefulness of the distinction depends upon one's goal. Popper's goal, according to Lakatos (1970), is 'a rational reconstruction of the growth of science in the world of ideas'. Thomas Kuhn is often thought of as a critic of Popper, but his goal is completely different. According to Lakatos (1970), he aims for: 'a description of change in the (normal) scientific mind'. To oversimplify a little, one might say that Popper is concerned with an idealized prescription for science, while Kuhn is concerned with a descriptive account of the practice of science.

It follows from Kuhn's goal that the demarcation between discovery and methodology is likely to be misleading. In *The Structure of Scientific Revolutions* (1970) he distinguishes between 'normal science' and 'revolutionary science'. During the phase of 'normal science' scientists are not so much seeking to falsify their hypotheses, as trying to solve puzzles using particular 'paradigms', or standard ways of interpreting phenomena. During 'revolutionary science', however, a paradigm is shown to be incapable of assimilating old and new observations. Hence a new paradigm is forced into being, frequently against the resistance of the old one. Kuhn is concerned with the processes which lead to the adoption of a new paradigm – an adoption which is neither sudden nor decisive. The central tenet of his theory is that an hypothesis should not be discarded until a better one becomes available.

In Reading 17, Kuhn discusses 'thought experiments' which enable the scientist to learn something both about his conceptual apparatus and the world of nature. Case studies are presented about paradigms of velocity. The thought experiments pose a conceptual conflict which Kuhn relates to developmental observations made by Piaget (see also Part II). The link between physical concepts and psychological data shows why the demarcation between discovery and methodology is essentially misleading when an attempt is made to account for change in scientific thought.

It may seem astonishing to modern readers to appreciate that Aristotle's concept of velocity, based on uniform motion, took no account of acceleration. It persisted for about 2,000 years. But there are jokes about speed which suggest that the concept is not intuitively comprehensible even by adults. Consider the following (freely adapted) dialogue between a policeman and a motorist, taken from Feynman's (1963) lectures on physics.

'Lady, you were going at 60 miles an hour!'
'That's impossible, sir, I was travelling for only seven minutes. It is ridiculous – how can I go 60 miles an hour when I wasn't going for an hour?'
'What we mean, lady, is this: if you kept on going the same way as you are going now, in the next hour you would go 60 miles.'
'Well, my foot was off the accelerator and the car was slowing down, so if I kept on going that way it would not go 60 miles.' OR 'If I kept on going the way I'm going now for one more hour, I would run into that wall at the end of the street.'

The Socratic policeman might continue:

'Yes, of course, before you went an hour, you would hit that wall, but if you went one second, you would go 88 feet; lady, you were going 88 feet per second, and if you kept on going, the next second it would be 88 feet, and the wall down there is no further than that.'
'Yes, but there's no law against going 88 feet per second. There is only a law against going 60 miles an hour.'

The difference in the two points of view is, of course, that the policeman is arguing in terms of 'average speed', and the motorist in terms of 'instantaneous velocity'. It is just this (apparently simple) difference between two concepts which lies at the heart of Kuhn's case studies. Other differences between conflicting paradigms could have been drawn from cosmology, evolution, or psycho-dynamics. The reader should consult Toulmin (1972) and Harris (1970) for similar conflicts over a wide range of science.

The impact between paradigms in the behaviour of children is illustrated in our next reading by Karmiloff-Smith and Inhelder. They provide developmental corroboration of Kuhn's thesis that the scientist does not readily relinquish a theory. Counter-examples to what the authors call 'theories in action' are not sought by children, and they only appear to recognize one as such when an implicit prediction is not confirmed. Their aim always appears to be to construct a unified theory which will account for both positive and negative instances. This behaviour precisely exemplifies a dictum of the German scientist and aphorist, Georg Lichtenberg (1742–99): 'One should not take note of contradictory experiences until there are enough of them to make constructing a new system worthwhile.' Science is not really like a game to be played according to fixed rules. One must have developed some sort of theory before testing counter-examples because only then can one begin to make sense of them. There is an analogy here to the understanding of negative sentences – without an affirmative context it is much more difficult to understand them (see Part II).

The reading by Wason which follows shows very similar findings with students who attempt to discover an unknown principle in an abstract task. The first experiment was published in 1960, and the results were interpreted within a Popperian framework. But, in fact, they corroborate Kuhn's thesis, and show that the findings of Karmiloff-Smith and Inhelder are by no means restricted to young children. The particular task used makes the experiments little more than instructive demonstrations. However, Mahoney (1976) has used it to test the reasoning skills of physicists, psychologists, and 'relatively uneducated Protestant ministers'. None found the task easy, but the scientists did worst – exactly the opposite to what might have been predicted. They developed hypotheses impulsively on scanty evidence (bold conjectures?), and kept returning to a consideration of those which had already been falsified by their performance. In other words, it would seem as if counter-examples were ignored because they would have complicated the process of acquiring a 'unified theory'.

In an independently conceived study, George Miller (1967) showed that if strings of symbols were not construed merely as positive and negative instances, then a different pattern of behaviour emerged. When the strings were interpreted as sentences in a language, the subjects did not merely seek to confirm their hypotheses – they tended to vary them. It would seem that such semantic support, provided by a model of grammar with reference, enabled the subjects to test the scope of their theories.

What happens when the content is made even more realistic? The answer is provided in the next reading, an article by Mynatt, Doherty, and Tweney. Their task simulated a scientific environment, but the results showed a tendency to confirm hypotheses, and avoid counter-examples, even when the subjects had been given instructions about the importance of disconfirmation in scientific procedure. To a large extent, these findings parallel those of Wason. Unlike Miller's study, the role of semantic support did not apparently help performance. And this prompts us to speculate about the kind of support which checks an impulsive desire to confirm one's own hypotheses. Miller was able to simulate a language, and it would seem that this provides a vital cue to accurate reasoning. On the other hand, the subjects in the experiment by Mynatt, Doherty, and Tweney were unfamiliar with scientific methodology, and hence a scientific context did not provide a realm of content appropriate for the consideration of counter-examples. Their subjects were able to appreciate the force of one such example (unlike many of Wason's subjects faced with a completely abstract task), but they did not actively seek one.

The importance of content, and the way in which it provides a means of coding the environment, is not restricted to the disconfirmation of hypotheses. Quantitative estimates about events with which we are not directly familiar are notoriously unreliable because they are frequently based on a superficial image. Malcolm (1958) tells the following riddle used by Wittgenstein to show how we are deceived by surface features: 'Suppose that a cord were stretched tightly round the earth at the equator. Now suppose that a piece one yard long was added to the cord. If the cord were kept taut, how much above the surface of the earth would it be?' Everybody in the class said that the distance would be so minute that it would be imperceptible. In fact, the actual distance would be nearly six inches. We do not code the problem mathematically – the circumference of the earth seems incommensurable with an extra yard: there is a total lack of resemblance between the two quantities. But a superficial resemblance can be just as misleading. The next reading by Tversky and Kahneman shows that individuals tend not to detect bias in their quantitative estimates because they lack an appropriate code for such judgments. They are prejudiced by a 'representative fact': they take a resemblance between A and B as the basis for inferring a relationship between them (see Introduction to Part I). A pervasive bias of this kind holds for most individuals over a wide range of statistical concepts.

Rosenthal and Gaito (1963), cited by Bakan (1967), have demonstrated that research psychologists appear to misunderstand the statistical basis of hypothesis testing. The psychologists claimed that they would place greater 'confidence' in experimental results with a large sample size than with a small sample size when the probability value of rejecting the null hypothesis was held constant. This is a mistake because the probability of rejecting the null hypothesis automatically increases as a function of the number of observations. Hence, rationally, more 'confidence' should have been attributed to the experimental results with a small sample size. The probability value is evidently wrongly interpreted as a measure of 'confidence', rather than reflecting an *a priori* decision on which to reject the null hypothesis. The error is an instructive one, and it is not inconsistent with Tversky and Kahneman's emphasis on the importance of large samples in research.

All of the readings in this Part show confusions which arise in the interpretation of hypotheses and theories. Their scope is wide. But if any general conclusion can be drawn from them it is that even highly educated adults rely upon intuitive considerations rather than the appropriate abstract principles. In the absence of the appropriate code, individuals rely upon their own experience, derived from familiar content, in making an inference or judgment. Their dilemma is epitomized by the difficulties which many find in reading philosophy. In spite of the fact that much philosophizing assumes no specialized knowledge, many individuals tend to lose the thread of the argument because they cannot relate the topics to their daily experience.

16. On hypotheses[1]

K. R. Popper

. . . Early during this period [after the First World War] I developed further my ideas about the *demarcation between scientific theories* (like Einstein's) *and pseudo-scientific theories* (like Marx's, Freud's, and Adler's). It became clear to me that what made a theory, or a statement, scientific was its power to rule out, or exclude, the occurrence of some possible events – to prohibit, or forbid, the occurrence of these events. Thus *the more a theory forbids, the more it tells us.*

Although this idea is closely related to that of the 'informative content' of a theory, and contains the latter idea in a nutshell, I did not, at the time, develop it beyond this point. I was, however, much concerned with the problem of *dogmatic thinking and its relation to critical thinking.* What especially interested me was the idea that dogmatic thinking, which I regarded as prescientific, was a stage that was needed if critical thinking was to be possible. Critical thinking must have before it something to criticize, and this, I thought, must be the result of dogmatic thinking.

I shall say here a few more words on the *problem of demarcation* and my solution.

(1) As it occurred to me first, the problem of demarcation was not the problem of demarcating science from metaphysics but rather the problem of demarcating science from pseudo-science. At the time I was not at all interested in metaphysics. It was only later that I extended my *criterion of demarcation* to metaphysics.

(2) My main idea in 1919 was this. If somebody proposed a scientific theory he should answer, as Einstein did, the question: 'Under what conditions would I admit that my theory is untenable?' In other words, what conceivable facts would I accept as refutations, or falsifications, of my theory?

(3) I had been shocked by the fact that the Marxists (whose central claim was that they were social scientists) and the psychoanalysts of all schools were able to interpret any conceivable event as a verification of their theories. This, together

[1] Excerpts from K. R. Popper, *Unended Quest* (Glasgow: Fontana/Collins, 1976). All footnotes have been omitted.

264

with my criterion of demarcation, led me to the view that only attempted refutations which did not succeed *qua* refutations should count as 'verifications'.

(4) I still uphold (2). But when a little later I tentatively introduced the idea of *falsifiability (or testability or refutability) of a theory as a criterion of demarcation*, I very soon found that every theory can be 'immunized' (this excellent term is due to Hans Albert) against criticism. If we allow such immunization, then every theory becomes unfalsifiable. Thus we must exclude at least some immunizations.

On the other hand, I also realized that we must not exclude all immunizations, not even all which introduced *ad hoc* auxiliary hypotheses. For example the observed motion of Uranus might have been regarded as a falsification of Newton's theory. Instead the auxiliary hypothesis of an outer planet was introduced *ad hoc*, thus immunizing the theory. This turned out to be fortunate; for the auxiliary hypothesis was a testable one, even if difficult to test, and it stood up to tests successfully.

All this shows not only that some degree of dogmatism is fruitful, even in science, but also that logically speaking falsifiability, or testability, cannot be regarded as a very sharp criterion. Later, in my *Logik der Forschung*, I dealt with this problem very fully. I introduced *degrees of testability*, and these turned out to be closely related to (degrees of) *content*, and surprisingly fertile: increase of content became the criterion for whether we should, or should not, tentatively adopt an auxiliary hypothesis.

In spite of the fact that all this was clearly stated in my *Logik der Forschung* of 1934, a number of legends were propagated about my views. First, that I had introduced falsifiability as a meaning criterion rather than a criterion of demarcation. Secondly, that I had not seen that immunization was always possible, and had therefore overlooked the fact that since all theories could be rescued from falsification none could simply be described as 'falsifiable'. In other words my own results were, in these legends, turned into reasons for rejecting my approach.

(5) As a kind of summary it may be useful to show, with the help of examples, how various types of theoretical systems are related to testability (or falsifiability) and to immunization procedures.

(a) There are metaphysical theories of a *purely existential* character (discussed especially in *Conjectures and Refutations* [1963]).

(b) There are theories like the psychoanalytic theories of Freud, Adler, and Jung, or like (sufficiently vague) astrological lore.

(c) There are what one might call 'unsophisticated' theories like 'All swans are white' or the geocentric 'All stars other than the planets move in circles.' Kepler's laws may be included (though they are in many senses highly sophisticated). These theories are falsifiable, though falsifications can, of course, be evaded: immunization is *always* possible. But the evasion would usually be dishonest: it would consist, say, in denying that a black swan was a swan, or that it was black; or that a non-Keplerian planet was a planet.

(d) The case of Marxism is interesting. As I pointed out in my *Open Society*, one may regard Marx's theory as refuted by events that occurred during the Russian Revolution. According to Marx the revolutionary changes start at the bottom, as it were: means of production change first, then social conditions of production, then political power, and ultimately ideological beliefs, which change last. But in the Russian Revolution the political power changed first, and then the ideology (Dictatorship plus Electrification) began to change the social conditions and the means of production from the top. The reinterpretation of Marx's theory of revolution to evade this falsification immunized it against further attacks, transforming it into the vulgar-Marxist (or socioanalytic) theory which tells us that the 'economic motive' and the class struggle pervade social life.

(e) There are more abstract theories, like Newton's or Einstein's theories of gravitation. They are falsifiable – say, by not finding predicted perturbations, or perhaps by a negative outcome of radar tests replacing solar eclipse observations. But in their case a *prima facie* falsification *may* be evaded, not only by uninteresting immunizations but also, as in the Uranus-Neptune kind of case, by the introduction of testable auxiliary hypotheses, so that the empirical content of the system – consisting of the original theory plus the auxiliary hypothesis – is greater than that of the original system. We may regard this as an increase of informative content – as a case of *growth* in our knowledge. There are, of course, also auxiliary hypotheses which are merely evasive immunizing moves. They decrease the content. All this suggests the *methodological rule* not to put up with any content-decreasing manoeuvres (or with 'degenerating problem shifts', in the terminology of Imre Lakatos). . .

Konrad Lorenz [1966] is the author of a marvellous theory in the field of animal psychology, which he calls 'imprinting'. It implies that young animals have an inborn mechanism for jumping to unshakable conclusions. For example, a newly hatched gosling adopts as its 'mother' the first moving thing it sets eyes on. This mechanism is well adapted to normal circumstances, though a bit risky for the gosling. (It may also be risky for the chosen foster parent, as we learn from Lorenz.) But it is a successful mechanism under normal circumstances; and also under some which are not quite normal.

The following points about Lorenz's 'imprinting' are important:

(1) It is a process – not the only one – of learning by observation.

(2) The problem solved under the stimulus of the observation is inborn; that is, the gosling is genetically conditioned to look out for its mother: it expects to see its mother.

(3) The theory or expectation which solves the problem is also to some extent inborn, or genetically conditioned: it goes far beyond the actual observation, which merely (so to speak) releases or triggers the adoption of a theory which is largely preformed in the organism.

(4) The learning process is *nonrepetitive*, though it may take a certain amount of time (a short time), and involve often some activity or 'effort' on the part of the organism; it therefore may involve a situation not too far removed from that normally encountered. I shall say of such nonrepetitive learning processes that

they are 'noninductive', taking repetition as the characteristic of 'induction'. (The theory of nonrepetitive learning may be described as *selective* or Darwinian, while the theory of inductive or repetitive learning is a theory of *instructive* learning; it is Lamarckian.) Of course, this is purely terminological: should anybody insist on calling imprinting an inductive process I should just have to change my terminology.

(5) The observation itself works only like the turning of a key in a lock. Its role is important, but the highly complex result is almost completely preformed.

(6) Imprinting is an irreversible process of learning; that is, it is not subject to correction or revision.

Of course I knew nothing in 1922 of Konrad Lorenz's theories (though I had known him as a boy in Altenberg, where we had close friends in common). I shall here use the theory of imprinting merely as a means of explaining my own conjecture, which was similar yet different. My conjecture was not about animals (though I was influenced by C. Lloyd Morgan [1894] and even more by H. S. Jennings [1906]) but about human beings, especially young children. It was this.

Most (or perhaps all) learning processes consist in theory formation; that is, in the formation of expectations. The formation of a theory or conjecture has always a 'dogmatic', and often a 'critical', phase. This dogmatic phase shares, with imprinting, the characteristics (2) to (4), and sometimes also (1) and (5), but not normally (6). The critical phase consists in giving up the dogmatic theory under the pressure of disappointed expectations or refutations, and in trying out other dogmas. I noticed that sometimes the dogma was so strongly entrenched that no disappointment could shake it. It is clear that in this case – though only in this case – dogmatic theory formation comes very close to imprinting, of which (6) is characteristic. However, I was inclined to look on (6) as a kind of neurotic aberration (even though neuroses did not really interest me: it was the psychology of discovery I was trying to get at). This attitude towards (6) shows that what I had in mind was different from imprinting, though perhaps related to it.

I looked on this method of theory formation as a method of learning by trial and error. But when I called the formation of a theoretical dogma a 'trial', *I did not mean a random trial*.

It is of some interest to consider the problem of the randomness (or otherwise) of trials in a trial-and-error procedure. Take a simple arithmetical example: division by a number (say, 74,856) whose multiplication table we do not know by heart is usually done by trial and error; but this does not mean that the trials are random, for we do know the multiplication tables for 7 and 8. Of course we could programme a computer to divide by a method of selecting *at random* one of the ten digits 0, 1, . . . 9, as a trial and, in case of error, one of the remaining nine (the erroneous digit having been excluded) by the same random procedure. But this would obviously be inferior to a more systematic procedure: at the very least we should make the computer notice whether its first trial was in error because the selected digit was too small or because it was too big, thus reducing the range of digits for the second selection.

To this example the idea of randomness is in principle applicable, because of every step in long division there is a selection to be made from a well-defined set of possibilities (the digits). But in most zoological examples of learning by trial and error the range or set of possible reactions (movements of any degree of complexity) is not given in advance; and since we do not know the elements of this range we cannot attribute probabilities to them, which we should have to do in order to speak of randomness in any clear sense.

Thus we have to reject the idea that the method of trial and error operates in general, or normally, with trials which are *random*, even though we may, with some ingenuity, construct highly artificial conditions (such as a maze for rats) to which the idea of randomness may be applicable. But its mere applicability does not, of course, establish that the trials are in fact random: our computer may adopt with advantage a more systematic method of selecting the digits; and a rat running a maze may also operate on principles which are not random.

On the other hand, in any case in which the method of trial and error is applied to the solution of such a problem as the problem of adaptation (to a maze, say), the trials are as a rule not determined, or not completely determined, by the problem; nor can they anticipate its (unknown) solution otherwise than by a fortunate accident. In the terminology of D. T. Campbell [1960], we may say that the trials must be 'blind' (I should perhaps prefer to say they must be 'blind to the solution of the problem'). It is not from the trial but only from the critical method, the method of error elimination, that we find, *after* the trial – which corresponds to the dogma – whether or not it was a lucky guess; that is, whether it was sufficiently successful in solving the problem in hand to avoid being eliminated for the time being.

Yet the trials are not always quite blind to the demands of the problem: the problem often determines the range from which the trials are selected (such as the range of the digits). This is well described by David Katz [1937]: 'A hungry animal divides the environment into edible and inedible things. An animal in flight sees roads of escape and hiding places.' Moreover, the problem may change somewhat with the successive trials; for example, the range may narrow. But there may also be quite different cases, especially on the human level; cases in which everything depends upon an ability to break through the limits of the assumed range. These cases show that the selection of the range itself may be a trial (an unconscious conjecture), and that critical thinking may consist not only in a rejection of any particular trial or conjecture, but also in a rejection of what may be described as a deeper conjecture – the assumption of the range of 'all possible trials'. This, I suggest, is what happens in many cases of 'creative' thinking.

What characterizes creative thinking, apart from the intensity of the interest in the problem, seems to me often the ability to break through the limits of the range – or to vary the range – from which a less creative thinker selects his trials. This ability, which is a critical ability, may be described as *critical imagination*. It is often the result of culture clash, that is, a clash between ideas, or frameworks of ideas. Such a clash may help us to break through the ordinary bounds of our imagination.

Remarks like this, however, would hardly satisfy those who seek for a psychological theory of creative thinking, and especially of scientific discovery. For what they are after is a theory of *successful* thinking.

I think that the demand for a theory of successful thinking cannot be satisfied, and that it is not the same as the demand for a theory of creative thinking. Success depends on many things – for example on luck. It may depend on meeting with a promising problem. It depends on not being anticipated. It depends on such things as a fortunate division of one's time between trying to keep up-to-date and concentrating on working out one's own ideas.

But it seems to me that what is essential to 'creative' or 'inventive' thinking is a combination of intense interest in some problem (and thus a readiness to try again and again) with highly critical thinking; with a readiness to attack even those presuppositions which for less critical thought determine the limits of the range from which trials (conjectures) are selected; with an imaginative freedom that allows us to see so far unsuspected sources of error: possible prejudices in need of critical examination.

(It is my opinion that most investigations into the psychology of creative thought are pretty barren – or else more logical than psychological. For criticial thought, or error elimination, can be better characterized in logical terms that in psychological terms.)

A 'trial' or a newly formed 'dogma' or a new 'expectation' is largely the result of inborn *needs* that give rise to specific *problems*. But it is also the result of the inborn need to form expectations (in certain specific fields, which in their turn are related to some other needs); and it may also be partly the result of disappointed earlier expectations. I do not of course deny that there may also be an element of personal ingenuity present in the formation of trials or dogmas, but I think that ingenuity and imagination play their main part in the *critical process of error elimination*. Most of the great theories which are among the supreme achievements of the human mind are the offspring of earlier dogmas, plus criticism.

What became clear to me first, in connection with dogma formation, was that children – especially small children – urgently need discoverable regularities around them; there was an inborn need not only for food and for being loved but also for discoverable structural invariants of the environment ('things' are such discoverable invariants), for a settled routine, for settled expectations. This infantile dogmatism has been observed by Jane Austen: 'Henry and John were still asking every day for the story of Harriet and the gipsies, and still tenaciously setting [Emma]. . . right if she varied in the slightest particular from the original recital.' There was, especially in older children, enjoyment in variation, but mainly within a limited range or framework of expectations. Games, for example, were of this kind; and the rules (the invariants) of the game were often almost impossible to learn by mere observation.

My main point was that the dogmatic way of thinking was due to an inborn need for regularities, and to inborn mechanisms of discovery; mechanisms which make us search for regularities. And one of my theses was that if we speak glibly of 'heredity and environment' we are liable to underrate the over-whelming role of heredity – which, among other things, largely determines what aspects of its objective environment (the ecological niche) do or do not belong to an animal's subjective, or biologically significant, environment.

I distinguished three main types of learning process, of which the first was the fundamental one:

(1) Learning in the sense of discovery: (dogmatic) formation of theories or expectations, or regular behaviour, checked by (critical) error elimination.

(2) Learning by imitation. This can be shown to be a special case of (1).

(3) Learning by 'repetition' or 'practising', as in learning to play an instrument or to drive a car. Here my thesis is that (a) there is no genuine 'repetition' but rather (b) change through error elimination (following theory formation) and (c) a process which helps to make certain actions or reactions automatic, thereby allowing them to sink to a merely physiological level, and to be performed without attention.

The significance of inborn dispositions or needs for discovering regularities and rules may be seen in the child's learning to speak a language, a process that has been much studied. It is, of course, a kind of learning by imitation; and the most astonishing thing is that this very early process is one of trial and critical error elimination, in which the critical error elimination plays a very important role. The power of innate dispositions and needs in this development can best be seen in children who, owing to their deafness, do not participate in the speech situations of their social environment in the normal way. The most convincing cases are perhaps children who are deaf *and* blind like Laura Bridgman – or Helen Keller, of whom I heard only at a later date. Admittedly, even in these cases we find social contacts – Helen Keller's contact with her teacher – and we also find imitation. But Helen Keller's imitation of her teacher's spelling into her hand is far removed from the ordinary child's imitation of sounds heard over a long period, sounds whose communicative function can be understood, and responded to, even by a dog.

The great differences between human languages show that there must be an important environmental component in language learning. Moreover, the child's learning of a language is almost entirely an instance of learning by imitation. Yet reflection on various biological aspects of language shows that the genetic factors are much more important. Thus I agree with the statement of Joseph Church [1961]: 'While some part of the change that occurs in infancy can be accounted for in terms of physical maturation, we know that maturation stands in a circular, feedback relationship to experience – the things the organism does, feels, and has done to it. This is not to disparage the role of maturation; it is only to insist that we cannot view it as a simple blossoming of predestined biological characteristics.' Yet I differ from Church in contending that the genetically founded maturation process is much more complex and has much greater influence than the releasing signals and the experience of receiving them, though no doubt a certain minimum of this is needed to stimulate the 'blossoming'. Helen Keller's grasping that the spelled word 'water' meant the thing which she could feel with her hand and which she knew so well had, I think, some similarity with 'imprinting'; but there are also many dissimilarities. The similarity was the ineradicable impression made on her, and the way in which a single experience released pent-up dispositions and needs. An obvious dissimilarity was the tremendous range of variation which the experience opened up for her, and which led in time to her mastery of language.

In the light of this I doubt the aptness of Church's comment: 'The baby does not walk because his "walking mechanisms" have come into flower, but because he has achieved a kind of orientation to space whereby walking becomes a possible mode of action.' It seems to me that in Helen Keller's case there was no orientation in linguistic space or, at any rate, extremely little, prior to her discovery that the touch of her teacher's fingers denoted water, and her jumping to the conclusion that certain touches may have denotational or referential significance. What must have been there was a readiness, a disposition, a need, to interpret signals; and a need, a readiness, to learn to use these signals by imitation, by the method of trial and error (by nonrandom trials and the critical elimination of spelling errors).

It appears that there must be inborn dispositions of great variety and complexity which cooperate in this field: the disposition to love, to sympathize, to emulate movements, to control and correct the emulated movements; the disposition to use them, and to communicate with their help; the disposition to use language for receiving commands, requests, admonitions, warnings; the disposition to interpret descriptive statements, and to produce descriptive statements. In Helen Keller's case (as opposed to that of normal children) most of her information about reality came through language. As a consequence she was unable for a time to distinguish clearly between what we might call 'hearsay' and experience, and even her own imagination: all three came to her in terms of the same symbolic code.

The example of language learning showed me that my schema of a natural sequence consisting of a dogmatic phase followed by a critical phase was too simple. In language learning there is clearly an inborn disposition to correct (that is, to be flexible and critical, to eliminate errors) which after a time peters out. When a child, having learned to say 'mice' uses 'hice' for the plural of 'house', then a disposition to find regularities is at work. The child will soon correct himself, perhaps under the influence of adult criticism. But there seems to be a phase in language learning when the language structure becomes rigid – perhaps under the influence of 'automatization', as explained in 3(c) above.

I have used language learning merely as an example from which we can see that imitation is a special case of the method of trial and error elimination. It is also an example of the cooperation between phases of dogmatic theory formation, expectation formation, or the formation of behavioural regularities, on the one hand, and phases of criticism on the other.

But although the theory of a dogmatic phase followed by a critical phase is too simple, it is true that *there can be no critical phase without a preceding dogmatic phase, a phase in which something – an expectation, a regularity of behaviour – is formed, so that error elimination can begin to work on it.*

This view made me reject the psychological theory of learning by induction, a theory to which Hume adhered even after he had rejected induction on logical grounds. (I do not wish to repeat what I have said in *Conjectures and Refutations* about Hume's views on habit.) It also led me to see that there is no such thing as an unprejudiced observation. All observation is an activity with an aim (to find, or to check, some regularity which is *at least* vaguely conjectured); an activity guided by poblems, and by the context of expectations (the 'horizon of expectations' as I later called it). There is no such thing as passive experience; no passively impressed association of impressed ideas. Experience is the result of active exploration by the organism, of the search for regularities or invariants. There is no such thing as a perception except in the context of interests and expectations, and hence of regularities or 'laws'.

All this led me to the view that conjecture or hypothesis must come before observation or perception: we have inborn expectations; we have latent inborn knowledge, in the form of latent expectations, to be activated by stimuli to which we react as a rule while engaged in active exploration. All learning is a modification (it may be a refutation) of some prior knowledge and thus, in the last analysis, of some inborn knowledge.

It was this psychological theory which I elaborated, tentatively and in a clumsy terminology, between 1921 and 1926. It was this theory of the formation of our knowledge which engaged and distracted me during my apprenticeship as a cabinetmaker.

One of the strange things about my intellectual history is this. Although I was at the time interested in the contrast between dogmatic and critical thinking, and although I looked upon dogmatic thinking as prescientific (and, where it pretends to be scientific, as 'unscientific'), and although I realized the link with the falsifiability criterion of demarcation between science and pseudoscience, I did not appreciate that there was a connection between all this and the problem of induction. For years these two problems lived in different (and it appears almost watertight) compartments of my mind, even though I believed that I had solved the problem of induction by the simple discovery that induction by repetition did not exist (any more than did learning something new by repetition): the alleged inductive method of science had to be replaced by the method of (dogmatic) trial and (critical) error elimination, which was the mode of discovery of all organisms from the amoeba to Einstein.

Of course I was aware that my solutions to both these problems – the problem of demarcation, the problem of induction – made use of the same idea: that of the separation of dogmatic and critical thinking. Nevertheless the two problems seemed to me quite different; demarcation had no similarity with Darwinian selection. Only after some years did I realize that there was a close link, and that the problem of induction arose essentially from a mistaken solution of the problem of demarcation – from the mistaken belief that what elevated science over pseudoscience was the 'scientific method' of finding true, secure, and justifiable knowledge, and that this method was the method of induction: a belief that erred in more ways than one. . .

17. A function for thought experiments[1]

Thomas S. Kuhn

Thought experiments have more than once played a critically important role in the development of physical science. The historian, at least, must recognize them as an occasionally potent tool for increasing man's understanding of nature. Nevertheless, it is far from clear how they can ever have had very significant effects. Often, as in the case of Einstein's train struck by lightning at both ends, they deal with situations that have not been examined in the laboratory.[2] Sometimes, as in the case of the Bohr–Heisenberg microscope, they posit situations that could not be fully examined and that need not occur in nature at all.[3] That state of affairs gives rise to a series of perplexities, three of which will be examined in this paper through the extended analysis of a single example. No single thought experiment can, of course, stand for all of those which have been historically significant. The category, thought experiment, is in any case too broad and too vague for epitome. Many thought experiments differ from the one examined here. But his particular example, being drawn from the work of Galileo, has an interest all its own, and that interest is increased by its obvious resemblance to certain of the thought experiments which proved effective in the twentieth-century reformulation of physics. Though I shall not argue the point, I suggest the example is typical of an important class.

The main problems generated by the study of thought experiments can be

---

[1] First published in T. S. Kuhn, *Mélanges Alexandre Koyné*, II, *L'aventure de l'esprit* (Paris: Hermann, 1964), 307–34.

[2] The famous train experiment first appears in Einstein's (1916) popularization of relativity theory. In the fifth (1920) edition, which I have consulted, the experiment is described on pp. 14–19. Notice that this thought experiment is only a simplified version of the one employed in Einstein's first (1905) paper on relativity. In that original thought experiment only one light signal is used, mirror reflection taking the place of the other.

[3] W. Heisenberg (1927); N. Bohr (1928). The argument begins by treating the electron as a classical particle and discusses its trajectory both before and after its collision with the photon that is used to determine its position or velocity. The outcome is to show that these measurements cannot be carried through classically and that the initial description has therefore assumed more than quantum mechanics allows. That violation of quantum mechanical principles does not, however, diminish the thought experiment's import.

formulated as a series of questions. First, since the situation imagined in a thought experiment clearly may not be arbitrary, to what conditions of verisimilitude is it subject? In what sense and to what extent must the situation be one that nature could present or has in fact presented? That perplexity, in turn, points to a second. Granting that every successful thought experiment embodies in its design some prior information about the world, that information is not itself at issue in the experiment. On the contrary, if we have to do with a real thought experiment, the empirical data upon which it rests must have been both well known and generally accepted before the experiment was even conceived. How, then, relying exclusively upon familiar data, can a thought experiment lead to new knowledge or to new understanding of nature? Finally, to put the third question most briefly of all, what sort of new knowledge or understanding can be so produced? What, if anything, can scientists hope to learn from thought experiments?

There is one rather easy set of answers to these questions, and I shall elaborate it, with illustrations drawn from both history and psychology, in the two sections immediately to follow. Those answers – which are clearly important but, I think, not quite right – suggest that the new understanding produced by thought experiments is not an understanding of *nature* but rather of the scientist's *conceptual apparatus*. On this analysis, the thought experiment's function is to assist in the elimination of prior confusion by forcing the scientist to recognize contradictions that had been inherent in his way of thinking from the start. Unlike the discovery of new knowledge, the elimination of existing confusion does not seem to demand additional empirical data. Nor need the imagined situation be one that actually exists in nature. On the contrary, the thought experiment whose sole aim is to eliminate confusion is subject to only one condition of verisimilitude. The imagined situation must be one to which the scientist can apply his concepts in the way he has normally employed them before.

Because they are immensely plausible and because they relate closely to philosophical tradition, these answers require detailed and respectful examination. In addition, a look at them will supply us with essential analytic tools. Nevertheless, they miss important features of the historical situation in which thought experiments function, and the last two sections of this paper will therefore seek answers of a somewhat different sort. Section III, in particular, will suggest that it is significantly misleading to describe as 'self-contradictory' or 'confused' the situation of the scientist prior to the performance of the relevant thought experiment. We come closer if we say that thought experiments assist scientists in arriving at laws and theories different from the ones they had held before. In that case, prior knowledge can have been 'confused' and 'contradictory' only in the rather special and quite unhistorical sense which would attribute confusion and contradiction to all the laws and theories which scientific progress has forced the profession to discard. Inevitably, however, that description suggests that the effects of thought experimentation, even though it presents no new data, are much closer to those of actual experimentation than has usually been supposed. Section IV will attempt to suggest how this could be the case.

I

The historical context within which actual thought experiments assist in the reformulation or readjustment of existing concept is inevitably extraordinarily complex. I therefore begin with a simpler, because nonhistorical, example, choosing for the purpose a conceptual transposition induced in the laboratory by the brilliant Swiss child psychologist Jean Piaget. Justification for this apparent departure from our topic will appear as we proceed. Piaget dealt with children, exposing them to an actual laboratory situation and then asking them questions about it. In slightly more mature subjects, however, the same effect might have been produced by questions alone in the absence of any physical exhibit. If those same questions had been self-generated, we would be confronted with the pure thought-experimental situation to be exhibited in the next section from the work of Galileo. Since, in addition, the particular transposition induced by Galileo's experiment is very nearly the same as the one produced by Piaget in the laboratory, we may learn a good deal by beginning with the more elementary case.

Piaget's (1946) laboratory situation presented children with two toy cars of different colours, one red and the other blue.[4] During each experimental exposure both cars were moved uniformly in a straight line. On some occasions both would cover the same distance but in different intervals of time. In other exposures the times required were the same, but one car would cover a greater distance. Finally, there were a few experiments during which neither the distances nor the times were quite the same. After each run Piaget asked his subjects which car had moved faster and how the child could tell.

In considering how the children responded to the questions, I restrict attention to an intermediate group, old enough to learn something from the experiments and young enough so that its responses were not yet those of an adult. On most occasions the children in this group would describe as 'faster' the car that reached the goal first or that had led during most of the motion. Furthermore, they would continue to apply the term in this way even when they recognized that the 'slower' car had covered more ground than the 'faster' during the same amount of time. Examine, for example, an exposure in which both cars departed from the same line but in which the red started later and then caught the blue at the goal. The following dialogue, with the child's contribution in italics, is then typical. 'Did they leave at the same time? – *No, the blue left first.* – Did they arrive together? – *Yes.* – Was one of the two faster, or were they the same? – *The blue went more quickly.*'[5] Those responses manifest what for simplicity I shall call the 'goal-reaching' criterion for the application of 'faster'.

---

[4] J. Piaget (1946), particularly chapters VI and VII). The experiments described below are in the latter chapter.
[5] *Ibid.* p. 160, my translation.

If goal-reaching were the only criterion employed by Piaget's children, there would be nothing that the experiments alone could teach them. We would conclude that their concept of 'faster' was different from an adult's but that, since they employed it consistently, only the intervention of parental or pedagogic authority would be likely to induce change. Other experiments, however, reveal the existence of a second criterion, and even the experiment just described can be made to do so. Almost immediately after the exposure recorded above, the apparatus was readjusted so that the red car started very late and had to move especially rapidly to catch the blue at the goal. In this case, the dialogue with the same child went as follows. 'Did one go more quickly than the other? – *The red.* – How did you find that out? – *I WATCHED IT*'.[6] Apparently, when motions are sufficiently rapid, they can be perceived directly and as such by children. (Compare the way adults 'see' the motion of the second hand on a clock with the way they observe the minute hand's change of position.) Sometimes children employ that direct perception of motion in identifying the faster car. For lack of a better word I shall call the corresponding criterion 'a perceptual blurriness'.

It is the coexistence of these two criteria, goal-reaching and perceptual blurriness, that makes it possible for the children to learn in Piaget's laboratory. Even without the laboratory, nature would sooner or later teach the same lesson as it has to the older children in Piaget's group. Not very often (or the children could not have preserved the concept for so long) but occasionally nature will present a situation in which a body whose directly perceived speed is lower nevertheless reaches the goal first. In this case the two clues conflict; the child may be led to say that both bodies are 'faster' or both 'slower' or that the same body is both 'faster' and 'slower'. That experience of paradox is the one generated by Piaget in the laboratory with occasionally striking results. Exposed to a single paradoxical experiment, children will first say one body was 'faster' and then immediately apply the same label to the other. Their answers become critically dependent upon minor differences in the experimental arrangement and in the wording of the questions. Finally, as they become aware of the apparently arbitrary oscillation of their responses, those children who are either cleverest or best prepared will discover or invent the adult conception of 'faster'. With a bit more practice some of them will thereafter employ it consistently. Those are the children who have learned from their exposure to Piaget's laboratory.

Only, to return to the set of questions which motivate this inquiry, what shall we say they have learned and from what have they learned it? For the moment I restrict myself to a minimal and quite traditional series of answers which will provide the point of departure for section III. Because it included two independent criteria for applying the conceptual relation 'faster', the mental

[6] *Ibid.* p. 161, my emphasis. In this passage I have rendered 'plus fort' as 'more quickly'; in the previous passage the French was 'plus vite'. The experiments themselves indicate, however, that in this context, though perhaps not in all, the answers to the questions 'plus fort?' and 'plus vite?' are the same.

apparatus which Piaget's children brought to his laboratory contained an implicit contradiction. In the laboratory the impact of a novel situation, including both exposures and interrogation, forced the children to an awareness of that contradiction. As a result, some of them changed their concept of 'faster', perhaps by bifurcating it. The original concept was split into something like the adult's notion of 'faster' and a separate concept of 'reaching-goal-first'. The children's conceptual apparatus was then probably richer and certainly more adequate. They had learned to avoid a significant conceptual error and thus to think more clearly.

Those answers, in turn, supply another, for they point to the single condition that Piaget's experimental situations must satisfy in order to achieve a pedagogic goal. Clearly those situations may not be arbitrary. A psychologist might, for quite different reasons, ask a child whether a tree or a cabbage were faster; furthermore, he would probably get an answer;[7] but the child would not learn to think more clearly. If he is to do that, the situation presented to him must, at the very least, be relevant. It must, that is, exhibit the cues which he customarily employs when he makes judgments of relative speed. On the other hand, though the cues must be normal, the full situation need not. Presented with an animated cartoon showing the paradoxical motions, the child would reach the same conclusions about his concepts, even though nature itself were governed by the law that faster bodies always reach the goal first. There is, then, no condition of physical verisimilitude. The experimenter may imagine any situation he pleases so long as it permits the application of normal cues.

II

Turn now to an historical, but otherwise similar, case of concept revision, this one again promoted by the close analysis of an imagined situation. Like the children in Piaget's laboratory, Aristotle's *Physics* and the tradition that descends from it give evidence of two disparate criteria used in discussions of speed. The general point is well known but must be isolated for emphasis here. On most occasions Aristotle regards motion or change (the two terms are usually interchangeable in his physics) as a change of state. Thus 'every change is *from* something to something – as the word itself *metabole* indicates' (Aristotle, 1930, II, 224^{b}35–225^{a}1). Aristotle's reiteration of statements like this indicates that he normally views any noncelestial motion as a finite completed act to be grasped as a whole. Correspondingly, he measures the amount and speed of a motion in terms of the parameters which describe its end points, the *termini a quo* and *ad quem* of medieval physics.

The consequences for Aristotle's notion of speed are both immediate and obvious. As he puts it himself, 'The quicker of two things traverses a greater magnitude in an equal time, an equal magnitude in less time, and a greater magnitude in less time' (1930 II, 232^{a}25–7). Or elsewhere, 'There is equal velocity

---

[7] Questions just like this one have been used by Charles E. Osgood (Osgood, Suci, and Tannenbaum, 1957) to obtain what he calls the 'semantic profile' of various words.

where *the same* change is accomplished in an equal time' (1930, II, 249ᵇ4–5). In these passages, as in many other parts of Aristotle's writings, the implicit notion of speed is very like what we should call 'average speed', a quantity we equate with the ratio of total distance to total elapsed time. Like the child's goal-reaching criterion, this way of judging speed differs from our own. But, again, the difference can do no harm so long as the average-velocity criterion is itself consistently employed.

Only, again like Piaget's children, Aristotle is not, from a modern viewpoint, everywhere entirely consistent. He, too, seems to possess a criterion like the child's perceptual blurriness for judging speed. In particular, he does occasionally discriminate between the speed of a body near the beginning and near the end of its motion. For example, in distinguishing natural or unforced motions, which terminate in rest, from violent motions, which require an external mover, he says: 'But whereas the velocity of that which comes to a standstill seems always to increase, the velocity of that which is carried violently seems always to decrease' (1930, II, 230ᵇ23–5). Here, as in a few similar passages, there is no mention of endpoints, of distance covered, or of time elapsed. Instead, Aristotle is grasping directly, and perhaps perceptually, an aspect of motion which we should describe as 'instantaneous velocity' and which has properties quite different from average velocity. Aristotle, however, makes no such distinction. In fact, as we shall see in section III, important substantive aspects of his physics are conditioned by his failure to discriminate. As a result, those who use the Aristotelian concept of speed can be confronted with paradoxes quite like those with which Piaget confronted his children.

We shall examine in a moment the thought experiment which Galileo employed to make these paradoxes apparent, but must first note that by Galileo's time the concept of speed was no longer quite as Aristotle had left it. The well-known analytic techniques developed during the fourteenth century to treat latitude of forms had enriched the conceptual apparatus available to students of motion. In particular, it had introduced a distinction between the total velocity of a motion, on the one hand, and the intensity of velocity at each point of the motion, on the other. The second of these concepts was very close to the modern notion of instantaneous velocity; the first, though only after some important revisions by Galileo, was a long step towards the contemporary concept of average velocity.[8] Part of the paradox implicit in Aristotle's concept of speed was eliminated during the Middle Ages, two centuries and a half before Galileo wrote.

That medieval transformation of concepts was, however, incomplete in one important respect. Latitude of forms could be used for the comparison of two different motions only if they both had the same 'extension', i.e. covered the same distance or consumed the same time. Richard Swineshead's statement of the Mertonian Rule should serve to make apparent this too often neglected limitation: If an increment of velocity were uniformly acquired, then 'just as

[8] For a detailed discussion of the entire question of the latitude of forms, see Marshall Clacett (1959, Part II).

much space would be traversed by means of that increment . . . as by means of the mean degree [or intensity of velocity] of that increment, assuming something were to be moved with that mean degree [of velocity] throughout the whole time' (Clacett, 1959, p. 290). Here the elapsed time must be the same for both motions, or the technique for comparison breaks down. If the elapsed times could be different, then a uniform motion of low intensity but long duration could have a greater total velocity than a more intense motion (i.e. one with greater instantaneous velocity) that lasted only a short time. In general, the medieval analysts of motion avoided the potential difficulty by restricting their attention to comparisons which their techniques could handle. Galileo, however, required a more general technique and in developing it (or at least in teaching it to others) he employed a thought experiment that brought the full Aristotelian paradox to the fore. We have two assurances that the difficulty was still very real during the first third of the seventeenth century. Galileo's pedagogic acuteness is one – his text was directed to real problems. More impressive, perhaps, is the fact that Galileo did not always succeed in evading the difficulty himself.[9]

The relevant experiment is produced almost at the start of 'The First Day' in Galileo's *Dialogue concerning the Two Chief World Systems* (1953, pp. 22–7). Salviati, who speaks for Galileo, asks his two interlocutors to imagine two planes, CB vertical and CA inclined, erected the same vertical distance over a horizontal plane, AB. To aid the imagination Salviati includes a sketch like the one below. Along these two planes, two bodies are to be imagined sliding or rolling without friction from a common starting point at C. Finally, Salviati asks his interlocutors to concede that, when the sliding bodies reach A and B respectively, they will have acquired the same impetus or speed, i.e. the speed necessary to carry them again to the vertical height from which they started.[10] That request also is granted, and Salviati proceeds to ask the participants in the dialogue which of the two bodies moves faster. His object is to make them realize that, using the concept of speed then current, they can be forced to admit that motion along the perpendicular is simultaneously faster than, equal in speed to, and slower than the motion along the incline. His further object is, by the impact of this paradox, to make his interlocutors and readers realize that speed ought not to be attributed to the whole of a motion, but rather to its parts. In

[9] The most significant lapse of this sort occurs in 'The Second Day' (Galileo, 1953, pp. 199–201). Galileo there argues that no material body, however light, will be thrown from a rotating earth even if the earth rotates far faster than it does. That result (which Galileo's system requires – his lapse, though surely not deliberate, is not unmotivated) is gained by treating the terminal velocity of a uniformly accelerated motion as though it were proportional to the distance covered by the motion. The proportion is, of course, a straightforward consequence of the Mertonian Rule, but it is applicable only to motions that require the same time. Drake's notes to the passage should also be examined since they supply a somewhat different interpretation.

[10] Galileo makes somewhat less use of this concession than I shall below. Strictly speaking, his argument does not depend upon it if the plane CA can be extended beyond A and if the body rolling along the extended plane continues to gain speed. For simplicity I shall restrict my systematized recapitualtion to the unextended plane, following the lead supplied by Galileo in the first part of his text.

short, the thought experiment is, as Galileo himself points out, a propaedeutic to the full discussion of uniform and accelerated motion that occurs in 'The Third Discourse' of his *Two New Sciences*.

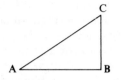

The argument itself I shall considerably condense and systematize since the detailed give and take of the dialogue need not concern us. When first asked which body is faster, the interlocutors give the response we are all drawn to though the physicists among us should know better. The motion along the perpendicular, they say, is obviously the faster.[11] Here, two of the three criteria we have already encountered combine. While both bodies are in motion, the one moving along the perpendicular is the 'more blurred'. In addition, the perpendicular motion is the one that reaches its goal first.

This obvious and immensely appealing answer immediately, however, raises difficulties which are first recognized by the cleverer of the interlocutors, Sagredo. He points out (or very nearly – I am making this part of the argument slightly more binding than it is in the original) that the answer is incompatible with the initial concession. Since both bodies start from rest and since both acquire the same terminal velocity, they must have the same mean speed. How then can one be faster than the other? At this point Salviati re-enters the discussion, reminding his listeners that the faster of two motions is usually defined as the one that covers the same distance in a lesser time. Part of the difficulty, he suggests, arises from the attempt to compare two motions that cover different distances. Instead, he urges, the participants in the dialogue should compare the times required by the two bodies in moving over a common standard distance. As a standard he selects the length of the vertical plan CB.

This, however, only makes the problem worse. CA is longer than CB, and the answer to the question, which body moves faster, turns out to depend critically upon where, along the incline CA, the standard length CB is measured. If it is measured down from the top of the incline, then the body moving on the perpendicular will complete its motion in less time than the body on the incline requires to move through a distance equal to CB. Motion along the perpendicular is therefore faster. On the other hand, if the standard distance is measured up from the bottom of the incline, the body moving on the perpendicular will need more time to complete its motion than the body on the incline will need to move through the same standard distance. Motion along the perpendicular is therefore slower. Finally, Salviati argues, if the distance CB is

[11] Anyone who doubts that this is a very tempting and natural answer should try Galileo's question, as I have, on graduate students of physics. Unless previously told what will be involved, many of them give the same answer as Salviati's interlocutors.

laid out along some appropriate internal part of the incline, then the times required by the two bodies to traverse the two standard segments will be the same. Motion on the perpendicular has the same speed as that on the incline. At this point the dialogue has provided three answers, each incompatible with both the others, to a single question about a single situation.

The result, of course, is paradox, and that is the way, or one of them, in which Galileo prepared his contemporaries for a change in the concepts employed when discussing, analysing, or experimenting upon motion. Though the new concepts were not fully developed for the public until the appearance of the *Two New Sciences*, the *Dialogue* already shows where the argument is headed. 'Faster' and 'speed' must not be used in the traditional way. One may say that at a particular instant one body has a faster instantaneous speed than another body has at that same time or at another specified instant. Or one may say that a particular body traverses a particular distance more quickly than another traverses the same or some other distance. But the two sorts of statements do not describe the same characteristics of the motion. 'Faster' means something different when applied on the one hand, to the comparison of instantaneous rates of motion at particular instants, and, on the other, to the comparison of the times required for the completion of the whole of two specified motions. A body may be 'faster' in one sense and not in the other.

That conceptual reform is what Galileo's thought experiment helped to teach, and we can therefore ask our old questions about it. Clearly, the minimal answers are the same ones supplied when considering the outcome of Piaget's experiments. The concepts which Aristotle applied to the study of motions were, in some part, self-contradictory, and the contradiction was not entirely eliminated during the Middle Ages. Galileo's thought experiment brought the difficulty to the fore by confronting readers with the paradox implicit in their mode of thought. As a result, it helped them to modify their conceptual apparatus.

If that much is right, then we can also see the criterion of verisimilitude to which the thought experiment had necessarily to conform. It makes no difference to Galileo's argument whether or not bodies actually execute universally accelerated motion when moving down inclined and vertical planes. It does not even matter whether, when the heights of these planes are the same, the two bodies actually reach equal instanteous velocities at the bottom. Galileo does not bother to argue either of the points. For his purpose in this part of the *Dialogue*, it is quite sufficient that we may suppose these things to be the case. On the other hand, it does not follow that Galileo's choice of the experimental situation could be arbitrary. He could not, for example, usefully have suggested that we consider a situation in which the body vanished at the start of its motion from C and then reappeared shortly afterwards at A without having traversed the intervening distance. That experiment would illustrate limitations in the applicability of 'faster', but, at least until the recognition of quantum jumps, those limitations would not have been informative. From them, neither we nor Galileo's readers could learn anything about the concepts traditionally employed. Those concepts were never intended to apply in such a case. In short, if this sort of thought experiment is to be effective, it must allow those who perform or study it to employ concepts in the same ways they have been employed before. Only if that condition is met can the thought experiment confront its audience with unanticipated consequences of their normal conceptual operations.

III

Up to this point, essential parts of my argument have been conditioned by what I take to be a philosophical position traditional in the analysis of scientific thought since at least the seventeenth century. If a thought experiment is to be effective, it must, as we have already seen, present a normal situation, i.e. a situation which the man who analyses the experiment feels well equipped by prior experience to handle. Nothing about the imagined situation may be entirely unfamiliar or strange. Therefore, if the experiment depends, as it must, upon prior experience of nature, that experience must have been generally familiar before the experiment was undertaken. This aspect of the thought-experimental situation has seemed to dictate one of the conclusions that I have so far consistently drawn. Because it embodies no new information about the world, a thought experiment can teach nothing that was not known before. Or, rather, it can teach nothing about the world. Instead, it teaches the scientist about his mental apparatus. Its function is limited to the correction of previous conceptual mistakes.

I suspect, however, that some historians of science may be uneasy about this conclusion, and I suggest that others should be. Somehow, it is too reminiscent of the familiar position which regards the Ptolemaic theory, the phlogiston theory, or the caloric theory as mere errors, confusions, or dogmatisms which a more liberal or intelligent science would have avoided from the start. In the climate of contemporary historiography, evaluations like these have come to seem less and less plausible, and that same air of implausibility infects the conclusion I have so far drawn in this paper. Aristotle, if no experimental physicist, was a brilliant logician. Would he, in a matter so fundamental to his physics, have committed an error so elementary as the one we have attributed to him? Or if he had, would his successors, for almost two millennia, have continued to make the same elementary mistake? Can a logical confusion be all that is involved, and can the function of thought experiments be so trivial as the entire point of view implies? I believe that the answer to all of these questions is no, and that the root of the difficulty is our assumption that, because they rely exclusively upon well-known data, thought experiments can teach nothing about the world. Though the contemporary epistemological vocabulary supplies no truly useful locutions, I want now to argue that from thought experiments most people learn about their concepts and the world together. In learning about the concept of speed Galileo's readers also learn something about how bodies move. What happens to them is very similar to what happens to a man, like Lavoisier, who must assimilate the result of a new unexpected experimental discovery.[12]

In approaching this series of central points, I first ask what can have been meant when we described the child's concept of faster and the Aristotelian concept of speed as 'self-contradictory' or 'confused'. 'Self-contradictory', at least, suggests that these concepts are like the logician's famous example, square-circle, but that cannot be quite right. Square-circle is self-contradictory in the sense that it could not be exemplified in any possible world. One cannot even imagine an object which would display the requisite qualities. Neither the child's concept nor Aristotle's, however, are contradictory in that sense. The child's concept of faster is repeatedly exemplified in our own world; contradiction arises only when the child is confronted with that relatively rare sort of motion in which the perceptually *more* blurred object *lags* in reaching the goal. Similarly, Aristotle's concept of speed, with its two simultaneous criteria, can be applied without difficulty to most of the motions we see about us. Problems arise only for that class of motions, again rather rare, in which the criterion of instantaneous velocity and the criterion of average velocity lead to contradictory responses in qualitative applications. In both these cases the concepts are contradictory only in the sense that the individual who employs them *runs the risk* of self-contradiction. He may, that is, find himself in a situation where he can be forced to give incompatible answers to one and the same question.

That, of course, is not what is usually meant when the term 'self-contradictory' is applied to a concept. It may well, however, be what we had in mind when we described the concepts examined above as 'confused' or 'inadequate to clear thought'. Certainly those terms fit the situation better. They do, however, imply a standard for clarity and adequacy that we may have no right to apply. Ought we demand of our concepts, as we do not and could not of our laws and theories, that they be applicable to any and every situation that might conceivably arise in any possible world? Is it not sufficient to demand of a concept, as we do of a law or theory, that it be unequivocally applicable in every situation which we expect ever to encounter?

To see the relevance of those questions, imagine a world in which all motions occur at uniform speed. (That condition is more stringent than necessary, but it will make the argument clearer. The requisite weaker condition is that no body which is 'slower' by either criterion shall ever overtake a 'faster' body. I shall call motions which satisfy this weaker condition 'quasi-uniform'.) In a world of that sort the Aristotelian concept of speed could never be jeopardized by an actual physical situation, for the instantaneous and average speed of any motion would always be the same.[13] What, then, would we say if we found a scientist in this

---

[12] That remark presumes an analysis of the manner in which new discoveries emerge, for which see Kuhn (1962).

[13] One can also imagine a world in which the two criteria employed by Piaget's children would never lead to contradiction, but it is more complex, and I shall therefore make no use of it in the argument that follows. Let me, however, hazard one testable guess about the nature of motion in that world. Unless copying their elders, children who view motion in the way described above should be relatively insensitive to the importance of a handicap to the winning of a race. Instead,

imaginary world consistently employing the Aristotelian concept of speed? Not, I think, that he was confused. Nothing could go wrong with his science or logic because of his application of the concept. Instead, given our own broader experience and our correspondingly richer conceptual apparatus, we would likely say that, consciously or unconsciously, he had embodied in his concept of speed his expectation that only uniform motions would occur in his world. We would, that is, conclude that his concept functioned in part as a law of nature, a law that was regularly satisfied in his world but that would only occasionally be satisfied in our own.

In Aristotle's case, of course, we cannot say quite this much. He did know, and occasionally admits, that falling bodies, for example, increase their speeds as they move. On the other hand, there is ample evidence that Aristotle kept this information at the very periphery of his scientific consciousness. Whenever he could, which was frequently, he regarded motions as uniform or as possessing the properties of uniform motion, and the results were consequential for much of his physics. In section II, for example, we examined a passage from the *Physics* which can pass for a definition of 'faster motion': 'The quicker of two things traverses a greater magnitude in an equal time, an equal magnitude in less time and a greater magnitude in less time.' Compare this with the passage that follows it immediately: 'Suppose that A is quicker than B. Now since of two things that which changes sooner is quicker, in the time FG, in which A has changed from C to D, B will not yet have arrived at D but will be short of it' (1930, 232ª28–31). This statement is no longer quite a definition. Instead it is about the physical behaviour of 'quicker' bodies, and, as such, it holds only for bodies that are in uniform or quasi-uniform motion.[14] The whole burden of Galileo's thought experiment is to show that this statement and others like it – statements which seem to follow inevitably from the only definition the traditional concept 'faster' will support – do not hold in the world as we know it and that the concept therefore requires modification.

Aristotle nevertheless proceeds to build his view of motion as quasi-uniform deeply into the fabric of his system. For example, in the paragraph just after that from which the preceding statements are taken, he employs those statements to show that space must be continuous if time is. His argument depends upon his assumption, implicit above, that, if a body B lags behind another body A at the end of a motion, it will have lagged at another body A at the end of a motion, it will have lagged at all intermediate points. In that case, B can be used to divide the space and A to divide the time. If one is continuous, the other must be too (1930, 232ᵇ21–233ª13). Unfortunately, however, the assumption need not hold if, for example, the slower motion is decelerating and the faster accelerating, yet Aristotle sees no need to bar motions of that sort. Here again his argument

everything should seem to depend upon the violence with which arms and legs are moved.

[14] Actually, of course, the first passage cannot be a definition. Any one of the three conditions there stated could have that function, but taking the three to be equivalent, as Aristotle does, has the same physical implications which I here illustrate from the second passage.

depends upon his attributing to all movements the qualitative properties of uniform change.

The same view of motion underlies the arguments by which Aristotle develops his so-called quantitative laws of motion.[15] For illustration, consider only the dependence of distance covered on the size of the body and upon elapsed time: 'If, then, A the movement has moved B a distance C in a time D, then in the same time the same force A will move 1/2 B twice the distance C, and in 1/2 D it will move 1/2 B the whole distance C: for thus the rules of proportion will be observed' (1930, 249^b 30–250^a 4). With both force and medium given, that is, the distance covered varies directly with time and inversely with body size.

To modern ears this is inevitably a strange law, though perhaps not so strange as it has usually seemed.[16] But given the Aristotelian concept of speed – a concept that raises no problems in most of its applications – it is readily seen to be the only simple law available. If motion is such that average and instantaneous speed are identical, then, *ceteris paribus*, distance covered must be proportional to time. If, in addition, we assume with Aristotle (and Newton) that 'two forces each of which separately moves one of two weights a given distance in a given time . . . will move the combined weights an equal distance in an equal time' (1930, 250^{a}25–8), then speed must be some function of the ratio of force to body size. Aristotle's laws follow directly by assuming the function to be the simplest one available, i.e. the ratio itself. Perhaps this does not seem a legitimate way to arrive at laws of motion, but Galileo's procedures were very often identical.[17] In this particular respect what principally differentiated Galileo from Aristotle is that the former started with a different conception of speed. Since he did not see all motions as quasi-uniform, speed was not the only measure of motion that could change with applied force, body size, and so on. Galileo could consider variations of acceleration as well.

These examples could be considerably multiplied, but my point may already be clear. Aristotle's concept of speed, in which something like the separate modern concepts of average and instantaneous speed were merged, was an integral part of his entire theory of motion and had implications for the whole of

[15] These laws are always described as 'quantitative', and I follow that usage. But it is hard to believe they were meant to be quantitative in the sense of that term current in the study of motion since Galileo. Both in antiquity and the Middle Ages men who regularly thought measurement relevant to astronomy and who occasionally employed it in optics discussed these laws of motion without even a veiled reference to any sort of quantitative observation. Furthermore, the laws are never applied to nature except in arguments which rely on *reductio ad absurdum*. To me their intent seems qualitative – they are a statement, using the vocabulary of proportions, of several correctly observed qualitative regularities. This view may appear more plausible if we remember that after Eudoxus even geometric proportion was regularly interpreted as non–numerical.

[16] For cogent criticism of those who find the law merely silly, see Toulmin (1959, particularly fn. 1).

[17] For example, 'When, therefore, I observe a stone initially at rest falling from an elevated position and continually acquiring new increments of speed, why should I not believe that such increases take place in a manner which is exceedingly simple and rather obvious to everybody? If now we examine the matter carefully we find no addition or increment more simple than that which repeats itself always in the same manner' (Galileo, 1946, pp. 154–5). Galileo, however, did proceed to an experimental check.

his physics. That role it could play because it was not simply a definition, confused or otherwise. Instead, it had physical implications and acted in part as a law of nature. Those implications could never have been challenged by observation or by logic in a world where all motions were uniform or quasi-uniform, and Aristotle acted as though he lived in a world of that sort. Actually, of course, his world was different, but his concept nevertheless functioned so successfully that potential conflicts with observation went entirely unnoticed. And while they did so – until, that is, the potential difficulties in applying the concept began to become actual – we may not properly speak of the Aristotelian concept of speed as confused. We may, of course, say that it was 'wrong' or 'false' in the same sense that we apply those terms to outmoded laws and theories. In addition, we may say that, because the concept was false, the men who employed it were *liable to become confused*, as Salviati's interlocutors did. But we cannot, I think, find any intrinsic defect in the concept by itself. Its defects lay not in its logical consistency but in its failure to fit the full fine-structure of the world to which it was expected to apply. That is why learning to recognize its defects was necessarily learning about the world as well as about the concept.

If the legislative content of individual concepts seems an unfamilar notion, that is probably because of the context within which I have approached it here. To linguists the point has long been familiar, if controversial, through the writings of B. L. Whorf (1956). Braithwaite (1953, pp. 50–87), following Ramsey, has developed a similar thesis by using logical models to demonstrate the inextricable mixture of law and definition which must characterize the function of even relatively elementary scientific concepts (see also Quine, 1953, pp. 20–46). Still more to the point are the several recent logical discussions of the use of 'reduction sentences' in forming scientific concepts. These are sentences which specify (in a logical form that need not here concern us) the observational or test conditions under which a given concept may be applied. In practice, they closely parallel the contexts in which most scientific concepts are actually acquired, and that makes their two most salient characteristics particularly significant. First, several reduction sentences – sometimes a great many – are normally required to supply a given concept with the range of application required by its use in scientific theory. Second, as soon as more than one reduction sentence is used to introduce a single concept, those sentences turn out to imply 'certain statements which have the character of empirical laws. . . Sets of reduction sentences combine in a peculiar way the functions of concept and of theory formation.'[18] That quotation, with the sentence that precedes it, very nearly describes the situation we have just been examining.

We need not, however, make the full transition to logic and philosophy of science in order to recognize the legislative function of scientific concepts. In another guise it is already familiar to every historian who has studied closely the evolution of concepts like element, species, mass, force, space, caloric, or energy.[19] These and many other scientific concepts are invariably encountered

---

[18] Hempel (1952). The fundamental discussion of reduction sentences is in Carnap (1936, 1937).
[19] The cases of caloric and of mass are particularly instructive, the first because it parallels the case

within a matrix of law, theory, and expectation from which they cannot be altogether extricated for the sake of definition. To discover what they mean the historian must examine both what is said about them and also the way in which they are used. In the process he regularly discovers a number of different criteria which govern their use and whose coexistence can be understood only by reference to many of the other scientific (and sometimes extra-scientific) beliefs which guide the men who use them. It follows that those concepts were not intended for application to any possible world, but only to the world as the scientist saw it. Their use is one index of his commitment to a larger body of law and theory. Conversely, the legislative content of that larger body of belief is in part carried by the concepts themselves. That is why, though many of them have histories of the sciences in which they function, their meaning and their criteria-for-use have so often and so drastically changed in the course of scientific development.

Finally, returning to the concept of speed, notice that Galileo's reformulation did not make it once and for all logically pure. No more than its Aristotelian predecessor was it free from implications about the way nature must behave. As a result, again like Aristotle's concept of speed, it could be called in question by accumulated experience, and that is what occurred at the end of the last century and the beginning of this one. The episode is too well known to require extended discussion. When applied to accelerated motions, the Galilean concept of speed implies the existence of a set of physically unaccelerated spatial reference systems. That is the lesson Newton's bucket experiment, a lesson which none of the relativists of the seventeenth and eighteenth centuries were able to explain away. In addition, when applied to linear motions, the revised concept of speed used in this paper implied the validity of the so-called Galilean transformation equations, and these specify physical properties, for example the additivity of the velocity of matter or of light. Without benefit of any superstructure of laws and theories like Newton's, they provided immensely significant information about what the world is like.

Or, rather, they used to do so. One of the first great triumphs of twentieth-century physics was the recognition that that information could be questioned and the consequent recasting of the concepts of speed, space, and time. Furthermore, in that reconceptualization thought experiments again played a vital role. The historical process we examined above through the work of Galileo has since been repeated with respect to the same constellation of concepts. Perfectly

discussed above, the second because it reverses the line of development. It has often been pointed out that Sadi Carnot derived good experimental results from the caloric theory because his concept of heat combined characteristics that later had to be distributed between heat and entropy. (See my exchange with V. K. La Mer, *American Journal of Physics*, **22** (1954), 20–7, **23** (1955), 91–5, 95–102, and 387–9. The last of these items formulates the point in the way required here.) Mass, on the other hand, displays an opposite line of development. In Newtonian theory inertial mass and gravitational mass are separate concepts, measured by distinct means. An experimentally tested law of nature is needed to say that the two sorts of measurements will always, within instrumental limits, give the same results. According to general relativity, however, no separate experimental law is required. The two measurements *must* yield the same result because they measure the same quantity.

possibly it may occur again, for it is one of the basic processes through which the sciences advance.

IV

My argument is now very nearly complete. To discover the element still missing, let me briefly recapitulate the main points discussed so far. I began by suggesting that an important class of thought experiments functions by confronting the scientist with a contradiction or conflict implicit in his mode of thought. Recognizing the contradiction then appeared an essential propaedeutic to its elimination. As a result of the thought experiment, clear concepts were developed to replace the confused ones that had been in use before. Closer examination, however, disclosed an essential difficulty in that analysis. The concepts 'corrected' in the aftermath of thought experiments displayed no *intrinsic* confusion. If their use raised problems for the scientist, those problems were like the ones to which the use of any experimentally based law or theory would expose him. They arose, that is, not from his mental equipment alone but from difficulties discovered in the attempt to fit that equipment to previously unassimilated experience. Nature rather than logic alone was responsible for the apparent confusion. This situation led me to suggest that from the sort of thought experiment here examined the scientist learns about the world as well as about his concepts. Historically their role is very close to the double one played by actual laboratory experiments and observations. First, thought experiments can disclose nature's failure to conform to a previously held set of expectations. In addition, they can suggest particular ways in which both expectation and theory must henceforth be revised.

But how – to raise the remaining problem – can they do so? Laboratory experiments play these roles because they supply the scientist with new and unexpected information. Thought experiments, on the contrary, must rest entirely on information already at hand. If the two can have such similar roles, that must be because, on occasions, thought experiments give the scientist access to information which is simultaneously at hand and yet somehow inaccessible to him. Let me now try to indicate, though necessarily briefly and incompletely, how this could be the case.

I have elsewhere pointed out that the development of a mature scientific specialty is normally determined largely by the closely integrated body of concepts, laws, theories, and instrumental techniques which the individual practitioner acquires from professional education.[20] That time-tested fabric of belief and expectation tells him what the world is like and simultaneously defines the problems which still demand professional attention. Those problems are the ones which, when solved, will extend the precision and scope of the fit between existing belief, on the one hand, and observation of nature, on the other. When problems are selected in this way, past success ordinarily ensures

[20] For incomplete discussions of this and the following points see Kuhn (1961a, b). The whole subject is treated more fully and with many additional examples in Kuhn (1970).

future success as well. One reason why scientific research seems to advance steadily from solved problem to solved problem is that professionals restrict their attention to problems defined by the conceptual and instrumental techniques already at hand.

That mode of problem selection, however, though it makes short-term success particularly likely, also guarantees long-run failures that prove even more consequential to scientfic advance. Even the data that this restricted pattern of research presents to the scientist never entirely or precisely fit his theory-induced expectations. Some of those failures-to-fit provide his current research problems; but others are pushed to the periphery of consciousness and some are suppressed entirely. Usually that inability to recognize and confront anomaly is justified in the event. More often than not minor instrumental adjustments or small articulations of existing theory ultimately reduce the apparent anomaly to law. Pausing over anomalies when they are first confronted is to invite continual distraction.[21] But not all anomalies do respond to minor adjustments of the existing conceptual and instrumental fabric. Among those which do not are some which, either because they are particularly striking or because they are educed repeatedly in many different laboratories cannot be indefinitely ignored. Though they remain unassimilated, they impinge with gradually increasing force upon the consciousness of the scientific community.

As this process continues, the pattern of the community's research gradually changes. At first, reports of unassimilated observations appear more and more frequently in the pages of laboratory notebooks or as asides in published reports. Then more and more research is turned to the anomaly itself. Those who are attempting to make it lawlike will increasingly quarrel over the meaning of the concepts and theories which they have long held in common without awareness of ambiguity. A few of them will begin critically to analyse the fabric of belief that has brought the community to its present impasse. On occasions even philosophy will become a legitimate scientific tool, which it ordinarily is not. Some or all of these symptoms of community crisis are, I think, the invariable prelude to the fundamental reconceptualization that the removal of an obdurate anomaly almost always demands. Typically, that crisis ends only when some particularly imaginative individual, or a group of them, weaves a new fabric of laws, theories, and concepts, one which can assimilate the previously incongruous experience and most or all of the previous assimilated experience as well.

This process of reconceptualization I have elsewhere labelled scientific revolution. Such revolutions need not be nearly so total as the preceding sketch implies, but they all share with it one essential characteristic. The data requisite for revolution have existed before at the fringe of scientific consciousness; the emergence of crisis brings them to the centre of attention; and the revolutionary reconceptualization permits them to be seen in a new way.[22] What was vaguely

[21] Much evidence on this point is to be found in Polanyi (1958, particularly ch. 9).

[22] The phrase 'permits them to be seen in a new way' must here remain a metaphor though I intend it quite literally. Hanson (1958, pp. 4–30) has already argued that what scientists see depends upon their prior beliefs and training, and much evidence on this point will be found in Kuhn (1970).

known in spite of the community's mental equipment before the revolution is afterwards precisely known because of its mental equipment.

That conclusion, or constellation of conclusions, is, of course, both too grandiose and too obscure for general documentation here. I suggest, however, that in one limited application a number of its essential elements have been documented already. A crisis induced by the failure of expectation and followed by revolution is at the heart of the thought-experimental situations we have been examining. Conversely, thought experiment is one of the essential analytic tools which are deployed during crisis and which then help to promote basic conceptual reform. The outcome of thought experiments can be the same as that of scientific revolutions: they can enable the scientist to use as an integral part of his knowledge what that knowledge had previously made inaccesible to him. That is the sense in which they change his knowledge of the world. And it is because they can have that effect that they cluster so notably in the works of men like Aristotle, Galileo, Descartes, Einstein, and Bohr, the great weavers of new conceptual fabrics.

Return now briefly and for the last time to our own experiments, both Piaget's and Galileo's. What troubled us about them was, I think, that we found implicit in the pre-experimental mentality laws of nature which conflicted with information we felt sure our subjects already possessed. Indeed, it was only because they possessed the information that they could learn from the experimental situation at all. Under those circumstances we were puzzled by their inability to see the conflict; we were unsure what they had still to learn; and we were therefore impelled to regard them as confused. That way of describing the situation was not, I think, altogether wrong, but it was misleading. Though my own concluding substitute must remain partly metaphor, I urge the following description instead.

For some time before we encountered them, our subjects had, in their transactions with nature, successfully employed a conceptual fabric different from the one we use ourselves. That fabric was time-tested; it had not yet confronted them with difficulties. Nevertheless, as of the time we encountered them, they had at last acquired a variety of experience which could not be assimilated by their traditional mode of dealing with the world. At this point they had at hand all the experience requisite to a fundamental recasting of their concepts, but there was something about the experience which they had not yet seen. Because they had not, they were subject to confusion and were perhaps already uneasy.[23] Full confusion, however, came only in the thought-experimental situation, and then it came as a prelude to its cure. By transforming felt anomaly to concrete contradiction, the thought experiment informed our subjects what was wrong. That first clear view of the misfit between experience and implicit expectation provided the clues necessary to set the situation right.

What characteristics must a thought experiment possess if it is to be capable of

---

[23] Piaget's children were, of course, not uneasy (at least not for relevant reasons) until his experiments were exhibited to them. In the historical situation, however, thought experiments are generally called forth by a growing awareness that something somewhere is the matter.

these effects? One part of my previous answer can still stand. If it is to disclose a misfit between traditional conceptual apparatus and nature, the imagined situation must allow the scientist to employ his usual concepts in the way he has employed them before. It must not, that is, strain normal usage. On the other hand, the part of my previous answer which dealt with physical verisimilitude now needs revision. It presumed that thought experiments were directed to purely logical contradiction or confusions; any situation capable of displaying such contradictions would therefore suffice; there was then no condition of physical verisimilitude at all. If, however, we suppose that nature and conceptual apparatus are jointly implicated in the contradiction posed by thought experiments, a stronger condition is required. Though the imagined situation need not be even potentially realizable in nature, the conflict deduced from it must be one that nature itself could present. Indeed, even that condition is not quite strong enough. The conflict which confronts the scientist in the experimental situation must be one that, however unclearly seen, has confronted him before. Unless he has already had that much experience, he is not yet prepared to learn from thought experiments alone.

18. 'If you want to get ahead, get a theory'[1]

Annette Karmiloff-Smith and Bärbel Inhelder

Introduction

How can we go about understanding children's processes of discovery in action?
Do we simply postulate that dynamic processes directly reflect underlying
cognitive structures or should we seek the productive aspects of discovery in the
interplay between the two? This is not an entirely new concern in the Genevan
context since in the preface of *The Growth of Logical Thinking* (Inhelder and
Piaget, 1958) it was announced rather prematurely that 'the specific problem of
experimental induction analysed from a functional standpoint (as distinguished
from the present structural analysis) will be the subject of a special work by the
first author'. Two decades have elapsed. With hindsight it is realized how much
more experimentation and reflection were required to undertake the structural
analysis. Operational structures are clearly an important part of the picture.
They provide the necessary interpretative framework to infer the lower and
upper limits of the concepts a child can bring to bear on a task. But they
obviously do not suffice to explain all facets of cognitive behaviour.

Our first experiments that focused directly on processes were undertaken as
part of some recent work on learning (Inhelder, Sinclair, and Bovet, 1974). The
results illustrated not only the dynamics of interstage transitions but also the
interaction between the child's various subsystems belonging to different
developmental levels. Though the learning experiments were process-oriented,
they failed to answer all our questions (Cellérier, 1972; Inhelder, 1972). What
still seemed to be lacking were experiments on children's spontaneous organizing activity in goal-oriented tasks with relatively little intervention from the
experimenter. The focus is not on success or failure *per se* but on the interplay
between action sequences and children's 'theories-in-action', i.e. the implicit
ideas or changing modes of representation underlying the sequences. Although
what happens in half an hour cannot be considered simply as a miniature version
of what takes place developmentally, it is hoped that an analysis of the processes

---

[1] Excerpts from the paper in *Cognition*, **3** (1974/5), 195–212.

of microdevelopment will later enable us to take a new look at macrodevelopment. . .

Experimental procedure

Subjects were requested to 'balance so that they do not fall' a variety of blocks across a narrow bar, a 1×25 cm metal rod fixed to a piece of wood. There were seven types of blocks, with several variants under each type. Some were made of wood, others of metal, some were 15 cm long, others 30 cm. One example of each type is illustrated in figure 1. Type A blocks had their weight evenly distributed; B blocks consisted of two identical overlapping blocks glued together, weight being evenly distributed in each block. In A and B blocks, the centre of gravity thus coincided with the geometric centre of the length of the solid as a whole. We shall refer to A and B types as 'length blocks' since dividing the length in half gives the point of balance. The child can succeed without being aware that weight is involved. C types consisted of a block glued to a thin piece of plywood; D types were similar, except that the plywood was much thicker and thus the weight of the glued block had less effect. We shall call C and D types 'conspicuous weight blocks' since the asymmetrical distribution of the weight could readily be inferred. E blocks were invisibly weighted with metal inside one end, and F types had a cavity at one end into which small blocks of various weights could be inserted. E and F types will be referred to as 'inconspicuous weight blocks'. An 'impossible' block (G type) was also used which could not be balanced without counterweights.

The experiment took place in two phases. In phase I, subjects were left free to choose the order in which they wished to balance each block separately on the bar. It was hoped in this way to gain insight into the ways in which children spontaneously endeavour to apprehend the various properties of the blocks: whether they group analogous blocks together, how they transfer successful action sequences from one block to another, and how they regulate their actions after success or failure. Once each block had been placed in equilibrium, children were requested to repeat certain items in a new order proposed by the experimenter. As an experimental precaution to make sure that no psychomotor difficulties would affect the results, subjects were first asked to balance two identical cylinders (2 cm diameter) one on top of the other.

When analysing the results of phase I, it was hypothesized that children interpret the results of their actions on the blocks in two very different ways: either in terms of success or failure to balance the blocks which will be referred to as positive or negative *action-response*, or in terms of confirmation or refutation of a theory-in-action, which will be called positive or negative *theory-response*. A negative theory-response, for instance, implies contradiction of a theory either through failure to balance when the theory would predict success, or through successful balancing when the theory would predict failure. In other words, the same result was interpreted by children either as positive action-response or as negative theory-response and *vice versa*.

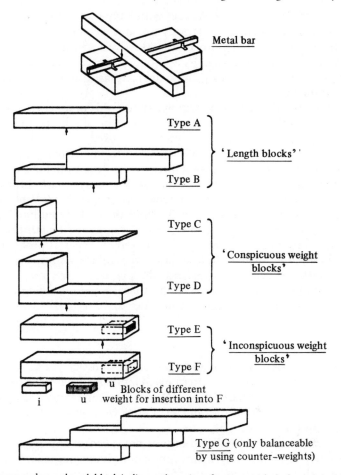

Figure 1. Arrow underneath each block indicates the point of contact with the bar when the block is in equilibrium. For Type F blocks, this point is a function of the weight of the blocks to be inserted into the cavity

Phase II focused on this problem. About half of the phase I subjects in each age group were interviewed again some twelve months later. The purpose was twofold. First, to verify the cross-sectional analysis, the interpretative hypotheses we had made, as well as to determine the progress achieved by each subject. Secondly, since we now had a detailed description of the phase I developmental trends, we wanted to intervene rather more systematically in phase II by providing increased opportunity for positive and negative action- and theory-response, in order to study their interplay during the course of a session. Apart from balancing each of the blocks separately on the bar, subjects were also asked to leave one block in balance and try to balance in front of it on the same bar another block that looked similar but which had a strikingly different centre of gravity (e.g. A types with E types), to add to blocks already in balance several small cubes of various size and weight, etc.

In both phases, a written protocol was taken by one observer and a continuous commentary was tape-recorded by a second observer on all the child's actions, corrections, hesitations, long pauses, distractions, gross eye movements and verbal comments.

Unlike many other problem solving studies, this new series of experiments did not strive to keep tasks untainted by conceptual aspects. Indeed, we purposely chose situations in which physical, spatial or logical reasoning was involved but which we had already analysed from a structural point of view, thus providing additional means for interpreting data. Both for constructing the material and interpreting results of the block-balancing task information was used from previous research (e.g. Inhelder and Piaget, 1958; Vinh Bang, 1968; Piaget and Garcia, 1974; Piaget, 1973) about the underlying intellectual operations and children's modes of interpreting weight and length problems.

The exact order of presentation of items and the types of problems set were not standardized in advance. Indeed, just as the child was constructing a theory-in-action in his endeavour to balance the blocks, so we, too, were making on-the-spot hypotheses about the child's theories and providing opportunities for negative and positive responses in order to verify our own theories.

Population

Sixty-seven children between the ages of 4;6 and 9;5 years from a Geneva middle-class state school were interviewed individually. Phase I covered forty-four subjects; twenty-three of these children were interviewed again in phase II. Five young subjects between 18 and 39 months were observed in provoked play sessions with the blocks.

In the results, some rough indications are given of the ages at which the various action sequences and theories-in-action are encountered, but this should not imply that the processes described are considered to be stage-bound. Twenty-two subjects from this experiment were also asked to perform quite a different task, that of constructing toy railway circuits of varying shapes, and it was quite clear that children interpreting success or failure as theory-responses in one task might be interpreting success or failure as action-responses in the other task. Furthermore, similar action sequences for block-balancing were encountered not only in many children of the same age but also during the course of a session with children of very different ages. On the basis of children's verbal explanations of the relevant physical laws, the development trend falls into neat stages. If the analysis is based on children's goal-oriented actions, this is not so obviously the case. However, both the nature and the order of action sequences as described in our results were overwhelmingly confirmed by changes during sessions as well as the longitudinal results of phase II

Observational data

We felt it would instructive to have an indication of how very small children go about balancing blocks. Accordingly, five subjects between 18 and 39 months were observed in provoked play sessions with our experimental material. This led us to interpret the older subjects' seemingly anomalous behaviour in conflict situations as rather clear-cut regressions to earlier patterns. None of the five subjects failed in balancing the two cylinders used for checking psychomotor problems. As far as the experimental blocks were concerned, it was possible to coax the children into trying to balance a few blocks, but only for very short periods of time. Nevertheless, what they did was often organized. The following was the basic pattern: Place the block in physical contact with the bar at *any* point (e.g. extremities, centre, pointed edge, side etc.), let go, repeat. Their attention was frequently diverted to the noise made by the falling block; indeed, the two youngest subjects rapidly made their goal that of causing a loud noise. Gradually, with the first chance successes on the 15 cm 'length blocks' (easier than the 30 cm ones), the three oldest subjects (32–39 months) lengthened their action sequences in a systematic way, as follows: Place the block at any point of physical contact with the bar, push hard with finger above that point of contact, let go, repeat immediately. However, these subjects did not move the block to another point of contact before letting go, although they had consistently done so when trying to balance the two cylinders or when building towers or houses with wooden cubes. It would appear that in such cases they were simply forming the parallel plane surfaces; in other words the problem of finding the appropriate point of contact between two objects of different shape did not arise. Nonetheless, even though the subjects placed the blocks at random points of contact, further development of action sequences by pushing on the block above the point of contact (i) seemed to denote that the need for spatio-physical contact had become clearer for the child, his finger acting somewhat like a nail and thus simplifying the balancing problem and (ii) provided the child with an indication through diffuse proprioceptive information of the fact that blocks have properties that counteract his actions.

The experimental material was in fact designed to allow for proprioceptive information. In previous research (e.g. Inhelder and Piaget, 1958; Vinh Bang, 1968) on equilibrium with a fixed fulcrum, subjects could only obtain visual information which then had to be expressed via another mode of representation.

Experimental data

Unlike previous Genevan research articles in which extensive quotations were given from what children said, the study's protocols consist mainly of detailed descriptions of children's actions. We shall, however, occasionally refer to children's spontaneous comment when it is particularly illustrative. Here we will describe those action sequences that were encountered among most children of a given age and repeated several times by each child on the various blocks.

Many of the subjects in the experiment proper started the session in a similar way to the young subjects just described in the observational data. However, what seemed to take place developmentally between 18 and 39 months was observed during part of a single session among 4- to 6-year-olds. Thus the initial approach was as follows: Place block at any point of contact, let go. This was immediately followed by a second attempt with the same block: Place at any point of contact, push hard above the point, let go. As the block kept on falling, the children gradually discovered through their act of pushing that the object had properties independent of their actions on it. Negative response sparked off a change from an action plan purely directed at the goal of balancing, to a subgoal of discovering the properties of the object in order to balance it. These children then undertook a very detailed exploration of each block trying one dimension after another, as follows: Place the block lengthwise, widthwise, upended one way, then the other and so forth. Such sequences were repeated several times with each block. Although the order of the dimensions tried out differed from one child to the next, each child's exploration of the various dimensions became more and more systematic. Yet only one point of contact was tried for each dimension – for quite some time the children would never change the point of contact along any one dimension. Frequently, even when children were successful in balancing an item on one dimension (e.g. at the geometric centre of length-blocks or along the length of the bar), they went on exploring the other dimensions of each block. It was as if their attention were momentarily diverted from the goal of balancing to what had started out as a subgoal, i.e. the search for means. One could see the children oscillating between seeking the goal and seeking to 'question' the block. Successful balancing was certainly registered since, in the course of their investigation of the blocks, the children returned more and more frequently to the dimension that had yielded the solution. Yet they continued to explore, as if seeking an alternative solution. Although such behaviour seems to indicate that the child is beginning to differentiate between his own actions and the properties of the block, this seeking for alternative solutions may be interpreted to mean that the child does not yet understand that a physical law, unalterable by his action, governs the object's behaviour. We hypothesize that during his exploration the child is endeavouring to make a sort of 'catalogue' of the different actions he may make on the blocks; once he has set the limits of these actions, he is then in a position to narrow them down to those that appear to be more relevant to his goal.

More advanced subjects did not lose sight of their goal; once they found a solution, they registered the positive response and no longer explored the block in any observable way. As balancing of length blocks became progressively easier, children attempted to balance all items on their longest, flat dimension, only reverting to 'exploration' and even to 'pushing hard above the contact point' when grappling with the difficult item G.

After opting for the longest dimension and retaining some form of representation of a previously balanced block on that dimension, children began their first real search for the effective point of balance. Here is where spatial symmetry, already so prevalent in young children's behaviour in solving other problems, is used by the child as possibly relevant for success. Action sequences were as follows: first place more or less symmetrically on the support bar, i.e. close to the geometric centre, correct in the right direction guided by the sensation of falling (adjustments were rarely made in the wrong direction), readjust in the other direction (corrections were frequently excessive), continue correcting back and forth but gradually more carefully until equilibrium is achieved.

It was suggested that for some time children treat the problem as one not governed by a physical law. By contrast, what was particularly apparent at the next level, either developmentally or later in a session, was that *all* blocks were systematically first tried at their geometric centre. Almost all children aged 6–7;5 and also some younger subjects, did this. Here we witness the beginnings of an important theory-in-action (i.e. spatial symmetry or as the children put it 'I'll try the middle first', '. . . half-way along'), which was generalized to all blocks and was to pervade behaviour at the next level. Action sequences ran as follows: Place at geometric centre, release hold very slightly to observe result, correct very slightly, correct a little more, return carefully to geometric centre, repeat until balance is achieved. Depending on the block, the further the child had to move away from the geometric centre, the more often he returned to it before further adjusting. These frequent returns to the geometric centre seem to denote that the child is using a form of spatial notation as a known location from which to orient his corrections and are an obvious prelude to the 'geometric centre theory' that develops next.

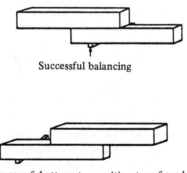

Successful balancing

Unsuccessful attempt – position transferred
from previous success

Figure 2

Another important change took place at this level. The children no longer seemed to be merely registering the fact of balance but beyond that something about the balancing position of the block. The new action sequence, which alternated with the one described previously, was as follows: First place at geometric centre, next place at the point of contact corresponding to the previous success (irrespective as yet of the differences between the two blocks and often far removed from possible empirical success – see figure 2), return to geometric centre, continue as in previous sequence. At this point, some corrections were made away from the centre of gravity, a feature to be discussed later. Notable in the various action sequences of these children was the interplay between the endeavour to use information acquired from previous actions and the gradual introduction of a coherent, analogous approach to *all* items.

Interestingly enough, most of those subjects who had been successful in balancing conspicuous or inconspicuous weight blocks because they had been concentrating on the goal, began later in the session to experience serious difficulties in repeating the successful action as their attention shifted to the means. They now placed the very same blocks more and more systematically at the geometric centre, with only very slight corrections around this point. They showed considerable surprise at not being able to balance the blocks a second time ('Heh, what's gone wrong with this one, it worked before'). This was in fact to be the dominating behavioural pattern for a long period to follow, either during the session or developmentally. Action sequences then became reduced to: Place carefully at geometric centre, correct very slightly around this centre, abandon all attempts, declaring the object as 'impossible' to balance. It is interesting to note that the child remained unflinchingly at the geometric centre and completely ignored the proprioceptive messages that had proved useful earlier. What is striking is that when these very same subjects were asked to close their eyes and attempt to balance inconspicuous weight blocks, success was very rapid. But once they reopened their eyes, they again resolutely tried the geometric centre and expressed surprise at their blind success. In fact we observed more failures to balance blocks among 5;6- to 7;5-year-olds than among 4;5- to 5;5-year-olds. How can this be explained? It would appear that a strong theory-in-action, i.e. that the centre of gravity necessarily coincides with the geometric centre of an object (or as one child put it 'things always balance in the middle' though others did not express verbally what was obvious in their actions), pervaded the actions of the older children. Not only did they place all blocks at their geometric centre with substantially no corrections of the position, but when asked to add small blocks of varying shapes and sizes to blocks already in balance, they added up to ten blocks precariously one on top of the other at the geometric centre rather than distributing them at the extremities, as did both the younger subjects ('it's like a see-saw, you put a block at each end') and those 8- to 9-year-olds who placed blocks equidistant from the point of contact.

If this 'geometric centre theory' is so pervasive and persistent despite negative theory-response (blocks fall when placed at the centre or balance at points other than the centre), how does the child ever come to change it? We postulate three interacting causes: (1) The ever-increasing pattern emerging from counter-examples, (2) changes taking place in the child's *general* conceptual competence and (3) the integration of the earlier proprioceptive information into a theory-in-action. Let us take up each of these points separately.

Frequent counter-examples do not alone induce a change in the child's behaviour. If they did, then progress could be achieved by simply providing a large number of counter-examples. The child must first form a unifying rule based on regular patterns he has observed: in this study, the geometric centre theory, which in fact accounts adequately for some blocks and for many situations in his daily life. Only when this theory is really consolidated and generalized, is he ready to recognize some form of unifying principle for the counter-examples which he earlier rejected as mere exceptions ('impossible to balance').

One obvious reason for giving up the geometric centre theory would be that the child considers weight and no longer exclusively length as being relevant. From previous studies, it is known that around 7 years children consider weight to be a significant property in problems involving equilibrium, and it is not until even later that the child differentiates between weight as an absolute property and weight as a force. Is this to imply that younger children are unaware that objects can be heavy or light or that imbalance is caused by heaviness? No, but what younger children do not understand is that weight plays a role in situations of *balance*. As the child attains conservation of weight and recognizes weight as being relevant in other situations, so in recognizing the regularity of counter-examples he looks by way of explanation for some aspect other than length, i.e. weight ('Oh, it's always just the opposite of what I expect . . . maybe it's this block glued to the end here'). And the first corrections away from the geometric centre took place with conspicuous weight blocks (type D) while inconspicuous weight blocks were still resolutely centred.

Though children may not have a conceptual understanding of the role of weight in equilibrium, it should be recalled that the younger children did react to weight communicated proprioceptively. It thus seems plausible that once weight is considered to be relevant, the prorioceptive information is integrated gradually into the child's theory-in-action. Interestingly enough, many corrections at this level were made away from the centre of gravity, denoting that the correction did not stem from proprioceptive information but from a conceptualized need for a change of position. Younger subjects relying on proprioceptive information alone rarely if ever made corrections in the wrong direction.

We have seen that three interrelating factors seem to bring about corrections to the weight items as distinct from the length items. Once this happens, do children then easily change their geometric centre theory and opt for a new and broader one? It is hypothesized that for some time they tend to hold on to the earlier theory. Among the conspicious weight blocks, for instance, type D (thick plywood base) were clearly easier for these subjects than type C (thin plywood base on which the weight of the glued block has more effect), because the centre of gravity of D blocks is much closer to the geometric centre than in C blocks. Correcting a D block from its geometric centre to its point of equilibrium is thus less of a challenge to the child's geometric centre theory than a C block which balances much nearer its extremity.

Furthermore, even when adjusting all conspicuous weight blocks children continued resolutely to centre the inconspicuous weight blocks. It would thus appear that the geometric centre theory was not abandoned when the child started taking negative responses and weight into account; it was retained for most situations where the theory could still hold true and a new theory, quite independent of it, was developed to deal with the most obvious exceptions. Length and weight were thus considered independently, which was apparent not only from the child's actions but also from the explanations he gave at the end of a session. For length blocks, weight was considered to play no role and symmetry of length was the sole property invoked; for conspicuous weight items, weight was used in the explanation. (For A blocks: 'it's the same length each side, there's no weight'; for C blocks: 'it's heavy on one side and long on the other . . . no in this one (D) there's weight all the way along the bar, in that one (C) there's only weight where the block is'.)

Gradually, and often almost reluctantly, the 7- to 8-year-olds began to make corrections also on the inconspicuous weight blocks. It is to be recalled that 4- to 5-year-olds did this immediately, but for different reasons. Whereas the young subjects were relying solely on the proprioceptive information, the older subjects (7;5–8;6 years) provided explicit references not only to equal length but simultaneously to equal weight for all items balanced at their geometric centre (types A and B). Previously length alone had sufficed to explain equilibrium. At this point, we observed many pauses during action sequences on the inconspicuous weight items: Place at geometric centre, correct slightly, pause, lift object, rotate object, pause, place at geometric centre, correct position slightly, release hold slightly, readjust carefully, pause longer, glance at a conspicuous weight item, pause, place again slowly at geometric centre, shake head, glance again at conspicuous weight item, then suddenly correct continuously and rapidly in the right direction until balance is achieved. Repetition of a success was thereafter immediate, even if the object was rotated. As the children were now really beginning to question the generality of their geometric centre theory, a negative response at the geometric centre sufficed to have the child rapidly make corrections towards the point of balance. We obviously do not mean to imply that he had a full, explicit understanding of the inverse relationship of weight and distance, but simply that he now implicitly understood the importance of both length and weight.

. . . A number of other apparently minor aspects of behaviour seem important. There is for example the manner in which children held the blocks. The very youngest children and many others at the outset of a session tended to hold blocks from above in one hand when trying to balance them and then to push with the same hand on the block above the point of contact. Next children tended to hold the blocks at each extremity with both hands, which is a much more informative method proprioceptively. Thus, the rather diffuse proprioceptive information by pushing with one hand above the point of contact, became a definite feeling of heaviness in one of the child's hands, indicating the side on which the block would fall (see figure 3). However, the child gradually seemed to realize that one of his hands was in fact superfluous. As his attention moved from his own actions on the blocks to the properties of the blocks, the child attempted (not without difficulty) to replace his hand by placing a small cube on top of the block as a counter-weight, or replaced his other hand by a cube underneath the block; thus providing a second support. The latter was not satisfactory for the child since the small cubes were purposely all lower or higher than the vertical distance between the table and the point of support: thus the block remained slanted. This again reinforced the need for either the use of counter-weights (rarely used spontaneously, except by the older subjects) or for corrections of the point of contact along the dimension chosen.

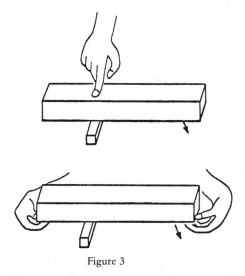

Figure 3

A second aspect was the order in which subjects chose to treat items in phase I where choice of order was left to the child. Many children (including all the youngest but also a certain proportion in the other age groups up to 7 years) chose blocks closest to them on the table in a haphazard order, not bothering to group identical or similar ones together. It was as if each block constituted a separate problem for them and as if there was no anticipation of the differences in complexity nor any effort to transfer acquired information intentionally during these initial attempts. Furthermore, when, after completing the free choice session, we then imposed a more 'informative' order (e.g. following C by D) children did finally begin to make transfers from one block to another. Only very gradually during a session, or more systematically for older subjects (as of roughly 7 years and including all subjects above 8;7 years), did children from the outset stretch out for blocks so as to group them in an organized fashion. When the children dealt with two seemingly analogous blocks, either spontaneously or because of the experimenter's imposed order, there were many erroneous yet informative transfers from one item to the next.

Discussion

What are the processes of discovery in history, in ontongenesis and during an experimental session? In his interesting book on Darwin's creativity, Gruber (1974) suggests that 'there is nothing necessarily creative in being immediately trapped by every original thought one has'. Indeed, in our particular field of inquiry, the processes of cognitive discovery involve far more than simply isolating the properties of weight and length. We have seen that action sequences are not merely a reflection of the child's implicit theories. The very organization and reorganization of the actions themselves, the lengthening of their sequences, their repetition and generalized application to new situations give rise to discoveries that will regulate the theories, just as the theories have a regulating effect on the action sequences. What is the role of experience or of the object's 'responses' in generating change?

It may seem surprising that an event as obvious as the falling of a block is not always clearly evaluated as negative theory-response but merely as negative action-response. While the child is solely success-oriented, all balancing – irrespective of which block – will be read as 'positive' information and all falling of blocks as 'negative'. However, if considered from the standpoint of theories-in-action, then the child's interpretation of the object's 'response' will depend on the block. For instance, for a child with the geometric centre theory, conspicuous or inconspicuous weight blocks in balance will, when not rejected as mere exceptions, be read as negative theory-response since such balancing indeed counteracts the child's theory-in-action. On the contrary, the balancing of a length block and the falling of any block placed at a point outside the geometric centre will be read by the child as positive (positive to his theory, though not immediately to his goal). And the reading of identical events can change from positive to negative or *vice versa* as the child modifies his theories.

Positive and negative action- and theory-responses seem to have varying roles at different times. While the child is exclusively success-oriented, i.e. concentrating on balancing, positive action-response is all-important. It encourages the child's natural tendency to repeat successful actions. Then gradually negative action-response shifts the child's attention to the means, i.e. 'how to balance'. At this point we witness experimentation for experimentation's sake; for attending to the means implies seeking knowledge of the approximate range of possible actions on an object. Koslowski and Bruner (1972) found a similar phenomenon when experimenting on young babies' use of a rotating level to obtain a distant object. The authors report a stage when babies continued experimenting with the various movements of the lever, thus becoming 'enmeshed in the means', ignoring the goal which they had meanwhile moved within their reach, whereas previously they had been solely goal-oriented.

As the child gradually begins to construct a theory for interpreting the regularity of positive action-responses, these become positive theory-responses. Negative responses remain action-responses until the child's theory is generalized and consolidated, after which they progressively become negative theory-responses, once the child becomes aware of their regularity. A futher important fact is that younger subjects make use of proprioceptive information in an uncontaminated fashion since they have not yet developed a unifying theory. For the more advanced subject the object's 'behaviour' is evaluated conceptually, and they are only able to use the proprioceptive information if they close their eyes.

As long as the child is predominantly success-oriented, there are rarely any pauses in his action sequences. As his attention shifts to means, however, pauses become more and more frequent in the course of the sequence. Only when goal and means are considered simultaneously do pauses *precede* action. Such differences in the occurrence of pauses are potentially meaningful for the observer.

Although negative responses are a necessary condition for progress, they are clearly not a sufficient one; in order to be effective, such responses must counteract a powerful theory-in-action, such as the geometric centre theory. It should be noted in passing that we purposely chose to speak of 'theories' and not of 'hypotheses' since the latter tend to have the connotation of intentionally seeking to verify. Previous research (Inhelder and Piaget, 1958) showed that the formal operational child was frequently capable of attempting to test hypotheses and verify theories by deliberately seeking counter-examples. In those experiments, however, tasks were often well beyond the capacities of the concrete operational child; his experimental method was therefore defined in terms of what was lacking as compared to the formal operational child. Our present research was aimed at elucidating the *positive* aspects of the younger child's behaviour by using simpler situations and looking more closely at how he goes about his task. Our observations indicate that the younger child does not intentionally *seek* counter-examples; rather, children in this research, whatever their theory-in-action (from the elementary need for physical contact to the more sophisticated geometric centre theory) constructed and generalized theories, and gradually *recognized* counterexamples. However, the earlier claim (Inhelder and Piaget, 1958) that 'at the concrete level, the child does not formulate any hypotheses' needs to be reconsidered in the light of the strong tendency of our children to act under the guidance of a powerful theory-in-action which involves far more than mere observation of immediate empirical reality. Nonetheless, their theories remain implicit, since the younger child clearly cannot reflect on hypothetical situations which might confirm or refute his theory. Indeed, although the child's action sequences bear eloquent witness to a theory-in-action implicit in his behaviour, this should not be taken as a capacity to conceptualize explicitly on what he is doing and why. Recent experimental work (Piaget 1974a, 1974b) has confirmed that a developmental gap exists between succeeding in action and being capable of explaining it.

Our present analysis is focused less on particular, explicit notions than on the gradual unification of ideas as observed in action sequences. There is no doubt that the generalized application of a theory will ultimately lead to discoveries which in turn serve to create new or broader theories. However, it seems possible for the child to experience surprise and to question his theory only if the prediction he makes emanates from an already powerful theory expressed in action. Our observations indicate that children hold on to their initial theory for as long as they can. Even when they finally do take counter-examples into consideration, they first prefer to create a new theory, quite independent of the first one, before finally attempting to unify all events under a single, broader theory.

The tendency to explain phenomena by a unified theory, the most general or simplest one possible, appears to be a natural aspect of the creative process, both for the child and the scientist. The construction of false theories or the over-generalization of limited ones are in effect productive processes. Over-generalization, a sometimes derogatory term, can be looked upon as the *creative simplification* of a problem by ignoring some of the complicating factors (such as weight in our study). This is implicit in the young child's behaviour but could be intentional in the scientist's. Overgeneralization is not only a means to simplify but also to unify; it is thus not surprising that the child and the scientist often refuse counter-examples since they complicate the unification process. However, to be capable of unifying positive examples implies that one is equally capable of attempting to find a unifying principle to cover counter-examples.

The history of physics abounds in examples analogous to those we have observed among children. Dugas (1950) recalls that the really creative scientists were those who did not merely study the positive examples of well-known principles but who endeavoured to *extend* the principles to other phenomena. It is in this way that scientists, and children, are able to discover new properties which in turn make it possible for new theories to be constructed. And psychology experiments on adults (Claparède, 1934; Miller, Gallanter, and Pribam, 1960; Wason and Johnson-Laird, 1972) illustrate the general tendency to construct powerful, yet often inappropriate, hypotheses which adults try to verify rather than to falsify. This temporarily blinds the adult to counter-examples which should actually suffice to have them reject their hypothesis immediately. Our present results on young children seem to point to the fact that constructing and extending a powerful theory-in-action is a very general aspect of discovery which has a deep-rooted function. . .

19. 'On the failure to eliminate hypotheses . . .' – a second look [1]

P. C. Wason

It is easy to obtain confirmations or verifications for nearly every theory – if we look for confirmation.

Popper

In my paper, 'On the failure to eliminate hypotheses in a conceptual task' (Wason, 1960), I discussed an experiment about the extent to which people acquire confirming and disconfirming evidence for their beliefs about a rule.

The subjects were told that the series, 2 4 6, conformed to a simple rule which they had to discover by generating successive series of their own. After each series they were told only whether their numbers conformed to the rule which was 'numbers in increasing order of magnitude'.

The paper provoked some criticism, e.g. 'the subjects' task is misleading' (Wetherick, 1962); 'we question whether the model is an appropriate one' (L. H. Shaffer, personal communication). Two points especially aroused suspicion and anxiety: 1. The rule was deemed grossly unfair in the sense that few subjects would consider order of magnitude to be a rule. 2. The generation of a large number of positive instances of a hypothesis does not increase the probability of its correctness, i.e. confirming evidence alone is completely useless. It seems that the rationale of the experiment was not made clear. This second look attempts both to clarify its aims and to discuss some subsequent research.

Unlike most concept attainment tasks the point was not to see whether the subjects discovered the rule. The point was to see how they behaved when their hypotheses had been corroborated by confirming evidence. This aim necessitates a task in which a number of plausible hypotheses, other than the correct rule, will spontaneously occur to the subjects. These hypotheses should be more specific than the correct rule, but any series of numbers which satisfy them should also satisfy the correct rule, i.e. these hypotheses should entail the rule. Hence the very general 'unfair' rule was selected in order to facilitate more

[1] First published in P. C. Wason and P. N. Johnson-Laird, *Thinking and Reasoning* (Harmondsworth, Middx.: Penguin, 1968).

307

specific hypotheses such as, 'an equal interval between three ascending numbers' (arithmetic progression).

What can the subjects do with their hypotheses? Suppose a subject had entertained the hypothesis, 'intervals of two between ascending numbers', on the strength of these confirming instances: 8 10 12, 15 17 19, 20 22 24. He could announce his hypothesis to the experimenter as being the rule, or he could generate a series such as 3 6 9 in order to test his hypothesis. If he is told that such a series conforms to the rule, as this one does, then he has eliminated 'intervals of two' decisively. Thus the subject can either offer his hypotheses to the experimenter for judgment and wait for him to say, 'that isn't the rule', or 'that is the rule', or he can acquire this knowledge by himself by the internalized process of elimination which De Groot (1965), in a different context, calls 'negative proof'. This consists essentially in an attempt to refute one's own hypotheses rather than simply trying to confirm them. It is clearly the sort of procedure which occurs in a scientist's thinking and experimenting. In real life inferences can only be assessed in relation to the evidence for them – there is no authority to pronounce them right or wrong.

The task was intended to simulate the understanding of an event for which several superficial explanations are possible. Since the real explanation would be merely a concealed component in the superficial ones it will most frequently defy detection until the more obvious characteristics have been varied. The analogy is not to creative thinking but to the search for simplicity, in the sense of minimal assumptions.

Although the task is artificial it does possess two novel features. The correct rule cannot be proved but any incorrect hypothesis can be disproved. Moreover, an infinite number of series exemplifying any hypothesis can be generated. The subject cannot run out of numbers which confirm his hypotheses. Secondly, the subject is not shown stimuli from which he can select instances as possible evidence. He has to generate both his own hypotheses and his own evidence.

The details of the experiment and the quantitative treatment of the results may be found in the original paper. Only an outline will be given here. The subjects, twenty-nine undergraduates, were told that the rule was concerned with a relation between three numbers, and it was stressed that they were to announce their hypotheses about it only when they were highly confident that they were correct. At each trial the subjects wrote down both their series and their reasons for choosing it on a record sheet. The experimenter said each time either, 'those numbers conform to the rule', or 'those numbers do not conform to the rule', according to whether they were in an increasing order of magnitude. If the correct rule was announced, the experiment was concluded. If an incorrect rule was announced, the subjects were told it was wrong and asked to carry on with the task. The session continued until the correct rule was announced, or the time exceeded forty-five minutes, or the subject gave up.

Twenty-two out of the twenty-nine subjects announced at least one incorrect rule, nine of these announced a second incorrect rule, and two of these nine announced a third incorrect rule. Six subjects announced the correct rule without any incorrect ones, and the results showed that these subjects varied their hypotheses much more frequently than those who announced one incorrect rule. Six representative protocols are given below, the first three from subjects who announced the correct rule without any incorrect ones, and the last three from those who made one or more incorrect announcements. The words which follow each series are the hypotheses, and the announcement of rules is printed in italics.

Examples of the protocols

No. 1. Female, aged 25

12 24 36: unit figures are even and increase in twos; 8 10 12: even numbers increasing in twos; 2 6 10: even numbers increasing in fours; 6 4 2: even numbers decreasing in twos; 2 6 8: even numbers ascending; 8 54 98: even numbers ascending; 1 17 23: ascending numbers; 1 18 23: ascending numbers; 1 2 3: ascending numbers.
The rule is ascending numbers (9 minutes).

No. 2. Female, aged 21

3 6 9: three goes into the second figure twice and into the third figure three times; 2 4 8: perhaps the figures have to have an L.C.D.; 2 4 10: same reason; 2 5 10: the second number does not have to be divided by the first one; 10 6 4: the highest number must go last; 4 6 10: the first number must be the lowest; 2 3 5: it is only the order that counts; 4 5 6: same reason; 1 7 13: same reason.
The rule is that the figures must be in numerical order (16 minutes).

No. 3. Male, aged 25

8 10 12: continuous series of even numbers; 14 16 18: continuous series of even numbers; 20 22 24: continuous series of even numbers; 3 5 7: continuous series of odd numbers; 1 2 3: continuous series but with smaller intervals; 3 2 1: reverse; 2 4 8: doubling series; 2 2 4: two numbers the same; 6 4 2: reverse of original numbers; 1 9 112: simple ascending numbers.
The rule is any ascending series of different numbers (10 minutes).

No. 4. Female, aged 19

8 10 12: two added each time; 14 16 18: even numbers in order of magnitude; 20 22 24: same reason; 1 3 5: two added to preceding number.
The rule is that by starting with any number two is added each time to form the next number.
2 6 10: middle number is the arithmetic mean of the other two; 1 50 99: same reason.
The rule is that the middle number is the arithmetic mean of the other two.
3 10 17: same number, seven, added each time; 0 3 6: three added each time.
The rule is that the difference between two numbers next to each other is the same.
12 8 4: the same number is subtracted each time to form the next number.
The rule is adding a number, always the same one to form the next number.
1 4 9: any three numbers in order of magnitude.
The rule is any three numbers in order of magnitude (17 minutes).

No. 5. Female, aged 19

1 3 5: add two to each number to give the following one; 16 18 20: to test the theory that it is simply a progression of two. These are chosen so that they are more complex and not

merely simple numbers; 99 101 103: to test the progression of two theory, using odd numbers.

As these numbers can hardly have any other connection, unless it is very remote, the rule is a progression of adding two, in other words either all even or all odd numbers.

1 5 9: the average of the two numbers on the outside is the number between them.

The rule is that central figure is the mean of the two external ones.

6 10 14; difference between the first two numbers, added to the second number gives the third; 7 11 15: to test this theory; 2 25 48: to test this theory.

The rule is that the difference between the first two figures added to the second figure gives the third.

7 9 11, 11 12 13, 12 9 8, 77 75 71

Subject gives up (45 minutes).

No. 6. Male, aged 23

8 10 12: step interval of two; 7 9 11: with numbers not divisible by two; 1 3 5: to see if rule may apply to numbers starting at two and upwards; 3 5 1: the numbers do not necessarily have to be in ascending or descending order; 5 3 1: could be in descending order.

The rule is that the three numbers must be in ascending order separated by intervals of two.

11 13 15: must have one number below ten in the series; 1 6 11: ascending series with regular step interval.

The rule is that the three numbers must be in an ascending series and separated by regular step intervals.

The rule is that the first number can be arbitrarily chosen; the second number must be greater than the first and can be arbitrarily chosen; the third number is larger than the second by the same amount as the second is larger than the first.

1 3 13: any three numbers in ascending order.

The rule is that the three numbers need have no relationship with each other, except that the second is larger than the first, and the third larger than the second (38 minutes).

It will be noted that in the first three protocols specific hypotheses are first of all considered, i.e. 'numbers increasing in intervals of two', 'successive multiples', and 'a continuous series of even numbers'. But in each case these hypotheses are eliminated by the second, third or fourth series. On the other hand, in the last three protocols examples of fixated behaviour can be found. In No. 4 virtually the same rule of arithmetic progression is announced three times in different terms. Similarly, in No. 5 the same rule is announced twice. In No. 6 a particularly interesting phenomenon occurs which was exhibited by two other subjects. The same rule is merely reformulated after it had been pronounced wrong, but before generating any further series. It would seem that in such cases there was an almost obsessional regard for verbal precision.

The most frequent incorrect rules were 'numbers increasing in intervals of two', 'increasing multiples of the first number', 'consecutive even numbers' and 'arithmetic progression'. A few rules were announced only once or twice throughout the task, e.g. 'arithmetic or geometric progression', 'the second number is the first number plus one and the third is the first number plus four'. (It is of interest to note that the latter rule is contradicted by the initial series, 2 4 6.)

After the announcement of an incorrect rule it would be expected, on a rational basis, that a high proportion of the immediately succeeding series would be inconsistent with the rule just announced, i.e. subjects would relinquish their hypotheses. In fact, over the entire experiment, sixteen such series were consistent and fifteen inconsistent with the rule announced. This experiment stongly suggested that the subjects were either unwilling, or unable to eliminate their hypotheses in this task.

In order to get more insight into the subjects' behaviour I conducted two further experiments. The first one, carried out in 1960, tried to determine whether subjects were merely unwilling to eliminate their hypotheses. One group of subjects was given ten shillings and told they could keep it if they announced the correct rule, but would forfeit half-a-crown for every incorrect rule announced. A control group did the same task without the money. The financial incentive only had the effect of significantly increasing the number of series generated before making an announcement. It appeared to have no effect on the tendency to announce incorrect rules as such. One subject remarked sourly, 'Dr Wason, the average subject is more concerned with pleasing the experimenter than with making money.' The failure to eliminate does not seem to be due to lack of motivation.

In the second experiment, which was carried out at Harvard in 1963, with the assistance of Martin Katzman, an improved technique was used. The twenty-two subjects (students) were told that they could announce only one rule during the task. If an incorrect rule was announced, they were not told it was wrong, but were asked, 'if you were wrong, how could you find out?' This question was asked in sixteen cases, i.e. to 73 per cent of the sample. Nine subjects replied that they would continue to generate series consistent with their hypotheses and wait for one to be negative; two replied that they would try out other hypotheses; two that they would generate series inconsistent with their hypotheses (the rational answer); three replied that no other rules were possible. 'I can't be wrong since my rule is correct for those numbers.' 'Rules are relative. If you were the subject and I were the experimenter then I should be right.' One subject did not make any announcement. Unfortunately he developed psychotic symptoms in the middle of the experiment and had to be removed by ambulance. Nothing similar has occurred with any other subject before or since. The present task seems to demand a level of functioning which most people readily tolerate, but it may impose severe strain on a few predisposed individuals: numbers and number-systems, for instance, sometimes have a peculiar fascination for people suffering from schizophrenia.

These subsidiary experiments suggest that in an abstract task most people are unable to use the procedure of negative proof – it would appear to be a totally alien concept. In 1961 Tirril Gatty did an experiment concerned mainly with correlations between behaviour in the task and the personality variables of 'rigidity', 'flexibility', 'ascendancy' and 'submissiveness'. None of the correlations approached significance. However, in an ingenious pilot study the subjects (students) were given an 'eliminative set', i.e. an instruction to discover the possible rules which *could* hold for the series, 2 4 6, other than the particular rule which the experimenter had in mind. The subjects were told to announce these 'not-rules' only when they were highly confident that they had discovered them. They were also told that if, in performing their main task, they happened to become completely confident about the correct rule, they were to announce that as well. Thus the subjects were alerted to the possibility of different rules, and invited directly to eliminate hypotheses.

These instructions had little effect. Six out of the eleven subjects announced at least one incorrect hypothesis as being *the correct rule*. These incorrect hypotheses were of the same type as those in my original experiment. The 'not-rules' were also similar but a few were more idiosyncratic, e.g. 'each number has the same number of digits', 'all the numbers must be different'. It is of interest to note that this latter rule is even more general than the correct one. Three subjects reformulated their 'not-rules', two doing so twice. Five subjects, in spite of the instructions, generated series to confirm a hypothesis first of all, and only then attempted to eliminate. Only two of the eleven subjects appreciated that one series was sufficient to prove conclusively that a hypothesis was incorrect. It would seem that the positive set is so strong in this task that specific instructions to eliminate do not break it.

What does apparently diminish this set, to some extent, is the initial presentation of a negative rather than a positive series, i.e. a series which does not conform to the rule. In 1962 Barbara Thompson retained the same rule, numbers in increasing order of magnitude, but gave her subjects the negative series, 7 5 3, with instructions to discover what relation must exist between three numbers in order for them not to conform to the rule. Similarly, Wetherick (1962) presented the negative series, 4 2 6, and instructed his subjects to discover the rule. In neither of these experiments were the results significant, but in both there was a trend suggesting that it is helpful to start with a negative series. The results, of course, are hardly surprising because a series which is not in increasing order of magnitude would be very likely to alert the subject to the possibility of order being relevant. Numbers, by convention, generally go up rather than down. The rule, instead of being an implicit component in a more specific hypothesis, becomes a factor of obvious importance.

All these experiments have been concerned with a relation between three numbers. In 1962 Jonathan Penrose attempted to generalize the problem in a pilot study by using as his task the inverted form of the game of 'Twenty Questions'. In the ordinary game a person asks questions of increasing specificity in order to discover a particular object. In the inverted game a person thinks of a logical class which another person has to discover by finding out whether objects fall under it. Penrose selected the class of 'living things' (analogous to numbers in increasing order of magnitude), and gave as the initial instance 'a Siamese cat' (analogous to the series 2 4 6). The subjects (students) were instructed to keep a written record of both their instances and their hypotheses. They were told to announce the class only when they were highly confident they had discovered it.

Only three out of the ten subjects announced the correct class without announcing any incorrect ones. 47·1 per cent of their instances confirmed their hypotheses and 52·9 per cent disconfirmed them. On the other hand, 86·5 per cent of the instances generated by the remaining subjects confirmed their hypotheses and only 13·5 per cent disconfirmed them. All the instances generated by the successful subjects, which resulted in the refutation of an hypothesis, led to consistent changes of hypotheses. But among the unsuccessful subjects there were eleven cases in which hypotheses were retained although logically excluded by one or more instances. A few cases of extreme fixedness of behaviour were observed. For example, one subject only changed his hypothesis from 'pets' to 'animals' over a period of twelve trials. These results suggest that the phenomena observed in the previous experiments are not specific to numbers.

In spite of the small samples used in these experiments, there would appear to be compelling evidence to indicate that even intelligent individuals adhere to their own hypotheses with remarkable tenacity when they can produce confirming evidence for them. What makes people so narrow minded and so cognitively prejudiced? Why did they find these trivial games so difficult?

One answer is that these tasks are simply *Einstellung* problems similar to Luchins's (1942) jar problems. The subjects appeared to display rigid or fixated patterns of behaviour because they failed to overcome the set created by their confirming evidence. In my original experiment, however, a hypothesis such as arithmetic progression might have been announced out of desperation – simply because the subject could not imagine any more general rule. Indeed, Wetherick has argued that hypotheses are not directly eliminated at all, but are only changed when another more general rule comes to mind (Wetherick, 1962; Wason, 1962). This argument is perhaps plausible when an individual progresses from relatively specific hypotheses, e.g. 'increasing intervals of two', to more general ones, e.g. 'arithmetic progression'. But it loses much of its force when the progression is in the opposite direction – when simple hypotheses are eliminated and more complex and vulnerable hypotheses are conceived. These cases are rare but they are of the greatest interest. A beautiful example was observed by Gatty (1961). One of her subjects generated eight series and at the same time eliminated these hypotheses, 'increasing intervals of two' and 'the second number is the first number times two, and the third is the second number plus two'. He then announced this hypothesis as the rule: 'the first and second numbers are random but the third is the second plus two.' On being told it was wrong he next acquired further evidence (six series) and announced this hypothesis as the rule: 'the first and second numbers are random but the first is smaller than the second, and the third is the second plus two.' On being told that it was also wrong he proceeded as follows:

261 263 101, 3 17 17, 51 53 56, 671 671 3, 671 673 900, 42 43 45, 41 43 42, 41 43 67, 67 43 45. *The rule is that either the first number equals the second minus two, and the third is random but greater than the second, or the third number equals the second plus two, and the first is random but less than the second.* (Subject gives up: 50 minutes.)

It seems highly probable that this subject could have conceived other hypotheses, as complex and as arbitrary as those which he announced, had he not been bemused by the confirming evidence for his own hypotheses. It was just this evidence which provided a sufficient warrant to make his particular hypotheses seem correct. There is no suggestion in his protocol that he was in any way bereft of ideas, or lacking in originality.

If one knows the correct rule in advance, then of course the subjects' behaviour may seem quixotic and absurd. It is only by doing the task or by watching someone else perform it, that one can really appreciate the helpless predicament into which the subjects so easily fall. At the end of the session in my original experiment the majority of the subjects, who had announced incorrect rules, were surprised and amused by what they recognized to be their own stupidity, but they claimed the experience, far from being humiliating, was both instructive and even cathartic. On the other hand, those subjects who announced the correct rule without announcing any incorrect ones, adopted an air of bland condescension and could not see any point in the experiment.

In the real world, as opposed to the psychological laboratory, the fixated obsessional behaviour of some of the subjects would be analagous to that of a person who is thinking within a closed system – a system which defies refutation. These experiments demonstrate, on a minature scale, how dogmatic thinking and the refusal to entertain the possibility of alternatives can easily result in error.

20. Confirmation bias in a simulated research environment: an experimental study of scientific inference [1]

Clifford R. Mynatt, Michael E. Doherty, and Ryan D. Tweney

. . . Numerous counter-arguments to Hume's sceptical conclusions about scientific inference have been proposed (see Salmon, 1967), one of the more widely accepted being Popper's (1959, 1963) falsification position. Given a conditional statement of the form 'if p then q', showing that q is true does not establish either the truth or falsity of p. However, if q is false, then p must be false. Since nearly all scientific propositions are of this form, where p is a general theory or law and q a predicted event, Popper argues that the only justifiable inference from data about such propositions is whether or not they have been falsified. He concludes that scientists should not attempt to confirm hypotheses, but rather should conduct research so as to maximize the likelihood of disconfirmation.

A related position, based on pragmatic and historical rather than logical considerations, is Platt's (1964) 'strong inference' strategy. This consists of first generating multiple hypotheses relevant to a particular phenomenon and then performing experimental tests to eliminate (i.e. falsify) as many of these as possible. The procedure involves a cycle of multiple hypotheses, experimental elimination of hypotheses, new multiple hypotheses, etc. Platt urges that, above all, the scientist should not concentrate upon the confirmation of a single, favourite hypothesis and thereby become wedded to an incorrect theory. Popper's and Platt's prescriptions for scientific inquiry differ in one important respect. Popper exhorts the scientist to direct his attention to a particular kind of data search, i.e. data inconsistent with the particular hypothesis under test. Platt accepts the utility of falsification, but stresses that it should be done in the context of multiple alternative hypotheses.

Both theories raise important questions about the actual behaviour of scientists (and, indeed, people in general) which cannot be answered adequately by either logical or historical analysis. One question is whether disconfirmatory evidence is sought or recognized; a second is whether alternative hypotheses are sought or examined. Anecdotal evidence seems to suggest that the answer to both questions may be 'no'. Examples abound of scientists clinging to pet

[1] Excerpts from the paper in *Quarterly Journal of Experimental Psychology*, **29** (1977), 85–95.

theories and refusing to seek alternatives in the face of large amounts of contradictory data (see Kuhn, 1970). Objective evidence, however, is scant.

Wason (1968) [see Reading 9 above] has conducted several experiments on
inferential reasoning in which subjects were given conditional rules of the form
'if p then q', where p was a statement about one side of a stimulus card and q a
statement about the other side. Four stimulus cards, corresponding to p, not-p,
q, and not-q were provided. The subjects' task was to indicate those cards – and
only those cards – which had to be turned over in order to determine if the rule
was true or false. Most subjects chose only p, or p and q. The only cards that can
falsify the rule, however are p and not-q. Since the not-q card is almost never
selected, the results indicate a strong tendency to seek confirmatory rather than
disconfirmatory evidence. This bias for selecting confirmatory evidence has
proved remarkable difficult to eradicate (see Wason and Johnson-Laird, 1972,
pp. 171–201).

In another set of experiments, Wason (1960, Reading 19) also found evidence
of failure to consider alternative hypotheses. . . With some notable exceptions,
what subjects did not do was to generate and eliminate alternative rules in a systematic fashion. Somewhat similar results have been reported by Miller (1967).
Finally, Mitroff (1974), in a large-scale nonexperimental study of NASA scientists, reports that a strong confirmation bias existed among many members of this
group. He cites numerous examples of these scientists' verbalizations of their own
and other scientists' obduracy in the face of data as evidence for this conclusion.

All the above evidence suggests that a bias in favour of confirmatory evidence
may be a general characteristic of human reasoning. This bias may be expressed
either as a failure to seek or utilize data which are inconsistent with a single
hypothesis under test, contrary to Popper's falsification strategy, or it may be
expressed as a failure to seek or utilize evidence for alternative hypotheses,
contrary to Platt's strong inference strategy.

Unfortunately, there has been little experimental research on reasoning and
inference processes in settings which resemble real world situations such as
those in which scientific inquiry occurs. The Wason research, which appears to
us to be dealing most closely with the type of reasoning involved in scientific
inference, has utilized relatively content-free tasks which lack much of the
concrete quality of science as it occurs in the real world. Indeed, in at least one
situation in which subjects were given a realistic, non-abstract task (Johnson-
Laird, Legrenzi, and Legrenzi, 1972), they seemed quite capable of seeking and
utilizing falsifying information. It is not known, however, what specific task
requirements are necessary to produce this result.

The purpose of the present study is to investigate inference behaviour in a
setting designed to resemble the conditions under which actual science is done.
It poses two questions. First: Do subjects tend to select situations for testing
their hypotheses which allow only confirmatory observations rather than selecting situations which allow alternative hypotheses to be tested? Second: Do
subjects who obtain direct falsifying evidence change hypotheses?

A fairly complex, dynamic environment was employed in which subjects were able to test concrete hypotheses by selecting various experiments to perform. Some of these experiments could, given a particular hypothesis, produce only confirmatory evidence for that hypothesis. Other experiments allowed the subject to test alternative hypotheses. One allowed direct falsification.

Method

The simulated scientific environment was designed as a controlled setting in which the behaviour of subjects could be closely monitored and which would mirror the qualities of actual research situations. The following general characteristics were deemed necessary for any such system:

1. The environment should have an 'object quality'. That is, events and objects should have a perceptual 'reality' similar to events and objects in the real world.

2. The environment should be lawful. A few simple equations should describe fully the relationships among the elements of the system.

3. The environment should appear complex. The simplicity of the underlying laws should be apparent only after a large amount of careful observations and experimentation.

4. The environment should be dynamic and interactive. Subjects should be able to make observations, plan and carry out experiments, etc.

5. The attempt to understand the environment should be interesting and challenging.

These characteristics were implemented by using an on-line computer which allowed the artificial research environment to be visually displayed to subjects and to be manipulated by them in an interactive mode. The subjects were forty-five undergraduates drawn from the Introductory Psychology subject pool at Bowling Green State University. . . The computer program allowed stationary figures with one of three different shapes (triangles, squares, or discs) to be displayed. Each stationary figure had one of two different brightness levels: all points enclosed by the figure lit or half of the points enclosed by the figure lit. These levels will be identified subsequently as the ratio of the number of points lit to total points, that is, 1·0 and 0·5, respectively. A particular arrangement of figures will be referred to as a 'screen'. Each such screen corresponds to one view of the total imaginable universe defined by the laws of the system.

A programmed keyboard command could be used by subjects to cause a small lighted dot or 'particle' to move by small steps from a fixed position in the upper left corner of each screen at a speed of approximately 0·6 cm/sec toward any point on the screen. A circular, non-visible boundary extended 4·2 cm beyond the geometric centres of some of the figures. Whenever a particle encountered a boundary, its motion ceased. Only figures with brightness ratios of 0·5 had such boundaries. All other aspects of the stationary figures, such as size, shape, location, etc., had no effect on particle motion and, hence, were irrelevant cues.

Procedure

Subjects were given printed instructions on how to use the keyboard, then shown the first screen which contained an 0·5 triangle, a 1·0 square, and a 1·0 disc. They could fire as many particles as they wished at any part of the screen, following which they were asked to write down an hypothesis which would account for the motion of the particles.

They were then shown a second screen on which were several 1·0 squares and discs, an 0·5 triangle, and a 1·0 triangle in close proximity to an 0·5 disc (see figure 1). The last two features were so close together that the triangle was completely inside the boundary of the disc and were arranged so that the disc was behind the triangle, relative to the location from which particles were fired. Subjects again fired as many particles as they wished and were instructed to write down an hypothesis which would account for the motion of the particles on both of the first two screens. They were told that this hypothesis could be the same as their first one, or that it could be different if evidence from the second screen had changed their minds. This hypothesis will be identified subsequently as the subjects' 'initial hypothesis'.

The purpose of the first two screens was to make probable the occurrence of hypotheses focusing on triangles. Shape and brightness were confounded on both screens, and we assumed that shape would be the more salient cue.

Subjects were then randomly assigned to one of three instructional treatments:

1. *Instructions to confirm*. Subjects were given written instructions which stated that the basic job of a scientist was to confirm theories and hypotheses. They were given an historical example of such a confirmation and told to try to confirm their hypotheses about particle motion.

2. *Instructions to disconfirm*. These were identical to the confirmation instructions except that subjects were told that the basic job of a scientist was to disprove or disconfirm theories and hypotheses. An historical example of scientific disconfirmation was given and subjects were instructed to attempt to disconfirm their hypotheses.

3. *Instructions to test*. These were identical to the preceding instructions except that subjects were simply told that the job of a scientist was to 'test theories and hypotheses', and that they were to test their own hypotheses about particle motion. They were given no further examples or instructions.

Dependent variables

Paired screen choices

After assignment to an instructional treatment, all subjects were shown ten pairs of photographs of screens and asked to choose the one member of each pair on which they would prefer to fire additional particles to obtain more evidence concerning their hypothesis. Six of the pairs were designed so that, given a triangle hypothesis, one of the screens could produce only confirmatory evidence (see table 1). For example, on pair 9, screen A contained a single 0·5 triangle and screen B contained a single 0·5 disc. The subjects could choose a screen, (A), which contained a feature similar to features which had apparently stopped particles on the first two screens; or they could choose a screen, (B), with a feature which had not been previously encountered in isolation. Subjects who were seeking confirmatory evidence for the hypothesis 'Triangles stop the particle' should, therefore, choose (A) over (B). The other four pairs were designed so that neither screen would be more likely than the other to produce confirmatory evidence.

INPUT PARTICLE DIRECTION?

Figure 1. Second screen
Note. Textured features are those having 0·5 brightness levels. Particles were fired from the grid in the upper left of the screen.

Subjects who were attempting to test alternatives to a triangle hypothesis should show a very different set of choice responses. On pair 9, for example, such a subject should not select screen A (a single 0·5 triangle). Rather, he should select screen B (a single 0·5 disc), since he can on this screen test the hypothesis that some characteristic of the features other then triangularity affects particle motion (e.g. brightness ratio). It should be noted that one screen, 5-B, can provide absolute, unambiguous disconfirmation of a triangle hypothesis. On this screen, a particle would travel completely through the 1·0 triangle.

Table 1. Paired screen descriptions

Pair no.		Screen A		Screen B
1	†	0·5 disc; 1·0 square	*	0·5 triangel; 1·0 square
2	*	0·5 triangle	†	0·5 square
3		1·0 square; 1·0 disc		1·0 square; 1·0 square
4	†	0·5 disc; 0·5 disc	*	0·5 disc; 0·5 triangle
5		0·5 triangle	‡	1·0 triangle
6		1·0 square		1·0 disc
7	*	1·0 triangle; 0·5 square	†	1·0 disc; 0·5 square
8		1·0 square		1·0 disc; 1·0 disc
9	*	0·5 triangle	†	0·5 disc
10	†	1·0 disc; 0·5 disc	*	0·5 triangle; 1·0 disc

Note. For all screens, the particle firing grid was in the upper left corner as in figure 1. All stationary figures were positioned in the lower middle or the lower right corner of the screens. When two figures were present, the distance between the centres of the figures was approximatly 2 cm (e.g. the disc and triangle in the lower right corner of the screen shown in figure 1).

* Confirmatory choices for subjects with triangle hypotheses.
† A particle fired at the figures on this screen would stop, providing evidence for an alternative to a triangle hypothesis.
‡ A particle fired at the triangle on this screen would not stop, logically disconfirming a triangle hypothesis.

Free responses

After the paired screen tasks, subjects were given the opportunity to fire particles on either chosen or non-chosen screens, but only one member of each pair (a restriction some subjects ignored). They were instructed to record what happened on each firing; whether or not their hypotheses changed and, if so, why; and, after firing as many particles as they wished on as many of the ten screens as they wished, to write down their final hypotheses. All subject input to the computer was automatically recorded. Thus, it was possible to determine, for example, whether a subject had ever observed the particle stopping on one of the screens not containing the triangles (e.g. 9-B).

Results

Subjects were first categorized by their initial hypotheses. Three categories were used: (a) Triangle, which included hypotheses with at least some mention of triangularity but no mention of brightness; (b) Brightness, which included hypotheses with any mention at all of brightness; and (c) Other. Across conditions, twenty subjects had initial triangle hypotheses; twelve subjects had initial brightness hypotheses; and thirteen subjects had initial hypotheses which were classified as 'other'. Of the twenty subjects classified as having initial triangle hypotheses, none mentioned brightness and fifteen mentioned nothing other than triangularity. These twenty subjects are of primary interest since the paired screen task was designed for subjects with a triangle hypothesis.

Paired screen data

The paired screen choice data for the twenty subjects with initial triangle hypotheses are shown in table 2. The choice data were collapsed across the three conditions, producing an overall mean proportion of confirmatory choices of 0·71. This mean proportion differed significantly from an expected mean proportion of 0·50 under a null hypothesis of random choice ($t = 4·31$, $df = 19$, $p <$ 0·01). That this effect was due to the subjects' initial hypothesis, and not to some artifact of the choice procedure, is demonstrated by the fact that the comparable proportions for subjects with initial brightness hypotheses (0·44 across conditions) and other hypotheses (0·47 across conditions) did not differ from an expected mean proportion of 0·50. The tendency to choose confirmatory screens was present from the very first pair of screens. Fifteen of the twenty subjects chose screen B (a confirmatory choice) on pair 1.

Table 2. Paired screen choice data for subjects with initial triangle hypotheses (N= 20)

Condition	
Test	n= 7
	0·71
Disconfirm	n= 6
	0·70
Confirm	n= 7
	0·71
Overall mean proportion= 0·71	

Note. Cell entries are numbers of subjects (n) in each condition who had an initial triangle hypothesis, and the mean proportion of confirmatory choices for these subjects.

Free response data

The free response data of the twenty subjects with initial triangle hypotheses were examined with three questions in mind:

1. Did subjects obtain evidence logically falsifying a triangle hypothesis by firing a particle on screen 5–B at the 1·0 triangle?

2. Did subjects make observations which would unambiguously support alternative hypotheses by firing a particle on a screen where a figure other than a triangle stopped the particle motion?

3. If subjects obtained evidence of the type described in (1) and (2), what changes, if any, did they make in their incorrect initial hypotheses?

Final hypotheses were categorized as being: (a) correct or partially correct (i.e. brightness clearly identified as the only variable influencing particle motion or some mention of brightness but with irrelevant variables added); or (b) incorrect. Any of the twenty subjects whose final hypothesis is in category (a) has, of course, changed his hypothesis. The relevant data are summarized in table 3.

Table 3. Free response data for subjects with initial triangle hypotheses (N = 20)

Free response choices	Correct or partially correct	Incorrect
No Fal No Alt	2	2
No Fal Alt	2	3
Fal No Alt	0	0
Fal Alt	10	1

Note. Fal Means that the subject fired a particle at the triangle on screen 5-B and has therefore received evidence falsifying a triangle hypothesis. Alt means that the subject fired a particle at a 0·5 brightness, non-triangular feature and has therefore received evidence supportive of an alternative to a triangle hypothesis.

Of the eleven subjects who made logically falsifying observations, ten had final hypotheses which were correct or partially correct. Of the nine who did not make a falsifying observation, only four achieved a correct or partially correct final hypothesis. These differences are significant using a chi-square test ($\chi^2 = 5\cdot08$, $df = 1$, $p < 0\cdot05$).

Final hypothesis data

All subjects, regardless of initial hypothesis, were categorized by their final hypotheses. The same two categories (correct or partially correct, and incorrect) were again used. These data are shown in table 4. A χ^2 test of the frequencies in the Confirm and Disconfirm conditions approached, but did not reach, significance ($\chi^2 = 3\cdot39$, $df = 1$, $p < 0\cdot10$).

Initial vs. final hypothesis data

Finally, all subjects were categorized by both initial and final hypotheses. The same categories as above were used. There were no significant differences across instructional treatments and the data were collapsed across treatments. These data are shown in table 5. A chi-square test of the frequencies in table 5 was significant ($\chi^2 = 13.42$, $df = 2$, $p < 0.01$).

Table 4. Final hypotheses data for all subjects (N = 45)

Condition	Correct or partially correct	Incorrect
Test	11	4
Disconfirm	11	4
Confirm	6	9
Overall	28	17

Note. Cell entries are number of subjects in each category.

Table 5. Initial and final hypotheses for all subjects (N = 45)

| | Final hypothesis | |
Initial hyppothesis	Correct or partially correct	Incorrect
Brightness	11	1
Triangle	14	6
Other	3	10
Overall	28	17

Note. Cell entries are number of subjects in each category across all three conditions.

Discussion

Two major conclusions can be drawn from these results. First, there is substantial evidence from the paired screen choice data that subjects failed to consider alternative hypotheses. Subjects who started with triangle hypotheses, regardless of which condition they were in, chose at a much higher than chance rate screens which could only confirm such hypotheses. Thus, they did not, in general, choose screens which would allow them to test alternatives to their initial hypotheses (e.g. by choosing screens with a square or disc). These results, which are remarkably similar to those found by Wason (1960, Reading 19), suggest that confirmation bias of this sort may be a general cognitive process which is not limited to abstract tasks. Wason's subjects generally failed to test alternatives when attempting to recover a numerical rule, just as our subjects failed to test alternatives when trying to discover the laws of our artificial universe.

Second, while the paired screen choice data provide strong support for a bias involving failure to consider alternative hypotheses, the free response data indicated that subjects could use falsifying data once they got it. Among those subjects who had an initial triangle hypothesis, nearly all (91 per cent) who obtained unambiguous falsifying evidence for this hypothesis changed to a correct or partially correct hypothesis. Less than half (44 per cent) of such subjects who did not obtain falsifying evidence reached a correct or partially correct solution. Thus, if confronted with unambiguous falsification, subjects appeared to appreciate its impact. It is interesting to note in this context that 92 per cent of the subjects who mentioned brightness in their initial hypotheses had at least a partially correct final hypothesis. Almost exactly the same percentage, 91 per cent, of subjects who had initial triangle hypotheses, but got disconfirming evidence, had at least a partially correct final hypothesis.

These two conclusions are reinforced by the results of a subsequent replication experiment. Thirty subjects were run under test condition 'Instructions' and produced data almost identical to those of the original study. For initial triangle hypothesis subjects (N = 18), the mean proportion of confirmation choices was 0·70. Among these subjects, those who received falsifying evidence were again significantly more likely to achieve a correct final hypothesis than were those who did not make a falsifying observation.

These findings have several implications with respect to both the methodology of falsification and previous research on confirmation bias. Wason (1968) suggests that his data from the 'selection task' indicate that people have difficulty understanding the logic of falsification [see Reading 7 above]. Our subjects experienced no such difficulty. When confronted with unambiguous falsifying evidence, they utilized it in precisely the correct way – by rejecting their incorrect hypotheses, just as Popper says they should. Our subjects did not, on the other hand, appear to look for and test alternative hypotheses. Thus, at least in the absence of explicit training or experience, people may not utilize anything like the multiple hypothesis approach advocated by Platt. Such a failure to look for alternative hypotheses becomes even more interesting when the relationship in the present study between initial and final hypotheses is examined. Of those subjects whose initial hypothesis at least mentioned brightness as a possible variable, nearly all (92 per cent) arrived at a correct or partially correct final hypothesis. Only about half (52 per cent) of the subjects whose initial hypothesis did not mention brightness arrived at a correct or partially correct solution. This indicates that the hypothesis generation stage in an inference process may be of critical importance. If an initial hypothesis is totally incorrect and misleading, and if alternatives are not considered, then arriving at a correct hypothesis may be very difficult. On the other hand, the effect of confirmation bias may not be so disadvantageous if the initial hypothesis is at least partly correct.

Platt's strong inference model should be considered in the light of the results of this experiment, although much more research must be done before too much is claimed. Three aspects of the results are relevant to Platt's approach. The first is the relative success of subjects who attended to the correct dimension in the hypothesis generation stage. The probability of doing so should be considerably enhanced if multiple hypotheses are explicitly tested. The second is the failure of subjects to choose test screens allowing the test of alternative hypotheses. The explicit formulation of multiple hypotheses should preclude the operation of this source of confirmation bias. Third, subjects in this study used falsifying evidence when they obtained it. Thus, Platt's model, which assumes some ability to falsify, is at least not demanding the impossible, even of naïve subjects. Whether subjects can readily design experiments to falsify, which is what Platt prescribes, is unclear. However, the weakness of the instructional manipulation suggests that such behaviour is very difficult to elicit.

21. Judgment under uncertainty: heuristics and biases[1]

Amos Tversky and Daniel Kahneman

Many decisions are based on beliefs concerning the likelihood of uncertain events such as the outcome of an election, the guilt of a defendant, or the future value of the dollar. These beliefs are usually expressed in statements such as 'I think that . . .', 'chances are . . .', 'it is unlikely that . . .', and so forth. Occasionally, beliefs concerning uncertain events are expressed in numerical form as odds or subjective probabilities. What determines such beliefs? How do people assess the probability of an uncertain event or the value of an uncertain quantity? This article shows that people rely on a limited number of heuristic principles which reduce the complex tasks of assessing probabilities and predicting values to simpler judgmental operations. In general, these heuristics are quite useful, but sometimes they lead to severe and systematic errors.

The subjective assessment of probability resembles the subjective assessment of physical quantities such as distance or size. These judgments are all based on data of limited validity, which are processed according to heuristic rules. For example, the apparent distance of an object is determined in part by its clarity. The more sharply the object is seen, the closer it appears to be. This rule has some validity, because in any given scene the more distant objects are seen less sharply than nearer objects. However, the reliance on this rule leads to systematic errors in the estimation of distance. Specifically, distances are often overestimated when visibility is poor because the contours of objects are blurred. On the other hand, distances are often underestimated when visibility is good because the objects are seen sharply. Thus, the reliance on clarity as an indication of distance leads to common biases. Such biases are also found in the intuitive judgment of probability. This article describes three heuristics that are employed to assess probabilities and to predict values. Biases to which these heuristics lead are enumerated, and the applied and theoretical implications of these observations are discussed.

[1] Excerpts from the paper in *Science*, **185** (1974), 1124–31. © 1974 the American Association for the Advancement of Science.

Representativeness

Many of the probabilistic questions with which people are concerned belong to one of the following types: What is the probability that object A belongs to class B? What is the probability that event A originates from process B? What is the probability that process B will generate event A? In answering such questions, people typically rely on the representativeness heuristic, in which probabilities are evaluated by the degree to which A is representative of B, that is, by the degree to which A resembles B. For example, when A is highly representative of B, the probability that A originates from B is judged to be high. On the other hand, if A is not similar to B, the probability that A originates from B is judged to be low.

For an illustration of judgment by representativeness, consider an individual who has been described by a former neighbour as follows: 'Steve is very shy and withdrawn, invariably helpful, but with little interest in people, or in the world of reality. A meek and tidy soul, he has a need for order and structure, and a passion for detail.' How do people assess the probability that Steve is engaged in a particular occupation from a list of possibilities (for example, farmer, salesman, airline pilot, librarian, or physician)? How do people order these occupations from most to least likely? in the representativeness heuristic, the probability that Steve is a librarian, for example, is assessed by the degree to which he is representative of, or similar to, the stereotype of a librarian. Indeed, research with problems of this type has shown that people order the occupations by probability and by similarity in exactly the same way (Kahneman and Tversky, 1973). This approach to the judgment of probability leads to serious errors, because similarity, or representativeness, is not influenced by several factors that should affect judgments of probability.

Insensitivity to prior probability of outcomes

One of the factors that has no effect on representativeness but should have a major effect on probability is the prior probability, or base-rate frequency, of the outcomes. In the case of Steve, for example, the fact that there are many more farmers than librarians in the population should enter into any reasonable estimate of the probability that Steve is a librarian rather than a farmer. Considerations of base-rate frequency, however, do not affect the similarity of Steve to the stereotypes of librarians and farmers. If people evaluate probability by representativeness, therefore, prior probabilities will be neglected. This hypothesis was tested in an experiment where prior probabilities were manipulated (Kahneman and Tversky, 1973). Subjects were shown brief personality descriptions of several individuals, allegedly sampled at random from a group of a hundred professionals – engineers and lawyers. The subjects were asked to assess, for each description, the probability that it belonged to an engineer rather than to a lawyer. In one experimental condition, subjects were told that the group from which the descriptions had been drawn consisted of seventy engineers and thirty lawyers. In another condition, subjects were told that the group consisted of thirty engineers and seventy lawyers. The odds that any particular description belongs to an engineer rather than to a lawyer should be higher in the first condition, where there is a majority of engineers, than in the second condition, where there is a majority of lawyers. Specifically, it can be shown by applying Bayes's rule that the ratio of these odds should be $(0.7/0.3)^2$, or 5.44, for each description. In a sharp violation of Bayes's rule, the subjects in the two conditions produced essentially the same probability judgments. Apparently, subjects evaluated the likelihood that a particular description belonged to an engineer rather than to a lawyer by the degree to which this description was representative of the two stereotypes, with little or no regard for the prior probabilities of the categories.

The subjects used prior probabilities correctly when they had no other information. In the absence of a personality sketch, they judged the probability that an unknown individual is an engineer to be 0.7 and 0.3, respectively, in the two base-rate conditions. However, prior probabilities were effectively ignored when a description was introduced, even when this description was totally uninformative. The responses to the following description illustrate this phenomenon: 'Dick is a 30-year-old man. He is married with no children. A man of high ability and high motivation, he promises to be quite successful in his field. He is well liked by his colleagues.' This description was intended to convey no information relevant to the question of whether Dick is an engineer or a lawyer. Consequently, the probability that Dick is an engineer should equal the proportion of engineers in the group, as if no description had been given. The subjects, however, judged the probability of Dick being an engineer to be 0.5 regardless of whether the stated proportion of engineers in the group was 0.7 or 0.3. Evidently, people respond differently when given worthless evidence. When no specific evidence is given, prior probabilities are properly utilized; when worthless evidence is given, prior probabilities are ignored.

Insensitivity to sample size

To evaluate the probability of obtaining a particular result in a sample drawn from a specified population, people typically apply the representativeness heuristic. That is, they assess the likelihood of a sample result, for example, that the average height in a random sample of ten men will be 6 feet (180 centimetres), by the similarity of this result to the corresponding parameter (that is, to the average height in the population of men). The similarity of a sample statistic to a population parameter does not depend on the size of the sample. Consequently, if probabilities are assessed by representativeness, then the judged probability of a sample statistic will be essentially independent of sample size. Indeed, when subjects assessed the distributions of average height for samples of various sizes, they produced identical distributions. For example, the probability of obtaining an average height greater than 6 feet was assigned the same value for samples of 1,000, 100, and 10 men (Kahneman and Tversky,

1972). Moreover, subjects failed to appreciate the role of sample size even when it was emphasized in the formulation of the problem. Consider the following question:

A certain town is served by two hospitals. In the larger hospital about forty-five babies are born each day and in the smaller hospital about fifteen babies are born each day. As you know, about 50 per cent of all babies are boys. However, the exact percentage varies from day to day. Sometimes it may be higher than 50 per cent sometimes lower.

For a period of one year, each hospital recorded the days on which more than 60 per cent of the babies born were boys. Which hospital do you think recorded more such days?

The larger hospital (21).
The smaller hospital (21).
About the same (that is, within 5 per cent of each other) (53).

The values in parentheses are the number of undergraduate students who chose each answer.

Most subjects judged the probability of obtaining more than 60 per cent boys to be the same in the small and in the large hospital, presumably because these events are described by the same statistic and are therefore equally representative of the general population. In contrast, sampling theory entails that the expected number of days on which more than 60 per cent of the babies are boys is much greater in the small hospital than in the large one, because a large sample is less likely to stray from 50 per cent. This fundamental notion of statistics is evidently not part of people's repertoire of intuitions.

A similar insensitivity to sample size has been reported in judgments of posterior probability, that is, of the probability that a sample has been drawn from one population rather than from another. Consider the following example:

Imagine an urn filled with balls, of which $\frac{2}{3}$ are of one colour and $\frac{1}{3}$ of another. One individual has drawn five balls from the urn, and found that four were red and one was white. Another individual has drawn twenty balls and found that twelve were red and eight were white. Which of the two individuals should feel more confident that the urn contains $\frac{2}{3}$ red balls and $\frac{1}{3}$ white balls, rather than the opposite? What odds should each individual give?

In this problem, the correct posterior odds are 8 to 1 for the 4 : 1 sample and 16 to 1 for the 12 : 8 sample, assuming equal prior probabilities. However, most people feel that the first sample provides much stronger evidence for the hypothesis that the urn is predominantly red, because the proportion of red balls is larger in the first than in the second sample. Here again, intuitive judgments are dominated by the sample proportion and are essentially unaffected by the size of the sample, which plays a crucial role in the determination of the actual posterior odds (Kahneman and Tversky, 1972). In addition, intuitive estimates of posterior odds are far less extreme than the correct values. The underestimation of the impact of evidence has been observed repeatedly in problems of this type. It has been labelled 'conservatism'.

Misconceptions of chance

People expect that a sequence of events generated by a random process will represent the essential characteristics of that process even when the sequence is short. In considering tosses of a coin for heads or tails, for example, people regard the sequence H-T-H-T-T-H to be more likely than the sequence H-H-H-T-T-T, which does not appear random, and also more likely than the sequence H-H-H-H-T-H, which does not represent the fairness of the coin (Kahneman and Tversky, 1972). Thus, people expect that the essential characteristics of the process will be represented, not only globally in the entire sequence, but also locally in each of its parts. A locally representative sequence, however, deviates systematically from chance expectation: it contains too many alternations and too few runs. Another consequence of the belief in local representativeness is the well-known gambler's fallacy. After observing a long run of red on the roulette wheel, for example, most people erroneously believe that black is now due, presumably because the occurrence of black will result in a more representative sequence than the occurrence of an additional red. Chance is commonly viewed as a self-correcting process in which a deviation in one direction induces a deviation in the opposite direction to restore the equilibrium. In fact, deviations are not 'corrected' as a chance process unfolds, they are merely diluted.

Misconceptions of chance are not limited to naïve subjects. A study of the statistical intuitions of experienced research psychologists (Tversky and Kahneman, 1971) revealed a lingering belief in what may be called the 'law of small numbers', according to which even small samples are highly representative of the populations from which they are drawn. The responses of these investigators reflected the expectation that a valid hypothesis about a population will be represented by a statistically significant result in a sample – with little regard for its size. As a consequence, the researchers put too much faith in the results of small samples and grossly overestimated the replicability of such results. In the actual conduct of research, this bias leads to the selection of samples of inadequate size and to overinterpretation of findings.

Insensitivity to predictability

People are sometimes called upon to make such numerical predictions as the future value of a stock, the demand for a commodity, or the outcome of a football game.Such predictions are often made by representativeness. For example, suppose one is given a description of a company and is asked to predict its future profit. If the description of a company is very favourable, a very high profit will appear most representative of that description; if the description is mediocre, a mediocre performance will appear most representative. The degree to which the description is favourable is unaffected by the reliability of that description or by the degree to which it permits accurate prediction. Hence, if people predict solely in terms of the favourableness of the description, their predictions will be insensitive to the reliability of the evidence and to the expected accuracy of the prediction.

This mode of judgment violates the normative statistical theory in which the extremeness and the range of predictions are controlled by considerations of predictability. When predictability is nil, the same prediction should be made in all cases. For example, if the descriptions of companies provide no information relevant to profit, then the same value (such as average profit) should be predicted for all companies. If predictability is perfect, of course, the values predicted will match the actual values and the range of outcomes. In general, the higher the predictability, the wider the range of predicted values.

Several studies of numerical prediction have demonstrated that intuitive predictions violate this rule, and that subjects show little or no regard for considerations of predictability (Kahneman and Tversky, 1973). In one of these studies, subjects were presented with several paragraphs, each describing the performance of a student teacher during a particular practice lesson. Some subjects were asked to *evaluate* the quality of the lesson described in the paragraph in percentile scores, relative to a specified population. Other subjects were asked to *predict*, also in percentile scores, the standing of each student teacher five years after the practice lesson. The judgments made under the two conditions were identical. That is, the prediction of a remote criterion (success of a teacher after five years) was identical to the evaluation of the information on which the prediction was based (the quality of the practice lesson). The students who made these predictions were undoubtedly aware of the limited predictability of teaching competence on the basis of a single trial lesson five years earlier; nevertheless, their predictions were as extreme as their evaluations.

The illusion of validity

As we have seen, people often predict by selecting the outcome (for example, an occupation) that is most representative of the input (for example, the description of a person). The confidence they have in their prediction depends primarily on the degree of representativeness (that is, on the quality of the match between the selected outcome and the input) with little or no regard for the factors that limit predictive accuracy. Thus, people express great confidence in the prediction that a person is a librarian when given a description of his personality which matches the stereotype of librarians, even if the description is scanty, unreliable, or outdated. The unwarranted confidence which is produced by a good fit between the predicted outcome and the input information may be called the illusion of validity. This illusion persists even when the judge is aware of the factors that limit the accuracy of his predictions. It is a common observation that psychologists who conduct selection interviews often experience considerable confidence in their predictions, even when they know of the vast literature that shows selection interviews to be highly fallible. The continued reliance on the clinical interview for selection, despite repeated demonstrations of its inadequacy, amply attests to the strength of this effect.

The internal consistency of a pattern of inputs is a major determinant of one's confidence in predictions based on these inputs. For example, people express more confidence in predicting the final grade-point average of a student whose first-year record consists entirely of B's than in predicting the grade-point average of a student whose first year record includes many A's and C's. Highly consistent patterns are most often observed when the input variables are highly redundant or correlated. Hence, people tend to have great confidence in predictions based on redundant input variables. However, an elementary result in the statistics of correlation asserts that, given input variables of stated validity, a prediction based on several such inputs can achieve higher accuracy when they are independent of each other than when they are redundant or correlated. Thus, redundancy among inputs decreases accuracy even as it increases confidence, and people are often confident in predictions that are quite likely to be off the mark (Kahneman and Tversky, 1973).

Misconceptions of regression

Suppose a large group of children has been examined on two equivalent versions of an aptitude test. If one selects ten children from among those who did best on one of the two versions, their performance on the second version will usually be found somewhat disappointing. Conversely, if one selects ten children from among those who did worst on one version, they will be found, on the average, to do somewhat better on the other version. More generally, consider two variables X and Y which have the same distribution. If one selects individuals whose average X score deviates from the mean of X by k units, then the average of their Y scores will usually deviate from the mean of Y by less than k units. These observations illustrate a general phenomenon known as regression towards the mean, which was first documented by Galton more than a hundred years ago.

In the normal course of life, one encounters many instances of regression toward the mean, in the comparison of the height of fathers and sons, of the intelligence of husbands and wives or of the performance of individuals on consecutive examinations. Nevertheless, people do not develop correct intuitions about this phenomenon. First, they do not expect regression in many contexts where it is bound to occur. Second, when they recognize the occurrence of regression, they often invent spurious causal explanations for it (Kahneman and Tversky, 1973). We suggest that the phenomenon of regression remains elusive because it is incompatible with the belief that the predicted outcome should be maximally representative of the input, and, hence, that the value of the outcome variable should be as extreme as the value of the input variable.

The failure to recognize the import of regression can have pernicious consequences, as illustrated by the following observation. In a discussion of flight training, experienced instructors noted that praise for an exceptionally smooth landing is typically followed by a poorer landing on the next try, while harsh criticism after a rough landing is usually followed by an improvement on the next try. The instructors concluded that verbal rewards are detrimental to learning, while verbal punishments are beneficial, contrary to accepted psychological doctrine. This conclusion is unwarranted because of the presence of regression toward the mean. As in other cases of repeated examination, an improvement will usually follow a poor performance and a deterioration will usually follow an outstanding performance, even if the instructor does not respond to the trainee's achievement on the first attempt. Because the instructors had praised their trainees after good landings and admonished them after poor ones, they reached the erroneous and potentially harmful conclusion that punishment is more effective than reward.

Thus, the failure to understand the effect of regression leads one to overestimate the effectiveness of punishment and to underestimate the effectiveness of reward. In social interaction as well as in training, rewards are typically administered when performance is good, and punishments are typically administered when performance is poor. By regression alone, therefore, behaviour is most likely to improve after punishment and most likely to deteriorate after reward. Consequently, the human condition is such that, by chance alone, one is most often rewarded for punishing others and most often punished for rewarding them. People are generally not aware of this contingency. In fact, the elusive role of regression in determining the apparent consequences of reward and punishment seems to have escaped the notice of students of this area.

Availability

There are situations in which people assess the frequency of a class or the probability of an event by the ease with which instances or occurrences can be brought to mind. For example, one may assess the risk of heart attack among middle-aged people by recalling such occurrences among one's acquaintances. Similarly, one may evaluate the probability that a given business venture will fail by imagining various difficulties it could encounter. This judgmental heuristic is called availability. Availability is a useful clue for assessing frequency or probability, because instances of large classes are usually recalled better and faster than instances of less frequent classes. However, availability is affected by factors other than frequency and probability. Consequently, the reliance on availability leads to predictable biases, some of which are illustrated below.

Biases due to the retrievability of instances

When the size of a class is judged by the availability of its instances, a class whose instances are easily retrieved will appear more numerous than a class of equal frequency whose instances are less retrievable. In an elementary demonstration of the effect, subjects heard a list of well-known personalities of both sexes and were subsequently asked to judge whether the list contained more names of men than of women. Different lists were presented to different groups of subjects. In some of the lists men were relatively more famous than the women, and in others the women were relatively more famous than the men. In each of the lists, the subjects erroneously judged that the class (sex) that had the more famous personalities was the more numerous (Tversky and Kahneman, 1973).

In addition to familiarity, there are other factors, such as salience, which affect the retrievability of instances. For example, the impact of seeing a house burning on the subjective probability of such accidents is probably greater than the impact of reading about a fire in the local paper. Furthermore, recent occurrences are likely to be relatively more available than earlier occurrences. It is a common experience that the subjective probability of traffic accidents rises temporarily when one sees a car overturned by the side of the road.

Biases due to the effectiveness of a search set

Suppose one samples a word (of three letters or more) at random from an English text. Is it more likely that the word starts with r or that r is the third letter? People approach this problem by recalling words that begin with r (road) and words that have r in the third position (car) and assess the relative frequency by the ease with which words of the two types come to mind. Because it is much easier to search for words by their first letter than by their third letter, most people judge words that begin with a given consonant to be more numerous than words in which the same consonant appears in the third position. They do so even for consonants, such as r or k, that are more frequent in the third position than in the first (Tversky and Kahneman, 1973).

Different tasks elicit different search sets. For example, suppose you are asked to rate the frequency with which abstract words (thought, love) and concrete words (door, water) appear in written English. A natural way to answer this question is to search for contexts in which the word could appear. It seems easier to think of contexts in which an abstract concept is mentioned (love in love stories) than to think of contexts in which a concrete word (such as door) is mentioned. If the frequency of words is judged by the availability of the contexts in which they appear, abstract words will be judged as relatively more numerous than concrete words. This bias has been observed in a recent study (Galbraith and Underwood, 1973), which showed that the judged frequency of occurrence of abstract words was much higher than that of concrete words, equated in objective frequency. Abstract words were also judged to appear in a much greater variety of contexts than concrete words. . .

Illusory correlation

Chapman and Chapman (1967) have described an interesting bias in the judgment of the frequency with which two events co-occur. They presented naïve judges with information concerning several hypothetical mental patients. The data for each patient consisted of a clinical diagnosis and a drawing of a person made by the patient. Later the judges estimated the frequency with which each diagnosis (such as paranoia or suspiciousness) had been accompanied by various features of the drawing (such as peculiar eyes). The subjects markedly over-estimated the frequency of co-occurrence of natural associates, such as sus-piciousness and peculiar eyes. This effect was labelled illusory correlation. In their erroneous judgments of the data to which they had been exposed, naïve subjects 'rediscovered' much of the common but unfounded, clinical lore con-cerning the interpretation of the draw-a-person test. The illusory correlation effect was extremely resistant to contradictory data. It persisted even when the correlation between symptom and diagnosis was actually negative, and it pre-vented the judges from detecting relationships that were in fact present.

Availability provides a natural account for the illusory correlation effect. The judgment of how frequently two events co-occur could be based on the strength of the associative bond between them. When the association is strong, one is likely to conclude that the events have been frequently paired. Con-sequently, strong associates will be judged to have occurred together frequently. According to this view, the illusory correlation between suspiciousness and peculiar drawing of the eyes, for example, is due to the fact that suspiciousness is more readily associated with the eyes than with any other part of the body.

Lifelong experience has taught us that, in general, instances of large classes are recalled better and faster than instances of less frequent classes; that likely occurrences are easier to imagine than unlikely ones; and that the associative connections between events are strengthened when the events frequently co-occur. As a result, man has at his disposal a procedure (the availability heuristic) for estimating the numerosity of a class, the likelihood of an event, or the frequency of co-occurrences, by the ease with which the relevant mental oper-ations of retrieval, construction, or association can be performed. However, as the preceding examples have demonstrated, this valuable estimation procedure results in systematic errors.

Adjustment and anchoring

In many situations, people make estimates by starting from an initial value that is adjusted to yield the final answer. The initial value, or starting point, may be suggested by the formulation of the problem, or it may be the result of a partial computation. In either case, adjustments are typically insufficient (Slovic and Lichtenstein, 1971). That is, different starting points yield different estimates, which are biased toward the initial values. We call this phenomenon anchoring.

Insufficient adjustment

In a demonstration of the anchoring effect, subjects were asked to estimate various quantities, stated in percentages (for example, the percentage of African countries in the United Nations). For each quantity, a number between 0 and 100 was determined by spinning a wheel of fortune in the subjects' presence.

The subjects were instructed to indicate first whether that number was higher or lower than the value of the quantity, and then to estimate the value of the quantity by moving upward or downward from the given number. Different groups were given different numbers for each quantity, and these arbitrary numbers had a marked effect on estimates. For example, the median estimates of the percentage of African countries in the United Nations were 25 and 45 for groups that received 10 and 65, respectively, as starting points. Payoffs for accuracy did not reduce the anchoring effect.

Anchoring occurs not only when the starting point is given to the subject, but also when the subject bases his estimate on the result of some incomplete computation. A study of intuitive numerical estimation illustrates this effect. Two groups of high school students estimated, within five seconds, a numerical expression that was written on the blackboard. One group estimated the product

$$8 \times 7 \times 6 \times 5 \times 4 \times 3 \times 2 \times 1$$

while another group estimated the product

$$1 \times 2 \times 3 \times 4 \times 5 \times 6 \times 7 \times 8$$

To answer rapidly such questions, people may perform a few steps of computation and estimate the product by extrapolation or adjustment. Because adjustments are typically insufficient, this procedure should lead to underestimation. Furthermore, because the result of the first few steps of multiplication (performed from left to right) is higher in the descending sequence than in the ascending sequence, the former expression should be judged larger than the latter. Both predictions were confirmed. The median estimate for the ascending sequence was 512, while the median estimate for the descending sequence was 2,250. The correct answer is 40,320. . .

Discussion

This article has been concerned with cognitive biases that stem from the reliance on judgmental heuristics. These biases are not attributable to motivational effects such as wishful thinking or the distortion of judgments by pay-offs and penalties, Indeed, several of the severe errors of judgment reported earlier occurred despite the fact that subjects were encouraged to be accurate and were rewarded for the correct answers.

The reliance on heuristics and the prevalence of biases are not restricted to laymen. Experienced researchers are also prone to the same biases – when they think intuitively. For example, the tendency to predict the outcome that best represents the data, with insufficient regard for prior probability, has been observed in the intuitive judgments of individuals who have had extensive training in statistics. Although the statistically sophisticated avoid elementary errors, such as the gambler's fallacy, their intuitive judgments are liable to similar fallacies in more intricate and less transparent problems.

It is not surprising that useful heuristics such as representativeness and availability are retained, even though they occasionally lead to errors in prediction or estimation. What is perhaps surprising is the failure of people to infer from lifelong experience such fundamental statistical rules as regression toward the mean, or the effect of sample size on sampling variability. Although everyone is exposed, in the normal course of life, to numerous examples from which these rules could have been induced, very few people discover the principles of sampling and regression on their own. Statistical principles are not learned from everyday experience because the relevant instances are not coded appropriately. For example, people do not discover that successive lines in a text differ more in average word length than do successive pages, bacause they simply do not attend to the average word length of individual lines or pages. Thus, people do not learn the relation between sample size and sampling variability, although the data for such learning are abundant.

The lack of an appropriate code also explains why people usually do not detect the biases in their judgments of probability. A person could conceivably learn whether his judgments are externally calibrated by keeping a tally of the proportion of events that actually occur among those to which he assigns the same probability. However, it is not natural to group events by their judged probability. In the absence of such grouping it is impossible for an individual to discover, for example, that only 50 per cent of the predictions to which he has assigned a probability of 0·9 or higher actually came true.

The empirical analysis of cognitive biases has implications for the theoretical and applied role of judged probabilities. Modern decision theory regards subjective probability as the quantified opinion of an idealized person. Specifically, the subjective probability of a given event is defined by the set of bets about this event that such a person is willing to accept. An internally consistent, or coherent, subjective probability measure can be derived for an individual if his choices among bets satisfy certain principles, that is, the axioms of the theory. The derived probability is subjective in the sense that different individuals are allowed to have different probabilities for the same event. The major contribution of this approach is that it provides a rigorous subjective interpretation of probability that is applicable to unique events and is embedded in a general theory of rational decision. . .

Part V

Inference and Comprehension

Introduction to inference and comprehension

Conscious deductions occur relatively rarely in everyday life, but automatic and implicit inferences are an inevitable part of many processes, especially those involved in perception. This point was stressed by Helmholtz over a century ago but largely forgotten until recent times. Helmholtz wrote:

The psychological activities that lead us to infer that there in front of us at a certain place there is a certain object of a certain character, are generally not conscious activities, but unconscious ones. In their result they are equivalent to a *conclusion*, to the extent that the observed action on our senses enables us to form an idea as to the possible cause of this action; although as a matter of fact, it is invariably simply the nervous stimulations that are perceived, that is, the actions, but never the external objects themselves. But what seems to differentiate them from a conclusion, in the ordinary sense of the word, is that a conclusion is an act of conscious thought. An astronomer, for example, comes to real conclusions of this sort, when he computes the positions of the stars in space, their distances, etc., from the perspective images he has had of them at various times and as they are seen from different parts of the orbit of the earth. His conclusions are based on conscious knowledge of the laws of optics. In the ordinary acts of vision this knowledge of optics is lacking. Still it may be permissible to speak of the psychic acts of ordinary perception as *unconscious conclusions*, thereby making a distinction of some sort between them and so-called conscious conclusions. And while it is true that there has been, and probably always will be, a measure of doubt as to the similarity of the psychic activity in the two cases, there can be no doubt as to the similarity between the results of such unconscious conclusions and those of conscious conclusions. (Helmholtz, reprint 1963)

In commenting on this passage Gregory (1970) wonders why the inferential view of perception has tended in the past not to be very popular among psychologists. The answer appears to be that it was vigorously challenged by William James (1890, vol. ii) as superfluous, and subsequently ignored by those psychologists who were primarily concerned with observable behaviour.

Perception is very complicated. Following Helmholtz we might consider that all the processes that mediate it are 'unconscious inferences'. However, we shall be considering here not so much the elementary sensory and perceptual processes involved in building up percepts but more the role of inference in

341

understanding what one perceives whether it is an object in the world, a visual scene, or a linguistic expression. We will be concerned with inference as a combination or transformation of elements of meaning – presumably represented mentally in some symbolic form – in order to obtain new propositional information.

Let us consider an example to clarify matters. If you are visiting a friend's house and open an interior door, you will expect to see a room of some sort. If you enter and turn about you will expect to see an orderly progression of walls, furniture, windows, doors, etc. And, indeed, if all goes well, your phenomenal experience will be just so, with a smooth sense of continuity as you move around in the room even if it is one that you have never before entered. The system mediating this continuity, and the set of everyday expectations that you have about the world, clearly relies on knowledge. It necessitates an organized system of knowledge about the world. Such knowledge can be put to use in manifold tasks that can be subsumed under the general rubric of making sense of the world or of descriptions of it.

How can we best think of the organization of such knowledge? One interesting hypothesis is Minsky's notion of a 'frame', which he outlines in the first reading in this Part. A frame is a structured piece of knowledge about some typical entity or state of affairs. It is an analogue in Artificial Intelligence of the notion of a 'prototype', which we encountered in Part III. Strictly speaking, a frame is more like a particular view of a prototype, and the prototype as a whole is represented by a frame-system, i.e. a set of frames with rules about how one moves from one frame to another.

There are three important components that the idea of a frame adds to the idea of a prototype. First, a frame contains 'slots' (or 'terminals' in Minsky's terminology) into which go the specific values of a given instance of the relevant entity. Thus, a particular room will have a specific size, a specific layout, a specific texture and colour, and so on. Second, the values of many such slots will often be specified by default: if no information is available about them, the frame will specify a typical or ideal value. Thus, the frame for a room in a house will specify at least one door, at least one window, and so on. Third, the frame makes explicit the structure of the information it contains: Minsky uses the sort of structured notions introduced in Winston's paper (Part III, Reading 12).

We may reinterpret the notion of a 'prototype' described by Rosch: it is simply a frame that takes all the default values for its relevant variables – a typical bird is specified by default to fly, to sing, and to lay its eggs in a nest, etc. A new virtue of prototypes now emerges: they allow a considerable economy in perception and communication. Once a relevant frame has been retrieved in understanding a percept or a description, then it is necessary only to pay attention to its unusual or abnormal features, the customary values can be filled in by default.

The notion of a frame is a peculiarly ubiquitous one: as Minsky shows, it crops up in a variety of guises within language – there are syntactic, semantic, and narrative frames. Yet, it is also a promise rather than an actuality: few programs making use of frames have been implemented. Likewise, the theory is difficult to test empirically: perhaps the nearest that psychology has come to providing empirical evidence about frames is in Johansson's (1971) ingenious studies of the perception of movement. He has found, for example, that small lights fixed only to the major joints of a man are sufficient to enable subjects to perceive a man walking in a dark room. Such cues seem sufficient to retrieve the 'walking' frame. However, Marr and Nishihara (1976) have argued that frames are not sufficiently flexible to mediate perception; and Johansson's results are even more compatible with their theory of the perception of three-dimensional shapes, which is based on identifying the important axes of figures and their constituent parts. In our view, Marr and Nishihara's theory predicts that lights at major joints would facilitate this process, whereas lights in the middle of limbs would not, and indeed Johansson reports that the latter do not give rise to the perception of a man walking. Nevertheless, the general idea of a frame-cum-prototype is not so easily abandoned: the Marr and Nishihara theory relies on a hierarchy of prototypical three-dimensional shapes which it uses to match against the visual image in order to identify objects.

It may happen, of course, that a perceiver cannot retrieve any frame or prototype relevant to what he sees. What exactly, for example, is the object depicted in figure 1? The reader presumably has no difficulty in perceiving what is depicted in that he recognizes a bent wire with a hoop in it, a prong at one end, and a receptacle at the other end. But, like an embarrassed recipient of 'the unknown wedding gift', he has no idea what the thing is for. Its function is obscure, and hence the object cannot be identified; in fact, it is a utensil designed for stoning olives. Bransford and McCarrell in the second reading of this Part bring out the importance of the identification of function, and introduce some further splendid artifacts that are easy to perceive but hard to comprehend.

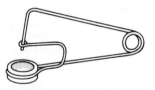

Figure 1. An object with a readily identifiable three-dimensional shape, but an obscure function.

We remarked in the Introduction to conceptual thinking (Part III) that many artifacts are defined by a common function rather than a common form, and this theme is taken up by George Miller in Reading 24 in this Part. The ability to name an object is a prerequisite for linguistic performance, and Miller argues for an analysis of the meanings of object names that includes a specification of perceptual characteristics and function. He shows how functional information implicates the notion of *possibility* which, in turn, requires an inference based on knowledge. Thus, even in the lowly task of verbal identification there is a role for implicit inference. The distinction between perceptual and functional information is borne out by neurological data. Warrington and Taylor (1973) have shown that lesions in the left parietal lobe can make it difficult for a patient to discern the use or purpose of an object, though they can perceive its three-dimensional shape; lesions in the right parietal lobe give rise to the opposite phenomena.

The notion that inference plays a role in comprehension of discourse proper can be traced back at least to Bartlett's (1932) study of remembering. When such studies began to be made again in the light of the revival of interest in language, two main research strategies were adopted. On the one hand, experimenters wrote texts that embodied the premises of explicit deductions in order to investigate whether the conclusion was drawn as part of the normal process of comprehension. For example, Frase (1969, 1972) presented his subjects with passages including such information as:

> The Fundalas are hill people in Ugala.
> Hill people are very religious.
> In Ugala religious people are often outcasts.

The subjects' task was to underline those parts of the passage containing information necessary to draw a conclusion typed at the end:

> The Fundalas are often outcasts.

Sentences outside this chain of inference were very poorly recalled. On the other hand, experimenters examined the effects of providing or denying their subjects key pieces of information about a text in order to determine the effects on comprehension. Thus, a mere knowledge of the title of a passage can exert a striking comparable effect as Dooling and Lachman (1971) have shown. A suitably vague passage such as:

With hocked gems financing him our hero bravely defied all scornful laughter that tried to prevent his scheme. Your eyes deceive he had said; an egg not a table correctly typifies this unexplored planet. Now, three sturdy sisters sought proof forging along sometimes through calm vastness yet more often over turbulent peaks and valleys. Days became weeks, as many doubters spread fearful rumours about the edge. At last from nowhere welcome winged creatures appeared signifying momentous success.

Such a passage illustrates how the process of comprehension can be a matter of problem solving. What is the hero's *scheme*? In what sense can the *sisters* forge along through a vastness? What is the nature of the *edge* about which rumours were spread? What are the *winged creatures* and how does their appearance signify a success? Most of these problems are immediately resolved if you are told that the title of the passage is, 'Christopher Columbus discovering America.' Dooling and Lachman found that the number of words correctly recalled from the text was superior when a subject was originally presented with both the passage and its title. The effect occurred even when the passage was in a scrambled order – a finding which suggests that the problematic aspect of the text is the interpretation of such noun phrases as *his scheme, three sturdy sisters, the edge,* and *welcome winged creatures.*

The most sustained investigations of this sort have been carried out by Bransford and his colleagues, and Reading 23 by Bransford and McCarrell brings together the results of a number of experiments showing that comprehension invariably entails going beyond explicit linguistic information in order to make a coherent interpretation. Walter Kintsch and his colleagues have also carried out experiments on inferences and comprehension (see Kintsch, 1974). They have investigated their subjects' ability to remember inferred information in comparison to the same information presented explicitly. Thus, for example, a subject might be presented with the following passage:

> A burning cigarette was carelessly discarded. The fire destroyed many acres of virgin forest

and then asked to evaluate as true or false the statement:

> The discarded cigarette caused the fire.

An inference is necessary in this case; it is unnecessary where the text has made the information explicit:

> A carelessly discarded burning cigarette started a fire. The fire destroyed many acres of virgin forest.

After a relatively short delay of about fifteen minutes, there ceased to be any difference in the time taken to evaluate test sentences whether the relevant information had been presented implicitly or explicitly. This finding is consistent with Kintsch's view that once a proposition has been stored in memory it no longer matters whether it was inferred or read. On the basis of errors in recall, Fredericksen (1972) in a comparable study has argued that some inferences occur while subjects are reading texts, others occur as part of the reconstruction of events involved in recalling the text. Likewise, Thorndyke (1976) has found that implicitly inferred information is likely to give rise to 'false alarms' in an unexpected recognition test of the sentences that occurred in a text.

The psychological studies of implicit inference during linguistic comprehension have the nature of empirical 'existence proofs': they establish the existence of the phenomenon rather than reveal the basis of its operation. For an analysis of underlying mechanisms we must begin by considering the different sorts of inference that occur. Certain inferences may be necessary simply to grasp the meaning of sentences. Consider an example that Miller discusses in Reading 24:

> The Smiths saw the Rocky Mountains flying to California.

Most people normally understand this sentence to mean that it was the Smiths who were flying to California. (Children of about 4 years old are more likely to make the opposite interpretation of such sentences, as Til Wykes, a student at Sussex University, has found in an unpublished experiment.) The standard linguistic explanation of the resolution of such ambiguities is by way of the device of 'selectional restrictions' introduced by Katz and Fodor (1963). They proposed that the meaning of a verb is represented in the lexicon together with information about the sorts of noun phrase with which it can occur. Thus, for example, the verb *to kick* has such a 'selectional restriction' on its grammatical object: it must be a physical entity of some sort. When an ambiguous word such as *ball*, which may mean a round physical object or a social occasion for dancing, occurs as the grammatical object of the verb:

> He *kicked the ball*

its ambiguity is resolved because only the 'physical object' sense of *ball* is compatible with the selectional restriction of the verb, *to kick*. The mechanism of selectional restrictions has been adopted by a variety of workers (including Winograd) in a variety of disciplines. However, a number of criticisms have been levelled at the theory (see, e.g. Savin, 1973). The most serious objection for our purposes is that there does not seem to be any selectional restrictions that can rule out mountains flying – after all, in another context the idea may be perfectly sensible, 'As the Smiths looked out of their spaceship they saw the Rocky Mountains flying past them.' Hence, Miller argues in his paper that listeners rely on their practical knowledge in order to infer that it is the Smiths who were flying to California.

It is useful to distinguish between the *meaning* of a sentence and the *significance* of its utterance in speech or writing (see Johnson-Laird, 1977). Any competent speaker of the English language understands the meaning of a sentence such as:

> The men object to their new rates of pay

but it has little or no significance beyond the fact that it is used to illustrate a point about language. Inference plays a role in retrieving the meaning of a sentence, as Miller shows, and it plays a still more important part in grasping the significance of its utterance. We shall illustrate the point by considering two aspects of significance: reference and illocutionary force.

In order to grasp the significance of an utterance, you must at least know to whom it refers. An initial source of difficulty may be the systematic ambiguity of the definite (*the*) and the indefinite articles (*a*, *an*). The following passage:

> An African elephant is the largest animal in the jungle. This elephant lives mainly off leaves. Nevertheless, it terrorizes the other animals in the jungle

could be referring to African elephants in general, and accordingly continue:

> Last week *one* went on the rampage in our village.

Alternatively, the passage could be referring to a specific elephant, and accordingly continue:

> Last week *it* went on the rampage in our village.

The conditions that an utterance must satisfy in order to identify a specific individual have not yet been completely codified. According to Vendler (1967), one clear cue is the use of a verb in the past tense making reference to a definite time. Thus, 'He flew a kite', apparently identifies a specific kite, whereas, 'He can fly a kite', need not. But this distinction is susceptible to the following critique developed by Stenning (1977). The sequence:

> He flew a kite.
> The kite was a birthday present

does indeed suggest that *a kite* identifies a specific object to which subsequent reference is made by *the kite*. However, consider the following alternative text:

> He flew a kite.
> In fact, he flew several.
> The kite was a birthday present.

Here, *a kite* no longer seems to identify a specific object and there is something rather odd about the use of the definite article in the last sentence. Stenning argues that the real meaning of the indefinite article is merely *at least one* (the existential quantifier of formal logic), and that the actual identification of a specific entity transcends the mere meaning of sentences and depends on the actual situations to which they apply. An identification requires the statement in which an indefinite noun phrase occurs to be true, and as a matter of pragmatic fact to be true of a unique entity. One bonus of this analysis is that it enables definite noun phrases to be treated simply as referring to *all* (the universal quantifier of formal logic) the members of the set established by such indefinite noun phrases. In some cases the set will have several members (e.g. 'the kites'), and in other cases the set will have a single member (e.g. 'the kite'). This is an ingenious solution; the psychologist should note that it simplifies semantics by placing a greater load on implicit inference, since it is necessary to take into account what one knows about the relevant situation in order to grasp whether a specific entity has been identified by an indefinite noun phrase.

Many discourses begin by identifying a specific referent, and once such an 'anchor' has been laid down, a whole chain of identification–reference links can be built up (see Vendler, 1967). Such a process is illustrated in table 1. It will be noted that an identifying expression generally precedes its corresponding referring expression except where a reference can be made directly because the existence of the relevant entity can be inferred from what is already known.

The ways in which links of this sort are established is a topic investigated by H. H. Clark in Reading 25 in this Part. He argues that such links require a 'bridging' inference to be made, and that these inferences depend on the conventional distinction between 'given' and 'new' information. Language provides a variety of means of distinguishing between what is taken for granted by a speaker (the 'given') and what is being introduced for the first time (the 'new'). A speaker may well reply to a question such as:

> Who did the striptease at the party?

using a cleft-sentence:

It was Mary who did the striptease

which marks a clear boundary between new (*it was Mary*) and given (*who did the striptease*). The same distinction can be conveyed by intonation contour. Clark argues that there is a convention that a speaker should respect the mechanisms for distinguishing given and new information, and ensure that information marked as given is truly common to him and his addressee and that information marked as new truly introduces material novel to the addressee. A speaker's respect for this convention enables a listener to draw those inferences necessary to establish a variety of links left implicit in actual utterances. In particular, the specification of referents can rely on the fact that the listener will search back in his memory for their identification. It is in this way that the reference of *the couple* in the example above is determined: the listener knows that he has the necessary information to determine it because the speaker will have respected the given–new contract. But, as Garrod and Sanford (1977) have shown, the remoter the relation between noun phrases the longer it takes to read a passage,

Table 1. A chain of identification-reference links based on an initial 'anchor' at the beginning of a text

Text	Interpretation
Jerome has recently married.	'Jerome' refers to an individual because it is a proper noun. This individual is the 'anchor':
His wife is from	'His wife' refers to an individual (cf. 'Jerome wants his wife to be a wealthy widow') because she is in the relation of marriage to the 'anchor'. This inference depends, in turn, on the assumption of coherence in the text – no other coherent referent for 'his wife' has been established in the previous text.
a small town out West.	'A small town' identifies a specific town since an individual is from it.
The town recently elected a new mayor.	'The town' refers to the previously identified town. 'A new mayor' identifies a specific mayor because he has been elected by a town that has been identified and referred to, and towns have only one mayor. The subtle shift in the meaning of 'town' should be noted, however.
It was through him	'Him' refers to the previously identified mayor – perhaps because the only other possible candidate was last referred to far back in the text.
that the couple met.	'The couple' refers to two individuals, Jerome and his wife, since it is an expression that commonly refers to married couples. This interpretation clinches the previous reference for 'him'.

presumably because the bridging inference is time-consuming. Clark emphasizes the role of bridging in establishing a variety of other sorts of connections between linguistic expressions, and provides a useful taxonomy of them.

The principles governing identification and reference apply to many usages of pronouns. Hence, pronouns typically refer to entities that have already been identified, i.e. to 'given' information:

When John entered the room, *he* was surprised to find *it* empty.

However, one clear exception to this principle is if a subordinate clause precedes the main clause:

When he entered it, John was surprised to find the room empty.

Bever (1970) has argued that this linguistic principle merely reflects a more general psychological principle:

A symbol 'S1' can stand for 'S2' if (a) the prior connection is known or (b) there is an indication that a connection is about to be established.

The cue in case (b) is simply that the clause is recognizably a subordinate one. One problem, however, is (as Bever recognizes) that there are sentences whose interpretation is hard to explain on the basis of this principle. Thus, it seems less binding when the object or indirect object of a sentence is initially pronominalized:

The butler brought it to them when the directors asked for coffee.

The root of the matter is probably that the linguistic constraints on pronominalization will never in themselves suffice to determine the referents of pronouns except in a few limited cases.

We can illustrate the problem by considering the way in which Winograd's (1972) program for understanding natural language seeks to determine the reference of *it*. In assigning candidates to the list of potential referents, the procedure for *it* works according to the following rules. If the pronoun has already occurred in the same or the previous sentence, then *it* is taken to have the same reference as before. Where *it* occurs as part of a complicated noun phrase (e.g. 'a block which is bigger than anything which supports *it*'), then it is taken to refer to the same entity as the head of the noun phrase (*a block* in the example above). Otherwise, there is the following rank order of preferences: a 'new' referent in the sentence, its subject, its object, a noun phrase in a prepositional phrase or a subsidiary clause. Thus, in 'Does the box contain a block? And is *it* red?' *it* will be taken to refer to the block, because 'the box' plainly refers to a given referent. In a series of unpublished studies, Til Wykes has found that $4\frac{1}{2}$-year-old children often perform in a way that resembles Winograd's program. For example, given a sentence such as:

I put the pencil in my pocket and because it had a hole it fell out

the children tend to treat the first *it* as referring to the pencil – the object of the sentence takes precedence over the noun phrase within the prepositional phrase, and they treat the second *it* as coreferential with the first. Adults, of course, use their general knowledge in order to infer the appropriate referents. Kate Ehrlich has found in an unpublished study carried out with adult subjects at Sussex University that the complexity of the inference affects the assignment of referents. It is easier to cope with a sentence such as:

Sam lent his car to Jim because he didn't use it

than with a sentence such as:

Sam lent his car to Jim because he had taken up cycling.

In order to grasp the significance of an utterance, the listener must do more than establish referents. He must at least in part determine the speaker's intention in uttering the sentence. As a minimum, he must determine the *illocutionary force* of the utterance. This concept was introduced by the philosopher, J. L. Austin (1962), in order to capture the idea that sentences are uttered in order to achieve such aims as making a statement, asking a question, issuing an order. Such speech acts should not be confused with the syntactic categories of declarative, interrogative, and imperative sentences. Declaratives do tend to be used to make statements, but the correlation is far from perfect. One can make a statement using an interrogative (e.g. 'Do you know that I am 92 years old?'). Moreover, a common type of misunderstanding is to fail to grasp the illocutionary force of an utterance:

A. Can you tell me the time?
B. Yes.

This response takes the interrogative as asking a question instead of as making a request: such misunderstandings are quite common in daily life, and they also appear characteristically among schizophrenics (see the examples reported in Mayer, 1972). It is sometimes not appreciated that determining the illocutionary force of an utterance is *always* a matter of inference. Certain linguists such as Ross (1970), for instance, have implied that the force of a statement can be made explicit by some such formula as:

I say to you that . . .

However, whether a speaker really means what he says or is merely joking, play-acting, or giving linguistic examples, is something that invariably requires a listener to take into account his knowledge of the speaker, the linguistic context, and the general circumstances of the utterance. No matter how ornate a formula of the form: 'I swear to you that I really am asserting that . . .', the speaker could always be joking. It is not without interest here that potential suicides often complain that no one treats their remarks seriously (Sudnow, 1972) – a phenomenon that would be impossible if language allowed you to convey that you really mean what you say.

Since we have raised the topic of speaking, we should mention that inference clearly plays a role here as well, if only because a speaker must make inferences about what a listener is likely to infer in order to attempt to ensure that his remarks will be interpreted correctly. Such a task is clearly a demanding one, and there is a characteristic asymmetry between speaking and listening. Speakers are often satisfied with an utterance from which an intended inference can be drawn but fail to appreciate that other unintended inferences are equally feasible:

> I am delighted to welcome Mr X to open our fete.
> We couldn't get a better man.

The same phenomenon is apparent in writing (see Parsons, 1969):

> Completing an impressive ceremony, the Admiral's lovely daughter smashed a bottle of champagne over her stern as she slid gracefully down the slipways.

In general, the significance of an utterance is inferred on the basis of five main components:

1. Its meaning.
2. Its linguistic context.
3. Its social and physical circumstances, including a knowledge of the speaker.
4. A knowledge of the conventions governing discourse.
5. General knowledge.

The structure of discourse is presumably determined by a complicated interplay of these factors. Linguists have proposed 'text grammars' that apply to units of discourse larger than the sentence (see, e.g. Van Dijk, 1972; but also Dascal and Margalit, 1974; and Stenning, 1977, for a critique). Undoubtedly, there are linguistic elements that make for cohesion and provide signposts to the structure of a text (see Meyer, 1975; Halliday and Hasan, 1976); there may even be rules structuring the sequence of information in stories (Rumelhart, 1975). However, sociologists, and particularly the so-called 'ethnomethodologists', have studied what actually happens in real conversations, and their descriptive accounts establish beyond any reasonable doubt that no purely linguistic analysis is going to elucidate the way discourse is structured (see, e.g. Schegloff, 1972; Schegloff and Sachs, 1973; Sachs, Schegloff, and Jefferson, 1974). The point may be best established by considering the conventions governing discourse, and the role of general knowledge in interpreting utterances.

Part of a speaker's linguistic competence is his ability to engage in discourse according to the conventions of his culture. The philosopher, Paul Grice, has formulated *some* of the conventions for our culture in a set of precepts, or conventional maxims, that are summarized in table 2. Perhaps the best evidence that such maxims are normally followed implicitly – with varying degrees of success – is the way in which deliberate breaches of them are interpreted, that is, the inferences that a listener draws from such violations. A statement that is blatantly irrelevant:

A. How old are you?

B. Nice weather we've been having

leads to the inference that a relevant answer is unspeakable. A statement that is deliberately uninformative may be a way of putting someone in their place:

You're a doctor, not a pregnant woman

or it may lead to a more interesting deduction

Fred is either a spy or he isn't.

∴ The speaker does not know that Fred is not a spy.

∴ Fred may be a spy.

Indeed, on occasion the uninformative utterance can have the most alarming implications, as in the Charles Addams cartoon of the nurse reassuring the expectant father with the striking news:

Congratulations, it's a baby!

Table 2. The principles of conversation proposed by Grice (1975)

The cooperative principle:	Make your conversational contribution such as is required by the accepted purpose or direction of the exchange in which you are engaged.

Specific conversational maxims:

Quantity:	Make your contribution as informative as is required – neither too much nor too little information.
Quality:	Don't say what you believe to be false. Don't say what you lack evidence for.
Relation:	Be relevant.
Manner:	Avoid obscurity and ambiguity. Be orderly and brief.

Grice's maxims are intuitive and incomplete. An idea of how much they entail can be gathered from Clark's paper, which is an exploration of the maxim: be orderly. The full implications of the conventions governing discourse are likely to be best understood by attempting to construct computer models of them. Some preliminary attempts to model discourse have been made in Artificial Intelligence (see Power, 1974; Davey and Longuet-Higgins, 1977), but the main focus of current work is the representation of general knowledge.

The initial step was Winograd's (1972) assumption that the comprehension of discourse requires 'a deep knowledge of the subject being discussed'. Such knowledge plays an important role in resolving ambiguities and in determining the referents of expressions, and this role can be modelled with some success in

PLANNER-like languages. They allow knowledge to be represented in a procedural form that facilitates the making of inferences (see the account of PLANNER in Part I, Reading 4). Although Winograd failed to follow his own philosophy in handling pronouns, Charniak (1973) has shown that it is very relevant both to them and to other aspects of discourse.

Consider, for example, the following simple children's story:

> Janet needed some money. She got her piggy bank and started to shake it. Finally some money came out.

If you are asked why Janet shook her piggy bank, you would probably reply: in order to get the money out. This answer is something that you have inferred from your knowledge of piggy banks. However, such common-sense inferences are not enough, and Charniak suggests that there are certain routines, triggered by specific concepts, which specify a set of relevant inferences. An important part of knowledge, for example, concerns the sequence of events that occurs in certain stereotyped circumstances such as having a meal in a restaurant, shopping at a supermarket, making a journey by train, etc. What seems to be required is another variation on Minsky's 'frame' idea, and such a theory is developed by Schank and Abelson in the final reading of this Part. They have written a computer program that represents the 'scripts' of some stereotyped activities and that uses this information in order to make inferences in understanding stories. The possession of a script allows a speaker to leave many things unsaid with the certainty that the listener will fill in such gaps by default. For example, it is unnecessary to state explicitly that a customer in a restaurant eats the food he has ordered. In accordance with Grice's conventions, it is only necessary to describe such untoward circumstance as, say, the customer refusing to eat his meal.

The work of Schank and Abelson represents a rare case of cooperation between a member of the artificial intelligentsia and a psychologist, and it is a nice illustration of the way in which the two disciplines can reinforce each other. Thus, a psychologist is likely to ask where scripts come from and how they are learnt. Schank and Abelson have recourse to the notion of 'plans' (cf. Miller, Galanter, and Pribram, 1960), that is, general methods for human beings to achieve their goals. There is thus a resemblance between a plan and a consequent theorem in a PLANNER language: given a particular goal, the plan specifies ways to achieve it. A plan can be used to make sense of discourse; it can also be used to try to construe people's behaviour within a causal or intentional framework and might thus play an important role in 'attribution' theory, that part of social psychology concerned with the perception of other people's intentions and reasons for action (see Kelley, 1973). If a particular sequence of subcomponents (Schank and Abelson call them 'deltacts') is frequently used in order to achieve a goal, it is likely to crystallize into a script.

We have paid tribute to Bartlett's (1932) early work on understanding and remembering prose. It is fitting that this final reading should close by reporting the results of an experimental study of remembering and by proposing the outlines of a theory that accounts for the drift towards 'prototypes' that Bartlett himself observed.

22. Frame-system theory[1]

Marvin Minsky

Here is the essence of the frame theory: When one encounters a new situation (or makes a substantial change in one's view of a problem), one selects from memory a structure called a *frame*. This is a remembered framework to be adapted to fit reality by changing details as necessary.

A *frame* is a data-structure for representing a stereotyped situation like being in a certain kind of living room or going to a child's birthday party. Attached to each frame are several kinds of information. Some of this information is about how to use the frame. Some is about what one can expect to happen next. Some is about what to do if these expectations are not confirmed.

We can think of a frame as a network of nodes and relations. The 'top levels' of a frame are fixed, and represent things that are always true about the supposed situation. The lower levels have many *terminals* – 'slots' that must be filled by specific instances or data. Each terminal can specify conditions its assignments must meet. (The assignments themselves are usually smaller 'sub-frames'.) Simple conditions are specified by *markers* that might require a terminal assignment to be a person, an object of sufficient value, or a pointer to a subframe of a certain type. More complex conditions can specify relations among the things assigned to several terminals.

Collections of related frames are linked together into *frame-systems*. The effects of important actions are mirrored by *transformations* between the frames of a system. These are used to make certain kinds of calculations economical, to represent changes of emphasis and attention, and to account for the effectiveness of 'imagery'.

For visual scene analysis, the different frames of a system describe the scene from different viewpoints, and the transformations between one frame and another represent the effects of moving from place to place. For nonvisual kinds of frames, the differences between the frames of a system can represent actions, cause-effect relations, or changes in conceptual viewpoint. *Different frames of a*

[1] This paper originally appeared in R. C. Schank and B. L. Nash-Webber (eds.) *Theoretical Issues in Natural Language Processing*. Preprints of a conference at MIT (June 1975).

system share the same terminals; this is the critical point that makes it possible to coordinate information gathered from different viewpoints.

Much of the phenomenological power of the theory hinges on the inclusion of expectations and other kinds of presumptions. A *frame's terminals are normally already filled with 'default' assignments*. Thus, a frame may contain a great many details whose supposition is not specifically warranted by the situation. These have many uses in representing general information, most likely cases, techniques for by-passing 'logic', and ways to make useful generalizations.

The default assignments are attached loosely to their terminals, so that they can be easily displaced by new items that fit better the current situation. They thus can serve also as 'variables' or as special cases for 'reasoning by example', or as 'textbook cases', and often make the use of logical quantifiers unnecessary.

The frame-systems are linked, in turn, by an *information retrieval network*. When a proposed frame cannot be made to fit reality – when we cannot find terminal assignments that suitably match its terminal marker conditions – this network provides a replacement frame. These interframe structures make possible other ways to represent knowledge about facts, analogies, and other information useful in understanding.

Once a frame is proposed to represent a situation, a *matching* process tries to assign values to each frame's terminals, consistent with the markers at each place. The matching process is partly controlled by information associated with the frame (which includes information about how to deal with surprises) and partly by knowledge about the system's current goals. There are important uses for the information, obtained when a matching process fails; it can be used to select an alternative frame that better suits the situation.

Local and global theories for vision

When we enter a room we seem to see the entire scene at a glance. But seeing is really an extended process. It takes time to fill in details, collect evidence, make conjectures, test, deduce, and interpret in ways that depend on our knowledge, expectations and goals. Wrong first impressions have to be revised. Nevertheless, all this proceeds so quickly and smoothly that it seems to demand a special explanation.

Would parallel processing help? This is a more technical question than it might seem. At the level of detecting elementary visual features, texture elements, stereoscopic and motion-parallax cues, it is obvious that parallel processing might be useful. At the level of grouping features into objects, it is harder to see exactly how to use parallelism, but one can at least conceive of [certain perceptual tasks] performed in a special parallel network.

At 'higher' levels of cognitive processing, however, one suspects fundamental limitations in the usefulness of parallelism. Many 'integral' schemes were proposed in the literature on 'pattern recognition' for parallel operations on pictorial material – perceptrons, integral transforms, skeletonizers, and so forth. These mathematically and computationally interesting schemes might quite possibly serve as ingredients of perceptual processing theories. But as ingredients only! Basically, 'integral' methods work only on isolated figures in two dimensions. They fail disastrously in coping with complicated, three-dimensional scenery.

The new, more successful symbolic theories use hypothesis formation and confirmation methods that seem, on the surface at least, more inherently serial. *It is hard to solve any very complicated problem without giving essentially full attention, at different times, to different subproblems.* Fortunately, however, beyond the brute idea of doing many things in parallel, one can imagine a more serial process that deals with large, complex, symbolic structures as units. This opens a new theoretical 'niche' for performing a rapid selection of large substructures; in this niche our theory hopes to find the secret of speed, both in vision and in ordinary thinking.

Seeing a cube

In the tradition of Guzman (1968) and Winston [see Reading 12], we assume that the result of looking at a cube is a structure something like that in figure 1. The substructures A and B represent details or decorations on two faces of the cube. When we move to the right, face A disappears from view, while the new face decorated with C is seen. If we now had to analyse the scene from the start, we would have to

(1) lose the knowledge about A,
(2) recompute B, and
(3) compute the description of C.

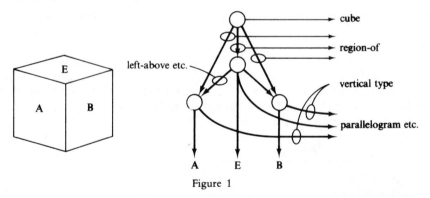

Figure 1

But since we know we moved to the right, we can save B by assigning it also to the 'left face' terminal of a second cube-frame. To save A (just in case!) we connect it also to an extra, invisible face-terminal of the new cube-schema as in figure 2. If later we move back to the left, we can reconstruct the first scene without any perceptual computation at all: just restore the top–level pointers to the first cube-frame. We now need a place to store C; we can add yet another invisible face to the right in the first cube-frame (see figure 3). We could extend this to represent further excursions around the object. This would lead to a more comprehensive frame-system, in which each frame represents a different 'perspective' of a cube. In figure 4 there are three frames corresponding to 45-degree MOVE-RIGHT and MOVE-LEFT actions. If we pursue this analysis, the resulting system can become very large; more complex objects need even more different projections. It is not obvious either that all of them are normally necessary or that just one of each variety is adequate. It all depends.

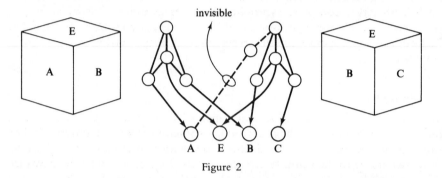

Figure 2

It is not proposed that this kind of complicated structure is recreated every time one examines an object. It is imagined instead that a great collection of frame-systems is stored in permanent memory, and one of them is evoked when evidence and expectation make it plausible that the scene in view will fit it. How are they acquired? We propose that if a chosen frame does not fit well enough, and if no better one is easily found, and if the matter is important enough, then an adaptation of the best one so far discovered will be constructed and remembered for future use.

Each frame has terminals for attaching pointers to substructures. Different frames can share the same terminal, which can thus correspond to the same physical feature as seen in different views. This permits us to represent, in a single place, view-independent information gathered at different times and places. This is important also in non-visual applications.

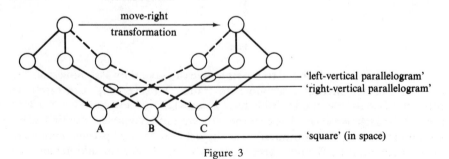

Figure 3

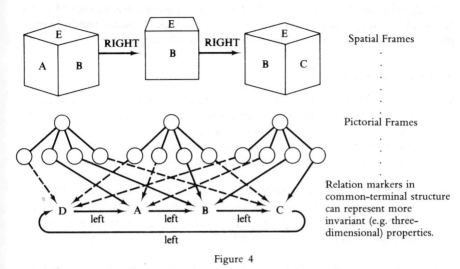

Figure 4

The matching process which decides whether a proposed frame is suitable is controlled partly by one's current goals and partly by information attached to the frame; the frames carry terminal markers and other constraints, while the goals are used to decide which of these constraints are currently relevant. Generally, the matching process could have these components:

(1) A frame, once evoked on the basis of partial evidence or expectation, would first direct a test to confirm its own appropriateness, using knowledge about recently noticed features, loci, relations, and plausible subframes. The current goal list is used to decide which terminals and conditions must be made to match reality.

(2) Next it would request information needed to assign values to those terminals that cannot retain their default assignments. For example, it might request a description of face C, if this terminal is currently unassigned, but only if it is not marked 'invisible'. Such assignments must agree with the current markers at the terminal. Thus, face C might already have markers for such constraints or expectations as:

Right-middle visual field.
Must be assigned.
Should be visible; if not, consider moving right.
Should be a cube-face subframe.
Share left vertical boundary terminal with face B.
If failure, consider box-lying-on-side frame.
Same background colour as face B.

(3) Finally, if informed about a transformation (e.g. an impending motion) it would transfer control to the appropriate other frame of that system.

Within the details of the control scheme are opportunities to embed many kinds of knowledge. When a terminal-assigning attempt fails, the resulting error message can be used to propose a second-guess alternative.

Is vision symbolic?

Can one really believe that a person's appreciation of three-dimensional structure can be so fragmentary and atomic as to be representable in terms of the relations between parts of two-dimensional views? Let us separate, at once, the two issues: is imagery *symbolic*? and is it based on *two-dimensional* fragments? The first problem is one of degree; surely everyone would agree that at *some* level vision is essentially symbolic. The quarrel would be between certain naive conceptions on one side – in which one accepts seeing *either* as picture-like *or* as evoking imaginary solids – against the confrontation of such experimental results of Piaget and Inhelder (1956) and others in which many limitations that one might fear would result from symbolic representations are shown actually to exist.

As for our second question: the issue of two- vs. three-dimensions evaporates at the symbolic level. The very concept of dimension becomes inappropriate. Each type of symbolic representation of an object serves some goals well and others poorly. If we attach the relation labels *left-of, right-of*, and *above* between parts of the structure, say, as markers on *pairs* of terminals, certain manipulations will work out smoothly; for example, some properties of these relations are 'invariant' if we rotate the cube while keeping the same face on the table. Most objects have 'permanent' tops and bottoms. But if we turn the cube on its side such predictions become harder to make; people have great difficulty keeping track of the faces of a six-coloured cube if one makes them roll it around in their mind. If one uses instead more 'intrinsic' relations like *next-to* and *opposite-to*, then turning the object on its side disturbs the 'image' much less.

Seeing a room

Visual experience seems continuous. One reason is that we move continuously. A deeper explanation is that our 'expectations' usually interact smoothly with our perceptions. Suppose you were to leave a room, close the door, turn to reopen it, and find an entirely different room. You would be shocked. The sense of change would be hardly less striking if the world suddenly changed before your eyes. A naive theory of phenomenological continuity is that we see so quickly that our image changes as fast as does the scene. There is an alternative theory: the changes in one's frame-structure representation proceed at their own pace; the system prefers to make small changes whenever possible; and the illusion of continuity is due to the persistence of assignments to *terminals common to the different view-frames*. Thus, continuity depends on the confirmation of expectations which in turn depends on rapid access to remembered knowledge about the visual world.

Just before you enter a room, you usually know enough to 'expect' a room rather than, say, a landscape. You can usually tell just by the character of the door. And you can often select in advance a frame for the new room. Very often, one expects a certain particular room. Then many assignments are already filled in.

The simplest sort of room–frame candidate is like the inside of a box. Following our cube-model, the room-frame might have the top-level structure shown in figure 5.

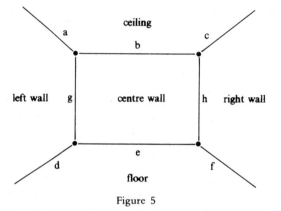

Figure 5

One has to assign to the frame's terminals the things that are seen. If the room is familiar, some are already assigned. If no expectations are recorded already, the first priority might be locating the principal geometric landmarks.

To fill in LEFT WALL one might first try to find edges a and d and then the associated corners ag and gd. Edge g, for example, is usually easy to find because it should intersect any eye-level horizontal scan from left to right. Eventually, ag, gb, and ba must not be too inconsistent with one another – because they are the same physical vertex.

However the process is directed, there are some generally useful knowledge-based tactics. It is probably easier to find edge e than any other edge, because if we have just entered a normal rectangular room, then we may expect that

Edge e is a horizontal line.
It is below eye level.
It defines a floor-wall texture boundary.

Given an expectation about the size of a room, we can estimate the elevation of e, and *vice versa*. In outdoor scenes, e is the horizon and on flat ground we can expect to see it at eye-level. If we fail quickly to locate and assign this horizon, we must consider rejecting the proposed frame: either the room is not normal or there is a large obstruction.

The room-analysis strategy might try next to establish some other landmarks. Given e, we next look for its left and right corners, and then for the verticals rising from them. Once such gross geometrical landmarks are located, we can guess the room's general shape and size. This might lead to selecting a new frame better matched to that shape and size, with additional markers confirming the choice and completing the structure with further details.

Scene analysis and subframes

If the new room is unfamiliar, no pre-assembled frame can supply fine details; more scene analysis is needed. Even so, the complexity of the work can be reduced, given suitable subframes for constructing hypotheses about sub-structures in the scene. How useful these will be depends both on their inherent adequacy and on the quality of the expectation process that selects which one to use next. One can say a lot even about an unfamiliar room. Most rooms are like boxes, and they can be categorized into types: kitchen, hall, living room, theatre, and so on. One knows dozens of kinds of rooms and hundreds of particular rooms; one no doubt has them structured into some sort of similarity network for effective access.

A typical room-frame has three or four visible walls, each perhaps of a different 'kind'. One knows many kinds of walls: walls with windows, shelves, pictures, and fireplaces. Each kind of room has its own kinds of walls. A typical wall might have a 3 × 3 array of region-terminals (left–centre–right) × (top–middle–bottom) so that wall-objects can be assigned qualitative locations. One would further want to locate objects relative to geometric interrelations in order to represent such facts as 'Y is a little above the centre of the line between X and Z.'

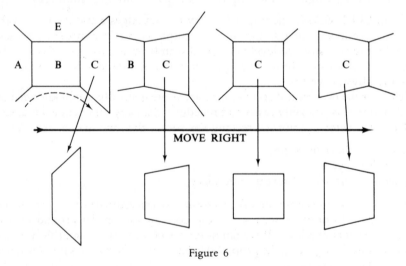

Figure 6

In three dimensions, the location of a visual feature of a subframe is ambiguous, given only eye direction. A feature in the middle of the visual field could belong either to a Centre Front Wall object or to a High Middle Floor object; these attach to different subframes. The decision could depend on reasoned evidence for support, on more directly visual distance information derived from stereo disparity or motion-parallax, or on plausibility information derived from other frames: a clock would be plausible only on the wall-frame while a person is almost certainly standing on the floor.

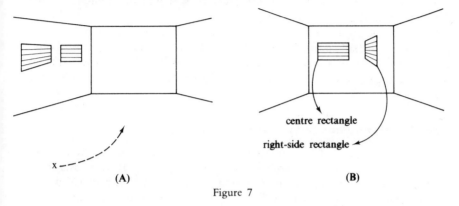

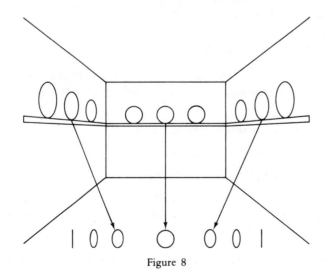

Figure 7

Given a box-shaped room, lateral motions induce orderly changes in the quadrilateral shapes of the walls as in figure 6. A picture-frame rectangle, lying flat against a wall, should transform in the same way as does its wall. If a 'centre-rectangle' is drawn on a left wall it will *appear* to project out because one makes the default assumption that any such quadrilateral is actually a rectangle hence must lie in a plane that would so project. In figure 7(A), both quadrilaterals could 'look like' rectangles, but the one to the right does not

Figure 8

match the markers for a 'left rectangle' subframe (these require, e.g. that the left side be longer than the right side). That rectangle is therefore represented by a centre-rectangle frame, and seems to project out as though parallel to the centre wall.

Thus we must not simply assign the label 'rectangle' to a quadrilateral but to a *particular frame of a rectangle-system*. When we move, we expect whatever space-transformation is applied to the top-level system will be applied also to its subsystems as suggested in figure 7(B).

Similarly the sequence of elliptical projections of a circle contains congruent pairs that are visually ambiguous as shown in figure 8. But because wall objects usually lie flat, we assume that an ellipse on a left wall is a left-ellipse, expect it to transform the same way as the left wall, and are surprised if the prediction is not confirmed.

Default assignment

While both seeing and imagining result in assignments to frame-terminals, imagination leaves us wider choices of detail and variety of such assignments. Frames are probably never stored in long-term memory with unassigned terminal values. Instead, what really happens is that frames are stored with weakly-bound default assignments at every terminal. These manifest themselves as often useful but sometimes counter-productive stereotypes.

Thus in the sentence 'John kicked the ball', you probably cannot think of a purely abstract ball, but must imagine characteristics of a vaguely particular ball; it probably has a certain default size, default colour, default weight. Perhaps it is a descendant of one you first owned or were injured by. Perhaps it resembles your latest one. In any case your image lacks the sharpness of presence because the processes that inspect and operate upon the weakly-bound default features are very likely to change, adapt, or detach them.

Words, sentences, and meanings

The concepts of frame and default assignment seem helpful in discussing the phenomenology of 'meaning'. Chomsky (1957) points out that such a sentence as

(A) Colourless green ideas sleep furiously

is treated very differently from the nonsentence

(B) Furiously sleep ideas green colourless

and suggests that, because both are 'equally nonsensical', what is involved in the recognition of sentences must be quite different from what is involved in the appreciation of meanings.

There is no doubt that there are processes especially concerned with grammar. Since the meaning of an utterance is 'encoded' as much in the positional and structural relations between the words as in the word choices themselves, there must be processes concerned with analysing those relations in the course of building the structures that will more directly represent the meaning. What makes the words of (A) more effective and predictable than (B) in producing such a structure – putting aside the question of whether that structure should be called semantic or syntactic – is that the word-order relations in (A) exploit the (grammatical) conventions and rules people usually use to induce others to make assignments to terminals of structures. This is entirely consistent with grammatical theories. A generative grammar would be a summary description of the *exterior* appearance of those frame rules – or their associated processes – while the operators of transformational grammars seem similar enough to some of our frame transformations.

We certainly cannot assume that 'logical' meaninglessness has a precise psychological counterpart. Sentence (A) can certainly generate an image. The dominant frame is perhaps that of someone sleeping; the default system assigns a particular bed, and in it lies a mummy-like shape-frame with a transluscent green colour property. In this frame there is a terminal for the character of the sleep – restless, perhaps – and 'furiously' seems somewhat inappropriate at that terminal, perhaps because the terminal does not like to accept anything so 'intentional' for a sleeper. 'Idea' is even more disturbing, because one expects a person, or at least something animate. One senses frustrated procedures trying to resolve these tensions and conflicts more properly, here or there, into the sleeping framework that has been evoked.

Utterance (B) does not get nearly so far because no subframe accepts any substantial fragment. As a result no larger frame finds anything to match its terminals, hence finally, no top level 'meaning' or 'sentence' frame can organize the utterance as either meaningful or grammatical. By combining this 'soft' theory with gradations of assignment tolerances, one could develop systems that degrade properly for sentences with 'poor' grammar rather than none; if the smaller fragments – phrases and subclauses – satisfy subframes well enough, an image adequate for certain kinds of comprehension could be constructed anyway, even though some parts of the top level structure are not entirely satisfied. Thus, we arrive at a qualitative theory of 'grammatical': if the top levels are satisfied but some lower terminals are not we have a meaningless sentence; if the top is weak but the bottom solid, we can have an ungrammatical but meaningful utterance.

Discourse

Linguistic activity involves larger structures than can be described in terms of sentential grammar, and these larger structures further blur the distinctness of the syntactic–semantic dichotomy. Consider the following fable, as told by W. Chafe (1972a):

There was once a wolf who saw a lamb drinking at a river and wanted an excuse to eat it. For that purpose, even though he himself was upstream, he accused the lamb of stirring up the water and keeping him from drinking. . . .

To understand this, one must realize that the wolf is lying. To understand the key conjunctive 'even though' one must realize that contamination never flows upstream. This in turn requires us to understand (among other things) the word 'upstream' itself. Within a declarative, predicate-based 'logical' system, one might try to formalize 'upstream' by some formula like:

[A upstream B] AND [Event T, Stream muddy at A]

$$\Rightarrow$$

[Exists [Event U, Stream muddy at B]] AND [Later U, T]

[That is, if A is upstream from B and there is an event making the stream muddy at A, then later the stream will be muddy at B.]

But an adequate definition would need a good deal more. What about the fact that the order of things being transported by water currents is not ordinarily changed? A logician might try to deduce this from a suitably intricate set of 'local' axioms, together with appropriate 'induction' axioms. I propose instead to represent this knowledge in a structure that automatically translocates spatial descriptions from the terminals of one frame to those of another frame of the same system. While this might be considered to be a form of logic, it uses some of the same mechanisms designed for spatial thinking.

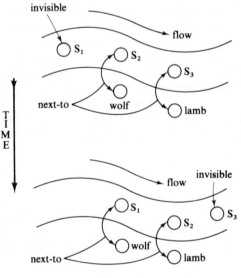

Figure 9

In many instances we would handle a change over time, or a cause–effect relation, in the same way as we deal with a change in position. Thus, the concept *river-flow* could evoke a frame-system structure something like the following, where S_1, S_2, and S_3 are abstract slices of the flowing river shown in figure 9.

There are many more nuances to fill in. What is 'stirring up' and why would it keep the wolf from drinking? One might normally assign default floating objects to the Ss, but here S_3 interacts with 'stirring up' to yield something that 'drink' does not find acceptable. Was it 'deduced' that stirring river-water means that S_3 in the first frame should have 'mud' assigned to it; or is this simply the default assignment for stirred water?

Almost any event, action, change, flow of material, or even flow of information can be represented to a first approximation by a two-frame generalized event. The frame-system can have slots for agents, tools, side-effects, preconditions, generalized trajectories, just as in 'case grammar' (Fillmore, 1968), but we have the additional flexibility of representing changes explicitly. To see if one has understood an event or action, one can try to build an appropriate instantiated frame-pair.

However, in representing changes by simple 'before-after' frame-pairs, we can expect to pay a price. Pointing to a pair is not the same as describing their differences. This makes it less convenient to do planning or abstract reasoning; there is no explicit place to attach information about the transformation. As a second approximation, we could label pairs of nodes that point to corresponding terminals, obtaining a structure like Winston's 'comparison-nodes', or we might place at the top of the frame-system information describing the differences more abstractly. Something of this sort will be needed eventually.

Scenarios

We condense and conventionalize, in language and thought, complex situations and sequences into compact words and symbols. Some words can perhaps be 'defined' in elegant, simple structures, but only a small part of the meaning of 'trade' is captured by:

first frame		second frame	
A has X	B has Y	B has X	A has Y

$\rightarrow$

Trading normally occurs in a social context of law, trust and convention. Unless we also represent these other facts, most trade transactions will be almost meaningless. It is usually essential to know that each party usually wants both things but has to compromise. It is a happy but unusual circumstance in which each trader is glad to get rid of what he has. To represent trading strategies, one could insert the basic manoeuvres right into the above frame-pair scenario: In order for A to make B want X more (or want Y less) we expect him to select one of the familiar tactics:

Offer more for Y.
Explain why X is so good.
Create favourable side-effect of B having X
Disparage the competition.
Make B think C wants X.

These only scratch the surface. Trades usually occur within a scenario tied together by more than a simple chain of events each linked to the next. No single such scenario will do; when a clue about trading appears it is essential to guess which of the different available scenarios is most likely to be useful.

Charniak (1972) studied questions about transactions that seem easy for people to comprehend yet obviously need rich default structures. We find in elementary school reading books such stories as:

Jane was invited to Jack's birthday party.
She wondered if he would like a kite.
She went to her room and shook her piggy bank.
It made no sound.

We first hear that Jane is invited to Jack's birthday party. Without the party scenario, or at least an invitation scenario, the second line seems rather mysterious:

She wondered if he would like a kite.

To explain one's rapid comprehension of this, we make a somewhat radical proposal: to represent explicitly, in the frame for a scenario structure, pointers to a collection of the most serious problems and questions commonly associated with it. In fact, we shall consider the idea that the frame terminals are exactly those questions. Thus, for the birthday party:

Y must get P for X .... Choose P!
X must like P .... Will X like P?
    Buy P .... Where to buy P?
    Get money to buy P .... Where to get money?
    (Sub-questions of the 'present' frame?)
Y must dress up .... What should Y wear?

Certainly these are one's first concerns when one is invited to a party.

The reader is free to wonder whether this solution is acceptable. The question 'Will X like P?' certainly matches 'She wondered if he would like a kite?' and correctly assigns the kite to P. But is our world regular enough that such question sets could be pre-compiled to make this mechanism often work smoothly? The answer is mixed. We do indeed expect many such questions; we surely do not expect all of them. But surely 'expertise' consists partly in not having to realize, *ab initio*, what are the outstanding problems and interactions in situations. Notice, for example, that there is *no* default assignment for the present in our party scenario frame. This mandates attention to that assignment problem and prepares us for a possible thematic concern. In any case, we probably need a more active mechanism for understanding 'wondered' which can apply the information currently in the frame to produce an expectation of what Jane will think about. The key words and ideas of a discourse evoke substantial thematic or scenario structures, drawn from memory with rich default assumptions.

In any event, the individual statements of a discourse lead to temporary representations – which seem to correspond to what contemporary linguists call [semantically interpreted] 'deep structures' – which are then quickly rearranged or consumed in elaborating the growing scenario representation. In order of 'scale,' among the ingredients of such a structure there might be these kinds of levels:

Syntactic frames – mainly verb and noun structures. Prepositional and word-order indicator conventions.

Semantic frames – action-centred meanings of words. Qualifiers and relations concerning participants, instruments, trajectories and strategies, goals, consequences and side-effects.

Thematic frames – scenarios concerned with topics, activities, portraits, setting. Outstanding problems and strategies commonly connected with topics.

Narrative frames – skeleton forms for typical stories, explanations, and arguments. Conventions about foci, protagonists, plot forms, development, etc., designed to help a listener construct a new, instantiated thematic frame in his own mind.

Requests to memory

We can now imagine the memory system as driven by two complementary needs. On one side are items demanding to be properly represented by being embedded into larger frames; on the other side are incompletely filled frames demanding terminal assignments. The rest of the system will try to placate these lobbyists, but not so much in accord with 'general principles' as in accord with special knowledge and conditions imposed by the currently active goals. When a frame encounters trouble – when an important condition cannot be satisfied – something must be done. We envision the following major kinds of accommodation to trouble.

Matching. When nothing more specific is found, we can attempt to use some 'basic' associative memory mechanism. This will succeed by itself only in relatively simple situations, but should play a supporting role in the other tactics.

Excuse. An apparent misfit can often be excused or explained. A 'chair' that meets all other conditions but is much too small could be a 'toy.'

Advice. The frame contains explicit knowledge about what to do about the trouble. Below, we describe an extensive, learned 'similarity network' in which to embed such knowledge.

Summary. If a frame cannot be completed or replaced, one must give it up. But first one must construct a well-formulated complaint or summary to help whatever process next becomes responsible for reassigning the subframes left in limbo.

Matching

When replacing a frame, we do not want to start all over again. How can we remember what was already 'seen'? We consider here only the case in which the system has no specific knowledge about what to do and must resort to some 'general' strategy. No completely general method can be very good, but if we could find a new frame that shares enough terminals with the old frame, then some of the common assignments can be retained, and we will probably do better than chance.

The problem can be formulated as follows: let E be the cost of losing a certain already assigned terminal and let F be the cost of being unable to assign some other terminal. If E is worse than F, then any new frame should retain the old subframe. Thus, given any sort of priority ordering on the terminals, a typical request for a new frame should include:

(1) Find a frame with as many terminals in common with [a, b, . . ., z] as possible, where we list high priority terminals already assigned in the old frame.

But the frame being replaced is usually already a subframe of some other frame and must satisfy the markers of *its* attachment terminal, lest the entire structure be lost. This suggests another form of memory request, looking upward rather than downward:

(2) Find or build a frame that has properties [a,b, . . ., z]

If we emphasize differences rather than absolute specifications, we can merge (2) and (1):

(3) Find a frame that is like the old frame except for certain differences [a,b, . . ., z] between them.

One can imagine a parallel-search to handle (1) and (2) if the terminals or properties are simple atomic symbols. . . . Unfortunately, there are so many ways to do this that it implies no specific design requirements.

Although (1) and (2) are formally special cases of (3), they are different in practice because complicated cases of (3) require knowledge about differences. In fact (3) is too general to be useful as stated, and we will later propose to depend on specific, learned, knowledge about differences between pairs of frames rather than on broad, general principles.

It should be emphasized again that we must not expect magic. For difficult, novel problems a new representation structure will have to be constructed, and this will require application of both general and special knowledge.

Excuses

We can think of a frame as describing an 'ideal'. If an ideal does not match reality because it is 'basically' wrong, it must be replaced. But it is in the nature of ideals that they are really elegant simplifications; their attractiveness derives from their simplicity, but their real power depends upon additional knowledge about interactions between them. Accordingly we need not abandon an ideal because of a failure to instantiate it, provided one can explain the discrepancy in terms of such an interaction. Here are some examples in which such an 'excuse' can save a failing match:

Occlusion. A table, in a certain view, should have four legs, but a chair might occlude one of them. One can look for things like shadows to support such an excuse.

Functional variant. A chair-leg is usually a stick, geometrically; but more important, it is *functionally* a support. Therefore, a strong centre post, with an adequate base plate, should be an acceptable replacement for all the legs. Many objects are multiple purpose and need functional rather than physical descriptions.

Broken. A visually missing component could be explained as in fact physically missing, or it could be broken. Reality has a variety of ways to frustrate ideals.

Parasitic contexts. An object that is just like a chair, except in size, could be (and probably is) a toy chair. The complaint 'too small' could often be so interpreted in contexts with other things too small, children playing, peculiarly large 'grain', and so forth.

In most of those examples, the kinds of knowledge to make the repair – and thus salvage the current frame – are 'general' enough usually to be attached to the thematic context of a superior frame.

Advice and similarity networks

In moving about a familiar house, we already know a dependable structure for 'information retrieval' of room frames. When we move through door D, in room X, we expect to enter room Y (assuming D is not the exit). We could represent this as an action transformation of the simplest kind, consisting of pointers between pairs of room frames of a particular house system.

When the house is not familiar, a 'logical' strategy might be to move up a level of classification: when you leave one room, you may not know which room you are entering, but you usually know that it is *some room*. Thus, one can partially evade lack of specific information by dealing with *classes* – and one has to use *some* form of abstraction or generalization to escape the dilemma of Bartlett's (1932) commander. [Bartlett cites Napoleon's remark: 'Those who form a picture of everything are unfit to command.' A commander who did envisage a battle in such a way would find, as Bartlett points out, that his picture would have gone awry soon after the opposing forces had joined. He would have nothing in reserve except another picture, and so on.]

Winston (see Reading 12) has proposed a way to construct a retrieval system that can represent classes but has additional flexibility. His retrieval pointers can be made to represent goal requirements and action effects as well as class memberships.

> What does it mean to expect a chair? Typically, four legs, some assortment of rungs, a level seat, an upper back. One expects also certain relations between these 'parts'. The legs must be below the seat, the back above. The legs must be supported by the floor. The seat must be horizontal, the back vertical, and so forth.
>
> Now suppose that this description does not match; the vision system finds four legs, a level plane, but no back. The 'difference' between what we expect and what we see is 'too few backs'. This suggests not a chair, but a table or a bench.

Winston proposes pointers from each description in memory to other descriptions, with each pointer labelled by a difference marker. Complaints about mismatch are matched to the difference pointers leaving the frame and thus may propose a better candidate frame. Winston calls the resulting structure a *similarity network*.

Is a similarity network practical? At first sight, there might seem to be a danger of unconstrained growth of memory. If there are N frames, and K kinds of differences, then there could be as many as $K \times N \times N$ interframe pointers. One might fear that:

(1) If N is large, say 10^7, then $N \times N$ is very large – of the order of 10^{14} – which might be impractical, at least for human memory.
(2) There might be so many pointers for a given difference and a given frame that the system will not be selective enough to be useful.
(3) K itself might be very large if the system is sensitive to many different kinds of issues.

But, according to contemporary opinions (admittedly, not very conclusive) about the rate of storage into human long-term memory there are probably not enough seconds in a lifetime to cause a saturation problem.

So the real problem, paradoxically, is that there will be too few connections. One cannot expect to have enough time to fill out the network to saturation. Given two frames that should be linked by a difference, we cannot count on that pointer being there; the problem may not have occurred before. However, in the next section we see how partially to escape this problem.

Clusters, classes, and a geographic analogy

To make the similarity network more 'complete,' consider the following analogy. In a city, any person should be able to visit any other; but we do not build a special road between each pair of houses; we place a group of houses on a 'block'. We do not connect roads between each pair of blocks; but have them share streets. We do not connect each town to every other; but construct main routes, connecting the centres of larger groups. Within such an organization, each member has direct links to some other individuals at his own 'level', mainly to nearby, highly similar ones; but each individual has also at least a few links to 'distinguished' members of higher-level groups. The result is that there is usually a rather short sequence between any two individuals, if one can but find it.

At each level, the aggregates usually have distinguished foci or *capitols*. These serve as elements for clustering at the next level of aggregation. There is no non-stop airplane service between New Haven and San Jose because it is more efficient overall to share the 'trunk' route between New York and San Francisco, which are the capitols at that level of aggregation.

The nonrandom convergences and divergences of the similarity pointers, for each difference d, thus tend to structure our conceptual world around

(1) the aggregation into d-clusters
(2) the selection of d-capitols.

Note that it is perfectly all right to have *several capitols in a cluster*, so that there need be no one attribute common to them all. The 'crisscross resemblances' of Wittgenstein (1958) are then consequences of the local connections in our similarity network, which are surely adequate to explain how we can feel as though we know what is a chair or a game – yet cannot always define it in a 'logical' way as an element in some class-hierarchy or by any other kind of compact, formal, declarative rule. The apparent coherence of the conceptual aggregates need not reflect explicit definitions, but can emerge from the success-directed sharpening of the difference-describing processes.

The selection of capitols corresponds to selecting stereotypes or typical elements whose default assignments are unusually useful. There are many forms of chairs, for example, and one should choose carefully the chair-description frames that are to be the major capitols of chairland. These are used for rapid matching and assigning priorities to the various differences. The lower priority features of the cluster centre then serve either as default properties of the chair types or, if more realism is required, as dispatch pointers to the local chair villages and towns.

Difference pointers could be 'functional' as well as geometric. Thus, after rejecting a first try at 'chair' one might try the functional idea of 'something one can sit on' to explain an unconventional form. This requires a deeper analysis in terms of forces and strengths. Of course, that analysis would fail to capture toy chairs, or chairs of such ornamental delicacy that their actual use would be unthinkable. These would be better handled by the method of excuses, in which one would by-pass the usual geometrical or functional explanations in favour of responding to contexts involving art or play.

Analogies and alternative descriptions

Suppose your car battery runs down. You believe that there is an electricity shortage and blame the generator.

The generator can be represented as a mechanical system: the rotor has a pulley wheel driven by a belt from the engine. Is the belt tight enough? Is it even there? The output, seen mechanically, is a cable to the battery or whatever. Is it intact? Are the bolts tight? Are the brushes pressing on the commutator?

Seen electrically, the generator is described differently. The rotor is seen as a flux-linking coil, rather than as a rotating device. The brushes and commutator are seen as electrical switches. The output is current along a pair of conductors leading from the brushes through control circuits to the battery.

The differences between the two frames are substantial. The entire mechanical chassis of the car plays the simple role, in the electrical frame, of one of the battery connections. The diagnostician has to use both representations. A failure of current to flow often means that an intended conductor is not acting like one. For this case, the basic transformation between the frames depends on the fact that electrical continuity is in general equivalent to firm mechanical attachment. Therefore, any conduction disparity revealed by electrical measurements should make us look for a corresponding disparity in the mechanical frame. In fact, since 'repair' in this universe is synonymous with 'mechanical repair', the diagnosis *must* end in the mechanical frame. Eventually, we might locate a defective mechanical junction and discover a loose connection, corrosion, wear, or whatever.

One cannot expect to have a frame exactly right for any problem or expect always to be able to invent one. But we do have a good deal to work with, and it is important to remember the contribution of one's culture in assessing the complexity of problems people seem to solve. *The experienced mechanic need not routinely invent*; he already has engine representations in terms of ignition, lubrication, cooling, timing, fuel mixing, transmission, compression, and so forth. Cooling, for example, is already subdivided into fluid circulation, air flow, thermostasis, etc. Most 'ordinary' problems are presumably solved by systematic use of the analogies provided by the transformations between pairs of these structures. The huge network of knowledge, acquired from school, books, apprenticeship, or whatever is interlinked by difference and relevancy pointers. No doubt the culture imparts a good deal of this structure by its conventional *use of the same words* in explanations of different views of a subject.

Summaries: using frames in heuristic search

Over the past decade, it has become widely recognized how important are the details of the representation of a 'problem space'; but it was not so well recognized that descriptions can be useful to a program, as well as to the person writing the program. Perhaps progress was actually retarded by ingenious schemes to avoid explicit manipulation of descriptions. Especially in 'theorem-proving' and in 'game-playing' the dominant paradigm of the past might be schematized so:

> The central goal of a theory of problem solving is to find systematic ways to reduce the extent of the search through the problem space.

Sometimes a simple problem is indeed solved by trying a sequence of 'methods' until one is found to work. Some harder problems are solved by a sequence of local improvements, by 'hill-climbing' within the problem space. But even when this solves a particular problem, it tells us little about the problem-space; hence yielding no improved future competence. The best-developed technology of Heuristic Search is that of game-playing using tree-pruning, plausible-move generation, and terminal-evaluation methods. But even those systems that use hierarchies of symbolic goals do not improve their understanding or refine their understanding or refine their representations. But there is a more mature and powerful paradigm:

> The primary purpose in problem solving should be better to understand the problem space, to find representations within which the problems are easier to solve. The purpose of search is to get information for this reformulation, not – as is usually assumed – to find solutions; once the space is adequately understood, solutions to problems will more easily be found.

The value of an intellectual experiment should be assessed along the dimension of success–partial success–failure, or in terms of 'improving the situation' or 'reducing a difference'. An application of a 'method', or a reconfiguration of a representation can be valuable if it leads to a way to improve the *strategy* of subsequent trials. Earlier formulations of the role of heuristic search strategies did not emphasize these possibilities, although they are implicit in discussions of 'planning.'

Papert (1972; see also Minsky 1970) is correct in believing that the ability to diagnose and modify one's own procedures is a collection of specific and important 'skills'. *Debugging*, a fundamentally important component of intelligence, has its own special techniques and procedures. Every normal person is pretty good at them or otherwise he would not have learned to see and talk. Goldstein (1974) and Sussman (1973) have designed systems which build new procedures to satisfy multiple requirements by such elementary but powerful techniques as:

(1) Make a crude first attempt by the first order method of simply putting together procedures that *separately* achieve the individual goals.
(2) If something goes wrong, try to characterize one of the defects as a *specific* (and undesirable) kind of interaction between two procedures.

(3) Apply a 'debugging technique' that, according to a record in memory, is good at repairing that *specific kind* of interaction.

(4) Summarize the experience, to add to the 'debugging techniques library' in memory.

These might seem simple-minded, but if the new problem is not too radically different from the old ones, then they have a good chance to work, especially if one picks out the right first-order approximations. If the new problem *is* radically different, one should not expect *any* learning theory to work well. Without a structured cognitive map – without the 'near misses' of Winston (Reading 12), or a cultural supply of good training sequences of problems – we should not expect radically new paradigms to appear magically whenever we need them.

23. A sketch of a cognitive approach to comprehension: some thoughts about understanding what it means to comprehend[1]

John D. Bransford and Nancy S. McCarrell

In reading, when I come upon an unfamiliar word or phrase I have a sensation of derailment. Some process that usually flows along smoothly has been interrupted. Some expected click of my mechanism has failed to occur. It has always seemed to be the principal task of psychology to discover the nature of this click. The meaningful linguistic form must set off some characteristic immediate effect in the person who understands. What is the substantial nature of this effect? (Brown, 1958, p. 82)

Brown describes the question that intrigues us: What happens when we comprehend? Obviously, this question is extremely complex and, as Huey (1968), notes, involves 'very many of the most intricate workings of the human mind' (p. 6). We do not presume to provide an adequate answer, but we do hope to raise particular questions about comprehension that may provoke further discussion and research.

Brown notes that psychologists' search for the 'click of comprehension' led them to ask how linguistic symbols give rise to meanings. Classical accounts generally dealt with individual words and their referents. . . . Linguistic communication generally does not involve isolated words, but rather sentences, and a sentence's meaning is not equivalent to the summed meanings of its component words (cf. Miller, 1965; Neisser, 1967). Similarly, our perception of the world is rarely confined to identification of an individual object in isolation, but instead includes perception of an object's role in events. For example, the object in figure 1(a) is usually perceived as a man running (maybe for a touchdown). The same object is perceived as a man chasing in figure 1(b), and in figure 1(c) the role is again changed.

[1] An edited excerpt of the paper. Reprinted with the permission of the authors and publishers from W. B. Weimar and D. S. Palermo (eds.) *Cognition and the Symbolic Processes* (Hillsdale, N. J.: Lawrence Erlbaum Associates, 1975), pp. 189–229.

Referent approaches were reasonable insofar as they attempted to tie some aspects of meaning to perceptual experience, but they fail because they assume an inadequate analysis of the information available from the perceptual world. Perception affords more than information about the characteristics of individual objects; it affords information about the spatio-temporal *relations* among entities that characterize dynamic perceptual events (cf. E. J. Gibson, 1969; J. J. Gibson, 1966). We shall sketch some implications of an approach to perception that focuses on information about relations rather than isolated entities, and suggest how this orientation yields results that may help us better understand linguistic comprehension.

(a)

(b)

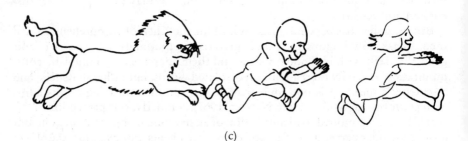

(c)

Figure 1 (a), (b), and (c). Object perception as a function of its role in events

We shall presuppose all abstract, relational information necessary to detect surfaces and entities, and shall concentrate on relational information among entities that render them meaningful. We begin by illustrating how relational information is important for understanding entities in our perceptual world.

Meaningful entities versus brute things

What do we know when an entity is meaningful for us? Dewey (1963) notes that 'Our chief difficulty in answering this question lies in the thoroughness with which the lesson of familiar things has been learned. Thought can more easily traverse an unexplored region than it can undo what has been so thoroughly done as to be ingrained in unconscious habit' (p. 138). A simple way to overcome some lessons of the familiar is to begin with unfamiliar entities and ask about the nature of information involved in conferring meaning upon them. This illustrates how meaning arises from perceiving an entity's participation in various events. Figure 2(a) illustrates an artificial entity. Some Ss (subjects) refer to it as a 'bumpy lump' and others as the back of a bear's head. The Ss thus attempt to confer meaning upon it (Bartlett's (1932) 'effort after meaning'; Piaget's (1952) 'assimilation'), but their understanding can be manipulated by viewing the entity's role in events. Figure 2(b) illustrates one sequence of events that gives the entity meaning; figure 2(c) illustrates a different meaning arising from a different sequence of events. Meanings for figures 2(b) and 2(c) both arise from viewing the entity in different contexts of usage. Figure 2(d) confers yet a different meaning on the artificial entity. Here the context is not one of usage, but rather specifies information about the entity's genesis from an organism's foot (i.e. it is a footprint). These examples illustrate that information about entities involves knowledge about their relations to other things that we know.

Figure 2 (a). An artificial entity

Figure 3(a) illustrates another set of relatively unknown objects. Rather than being artificial, however, they are drawings of real ones. Most people remain puzzled even when presented with the real things. These objects become more meaningful when one understands that they are tools designed to perform special functions. The appropriate functions for each object are provided in figure 3(b). These examples illustrate that information about an isolated object is not sufficient to allow an organism to grasp its meaning. . . .

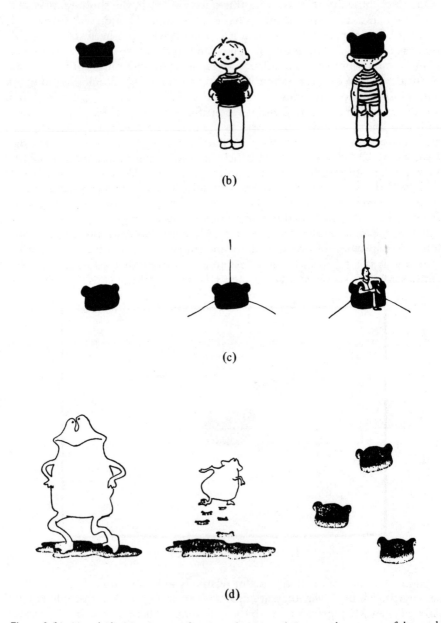

(b)

(c)

(d)

Figure 2 (b), (c) and (d). Meaning as a function of entities relating to other aspects of the world

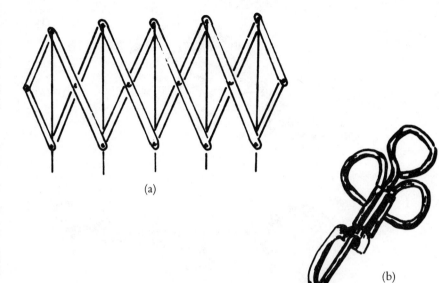

(a)

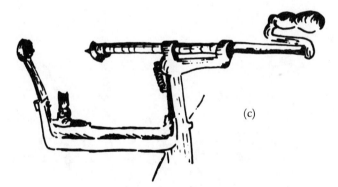

(b)

(c)

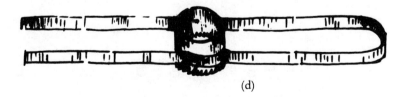

(d)

Figure 3 (a). Drawings of real 'incomprehensible' objects

(b)

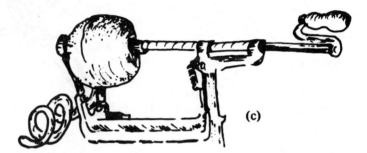

(c)

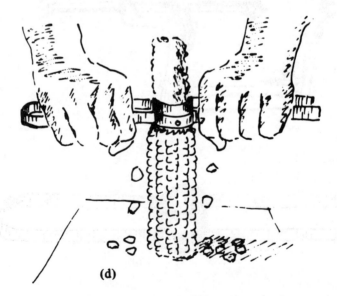

(d)

Figure 3 (b). Contexts for objects in figure 3 (a). Parallel line drawer–marker (a) is not pictured

Structural constraints and meaningfulness

The claim that objects become meaningful as a function of perceived interrelations with other objects (including ourselves) is not a claim that the relation between the isolated object and its potential meanings is arbitrary. On the contrary, the object's characteristics in isolation (e.g. what it looks like, is made of) constrain the types of events in which it might be involved.

The notion of a nonarbitrary relation between what something looks like and what it means is related to J. J. Gibson's (1966) notion of affordances. Certain objects and their properties provide visual information for the activities and interactions they afford. So, for example, sharp objects afford piercing, certain extensions (e.g. handles) afford grasping, hardness affords pounding, and roundness affords rolling. . . .

Of course, an object's physical form is not only nonarbitrarily related to possible relations with the organism who is the knower, but is also nonarbitrarily related to acts, interactions, and functions involving other objects in its environment. For example, a snake, infant, rabbit, human adult, and toy truck move across a surface in different manners. In each case, the organism's structure and posture provide support for the particular type of movement that takes place. Similarly, an object like a bed affords comfortable reclining, and its structure is clearly nonarbitrarily related to its use. Its structure will systematically vary according to the structure of the organisms (e.g. dog vs. human) that use it. And a structure's function may vary according to environmental context. Thus a wire cage supported by a single metal pole attached to a floor would not be a likely candidate for a bed for a human adult because it does not afford comfortable sleeping. However, if the wire frame is presented as a bed for an astronaut free of gravity, its affordance value for sleeping is more readily understood. The unfamiliar objects presented in figure 2 provide additional examples of the nonarbitrary relation between structure and function. Their structures place considerable constraints on their possible meanings. None of our informants entertained hypotheses about these objects being edible, sleep-on-able, and the like.

That physical properties may have meaningful implications is important for considerations of perceptual learning, because it suggests that relational information that allows objects to become meaningful also affects what perceptual characteristics are learned. Most researchers in perceptual learning have realized the importance of relations and concentrated on the acquisition of relationally derived distinctive features that serve to differentiate stimuli from other structurally similar ones (e.g. Garner, 1966). But there are other types of relations besides those which occur between structurally similar stimuli, and these too should affect what is learned. For example, one may learn to appreciate unique perceptual characteristics of the different scissors in figure 4 by noting how they differ from one another (i.e. by acquiring the perceptual features that differentiate the objects from one another) or, each scissor's unique structure can be meaningfully apprehended by better understanding the relations between the structures and the particular functions that each scissors was designed to perform. Table 1 summarizes appropriate functions for the scissors in figure 4. This example suggests that not only may physical structures have implications for objects' interrelations with other objects, but also that such interrelations may affect what is noticed about physical structure. . . .

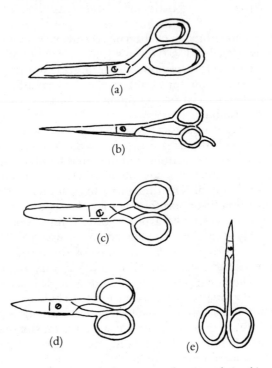

Figure 4. Scissors: an exercise in structure–function relationships

Linguistic comprehension

We have suggested that comprehension of perceptual events often involves assumptions about circumstances (e.g. instigating forces) that may not be immediately perceivable in the environment, and that the comprehender's knowledge of abstract constraints on entities and relations directs the assumptions or cognitive contributions he makes in order to understand. We think that – to an even greater extent than in perceptual comprehension – linguistic comprehension involves cognitive contributions on the part of the comprehender. The remaining sections consider some cognitive contributions that appear to accompany 'clicks of comprehension', and argue that the ability to make appropriate contributions depends on the comprehender's currently activated knowledge of his world. . . .

Table 1. Scissors: an exercise in structure–function relationships

Structure	Function
(a) Dressmaker shears	
heavy	because of heavy use.
one hole larger than other	so that two or three fingers will fit in larger hole – allows greater steadiness as one cuts cloth on flat surface.
blades off-centred and aligned with finger hole edge	so that blade can rest on table surface as cloth is cut – again, greater steadiness.
(b) Barber shears	
very sharp	to cut thin material; i.e. hair.
pointed	permits blades to snip close to scalp and to snip very small strands of hair.
hook on finger hole	a rest for one finger which allows scissors to be supported when held at various angles – hence greater manoeuvrability.
(c) Pocket or children's scissors	
blunt ends	so scissors can be carried in pocket without cutting through cloth; so children can handle without poking themselves or others.
short blades	allows greater control by the gross motor movements of the child just learning to cut.
(d) Nail scissors	
wide and thick at pivot point	to withstand pressure from cutting thick and rigid materials; i.e. nails.
slightly curved blades	to cut slightly curved nails.
(e) Cuticles scissors	
very sharp blade	to cut semi-elastic materials; i.e. skin of cuticles.
small, curved blades	to allow manoeuvrability necessary to cut small curved area.
long extension from finger holes to joint	as compensation for short blades, necessary for holding.

Our arguments will include the following considerations: (a) that Ss do make cognitive contributions while comprehending; (b) that certain contributions are prerequisites for achieving a click of comprehension; (c) that knowledge of abstract constraints on entities and relations plays an important role in determining Ss' contributions; and (d) that meaning is the result of such contributions and is best viewed as something that is 'created' rather than stored and retrieved. Following this, we shall consider some implications of the present approach.

Some considerations of the information available when we comprehend

That linguistic inputs might be viewed as cues or instructions to create meanings implies that semantic descriptions created by Ss may not always correspond to the information a sentence 'expresses directly.' The semantic descriptions created by Ss may often include more information than was expressed in a sentence, and the same inputs may result in different semantic descriptions depending on the cognitive contributions that the comprehender makes. This section reviews studies supporting this view.

Consider the following two sentences: (1) *Three turtles rested beside a floating log and a fish swam beneath them.* (2) *Three turtles rested on a floating log and a fish swam beneath them.* Both sentences express a spatial relation between the log and the turtles (either *on* or *beside*) and both express a relation between the fish and the turtles (namely, that the fish swam *beneath* the turtles).

Bransford, Barclay, and Franks (1972) reasoned that although the linguistic propositions underlying the two sentence types were similar, the semantic descriptions constructed by Ss might nevertheless differ. Thus, for sentence (2), Ss' knowledge of spatial relations should allow the inference that the fish swam beneath the log as well as the turtles (since the turtles were on the log), but the same inference should be less probable for Ss hearing sentence (1). Memory data supported the hypothesis that sentences like (1) and (2) may result in different semantic descriptions. Subjects hearing sentences like (2) were likely to think that they had actually heard novel sentences that expressed the probable inference (e.g. *Three turtles rested on a floating log and a fish swam beneath it*); whereas Ss hearing sentences like (1) were less likely to think that they had heard its novel counterpart (e.g. *Three turtles rested beside a floating log and a fish swam beneath it*). These data suggest that Ss used the linguistic inputs to create semantic descriptions of situations and that these descriptions often included more information than the input sentence directly expressed.

An obvious extension of the notion that Ss use linguistically communicated information to construct spatial descriptions of situations is that the same sentences may result in different semantic descriptions depending on the contextual information available to each S. A pilot study conducted by Bransford, Johnson, and Solomon evaluated this idea. Two groups of Ss saw two different pictorial contexts. Group I saw the picture in figure 5(a), whereas group II saw the picture in figure 5(b). All Ss were told that these were pictures of a farmhouse and a hill. Both groups were then read the same linguistic passage and asked to try to understand it. In the passage, entities were described in terms of their relation to the farmhouse and the hill. For example, the passage contained the following two sentences: (3) *The pond was to the right of the farmhouse;* (4) *The forest was to the left of the hill.* Such sentences should have different implications depending upon the initial context from which Ss viewed them. Thus Ss seeing picture (b) might assume that anything to the right of the farmhouse was also to the right of the hill, and *vice versa*, hence they should be likely to think they had heard the novel sentences (5) *The pond was to the right of the hill;* and (6) *The forest was to the left of the farmhouse*. However, Ss seeing picture (a) should be less likely to make such inferences, since, for example, the pond could be to the right of the farmhouse and yet in front of the hill.

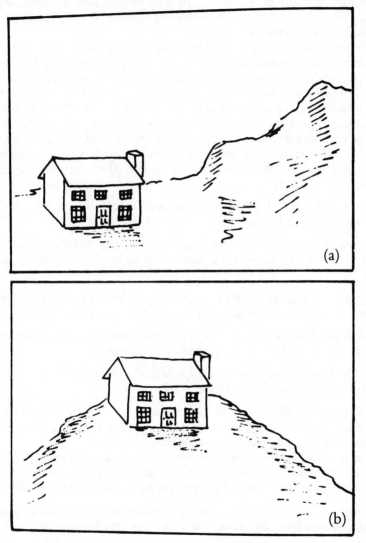

Figure 5 (a) and (b). Two different contexts for farm passage

Recognition data suggested that Ss did indeed create different semantic descriptions as a function of the initial context from which they viewed the linguistic passages. The Ss seeing picture (b) were generally unable to differentiate sentences that were actually heard, e.g. (3) (4), from novel but appropriate sentences like (5) and (6). However Ss seeing picture (a) were able to differentiate such sentences quite well. Note that if only the linguistic input were stored, both groups should have performed in an equivalent manner since the passages they heard were identical. That their performance did differ suggests that the information acquired from the input sentences depended upon the initial contexts from which they were viewed.

Of course, it is likely that Ss make assumptions about (and 'remember') things other than inferred spatial relations among objects mentioned in the input sentences. For example, they may assume the existence of objects never mentioned in the sentence, or they may elaborate the consequences that particular inputs seem to imply. Johnson, Bransford, and Solomon (1973) showed that Ss make assumptions about objects never mentioned in sentences – in this case, the objects were those generally necessary to perform certain acts. The Ss were read a series of very short descriptions. Experimental Ss were read stories designed to suggest particular inferences about instruments used to carry out the actions. For example:

> John was trying to fix the bird house. He was *pounding the nail* when his father came out to watch him and to help him do the work.

For the control group, the same story frames were used but in each case a verb was changed so that no object was implied or so that the implied object was different:

> John was trying to fix the bird house. He was *looking for* the nail when his father came out to watch him and to help him do the work.

At recognition, both groups of Ss were presented with the same sentences. The critical instrument-inference item for the above story was:

> John was using the *hammer* to fix the bird house when his father came out to watch him and to help him do the work.

The Ss hearing the first version of the story were quite likely to think that they had actually heard the recognition foil, but Ss hearing the second version were quite sure that they had not heard it before.

The same study investigated false recognition memory for another class of inferences: those dealing with perceived consequences of input events. Once again, Ss were read brief stories. The experimental group heard stories like this:

> The river was narrow. A beaver hit the log that a turtle was sitting on and the log flipped over from the shock. The turtle was very surprised by the event.

If you think about this situation for a moment, you will realize that a probable consequence of the log's flipping over is that the turtle would get knocked into the water.

A control group heard the identical story, except that the turtle was *beside* the log rather than on it. After acquisition, both groups heard the same recognition foil: *A beaver hit the log and knocked the turtle into the water.* Once again most *S*s in the experimental group were quite sure that they had actually heard this sentence whereas *S*s in the control group felt that they had not heard it before.

These studies suggest that information 'directly expressed' by sentences cannot always be equated with the information available to the comprehender. Comprehenders do not simply store the information underlying sentences, but instead use linguistic inputs in conjunction with other information to update their general knowledge of the world. These considerations apply not only to individual sentences but also to sets of sentences. Thus, *S*s often use information expressed by a number of individual sentences (often ones which are nonadjacent) to form wholistic semantic descriptions containing more information than any particular acquistion sentence expressed (e.g., Barclay, 1973; Bransford and Franks, 1971; Potts, 1971). Such studies support arguments made previously by Wundt that 'the mind of the hearer is just as active in transforming and creating as the mind of the speaker' (cf. Blumenthal, 1970, p. 37) and that it is the apperceptive constructive processes that organize the input events. We are thereby reminded that an adequate approach to comprehension must consider the cognitive contributions of the comprehender as well as the linguistic characterizations of input sentences. But we need a clearer picture of the role that particular cognitive contributions may play.

Cognitive contributions that are necessary in order to comprehend

A reasonable interpretation might be that *S*s first comprehend sentences and *then* make cognitive contributions such as elaborating spatial implications, inferring probable consequences, and so forth. One might therefore suppose that cognitive processing takes over *after* something called 'linguistic comprehension' takes place. But our view of linguistic knowledge as abstract cues or instructions used to create meanings denies that one's knowledge of language incorporates knowledge of meaning – in the sense of meaning sufficient to produce a click of comprehension. Comprehension results only when the comprehender has sufficient nonlinguistic information to use the cues specified in linguistic input to create some semantic content that allows him to understand. In actuality, there are undoubtedly many levels at which one can understand utterances. Nevertheless, there appears to be some minimum level below which *S*s will fail to call sentences 'comprehensible'. This suggests that one may have knowledge of language and yet fail to understand utterances unless one is able to activate appropriate nonlinguistic knowledge. This section considers some studies that investigate this idea.

Bransford and Johnson (1972, 1973) sought to manipulate *S*s' abilities to comprehend by varying the availability of prerequisite information. For example, consider the following passage (which was read to *S*s) and imagine that you are to try to recall it after it is read:

If the balloons popped the sound wouldn't be able to carry since everything would be too far away from the correct floor. A closed window would also prevent the sound from carrying, since most buildings tend to be well insulated. Since the whole operation depends upon a steady flow of electricity, a break in the middle of the wire would also cause problems. Of course, the fellow could shout, but the human voice is not loud enough to carry that far. An additional problem is that a string could break on the instrument. Then there could be no accompaniment to the message. It is clear that the best situation would involve less distance. Then there would be fewer potential problems. With face to face contact, the least number of things could go wrong.

One group (No Context–1) heard the passage (read once through) and were then asked to rate it on a 7-point comprehension scale. Following that, they were asked to recall as much as they could. Table 2 indicates that these Ss rated the passage as very incomprehensible and showed very poor recall. A second group (Appropriate Context) heard the same tape-recorded passage, but they saw the picture in figure 6 for thirty seconds before the passage was read. Note that the passage does not simply describe the picture, but instead specifies events that could happen given the picture as a conceptual base. The Ss seeing this picture rated the passage very comprehensible and showed a 100 per cent increase in recall over the No Context group (see table 2). This picture had to be made available to Ss *before* they heard the passage, however. A third group (Context After Ss) received the appropriate context picture after hearing the passage, and table 2 shows that this did not appreciably augment their comprehension and recall scores relative to the No Context group. And the ability to comprehend the passage was not simply an effect of mere repetition of information: a fourth group (No Context–2) heard the passage (without context) twice in succession. Nevertheless, they still exhibited poor comprehension and recall scores.

Table 2. Mean comprehension ratings and recall scores
for experiment on the 'balloon passage'

	No Context–1	No Context–2	Context After	Partial Context	Context Before
Comprehension	2.30	3.60	3.30	3.70	6.10
Recall	3.60	3.80	3.60	4.00	8.00

A fifth group was also run in the experiment. These Ss (Partial Context Ss) saw the picture in figure 7 for thirty seconds before the passage was read. Note that the picture contained the same concrete elements as the appropriate context figures, but the relations among the elements were changed. Table 2 shows that Ss seeing the second picture did not benefit from it. They still exhibited very low comprehension and recall scores. We shall return to consider why the appropriate context helped Ss comprehend the passage and why the second picture failed to help them, but first, consider some additional studies that attempt to manipulate Ss ability to comprehend.

The preceding passage referred to a particular situation with which few people were likely to have had contact. However, the importance of prerequisite knowledge is applicable to situations where the semantic prerequisites are available from Ss' prior knowledge, but are not activated at the time the passage is heard. Consider the following passage and imagine again that you are to try to recall what you heard.

The procedure is actually quite simple. First you arrange things into different groups. Of course one pile may be sufficient depending on how much there is to do. If you have to go somewhere else due to lack of facilities that is the next step, otherwise you are pretty well set. It is important not to overdo things. That is, it is better to do too few things at once than too many. In the short run this may not seem important but complications can easily arise. A mistake can be expensive as well. At first the whole procedure will seem complicated. Soon, however, it will become just another facet of life. It is difficult to foresee any end to the necessity for this task in the immediate future, but then one never can tell. After the procedure is completed one arranges the materials into different groups again. Then they can be put into their appropriate places. Eventually they will be used once more and the whole cycle will then have to be repeated. However, that is a part of life.

Now read the passage again, but with the knowledge that the topic is *washing clothes*. Results of two such experiments are shown in table 3. The Ss in the No Topic group showed poor comprehension and recall scores, as did Ss who received information that the passage was about washing clothes *after* hearing the passage but just before recall. The Ss in the Topic Before groups showed

Figure 6. Appropriate context for balloon passage

Figure 7. Partial context for balloon

higher comprehension and recall scores. Note that prior knowledge is not sufficient to assure comprehension. This knowledge must be activated if one is to understand.

Table 3. Mean comprehension ratings and recall scores for
two different experiments on passages about 'washing clothes'

	Experiment 1			Experiment 2	
	No Topic	Topic After	Topic Before	Topic After	Topic Before
Comprehension	2.29	2.12	4.50	3.40	5.27
Recall	2.82	2.65	5.83	3.30	7.00

A third experiment by Bransford and Johnson (1973) is also relevant. Ss were read the following passage after informing them that its title was *Watching a peace march from the fortieth floor:*

The view was breathtaking. From the window one could see the crowd below. Everything looked extremely small from such a distance, but the colourful costumes could still be seen. Everyone seemed to be moving in one direction in an orderly fashion and there seemed to be little children as well as adults. The landing was gentle and luckily the atmosphere was such that no special suits had to be worn. At first there was a great deal of activity. Later, when the speeches started, the crowd quieted down. The man with the television camera took many shots of the setting and the crowd. Everyone was very friendly and seemed to be glad when the music started.

After hearing the passage, Ss were asked to recall it. Most sentences were recalled well except for the one about 'the landing'. There was extremely low recall for this sentence, and Ss noted that there was one sentence (i.e. about a landing) that they could not understand. Even when presented with a 'cue outline' e.g. Luckily the landing —— and the atmosphere ——), Ss exhibited very low ability to remember what this sentence was about.

A second group of Ss heard the identical passage but with a different title: *A space trip to an inhabited planet.* These Ss showed much better free recall of 'the landing' sentence than did the first group, as well as greater ability to fill in the gaps in the cue outline presented above (see Bransford and Johnson, 1973). These results suggest that a sentence that would be comprehensible in isolation (i.e. 'the landing' sentence) can become incomprehensible when viewed from an inappropriate context, and that such incomprehensibility has a marked effect on ability to recall. The results also illustrate that the same passage, when viewed from different contexts, can be interpreted as meaning very different things.

Evidence for cognitive contributions that allow one to comprehend

The preceding studies demonstrate that one can have knowledge of language and yet fail to understand utterances if one is unable to activate appropriate knowledge of the world. But it could be argued that these are contrived situations (which they are) and that one's ability to comprehend a multitude of sentences in isolation suggests the existence of other, more natural, linguistic processes that usually take place when one comprehends. We contend that sentences which are and are not comprehensible in isolation differ *not* in terms of necessary cognitive contributions, but rather in terms of the ease with which such contributions can be made. In this section we present evidence suggesting that Ss do frequently make cognitive contributions *in order to understand* sentences. Our evidence will still be based on sentences which, although comprehensible in isolation, are still rather difficult and perhaps not 'normal'. We begin with such sentences for the same reasons that Bühler and his colleagues apparently did (cf. Blumenthal, 1970): They allow an opportunity for otherwise unconscious processes to be observed. In later sections we will consider more 'normal' sentences as well.

An experiment by McCarrell, Bransford, and Johnson suggests that Ss spontaneously specify certain cognitive conditions while comprehending sentences. Two parallel sets of target sentences were constructed. One set was composed of sentences designed to elicit special assumptions (SA sentences) (e.g. *The floor was dirty because Sally used the mop; The shirt looked terrible because Jane ironed it; John missed the bus because he knew he would have to walk to school*). The second set included similar sentences that were more 'self-contained' (SC sentences) in that fewer special assumptions had to be made (e.g. *The floor was dirty so Sally used the mop; The shirt looked terrible so Jane ironed it; John missed the bus so he knew he would have to walk to school*). For the SA sentences Ss are forced into specifying how a state or event (e.g., dirty floor, terrible looking dress, missed bus) could result from a preceding action or idea (e.g. mopping, ironing, knowing about having to walk). Most Ss assume that such relations can take place if, for example, the mop was dirty, Sally was a poor ironer, and John wanted to walk to school.

The SA and SC target sentences were embedded in short story frames and read to Ss. Either an SA or its SC counterpart was presented in the identical story frame. After hearing the series, Ss were asked to recognize which *exact* sentences they had actually heard during acquisition. The question was the degree to which Ss would falsely recognize novel sentences that expressed probable assumptions (e.g. *The mop was dirty before Sally washed the floor; John wanted to walk to school so he purposefully missed the bus, etc.*) as a function of whether Ss had heard an SA or SC form. The Ss hearing an SA form were quite likely falsely to recognize such sentences, whereas those hearing an SC form were not likely to think they had heard them before.

A pilot study has investigated the effects of cognitive contributions on the free recall of sentences. Our reasoning was that if certain sentences (e.g. (1) *The shirt looked terrible because Jane ironed it;* (2) *The mirror shattered because the child grabbed the broom*) require elaborative contributions *(elaboratives)*, they might stand out from other sentences more than their easy counterparts *(easies)* (e.g. (3) *The shirt looked terrible so Jane ironed it;* (4) *The mirror shattered so the child grabbed the broom*). Hence, *elaboratives* might be more likely to be recalled. Using a within-Ss design, we presented Ss with sentences such as (1) and (4) and other Ss with sentences such as the counterparts (2) and (3). *Elaborative* sentences were recalled more frequently than their *easy* counterparts, hence supporting the notion that there is some psychological reality to cognitive elaborations that take place when we comprehend. Of course, one might argue, that the *elaborative* sentences were simply 'unusual' and that this accounts for their high recall. But not all 'unusual' sentences result in high recall, as the next study shows.

A third experiment reminds us that certain cognitive contributions may be necessary in order to allow one to comprehend. The immediately preceding study used *elaboratives* and *easy* sentences that were ultimately comprehensible to Ss who were able to make appropriate cognitive specifications that permitted them to comprehend. In the present study, we designed sentences for which it was unlikely that Ss could specify appropriate conditions unless provided with cues from E (experimenter). The study compared recall of these *difficult* sentences with recall of sentences that were *easy* to comprehend. Examples of *easy* and *difficult* sentences are provided below:

> Easy: The office was cool because the windows were closed.
>   The car was moved because he had no change.
> Difficult: The trip was not delayed because the bottle shattered.
>   The haystack was important because the cloth ripped.

Note that both the *easy* and *difficult* sentences were constructed by linking easily comprehended, simple sentences by *because*. The differential difficulty of the two sentence sets thus arises from the differential ease with which Ss could specify situations in which the *because* relation between the simple sentences could make sense.

Two groups were run: One group (No Context) received a list consisting of eight *easy* and eight *difficult* sentences, randomly intermixed. On the study trials, each sentence was preceded by the subject noun (e.g. the office, the car, the trip, the haystack). On the test trials, the subject nouns were available as retrieval cues. For this condition, *easy* sentences were recalled much better than were *difficult* sentences, with the advantage of the *easy* items persisting over three study-test trials.

The second group (Context) received conditions identical to those of the first except that each sentence was preceded by a context cue rather than a subject noun on the study trials. The contexts for the sentences above were *air-conditioning, parking meter, christening a ship,* and *parachutist,* respectively. They were designed to provide Ss with information that would allow them to grasp the *because* relation between the entities mentioned in each clause. The retrieval cues on the recall tests were the subject noun.

Presentation of the context cues eliminated the differential recall for *easy* and *difficult* sentences. The differential difficulty of these sentence classes was therefore not simply a function of the sentences *per se,* but rather of the ease with which Ss could specify conditions that would allow the *because* relations to be grasped.

Towards a characterization of the constraints governing the specifications subjects must make

Reasonable evidence suggests that the comprehender must frequently do considerable work to create situations that allow him to grasp the relations specified in input sentences, and that at least some specifications are necessary for the click of comprehension to occur. But such a statement still lacks cognitive content. Why do certain specifications permit comprehension and others result in failure? Do Ss randomly make assumptions, or are their assumptions somehow constrained? Do all sentences involve cognitive specifications on the comprehender's part, or are the sentences we have considered merely special cases that are different from those Ss normally hear? We cannot completely answer these questions, but in the present section we shall argue that they are worth asking, and we shall speculate on directions one might take in order to determine what adequate answers might be.

Constraints on entities entering into events

Consider a sentence which most Ss find initially anomalous and then comprehensible: *The man put the plane in the envelope.* Most Ss assume that the plane must be a toy one; and with this discovery, they comprehend. What is it that forces Ss to place special constraints on their interpretation of *plane*?

We have suggested that comprehending involves the grasping of relations, and in the above sentence, an important relation is '*x* is contained by *y*.' It seems reasonable that such a relation is known to involve size restrictions between a container and the contained, and that these restrictions force Ss to specify certain conditions (i.e. that it is a toy plane) that will allow such a relation to occur. Of course, Ss might choose to assume a large envelope rather than a small plane, but the latter is presumably more likely given our knowledge of the world . . . Size restrictions are, of course, but one of many restrictions on entities entering into events.

Instigating force as an abstract category underlying many events

As another example of the effect of relations (and their participating entities) on comprehension, consider the following sentences: *The wind broke the window; The ball broke the window.* These sentences are comprehended in different ways. Changes of state generally involve some instigating force responsible for the situation, and the verb *break* certainly involves a change of state (cf. Fillmore,

1971). Among other things, the comprehender is forced to assign a member of the category *instigating force* to the sentences above. . . .

Words as abstract constraints that guide meaning-making acts

. . . Putting a toy plane into an envelope presumably involves the use of hands, whereas putting a real airplane into a hanger necessitates a very different understanding of the word *put*. It appears reasonable to suggest that words and sentences specify some abstract conditions concerning the nature of the relations and the participating entities to be considered, and that it is the comprehender's ability to think (i.e. create situations such that the relations can be realized) that allows him to understand what the sentence might mean.

The conception of words as abstract constraints that guide meaning creation may help us understand how words can have so many different senses or meanings. If meaning results from Ss' creations of situations that permit the occurrence of certain relations specified in a sentence, a word should be interpreted differently as a function of its context. Consider, for example, the word *use*. One can use a rope, knife, box, etc., and in each case what one understands by *use* depends on the nature of the entities involved in the event *using*. Furthermore, the same entity can be used for different functions. Thus, to use a wooden box to carry books is different from using it to reach the ceiling; to use a rope to tie a package is different from using it to climb down from the third floor. And one uses a knife to cut bread in a different manner from using it to drive a screw into the wall. In each case the word *use* imposes abstract constraints on the nature of the event considered, but the entities involved affect the semantic content of the relation that comprehenders create.

Of course, not only may a word be interpreted differently as a function of its sentence context, but a whole sentence may also be understood differently as a function of the larger context in which it is heard. The following passage, read at normal speed, illustrates how overall context can affect Ss' understanding of the relations specified in a sentence:

The man was worried. His car came to a halt and he was all alone. It was extremely dark and cold. The man took off his overcoat, rolled down the window, and got out of the car as quickly as possible. Then he used all his strength to move as fast as he could. He was relieved when he finally saw the lights of the city, even though they were far away.

Immediately after hearing this passage, Ss were asked to answer two questions as quickly as possible: (1) Why did he take off his overcoat? (2) Why did he roll down the window? For both sentences the results were rather striking. The Ss generally took a very long time to answer (10–20 seconds), and they were unsure of the answers they gave (e.g. 'maybe he rolled down the window to check for oncoming traffic').

A second group of Ss was also run in the study. They heard the identical passage except that it contained one additional adjective which told them that the car was submerged (i.e. *His submerged car came to a halt* . . .). These Ss could answer the questions about the coat and the window very rapidly, and were quite certain of the answers they gave.

Evidently, the first group understood the relations between the man, coat, and window as one of temporal succession, and did not process the relations beyond that. The second group, however, understood these relations at a richer level than one of mere temporal succession, and hence could readily answer why the coat was removed (so he could swim more easily) and why he opened the window (to swim out). The same abstract constraints can therefore result in different meanings as a function of the contributions made by the S.

As a final example of abstract constraints that direct the comprehender to specify certain situations, consider relations such as *if . . . then* and *because*. These words direct Ss to attempt to specify situations in which one thing could follow from another, and this is often a difficult task. In sentences like *The mirror shattered because the child grabbed the broom,* Ss can assume that the child hit the mirror with the broom and broke it. But if Ss are presented with a sentence like *The haystack was important because the cloth ripped,* they have a much more difficult time specifying conditions that could permit the relation – unless a cue such as *parachute* is provided by E. Even with the cue, Ss must presumably make some additional cognitive specifications: that the parachute was *above* the haystack when it ripped, etc.

We think that the *because* and *if . . . then* relations make it difficult to comprehend the balloon passage presented earlier. For example, the sentence, *If the balloons popped the sound wouldn't be able to carry . . .* , was difficult to comprehend in isolation. One problem was that Ss had to decide what *sound* referred to, and the most likely candidate was that sound was something made by the balloons when they popped. But given this interpretation, it became difficult to understand why the sound could not carry. The Ss were forced to imagine some situation in which the relation made sense. They reported that they did come up with some conditions that allowed some sentences in the balloon passage to be comprehended, but that these situations then failed to specify conditions necessary for understanding subsequent sentences.

The Ss seeing the partial context picture were in a similar predicament. They knew that the balloons were being held by the boy, but again *sound* seemed to refer to the result of the balloons popping and therefore the question of why the sound did not carry had to be resolved. Some of these Ss also remarked that they could specify conditions allowing the comprehension of some sentences, but that they could not create an overall situation in which all the sentences of the passage made sense.

The Ss seeing the appropriate picture were in a different situation. They could understand that an implication of the balloons' popping would be that the speakers would fall and that *sound* referred to the noise from the speakers and not from the balloons. The picture also allowed them to calculate why the sound could not carry; namely, because the speakers would be too far away from the girl if they fell to the ground. In short, Ss seeing the appropriate context picture before hearing the passage were able to specify how the relations referred to in the utterances could be realized. The appropriate context picture was, therefore, not a static set of retrieval cues nor a mnemonic device into which Ss could 'plug' the input sentences; rather, it communicated information that allowed Ss to specify how certain relations could occur.

Conclusions

We have proposed that knowledge of language might fruitfully be conceptualized as knowledge of abstract cues or instructions that guide the comprehender. The semantic content of a particular linguistic message is created only as the comprehender, guided by the linguistic cues, specifies conditions under which the abstract relations can be realized given his knowledge of the world. A person may therefore have knowledge of a language and yet fail to comprehend an utterance because he is unable to make the necessary cognitive contributions. And the same sentences may be understood differently as a function of the cognitive contributions that different listeners make.

If the present approach is to be fruitful, an important future problem is the characterization of the abstract information specified by lexical items (plus certain rules of syntax), and the investigation of the manner by which this information is utilized by the comprehender to achieve the click of comprehension to which Brown (1958) referred. Some of our information about certain lexical items undoubtedly derives from information about events that they may refer to, or from information about the relations that a class of entities has to other aspects of the world. For example, we have suggested that events involve restrictions on the nature of the entities that enter into them and may require certain 'categories of information' (e.g. an instigating force, an instrument to carry out an action, etc.) that the comprehender must 'fill in'. Linguistic symbols that refer to such events or entities should activate information about such abstract specifications, and the symbols will differ in terms of the degree of specificity implied (e.g. a toy truck, a snake, and a human can move across a room, but only a human can walk). . . .

Our approach to comprehension focuses on the comprehender's ability to use his general knowledge to create situations that permit the relations specified in input sentences to be realized, or to postulate situations that allow perceptual events to be understood. In short, the ability to create some level of semantic content sufficient to achieve a click of comprehension depends upon the comprehender's ability to think. This leads us to attempt to characterize the abstract relational knowledge derived from perceptual experience, and to study how this information places cognitive constraints on one's ability to understand linguistic strings.

It is painfully obvious that the present paper has barely scratched the surface of the problem of comprehension. In fact, the more we study the area the more we discover what we do not know. In particular, we need to determine how our approach resembles and differs from those proposed by H. H. Clark (1974), Collins and Quillian (1972), Kintsch (1972), Rumelhart, Lindsay, and Norman

(1972) Schank (1972), Trabasso (1972), and Winograd (1972). Besides having the advantage of formal characterizations of their concepts, these authors raise many important questions that we have not considered here. We have no illusions about having answered how one achieves a click of comprehension. Our purpose has been to sketch a general orientation towards the problem, and to present some experimental paradigms that may help us study it in greater detail.

24. Practical and lexical knowledge[1]

George A. Miller

This paper is addressed to one aspect of what people know when they know the categories that are named by nominal expressions in their language. Although this may seem a relatively straightforward question, the range of opinions expressed about categorical knowledge by psychologists, linguists, philosophers, and others is too great for any simple summary. In order to stay within reasonable limits, therefore, the particular aspect to be discussed here concerns the possibility of making some reasonable division of that categorical knowledge into two parts, one part having to do with a person's general knowledge about the world and the things that happen in it, and another part having to do with the entailments that follow from a claim that something is a member or instance of a category. In order to talk about this possible division it is convenient to introduce the terms 'practical knowledge' and 'lexical knowledge', but that terminology should not be taken to represent a pre-judgment about their distinguishability.

The knowledge problem

Let us begin with an example. The sentence, *The Smiths saw the Rocky Mountains while they were flying to California,* is ambiguous, since it is not clear whether the Smiths, the Rocky Mountains, or both were flying to California when the sighting took place. Most people fail at first to notice the ambiguity, because the interpretation in which the Smiths are flying is far more salient than interpretations in which the Rocky Mountains are. The reason is obvious. Anyone who knows what mountains are knows that they do not fly.

This fact – that mountains do not fly – is practical knowledge. It is not a fact that can be discovered by consulting dictionaries and would not be included in any reasonable account of a person's lexical knowledge. Yet it affects the interpretation of the ambiguous sentence almost as directly and immediately as

[1] This paper is reprinted with the permission of the author and publishers from E. Rosch and B. B. Lloyd (eds.) *Cognition and Categorization* (Hillsdale, N. J.: Lawrence Erlbaum Associates, in press).

does any knowledge that would be conventionally regarded as lexical. Given that one's practical knowledge of mountains enters as directly as one's lexical knowledge of the word *mountains*, it is natural to ask how this is possible. Since practical knowledge must play an important role in most of the uses we make of language, we might even wonder whether any purpose is served by distinguishing two kinds of knowledge.

The advantage of distinguishing lexical from practical knowledge is that it helps to set manageable bounds on what phenomena a theory of linguistic communication can be expected to treat. There is more than enough to explain even if we limit our theorizing to the lexical meanings of words and phrases and their linguistic entailments. If we must also include a theory of knowledge in general, the theoretical task will become unmanageable. Moreover, the difference is readily illustrated. One feels that the relation of *John's children are asleep* to *John has children* is very different from its relation to *John is married*. In the latter case an inference can be justified by practical knowledge, but it lacks the requiredness of the former relation, which can be justified in terms of the linguistic meaning of *John's children*, in terms of lexical and linguistic knowledge.

Students of language are, therefore, strongly motivated to draw the distinction. But if we place practical knowledge outside the basic machinery of linguistic comprehension, we create the problem of explaining when and how it is invoked for interpretive purposes. That is what 'the knowledge problem' will be taken to mean in the present context.

The usual resolution of this problem consists of waving the hands vaguely toward a distant bridge that may someday need to be crossed. Perhaps the output of the linguistic component is passed on to some further cognitive component where practical knowledge is ready and waiting to add its contribution; how this interface could be achieved is left as a problem for future research. Its resolution is a matter of some psychological importance, however, because a language machine that does not interact smoothly with a person's practical knowledge will say little or nothing of importance about the central problems of cognitive psychology. The goal of the present paper is to propose one tentative hypothesis about this so-called knowledge problem, as much in hope of calling attention to it as of solving it.

A second example will move us a step closer to this goal. Imagine two people using a tree stump for a picnic lunch. One of them says *This stump is a good table*. The problem here, of course, is that a stump is not a table. How are we to explain the fact that *This stump is a good table* can be true at the same time that *This stump is a table*, literally interpreted, is false? Calling a stump a table doesn't make it one, but calling a stump a good table (or a poor table) is perfectly acceptable.

This example admits explanations either in terms of practical knowledge or in terms of lexical knowledge. We might say, for example, that in addition to knowing the lexical meaning of *table* a person has practical knowledge of the function that tables serve, and that this practical knowledge is somehow invoked in order to interpret a metaphorical extension of the lexical meaning.

Or, on the other hand, we might say that the mental lexicon includes two related but distinct meanings of *table*, the literal meaning and a more general meaning of *anything serving the function of a table*. Neither account has any explanatory force. The appeal to practical knowledge leaves unsettled how such knowledge is used to produce or evaluate metaphorical extensions. The appeal to lexical knowledge leaves unsettled how one recognizes that something can serve the function of a table. And the role of the evaluative adjective *good* in signalling the alleged metaphor or retrieving the alleged second meaning is left as a curious puzzle.

We are now squarely facing the theoretical 'knowledge problem' that I want to discuss. Before we can deal with it, however, we must introduce more of a framework in which to work.

Identifying instances

If we stay with the problem of the stump and the table, we might phrase it as follows. How are we to formulate a plausible procedure for recognizing instances of the category named by *table* that will accept both tables and stumps without destroying the conventional differences in meaning between *table* and *stump*? Before we can discuss possible answers, we need some way to talk about how we can identify instances of a category at all.

A common-sense view of the matter would be that, in order to determine whether some object is a table, you look at it to see whether it has the perceptual properties you have learned are characteristic of tables. That is to say, you look to see whether it is a rigid, three-dimensional object with a flat horizontal surface supported by one or more vertical legs. It is possible to reduce these perceptual criteria to a set of judgments based on the visual input. It is even possible to formulate the judgments in such a way that a computer can recognize instances in a visual field that is presented to it in an appropriate manner. If the necessary perceptual predicates are satisfied, the sentence *This is a table* is accepted as true; if not, the sentence is rejected as indeterminate or false.

There are problems, however. For example, people recognize that some tables are more typical than others, whereas the identification device just described would accept all instances as equivalent. Moreover, many category boundaries are vague and movable; an object that would be accepted as a table in one context may be identified as a bench on some other occasion. Or, again, the identification device described above would recognize tables only in their normal orientation, whereas people who encounter tables that are on end or upside down are still able to recognize them as tables. These difficulties – equivalence of instances, lack of vagueness, insensitivity to context, dependence on normal orientation – can all be overcome, but only at the cost of considerable complication in the identification process.

A major objection to a purely perceptual account of how instances are recognized is that it takes no account of the function that instances are expected to serve. For example, the same object may, at different times of day, serve as a breakfast table, coffee table, lunch table, kitchen table, dinner table, poker table.

Perceptual criteria are inadequate to distinguish among these various sub-categories of *table*. The natural solution would be functional: used for eating breakfast, used to serve coffee, and so on. But an identification device based solely on testing a set of perceptual criteria is ill-suited to recognize what functions an object might serve.

Given that a functional characterization is a necessary part of an identification device, one might wonder whether perceptual aspects could be dispensed with entirely. After all, a functional characterization of a table (as something used to support various objects used in eating, working, or playing games) goes a long way toward determining the acceptable shapes of tables. In some cases – a word like *ornament*, for example – any appearance is satisfactory as long as it serves the function that instances are expected to serve. But to abandon perceptual criteria completely leaves us without a sensible distinction between tables and stumps – a large, low, tree stump can serve all the functions of a picnic table (getting your feet under it is not an essential condition), and so should be an unquestioned instance. Or, to turn the problem around, how would *stump* be defined in functional terms? To dispense with the perceptual aspect of identification is to go too far. The present claim is merely that it must be supplemented by functional information.

Adding function to form may reduce the other problems we noted, but it does not solve them all. Just as there is a difference among instances in how much they look like tables are expected to look, so there are differences in how well they serve the function that tables are expected to serve. And just as the boundaries of what looks like a table are vague, so the boundaries of what can function as a table are vague. Nonequivalence of instances and vagueness still need to be explained. But one might argue plausibly that shifts in category boundaries are dependent on the function that an instance happens to be serving, and that the existence of normal orientations is entailed by functional requirements.

Vagueness of category boundaries, whether based on perceptual or functional criteria, is an unavoidable consequence of the nature of human perception and judgment. If machines were built to do the task, they could be given precise measurements to use in distinguishing, say, a table from a bench, or a cup from a bowl. But people must rely on uncertain estimates and so must judge whether the object in question is more like one category or more like another; the fact that people are able to judge degrees of similarity in this manner is well documented by hundreds of psychological experiments. The implication for our present discussion, however, is that identifying category membership is a matter of more or less, not a matter of all or nothing.

One might conclude that such uncertainties would greatly reduce the use-fulness of human language in just those boundary cases where precision seems most needed. In fact, however, it is no great inconvenience because we almost always identify an object relative to a set of alternative objects; the communicative purpose of identification is not to establish some absolute and timeless categorization, but simply to establish agreement as to what things or events we are referring to in a particular situation at a particular time.

The identification process must be relativistic, therefore, admitting both perceptual and functional tests and admitting degrees of typicality and vague boundaries. A psychologist must think both in terms of perceptual recognition and in terms of dispositions to respond to candidate instances in particular ways. The functional side of the picture has not been ignored by psychologists, particularly in studies of child language, but the formal theory of such criteria has lagged well behind the theory of perceptual recognition. This lag is particularly unfortunate for the knowledge problem because it leaves us with all the same uncertainties about function that we noted about practical knowledge. Is expected function part of lexical knowledge or part of practical knowledge? Can we use functional criteria to build a bridge between lexical and practical knowledge? As long as the role of functional knowledge remains unclear, these important questions must remain unanswered.

Form and function

We have argued that human categorization exploits relativistic judgments involving estimates of deviation from typical instances of the category. Will this fact explain how it is possible for people to call a stump a table without misunderstanding one another? Such an explanation would imply that a person makes a subjective judgment that a particular stump is sufficiently like a table to merit inclusion in that category. If a person does consider a stump to be a table on those grounds, however, it would surely be a poor instance. Yet in the example given above the picnicker did not say *This stump is a poor table.* On the contrary, he said *This stump is a good table,* where the adjective *good* plays an important role in marking the extended sense of *table.*

If the extension of the category *table* to include a tree stump is not to be explained in terms of category vagueness, perhaps we can explain it in terms of functional criteria. Such an explanation would imply that a person makes a subjective judgment that a particular stump serves the function of a table sufficiently well to merit inclusion in that category. Although this account is closer to what he probably means, it is still not precise. He does not mean that this tree stump is literally an instance of the category *table.* He means merely that the stump serves the functions of a table sufficiently well to justify calling it a table on this occasion. The adjective *good* signals that only functional criteria are involved.

If the identification device for *table* has both perceptual criteria P and functional criteria F, then presumably each candidate instance x is evaluated with respect to both. A conventional table should yield values for both $P(x)$ and $F(x)$ that are above the somewhat vague thresholds for inclusion in the category. Objects satisfying both kinds of criteria are literal tables. The meaning of *table* can be extended, however, by applying criteria of only one or the other kind. *Table* can be applied to a picture of a table, for example, even though a picture could not serve the function that tables are expected to serve; *table* can be applied to a packing case, for example, even though the box does not have the appearance that tables are expected to have. Objects satisfying only one kind of criterion are figurative tables.

Philosophers of language call evaluative adjectives like *good* syncategorematic because their meaning seems to change according to the noun they modify. In *a good chair, good* means *comfortable*; in *a good clock* it means *accurate*; in *a good view* it means *unrestricted*; and in *a good nurse* it means *skilful*; and so on. It would be footless to define *good* by listing all these possible interpretations as alternative senses, and therefore it is necessary to define it in terms of features of the head noun it modifies. *Good* can select a salient feature of the meaning of its noun and assign a positive evaluation to that feature. For example, the salient feature of the meaning of *red* is its colour, and *a good red* is one that has that colour in more than usual degree; the salient feature of the meaning of *knife* is that it is used for cutting, and *a good knife* is one that cuts well. Thus the salient feature that *good* evaluates may be either perceptual or functional. In some cases there is no salient feature. *Good electricity*, for example, seems odd without an explanation of why this instance is superior; out of context, all electricity is equally good electricity. *A good president*, on the other hand, leaves unresolved what particular feature of the meaning of *president* the speaker assigns his evaluation to: political skill, honesty, leadership, knowledge, personal appearance, etc. But many categories do have salient features that are known to provide the conventional basis for evaluating their instances.

Out of context, *a good table* is mildly ambiguous in much the way that *a good president* is ambiguous. It is not clear whether the speaker is evaluating an instance on the basis of form or function: whether it looks to more than average degree the way he expects tables to look, or serves unusually well the functions that he expects tables to serve. As applied to a picture, however, *a good table* can only express an evaluation on the basis of form; as applied to a tree stump, it can only express an evaluation on the basis of function.

In the case of tables, the functional criterion concerns what it is possible to do with a table. It may be important to distinguish this kind of functional information from information about what an instance is normally expected to do. *A good cook*, for example, is not a cook you can do something with, but is somebody who does something well. Until clearer reasons are found for drawing this distinction, however, both kinds of criteria will be considered together under a single rubric.

Our claim that both form and function enter into the definition of the category *table* seems to fit well with this analysis of the syncategorematic adjective *good* and yields a natural and plausible interpretation of *This stump is a good table*. However, we are still unable to say whether this use of *table* should be explained in terms of practical or lexical knowledge. If we think of functional information as part of our practical knowledge of tables, it falls on one side of the dichotomy; if we think of it as part of our lexical knowledge of *table*, it falls on the other.

True and possible

We will claim that functional information is part of lexical knowledge. That is to say, if P states the perceptual features of *table* and F states the functional features, the lexical entry for *table* would take this form:

Something x is a *table* if $P(x)$ is true or $F(x)$ is possible.

The candidate x is a literal table if both terms of the disjunction are satisfied, a figurative table if only one is. Since this general formulation is imagined to fit many nouns other than *table*, we are not really concerned here with the particular formulations of P and F. The terms of special interest are *true* and *possible*.

The importance of truth for the theory of meaning has long been recognized. It is sometimes stated in the form: 'To know what a sentence means is to know the conditions under which it would be true.' We have nothing to add to the vast literature on this topic, most of which is irrelevant to the substantive problems of psychology. In the present context *true* is used to denote a psychological procedure that involves attending to various perceptual aspects of a candidate instance x and judging whether they fall within the range of values specified by P.

The task, therefore, is to provide a comparable procedural account of *possible*. The technical literature on the modal concepts *possible* and *necessary* is almost as vast as that on *true* and *false*, and just as irrelevant to psychological theory. The following approach is intended to provide a plausible account in terms of cognitive operations.[2]

We wish to define an operator M that can take $F(x)$ as its argument and yield another statement, $M(F)$, to the effect that $F(x)$ is possible. We will assume that a person will say F is possible if he can derive it by applying what he knows to the current situation, or, failing that, if nothing that he knows yields not$F$. This formulation must be made more precise, but the general idea is that some action is possible, relative to the circumstances, if you know how to do it (if you can reduce it to procedures that you already know are possible under the circumstances) or if you do not know any reason why it could not be done. It is easier to think about procedural formulations, if we ask how plans might be derived for carrying them out, but the formulation should be more general – it should also apply to possible states of affairs, like *It may be raining in Chicago*. The relation 'derived', therefore, must be thought of as a general cognitive operation that a person uses to go from his practical knowledge and his assessment of the prevailing circumstances to some description of a state or course of action.

Let us denote various circumstances that might obtain as $c_0, c_1, c_2, \ldots, c_j, \ldots,$ where c_0 represents the circumstances that the person assumes to obtain. And let his system of practical knowledge be characterized by subsystems k_i which describe facts that he has learned, including general rules and principles, and also procedures for carrying out various actions that he knows he is able to perform under appropriate circumstances – walking, reading, driving a car, and so on. To

[2] This formulation is the result of collaboration with P. N. Johnson-Laird.

say that a person derives F is to say that when he searches through his practical knowledge, he finds a knowledge system k_i that can be applied to c_0 according to fixed rules to yield the statement of plan F. An enumeration of those fixed rules of derivation, of course, would be an information-processing theory of thinking. Although such theories have been explored, a complete account of human thinking in these terms is not presently available (even if it were, we could not summarize it here), but it would obviously include much more than the operations admitted in most systems of formal logic. Fortunately, our present needs are more modest, and can be served by simply postulating a relation '$\rightarrow$' such that $k_i(c_0) \rightarrow F$ can be taken to mean that applying knowledge k_i to circumstances c_0 yields F.

Now we can define an operator D_0 as follows:

$$D_0(F): (\exists k_i)\ [k_i(c_0) \rightarrow F]$$

This says that F is derived, relative to the circumstances c_0 that are assumed to obtain, if there is a system of knowledge k_i that can be applied to c_0 to yield F directly. [The existential quantifier, symbolized by '$\exists$', has the logical force of 'there is . . .' or 'there exists . . .'.] It is obvious that D_0 must depend on what the person knows – a person with considerable experience should see more ways to derive F than a novice would. It is also obvious that D_0 is not a satisfactory definition of M, even though the two notions are related. One difficulty is that a person may say F is possible, even when it is not possible under the prevailing circumstances, if he can see some way to modify the circumstances in order to make F possible. A second difficulty arises from the fact that people tend to think something is possible, even when they cannot derive it, if they see no reason why it is impossible. Let us consider these difficulties in turn.

In order to include the fact that a person can sometimes modify the circumstances in such a way as to make F possible, let us introduce F_j as follows:

$$F_j(c_0) = c_j$$

Then we can set up $D_0(F_j)$ as a subgoal. That is to say, we can define an operator D_j as follows:

$$D_j(F): (\exists F_j)[D_0(F_j)\ ]\ \&\ (\exists k_j)[k_i(c_j) \rightarrow F]$$

Of course, the derivation of F_j may also require modifications of c_0, in which case a further subgoal can be created. In this way a complex plan having several steps may be developed. For our present purposes, however, we can define D:

$$D(F): D_0(F)\ \text{or}\ D_j(F)$$

$D(F)$ means that the person can derive F by applying what he knows either to the existing circumstances or to circumstances that he could cause to exist.

In order to include the fact that a person will also assume something is possible if he knows no reason why it is impossible, we must consider notD (not$F$), which means that in his search for relevant knowledge he does not succeed in finding knowledge needed to derive not$F$. The operator notD raises questions about the exhaustiveness of the search, but we need not assume that something is really not derivable just because a person has not derived it. For psychological purposes, if he has not derived something, the fact that he could have derived it with further thought is not important. We must leave room for the kinds of mistakes that we know people often make.

We can now define M in terms of D:

M(F): D(F) or notD(notF), but not both.

The exclusive 'or' is required because people do not normally say that something that is necessary is merely possible.[3] That is to say, if F is thought to be possible, then notF is also thought to be possible. The definition of M respects this usage, since M(F) and M(notF) are equivalent.

This digression into a psychological theory of modal concepts must now be related to the problem with which we began, namely, how to include possible functions in the lexical entries for words like *table*. An expanded lexical entry for *table*, therefore, would look like this:

Something x is a table if $P(x)$ is true or if applying what you know to the circumstances either yields $F(x)$ or, alternatively, does not yield not$F(x)$.

We can think of the picnickers walking through the woods looking for something to use as a (figurative) table. They see a rock, but it does not have a sufficiently horizontal surface; the circumstances require using containers, and the laws of mechanics entail that their jars and glasses will not stand up on this rock. They do not derive $F(x)$ under these circumstances; the rock will not serve the functions of a table. They look further, find a large tree stump, derive $F(x)$ under the circumstances, and so proceed to set out their luncheon.

The knowledge that is invoked in order to determine whether F is possible can be as well formulated as the laws of mechanics or electricity, or even a moral code. Or it can represent nothing more than the systematized conclusions that a person has reached, perhaps unconsciously, on the basis of his previous experience with the function F under a variety of circumstances. But some such knowledge is required to determine whether F is possible, and it must be organized in such a way that, given F, practical knowledge can be searched rapidly for relevant subsystems k_i.

The knowledge problem again

The direction of our argument should now be obvious. If a person's knowledge is divided into two parts, practical and lexical, it is necessary to explain how practical knowledge can affect processes of linguistic comprehension. We first argued that the lexical knowledge associated with many nominal categories includes functional information. Next we argued that descriptions of expected

[3] F is necessary, N(F), would be defined as D(F) & notD(notF), where both conjuncts must be true. If M is defined with inclusive 'or', N implies M, which violates normal usage: it is odd to say that it is possible to obey the laws of gravity, for example.

functions must be stated modally, in terms of *possible*. Then we argued that judgments of possibility depend on systems of practical knowledge. The final step is to point out that this formulation provides a place in the lexical entry for the insertion of nonlexical, practical knowledge.

It is critically important to this conclusion to note that the expanded formulation given above for *table* does not specify which body of knowledge must be invoked. It is left as a problem for the language user to determine whether there is a k_i that, under the circumstances, yields not$F$; how well he will be able to do that will depend on how much he knows, how what he knows is organized for search, what he happens to think of while he is searching, and so on. And even if he does remember some information that yields not$F$ under the circumstances, he may (if his need is great enough) go on to consider ways to change the circumstances. But all that is outside the system of lexical knowledge. The definition merely provides a place where such practical knowledge is to be consulted.

We have, therefore, found a way for those who wish to draw a division between practical and lexical knowledge to do so without isolating the linguistic machinery from everything else a person knows and does. The solution requires that lexical knowledge include both form and function – that a lexical entry be sufficiently rich to include both information about form that can be judged true or false and information about function that can be judged possible or impossible. Just as the formal description provides a locus of interaction between perceptual processes and lexical choice, so the functional description provides a locus of interaction between practical knowledge and lexical choice. There is nothing in this solution that requires a theorist to divide knowledge into the practical and lexical varieties, of course, and for some purposes the division may be counter-productive. But when the division is advantageous, the knowledge problem cannot be used as an argument against adopting it.

In conclusion, a word about potential implications of this general line of argument for the more general problem of linguistic comprehension. Consider once more the initial example, *The Smiths saw the Rocky Mountains while they were flying to California.* It is also necessary to bring practical knowledge to bear on the interpretation of this sentence. How would we introduce it? There does not seem to be a convenient lexical slot: it is implausible that *mountain* should include functional information of the kind discussed for *table*. Perhaps we should shift attention to the verb *fly*. Some linguists would say that *Mountains fly* violates the selectional restrictions of *fly*, and that is true enough. But why does it violate the selectional restrictions? Do we assume some special semantic category of flyable objects from which mountains are excluded? Or do we assume some inferential process that finds a contradiction between flying and being part of the earth's surface?

The inferential process seems more plausible than an *ad hoc* list of flyable objects. Indeed, there may be an inferential base for all selectional restrictions, although in more regular cases it is probably not necessary to repeat the inferential process; in some cases the set of admissible subjects or objects of a verb seem to form a coherent class that can simply be remembered. But in other cases – and probably in most cases for young children – inferences based on practical knowledge and prevailing circumstances are the ultimate court of appeal.

But how should inferences about possibilities be introduced? In the case of *table* we argued for a lexical locus, but that alternative seems unavailable for *Mountains fly*. It is necessary to assume that questions about both truth and possibility are raised in the course of thinking about sentences as well as in the course of identifying instances of categories. Possibility may be the only consideration for sentences that ask questions or request actions; truth may be the only consideration for sentences that assert logical relations. It would go far beyond the limits set for this paper to develop the argument that practical knowledge is involved in understanding most sentences. Since the claim is hardly surprising even without development, however, it is sufficient for present purposes merely to point out that the analysis of lexical categories proposed here is but one aspect of the ubiquitous process of introducing practical knowledge into the comprehension of linguistic messages.

25. Bridging[1]

Herbert H. Clark

Nixon, not long before he was deposed, was quoted as saying at a news conference, 'I am not a crook.' We all saw immediately that Nixon shouldn't have said what he said. He wanted to assure everyone that he was an honest man, but the wording he used was to deny that he was a crook. Why should he deny that? He must have believed that his audience was entertaining the possibility that he was a crook, and he was trying to disabuse them of this belief. But in so doing, he was tacitly acknowledging that people were entertaining this possibility, and this was something he had never acknowledged before in public. Here, then, was a public admission that he was in trouble, and this signalled a change in his public posture. My inferences about Nixon's utterance stopped about there, but I am sure that the knowledgeable White House press corps went on drawing further inferences. In any event we all took this utterance a long way.

This is an example *par excellence* of a basic problem for theories of understanding natural language: How do listeners draw inferences from what they hear, what direction do they take their inferences, and when do they stop? In this particular example, at least most listeners began, tacitly, drawing the same line of inferences, but at a certain point, the lines diverged and went on to many different stopping points. But is this description general? Could listeners go on drawing inferences *ad infinitum*? And ultimately, is drawing inferences as a part of comprehension a describable process, one with specifiable constraints?

In this brief paper I would like to discuss a certain class of inferences in comprehension that may provide some general lessons about the problem of drawing inferences. The inferences I will discuss are ones the speaker intends the listener to draw as an integral part of the message, and so they are a rather special type. Following Grice's (1975) terminology, I will refer to them as implicatures, since they have all the characteristics of other implicatures. I will draw three lessons about these implicatures. (1) Implicatures of this kind originate in an

[1] This paper originally appeared in R. C. Schank and B. L. Nash-Webber (eds.) *Theoretical Issues in Natural Language Processing*. Preprints of a conference at MIT (June 1975).

411

implicit contract, of quite a specific sort, that the speaker and listener have agreed upon about the way they are to converse with each other. (2) These implicatures, though conveyed by language and a necessary part of the intended message, draw on one's knowledge of natural objects and events that goes beyond one's knowledge of language itself. (3) These implicatures are not indeterminate in length, but have a well-defined stopping rule.

Given–New Contract

The implicatures I am concerned with are a consequence of a speaker–listener agreement Susan Haviland and I have called the Given–New Contract (Clark and Haviland, 1974, in press; Haviland and Clark, 1974). English assertions draw a distinction between two kinds of information they convey, a distinction carried by the syntax and intonation alone. The first kind of information has been called Given information, since it is conventionally required to convey information the listener already knows; and the second kind has been called New information, since it is conventionally required to convey information that the listener doesn't yet know but that the speaker would like to get across. The point is, the Given–New distinction is a syntactic one, identifiable for sentences in isolation, and yet it serves a pragmatic function, that of conveying two types of information as far as the listener is concerned. For this distinction to be useful as a communicative device, therefore, the speaker and listener must agree to use it in the conventional way. The speaker must agree to try to construct his utterances so that the Given information contains information he believes the listener already knows and so that the New information contains information he believes the listener doesn't yet know. The listener, for his part, agrees to interpret each utterance on the assumption that the speaker is trying to do this.

Consider the sentence *It was Mary who left*. Syntactically, it is Given that someone left, that is, X *left*, and it is New that that someone was Mary, that is, $X \equiv Mary$. To deal with this sentence, the listener is assumed to use the following strategy. (1) He identifies the Given and the New. (2) He realizes he is expected to know already about a unique event of someone leaving, and so he searches back in memory for just such an event. When he finds it, say *E31 left* ('some entity labelled E31 left'), he calls this the Antecedent. (3) Since the listener assumes that X *left* was meant to refer to the Antecedent *E31 left*, he then replaces X in $X \equiv Mary$ by *E31* to form the new proposition *E31* $\equiv$ Mary. This he places in memory as what the speaker meant to assert in his utterance.

In the simplest case, the strategy just given will work without problems. Consider sequence (1):

(1) John saw someone leave the party early. It was Mary who left.

To simplify things, imagine that the listener hearing the second sentence has in episodic memory only the information conveyed by the first. In applying his strategy to the second sentence, the listener will search for an Antecedent for X

left, find an event of someone leaving in memory from the first sentence, and then integrate the New information into memory as he should.

In the more typical case, however, the listener will fail at step 2 of the strategy – he won't find such an Antecedent directly in memory. When this happens, he is forced to construct an Antecedent, by a series of inferences, from something he already knows. Consider sequence (2):

(2) In the group there was one person missing. It was Mary who left.

In this sequence the first sentence doesn't mention anyone's leaving, so there is no direct Antecedent for the Given information *X left* of the second sentence. The listener must therefore bridge the gap from what he knows to the intended Antecedent. He might note that it would follow that one person in the group would be missing if that person had left. It must be that the speaker was referring to that person by the Given information *X left* and that the listener was supposed to work this out by drawing this inference. In short, the listener assumes the speaker meant to convey two things: (1) the implicature *The one person was missing because that person left*, and (2) the latter clause contains the intended Antecedent of the Given information in the second sentence *X left*.

In its most general form, then, the Given–New Contract goes something like this:

Given–New Contract: The speaker agrees to try to construct the Given and New information of each utterance in context (a) so that the listener is able to compute from memory the unique Antecedent that was intended for the Given information, and (b) so that he will not already have the New information attached to the Antecedent.

The listener in turn knows, then, that the speaker expects him to have the knowledge and mental wherewithal to compute the intended Antecedent in that context, and so for him it becomes a matter of solving a problem. What bridge can he construct (1) that the speaker could plausibly have expected him to be able to construct and (2) that the speaker could plausibly have intended? The first part makes the listener assess principally what facts he knows and the second what implicatures he could plausibly draw.

Bridging – the construction of these implicatures – is an obligatory part of the process of comprehension. The listener takes it as a necessary part of understanding an utterance in context that he be able to identify the intended referents (in memory) for all referring expressions. All referring expressions are Given information, and so the listener feels it necessary to succeed in applying the strategy outlined above, since it identifies the intended referents. In most instances, the success of this strategy requires the listener to bridge, to construct certain implicatures, and so he takes these implicatures too as a necessary part of comprehension. In short, he considers implicatures to be intrinsic to the intended message, since without them the utterance could not refer.

Varieties of implicature

Bridging from previous knowledge to the intended Antecedent can take many forms. I will here give a brief taxonomy of bridges I have found in naturally occurring discourse. As before I will illustrate the bridges with two sentence sequences in which the first constitutes the entire episodic knowledge available for bridging to the second. What I say here, however, is meant to apply just as much to episodic information derived from nonlinguistic sources; the two-sentence sequences are just an expositional device. One more caveat. As with any taxonomy, this one is hardly complete. Indeed, it cannot be until one has a theory to account for the taxonomy itself.

Direct reference

Given information often makes direct reference to an object, event, or state just mentioned. These always force an implicature of some sort, even though it may be trivially simple. This class of bridging is well known:

Identity

(1) I met a man yesterday. The man told me a story.
(2) I ran two miles the other day. The run did me good.
(3) Her house was large. The size surprised me.

Pronominalization

(4) I met a man yesterday. He told me a story.
(5) I ran two miles the other day. It did me good.
(6) Her house was large. That surprised me.

Epithets

(7) I met a man yesterday. The bastard stole all my money.
(8) I ran two miles the other day. The whole stupid business bored me.
(9) Her house was large. The immensity made me jealous.

The implicature for these direct references is straightforward. For the identity in (1), the implicature is approximately this:

(1′) The Antecedent for *the man* is the entity referred to by 'a man'.

This implicature, though obvious, must be drawn for the second sentence in (1) to be complete; conceivably, *the man* could have referred to some other object, and so the listener is making a leap – perhaps only a millimetre leap – in drawing this implicature. The same implicatures arise in (2) and (3). As for the pronominalization in (4), the principle is the same, but the pronoun (*he*) uses only a subset of the properties that characterize the previously mentioned man. Indeed, there is a continuum of pronominalization, as for the noun phrase *an elderly gentleman: the elderly gentleman, the elderly man, the gentleman, the man, the oldster, the adult, the person,* and *he.* The 'pronouns' here range from full to sparse specification, but otherwise work like (1) and (1'). the epithets, on the other hand, add information about the referent, as in the implicature for (7):

(7') The Antecedent for *the bastard* is the entity referred to by 'a man'; that entity is also a bastard.

Epithets are surprisingly restricted in productivity, for not just anything will do. Replace *the bastard* in (7) by *the rancher,* or even by *the robber,* and the bridging does not go through; *the rancher* and *robber* seem to refer to someone other than the man.

One can also make direct reference to one or more members of a set, as in these examples:

Set membership

(10) I met two people yesterday. The woman told me a story.
(11) I met two doctors yesterday. The tall one told me a story.
(12) I swung three times. The first swing missed by a mile.

Here the Given information has an Antecedent that must be picked out uniquely from a previously mentioned set, and to pick it out, one must draw an implicature with several parts. For (10), the implicature is approximately this:

(10') One of the entities referred to by 'two people' is a woman and the other is not; this woman is the Antecedent of *the woman.*

The listener of (10) infers that the other person is not a woman since that is the only way the speaker could have picked out 'the woman' uniquely. There are similar implicatures for (11) and (12).

Indirect reference by association

Given information often has as its Antecedent some piece of information not directly mentioned, but closely associated with the object, event, or situation mentioned (see Chafe, 1972b). These 'associated' pieces of information vary in their predictability from the object, event, or situation mentioned – from absolutely necessary to quite unnecessary – although I will list only three levels:

Necessary parts

(13) I looked into the room. The ceiling was very high.
(14) I hit a home run. The swing had been a good one.
(15) I looked into the room. The size was overwhelming.

In (13), since all rooms have ceilings, and only one ceiling each, the ceiling can be definite with the following implicature:

(13') The room mentioned has a ceiling; that ceiling is the Antecedent of *the ceiling*.

Next consider associated parts that are only probable:

Probable parts

(16) I walked into the room. The windows looked out to the bay.
(17) I went shopping yesterday. The walk did me good.
(18) I left at 8 p.m. The darkness made me jumpy.

There is no guarantee that the room has windows, that going shopping means walking, or that it is dark at 8 p.m., but these are all probable or at least reasonable. The implicature of (16) is simply this:

(16') The room mentioned has windows; they are the Antecedent for *the windows*.

There are, however, associated parts that one would normally not think of and are only induced by the need for an Antecedent:

Inducible parts

(19) I walked into the room. The chandeliers sparkled brightly.
(20) I went shopping yesterday. The climb did me good.
(21) I left at 8 p.m. The haste was necessary given the circumstances.

Here we come to infer that the room had chandeliers, that going shopping included some climbing, and that the departure at 8 p.m. was hasty, but these were certainly not necessary parts of these objects, events, or states. For (19), the implicature would be this:

(19') The room mentioned had chandeliers; they are the Antecedent for *the chandeliers*.

Here, then is a clear case in which the search for an Antecedent induced the proposition that a particular part must be present. In normal comprehension, after reading *I walked into the room*, we would not spontaneously think of a chandelier in the room. The first part of (19') clearly only arises because of the second sentence in (19). On the other hand, notice that (19') is an implicature of precisely the same form as (16'). It is just that the first half of the implicature in (19') cannot be assumed either automatically or even probably.

Indirect reference by characterization

Often the Given information characterizes a role that something implicitly plays in an event or circumstance mentioned before, and these have a tremendous variety. First there are the necessary roles:

Necessary roles

(22) John was murdered yesterday. The murderer got away.
(23) I went shopping yesterday. The time I started was 3 p.m.
(24) I trucked the goods to New York. The truck was full.

The implicature for these is uncomplicated, as illustrated for (22):

(22′) Some one person performed John's murder; that person is the Antecedent for *the murderer*.

The first sentence in (22) does not claim that there was only one murderer, but the second sentence forces this implicature. Similarly, the verb *trucked* in (24) doesn't say there is only one truck, but the second sentence, as part of its implicature, forces this to be the case.

Then come the strictly optional roles:

Optional roles

(25) John died yesterday. The murderer got away.
(26) John was murdered yesterday. The knife lay nearby.
(27) John went walking at noon. The park was beautiful.

In (25), the implicature is something like this:

(25′) Some one person caused John to die; that one person is the Antecedent of *the murderer*.

In (26), the implicature is that John was stabbed to death with a knife, the instrument referred to by *the knife*, and in (27) the implicature is that where John went walking was in a park, the place referred to by *the park*.

These two categories – necessary and optional roles – cover a lot of ground. Most noun phrases, for example, are characterizing, in that they contain as part of their specification how they relate to other events. I have given unadorned noun phrases here, but of course they can become quite elaborate. *The murderer* could have been *the person who murdered John; the knife*, which is implicitly defined as a tool, could have been *the knife with which it was done;* and so on. English contains a range of cleft and pseudo-cleft sentences that often fill just this purpose, as in *The one who murdered John got away*, and *It was that man who murdered John*. Adjectives can carry out this characterizing function too, as in *The guilty party got away*. What these adjectives (e.g. *guilty*), relative clauses (e.g. *who murdered John*), and derived nouns (e.g. *the murderer*) do is pick out the role the intended Antecedent plays in the previously named events.

It is not easy to separate 'parts' from 'roles' in every instance. For example, the knife in (26) is conceived of not as a part of the action of murdering, as, say, 'stabbing' would be, but rather as a role in the action, as an instrument. I have considered the word *knife* to have implicitly within it the notion that it is an instrument, so it is a characterizing noun, like *murderer*, not simply a name of a nonfunctional class like *man*. Ultimately, however, this distinction may be impossible to maintain.

Reasons, causes, consequences, and concurrences

The Antecedent to the Given information of a sentence is often an event and not an object, and then it plays different types of roles with respect to previous events. Instead of being agents, objects, or instruments characterized with respect to previously mentioned events, this class of Antecedents gives reasons for, causes of, consequents to, or concurrences of previously mentioned events or states.

Reasons

(28) John fell. What he wanted to do was scare Mary.
(29) John came to the party. The one he expected to meet was Mary.
(30) John had a suit on. It was Jane he hoped to impress.

In each case the Antecedent of the Given information in the second sentence is contained in a *reason* for the first event. So the implicature for (28) is something like this:

(28') John fell for the reason that he wanted to do something; that something is the Antecedent to *what he wanted to do*.

Reasons always answer the question 'what for?' and the Antecedents in (28) – (30) all make use of this kind of reason to bridge from the first sentence's event or state.

Unlike reasons, causes answer the question 'How come?'

Causes

(31) John fell. What he did was trip on a rock.
(32) John came to the party. The one who invited him was Mary.
(33) John had a suit on. It was Jane who told him to wear it.

The implicature in (31) goes something like this:

(31') John fell because he did something; that something is the Antecedent for *what he did*.

This type of implicature works for (32) and (33) as well. In each case we infer a causal relation between the event presupposed by the Given information of the second sentence and the event mentioned in the first sentence.

Consequences

(34) John fell. What he did was break his arm.
(35) John came to the party early. The one he saw first was Mary.
(36) John met Sally. What he did was tell her about Bill.

The approximate implicature for (34) is as follows:

(34') John did something because he fell; that something is the Antecedent to *what he did.*

The sequences in (35) and (36) have similar implicatures, ones that also depend on the Antecedent's being taken as the consequence of the event mentioned in the first sentence.

Concurrences

(37) John is a Republican. Mary is slightly daft too.
(38) John is a Republican. Mary isn't so smart either.
(39) Alex went to a party last night. He's going to get drunk again tonight.

For (37) the implicature is approximately this (see Lakoff, 1971):

(37') All Republicans are slightly daft; therefore, John is slightly daft, which is the Antecedent to the Given information someone other than Mary is slightly daft.

In all three of these sequences, the listener is expected to draw the implicature that being in one state, or doing one event, necessarily entails the concurrence of another state, or event.

These are four general ways, then, in which the listener can bridge from an event or state mentioned in the first sentence to an Antecedent in the second. These bridging relations turn out to be very common, especially in narratives. The most common, perhaps, is the consequence, which pops up between one sentence and the next every time chronological order is conveyed. The Given information of the second sentence is taken as a consequence to the event mentioned in the first.

Determinacy in bridging

In principle, bridges need not be determinate. One could, if one had the time and inclination, build an infinitely long bridge, or sequence of assumptions, to link one event to the Antecedent of the next. In (39), for example, we assumed that every time Alex goes to a party he gets drunk. But we could have assumed instead that every time he goes to a party he meets women, and all women speak in high voices, and high voices always remind him of his mother, and thinking about his mother always makes him angry, and whenever he gets angry, he gets drunk. It takes very little imagination to add span after span to a bridge of this type.

Yet in a natural discourse, bridges are always determinate. Indeed, I suggest that they have a stopping rule that goes something like this: Build the shortest possible bridge that is consistent with the Given–New Contract. The listener assumes, based on this contract, that the speaker intended him to be able to compute a unique bridge from his previous knowledge to the intended antecedent of the present Given information. If the speaker was certain that the listener could do this, he must have intended the listener to take the shortest possible bridge consistent with previous knowledge, for that would make the bridge unique, as required. So in (39) the listener assumes the speaker intended him to infer no more than that every time Alex goes to a party he gets drunk, for this implicature makes the fewest assumptions yet is consistent with previous knowledge of parties, drinking, and even Alex. In short, the listener takes as the intended implicature the one that requires the fewest assumptions, yet whose assumptions are all plausible given the listener's knowledge of the speaker, the situation, and facts about the world.

The implicatures I have discussed here differ from the inferences we drew from Nixon's 'I am not a crook' in one important way. The implicatures I took up were intended by the speaker to be constructed by the listener, whereas the inferences from Nixon's blunder were not. With the implicatures, as with every other intended meaning, the speaker had a unique bridge in mind, and so the listener had something unique to try to figure out. But for Nixon's bobble, after the first unique and legitimate inference – denials presuppose that the audience does or could believe what is being denied – the inferences were completely unauthorized by the speaker. So bridging is determinate with a definite stopping rule, whereas unauthorized inferences typically are not.

This brings us, finally, to the issue of forward vs. backward inferences. When we hear the phrase *the room* in (19), we may begin imagining all sorts of things about this room, some necessary, but many others optional. All but the necessary inferences here, of course, are unauthorized. These 'forward' inferences differ radically from the 'backward' inferences forced by the phrase *the chandelier* in (19), for the speaker intended the listener to infer that the room had a chandelier. Both types of inferences occur, but only the latter type are fully determinate. I suggest that we might do well to study the determinate inferences first, for they may well give us a clue as to what sorts of unauthorized inferences would be likely to be drawn for a typical utterance.

26. Scripts, plans, and knowledge[1]

Roger C. Schank and Robert P. Abelson

Of what a strange nature is knowledge! It clings to the mind, when it has once seized on it, like a lichen on the rock.

— Frankenstein's Monster
(Mary Shelley, *Frankenstein or the Modern Prometheus*, 1818)

Preface

In an attempt to provide theory where there have been mostly unrelated systems, Minsky (1974, cf. Reading 22) recently described the work of Schank (1973a), Abelson (1973), Charniak (1972), and Norman (1972) as fitting into the notion of 'frames'. Minsky attempted to relate this work, in what is essentially language processing, to areas of vision research that conform to the same notion.

Minsky's frames paper has created quite a stir in Artificial Intelligence (e.g. Bobrow, 1975; Winograd, 1975). We find that we agree with much of what Minsky said about frames and with his characterization of our own work. The frames idea is so general, however, that it does not lend itself to applications without further specialization. This paper is an attempt to develop further the lines of thought set out in Schank (1975a) and Abelson (1973; 1975a). The ideas presented here can be viewed as a specialization of the frame idea. We shall refer to our central constructs as 'scripts'.

The problem

Researchers in natural language understanding have felt for some time that the eventual limit on the solution of the problem will be our ability to characterize knowledge of the world. Various researchers have approached world knowledge in various ways. Winograd (1972) dealt with the problem by severely restricting the world. This approach had the positive effect of producing a

[1] This paper originally appeared in the *Proceedings of the Fourth International Joint Conference on Artificial Intelligence*. Tbilisi, 1975.

421

working system and the negative effect of producing one that was only minimally extendable. Charniak (1972) approached the problem from the other end entirely and has made some interesting first steps, but because his work is not grounded in any representational system or any working computational system the restriction of world knowledge need not critically concern him.

Our feeling is that an effective characterization of knowledge can result in a real understanding system in the not too distant future. We expect that programs based on the theory we outline here and on our previous work on conceptual dependency and belief systems will combine with the MARGIE system (Schank, Goldman, Rieger, and Riesbeck, 1973; Riesbeck, 1975; Rieger, 1975) to produce a working understander. We see understanding as the fitting of new information into a previously organized view of the world. . . Earlier work has found various ways in which a word in a single sentence sets up expectations about what is likely to be found in the rest of the sentence. A single sentence and its corresponding conceptualizations set up expectations about what is to follow in the rest of a discourse or story. These expectations characterize the world knowledge that bears on a given situation, and it is these expectations that we wish to explore.

Scripts

A script, as we use it, is a structure that describes an appropriate sequence of events in a particular context. A script is made up of slots and requirements about what can fill those slots. The structure is an interconnected whole, and what is in one slot affects what can be in another. Scripts handle stylized everyday situations. They are not subject to much change, nor do they provide the apparatus for handling novel situations, as plans do (see below p. 428).

For our purposes, a script is a predetermined, stereotyped sequence of actions that define a well-known situation. A script is, in effect, a very boring little story. Scripts allow for new references to objects within them just as if these objects had been previously mentioned; objects within a script may take 'the' without explicit introduction because the script itself has already implicitly introduced them. (This can be found below, in the reference to 'the waitress' in a restaurant, for example.)

Stories can invoke scripts in various ways. Usually a story is a script with one or more interesting deviations.

(1) John went into the restaurant.
    He ordered a hamburger and a coke.
    He asked the waitress for the check and left.
(2) John went to a restaurant.
    He ordered a hamburger.
    It was cold when the waitress brought it.
    He left her a very small tip.
(3) Harriet went to a birthday party.

She put on a green paper hat.
Just when they sat down to eat the cake, a piece of plaster fell from the ceiling onto the table.
She was lucky, because the dust didn't get all over her hair.

(4) Harriet went to Jack's birthday party.
The cake tasted awful.
Harriet left Jack's mother a very small tip.

Paragraph (1) is an unmodified script. It is dull. It would be even duller if all the events in the standard restaurant script (see below) were included.

Paragraph (2) is a restaurant script with a stock variation, a customer's typical reaction when things go wrong.

Paragraph (3) invokes the birthday party script, but something wholly outside the range of normal birthday parties occurs – the plaster falls from the ceiling. This deviation from the script takes over the initiative in the narrative until the problem it raises is resolved, but the birthday script is still available in the indirect reference to the party hat and in the possibility that normal party activities be resumed later in the narrative. It seems natural for reference to be made to dust in the hair following the plaster's falling, which implies that there is a kind of script for falling plaster too. (This kind of script we call a vignette (Abelson, 1975a).) Notice that 'the ceiling' refers to an uninteresting 'room' script, which can be used for references to doors and windows that may occur. Thus it is possible to be in more than one script at a time.

Paragraph (4) illustrates the kind of absurdity that arises when an action from one script is arbitrarily inserted into another. That one feels the absurdity is an indication that scripts are in inadmissable competition. It is conceivable that with adequate introduction the absurdity in (4) could be eliminated.

With these examples, a number of issues have been raised. Let us at this point give a more extensive description of scripts. We have discussed previously (Schank, 1975b) how paragraphs are represented in memory as causal chains. This work implies that, for a story to be understood, inferences must connect each input conceptualization to all the others in the story that relate to it. This connection process is facilitated tremendously by the use of scripts.

Scripts are extremely numerous. There is a restaurant script, a birthday party script, a football game script, a classroom script, and so on. Each script has players who assume roles in the action. A script takes the point of view of one of these players, and it often changes when it is viewed from another player's point of view.

The following is a sketch of a script for a restaurant from the point of view of the customer. Actions are specified in terms of the primitive ACTs[2] of conceptual dependency theory (Schank, 1972).

[2] [Schank has proposed a theory of semantics in which the meanings of words are represented by semantic primitives. They include the following items: PTRANS – the transfer of the physical location of an object, ATRANS – the transfer of an abstract relation such as possession, MTRANS – the transfer of mental information, MOVE – movement of a body part, PROPEL – application of a physical force to an object, and MBUILD – the construction of new information.]

script: restaurant
roles: customer, waitress, chef, cashier
reason: to get food so as to go up in pleasure and down in hunger

scene 1: entering
          PTRANS self into restaurant
          ATTEND eyes to where empty tables are
          MBUILD where to sit
          PTRANS self to table
          MOVE sit down

scene 2: ordering
          ATRANS receive menu
          MTRANS read menu
          MBUILD decide what self wants
          MTRANS order to waitress

scene 3: eating
          ATRANS receive food
          INGEST food

scene 4: exiting
          MTRANS ask for check
          ATRANS receive check
          ATRANS tip to waitress
          PTRANS self to cashier
          ATRANS money to cashier
          PTRANS self out of restaurant

In this script, the instruments for performing an action might vary with circumstances. For example, in scene 2 the order might be spoken, or written down with predesignated numbers for each item, or even (in a foreign country with an unfamiliar language) indicated by pointing or gestures.

Each act sequence uses the principle of causal chaining (Schank, 1973b; Abelson, 1973). That is, each action results in conditions that enable the next to occur. To perform the next act in the sequence, the previous acts must be · completed satisfactorily. If they cannot be, the hitches must be dealt with. Perhaps a new action not prescribed in the script will be generated in order to get things moving again. This 'what-if' behaviour, to be discussed later, is an important component of scripts. It is associated with many of the deviations in stories such as paragraph (2).

In a text, new script information is interpreted in terms of its place in one of the causal chains within the script. Thus in paragraph (1) the first sentence describes the first action in scene 1 of the restaurant script. Sentence 2 refers to the last action of scene 2, and sentence 3 to the first and last actions of scene 4. The final interpretation of paragraph (1) contains the entire restaurant script, with specific statements filled in and missing statements (that he sat down, for example) assumed.

In paragraph (2), the first two sentences describe actions in scenes 1 and 2. Part of the third sentence is in the script as the first action of scene 3, but there is also the information that the hamburger is cold. The fourth sentence ('He left her a very small tip') is a modification of the third action of scene 4. The modifier, 'very small,' is presumably related to the unexpected information about the 'cold hamburger'. Even a stupid processor, checking paragraph (2) against the standard restaurant script, could come up with the low-level hypothesis that the small size of the tip must have something to do with the temperature of the hamburger, since these two items of information are the only deviations from the script. They must be related deviations, because if they were unrelated the narrative would have no business ending with two such unexplained features.

Of course we do not want our processor to be stupid. In slightly more complex examples, adequate understanding requires attention to the nature of deviations from the script. A more intelligent processor can infer from a cold hamburger that the INGEST in scene 3 will then violate the pleasure goal for going to a restaurant. The concept of a very small tip can be stored with the restaurant script as a what-if associated with violations of the pleasure goal.

The general form for a script, then, is a set of paths joined at certain crucial points that define the script. For restaurants the crucial parts are the INGEST and the ATRANS of money. There are many normal ways to move from point to point. Ordering may be done by MTRANSing to a waiter or by selecting and taking what you like (in a cafeteria). Likewise the ATRANS of money may be done by going to the cashier, or paying the waitress, or saying, 'Put it on my bill.' There are also paths to be taken when situations do not go as planned. Paragraphs (3) and (4) call up deviant paths in the birthday party script. All these variations indicate that a script is not a simple list of events but rather a linked causal chain; a script can branch into multiple possible paths that come together at crucial defining points.

To know when a script is appropriate, script headings are necessary. These headings define the circumstances under which a script is called into play. The headings for the restaurant script are concepts having to do with hunger, restaurants, and so on in the context of a plan of action for getting fed. Obviously contexts must be restricted to avoid calling up the restaurant script for sentences that use the word 'restaurant' as a place ('Fuel oil was delivered to the restaurant').

Scripts organize new inputs in terms of previously stored knowledge. In paragraph (1), many items that are part of the restaurant script are added to the final interpretation of the story. We do not need to say that a waitress took the customer's order or that he ate the hamburger. These ideas are firmly a part of the story because the restaurant script requires them. In understanding a story that calls up a script, the script becomes part of the story even when it is not spelled out. The answer to the question 'Who served John the hamburger?' seems obvious, because our world knowledge, as embodied in scripts, answers it.

What-ifs

There are at least three major ways in which scripts can be thrown off normal course. One is *distraction*, interruption by another script, such as the plaster's falling from the ceiling. We will not pursue here an analysis of the conditions and consequences of distraction. The other two ways, *obstacle* and *error*, are intimately connected with what-if behaviour. An obstacle to the normal sequence occurs when someone or something prevents a normal action from occurring or some usual enabling condition for the action is absent. An error occurs when the action is completed in an inappropriate manner, so that the normal consequences of the action do not come about.

In principle, every simple ACT in a standard script has potential obstacles and errors. We assume that, every time an obstacle or error occurs in a script that is being learned, the methods used to remove the obstacle or redeem the error are stored with the script as what-ifs. The result of many repetitions is that most of the common what-ifs are attached to the script.

Every obstacle has one or more characteristic what-ifs. In scene 2 of the restaurant script, if the waitress ignores the customer, he will try to catch her eye or call to her when she passes nearby. If he cannot make out the menu or needs further information, he will ask the waitress. If she does not speak his language, he will attempt to speak her language, or make gestures, or seek another customer to translate, or accept her suggestion of what to order. In scene 3, if the waitress does not bring the food, he will again try to catch her eye. If the food is not fit to eat, he will send it back.

Errors have a slightly different character from obstacles but follow the same general rules. Receiving the menu is an error if the waitress gives the customer yesterday's menu, or the breakfast instead of the dinner menu. Reading the menu may yield an error if the customer gets the wrong idea of what it says – say, he thinks filet mignon is a fish. Here it is up to the waitress to supply the what-if corrective. Deciding what to order may yield an error if the customer goes through the decision process but forgets the stored outcome. The what-if is to review the MBUILD ('Let's see now, what *did* I decide?') Giving the order to the waitress may be in error if she writes down something other than what the customer said, or omits a portion of it. The what-if is to repeat the order, asking the waitress whether she is sure she got all of it.

The SAM program

We have created a program SAM (Script Applier Mechanism) that uses scripts to make inferences in domains it knows about and have added it to the MARGIE program reported by Schank *et al*. (1973). . . SAM identifies the script to be used and fills in the identified script with the new inputs as they are received. It makes the inferences that are necessary to complete a causal chain between input conceptualizations. The resultant complex structure can then be queried by input English questions or be used to make summaries and paraphrases of the initial story. SAM was written by Chris Riesbeck, Richard Cullingford and Wendy Lehnert. Goldman's generation program (1975) is used to map the answers of paraphrases into English. It was modified for this purpose by Gerald DeJong and W. J. Stutzman. An example of SAM's input and output is:

Input:

John went to a restaurant. The hostess seated John. The hostess gave John a menu. The waiter came to the table. John ordered lobster. John was served quickly. John left a large tip. John left the restaurant.

Questions and answers:

Q: What did John eat?
A: LOBSTER.
Q: Who gave John the menu?
A: THE HOSTESS.
Q: Who gave John the lobster?
A: PROBABLY THE WAITER.
Q: Who paid the check?
A: PROBABLY JOHN.
Q: What happened when John went to the table?
A: THE HOSTESS GAVE HIM A MENU AND JOHN SAT DOWN.
Q: Why did John get a menu?
A: SO HE COULD ORDER.
Q: Why did John give the waiter a large tip?
A: BECAUSE HE WAS SERVED QUICKLY.

Paraphrase:

JOHN DECIDED HE WAS GOING TO GO TO A RESTAURANT. JOHN WENT TO A RESTAURANT. JOHN INDICATED TO THE HOST HE WOULD LIKE TO BE AT A TABLE. THE HOST INDICATED TO JOHN HE COULD GO TO A TABLE. JOHN WENT TO THE TABLE. THE HOST WENT TO THE TABLE. JOHN SAT DOWN IN THE CHAIR. JOHN GOT THE MENU FROM THE HOST. JOHN READ THE MENU. THE WAITER SAW JOHN WAS AT THE TABLE. THE WAITER WENT TO THE TABLE. JOHN ORDERED LOBSTER. THE CHEF PREPARED THE LOBSTER. THE WAITER GOT THE LOBSTER FROM THE CHEF. THE WAITER SERVED JOHN THE LOBSTER. JOHN ATE THE LOBSTER. JOHN INDICATED TO THE WAITER HE WOULD LIKE TO GET THE CHECK FROM HIM. JOHN GOT THE CHECK FROM THE WAITER. JOHN LEFT THE WAITER A LARGE TIP. JOHN PAID THE CHECK. JOHN LEFT THE RESTAURANT.

Summary:

JOHN WENT TO A RESTAURANT AND ATE LOBSTER.

This program runs on the PDP-10 at Yale. It currently has only a small amount of knowledge and a small vocabulary. But we feel encouraged that our script theory is workable because of the simplification in the inference process that has resulted from the use of scripts.

Plans

Plans are responsible for the deliberate behaviour that people exhibit. Plans describe the set of choices that a person has when he sets out to accomplish a goal. In listening to a discourse, people use plans to make sense of seemingly disconnected sentences. By finding a plan, an understander can make guesses about the intentions of an action in an unfolding story and use these guesses to make sense of the story.

Consider the following paragraph:

John knew that his wife's operation would be very expensive.
There was always Uncle Harry . . .
He reached for the suburban phone book.

How are we to make sense of such a paragraph? It makes no use of headings or the scripts they signal. It would be unreasonable to posit a 'paying for an operation' script with all the necessary acts laid out as in our restaurant script. But, on the other hand, the situation is not entirely novel, either. The problem of understanding this paragraph would not be significantly different if 'wife's operation' were changed to 'son's education' or 'down payment on the mortgage'. There is a general goal state in each case, raising a lot of money for a legitimate expense, and there is a generalized plan or group of plans that may lead to the goal state.

Plans start with one or more goals. A high-level goal is illustrated by the sequence:

John wanted to become king.
He went to get some arsenic.

A low-level goal is illustrated by:

John wanted to cut his steak.
He called to his wife in the kitchen.

A plan is a series of actions that will realize a goal. Often in order to realize one goal another must be decided on and a plan drawn up to achieve it. In the first example above, a goal to attain power is reduced to a goal to get arsenic. High-level goals are more interesting and we have concentrated on them first.

We define a 'deltact' as an action or a group of actions that leads to a desired state. Deltacts constitute subplans that are pursued because of their intended effects. There are five deltacts in the present system:

$\triangle$AGENCY   – a change in obligation to do something for somebody
$\triangle$CONT   – a change in the control of an object

$\triangle$KNOW   – a change in what an actor knows
$\triangle$PROX   – a change in the proximity relations of objects and actors
$\triangle$SOCCONT – a change in social control over a person or a situation

There is also a set of lower-level deltacts (Abelson, 1975a). Plans are made up of deltacts. When a collocation of deltacts is used often enough, it becomes a script.

A plan includes a set of planboxes, lists of actions that will yield state changes and the preconditions for these actions, along with a set of questions for choosing the appropriate planbox.

For instance, the TAKE plan has the goal of enabling the taker to do something with an object, whatever is generally done with it. To TAKE something you must be close to it, so either the object and the taker must be in the same location or the taker must use a subplan $\triangle$PROX. Either no one else must have CONTROL of the object or at least there must be no bad consequences in the taker's attempt to PTRANS the object to himself. The TAKE plan calls a PTRANS of the object if all the preconditions are positive.

But if, say, someone else CONTROLs the object, a plan for the taker's gaining CONTROL must be called. This subplan is $\triangle$CONT. $\triangle$CONT has a set of planboxes attached to it. These planboxes define a deltact just as inferences define a primitive ACT. A planbox is a list of primitive ACTs that will achieve a goal. Associated with each ACT are its preconditions, and a planbox checks them. A set of positive conditions allows the desired ACT. Negative conditions call up new planboxes or deltacts that have as their goal the resolution of the negative state.

Preconditions fall into three classes. A *controlled* precondition can be fixed when it is negative by doing an ACT. A negative *uncontrolled* precondition cannot be fixed, and another planbox must be tried. Negative *mediating* preconditions can be altered but require plans of their own to change. Mediating preconditions usually refer to the willingness of other parties to participate in plans. Further details on planboxes appear in Schank (1975c).

To see why an understander needs plans, consider the following sequence:

Willa was hungry.
She took out the Michelin Guide.

Most readers understand that Willa was using the Michelin Guide to find a good restaurant. But if the first sentence were subjected to straightforward inference (Rieger, 1975), predicting that Willa is likely to do something to enable herself to INGEST food, the second sentence would seem to answer this prediction only in the weird interpretation that she will eat the Michelin Guide. An understander will reject this in favour of any better path that it can find. The first sentence will be analysed for any goal that might generate a plan. 'Hungry' is listed in the dictionary as indicating the need for a plan to do a $\triangle$CONT of food. One means for gaining control of food is a restaurant. An enablement for this means is going to a restaurant, which requires $\triangle$PROX. This in turn requires knowing where you are going, which may require $\triangle$KNOW.

In the dictionary, all books are listed as means of satisfying $\triangle$KNOWs and the Michelin Guide is listed as a book. To complete the processing of this sequence it would, of course, be necessary to have the information that the Michelin Guide lists restaurants. Without this information, the sequence might be as nonsensical as 'Willa was hungry. She took out *Introduction to Artificial Intelligence.*'

With the information that the Michelin Guide is a source of knowledge about restaurants, we know why the second action was done and can predict future actions. We have transformed a seemingly disconnected sequence into one that provides the expectations that are so vital to understanding. If the next sentence is 'Willa got in her car', we will know that the plan is being effected. By using what we know about cars (that they are instruments of PTRANS) and the script for restaurants (that it starts with a PTRANS), we can make the inference that Willa is on her way to a restaurant. Some restaurant heading would still be required to initiate the restaurant script in its full glory.

The procedure of taking out the Michelin Guide when hungry, while seemingly novel, could conceivably be routine for a certain individual in a certain context. If we know that Willa is a gourmet tourist staying in Paris who enjoys going to a different restaurant every evening, then the procedure of looking in the Guide might become part of her restaurant script. For her there is a scene before scene 1 in which she ATTENDs to the Guide, MBUILDs a choice, and MTRANSes a reservation. A routinized plan can become a script, at least from the planner's point of view.

Conclusion and prognosis

It is clear that in order to understand one needs knowledge. Knowledge is a potentially unwieldy thing, so what we must do is determine the types of knowledge that there are and find out how to apply them. The SAM system is a first step at adding structured knowledge to the MARGIE system (Schank *et al.*, 1973). We are currently building up our knowledge base by adding more scripts to SAM. In addition we are adding a plan component PAM. These two programs should bring us up to the level of understanding simple stories about a large range of known domains.

But what about complex stories? Is the kind of understanding that humans exhibit on real stories likely to resemble the mechanisms to be found in SAM?

When a person reads a 300-page novel he does not (unless he is very unusual) remember all the conceptualizations stated in the story in the form of a giant causal chain. Rather he remembers the gist of the book. Maybe five or ten pages of summary could be extracted from him after reading the book. Previously we have said that Conceptual Dependency Theory will account for memory for gist of sentences. But it cannot be seriously proposed that this is all that is needed for gist of long and complex stories. Some other explanation must be given.

In a recent experiment, Abelson (1975b) showed that people remember stories better when they are asked to take some particular point of view (of one of the participants or of an observer in a particular place), and that what they remember is contingent on which point of view they had. The ramifications of this experiment for a theory of language understanding have to be that when people have a clue of what to forget they do better at remembering. In other words, good forgetting is the key to remembering. Likewise, if we want to build programs that remember, we had best teach them how to forget. One method of forgetting is simply not noticing levels of detail that are there. This can be done by treating the instruments for an action at a different level than the main ACTs that they explain. When looking at a story at one level of detail we would not see the level of detail underneath it unless specifically called upon to do so.

For example, consider the sentence, 'John went to New York by bus.' We have previously represented this sentence by a simple ACT (PTRANS), and an instrumental act (PROPEL). But it must be realized that as with any other script, questions could be answered about this sentence that were not specifically in it. Subjects all seem to agree that the answer to 'Was there a bus driver?' is 'Yes' and to 'Did John pay money to get on the bus?' is 'Probably.' This seems to indicate that the instrument of John's PTRANS is, in actuality, the entire bus script.

Should we, as understanders, go so far as to place the entire bus script in what we obtain from understanding the above sentence? The answer seems obvious. You do not want to do all that unless you need to, but you want to have quick access to it in case you need to.

Consider the following story:

John wanted some cheesecake. He decided to go to New York. He went to New York by bus. On the bus he met a nice old lady who he talked to about the prices in the supermarket. When he left the bus he thanked the driver for the ride and found the subway to go to Lindy's. On the subway he was reading the ads when suddenly he was robbed. He wasn't hurt though and he got off the train and entered Lindy's and had his cheesecake. When the check came, he said he couldn't pay and was told he would have to wash dishes. Later he went back to New Haven.

Ideally, our representation of this story should account for the fact that hearers of this story invariably forget the sentences about talking to the old lady and the bus driver, but always remember the mugging, its consequence of dishwashing, and the main goal of going to New York to eat cheesecake.

We propose to represent stories therefore in the following way: There will be a causal chain connecting the main events of the story. (Here the PTRANS to the restaurant, the INGEST, and the PTRANS back home.) Underneath each of these main events will be the instrumental script that underlies each of them (the bus script, the subway script, and the restaurant script). These scripts will be 'forgotten' to be reconstructed later, with the exception that any event that occurred within them that was not predicated by them will be placed on a 'weird list' to be specially remembered.

The final representation of a story will consist of the events connected directly to the goals and plans to realize those goals made by the participants. These goals will be tied to the events that actually occurred and to the weird events and their consequences. Thus four lists replace our original (and growing) causal chain. An event list (with script events left out); a goal list; a plan list; and a weird list. What these lists do is help us forget. And of course forgetting helps us remember.

There are two ways in which this occurs: by omission and by prototyping. Events which enter *none* of the four lists (such as the conversation with the old lady) are dropped entirely. (More precisely, they are retained only until the constructed final representation is transferred from working memory to long-term memory. Anything not in this final representation is lost.) Also, the event list and plan list are condensed by using pointers to prototypes. The details are thus 'normalized' (Bartlett, 1932); what is remembered is that a normal plan for satisfying such-and-such goal was used, including normal enactments of appropriate scripts. The function of the weird list is to mark the interesting departures from these normalities.

What we are saying then is that one of the major issues in Artificial Intelligence research must be the creation of the theory of forgetting. It simply is not possible to assume that people do, or that machines should, remember everything they encounter. In listening to a speaker, reading a book, or engaging in a conversation, people could not possibly remember everything they are told *verbatim*. In attempting to get the gist of a sequence, they must employ what we call *forgetting heuristics*. As part of these procedures, are heuristics that search out items of major importance. The selection of these major items is the key to forgetting. We do not really wish to assert that people could not possibly remember everything they hear. Rather we wish to find a procedure that will let us see only the major items, yet also find, with some difficulty, the thoughts or statements that underlie them, and the ideas that underlie those, and so on.

Thus, the key to understanding must be, in order to facilitate search among what has been understood, an organization of the new information in such a fashion as to seem to forget the unimportant material and to highlight the important material. Forgetting heuristics must do this for us. So the task before us is to establish what the most significant items in a text are likely to be, and then to establish the heuristics which will extract and remember exactly those items.

Part VI

Language, culture, and thinking

Introduction to language, culture, and thinking

The bushes twitched again. Lok steadied by the tree and gazed. A head and a chest faced him, half-hidden. There were white bone things behind the leaves and hair. The man had white bone things above his eyes and under the mouth so that his face was longer than a face should be. The man turned sideways in the bushes and looked at Lok along his shoulder. A stick rose upright and there was a lump of bone in the middle. Lok peered at the stick and the lump of bone and the small eyes in the bone thing over the face. Suddenly Lok understood that the man was holding the stick out to him but neither he nor Lok could reach across the river. He would have laughed if it were not for the echo of the screaming in his head. The stick began to grow shorter at both ends. Then it shot out to full length again.

The dead tree by Lok's ear acquired a voice.

'Clop!'

His ears twitched and he turned to the tree. By his face there had grown a twig: a twig that smelt of other, and of goose, and of the bitter berries that Lok's stomach told him he must not eat. This twig had a white bone at the end. There were hooks in the bone and sticky brown stuff hung in the crooks. His nose examined this stuff and did not like it. He smelled along the shaft of the twig. The leaves on the twig were red feathers and reminded him of goose. He was lost in a generalized astonishment and excitement. He shouted at the green drifts across the glittering water and heard Liku crying out in answer but could not catch the words. They were cut off suddenly as though someone had clapped a hand over her mouth. He rushed to the edge of the water and came back. On either side of the open bank the bushes grew thickly in the flood; they waded out until at their farthest some of the leaves were opening under water; and these bushes leaned over.

This strange passage is the way in which William Golding, an author of remarkable invention, creates the conceptual world of Neanderthal man in his novel *The Inheritors* (1955). It is an account of how Lok, one of a small band of Neanderthals, interprets the experience of being shot at with a bow and arrow by a member of a more advanced tribe. The pattern of thought of an alien people is, indeed, a topic of perennial fascination both to artists and scientists, and, as the passage from Golding's book shows, it is natural to associate a different way of thinking with differences in language (see Halliday, 1973, for a cogent linguistic

435

analysis of the novel). But, do people from different living cultures think in different ways?

The pioneers of anthropology had little doubt about the matter. A facile application of Darwinism led all too easily to the view that primitive societies were a reflection of primitive mentalities. Thus, Tylor (1964, first published 1865). Levy-Bruhl (1966, first published 1910), and others, argued that the thought of 'savages' was childlike, lacking in abstraction, confused, and so on and on. Other peoples' magical thinking is highly conspicuous; one's own is invisible. Magic in the savage world accordingly seemed ubiquitous, and Sir James Frazer considered it arose from erroneous conceptions of causality. He distinguished (1) *homeopathic* magic in which one event is supposed to cause another event of a similar sort, and (2) *contagious* magic where contact was supposed to provide the cause. (Even this distinction can be related to language, see Jakobson and Halle, 1956; Leach, 1976.) Later thinkers, such as Malinowski (1954) construed magical thinking as a form of irrationalism, a symbolic method of striving to control the uncontrollable. The pervasive view was accordingly that 'primitive' thought was pre-logical, animistic, and tolerant of self-contradiction.

How is it, for example, that an Azande potter will attribute to witchcraft cracks in his pots that arise during firing (Evans-Pritchard, 1937)? Or that an Australian tribe believes that a man's murderer can be identified by tugging at the victim's hairs and reciting the names of the suspects? (The name that occurs when the first hair comes out is that of the murderer, see Levi-Strauss, 1966, p. 185.) Such beliefs are similar in some respects to the ideas entertained by children about natural and social phenomena, as Piaget established in some of his early studies. Indeed, the allegedly childish nature of 'primitive' thinking has haunted theorists from Tylor and Levy-Bruhl to the more recent comparative psychologists, Werner and Kaplan (1956). Yet, as has been pointed out many times, it is a mistake to make judgments about thought *processes* on the basis of their *contents* (see, e.g. Boas, 1965, first published 1911; Levi-Strauss, 1966). Extraordinary beliefs follow quite logically from extraordinary premises. Moreover, you do not have to look very far even in a technological society for signs of 'magical' thinking. It is a rare individual indeed who is bereft of all such thoughts. They may even receive an institutional sanction within society. If you are tempted to be patronizing about a culture that has recourse to witch doctors, consider what one distinguished general practitioner writes of Western medicine:

Medicine in general practice has not really changed very much. Magic and antiquated science are its foundations. Certainly, new drugs like penicillin are an exception, but only partly so. Penicillin is very good at killing streptococci. A doctor sees a child with a streptococcal sore throat and prescribes this drug, and the child quickly recovers. But most sore throats are not caused by streptococci, they are caused by viruses. Viruses grow happily in the presence of penicillin, and the prescribing of this drug does not help a virus sore throat to recover, it will do so anyway within a few days. Nevertheless, many doctors prescribe penicillin for virus sore throats. Penicillin is known as a potent drug and a good treatment. The virus sore throat recovers within a few days without of course the help of the penicillin, but the penicillin has done something: the doctor has another grateful patient. (Malleson, 1973, p. 22)

An even more striking instance of magical thinking in modern medicine is the use of electro-convulsive therapy as a treatment for schizophrenia. The basis of the treatment appears to be a clear case of homeopathic and contagious magic. Epileptics seemed to be less likely to suffer from schizophrenia than non-epileptics, it was therefore considered a good idea to induce epileptic-like seizures in schizophrenics. In fact, however, the therapeutic effects of ECT are more marked on depression, for which it continues to be used, but no one knows whether its undoubted healing properties are due to a current being passed through the brain or simply to the faith in the treatment that is shared by doctor and patient. As Sutherland (1976) reports, when a faulty machine failed to deliver a shock, the psychiatrists failed to notice the failure or any difference in the 'effects' on their patients. Although it is important to establish therapies on a scientific basis, such knowledge is double-edged. Once a treatment is shown to be magical, doctors will lose faith in it and so too will their patients; thereupon it will cease to produce its beneficial effects. Perhaps one should only despise the use of magic in medicine where there is a scientifically tested alternative to it.

If magical thinking is so ubiquitous, it is natural to inquire into its origins and functions. The question of function has been answered by several generations of social (cultural) anthropologists and is of too large a scope to be considered here. We shall pursue only the question of underlying psychological mechanisms. For our purposes, magical thinking consists in the ascription of a causal relation in a case where there are no objective grounds for it, e.g. the witch's spell *causes* the crack in the pot, the name of the murderer *causes* the hair in the victim's head to come out. The exact nature of any causal claim is singularly obscure. Language is full of causal verbs such as *kill, show, give, inform,* but no semantic analysis of the everyday sense of causation has yet gained general acceptance (see Miller and Johnson-Laird, 1976, for a discussion of causation and a semantic analysis of causal verbs). However, most people have a well-developed propensity for positing causal relations between events. Common observation and experimental investigation (Jenkins and Ward, 1965) concur that in seeking to discover a pattern in events an observer will (too) readily construe them as causally related. It is all too easy to move from an observation of concomitant events to an interpretation that the first event is the cause of the second event. Hume established that this step was logically unwarranted on the basis of observation alone; modern physics has no need of recourse to the concept of cause. It is plausible to suppose that cause is essentially a conceptual relation: *it is not possible to have A without B*, where as Miller shows in Reading 24 in Part v, *possibility* involves a 'computation' based on knowledge. It is also plausible to suppose that a causal interpretation of the world is advantageous because it confers some power of prediction to its adherents. That this ability may turn out to be illusory does not necessarily negate its utility: fallacious theories are usually more useful than no theory at all. The ascription of causality is accordingly an interpretation of events, even in the case of the simple but powerful causal illusions of the laboratory (Michotte, 1963). Their rapid and automatic interpretation reflects the implicit nature of many causal inferences rather than an innate perceptual process (*pace* Michotte). In the interpretation of the events of daily life, it is almost invariable that in order to set them within a broader causal or intentional framework, it is necessary to go beyond what is explicitly given. An event does not have a unique interpretation – a fact that Geertz (1973b), echoing Ryle before him, has emphasized. You cannot literally see the difference between a wink and an involuntary twitch.

Turning to causal relations between classes of events – the true domain of the proto-theories of daily life – it is evident that very careful and systematic experimentation has to be carried out in order to test whether events of one sort truly cause events of another sort. In fact, observers will settle for meta-causal relations – A is a *possible* cause of B – which are almost impossible to test, and they will do so with a minimum of evidence. Thus, it was originally claimed that smoking is a possible cause of cancer largely on the basis of a correlation between smoking and cancer. Such a correlation, as the eminent statistician the late Sir Ronald Fisher pointed out, could be explained by some unknown constitutional factor predisposing an individual both to smoke and to succumb to cancer. In ordinary life, a correlation combined with 'common sense' is usually sufficient to lead to a causal claim.

In the first reading in this Part, Shweder delineates another potential mechanism underlying magical thinking: intelligent people ignorant of statistics fail to grasp the concept of correlation. They readily substitute a mere similarity between two states of affairs for an actual correlation between them. Reading 21 by Tversky and Kahneman in Part IV should have prepared the reader for such an eventuality. What is striking about Shweder's claim, however, is not that people untutored in statistics have difficulty with correlation, but the nature of the concept with which they replace it: resemblance between things. If this claim is true – and it certainly merits further rigorous testing, then homeopathic magic is almost unavoidable. Most people, regardless of their culture, will be prone to argue:

A resembles B
∴ A tends to be associated with B

Couple this conclusion with the principles of causal inference that we discussed earlier and one obtains:

A tends to be associated with B
A occurs before B
∴ A causes B

By these two inferential steps, men come to believe that witchcraft causes cracks in pots, or that penicillin cures a sore throat, or even perhaps that the experiences of early childhood play a crucial role in determining adult personality. Such propositions may, of course, be true – *that* is a matter for scientific testing. The point to be emphasized is that 'magical' thinking is simply a useful heuristic for generating ideas. We have pointed out the importance of metaphor and representative fact in solving problems: 'magical' thinking establishes a role for simile. The relation to language is hardly accidental; it is corroborated from an unexpected quarter. Charles Rycroft (1968) has argued that psychoanalysis is more a theory of semantics than an empirical science. It is, indeed, a mistake to confuse 'propositions about language' with 'propositions about the world'.

After a small beginning – the Cambridge expedition of anthropologists and psychologists to the Torres Straits at the turn of the century – cross-cultural studies have investigated most aspects of psychology, and the reader is referred to Lloyd (1972) and Cole and Scribner (1974) for excellent reviews of the literature. It is, of course, intrinsically interesting to learn that, for instance, when Wolof children (Senegal) are tested for conservation of the volume of liquid – a standard Piagetian procedure, they are apt to think that the experimenter has *magically* influenced the quantities of liquid in the test beakers: conservation increases considerably when they are allowed to pour the liquid for themselves (Bruner, Olver, and Greenfield, 1966). However, what is the ultimate purpose of cross-cultural studies? Is it no more than to establish similarities and differences in the cognitive functioning of peoples from different cultures or genetic groups?

One prevalent aim has been to identify the source of the mental 'deficit' in primitive thinking. This notion certainly pre-judges the issue, but is by no means held solely by prejudiced thinkers. There have been prejudiced psychologists (see Kamin, 1974, who ingeniously allows them to discredit themselves in their own words). But other psychologists have been genuinely convinced that 'primitive mentality' is truly a form of simple-mindedness. Their grounds include the anthropological evidence about magical thinking, a belief in the validity of certain empirical studies of cognition in other cultures, and erroneous views about their *own* culture and cognition. Thus, for example, Werner (1948) writes about 'primitive' languages in the following terms: 'One peculiarity of these languages is that the verbal classification of several single objects by means of one name common to all is not always dependent on any actual common likeness.' The fallacy, here, of course, is the assumption that this phenomenon is unique to 'primitive' langauges. It is in fact a feature common to English, Indo-European languages in general, and probably to all languages (see the Introduction to Part III for a specific consideration of the phenomenon).

It seems to be extremely easy for psychologists to establish a deficit in the thinking of people from an alien culture (or class). It would probably be equally easy for members of that culture (or class) to reverse the roles. Few of us would be capable of fashioning an arrowhead from stone, or making fire with a wooden drill (see Kroeber, 1961); most of us, like Elizabeth Bowen (1954), would find it all but impossible to commit to memory the many local names for an exotic flora. You may protest that you were never taught such things; a 'primitive' may protest that he was never taught any symbolic skills. It seems unlikely that there can ever be a test of mental ability that is fair for members of any culture. Only if it fails to reveal differences might we begin to suspect that it is truly 'culture free', but, as statisticians know, it is impossible to prove the null hypothesis. In this context, it is interesting to quote some remarks of Tulkin and Konner (cited by Flavell, 1977) on the experience of Western scientists who participated in some 'seminars' with Kalahari Bushmen on the topic of hunting:

As scientific discussions the seminars were among the most stimulating the Western observers had ever attended. Questions were raised and tentative answers (hypotheses) were advanced. Hypotheses were always labeled as to the degree of certainty with which the speaker adhered to them, which was related to the type of data on which the hypothesis was based. . . .
    The process of tracking, specifically, involves patterns of inference, hypothesis-testing, and discovery that tax the best inferential and analytic capacities of the human mind. Determining, from tracks, the movements of animals, their timing, whether they are wounded and if so how, and predicting how far they will go and in which direction and how fast, all involve repeated activation of hypotheses, trying them out against new data, integrating them with previously known facts about animal movements, rejecting the ones that do not stand up, and finally getting a reasonable fit, which adds up to meat in the pot.

The idea that there can be no 'culture-free' tests might seem to render cross-cultural studies pointless. At the very least, however, if a 'deficit' is discovered, a psychologist may investigate how – if desirable – it might be overcome. Michael Cole was in exactly this predicament, as he describes in Reading 28, when he was suddenly called upon to improve the education of tribal children in Liberia. His paper records how he and his colleagues gradually climbed out of the trap of assuming that the members of a culture must be in some way deprived because they were unable to perform certain (Western) tests of cognitive ability. Very often his subjects performed poorly as a result of a lack of familiarity with a problem, though this global description fails to do justice to the detailed causes that Cole and his colleagues have discovered.

A major mystery in cross-cultural work is why performance on Piaget's tests of conservation is often so poor. A bald interpretation of the results (reviewed by Dasen, 1972a) is that adults in non-Western cultures may not attain the level of 'concrete operations'. They may think, for example, that if liquid is poured from a standard container into a tall, thin container its quantity is thereby increased. As Cole remarks, an Australian aboriginal society that thereby thought to increase its water supply would have disappeared long ago. Yet, a satisfactory explanation for the experimental results has still to be formulated.

It is hardly surprising that when adults in 'primitive' cultures are asked to make more abstract inferences, they often are unable to do so. One very important factor appears to be whether or not an individual has attended school; and it is the effect of this variable that is a central topic of Reading 29, a cross-cultural study of deductive reasoning, by Sylvia Scribner. It appears to be school rather than culture *per se* that is the major determinant of performance. What Scribner goes on to suggest is that the formal approach necessary to cope with deductive problems is, in essence, a particular *genre* of language. It may be that school teaches one to grasp its underlying schema or at least to be sensitive to those cues (in the experimental situation and elsewhere) that suggest its relevance. The notion of a logical genre of discourse raises a more general question about the relations between language and thought.

The idea that language can determine thought has proved extremely attractive to a number of thinkers. The philosopher, Nietzsche, wrote 'By the grammatical structure of a group of languages everything runs smoothly for one kind of philosophical system, whereas the way is barred for certain other possibilities.' Bertrand Russell took very much the same sort of view when he attempted to show how Leibniz's philosophy was a direct consequence of his analysis of sentences into a subject–predicate structure (see Russell, 1900). Perhaps the most famous implicit invocation of the principle is in George Orwell's imaginary language, 'Newspeak', which featured in his novel *1984*. This is a language – almost a parody of C. K. Ogden's (1935) Basic English – in which it was supposed to be impossible to express certain ideas, with the ultimate aim of rendering it impossible to think them. (The principles of the language are spelled out in an appendix to the novel (Orwell, 1949).) As his essays on 'Politics and the English Language' and 'New Words' show, Orwell (1970a, b) certainly seems to have taken seriously the idea that language, and particularly its corrupted usage, has an important influence on the way people think. In this respect he resembles Karl Kraus, the scourge of the Viennese journalists, whose views on language also appear to have influenced the philosopher, Ludwig Wittgenstein (see Janik and Toulmin, 1973), who came to think that philosophers were bewitched by language (Wittgenstein, 1958).

The hypothesis that language influences thought has been applied not merely to metaphysics and politics, but also to the mundane world of everyday affairs. Its most notable exponent was Benjamin Lee Whorf (1956), who proposed a 'linguistic relativity' principle according to which the same physical events can give rise to a very different interpretation depending on the language of the observer:

We dissect nature along lines laid down by our native languages. The categories and types that we isolate from the world of phenomena we do not find because they stare every observer in the face; on the contrary, the world is presented in a kaleidoscopic flux of impressions which has to be organized by our minds – and this means largely by the linguistic systems in our minds. We cut nature up, organize it into concepts, and ascribe significances as we do, largely because we are parties to an agreement to organize it in this way – an agreement that holds throughout our speech community and is codified in the patterns of our language.

Whorf worked as an insurance inspector, but in his spare time he made a study of American Indian languages. He was greatly taken with the apparently 'timeless' nature of Hopi, and figure 1 illustrates the contrast he drew between that language and English.

Whorf's hypothesis has engendered much confusion, and many circular arguments. Its converse often seems more plausible. The fact, for example, that an Australian aboriginal language contains suffixes that locate events *across the river* or *this side of the river, up the hill* or *down the hill*, must surely reflect a preoccupation with such aspects of the terrain. It would be bizarre to claim that the existence of such suffixes has caused speakers to become preoccupied with these features of their local topography. Despite such arguments, Whorf's hypothesis has led to a considerable quantity of empirical research (see Miller and McNeill, 1969, for a comprehensive review of the earlier studies).

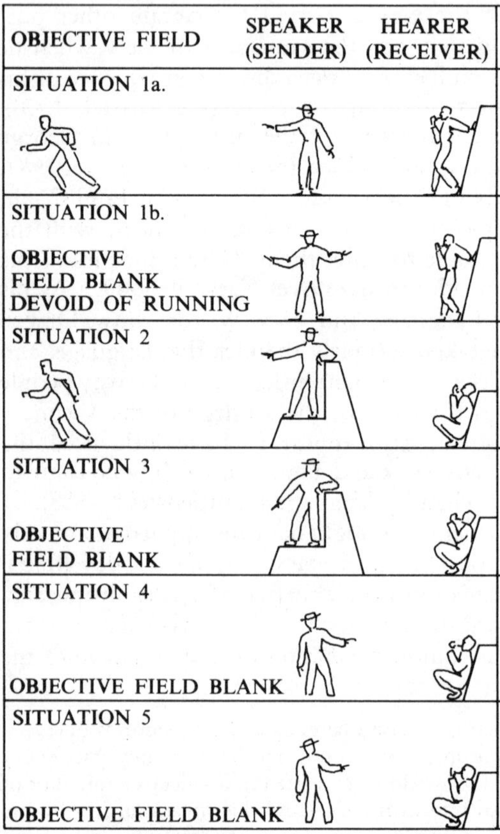

OBJECTIVE FIELD	SPEAKER (SENDER) HEARER (RECEIVER)	HANDLING OF TOPIC, RUNNING OF THIRD PERSON
SITUATION 1a.		ENGLISH...'HE IS RUNNING' HOPI... 'WARI'. (RUNNING. STATEMENT OF FACT)
SITUATION 1b. OBJECTIVE FIELD BLANK DEVOID OF RUNNING		ENGLISH...'HE RAN' HOPI... 'WARI' (RUNNING, STATEMENT OF FACT)
SITUATION 2		ENGLISH...'HE IS RUNNING' HOPI... 'WARI' (RUNNING, STATEMENT OF FACT)
SITUATION 3 OBJECTIVE FIELD BLANK		ENGLISH...'HE RAN' HOPI... 'ERA WARI' (RUNNING, STATEMENT OF FACT FROM MEMORY)
SITUATION 4 OBJECTIVE FIELD BLANK		ENGLISH...'HE WILL RUN' HOPI... 'WARIKNI' (RUNNING, STATEMENT OF EXPECTATION)
SITUATION 5 OBJECTIVE FIELD BLANK		ENGLISH...'HE RUNS' (E.G. ON THE TRACK TEAM) HOPI... 'WARIKNGWE' (RUNNING, STATEMENT OF LAW)

Figure 1. The contrast drawn by Whorf between a 'temporal' language (English) and a 'timeless' language (Hopi): he claimed that differences of time in English are differences in the kind of validity in Hopi (from Whorf, 1956)

In Reading 30, Eleanor Rosch presents a sustained critique of the hypothesis. As she rightly points out, there is no evidence for the strong version of the hypothesis – that language imposes upon its speakers a particular way of thinking about the world. A weaker formulation of the theory postulates that one language rather than another may render certain categories of events easier to remember. Verbal labels are known to affect the way visual stimuli are recalled (Carmichael, Hogan, and Walters, 1932); and similar results were reported for the memorability of colours as a function of the colour terms within a language (e.g. Lenneberg and Roberts, 1956). The design of such studies need no longer reflect the 'deficit' model of cross-cultural research. The investigator can be concerned to establish an interaction between culture and performance – to show the relative performance of speakers of different languages for different regions of the colour space. One language may facilitate recall of colours in the blue-green region, another language may facilitate recall of colours in the orange-red region. It is such interactions, as Rosch has emphasized, that will best help us to understand the contribution of culture to cognition. In fact, however, colour terminology turns out to have some remarkable properties. Berlin and Kay (1969) carried out a seminal investigation of colour terminology in a variety of languages, and established that there are 'focal' colours, very much analogous to 'prototypes' (see Part III). As Rosch shows, they appear to reflect the neurophysiology of colour vision and accordingly to provide a *universal* basis for colour terminology. There are other possible cognitive universals. For example, there are striking similarities between languages in the metaphorical use of adjectives denoting physical properties such as *hard, cold, straight,* to describe human traits (see Asch, 1961). Numerous studies of so-called 'phonetic symbolism' suggest that the sound quality of words may provide a universal basis for certain aspects of symbolism. Most people, for example, have little difficulty in guessing that the Chinese word *ch'ing* means *light* and *ch'ung* means *heavy,* rather than *vice versa* (see, e.g. Klank, Huang, and Johnson, 1971).

One of the most recent revivals of linguistic relativity has been in the area of sociolinguistics. The English sociologist, Basil Bernstein, has argued that there are two main linguistic 'codes'. There is a *restricted code* consisting of the simple predictable syntax used for conveying stereotyped thoughts, concrete particular meanings, greetings, expressions of good will, and so on. There is an *elaborated code* consisting of the less predictable syntax required for communicating more abstract and universal meanings. Bernstein claims that 'one of the effects of the class system is to limit access to elaborated codes' (Bernstein, 1973, p. 200). This thesis may account for the apparent difficulty that working-class children have in conventional schools; it has inspired a considerable amount of research. There does not seem, however, to be any very easy way for assigning utterances to the different categories of *code;* and there is no direct evidence that the predominant speech code of a class directly affects the thought processes of its members. Indeed, in the postscript to his collected papers Bernstein (1973) has stressed that he is now concerned with sociolinguistic codes (determined by social relations) rather than linguistic codes, and with the conditions in which a child will use the codes within his or her repertoire.

In fact, the contrast between the two sorts of code often seems to involve deixis, the presence of elements that can only be interpreted in context. The contrast is illustrated in the following two transcripts constructed to demonstrate the difference between the codes (Bernstein, 1973, p. 203):

1. Three boys are playing football and one boy kicks the ball   and it goes through the window   the ball breaks the window   and the boys are looking at it   and a man comes out and shouts at them   because they've broken the window   so they run away   and then that lady looks out of her window and she tells the boys off.
2. They're playing football   and he kicks it and it goes through there   it breaks the window and they're looking at it   and he comes out   and shouts at them   because they've broken it   so they run away   and then she looks out   and she tells them off.

The first version of the story shows the way in which a middle-class child uses a more elaborate code that relies much less on the context – a series of pictures – than the working-class child's restricted code. (One wonders to what extent children could imitate codes of other classes in such a task; Hudson (1968) found that apparently 'convergent' children, potential scientists, could become quite 'divergent' in tasks of creativity when they were asked to pretend that they were Bohemian artists.)

The view that an impoverished language is the basis of poor performance in school was urged most strongly a decade ago by various psychologists in the USA (e.g. Bereiter and Engelmann, 1966; Jensen, 1969). Thus, Bereiter and his colleagues argued that the language of ghetto children was not merely under-developed, but basically a nonlogical mode of expressive behaviour. Yet, there is no real evidence that ghetto children have an impoverished language. As William Labov (e.g. 1969) has shown most ingeniously, many misconceptions about the linguistic ability of such children are based on sociolinguistic aspects of interviewing. Even a highly skilled Black interviewer from Harlem will fail to elicit a real reflection of a child's mastery of the vernacular, if the test takes the form of a formal interview. Indeed, very similar factors appear to be at work here as in Cole's report of the difficulty of testing Kpelle farmers: it turns out that they have a highly verbal culture despite their inability to cope with a laboratory test of linguistic communication. Likewise, far from being an impoverished verbal community, the urban ghetto revolves around 'speech events which depend upon the competitive exhibition of verbal skills: sounding, singing, toasts, rifting, louding – a whole range of activities in which the individual gains status through his use of language' (Labov, 1969). As an example of the dialectical skill of an articulate speaker of the nonstandard English of the New York Black ghetto (with its special rules governing nega-tion, use of *it* for *there*, etc.), here is an extract of a long interview between Larry, a 15-year-old core member of the Jets, and John Lewis, one of Labov's col-leagues. The topic is what happens to you after you die:

LARRY: You know, like some people say if you're good an' shit, your spirit goin' t' heaven . . . 'n if you bad, your spirit goin' to hell. Well, bullshit! your spirit goin' to hell anyway, good or bad.
JL: Why?
LARRY: Why? I'll tell you why. 'Cause, you see, doesn't nobody really know that it's a God, y'know, 'cause I mean I have seen black gods, pink gods, white gods,

all color gods, and don't nobody know it's really a God. An' when they be sayin' if you good, you goin' t' heaven, tha's bullshit, 'cause you ain't goin' to no heaven, 'cause it ain't no heaven for you to go to.

The argument is playful: Larry is not really committed to any of his assertions. The trouble is, of course, that his *reductio ad absurdum* proves more than it should, yet when challenged on this point by the interviewer, Larry's reply is unanswerable:

> JL: Well, if there's no heaven, how could there be a hell?
> LARRY: I mean – ye-ah. Well, let me tell you, it ain't no hell, 'cause this is hell right here, y'know!
> JL: This is hell?
> LARRY: Yeah, this is hell right here!

It is difficult to resist the conclusion that language is more likely to reflect an individual's attitude to life (and schooling), perhaps absorbed from others of the same social class, than to mould such attitudes. Such a conclusion seems congruent with both Labov's and Bernstein's theories, despite the apparent conflicts between them. Yet, if language has no effect on thought processes, then what cognitive advantages accrue to those who possess it? It seems most plausible that language can provide an economic notation for conceptual 'computations' (see Fodor, 1976). Mental arithmetic with Roman numerals would be taxing; it would be impossible with an Aboriginal language in which explicit numbers cease at five. Whatever value linguistic powers are likely to grant to the powers of thought, it seems probable that it does so, not only by enabling people to communicate, but also by furnishing them with an articulated internal representation of the world. The role of internal representations in thought processes is the topic to be considered in the final Part of this book.

27. Likeness and likelihood in everyday thought: magical thinking and everyday judgments about personality[1]

Richard A. Shweder

In what terms should we understand the understandings of other peoples, and in what terms should we compare their understandings with our own? A moment's reflection on this central issue in the 'anthropology of thought' brings one up against the perplexing secondary question: what are we to make of another culture's apparently false knowledge? For example, how is the student of Azande culture to comprehend their attempts to cure epilepsy by eating the burnt skull of a red bush monkey, or their therapeutic application of fowl's excrement for cases of ringworm (see Evans-Pritchard, 1937; Tambiah, 1973)? A line of research conducted by Newcomb (1929), D'Andrade (1965, 1973, 1974), Chapman (1967), Chapman and Chapman (1967, 1969), Tversky and Kahneman (1971, 1973, Reading 21), and Shweder (1972a,b, 1975a,b, in press a,b,c) suggests one possible answer to this question, namely, the distinction between resemblance and correlation is collapsed in everyday thought. . . . As one researcher has put it, 'normal adults with no training in statistics' may lack a concept of correlation (Smedslund 1963).

The absence of a distinction between resemblance and correlation is familiar to anthropological fieldworkers. It is characteristic of magical thought systems. Evans-Pritchard, for example, in his classic volume on Zande magic, notes:

Generally the logic of therapeutic treatment consists in the selection of the most prominent external symptoms, the naming of the disease after some object in nature it resembles [e.g. the physical movements of bush monkeys resemble epileptic seizures; ringworm resembles fowl excrement] and the utilization of the object as the principal ingredient in the drug administered to cure the disease. The circle may even be completed by belief that the external symptoms not only yield to treatment by the object which resembles them but are caused by it as well. (1937, p. 487)

[1] Edited excerpts of the paper to appear in *Current Anthropology*. © 1977 The University of Chicago Press. The reader should note that the same issue of the journal contains commentaries on the paper, and the author's replies to them.

The very existence of magical thinking has posed a difficult interpretive problem for anthropological theory. Some scholars (e.g. Levi-Strauss, 1966) have viewed magic as a relatively effective set of procedures for acquiring knowledge and exercising control over one's environment, comparable to scientific canons of inquiry. Others (e.g. Malinowski, 1954) have viewed it as analogous to wish-fulfillment, an irrational symbolic attempt to influence uncontrollable events. Still others (e.g. Tambiah, 1973) have viewed magical thinking as a form of persuasive rhetoric, designed to arouse sentiments rather than to make claims about what goes with what in actual experience. This paper presents an alternative perspective. It will argue that magical thinking is an expression of a *universal disinclination* of normal adults to draw correlational lessons from their experience coupled with a *universal inclination* of normal adults to seek symbolic and meaningful connections (resemblances) among objects and events. Magical thinking is no less characteristic of our own mundane intellectual activities than it is characteristic of Zande curing practices.

Correlation and contingency are relatively complex concepts that are not spontaneously available to human thought (see e.g. Smedslund, 1963; Jenkins and Ward, 1965; Ward and Jenkins, 1965). Correlation relevant information is difficult for the human mind to organize into a format that lends itself to correlational manipulation, and correlational reasoning is typically avoided when most adults estimate what goes with what in their experience. (Using Piaget's terminology we might hypothesize that most adults in all cultures are not formal operational thinkers. Correlation and contingency are formal operational concepts, see e.g. Inhelder and Piaget, 1958). Instead most normal adults do as the Azande do. They rely on resemblance to estimate correlation.

This study examines this cognitive processing perspective on magical thinking by focusing upon everyday personality judgments. The study will show that the distinction between resemblance and correlation is ignored in everyday judgments about individual differences in conduct. When normal adults make personality assessments, items of conduct that *resemble* one another (e.g. smiles easily, introduces himself to strangers, likes parties) are typically said to covary over people *despite experience and available information to the contrary*. Magical thinking seems to be no more a feature of Zande beliefs that ringworm and fowl excrement go together than our own beliefs that self-esteem and leadership do. It is a universal aspect of everyday judgments about what goes with what in experience. The study suggests that anthropologists interested in thought may have mistaken a difference in the content of thought for a difference in mode of thought. Magical thinking, *as a practice*, is not a mode of thought that distinguishes one culture from another. Resemblance, not correlation, is a fundamental conceptual tool of the everyday ('savage?') mind. Most of us have a 'savage' mentality much of the time.

Intuitive and nonintuitive concepts in human thought

A useful distinction in the study of human thought is between intuitive and nonintuitive concepts. Concepts can be arranged along a continuum having to do with the relative ease with which they can be attained. More intuitive (so-called 'spontaneous') concepts are acquired even under highly degraded learning conditions, e.g. without explicit instruction, with a minimal amount of practice, and regardless of a desire to learn or the nature of reinforcements (see Seligman and Hager, 1972). Moreover, intuitive concepts seem to be available for use without conscious effort or reflection. In contrast, nonintuitive concepts require special learning conditions for their acquisition, e.g. massive instructional input, an orderly and explicit organization of learning trials, high motivation, etc. These learning conditions are more difficult to arrange. Consequently, nonintuitive concepts are less widely distributed (both within and across human populations) than intuitive concepts; they seem to be associated with deliberate, self-reflective intellectual activities.

Some concepts are so intuitive that they will be attained even under the most degraded of learning conditions and regardless of *variations* in physical, social or cultural environment. Developmental psychologists such as Price-Williams (1969) have alerted us to the relative ease with which children in all cultures come to have such concepts as 'object constancy' and 'reversibility' (see Piaget 1952, 1967).[2] It seems safe to conclude that normal adults in all cultures act on the implicit understanding that the external world has an independent existence. Normal adults in all cultures have the concept of object constancy; they make plans, negotiate agreements, predict events, etc. It also seems safe to conclude that normal adults in all cultures act on the implicit understanding that for any event there is an intellectual operation that compensates for it, cancels it or undoes it. Normal adults in all cultures have the concept of reversibility, e.g. breaches of social expectation are followed by excuses, verbal stratagems designed to reverse and undo the distress caused by misconduct. Normal adults in all cultures *easily* master the intuitive intellectual manipulations characteristic of *concrete* operational thought (as discussed by Piaget, 1967, *pace* Dasen, 1972a; see also Mehler and Bever, 1967).

The anthropological literature on the kinds of relationships expressed in folk definitions (e.g. Casagrande and Hale, 1967; Tyler, 1969) provides us with other examples of relatively intuitive concepts. It appears that 'relationship concepts' such as class inclusion, function, antonymy, synonymy, exemplification, part–whole, temporality, etc., are relatively easy to acquire and are universally mastered with or without reinforcement, deliberate training, etc., and regardless of variations in culture (also see Shweder and LeVine, 1975).

There is some controversy over whether concepts such as object constancy, reversibility, class inclusion or synonymy are merely elicited by experience (the innateness hypothesis), constructed out of experience (the Piagetian hypothesis)

---

[2] [Even gorillas can attain object constancy, as Margaret Redshaw has shown, personal communication to the editors.]

or received from experience (the learning theoretic hypothesis) (see e.g. Chomsky, 1968; Piaget, 1970; Putnam, 1975b). Nonetheless, such concepts are easy to acquire; the fact that they are universally attained is some evidence of this relative acquistional ease.

On the other hand, one can point to many nonintuitive concepts. They are relatively difficult to learn, and they are absent from the thinking of most normal adults. For example, many statistical concepts having to do with 'chance' and 'probability' are nonintuitive. Consider the following case. If I wager you that in a randomly selected group of *twenty-five* people, two of those people will be born on the same day of the year, the chances are slightly *in my favour* (Kemeny, Snell, and Thompson, 1966, pp. 134–41). Yet very few normal adults would refuse my request for heavy odds. For randomly composed groups of *forty* people, it is I who should offer you heavy odds, in fact, eight to one if you are foolish enough to stake the bet that no two people in the group will be born on the same day of the year. The intuitive mind boggles. Consider a second example of a nonintuitive problem in estimation. A piece of paper is folded in half. It is folded in half again and again. After 100 folds how thick will it be? Most readers will estimate a thickness of a few inches, perhaps a foot, and will be startled to discover (upon reflection) that the thickness will be greater than the distance between the earth and the moon.

The concept of correlation

Correlation is a nonintuitive concept. Like many statistical concepts, it is generally absent from the thinking of most normal adults including social scientists (see e.g. Smedslund 1963). Correlation is a relatively difficult concept to master. It is a second order relational concept expressing the relation between two relations. One way to describe the concept of correlation is as a comparison between two conditional probabilities (see Ward and Jenkins, 1965). Consider for example table 1, which is a 2 × 2 contingency table protraying hypothetical information about the correlation between a symptom (S) and a disease (D). One can estimate the correlation between the symptom and the disease by judging the extent to which the probability of having the disease, given that the patient has the symptom, *differs from* the probability of having the disease, given that the patient does *not* have the symptom. The judgment amounts to an estimate of

$$\frac{a}{a + b} - \frac{c}{c + d}$$

or alternatively

$$\frac{ad - bc}{(a + b)(c + d)}$$

In table 1 the correlation between the symptom and the disease is close to zero. Smedslund (1963) presented the information in table 1 to a group of Swedish nurses. He presented them with a pack of 100 cards supposedly representing 'excerpts from the files of 100 patients'. Each card indicated the presence or absence of the symptom and the presence or absence of the disease in ratios corresponding to the information in table 1. The nurses were asked to find out 'whether there is a relationship (connection)' between the symptom and the disease. They were told that they could study and organize the cards in any way they wished, *and that they could take notes*. Eighty-five per cent of the nurses claimed that there was a relationship between the symptom and the disease. Most of them justified their claim by pointing out that the number of cards in which the symptom and disease were both present (37) was 'the largest or was large'. Almost all the nurses found the task difficult.

Table 1. The relation between a symptom (S) and a disease (D) in the files of 100 hypothetical patients. Normal adults with no training in statistics generally think this information reveals a connection between the symptom and the disease (Smedslund, 1963)

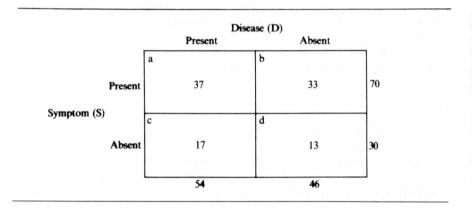

	Disease (D)		
	Present	Absent	
	a	b	
Present	37	33	70
Symptom (S)			
	c	d	
Absent	17	13	30
	54	46	

There are numerous ways to manipulate correlation relevant information in a noncorrelational way. Smedslund's nurses tended to focus upon joint occurrences of the symptom and the disease. A somewhat different misuse of correlation relevant information is reported by Ward and Jenkins (1965). College students were presented with contingency information concerning the relationship between cloud seeding and subsequent rainfall. One set of students focused upon *confirming* cases (the number of seed–rain days plus the number of no seed–no rain days) to estimate the success of cloud seeding programmes. They tended to ignore information about the number of no seed–rain days and seed–no rain days. Another set of students failed to *compare* conditional probabilities. They assessed the effectiveness of cloud seeding by the probability of rain for those days when clouds were seeded without comparing this conditional probability to the probability of rain for those days when clouds were not seeded.

The claim that correlation is not an intuitively available concept requires some clarification. Specifically, one must distinguish between a *disinclination* to think correlationally and an *incapacity* to think correlationally. It is *possible* to get American college students to think correlationally. Nonetheless, the conditions one has to contrive in order to elicit correlational thinking are rather special and quite unrepresentative of everyday life. For example, Ward and Jenkins (1965) discovered that when information is presented serially, namely 'on a trial by trial basis, as it usually occurs in the real world', only 17 per cent of their students display correlational thinking in their estimates of the effectiveness of cloud seeding. Moreover, explicit summary information in the form of 2 × 2 contingency tables has 'little influence on judgments when it was presented *after* they [the students] have followed a trial by trial presentation'. The only condition in which a majority of students display correlational thinking is when they receive summary information in the form of a 2 × 2 contingency table *without* prior trial by trial experience with the data. Most normal adults have the mental capacity to think correlationally. Nonetheless, they do not apply the concept in their everyday judgments. Because correlation is not an intuitively available concept, normal adults are not likely to master it without explicit instructions to do so. If all concepts were intuitive, educational environments and explicit training would not be necessary.

. . . As soon as events can be *meaningfully linked* to one another, magical thinking makes its appearance; normal adults substitute the readily available intuitive concept of resemblance for the unavailable nonintuitive concept of correlation. This substitution of 'propositions about language' for correlational propositions does not imply that magical thinking is *equivalent* to non-correlational thinking. Rather, magical thinking is one type of noncorrelational thinking. (Other types of noncorrelational thinking include the cognitive strategies just discussed above, e.g. the focus on confirming cases, etc.). In the light of the general disinclination of normal adults to manipulate information in a correlational way, magical thinking seems to occur when adults assess the degree of *empirical* relationship among objects or events that also *conceptually* affiliate or exclude one another in their minds. Thus what D'Andrade (1965) has called a 'hazard of science' is an appropriate definition for magical thinking. *Magical thinking can be defined as a confusion of 'propositions about the world with propositions about language'.*

Recent research by personality psychologists suggests that this confusion may characterize everyday judgments about personality. It has become increasingly apparent that the behavioural traits that play such an important role in our everyday descriptions of personality are not 'out there' waiting to be discovered, but are rather the creations of the magical mind.

The crisis in personality psychology: in search of the missing trait

It has become increasingly apparent that behaviour is not the place to search for everyday personality traits. Personality psychologists have tried; for the most part their efforts have not been rewarded (see e.g. Newcomb, 1929; Mischel, 1968; Fiske, 1974).

For years, personality psychologists have laboured to 'discover' everyday personality traits (e.g. dependency, aggressiveness, character strength) in behaviour (see e.g. Allport, 1937; Cattell, 1957; Norman, 1963). Encouraged by the assumption that everyday trait terms encode information about 'the relative frequencies of joint occurrences' of various 'behavioral dispositions in other persons' (Passini and Norman, 1966) they have searched around in behaviour for corresponding 'unities' or 'consistencies' in the way persons differ from one another over comparable situations. In pursuit of 'dependency' they have hoped to find that the *same* child prods his mother for attention *and* clings to her apron strings. In pursuit of 'introversion' they have hoped to find that the *same* adult is shy with strangers *and* prefers to work alone. In pursuit of 'character strength' they have hoped to find that self-reliance and responsibility go together or correlate.

In general, personality psychologists have failed in this quest (see e.g. Raush, Dittmann, and Taylor, 1959; Sears, 1963; Endler and Hunt, 1968; Mischel, 1968, 1973; Moos, 1969; Fiske, 1974). What they have discovered is that (1) *inter-observer reliability is difficult to attain* (see e.g. Bourne, 1976). For example, two observers of the *same* person agree very little in their answers to the question 'What's he like?' and are not more likely to agree with each other than observers of *different* persons. What they have discovered is that (2) *method variance is greater than person variance* (see e.g. Campbell and Fiske, 1959; Burton, 1970). Distinguishable qualities (e.g. 'being disagreeable' and 'promoting solidarity') typically show higher within method associations than parallel across method associations. For example, if 'being disagreeable' and 'promoting solidarity' are measured using two methods, a personality inventory and a projective test, 'being disagreeable' and 'promoting solidarity' will more positively correlate within the inventory data than 'promoting solidarity' correlates with *itself* across the two methods. In general, features of personality measuring instruments have been found to be more stable than features of the persons measured. What personality psychologists have also discovered is (3) that *hypothesized traits (e.g. friendliness, dominance) typically account for no more than 9–15 per cent of the diversity of individual differences over naturally occurring situations* (see Mischel, 1968, 1973 for an overview; also see Shweder 1972b, 1973). The more assertive child at the breakfast table is not the more assertive child in the playroom. Different situations affect different persons differentially.

. . . It is very difficult for us to accept the idea that everyday personality traits are not there to be discovered in behaviour, just as it is difficult for the Azande to accept the notion that fowl excrement does not cure ringworm. What our common resistance reveals is the pervasiveness of magical thinking and its power to influence our perceptions of reality. Everyday personality traits (e.g. dependent, aggressive, friendly) are not correlational patterns to be found in conduct; they are clusters of meaning evoked by conduct. Personality traits are symbols or interpretive categories that link together items of behaviour, and are linked to each other by *conceptual* relationships that have little to do with frequency and correlations. Nonetheless these conceptual affiliations (e.g. connections due to resemblance) dominate our understandings of what goes with what in the world of experience. As we shall see, resemblance, not correlation, is a primary conceptual tool of the 'everyday mind'.

However, before examining the absence of a distinction between resemblance and correlation in everyday judgments of personality it is important that we clarify what it means to say that everyday personality traits are interpretive categories.

How does behaviour give rise to meanings?

Personality traits may not be there to be found in behaviour, but they are part of a *language* of interpersonal comprehension designed to help us 'read' one another's conduct. They are the terms in which a person *qua* person acquires meaning. How does this everyday sense-making activity work? How does behaviour give rise to meanings? To what kinds of meanings does it give rise? To answer these questions, we must consider the sense-making process in general.

Behind every attribution of a personality trait is a hidden inference, usually an induction. Consider, for example, the following hypothetical conversation between two mothers:

'Your son is so self-confident.' (Inductive inference)
'Why do you say that?'
'I saw him organizing games in the playground.' (Minor inductive premise)
'Yes. I noticed that, but . . .'
'Well, children who organize games are usually self-confident.' (Major inductive premise)

There are two points to be made about this piece of everyday talk about personality. The first point is that the conversation is inductive (and not deductive) in form. It is contradictory to assert 'an oak, but not a tree'; it is not contradictory to assert, 'organizes games, but not self-confident'. The inference is not *entailed* by its premises (see e.g. Black, 1970, pp. 150–1). Alternative inferences are always possible without logical error. The second point is that this particular hypothetical example is somewhat artificial. One reason for this is that it is unduly laboured. A second reason is that it obscures our interpretive options.

The inductions of everyday life are rarely explicit. In fact, a notable feature of everyday talk about individual differences in conduct is its condensed and abbreviated form; everyday exchanges of words leave a lot unsaid. One or more of the premises (e.g. your son organizes games in the playground; children who organize games are usually self-confident) that support the inference (e.g. your son is self-confident) go unverbalized. Consequently, normal adults often talk 'as though' they had actually observed 'self-confidence' itself, and not merely the organizational initiative of a child. Sometimes they even fool themselves. They should not be permitted to fool us. Self-confidence cannot be observed; it can only be inferred.

Abbreviations and condensations can occur in everyday talk primarily because normal adults can count on context, and a shared body of knowledge, beliefs and presuppositions in the listener (what Ziff, 1972 calls a 'special program'; what anthropologists call 'culture') to contribute tacitly whatever information is required to make their utterances comprehensible (see e.g. Bransford and McCarrell, Reading 23) . . .

. . . Behavioural events are inherently ambiguous; they do not give their exclusive warrant to any particular interpretation (see e.g. Schachter and Singer, 1962; Geertz, 1973a, ch. 1; Goffman, 1974, ch. 12). In part, this is because all behavioural events simultaneously possess a number of features. They are the overt and physical movements of some actor. They are situationally located. They are temporally arranged with respect to other acts. They may be goal-oriented. They may be rule-governed (see e.g. Burke, 1969). To ask, 'Was it Bill (the actor) or the chair (a feature of the situation) that caused him to fall down?' is like asking Donald Hebb's rhetorical question, 'What contributes more to the area of a football field, its width or its length?' In the absence of *either* Bill *or* the chair, the specific event would not have occurred. *Bill* would not have tripped over *that* chair. The event is unique; it is a singular interaction effect, involving this particular actor, this particular situation, this particular goal, etc.

Nonetheless, in everyday thought, behavioural events are *assimilated* to one kind of interpretive language or another all the time. 'He tripped because he is clumsy.' 'I tripped because something got in my way' (see Jones and Nisbett, 1972).

There are many possible interpretive points of view for ascribing meaning to conduct. We often explain why someone behaved as he did (e.g. striking another person) by reference to a trait of the actor (e.g. he is aggressive). But we can also explain behaviour by reference to features of the situation (e.g. his apartment was too crowded), by reference to antecedent acts (e.g. he was struck first), by reference to goals (e.g. he was trying to establish his authority), by reference to rules (e.g. that's what's done in a boxing match), etc.

Although the choice of an interpretive point of view is guided by some well-understood psychological principles (see e.g. Kelley, 1967, 1972), the selection of a particular interpretive perspective is never *logically* warranted by behaviour itself. For example, one psychological principle might be formulated as follows: equate propositions about *variations* in behaviour with propositions about the *causes* of behaviour. In everyday thought, the chair will be perceived as the cause of Bill's fall if everyone who enters the room (including Bill) trips over it. However, if only Bill trips over it, he will be perceived as causally responsible for what is now interpreted as his own 'clumsiness'. To make attributions in this way is tantamount to what Campbell (1969) has called an '*a priori* preference for parsimony' and a 'presumptive bias in favor of main effects'. In both cases the event is identical, Bill tripped. Without Bill that trip would not have occurred. Without the chair that trip would not have occurred. Bill and the chair are both causally relevant *and equally so*, no matter how many other people do or do not happen to fall over the same object. The 'coincidence of two [or more] separate specific interaction effects' (e.g. ten people trip over the chair) is no logical warrant for the attribution of a general cause (e.g. it is the chair's fault!).

Behavioural events do not speak for themselves; they evoke meanings that are not to be found in the behaviour itself. The meaning may *seem* to be inextricably part of the event once an interpretation is made, but this phenomenological illusion of inherent meaning should not mislead us into thinking that meanings are discovered. The temptation to confuse one's interpretive categories with the events they describe is at the basis of magical thinking. . .

The creations of the magical mind

How do normal adults use their interpretive categories? . . . A series of cognitive experiments conducted by Shweder (1972b, 1975a, in press b) suggest the universality of magical thinking and its intimate relation to the absence of the concept of correlation in normal adults. The experiments concern everyday judgments about what goes with what across individual differences in conduct. Everyday personality traits are generally not there to be discovered in behaviour; nonetheless, the magical mind seems to 'discover' them all the time.

Experiment I: Resemblance and judgments of co-occurrence likelihood

Resemblance is not a good predictor of co–occurrence likelihood. Pairs of objects or events that are conceptually linked (red and pink, ringworm and fowl's excrement, draughty rooms and runny noses, anal retentiveness and miserliness, self-esteem and leadership) do not typically co–occur in one's experience.

. . . The first nonexperimental investigation to compare the structure ('what goes with what') of experience with (1) the structure of observer reports about experience *and* (2) the semantic structure of the observers' categories was carried out by D'Andrade (1974). He discovered that the actual correlations among the behavioural referents of a set of categories used for coding small group behaviour were relatively unstable and did not correspond to the semantic similarities among the category labels. However, semantic similarity was decisive for observers' estimates of what goes with what in their experience. D'Andrade's study is the prototype for the analysis presented below.

The lack of fit between resemblance and correlation is fortunate for our research enterprise. It makes it possible for *us* to distinguish the two concepts. We can ask: Do normal adults collapse the distinction when they report what goes with what in their experience? Which is the more important intellectual tool of the everyday mind, the concept of 'correlation' or the concept of 'resemblance'?

To answer these questions, Newcomb's (1929) study of extroverted and introverted social behaviour among boys at a summer camp was reanalysed. This study was selected because it consists of *both* daily records and observer ratings on the same twenty-six items of behaviour. This makes it possible to compare observers' *reports* of what goes with what and actual *data* (systematically collected by the observers themselves) on what goes with what.

In Newcomb's data daily records were kept on each boy ($N = 24$) by a counsellor who noted the presence of an item as soon after its occurrence as possible. An odd–even day reliability check on behaviour percentages produced a mean reliability coefficient of 0.78 over the twenty-six items of behaviour in the daily records. At the end of the camp session (twenty-four days), six observers, including the counsellor, rated the boys on a five-point scale for each of the twenty-six items. Their ratings were pooled in all analyses. The twenty-six behaviours included such items as 'speaks with confidence of his own abilities', 'takes the initiative in organizing games', 'spends more than an hour a day alone'. Newcomb's data consist of 110 intercorrelations among pairs of the twenty-six behaviours calculated separately for the daily records and again for the observer ratings. The percentage of days an item appeared in a boy's behaviour was used by Newcomb for calculating intercorrelations (what goes with what) in the daily records. . . Ten University of Chicago students in one of the present author's classes were asked to make paired-comparison judgments of conceptual similarity among pairs of the twenty-six interpretive categories. A seven-point scale was used for making these judgments. . .

The reanalysis of Newcomb's data was guided by the following question. When the actual correlation between a pair of behavioural categories *is unrelated to* the observers' beliefs about their similarity, what do the observers report? Do they report what actually goes with what in their experience, or do they report what resembles what in their pre-existing conceptual system? For example, observers believe that 'gives loud and spontaneous expressions of delight or disapproval' and 'talks more than his share of the time at the table' resemble each other as concepts. The actual correlation between the two items in the boys' daily records is only 0.08. Yet in the observer ratings of their experiences with the boys the correlation between the two items is 0.92. Despite experience to the contrary, in this case observers of behaviour seem to rely on the concept of resemblance to estimate what goes with what in their experience. How general is this tendency?

To answer this question, thirty-three item pairs were selected in which either the degree of conceptual resemblance of the student judges for the pair was *above* the mean of all pairs (4.1 on a seven-point scale) *and* the actual behaviour correlation (in the daily records for that pair) *below* the mean of all pairs (0.10), or the converse. The reanalysis consisted of a comparison of (a) the observers' reports, (b) the actual correlations between the pairs of behaviours, and (c) their conceptual resemblance. . . . The results of the comparison are presented in table 2. When the actual correlations are unrelated to pre-existing beliefs about resemblances ($r_s = -0.36$) the observers' reports of what goes with what replicate the beliefs about resemblance ($r_s = 0.84$) rather than the actual correlations ($r_s -0.27$). Normal adults are magical thinkers; they confuse propositions about resemblance with propositions about correlation.

Do these results reflect a general disinclination of normal adults to draw correlational lessons from their experience? On the basis of these results alone, one cannot tell. It is possible the results reflect the tendency of human memory to 'drift' in the direction of pre-existing conceptual schemata (D'Andrade 1974). The next two experiments, however, lend credence to the hypothesis that . . . a concept of correlation is absent in normal adults.

Table 2. The relations between the actual correlations between pairs of behaviours, observers' reports about the behaviours, and the conceptual resemblances between the behaviours (the statistic is Spearman's rank correlation coefficient)

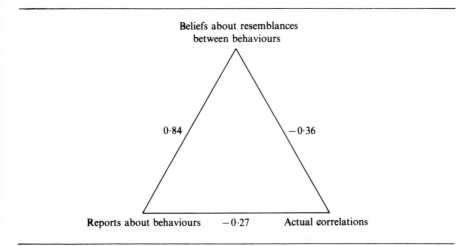

Beliefs about resemblances
between behaviours

0·84   −0·36

Reports about behaviours   −0·27   Actual correlations

Experiment II: Correlation relevant information is available but not utilized

. . . Normal adults have beliefs about the frequency with which various personality traits occur. Should they care to utilize these beliefs and to organize them properly, they have at their disposal all the information they need to compare conditional probabilities and to arrive at an estimate of the correlation between a pair of traits. For example, a characteristic pattern of frequency beliefs among American college students about the distribution of self-esteem and leadership 'out of 100 people in the general population' is shown in table 3. Twenty out of 100 people are thought likely to be leaders. Sixty-five out of 100 are thought likely to have self-esteem. Fifteen out of the twenty leaders are thought likely to have self-esteem, etc. . . .

In table 3 the conditional probability of being a leader given that you have self-esteem ($\frac{15}{65}$ or 0·23) is not much greater than the conditional probability of being a leader given that you lack self-esteem ($\frac{5}{35}$ or 0·14). Thus, the contingent relationship between self-esteem and leadership is only 0·09. Do normal adults take this information into account when they judge the extent to which self-esteem and leadership are related in experience? Most American college students claim that knowledge of whether or not someone has self-esteem does indeed enable them to predict whether or not that person is a leader. The claim is made despite information to the contrary. How typical is this failure?

A recent investigation by the author illustrates the difficulty of utilizing subjectively available frequency information to draw correlational inferences. Five women observers participated in the study. All five were University of Chicago students with professional experience observing and coding behavioural interactions between mothers and infants.

Table 3. A representative pattern of beliefs about the distribution of self-esteem and leadership over 100 people in the general population

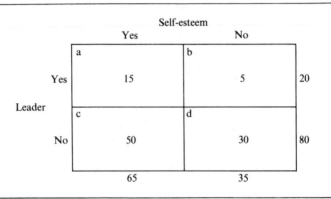

Judgments were elicited about the contingent relationship within each of twenty pairs of trait terms. Many of the trait terms appear in the personality psychology literature (see e.g. Norman, 1963; Smith, 1967). The pairs differed in the degree to which the judges believed that information about the presence or absence of the first trait enabled them to draw an inference about the presence or absence of the second trait. For example, the judges believed that knowledge of whether or not a person is 'compulsive' enabled them to predict whether or not he is 'adaptable', but they did *not* believe that an inference could be drawn from 'anxious' to 'quiet'. . . . They made their judgments on a scale ranging from 0 ('does not enable me to predict at all') to 100 ('enables me to predict perfectly') in ten-point intervals . . .

A second task was administered to elicit estimates from the judges concerning the marginal values of 2 × 2 contingency tables for each pair of traits. The judges were asked, for example, 'How many people out of 100 are tolerant?' A third task required the judges to estimate single conditional probabilities for each trait pair. For example, the judges were asked to 'think of all the people who are gentle. What percentage of gentle people are also good–natured?' These frequency estimates provided the information needed to construct a 2 × 2 contingency table (e.g. table 3) for each pair of traits for each judge. For each table the contingent relationship between the first and second trait was calculated using the contingency measure discussed earlier. As a reliability check all five judges were re-tested within three to seven days after the initial test session. Thus for each of twenty pairs of traits, for each of five judges, for each of two test sessions, we have (1) a score (ranging from 0 to 100) reflecting the pre-existing belief of the judge about the extent to which information about the first trait warrants an inference to the second trait, and (2) a measure of the contingent relationship among the two traits in the judge's own frequency information.

The data for . . . the twenty trait pairs were rank-ordered in two different ways: (1) by the degree to which the first trait was said to warrant an inference to the second trait, and (2) by the magnitude of the contingent relationship between the two traits. The rankings were generated separately for each test session, producing four rankings of the twenty trait pairs for each judge. For each judge, all possible pairs of the four rankings were compared using the Spearman rank order correlation coefficient (r_s).

The results of the rank order analysis are noteworthy in two respects. The first is that a judge's pre-existing beliefs about what predicts what are more stable than her estimates of the frequencies relevant to a correlation. Over all five judges, nearly one third (32 per cent) of such estimates were *internally inconsistent* in one test session or the other, or both. For example, consider the trait pair 'tense' and 'tolerant'. One judge estimated that out of 100 people, 70 are tense, and 75 are tolerant. This means, of course, that 30 are not tense, and 25 not tolerant. [This yields the marginal totals shown in table 4.] The judge then estimated that *of those people who are tense*, 10 per cent (or 7) are tolerant. But this is a glaring contradiction. The judge first claims that only 30 people out of 100 are *not tense*. Then the judge makes a conditional probability estimate that requires that there actually be at least 68 people (out of 100) who are *not tense*. [The reader will soon detect the contradiction if he tries to fill in the remaining cell values in table 4 without violating the marginal totals.]

Table 4. *An example of a judge's estimates of the marginal totals of a contingency table and her inconsistent estimates of the proportions of tolerant people among those who are tense.* [We have constructed this table to help the reader follow the argument in the text – Eds.]

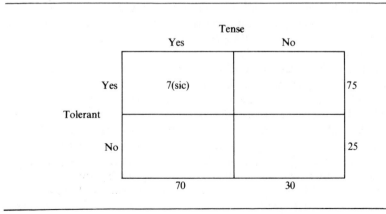

	Tense		
	Yes	No	
Tolerant Yes	7(sic)		75
Tolerant No			25
	70	30	

The second noteworthy feature of the rank order analysis concerns the degree of correspondence between variations in pre-existing beliefs about what predicts what and variations in the contingency coefficients derived from the estimates of the frequencies relevant to correlations. By dropping internally inconsistent pairs from the analysis, direct comparisons can be made between the two sets of scores both within and across test and retest conditions. When this is done the fit (r_s) between a judge's pre-existing beliefs about what predicts what and the contingency coefficients in that same judge's correlation relevant frequency information averages 0·39.

The results suggest that frequency information is neither consistently utilized, nor correlationally manipulated even when it is available. Normal adults seem disinclined to reason correlationally when they make claims about what predicts what in experience. They seem to lack a concept of correlation. Correlation relevant information is hard to think about. The concept of correlation is not intuitively available to the everyday mind.

Experiment III: It is hard to think correlationally

It has been remarked that the concept of correlation may be viewed as a comparison between two conditional probabilities, e.g. the likelihood that someone is a leader given that he has self-esteem, in contrast to the likelihood that he is a leader given that he lacks self-esteem. It has also been remarked that adults possess all the information needed to make such comparisons. They can estimate the number of leaders in the population, and the number of people with self-esteem. With somewhat more effort they can estimate the number of people possessing both characteristics, etc. The question arises, how easily can normal adults assemble their own correlation relevant frequency information and organize it into a format that makes it easy to compare conditional probabilities? Alternatively one may ask, is all relevant information about conditional probabilities equally accessible for correlational manipulation when adults claim that two traits go together in their experience?

The details of the present experiment need not concern us. In our current context it is only necessary to point out that the information concerning self-esteem and leadership in table 3 is the pattern of frequency belief for all twenty judges discussed below.

Notice that table 3 contains frequency information supporting the truth of each of four conditional assertions: (1) In general, people who are leaders have self-esteem (cells a, b). (2) In general, people who are not leaders have self-esteem (cells c, d). (3) In general, people lacking self-esteem are not leaders (cells b, d). (4) In general, people with self-esteem are not leaders (cells a, c).

Each of these four assertions, and four corresponding denials of these assertions (e.g. In general, people who are leaders lack self-esteem) were placed on 3 × 5 cards and presented in random order to University of Chicago students. The student judges were told they would be shown statements about the relationship between self-esteem and leadership in the general population. Judges were asked to read each statement, and then say whether it was true or false. Judges were told to respond as quickly and accurately as possible. Response times were recorded to a tenth of a second.

Table 5 displays the *differential* ease and accuracy with which the judges are able to think about each of the four conditional assertions (and their denials). The judges seem to have the easiest time processing the assertion (and denial) of: 'In general, people who are leaders have self-esteem.' Average response times are relatively short (3·98 seconds and 4·78 seconds, respectively), and the judgments of truth and falsity are invariably correct, *given the judges' own relevant frequency information* (see table 3, cells a, b).

Table 5. Comparison of the differential ease and accuracy with which twenty judges think about the truth or falsity of four conditional assertions (see table 3) and their denials

		Truth value (See table 3)	Per cent correct	Response time (seconds)
ertion	In general, people who are leaders have self-esteem.	True	100	3·98
ial	In general, people who are leaders lack self-esteem.	False	100	4·78
ertion	In general, people who are not leaders have self-esteem.	True	55	9·33
ial	In general, people who are not leaders lack self-esteem.	False	75	9·24
ertion	In general, people lacking self-esteem are not leaders.	True	75	8·53
ial	In general, people lacking self-esteem are leaders.	False	100	6·26
ertion	In general, people with self-esteem are not leaders.	True	60	6·88
ial	In general, people with self-esteem are leaders.	False	20	5·30

Judges are extraordinarily inaccurate (although relatively fast) in their response to the conditional assertion, 'In general, people with self-esteem are leaders.' They tend to say 'true', contrary to their own frequency estimates (see table 3, cells a, c). Judges are slow and not very accurate in their responses to the conditional assertion, 'In general, people who are not leaders have self-esteem.'

In general, the data in table 5 suggest that the requisite information for comparing conditional probabilities is *differentially* accessible. Some conditional assertions are just hard to think about at all. Under these circumstances, it does not seem surprising that judges do not consistently refer to their own relevant frequency information when they claim that two traits go together (or exclude one another). *The concept of correlation is not an intuitive concept of the everyday mind.*

Conceptual schematization

'Going togetherness' is the most general form of conceptual association among objects and events. It reflects the fact that everyday knowledge is a process of sorting out objects and events into interrelated symbolic complexes (categories, groupings, taxa, kinds, etc.). This section addresses the question: By means of what criteria are symbolic complexes formed? How are objects and events conceptually interrelated? How do everyday thinkers schematize their universe?

A related goal of this section is to clarify the notion of 'going together-ness' in everyday thought. It has been suggested that the nonintuitive concept of correlation does not play a significant part in everyday efforts to sort out objects and events into groupings. Everyday empirical claims about 'what goes with what' in experience typically turn out to be claims about *noncorrelational* rela-tionships among interpretive categories. Up to this point in this study, these noncorrelational relationships have been referred to as relationships of 'resemblance'. Unfortunately, 'resemblance' is a somewhat misleading term. It seems to suggest that interrelated items must 'have something in common'. 'Having something in common' is of course one of the ways in which objects and events can be said to conceptually relate to one another, but it is not the only way. In fact, its importance for everyday thought has probably been exag-gerated. As we shall see, symbolic complexes are held together by many intuitive relationships other than (but sometimes including) 'attribute shar-ing'. The term 'resemblance' *as used in this study* is meant to refer to this full set of intuitive ways in which objects and events are conceptually associated. 'Attri-bute sharing' is but one member of the set. The concept of correlation is not a member at all.

How are objects and events organized into symbolic complexes in everyday thought? Why is it that spiders and flies, backgammon and solitaire, mother's brother and father's sister's husband, self-esteem and leadership, go together in our thinking. One popular answer to this question (the so-called 'essentialist' response) claims that to be an element in a symbolic complex (a member of a category, an instance of a kind) is to manifest the essence of that symbolic complex (category, kind, class, taxa, etc.). From an 'essentialist' perspective, items go together because they jointly possess certain necessary and sufficient features (attributes, characteristics, etc.) that all members of the complex *have in common*. Propositions that are true of the complex as a whole are held to be true of each of the elements of the complex.

There are two rather trivial versions of this essentialist perspective on the formation of symbolic complexes. Sometimes it is argued that what all the elements of a category have in common is simply *the fact of having been grouped together*, as evidenced by their name, e.g. 'insects', 'games', 'uncles'. Categor-ization is reduced to labelling. Sometimes it is also argued that what all the elements of a category have in common is the *disjunction* or list of the elements of the category. Categorization is reduced to enumeration. According to these two versions of essentialism, there are no better or worse groupings of elements, and new elements can be added to a category at whim. Neither account need be taken seriously.

A more formidable version of essentialism, however, has many adherents in anthropology, especially among 'componential analysts' and 'ethno-scientists'. According to Lounsbury (1964) the motivation for a componential analysis is to arrive at 'uniform criteria' for assigning various elements (e.g. kin types) into particular classes (e.g. kinship categories). As Lounsbury remarks, the goal of a componential analysis is to produce a Boolean class product or conjunctive definition of everyday terms. . . . The taxonomist and the ethno-scientist imagine the existence of discrete (well-bounded) collections of objects that lend themselves to partitioning into exhaustive, mutually exclusive groupings (e.g. species) by a process of logical division that presupposes that at any higher taxonomic level the objects have something in common (e.g. the genus, that which makes the species like other species). At each taxonomic level in the partitioning process there is a search for an essence, that without which the objects in the grouping would be something else.

A difficulty with the essentialist view of category formation *as applied to everyday thought* is that it confuses the (somewhat utopian) *ideals* of a scientific (and formal) language with the communicative requirements of everyday language. It mistakenly believes that one special language of man can provide a model for all his languages.

Scientific languages are special, perhaps unique, in that they aspire to *universal* intelligibility. One way they do this is to strip language of its communicative reliance on the context and implicit culture linking speaker and listener. Essentialism, in fact, may be viewed as a recommendation for how to achieve precision and reduce communicative ambiguity free of context and culture (see Ziff, 1972; Shweder, 1976). The recommendation: multiply the terms in one's vocabulary until all the objects or events mentioned by those terms have been exhaustively partitioned into mutually exclusive, homogeneous (i.e. conjunctively defined) subsets. Imagine that the everyday term 'father' appears on a piece of paper before your eyes. What is being mentioned? A genitor? A priest? A god? One can't tell. Essentialism solves this 'problem' of multiple senses by splitting up the one term into many. $Father_1$ will mean 'male household head'. $Father_2$ will mean 'male sire', etc. According to the essentialist ideal, scientific language terms should have determinate meanings regardless of who utters them or the context in which they are uttered.

The difficulty with essentialism as an approach to everyday thought is that scientific languages are not satisfying models of everyday languages. One reason for this is that everyday languages do not attain their precision (and they can be very precise) by proliferating terms to label mutually exclusive senses. Rather, they rely on context and implicit understandings to clarify the *relevant* sense of a single term (see Black, 1963, for an example of the logical paradoxes that arise when context-dependent concepts are analysed as if they were context-free). Sitting together by a desk, 'pass me the red book', can have a precise referent. Abstracted out of context, 'the red book' might even be a magazine.

A second reason for the limited relevancy of essentialism is that everyday ambiguity sometimes has a point. Its elimination is not always the goal. On one's knees in a confessional, the ambiguity of 'father' (god, confessor) is in the service of the institution. Moreover, everyday language users often welcome the opportunity to be 'read' in more than one way. Ambiguity serves a social function; it allows messages to be transmitted without having to assume responsibility for one's words.

But perhaps the central reason scientific languages are inadequate models of everyday languages is that the various senses of everyday terms *overlap*, sometimes in complex ways. They are not mutually exclusive; they do not lend themselves to nonarbitrary 'splitting' (again see Ziff, 1972). Wittgenstein's (1958) critique of essentialism alerts us to the *possibility* that everyday categories are more appropriately conceptualized as a *continuum of merging senses* rather than a partitioned set of discrete meanings [see the quotation at the head of the introduction to Part III].

. . . Besides essentialism, and its image of partitioned subsets, there are at least two other major images of the way objects and events are organized into symbolic conplexes in everyday thought. The *polythetic* approach (see e.g. Wittgenstein, 1958; Beckner, 1959; Sokal, Reading 11; Needham, 1975) codifies the image of a merging continuum. The *prototype* approach (e.g. Berlin and Kay, 1969; Putnam, 1975a; Rosch, 1975a, and Reading 13) disrupts the continuum somewhat. It introduces the image of nodal, salient or exemplary members of a symbolic complex, around which other objects and events cluster or distribute.

The polythetic approach has certain shortcomings when applied to everyday judgments of conceptual relatedness. One difficulty is that the polythetic approach assigns equal status to all members of a category. Thus an important aspect of everyday *beliefs* about how objects and events sort into kinds is overlooked: everyday language users think that certain members of their symbolic complexes represent or stand for the category more faithfully than others. A sparrow is thought to be more 'bird-like' than a turkey; an apple is thought to be more 'fruit-like' than a watermelon (Rosch 1975a, Reading 13). In the minds of everyday language users, symbolic complexes are differentially typified by their elements; everyday thinkers have well-developed and reliable perceptions of category *prototypes*.

Casagrande and Hale (1967) alert us to a set of concepts (e.g. function, synonymy, provenience, class inclusion, similarity, etc.) that are intuitively available for arranging objects and events into symbolic complexes. All peoples think with these relationship concepts, and any one of these intuitive concepts *might* stand in for the nonintuitive concept of correlation (or contingency) when normal adults estimate what goes with what in their experience. Throughout this paper, in an omnibus way, I have referred to the collection of all these intuitive relationships as relationships of resemblance.

Nonetheless, in the personality domain one type of intuitive relationship concept seems to have a privileged position. Items of conduct are often said to go together because they jointly evoke an image of a symbolic behavioural type. For example, in 1969 the following items of conduct conceptually clustered together in the minds of American college students: 'feels that others are generally too conforming to conventional social expectations', 'demands pleasure and gratification for himself', 'feels his independence is very important'. The items clustered in this way because they worked together to evoke the image of a 'hippy'. The items could be interrelated as constituent parts of a symbolic whole, the image of the behavioural type. They were part of what it *meant* to be a hippy. Without the image of a 'hippy', 'demands pleasure and gratification' and 'feels his independence is very important' might not have been linked at all.

Intuitively available part–part and part–whole relationships of this type often replace the nonintuitive concept of correlation when normal adults judge that two items of conduct go together in behaviour. When American students are asked 'To what extent does gentleness and good-naturedness go together in people?' the question evokes in them such images as 'pastoral males bathed in sunlight', 'Santa Claus', 'barmaids', and 'old people'. This process of organizing items of conduct by means of images of behavioural types seems to be widely distributed across cultures. It certainly occurs in India as well as in the United States [see Shweder, 1972b]. People apparently estimate the degree to which items go together in behaviour by the ease with which they can bring to mind a higher order symbolic behavioural type in which the items compatibly fit as parts of the imagined whole (see Tversky and Kahneman, 1973, Reading 21, on the everyday use of 'availability heuristics' for estimating frequency under conditions of uncertainty). They seem to substitute one type of relationship for another. In this way, resemblance and correlation become merged in everyday thought.

Discussion

The goal of this final section is to anticipate some possible misunderstandings that may arise over what has been claimed.

1. It should be kept in mind that this paper has been concerned primarily with the kinds of concepts men employ to *organize and manipulate* information regardless of the content of the information processed. Evidence of a universal disinclination of the everyday mind to employ a concept like correlation is perfectly compatible with documented cross-cultural differences in the content of the categories into which objects and events are sorted. Fowl excrement and ringworm go together for the Azande, not Americans.

2. Documented evidence of a disinclination of normal adults to employ the concept of correlation has implications for our understanding of Piaget's theory of intellectual development. Although *under special circumstances* it is possible to elicit correlational reasoning from normal adults, the very need to contrive such circumstances suggests that the transition to formal operational thinking is not a spontaneous occurrence, and the transition to formal operational thinking (when it does occur) is to be explained in different theoretical terms than the transition to concrete operational thinking (which seems to occur universally and perhaps earlier than many suppose, see e.g. Mehler and Bever, 1967).

3. It would not be surprising if this study reminded some readers of late nineteenth-century accounts of the primitive mind. J. G. Frazer, for example, sorted magical thinking into two classes, homeopathic and contagious. The two

classes were defined by the confusion of concepts such as similarity and contiguity with the concept of causation. In effect, this study provides a cognitive processing basis for Frazer's insight and argues for the universality of the magical mode of thought.

4. There is a more profound sense in which the study is neo-Frazerian or neo-Tylorian (see Horton, 1967, 1968). It shares the following two assumptions (and only the following two assumptions) with these nineteenth-century evolutionists. (a) Normal adults in all cultures strive to understand, explain, and arrive at generalizations about the empirical relations among objects and events in their experience. *This is true regardless of the presence or absence of explicit, self-conscious scientific canons of objectivity and verification in their society (pace, Tambiah, 1973).* (b) Some of the concepts developed by normal adults to arrive at these generalizations are less adequate to the task than some of the concepts of Western scientists (Levi-Strauss, 1966, pp. 1–22 seems to agree but hedges). Resemblance is one of those inadequate concepts. It is a relatively poor index of contingent and correlational relationships in experience (in spite of Levi-Strauss's opinion to the contrary); yet it is relied upon when normal adults judge what goes with what in their lives. As a 'neo-Tylorian' might put it, magical thinking is inductive in its intent but mistaken in its conclusions. Unfortunately, these two neo-Tylorian or neo-Frazerian assumptions are easily misconstrued. I would clarify them in the following ways.

Firstly, to claim that all men are applied scientists (and rather poor ones at that) is not the same as asserting that men are only applied scientists. I have no quarrel with the caveat that investigators of thought should not confuse poetry with science, persuasion with induction, matters of value with matters of fact, or performative utterances with propositional utterances. I agree that it can only lead to misunderstanding to compare all these cognitive activities using the same yardstick. Truth and falsity, error and ignorance are not the only criteria available for assessing cognitive acts. For example, if it is the *goal* of mythological thought to use 'propositions about the world' to make 'propositions about language' (as Levi-Strauss, 1963, seems to suggest), it would be unjustified to interpret mythological formulations as confusions. But, it would be similarly misleading to interpret actual instances of erroneous inference, such as those discussed in this paper, as *intended* to be symbolic.

Secondly, cognitive acts cannot always be assessed using some *single* yardstick. It would be simplistic, and perhaps ethnocentric, to suggest that they can. Gellner (1973) makes the point that a feature of the 'savage' (everyday?) mind is 'the conflation of the descriptive, evaluative, identificatory, status-conferring, etc. roles of language'. To treat magical thinking as a form of thought in which 'propositions about language' are confused with 'propositions about the world' (i.e. to treat it as erroneous science) is not to deny the possibility that it also has other functions.

Finally, it is important to return to the distinction between intuitive and nonintuitive understandings, a distinction that is rarely respected in anthropological studies. The explicit canons of science in the West insist upon a sharp division between resemblance and contingency. Some might even argue that this formal recognition of the difference between face validity and all other types of validity is distinctive of Western scientific ideals. Nonetheless, it should be kept in mind that intuitive understandings are usually unaffected by nonintuitive reflection. (For example, Hume's epistemological dualism has had no influence on everyday intuitions that the world can be *directly* perceived). Despite our own scientific ideals, in everyday practice we are as magical as anyone. . .

28. An ethnographic psychology of cognition[1]

Michael Cole

Some presuppositions

Like many psychologists who currently engage in cross-cultural research, my introduction to this area of psychology was an accident of circumstances. Trained as a mathematical psychologist and possessing an active passport, I was available on short notice to go to Liberia on a project to improve the mathematics education of tribal children. At the time I embarked for Liberia, I had only a vague idea of its geographic location. My sponsors had an equally vague idea of my mission, and how it was to be accomplished.

As a graduate student, trained in the tradition of American psychology of learning, I arrived in Liberia with an invisible cargo of assumptions about human nature and human learning. Of course I knew a lot about the experimental method. I could properly design and execute a wide variety of experiments, collect the data in neat tables, and analyse those tables of numbers by a variety of statistical techniques. Like most of my colleagues, I was an environmentalist. I was willing to grant individual differences in all sorts of human attributes, including something loosely labelled intelligence, but I did not believe that any one race was likely to have more of that stuff than any other. More important, I was convinced that the psychological processes that people develop are very much a function of their early experiences; lacking certain experiences, various psychological processes are unlikely to develop, or at least, unlikely to develop fully. Finally, I knew that psychological tests and experiments are essential tools to understanding psychological processes. To learn about a child's level of conceptual development, I could use Piagetian conservation tasks that would tell me whether the child had made it into the concrete operational stage or not. Conservation performance also would indicate whether the child had developed such schemas as 'reversibility'. I could

[1] An edited version of the chapter in R. W. Brislin, S. Bochner, and W. J. Lonner (eds.) *Cross-cultural Perspectives on Learning*, I, *Cross-cultural Research and Methodology* (New York: Halsted Press, Wiley, 1975). Reprinted with the permission of the author and Sage Publications.

assess the development of mediated learning processes using one of several discrimination transfer designs. Subjects' abilities to classify and their abstract thinking abilities could be measured by a variety of classification tasks, and clustering in free recall would tell me about whether their memories were organized categorically. The number of experimental tools I could use and the number of hypothetical processes that I could study were legion. The only common denominator was the assumption that each experimental task was diagnostic of a particular cognitive process.

When I first arrived in Liberia, I spent a good deal of time travelling around the countryside asking people about the source of the mathematics difficulties which had prompted my trip. The answers I got from people who spent time around children (teachers, doctors, American mothers who had observed African children playing with their offspring) were consistent with expectations I had brought with me.

The list of things that the tribal children could not do, or did badly, was very long indeed. They could not tell the difference between a triangle and a circle because they experienced severe perceptual problems. This made the tribal child's task almost hopeless when it came to dealing with something like a child's jigsaw puzzle, explaining why 'Africans can't do puzzles'. I heard a lot about the fact that 'Africans don't know how to classify' and, of course, the well-known proclivity of African schoolchildren to learn by rote came in for a lot of discussion.

The source of these difficulties? A college physics teacher suggested that AID buy tinkertoys for every child in Liberia. Almost everyone had a favourite deficit in the child's experience which, if rectified, would greatly benefit the educational products of Liberian schools.

Both the collection of assumptions that I brought to Liberia as a result of my graduate education and the diagnoses of my hosts concerning the learning difficulties of Liberian students were very much a part of the times. This was the era in which America 'discovered' the disadvantaged child. In language very much like that applied to Kpelle children in Liberia, American scholars and educators offered explanations for the school difficulties of American minority groups and the poor (Riessman, 1962; Deutsch et al., 1967).

John Gay and I also sought the source of school difficulties in the child's home background. But it turned out, in retrospect, that we approached this problem with added assumptions that really were not a part of my psychological training and were not shared (or at least not taken into consideration) by the educators and psychologists with whom we talked. First, we assumed that, although Kpelle children lacked particular kinds of experiences routinely encountered by children, they were by no means lacking in experience. In fact, we explicitly began with the assumption that 'we must know more about the indigenous mathematics so that we can build effective bridges to the new mathematics that we are trying to introduce' (Gay and Cole, 1967). This assumption led us into an exploration of the way that numbers, geometrical forms, and logical operations are expressed in the Kpelle language. We also investigated situations in which the Kpelle measure, engage in arguments, and organize situations for the education of their children.

Our second, somewhat unprofessional, assumption was that people would be skilled at tasks they had to engage in often. This statement may seem patently obvious or trivial, but its consequences are neither. Eventually, it led me to reformulate the problem of the relation between experience and the development of cognitive processes, as I shall attempt to make clear presently. In the 1960s, it led us to discover that Kpelle people are masters at measuring rice. For this area of their experience, they have a highly developed vocabulary and a system of measurements that is completely consistent. When measuring distances or lengths, however, the vocabulary is less detailed, and we discovered that very often noninterchangeable units of length depended upon the kind of object or distance being measured.

Looking back at our early work, I find a great deal with which I can no longer agree. Too much of our thinking was imbued with the idea of cultural deprivation and its consequent cognitive deficits. Nevertheless, I can see now that our mixture of 'scientific' and 'common-sense' approaches to Kpelle mathematical behaviour pointed the way to our later work on culture and cognition. In particular, it led us to emphasize the situation–dependent nature of cognitive processes and the consequent need to combine ethnographic and experimental techniques in the study of culture and cognition.

Communicating: a psychologist's deficit is an ethnographer's skill

To illustrate the kind of paradox that concerns me when I go beyond standard psychological inferences to consider ethnographic evidence, I will describe part of an unpublished study conducted among the Kpelle of Liberia. Two adults are seated at a table. In front of each is a haphazardly arranged pile of ten sticks made of different kinds of wood of different shapes and sizes. A barrier is placed between the two men and one (to whom I shall refer as the speaker) is told to describe the sticks one at a time to his partner (the listener). One of the sticks is then chosen from a pre-assigned list, laid next to the barrier in front of the speaker, who describes the stick. After hearing the description, the listener tries to pick up the appropriate stick from his array. This process continues until all ten sticks have been placed by each man. They are then shown the array of ten pairs, errors are described and discussed, and the process repeated.

A set of sticks as I would describe them and as actually described by a Kpelle speaker is listed below in table 1.

What is striking about this man's performance (and it is representative of the performance of the many traditional Kpelle rice farmers who participated in this study) is that he is failing to include features in his description which, given the nature of the array, must be communicated if the message is to be unambiguously received.

When such results are obtained with young American children, they are usually interpreted as evidence that the child has failed to develop the capacity to take the listener's point of view. Some investigators would attribute the speaker's inadequacy to his failure to have developed beyond the stage of egocentric speech (Piaget, 1926). In the work of Bernstein (1961), or Krauss and Rotter (1968), it is hypothesized that the difficulty of lower-class children relative to middle-class children in a communication task similar to this one arises because of the minimal interactions between child and adult and because of deficiencies in lower-class language when it comes to the expression of abstract ideas. Both of these theoretical approaches are applicable to interpretation of our Kpelle subjects' behaviour. But are they reasonable? Do we really want to claim that a Kpelle adult is no more developed cognitively than a Genevan 6-year-old, or that the Kpelle language is deficient in its capacity to deal with abstract ideas?

Table 1

English description	Kpelle description 1	Kpelle description 2*
thickest straight wood	one of the sticks	one of the sticks
medium straight wood	one a large one	one of the sticks
hook	one of the sticks	stick with a fork
thin, curved bamboo	piece of bamboo	curved bamboo
thin, curved wood	one stick	one of the sticks
thin, straight bamboo	one piece of bamboo	small bamboo
long, fat bamboo	one of the bamboo	large bamboo
short thorny	one of the thorny	has a thorn
long thorny	one of the thorny sticks	has a thorn

* Actual order of presentation for trial 2 was different from that for trial 1.

These doubts are quickly reinforced by casual discussion with the subjects outside the experimental situation. They certainly seem to communicate very adequately, and about the time they have talked us into buying them a couple of bottles of beer, we may be very uncertain about just what was going on back in that experimental room.

Recourse to the ethnographic literature gives us even more cause for theoretical scepticism.

Among the many papers written by Evans-Pritchard about Zande culture is one entitled, 'Sanza, a characteristic feature of Zande language and thought' (1963). In this paper, Evans-Pritchard describes the way in which the Zande exploit the potential for ambiguity in speech in order to protect themselves against their supposedly hostile tribesmen. Evans-Pritchard gives many examples of Sanza, but one which we can all appreciate readily is the following:

A man says in the presence of his wife to his friend, 'friend, those swallows, how they flit about there.' He is speaking about the flightiness of his wife and in case she should understand the allusion, he covers himself by looking up at the swallows as he makes his seemingly innocent remark. His friend understands what he means and replies, 'yes, sir, do not talk to me about those swallows, how they come here, sir!' (What you say is only too true.) His wife, however, also understands what he means and says tartly, 'yes, sir, you leave that she (wife) to take a good she (wife), sir, since you married a swallow, sir!' (Marry someone else if that is the way you feel about it.) The husband looks surprised and pained that his wife should take umbrage at a harmless remark about swallows. He says to her, 'does one get touchy about what is above (swallows), madam?' She replies, 'ai, sir. Deceiving me is not agreeable to me. You speak about me. You will fall from my tree.' The sense of this reply is, 'you are a fool to try and deceive me in my presence. It is me you speak about and you are always going at me. I will run away and something will happen to you when you try to follow me.' (1963, p. 211)

Evans-Pritchard's formulation for a successful Sanza is as follows (1963, p. 222): 'The great thing . . . is to keep under cover and to keep open a line of retreat should the sufferer from your malice take offense and try to make trouble.' So successful are the Zande in following this practice, and so ubiquitous is the use of Sanza in everyday Zande speech, that our renowned Oxonian colleague is led to lament at the end of his article: 'It [Sanza] adds greatly to the difficulties of anthropological inquiry. Eventually the anthropologist's sense of security is also undermined, his confidence shaken. He learns the language, can say what he wants to say in it, and can understand what he hears; but then he begins to wonder whether he has really understood . . . he cannot be sure, and even they [the Zande] cannot be sure, whether the words do have a nuance or someone imagines that they do.' He closes by quoting the Zande proverb, 'Can one look into a person as one looks into an open-wove basket?'

It is important to mention that, while the particular form of ambiguous speech that Evans-Pritchard describes may have special features among the Zande, the use of rhetorical skills as a vehicle for controlling one's social environment is a very general feature of both nonliterate and literate societies alike (Albert, 1964; Labov, 1969).

I have picked these examples because they can serve as a vehicle for illustrating the ways in which anthropological and psychological approaches to the study of culture and cognition differ.

Consider first the example from Evans-Pritchard. It seems no more than good, common sense to recognize from the data presented that the Zande are subtle and complex thinkers who must consider a host of contingencies, including the viewpoint of their listeners, when deciding what they are going to say, to whom, and how. Assuming equal rhetorical skill among the Kpelle (and there is good evidence that this is so: Bellman, 1969), it seems equally obvious that there must be something wrong with the communication experiment. Perhaps the participants are deliberately shamming, or failing to understand what is expected of them. How could anyone who is an accomplished debater, a user of proverbs and subtle insults, be incompetent in such a simple task?

This style of interpretation has a long and honourable history in anthropology. Starting from the *assumption* of psychic unity, the anthropologist asserts that all human groups are sufficiently competent to carry out the many complex functions demanded of them by their culture and physical environment (Kroeber, 1948). Societies, of course, vary in the kinds of tasks that they pose their members, and environments vary in their physical features. The common-sense dictum that people will be skilful at tasks they experience often leads to the conclusion that there will be cultural differences in the activities eliciting skilled performance. But these are not differences in 'cognitive processes' in the sense that psychologists seem to mean. They are only differences in emphasis.

It may be asked, how could anyone fail to agree? The fact is that psychologists generally do fail to agree, both on the interpretation of our two examples, and on the problem of the relation between culture and cognitive processes in general.

I cannot give a detailed account of how these differences arose (for a slightly more expanded account, see Cole, Gay, Glick, and Sharp, 1971, chs. 1 and 6). The major points seem to be these:

(1) Psychologists as a group reject the use of naturally occurring behaviour sequences as a source of evidence about learning and thinking processes. The major line of objection can be seen in an example taken from Cole *et al*. (1971): A man sees black clouds on the horizon and says it is going to rain. Did he make an inference, or did he simply remember the association, black clouds = rain? Complicate the example. Suppose that a man uses instruments to measure wind velocity and barometric pressure. A certain combination of wind velocity and barometric pressure is observed, and he says it is going to rain. Did he make an inference? It would seem more likely than in the first case, but it is still possible that he simply remembered this case from an earlier experience. In fact, it is impossible to determine, without specific kinds of prior knowledge about the person and circumstances involved, whether a particular conclusion is a remembered instance from the past, or an example of inference based on present circumstances. Hence, evidence about the 'logic of an inference' obtained from anecdotes or naturally occurring instances is always open to alternative interpretation. Just as there are ambiguities when trying to decide what processes are involved in the prediction of rain, there are problems in deciding exactly what people are doing when they use Sanza. Sanza, by its nature, is designed to be ambiguous, but the ambiguity of interpretation for the psychologist is twofold. We not only need to know what the person 'really' meant, but we want to know if what he said represented 'thinking' or memory. Perhaps people learn a set stock of Sanzas. As children they observe the application of Sanzas by adults and then emulate their elders when the appropriate situation arises. In effect, it might be argued that Sanza requires little more than recall of ambiguous formulae.

(2) These kinds of difficulties led psychologists to *define* thinking as a new combination of previously learned elements, among which problem solving situations have been predominant. Bruner's (1957) definition of cognition as 'going beyond the information given' captures the essence of this approach which is shared by psychologists of a wide variety of theoretical persuasions. Such a definition seems to require experimentation in order to make statements about thinking.

(3) The dominant pattern of inference in psychology is to use data from experiments as evidence about the psychological processes of individuals and, statistically, about groups. These processes are treated as properties of individuals that are 'tapped' by the experimental procedures. It must be obvious from what I have said so far that I believe there is a very wide gulf between ethnographic and psychological approaches to the study of cognition. The two disciplines do not share the same data base: ethnographers rely for the most part on naturally occurring, mundane events, while psychologists rely on experiments. Ethnographers reject experiments as artificial, while psychologists avoid natural behaviour sequences as ambiguous.

The interpretation of failure to perform

In my opinion, the weakest aspect of current experimental psychological research in cross-cultural settings is the way that inferences are drawn from 'poor performance', instances in which subjects give the wrong answer.

I am referring to instances such as the failure of our Kpelle subjects to specify the critical attributes of the sticks about which they are asked to communicate. Given the pattern of inference current among developmental psychologists, we are led inexorably to the conclusion that Kpelle adults are egocentric, or in some other way deficient in the cognitive processes at their disposal. I believe this pattern of inference to be logically indefensible as it is ubiquitous. As one investigator stated recently: 'Experiments in developmental child language can show you what children *can* do at various ages, but you cannot conclude from that what children *cannot* do' (see the discussion on Mehler in Ingram, 1971, p. 154). I can add only that this same principle applies generally to comparative research, whether age, culture, or species is the contrast of concern.

The reason lack of performance (or a low score) leads to the inference of lack of capacity is that the conclusion so often seems 'reasonable'. When applied to children in a single culture, the fact that an older child remembers more words, communicates more accurately, and in general behaves more competently is only to be expected. After all, the child has matured! He *must* have acquired some new cognitive apparatus.

In the same fashion, comparisons involving cultural institutions become plausible. Comparative statements are commonly made by psychologists and some anthropologists, usually in terms of a theory of general cultural advancement as cultures become more modernized. Rarely are the cultural institutions and cultures compared viewed as 'different, but equal'. Schooling (Greenfield and Bruner, 1966), literacy (Goody and Watt, 1962), and acculturation (Doob, 1960) are all seen as providing people with new cognitive processes, new abilities, and new intellectual tools. It is claimed that, without extensive training, the mind is only capable of concrete thought; without writing, analytic thinking is not possible; without new technical challenges, culture and thought are stagnant.

The general consequence of this view that I have emphasized so far is that the 'deprived' groups (who lack formal schooling, who have not learned to write, and who lack Western technology) are seen as uniformly lacking in particular, 'developed' skills. Another consequence is that the cultural transition to the educated, literate, technological world is often conceived of as causing a *transformation* in cognitive processes. It is in this framework that Bernstein's ideas become plausible vehicles for explaining cultural differences in communication. And it is this framework which makes it possible for some people to suppose that traditional Kpelle adults are egocentric enough to be unable to take the point of view of their listeners.

It is on inferences of this type that the anthropologist and the psychologist part company. My objection to the anthropological treatment of experiments is that justified criticisms of the inference drawn from poor performance are combined with unjustified dismissal of culturally linked differences in performance. Data from psychological experiments, properly treated, are an important source of evidence about the applicability and limits of the doctrine of psychic unity. I also believe that proper cross-culture experimentation can greatly enrich our understanding of the development and structure of cognitive processes in general. But I do not believe that most cross-cultural experimentation fulfils our hopes for it.

An illustrative example

Let me briefly recount an example of a research programme in which pursuit to the causes of poor performance was instructive. My example concerns inference (see Cole *et al.*, 1971, ch. 6).

The enduring controversy over the existence or nonexistence of 'primitive mind' involved, among other things, an argument over whether it was the premises or laws of inference that differ among 'primitive' and 'civilized' peoples.

Starting with a device used to assess inferential processes in American children, we set out to study the development of inferential processes among the Kpelle of Liberia. The device we used is pictured in figure 1.

The problem is presented as follows.

First, the subject is taught that pushing the button on the left-hand panel will yield him a marble. Then he is taught that pushing the button on the right-hand panel will yield a ball bearing. Then, with the two side panels closed, he is taught that putting a ball bearing in a hole in the centre will yield him a piece of candy which he can see in a small window in the panel. Finally, all three panels are opened at once, and the subject is instructed to obtain the candy which he can keep and eat.

This problem has the nice feature of specifying the 'premises' (the way to get a marble and a ball bearing) from which a solution (get the candy) is to be reached and of ensuring that the subjects know these premises very well before they proceed to make the required inference.

When this problem was first presented to groups of traditional Kpelle (children and young adults), performance was very unimpressive. For example, only 15 per cent of the young adults spontaneously solved the problem and about half reached an incorrect solution.

Another experiment identified the general source of difficulty. When an analogous problem was constructed of matchboxes and a small locked chest, even small children were generally proficient performers. This suggests strongly that familiarity with the materials about which one is asked to reason is important if people are going to apply a cognitive skill they have. (It is almost certainly no coincidence that Wason and Johnson-Laird, 1972, come to this conclusion in their studies of reasoning among educated British adults.)

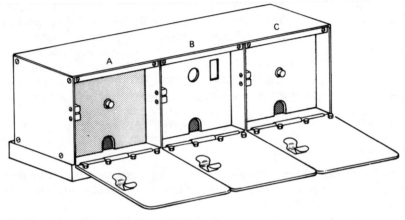

Figure 1

One additional study further localized the point in the problem where familiarity was important. Stages of the first two studies were pitted against each other. For example, keys were obtained from our fancy apparatus, one of which could open the locked box. It was shown that subjects who performed poorly did so because they did not deal effectively with the *first* link in the problem. Once they got started on the right track, the inference proceeded adequately, but the need to initiate a solution on an unfamiliar instrument seems to impede the whole process.

Here again is an instance where following up poor performance has been instructive. It comes as no surprise to the anthropologist that the subject has difficulty with 'that foreign contraption'. Such findings certainly fit with common observation that some nontechnological peoples have considerable difficulty when first encountering various kinds of machinery. But we are in a position to say more. First, we can demonstrate (rather than assert) that the people in question solve such problems under more familiar circumstances; for example, they are capable of making inferences. Second, we have isolated the point in the problem solving processes where difficulties occur: it is not just the presence of the funny device; it is a particular stage in having to work it that is the stumbling block.

Problems for the future

Looking back over almost a decade of our research on culture and cognition, I can see that it has been dominated by two classes of questions. At the start we were led to make two inquiries: what kinds of experiences promote the development of what kinds of intellectual processes? Are these experiences linked to particular cultural institutions that are of special importance? In answering these questions, I proceeded on the assumption of a close relationship between experimental technique and psychological process. Implicitly, I was using the experiments as an assessment technique: how much of process X is present in culture Y?

In the past few years, the question changed. I began to ask: What kinds of cultural experience promote the manifestation of intellectual processes in particular experimental situations? This question led us to ask another: What kinds of nonexperimental situations yield clues about the existence of abstract thinking, inference, memory, and a variety of cognitive processes? I became much more sceptical about the relation between experiment and process, resorting to the generalization that 'cultural differences in cognition reside more in the situations to which particular cognitive processes are applied than in the existence of a process in one cultural group and its absence in another' (Cole et al., 1971, p. 233).

I believe this statement to be true, but its acceptance should not obscure two important unresolved issues. First, are there identifiable deficits in cognitive processes arising from absence of specifiable experiences? Our methodological critique of current psychological experimental and inferential practices is not a denial of the possibility that there are cultural differences in the existence of cognitive processes. Such a blanket denial is not only premature, it is almost certainly wrong. Second, a demonstration that someone has the capacity to remember and form concepts is not a claim that there are no important cultural differences in cognition. Kpelle children often fail to remember well in school; they do not make 'obvious' inferences about the cause of hookworm; they do not generalize from $2 + 2 = 4$ and $4 + 4 = 8$. These difficulties may all result from a failure to apply existing capacities to the problem at hand, but they are no less real problems on that account.

I will consider these two issues in turn, emphasizing my belief that their resolution will depend upon a combination of ethnographic and experimental approaches.

On the existence of psychological processes

One of the really attractive aspects of cross-cultural research on cognition is that it seems to offer a natural laboratory in which to test a wide variety of hypotheses about the relation between experience and behaviour. Because most of us accept the general proposition that adult cognition arises out of an interaction of organism and environment, what could be more natural than the impulse to introduce some meaningful variation on the environment side of this proposed interactional system? It is within this framework that my colleagues and I undertook our studies of the influence of education on cognitive development. And it is within this framework that most of the major programmes of cross-cultural research have been conducted (e.g. Segall, Campbell, and Herskovits, 1966; Berry, 1971; Bruner, Olver, and Greenfield, 1966; Dasen, 1972a,b and many others).

I very much want to see this kind of research effort continued and expanded. I have been stimulated by the evidence that education, child-rearing practices, physical environment, and language can all influence cognitive behaviour. But from my presentation thus far, you can anticipate the uneasiness with which I greet conclusions that equate poor performance with lack or less of some general cognitive process. I will discuss only one of many lines of research about which I have many questions.

I want to examine the conclusions we can draw from the enormous and growing body of cross-cultural work using Piagetian tasks which is putatively relevant to the issue of whether certain cultures push cognitive growth further and faster than others. Leaving aside the question of whether or not formal educational experience is crucial to the development of concrete-operational thinking among traditional, nonliterate peoples (Greenfield and Bruner's work, 1966, would lead us to believe it is; Dasen, 1972a,b, would lead us to believe it is not sufficient), I am left wondering about the cognitive status of people who do not conserve. Consider, for example, research done among people who live in semi-arid locations where severe water shortages occur from time to time and natives' abilities to find scarce water are legendary (e.g. Aborigines). Are we to believe that Aborigine adults will store water in tall thin cans in order to 'have more water'; do they think they lose water when they pour it from a bucket into a barrel? I am tempted to believe that they would have disappeared long ago were this the case. I also find it difficult to believe that they cannot think through an action and its reverse. Yet if we are to extrapolate the interpretations of poor performance from Genevan children to Aborigine adults (note, I am not quarrelling with the *fact* that many Aborigine adults fail to make conservation responses in experimental situations), what else can we conclude?

Like Heron (1971), I am curious about the noncorrelation between performance on a Piagetian task and mathematical performance which takes for granted the operations assessed as absent. If schools promote cognitive growth, the tests which reflect this growth ought to discriminate between the relevant performances of the more and less developed students (according to the test criterion). Yet this was not so in the case of Heron's Zambian students, and we have no evidence that it is true in the other cases where conservation performance has been assumed indicative of cognitive development.

The failure of many Aborigine (and African) young adults to make conservation responses is a fact, but the interpretation of this fact seems quite problematic to me. In Europe and the United States, where all normal children eventually come to respond correctly across the whole spectrum of conservation problems, such a statement as '55 to 60 per cent of the 5- to 6-year-olds conserve' has a relatively clear interpretation: 55 to 60 per cent of the children have entered the concrete operational stage that *all* children *eventually* enter. The culture is homogeneous with respect to adult performance, but the various traditional societies we have been studying are *not* homogeneous with respect to their level of cognitive maturity as measured by conservation performance: some adults conserve, some do not.

What does it mean to claim that 'tribe X does not mature past the European 11-year stage' if 50 per cent of the members of tribe X conserve and 50 per cent do not? No one in tribe X is operating at the '11-year-old-level' and to speak of a 'levelling off of cognitive development' as if the statement applies to individuals is a serious mistake. Until we have some better idea of what induces some members of traditional societies to solve conservation problems while their neighbours do not, we cannot be certain about the significance of conservation tests as a tool for understanding the relation between culture and cognitive development.

I do not think that current research practices will resolve these difficulties. It is going to be necessary to get a much more detailed idea of exactly what kinds of past experiences are linked to particular kinds of conservation. A few investigators have explored the influence of variations in content and procedures on conservation (e.g. Price-Williams, 1969; Greenfield, 1966; Price-Williams, Gordon, and Ramirez, 1969). I think this is a step in the right direction, and the evidence so far clearly indicates that both procedural and content variations can have a marked effect on conservation performance (see also Dasen, 1972a,b). However, no one has carried out the systematic variations that Price-Williams (1967) advocates, and no one has made a study of a group's ecology and daily activities to determine if conservation-like principles are observable in any sphere.

On situational variation in the manifestation of cognitive processes

Although I have emphasized the problems of research focused on cultural variations in the existence and amount of general cognitive processes, the situational approach to the study of culture and cognition is also fraught with conceptual problems and empirical gaps, all the more so because it has received so little attention.

To begin with, a good deal of hard thinking must be devoted to clarifying the concepts of *cognitive process* and *situation*. So long as we conceive of a cognitive process in the context of a particular theory and the experiments which have been accepted as diagnostic, these questions do not often arise. But our current analysis forces them upon us. In the literature on cognition, and on culture and cognition in particular, the variety of terms that can be grouped under the labels 'process' and 'situation' is bewilderingly large. It is not at all clear what distinctions, if any, are intended by different terms. At times 'skill', 'mechanism', 'ability', 'capacity', and 'process' are used as if they were interchangeable. At other times there have been attempts to introduce systematic distinctions among these terms; Flavell and Wohlwill (1969), for example, suggest a distinction between 'mental operations' and 'mechanisms for processing input and output'; Donaldson (1963) talks about 'structural' and 'executive' errors. Our distinction between the existence and application of capacities is in this latter tradition. But like others, I have been guilty of vagueness (as, for example, in the discussion of the 'processes and skills' that underlie good free recall performance), and I will continue to be vague until we can specify criteria differentiating these terms.

Our problems with respect to the notion of situation are just as severe. At times situation has been used as roughly synonymous with 'experimental manipulation'. Here I would class the studies varying experimental materials (pictures versus objects, water versus soda pop), instructions, incentives, and the like. At other times, situation refers to the entire context of inquiry, as when we compare verbal duelling with a communication game. At present, we have no theory of situations to guide us; work from contemporary sociology (McHugh, 1968; Gumperz and Hymes, 1972) and perhaps some contemporary research in social psychology (Orne, 1970) might be used as a starting point.

In addition to definitional problems, we also need to consider what general form a theory of culture and cognition would take if situational factors are to be a part of the theory. At one extreme we can imagine a situational theory that is quite close to a general cognitive development or 'factor' approach: some cultural institutions promote the widespread use of one particular process (e.g. abstraction) while others promote its application in only a few, selected situations. An example might be provided by Gladwin's (1970) description of Puluwat navigators, who use an abstract star compass to help them get from island to island, but who fail to respond with sufficient abstractness to a Piagetian seriation task. This approach will often assume that one process (abstract, generalized) is developmentally 'higher' than another (concrete, rote).

A somewhat different approach to situational variations would emphasize differences in the application of cognitive skills to different domains of activity within a given culture in an attempt to determine what variables control the manifestation of different processes. A concrete example of the kind of research that I have in mind can be illustrated by reference to the work of Greenfield and Childs (1974) concerning whether or not learning to weave one of the three traditional Zinacantecan cloth patterns influenced a general ability to represent patterns. Research with girls (who know how to weave) and boys (who do not) demonstrated very little influence of weaving experience on any *generalized* ability to represent patterns, although girls were better than boys at copying details of given patterns. Greenfield and Childs also failed to obtain any marked influence of primary education on their pattern generalization task.

Why did learning to weave fail to have a generalized effect? Several possibilities exist. Citing Price-Williams, Gordon, and Ramirez (1969), Greenfield and Childs mention the possibility that the girls did not weave enough for their patterns to become generalized. Greenfield and Childs (1974, p. 29) prefer the explanation that 'practical experience develops specific component cognitive skills . . . whereas other more general cultural influences, economic activity for instance, develop generalized cognitive performance'.

I am unhappy with this explanation because it does not specify what is special about economic activity except that it is 'a general cultural influence'. But one of our tasks is to discriminate and order cultural influences in terms of their generality. Is economic activity inherently general, or will any 'general' activity do?

Let me make a suggestion which does not resort to invocation of general cultural influences, but which does offer some possibility of tying situational variation to a solid body of psychological data.

I would like to propose that the variety, as well as the amount, of practice with a particular subject matter is crucial to the wide application of cognitive skills. If there is a single, central lesson to be derived from years of research on learning sets, it is that animals (including man) learn generalized problem solving skills through repeated experience with different problems of the same type. Weavers in Zinacantecan learn three patterns. That is all there are. As Bruner, Goodnow, and Austin (1956) pointed out, concepts are essential as a means of handling large quantities of information. But what is essential if the domain of information is small and constant? As a test of these ideas, I propose another experiment on weaving, but I seek an area where some people know only one or two patterns, others know five or six, and still others know fifteen or twenty. I know of no such place when we speak of weaving cloth, but in Yucatan, Mexico, where I have worked recently, I know there are great varieties of multi-coloured patterns woven into hammocks. Some people know how to weave only a few patterns, some know how to weave many.

What I propose, then, is a study of the influence of weaving on pattern representation as a function of how many patterns a person can weave. I would be most interested in an outcome where the generality of pattern representation is a direct function of the number of patterns a person knows. Next I want to generalize this research strategy from the examples of ambiguous speech and communication performance which I presented at the outset of this paper. You can see that I am very impressed by the way traditional peoples seem to apply complex cognitive skills in social situations, while failing to use these skills in an experimental task. In the context of our weaving example, I would claim that social interactions provide for repeated practice with problems of the same type (getting someone to do a favour for you) but different content (different people, things, etc.). I would very much like some way to tie this speculation to experimentally replicable observations. This will require experiments that are *social* in content. I have no idea at the moment of how to proceed in this direction.

I am also anxious to explore other domains of daily activities with an eye to the variety of exemplars that they involve. Ethnographic descriptions of traditional farming and handicrafts emphasize the rudimentary technology and paucity of tools. Might it be that an important dimension of cultural differences will turn out to rest on the variability of tasks and tools that people must deal with?

These are very broad theoretical questions indeed. I have discussed them at some length because they make interpretable my insistence on combining ethnography with psychology in the service of understanding culture and cognition.

29. Modes of thinking and ways of speaking: culture and logic reconsidered[1]

Sylvia Scribner

> Our attitude towards what we listen to is determined by our habits. We expect things to be said in the way in which we are accustomed to talk ourselves: things that are said some other way do not seem the same at all but seem rather incomprehensible. . . Thus, one needs already to have been educated in the way to approach each subject.
>
> (Aristotle *Metaphysics* book II)

Of the many issues relating to culture and thought that have been a matter of scholarly concern in the last century, the question of whether industrialized and traditional people share the same logical processes has provoked the most bitter controversy. Initially centred within sociology and anthropology, the debate has largely shifted to the psychological arena. Here it has taken its most prominent form in the clash over the proper interpretation of cross-cultural Piagetian experiments on logical competencies: do they, or do they not, demonstrate the universality of logical structures of intelligence? (For a historical review of theoretical positions on cultural differences and logical thinking, see Cole and Scribner, 1974. Dasen, 1972a, provides a summary and analysis of cross-cultural Piagetian research.)

In the last few years, quite a different line of psychological evidence has become available. Following a time-honoured tradition in psychological laboratories (see Woodworth, 1938), a number of cross-cultural investigators have made use of syllogisms and other formal logical problems as tools for studying processes of inference in verbal thinking. While still in its early stages, this work has produced a coherent body of findings which suggest the fruitfulness of a new strategy in the pursuit of cultural influences on logical processes – a strategy uniting the psychological study of thinking processes with the ethnographic study of ways of speaking.

This paper reviews the principal findings of this research and offers a first, speculative framework for their interpretation. We begin with a brief description

[1] An edited version of a chapter to appear in R. O. Freedle (ed.) *Discourse Production and Comprehension* (Hillsdale, N. J.: Lawrence Erlbaum Associates, in press). Reprinted with the permission of the author and publishers.

of the studies that furnish the data for discussion, while Aristotle, the inventor of the syllogism and the analyst of discourse, waits in the wings.

Cross-cultural studies on verbal reasoning

Verbal logic problems were first used to investigate cultural influences on reasoning by the Soviet psychologist Luria (1971) and his colleagues in studies conducted in 1931–2 in remote regions of Uzbekistan, Central Asia. Inspired by Vygotsky's theory of mental development which holds that the specific characteristics of complex intellectual processes are determined by conditions of social life and practical activity, these psychologists sought to determine whether the social and economic reforms introduced in Uzbekistan after the revolution had effected changes in the perceptual and cognitive skills of the local people.

To investigate reasoning, Luria prepared simple syllogisms and used them in a semi-experimental, semi-interview format with four basic populations, differing in the extent to which they participated in modern social institutions: nonliterate Muslim women in remote villages who were not engaged in productive activity; nonliterate men in the same villages who carried on traditional modes of farming; young activists involved in collective farming, some of whom had minimal literacy training; women enrolled in courses at teacher training schools. Marked differences in performance between the 'traditional' and 'modern' groups (described below) were taken as confirmation of Vygotsky's theory.

Some decades later, Cole, Gay, Glick, and Sharp (1971) incorporated verbal logic problems in their extensive series of studies on learning and thinking among the Kpelle, a rice-farming tribal people in Liberia, West Africa. To determine the specific situational and experiential features affecting performance, they used a wide variety of problem materials (sentential and syllogistic problems), tasks (drawing conclusions or judging validity) and settings (individual interviews and group discussions). Comparative populations were nonliterate men and women in traditional occupations and young people with varying amounts of education in the English curricula of government and mission schools. Their finding of what appeared to be massive 'error' on the part of traditional populations prompted Scribner (1975) to undertake a series of recall studies among the Kpelle and Vai (a neighbouring people), seeking to test the hypothesis that failure to integrate and retain the information in the problems was the source of apparent 'nonlogical' performance.

In an attempt to further specify the effects of particular cultural factors on performance, Sharp and Cole (1975) replicated the Kpelle studies among Mayan-speaking and Spanish-speaking villagers in the Yucatan, Mexico. Comparison groups were rural and semi-urban, schooled and non-schooled adult and child populations. Finally, Cole and Scribner administered a set of syllogisms to a sample of 750 Vai adults as part of a project to investigate the cognitive consequences of literacy (the Vai Literacy Project is briefly described in Scribner and Cole, 1974).

The type of problem material used in these studies is illustrated in table 1. Considering the diversity of people, settings, tasks, and materials covered in these studies and of the special problems of 'nonreplicability' in cross-cultural research, the consistency of basic findings is impressive. Not only are quantitative results strikingly uniform from study to study, but certain qualitative aspects of performance are so similar that it is often difficult to distinguish the translated interview protocol of a Uzbekistanian from that of a Vai – cultural and geographical distance notwithstanding.

Table 1. Representative problems in cross-cultural studies on verbal reasoning

Central Asia

Cotton grows where it is hot and humid.
In the village it is hot and humid.
Does cotton grow there or not?

In the far north all bears are white.
Novaya Zemyla is in the far north.
What colours are the bears there?

West Africa

All people who own houses pay house tax.
Boima does not pay a house tax.
Does he own a house?

Some of the people we know are not in school.
All of the people we know are in Liberia.
Are all of the people in Liberia in schools?

Mexico

A dog and a horse are always together.
The horse is here now.
Where do you think the dog might be now?

So that Jose can carry corn from his farm to the town, he needs a cart and a horse.
He has the horse but doesn't have the cart.
Can Jose carry his corn from his farm?

Performance consistency with respect to problem solution is displayed in table 2, which summarizes findings in simplified form. (Luria's studies are omitted, since his method, adapted to each individual respondent, does not yield a 'tally' of scores). Basic comparisons are made with respect to the contrast feature of schooling/no schooling, the only characteristic of populations that was systematically investigated across studies. Two studies of US school-children are included to extend the range of comparisons. In several studies, social conditions made it possible to vary age and schooling independently and these studies are indicated by an asterisk.

Table 2. Summary of cross-cultural studies: Percentages of correct answers to verbal logic problems

	Nonschooled	Schooled
Cole, Gay, Glick, and Sharp (Kpelle)		
Study 3	35	91 (high school)
Study 4	61	100 (high school)
Study 5	65	
	64* (10–14 yrs)	82* (10–14 yrs, 2nd–3rd gr.)
		89* (10–14 yrs. 4th–6th gr.)
Scribner (Kpelle)		
Study 1	63	83 (jr high school)
Study 2	62	
Scribner (Vai)	52	
Cole and Scribner (Vai)	69	87 (all grades)
Sharp and Cole (Yucatecans)	45* (Mayan, trad. town)	73* (3rd gr. educ.)
	62* (Mayan, trans. town)	76* (4th gr. educ.)
		55 (1st–2nd gr.)
		78 (4th–6th gr.)
		97 (secondary school)
Scribner, Orasanu, Lazarov, Woodring (United States)		
Study 1		74 (2nd gr.)
		77 (5th gr.)
Study 2		72 (2nd gr.)
		74 (5th gr.)

* Indicates age-controlled studies.

Taken as a group, these studies appear to support a number of generalizations.

1. *In all cultures*, populations designated as 'traditional' or 'nonliterate' have just somewhat better than a chance solution rate across all types of problem material. (In the majority of studies cited, subjects were confronted with a two–choice judgment decision so that the 50 per cent level may be taken as a crude indicator of 'chance'). Absolute levels vary with tasks and materials.

2. *Within each culture* there is a large discrepancy in performance between schooled and nonschooled. The major jump seems to occur at levels of education as low as two to three years of school (Luria also reports 'educational effects' with minimal literacy training), and there is continued improvement at the second school and college level.

3. With schooling, there is little *between-culture* variation in performance for the cultures studied. Grade, rather than society, is most determinative of performance. The two studies of US elementary school children included in the table show the consistency of the grade-level/performance relationship.

A significant finding, not represented in the summary statistics of table 2, is that there was considerable diversity of performance among nonliterate adults.

Accuracy of solution varied from problem to problem (see Cole, *et al.* 1971; Scribner, 1975; and Sharp and Cole, 1975, for detailed problem analyses) and from population to population. These diversities constitute an important line of evidence for the argument developed in this paper. Nonetheless, the overall level of performance of nonschooled traditional people and the within-culture differences in performance between schooled and nonschooled groups suggest that logical problems pose special difficulties for traditional nonliterate people. Uniformities in patterns *across* cultures indicate that the source of these difficulties is not likely to reside in aspects of culture that are unique to any one of the given cultures.

Logical thinking versus logical error

Is the source of difficulty in these problems the fact that traditional people do not reason logically? Even minimal familiarity with daily life in these communities makes such a conclusion untenable with respect to everyday thinking. Levy-Bruhl (1966), who first formulated the notion of a 'different logic' characterizing primitive thought, specifically exempted the sphere of practical activity from this generalization.

Is it then the case that traditional people do not apply their logical skills to *verbal* material? Internal evidence from the experimental situation itself argues against such a notion. Many of the nonliterate people demonstrated in the course of the interviews that they were perfectly capable of valid inferential reasoning with information presented in the verbal mode. This is well illustrated in the following protocol from a Kpelle farmer:

Experimenter: If Sumo or Saki drinks palm wine, the Town Chief gets vexed. Sumo is not drinking palm wine. Saki is drinking palm wine. Is the Town Chief vexed?
    Subject: People do not get vexed with two persons.
       E: (Repeats the problem.)
       S: The Town Chief was not vexed on that day.
       E: The Town Chief was not vexed? What is the reason?
       S: The reason is that he doesn't love Sumo.
       E: He doesn't love Sumo? Go on with the reason.
       S: The reason is that Sumo's drinking is a hard time. That is why when he drinks palm wine, the Town Chief gets vexed. But sometimes when Saki drinks palm juice he will not give a hard time to people. He goes to lie down to sleep. At that rate people do not get vexed with him. But people who drink and go about fighting – the Town Chief cannot love them in the town.

While this man's answer is 'wrong' as far as the experimental problem is concerned, it is the outcome of an elegant piece of logical reasoning from new evidence. We can easily see this by recasting his statements into more traditional syllogistic form:

Sumo's drinking gives people a hard time. (Explicit premise)

Saki's drinking does not give people a hard time. (Explicit premise)
People do not get vexed when they are not given a hard time. (Explicit premise)
The Town Chief is a person. (Implicit premise)
Therefore, the Town Chief is not vexed at Saki. (Conclusion)

This is not an isolated example. Scribner (unpublished notes) analysed interviews with eight adults in one of the Cole *et al.* studies, each of whom had received at least three problems to solve. Wherever there was sufficient information to reconstruct the chain of reasoning leading to the answer it was found to follow logically from the evidence used by the subject.

The critical factor is that the 'evidence used by the subject', in many cases (as in the illustration given above), bore little resemblance to the evidence supplied in the experimental problem. Cole *et al.* (1971, p. 188) concluded: 'The subjects were (or seem to have been) responding to conventional situations in which their past experience dictated the answer. . . In short, it appears that the particular verbal context and content dictate the response rather than the arbitrarily imposed relations among the elements in the problem.'

Luria had earlier reported the same tendency for Uzbekistanians to respond in terms of direct personal experience. By manipulating the content of the problems, however, he demonstrated that where the subject matter was related to practical *knowledge* but did not deal with already known *facts*, responses were not merely verbalizations of conventional answers but were new conclusions reached through step-by-step reasoning from the problem premises. 'Reasoning and deduction . . . follow well-known rules . . . subjects make excellent judgments about facts without displaying any deviation from the 'rules' and revealing a great deal of worldly intelligence' (Luria, 1977).

These observations make it clear that inferences about a generalized incapacity of traditional people to reason logically are unwarranted. Moreover, they suggest that any inference about reasoning abilities of members of a traditional culture requires some specification of what they are reasoning *about*. Are subjects making their judgments on the basis of assertions made in the problem statements or are they drawing upon real world knowledge to generate conclusions? Is the *functional* evidence (the information actually used by the subject) the same or different from the *formal* evidence (the information supplied in the premises)? Fortunately, there are data which help us identify the functional evidence used in problem solutions; an examination of the nature of this evidence deepens our understanding of the factors affecting performance on logic problems.

'Empirical' vs. 'theoretical' explanations

In some studies, subjects were asked not only to draw conclusions but to justify or explain their answers as well. Scribner took these explanations as indicators of whether subjects were responding to the information contained in the problem or to information external to it. All statements that *explicitly* related the conclusion to the problem premises were coded as 'theoretical'; all statements justifying the conclusion on the basis of what the subject knew or believed to be true, and nonresponsive replies, were classified as 'empirical'. Examples of each will clarify the distinction.

The problem is:

> All people who own houses pay a house tax.
> Boima does not pay a house tax.
> Does Boima own a house?

A theoretical justification: 'If you say Boima does not pay a house tax, he cannot own a house.' An empirical justification: 'Boima does not have money to pay a house tax.'

Table 3 presents the proportion of theoretical explanations given by the principal comparative groups in four studies.

Table 3. Percentages of theoretical reasons for problem answers

	Nonschooled	Schooled
Scribner (Kpelle)	22·3	75·0 (students, jr high school)
Scribner (Vai)	8·3	—
Cole and Scribner (Vai)	29·5*	72·2* (adults, all grades)
Sharp and Cole (Yucatecans)		
Mayan, trad. town	43·0	75·9 (Mestizo adults, grs. 1–6)
Mayan, trans. town	58·5	46·5 (2nd gr.) 80·8 (4th–6th gr.) 97·4 (secondary school)
Scribner, Orasanu, Lazarov, Woodring (United States)		
Study 1		77·6 (2nd gr.) 93·2 (5th gr.)
Study 2		76·0 (2nd gr.) 95·1 (5th gr.)

* Sample from survey

Population differences here are even more marked than those relating to solution rates and again the dimension of schooling/nonschooling serves as a significant discriminator. Nonschooled villagers overwhelmingly support their answers by appeals to fact, belief or opinion. With comparable consistency, schooled groups adopt a theoretical approach to the task; even 7-year-old second graders in school systems known for emphasizing rote learning rather than the development of critical thinking tend to refer to what the problems *say* when asked to account for their answers. These data not only corroborate anecdotal reports of the several investigators, but document the pervasiveness of villagers' resort to the concrete example or particular circumstance. This appeal to real world knowledge and experience, which for the time being we will call 'empirical bias', is the single most prominent characteristic of villagers' performance and merits detailed analysis.

What is empirical bias? Some examples

As ordinarily used in studies on reasoning, empirical bias refers to the subtle effects of problem content which 'seduce' the reasoner from the formal task; it operates as a 'distractor'. In the cross–cultural research reported here such distracting effects are also found, but, among some traditional groups, empirical bias takes a new form: it operates as an 'organizer', characterizing the individual's entire mode of engagement with the material.

At an extreme, such bias is shown in a refusal of some individuals to engage in the reasoning task at all, on the grounds that the problems presented are, *in principle*, unanswerable. This is illustrated in the following protocol of a non-literate Kpelle farmer who has been presented with a description of this word game and shown how to solve a practice problem by 'listening to the words and taking them to the true' (a colloquial Kpelle expression). The problem:

> All Kpelle men are rice farmers.
> Mr Smith is not a rice farmer.
> Is he a Kpelle man?

The subject replies:

S: I don't know the man in person. I have not laid eyes on the man himself.
E: Just think about the statement.
S: If I know him in person, I can answer that question, but since I do not know him in person I cannot answer that question.
E: Try and answer from your Kpelle sense.
S: If you know a person, if a question comes up about him you are able to answer. But if you do not know the person, if a question comes up about him, it's hard for you to answer it.

This man firmly rejects the possibility of coming to a conclusion on the basis of propositions which make assertions about matters on which he has no personal information. He is not distinguishing between the process of drawing conclusions from statements asserting relationships and the process of evaluating information. At the same time, the protocol illustrates that his failure to grasp the nature of this reasoning task should not be confused with failure to adopt a hypothetical attitude. In fact, on several occasions this Kpelle man reasoned hypothetically (i.e. from a conditional statement) in his exposition of why he *couldn't* answer the question ('If you know a person . . . you are able to answer. . .'), but his hypothetical reasoning was within the empirical mode. One might say he was reasoning hypothetically about the *actual* while denying the possibility of reasoning hypothetically about the *postulated*.

Luria's (1977) transcripts have many such examples drawn from interviews with nonliterate Uzbekistanian women, who seem to have been the most isolated of the groups worked with thus far. To the problem: 'In the far north all bears are white; Novaya Zemyla is in the far north. What colour are the bears there?' the women often suggested, 'You should ask the people who have been there and seen them'; 'We always speak of only what we see; we don't talk about what we haven't seen.' These represent the extreme examples and were only occasionally encountered in contemporary studies, but no similar cases, to our knowledge, have been reported outside of the cross-cultural literature.

For the majority of traditional adults, empirical bias entered the problem solution process primarily as selector and editor of the 'evidence'. Personal knowledge and experience were used as (1) the criterion for acceptance or rejection of particular information conveyed in the premises, (2) the source of new information from which to derive a conclusion, (3) 'proof' or verification of a conclusion reached through use of problem information. These functions are illustrated in the following protocols from Vai respondents, all adult men and women without schooling.

Problem	*Answer and explanation*
Rejection of problem information	
(1) All women who live in Monrovia are married. Kemu is not married. Does she live in Monrovia?	Yes. Monrovia is not for any one kind of people, so Kemu came to live there. (denial of first premise)
(2) Some government officials are wealthy. All wealthy men are powerful. Are some government officials powerful?	No. Because all government officials are wealthy, but not all wealthy people have power. (denial of second premise)
Importing new evidence	
(3) All people who own houses pay house tax. Boima does not pay a house tax. Does he own a house?	Yes. Boima has a house but he is exempted from paying house tax. The government appointed Boima to collect house tax so they exempted him from paying house tax. (discussion indicated that this was exception proving the rule that all people pay house tax)
Verifying a conclusion Problem (3) above.	No. If he has a house, he would pay the government tax *as required by the Liberian government*. (factual corroboration)
(4) Some of the people we know are not in school. All of the people we know are in Liberia. Are all of the people in Liberia in school?	No. Because you said you know some people who do not go to school and *myself know a lot of them too*. (corroboration of the formal evidence by personal experience)

(5) All schools in Vai land are in a town.   Yes.
I know a school in Vai land.   All schools are in a town. A school *should*
Is it in a town?   be for the *fact human beings are attending it so
it can't be built in the bush*. (corroboration by
common sense)

As these examples show, evidence from the problem and evidence from personal knowledge can be interwoven in any designs to sustain a reasoning process and yield an inference.

For populations at the extreme end of formal education and/or modernity, theoretical approaches may be an all-or-none matter; at the extreme of rural isolation (as among Luria's Muslim women) empirical approaches may be all-or-none. In the present analysis, formal evidence in a problem controls performance of the schooled groups. The nonschooled groups show no such homogeneity: some respondents appear at either end of the spectrum, handling all problems empirically or, in fewer numbers, handling them all theoretically. The great majority have a mixed strategy, relying now on the formal information in the problem, now on evidence external to it. Adoption of a particular mode is influenced in varying degrees by specific features of the material, especially the factual status of the information supplied in the premises. Several problems in the Vai research evoked empirical responses from more than 75 per cent of respondents while others drew such responses from only 30 per cent of the sample. The fact that most nonliterate individuals respond theoretically to at least one problem demonstrates that while their approach to the task is dominated by empirical bias, it is not wholly controlled by it.

Empirical vs. theoretical explanations and wrong answers

The presence of within-subject as well as between-group variability in empirically and theoretically based answers raises an interesting possibility. If we separate out the problems in which individuals used evidence contained in the premises, as indicated by their theoretical justifications, we should expect to find a high proportion of correct answers. Indeed, theoretical responses should *invariably* be associated with correct responses, provided the subject is able to meet the logical demands of the problem. If people are making judgments on the basis of their own experience, however, as evidenced by empirical justifications, their conclusions could be either correct or incorrect, depending on the factual status of the information given in the problem.

To test this line of reasoning, we made a detailed problem-by-problem analysis of the relationship between explanations and answers for the first 100 respondents in a village picked at random from the current Vai survey study. This was a heterogeneous sample in which the majority of respondents were nonliterate, but it included some men literate in the indigenous Vai script and several individuals who had attended English school. Of the 600 cases (100 subjects × six syllogistic problems) there are 171 wrong answers, *but not a single case in which a theoretical reason is given for a wrong answer* (see table 4).

To determine the generality of this relationship for logical problems of a different type and for members of another culture, a similar analysis was made for the Sharp–Cole studies. Although, as we have seen, the distribution of empirical and theoretical explanations differs markedly from one group to another, the relationship between theoretical justifications and correct answers is robust. Summing across populations as well as problems, of 233 wrong answers to problems, only 17 are associated with theoretical reasons.

Table 4. Type of reason and error in problem solution

	Proportion of theoretical reasons with wrong answers	Proportion of empirical reasons with wrong answers
Sharp and Cole, 1975 (Mexico)		
Mayan, trad.	0·02	0·21
Mayan, trans.	0·01	0·15
Mestizo adults		
(elementary school)	(<0·01)	0·08
2nd gr. children	0·01	0·18
4th–6th gr. children	0·02	0·09
Secondary school students	(<0·01)	0·00
Scribner and Cole, 1975 (Africa)		
Vai adults	0·01	0·42

Not only is this relationship constant across groups, but it holds for *any given individual* within every population group: men and women from a traditional culture who give theoretical reasons on particular problems produce the logically correct answers on these problems, even though all their other answers may be wrong.

. . . While theoretical reasons almost always predict accuracy, empirical reasons, as we conjectured, were used to justify right as well as wrong answers. In some problems, the validly correct conclusions coincide with facts that would be known through direct personal experience, e.g. conclusions such as 'Not everyone in Liberia goes to school', derived from the premises 'Some of the people we know are not in school' and 'All of the people we know are in Liberia.' Correct answers on these problems could either represent reasoning about familiar situations or merely the person's assent to a true fact of life. In the absence of extended discussion with the subject, we cannot tell which process was involved. In contrast, other problems contained one or more premises that denied a commonly accepted truth, thus setting the valid problem conclusion into opposition with experienced reality. One problem in the Vai research asserted the 'absurd' proposition that 'All women who live in Monrovia (the capital city of Liberia) are married', the second proposition stated that 'Kemu is not married', and the question asked, 'Does Kemu live in Monrovia?' Respondents working from real-life knowledge-acquaintance with a particular Kemu, for example, or from the known fact that there *are* unmarried women in Monrovia – could arrive at an incorrect answer through logical reasoning.

. . . The significant comparative conclusion is that, in those instances where they deal with the problem as a formal 'theoretical' one, nonschooled nonliterate men and women display exactly the same logicality as adults and children exposed to Western-type schooling. In the sample at hand, when they are 'theoretical', they are virtually never wrong.

This evidence, of course, does not rule out the possibility of error attributable to reasoning processes or other sources. It is well known (Wason and Johnson-Laird, 1972; Henle, 1962) that even test-sophisticated US and British university students err on logic problems, depending on their structural complexity, content, and linguistic features. The present conclusion holds only for the problems used in the two studies analysed, and the degree of complexity they represent; it may be that the problem sample was weighted toward the structurally simple, 'easy' end of the spectrum. . .

The constancy of the relationship between theoretical approaches and accurate solutions represents the strongest evidence to date that traditional people can and do engage in valid deductive reasoning on verbal logic problems, provided they put brackets about what they know to be true and confine their reasoning to the terms of the problems. More often than not, traditional villagers fail to do just that, under conditions in which educated subjects almost always do just that. It appears characteristic for villagers to approach informally 'as a matter of course' a task that students approach formally 'as a matter of course'. Those living in the most rural and isolated towns bring to the arbitrary problems of the experiment a reasoning system, at play in everyday life, in which inference is intricately interwoven with evaluation and interpretation of semantic information; others, adopting a formal mode for some problems tend to lapse into the semantic-evaluative approach to other problems. Performance on the formal task is rarely free from intrusions of real-world knowledge.

The question originally motivating the research – what is the relation between cultural influences and verbal reasoning – involves us in the exploration of another: what is the relation between cultural experiences and empirical bias? How do we pin down the specific activities within a given cultural milieu that contribute to a 'break' between empirical approaches to everyday problems and theoretical approaches to problems whose subject matter does not 'count'?

Empirical bias: task dependent?

Before turning to some hypotheses suggested in the ethnographic literature, we would like to examine another set of cross-cultural experimental data involving somewhat different operations with syllogisms. Scribner (1975) conducted several studies among the Kpelle and Vai in which she asked subjects to *repeat* the syllogisms after they were read, or to *recall* them after they had been solved. Results from these studies help us to determine whether the phenomenon of empirical bias in the reasoning experiments was a function of the specific task demands set in those experiments. We know that, at least in some of the cultures studied, riddles and disputations are common forms of verbal exchange. It may be that the experimental situation conveyed to the subjects the implied expectation that cleverness – 'good argumentation' – was called for, and thus encouraged the production of culturally valued types of proof. No such expectation is implied, however, when subjects are asked to repeat as accurately as possible exactly what they have heard. In Scribner's initial studies conducted among the Kpelle, subjects were asked to repeat each syllogism on two occasions: once after having answered and explained it, and a second time, immediately after hearing the problem restated. In follow-up studies among the Vai, additional groups were added in which the only task was to repeat the syllogism in its entirety or sentence-by-sentence. In the one-sentence-at-a-time procedure, repetition was almost perfect, indicating that the surface structure of individual propositions did not pose any special encoding problems. In the other experimental condition recall errors were similar to those among the Kpelle (results are presented in table 5) and the discussion will be based on the Kpelle data.

Table 5. Percentages of problems with accurately recalled premises (Kpelle)*

	Both premises	One premise	No premise
Kpelle villagers (N = 87)	24·1	39·1	36·8
Kpelle students (N = 93)	48·4	31·2	20·4
U.S. students (N = 90)	69·5	26·3	4·2

* Data presented are from subjects' second recall involving repetition of problems immediately after they were read.

Recall was scored for preservation of meaning rather than verbatim accuracy; lexical substitutions, omissions, and changes in word order that did not change the meaning were scored as accurate. Even on this basis, recall of the problem as a whole was highly fragmentary; in only a small number of cases did villagers reproduce the sense of the problem as such. Information was omitted or transformed in such a way that implicative relationships were destroyed and questions posed that did not follow from what had gone before.

A Kpelle farmer attempts to recall:

Problem:
> All the stores in Kpelleland are in a town.
> Mr Ukatu's store is in Kpelleland.
> Is Mr Ukatu's store in a town?

First repeat:
> You told me Mr Ukatu came from his home
> and built his store in the Kpelleland. Then
> you asked me, is it in a town?

Second repeat (immediately after hearing problem reread):
>   All stores are in the land. Mr Ukatu's store
>   is the one in Kpelleland. Is it in the town?

In the first repetition the subject has assimilated the problem to a narrative form. He imported new information pertaining to a personally known Mr Ukatu ('came from his home and built his store'), but omitted the major premise entirely. In the second repetition, the surface form more closely approximates the syllogism, but the major proposition – that all stores in Kpelleland are built in towns – is still omitted. In each case, the question, 'Is Mr Ukatu's store in a town?' does not follow from the information reproduced and appears only as a question of fact, unrelated to the preceding material.

The most common classes of error included changes or omissions in quantifiers that converted generalizing statements into particular statements of fact, omission of entire premises and displacement of terms. These changes in many instances had the effect of 'destroying the syllogism as a unified system' (Luria, 1977) and replacing it with a series of discrete statements that shared the same topic but were not logically related to each other.

In a number of recall reproductions the hypothetical or theoretical status of the problem was converted to a factual status. 'Remembering' new information from personal experience was one form this conversion took; another was the rephrasing of the problem question such that it referred, not to the antecedent information, but to matters of belief or fact: 'Do you *think* he can be a bachelor?' 'Why is it Mr Zerby *cannot* make rice farm?' 'Then, Mr Ukatu's store, do you *know* it is in town?' '*For what reason do you think* any of them can be a bachelor?' 'All the people in Liberia, do you *believe* they are in schools?'

Replication recall studies with Kpelle and US students showed, as did the problem solving studies, both commonalities and differences with the villagers. Again, magnitude of error was considerably greater for unschooled villagers than for either student group. Educated subjects, both African and American, resembled villagers in that their most common form of error was confusion of quantifiers, and, like the villagers, they sometimes omitted entire premises and switched terms from one premise to another. The one class of errors students did not make was conversion to the factual. Even when their problem repetitions were inaccurate with respect to the originals, students almost invariably preserved their hypothetical status.

It appears that among population groups for whom logical relations do not control problem solving in the experimental situation, such relations often fail to control memory as well. The dominance of an empirical approach to problem solving is thus not necessarily a reflection of the fact that individuals are required to draw or justify conclusions. The recall data, taken together with evidence from earlier studies, suggests that more general processes of 'understanding' the material may underline both recall *and* solution.

In what follows, we will sketch one approach to the special characteristics of formal problems and what may be involved in understanding them. This approach is not in any way dictated by the evidence at hand, but it is offered as one framework within which to search for the relationship between culture and the formal approach to problem solving.

Schemas and genres

The theory of comprehension and sentence memory proposed by Bransford, Barclay, and Franks (1972) and Barclay (1973) provides a starting point for the integration of recall and problem solving findings. They maintain that, with the exception of the special case in which individuals are required to memorize the literal wording of sentences, memory for connected discourse is an active constructive process of comprehension. Comprehension involves relating or integrating the information presented in the individual sentences and assimilating it to existing lexical and nonlexical knowledge schemas. They have demonstrated experimentally that memory for a text may be 'richer' than the information explicitly contained in its constituent sentences – incorporating additional conceptual information from the schemas into which the material was assimilated.

Data from recall studies with syllogisms illustrate the converse case: memory for these connected sentences not only failed to incorporate new logical inferences but often failed to preserve the logical and conceptual information in the original. In Bransford and Barclay's terms, this may be interpreted as an indication that the material was not integrated and assimilated to pre-exisiting schemas.

This interpretation raises a general question: *What are* (how can we conceive the nature of) *the pre-existing schemas into which verbal logic problems can be assimilated?* If the information the problems contain is completely congruent with practical knowledge, their assimilation could follow the course of comprehension of other forms of connected discourse. (Recall Luria's excellent results with material involving practical knowledge but not directly related to people's own personal experiences.) If the relations the problems express are arbitrary, not consonant with or in opposition to accumulated knowledge, their assimilation into pre-existing schemas may militate *against*, rather than facilitate, comprehension, recall, and problem solving. Such assimilation would manifest itself in 'empirical bias', as pre-existing schemas become the field of operation for remembering and reasoning activities. For a formal or theoretical approach to be maintained, with operations restricted to the arbitrary terms of the problems, the schema to which the material is assimilated must be based on relationships rather than subject matter.

In addition to the concept of schemas, the general interpretive framework we would like to develop makes use of another analytic category, that of *genre*. Hymes (1974) has proposed that *genres* and *performances* be considered basic categories for the study of ways of speaking in different speech communities. As he uses the term, *genre* refers to stylistic structures or organized verbal forms with a beginning and an end, 'and a pattern to what comes between' (1974, p. 442). Greetings, farewells, riddles, proverbs, prayers, are among well-known elementary genres, and tales and myths representative of complex genres. *Performances* refers to the use of genres in particular contexts. Both genres and performances may vary from one speech community to another, and the relationship between them may vary as well: certain genres in certain communities may be context-bound while in others they range over diverse events and situations.

Let us entertain the proposition that verbal logic problems (along with other 'formal problems' which we shall not attempt to specify at this point) constitute a specialized language genre that stands apart from other genres in ways that may be difficult to define but are readily recognizable (just as poetry may be distinguished from prose by readers who may never exactly agree on what poetry 'is').

It is, of course, true that people do not 'speak in syllogisms' in any community we know of, but we have good authority for considering logic problems a specialized form of discourse. In one of his definitions of a syllogism, Aristotle referred to it as 'discourse in which certain things being stated, something other than what is stated follows of necessity from their being so' ('Prior analytics', quoted in Jager, 1963, p. 14). Or, again, he defined the component parts of the syllogism as premises, each of which is a 'form of speech which affirms or denies something' and is itself composed of terms which predicate something of something else (Bochenski, 1970, p. 45). Aristotle is here developing new terminology ('premises', 'terms') to talk about a language function that has hitherto not been isolated from the other functions in which it is ordinarily embedded. As Bochenski points out, new technical terminology was required to convey the distinction between two customarily related, but conceptually independent, aspects of sentences – the truth value they express (dependent on subject matter) and the relations authorizing necessary inferences that they express and that are independent of subject matter.

In ordinary discourse, these aspects interpenetrate. Discourse that uses language primarily to convey necessary relations between propositions constitutes what we have been calling the 'logical genre'. In its focus on topic-neutral relations rather than topic-bound content, the logical genre stands in contrast to other genres, both formal and informal (see Bricker, 1975, for an analysis of formal and informal Mayan speech genres).

With these constructs – *schema, genre, performance* – we can suggest an interpretation for the findings of both the memory and reasoning studies. Through experience with the genre (a socially evolved language structure) individuals develop a cognitive schema through which they assimilate increasingly varied and more complex examples of the genre. They will remember the form of a problem (the general relationship between premises) even when they forget the particular subjects and predicates used. In a reasoning task, they will grasp an example (e.g. approach a problem formally) even though they may not be able on a particular occasion to handle successfully its specific content.

An example from memory research makes this point more concretely. In societies in which narrative is a developed genre, recall of 'stories' will be facilitated by their assimilation to the narrative structure. This structure confers 'sense' on the presented material and serves as a guide to the retention and retrieval of the specific informational content in the given example. The narrative, like the formal problem, may be considered a socially evolved genre that individuals in varying degrees, depending on their own personal life experiences, acquire or, in Vygotsky's terms, internalize. Like narrative, when the formal problem's structure is internalized, it helps to make sense of the material presented and serves as a device that guides and constrains remembering and reasoning.

In the studies we have reviewed, there were some individuals who seem not to have developed the requisite schema for handling the type of discourse represented in the logic problem. They denied the sense of the question or failed to retain the logical system in their recall reproductions. The overwhelming bulk of respondents in all cultural groups, however, showed some grasp of the genre. For most nonschooled adults this was a transient phenomenon. Several possibilities exist here. Schemas may not be generalized across all content and may be more vulnerable to certain subject matters than others. Alternatively, or concurrently, the experimental or interview context may not have provided the appropriate cues to elicit the desired performance – the use of the logical genre (cf. Hymes, 1974).

We know very little about the social conditions which give rise to the logical genre, how cultures define the occasions for its use, through what experiences individuals acquire its schema. Within Western academic institutions, examples of the genre are not uncommon. Verbal and arithmetical problems would seem to fall into the class of problems whose content is arbitrary and whose meaning resides in the relationships expressed. If the teacher presents a problem: 'Johnny has one red apple and Mary has one red apple, how many apples do Johnny and Mary have altogether?' it will not do for a child to look around the room to see who else may have an apple or to question whether apples are really red. An empirical approach to the problem will not earn a passing grade. Specialized studies – algebra, geometry, chemistry – and other fields that use technical notational systems may be considered to present 'arbitrary problems' in the sense that the problems derive from a system outside the learner's own personal experience and must be taken in their own terms. It would be interesting to examine school curricula to find to what extent students must learn to work with other verbal problems that represent the genre of logical discourse.

More challenging is the question of what activities outside of school, and especially what activities in traditional cultures, might give rise to this form of discourse. Ryle (1963) has made the provocative suggestion that the 'logical idiom' arises when societies face pressures for 'special kinds of talk', especially involving commercial transactions, contracts and treaties, legal and administrative services. To our knowledge, no researches in the ethnography of speaking have yet identified and analysed examples of this genre, but it appears to be an important direction in which to carry studies of specialized language functions.

For the psychologist, the leading developmental question becomes that of specifying under what circumstances and as a result of what experiences individuals possessing this genre internalize it as a schema available for cognitive activities. The leading functional question becomes that of specifying the experimental conditions, as well as everyday conditions, under which a given example of this form of discourse is assimilated in the logical schema.

30. Linguistic Relativity[1]

Eleanor Rosch

Covert linguistic classifications

Language as metaphysics

The strongest and most inclusive form of the Whorfian hypothesis (and the only form, perhaps, that Whorf would today recognize) is that each language both embodies and imposes upon the culture a particular world view. Nature is, in reality, a kaleidoscopic continuum, but the units which form the basis of the grammar of each language serve both to classify reality into corresponding units and to define the fundamental nature of those units. . . The metaphysics implicit in the grammar of Standard Average European makes it sensible to analyse sentences, and thus reality, into agents, actions, and the objects, instruments, and results of actions; but such constructions, Whorf argues, are gross distortions when used as units of analysis for various American Indian languages. In support of his contentions, Whorf (1956) provides a variety of translations of statements in various Indian languages into English to show how unlike ours are the thought processes of speakers of those languages. Thus, in Apache, 'It is a dripping spring' is expressed by 'As water, or springs, whiteness moves downward.' In Shawnee, 'cleaning a gun with a ramrod' is 'direct a hollow moving dry spot by movement of tool'.

The Whorfian hypothesis is, at the least, intriguing: what is it like to live in a mental world in which there are no things or actions but only events, where there are no agents and acts, no separate space and time? Can we ever hope to communicate with people who have such a world view? At the most, the Whorfian view challenges our most fundamental beliefs. Are common-sense distinctions (such as that between object and action) which appear to us to be 'given' unequivocally by our senses, actually an illusion fostered by the grammar of English? Is Newtonian physics not a necessary first step in the

[1] An excerpt from the chapter in A. Silverstein (ed.) *Human Communication: Theoretical Perspectives* (Hillsdale, N. J.: Lawrence Erlbaum Associates, 1974). Reprinted with the permission of the authors and publishers.

development of physical theory, but merely a metaphor derived from the grammatical units of Standard Average European? Are the basic concepts of linguistics perhaps the only means by which we may hope to surmount the limitations of our own language and become able to analyse differences between languages, or are these concepts themselves only reifications of the grammar of our own language family?

Upon what evidence are such sweeping claims based? As a linguist, Whorf found the grammar of several American Indian languages to differ from English grammar to such an extent that literal translations between those languages and English made no sense. The literal translations, given above, of 'a dripping spring' and 'cleaning a gun with a ramrod' do, indeed, appear to be products of a very alien mode of thought. Of course, it is also true that all languages have somewhat different grammars, even the languages which Whorf calls 'Standard Average European'. However, notice that when we learn French, we are taught to translate 'Comment allez vous?' not literally as 'How go you?' but as the standard English greeting to which it corresponds, 'How are you?' And if a student translates 'le chat gris' as 'the cat grey', he is told he has made an error; in English, modifiers come before the noun, not after, and the correct rendition of the phrase in English is 'the grey cat'. Let us, however, try to take a Whorfian view of French and suppose that the order of noun and modifier is indicative of a difference in metaphysics. The French language, we may assert, defines the basic units of nature not as substantive things but as pervasive attributes such as colours, shapes, and sizes. What we see as a thing-with-attributes, the Frenchman sees as a specific local perturbation of a general Attribute; thus what we call a cat with a particular colour is, in French, a particular modification of the general colour manifold – some 'cat grey' as opposed, perhaps, to some 'fog grey'. Why should such interpretations seem absurd for French but not Hopi? Is it that we have other evidence for concluding that Frenchman are not that different from ourselves? If there were a sovereign Hopi nation to the south of the United States, might we today be learning in our classrooms not to make errors of literal translation in Hopi?

. . . In summary: the most dramatic form of the Whorfian hypothesis – the assertion that each language embodies and imposes upon the culture an implicit metaphysics – does not, in that form, appear to be an empirical statement. If it must be interpreted as meaning only that languages differ, then it is true but trivial. If it is to mean more than that, we find that we have no idea what the state of the world would 'look like' if the hypothesis were true, or, correspondingly, if it were false. The rest of this paper discusses successive attempts to reinterpret the Whorfian view into claims which are sufficiently specific that we can understand their meaning and test whether they are true or false.

Grammatical form class

The words (actually, the morphemes, or units of meaning) of any language can be divided into classes of grammatical equivalents on the basis of the positions which they can occupy in word sequences (such as sentences). The most basic units of grammar, which Whorf claimed formed the basis of the metaphysics of a language, are none other than the most general form classes of the languages – in English the parts of speech such as nouns, verbs, adjectives, and adverbs. Many form classes are more limited in scope than the basic 'parts of speech': gender defines classes of nouns in French; English nouns are either 'mass' (occur in the position 'Some X') or 'count' (occur in the position 'An X'); and in Navajo, verbs of handling take a different form depending on the nature of the objects handled. Obviously, form classes are not the same in all languages.

As long as form classes are considered only 'structural' (defined only by position of occurrence in sentences), they do not suggest important cognitive differences between speakers of different languages. However, Whorf and others have stressed that form classes also have semantic (meaning) correlates. Thus, nouns are seen as substances; verbs as actions; mass nouns as indefinite, uncontained, flowing masses of matter; count nouns as singular, self-contained objects; gender as masculine, feminine, and neuter; and Navajo verb stem classifiers as shape types (round, long granular, etc.). Generally, the members of a linguistic community are unconscious of the semantics of form class. For example, even in a relatively grammatically self-conscious society like ours, most people have never spontaneously noticed the distinction between mass and count nouns, nor ever thought about which English verbs can or cannot take the prefix 'un-'. Whorf speaks of the semantic correlates of form classes (he calls them 'cryptotypes') as the 'covert categories', the 'underlying concepts' of the language. In fact, it is the pervasive, covert influence of cryptotypes on thought which may be one relatively concrete interpretation of what it might mean for grammar to influence metaphysics.

The semantic interpretation of form class has not gone unchallenged. Descriptive linguistics considers the relation between structurally defined form classes and their semantic correlates highly dubious (cf. Fries, 1952). Semantic definitions of form class are always unclear or overextended; not all nouns are substances (e.g. 'space') nor all verbs active (e.g. 'hold'); mass nouns can come in discrete units ('some bread'), and count nouns can refer to fluid masses ('a martini'); masculine and feminine gender forms are used for innumerable gen-derless objects; and specific Navajo shape classifiers are used for abstractions ('news' takes the round classifier).

There is, however, undoubtedly a *partial* correlation between some form classes and some semantics. It would be to the advantage of individuals learning a language to be aware (at some level) of these partial correlations. Roger Brown (1958) has shown that even 4-year-old children can use structural syntactic cues for guessing the semantic referent of form classes. Brown showed the children pictures in which an action, a discrete object, and an unbounded flowing mass were depicted, introducing the picture either with 'This is a picture of latting' or 'of a latt' or 'of some latt'. The 4-year-olds easily identified the object by means of the form-class cue. A similar experiment was performed on the form-class gender by Ervin (1962). Italian speakers living in Boston were read nonsense syllables formed with Italian gender. When subjects were asked to rate the syllables on a series of adjective scales (called the semantic differential – cf. Osgood, Suci, and Tannenbaum, 1957), they rated the masculine gender syllables more similar to their ratings for 'man' than 'woman' and *vice versa*. Such experiments demonstrate that we can make use of what semantic information there is in form classes when we are learning and applying words. They do not, however, prove that speakers of languages with different sets of form classes take different views of the semantic nature of the world. After all, discrete solid objects and unbounded fluids, and male and female organisms, have quite different physical properties which all peoples might well be required to take equal account of whether or not their grammar makes such distinctions.

If we wished to test whether semantic aspects of form class do affect thought, what kinds of correlates or effects on thought might we look for? In fact, there has been little systematic consideration and little research concerning this issue. One possibility is that there is a 'metaphorical generalization' of the meaning from members of the form class to which it literally applies to members to which it does not apply literally at all. Thus, the French may really think of and treat tables as feminine, and the Navajo may consider news to be round. Whorf himself suggests this kind of interpretation when he claims that we read action into all words that are verbs, and, since all English sentences contain verbs, into every statement. 'We therefore read action into every sentence, even into "I hold it". . . . We think of it (i.e. holding) and even see it as an action because language formulates it in the same way as it formulates more numerous expressions, like "I strike it", which deals with movements and changes' (Whorf, 1956, p. 243). But *do* we read action into all verbs? How can we tell? One test would be to go to the natural logic of language use itself; if action is being 'read into' verbs like 'hold', they should be capable of occurring modified by action adverbs just as do 'true' action verbs. The actual state of such verbs is described by the philosopher Max Black: 'a man may strike slowly, jerkily, energetically, and so on. Now if somebody were to attach these adverbs to the verb "to hold" that would be sufficient indication that he was "reading action" into the verb. I suppose a child might say he was holding his hat slowly, and the poet is allowed a similar license; but otherwise the conceptual confusion is too gross to occur' (Black, 1959, pp. 252–3).

Are there *any* cases in which the partially correlated semantics of a form class are extended to other words that happen to be in that class? Is there a systematic way of studying such extensions so that we might conclude that it never happens? These intriguing questions remain entirely open to future investigation, and the interested student might well try using his intuition as a speaker of his own language to consider them.

Even if the semantic partial correlates of form class do not extend beyond the clear-cut cases, they may have effects on thought – one obvious possibility is that they continually draw the attention of speakers of the language to those aspects of the world which are the basis for the (even partial) form–class semantic distinctions. Such an effect would be most likely demonstrable in the case of a form class which was sufficiently salient linguistically and sufficiently correlated with a clear–cut semantic for it to be reasonable to expect speakers of the language to be influenced by habitual use of the class. Navajo shape classifiers appear to be just such a case. Use of verb stems which indicate shape in Navajo is obligatory linguistically, and such stems are very high frequency items in the language. For all objects that actually have a shape, the classifiers are used consistently – even English speakers new to the system perceive the classifiers to refer predictably to shape types. Most importantly, the classifier used for an object is not an invariable attribute of the object (as is generally the case with gender) but varies with the actual shape of the object at the time of reference. Thus, a rolled–up rug will take a different classifier from the same rug when it is lying flat (S. Ervin–Tripp, personal communication, 1972). It is reasonable to suppose that Navajo speakers are continually noticing shape when speaking and, thus, would be more likely to notice shape and to use shape as a basis of classification than speakers of a language which does not incorporate obligatory grammatical shape distinctions.

A test for this hypothesis was devised by Carroll and Casagrande (1958). Subjects were presented with a reference object and two other objects, each one resembling the standard by a different attribute. For example, the standard might be a red circle and the other objects a red square and a blue circle. Subjects were asked to choose which of the two objects was most like the standard. A variety of objects were used, incorporating all combinations of the attributes form, colour, and size. The basic hypothesis was that Navajo speakers would prefer to classify by form rather than by the other equally correct attributes. Three groups of children were tested: Navajo children whose dominant language was Navajo; Navajo children for whom English was the dominant language; and monolingual English speakers. As predicted, the Navajo-dominant Navajo preferred to classify on the basis of form; however, so did the English-speaking Boston children. English-dominant Navajo, on the other hand, preferred colour. These results are not unequivocal. They have been treated both as evidence against the Whorfian view – because English speakers, whose grammar does not call attention to form preferred form classifications just as much as the Navajo-dominant Navajo – and as evidence in support of Whorf – because the English-dominant Navajo, whose culture and early environment, but not language, were the most similar to that of the Navajo-dominant Navajo, preferred colour and not form. The reader might pause and consider what arguments might be offered on each side.

In fact, the results are probably even more difficult to interpret than has been supposed. Since the time of Carroll and Casagrande's experiments, a great many tests of colour-form preference in classification have been performed on a variety of populations, and a consistent but, to the present author, incomprehensible pattern of results has emerged. Around the world, the younger the subject and/or the less Western schooling he has received the more likely he is to use colour as the basis of classification in the kind of 'triads' test used by Carroll and Casagrande (see Serpell, 1969, for a review of studies). However, it is just young children and non-Western peoples who appear to be the populations least likely to classify by colour in more naturalistic contexts. It is the technologically less advanced cultures which appear to have smaller colour vocabularies and less cultural concern with colour distinctions and coordinations (see Berlin and Kay, 1969, and the latter part of the present paper). Young children in Western cultures only come to use colour terms correctly and consistently at about the age when they begin to prefer form classification in the colour-form preference triads (Heider, 1971; Istomina, 1963). Further evidence comes from a study of the published diaries of the language development of individual children (usually kept by fond linguist parents). Clark (1973) has examined all of the diary examples of young children's overgeneralizations of words – that is, of cases where a child applies a newly learned word to a variety of things to which that word does not actually apply in the adult language (e.g. calling all animals 'dogs' or all men 'daddy'). Clark was interested in finding out the attributes by which children generalize meaning. What is relevant to the present issue is that, in all of the diary literature, there is not one single instance reported in which a child seemed to overgeneralize a word on the basis of colour! So classifying by colour or form on the triad type of test may well be the result of factors very specific to operations and cognitions in that test situation and may not reflect any tendency to use either attribute as the basis of classification in any other context.

Navajo shape-classifying verb stems appeared to be a case ideally suited to a demonstration of the effect of grammatical form class on attention. However, preference for form over colour in a triad classification task may involve too crude a hypothesis or may be too task-specific to test the issue. The interested reader might try to think of a more reasonable test. Does anything in the literature on perception, memory, learning, problem solving, or other human cognitive functions suggest such a test? Unfortunately, at present, the evidence concerning the effects of form class on attention remains equivocal.

If the semantics of form class provide the cryptotypes – the underlying categorization of reality – for speakers of a language, then at the very least, at some cognitive level, speakers of the language should code form classes as categories. Overt semantic categories have been shown to have several reliable effects on human memory – do categories consisting of form classes have similar effects?

One such effect occurs in the kind of experiment called 'free recall'. A subject is read a list of ordinary words and then attempts to recall the words in any order he wishes. The list may consist of random, unrelated words, or it may contain a number of words from the same semantic categories (for example, flowers, animals, musical instruments). When subjects receive a 'categorized' word list, they remember more words than in uncategorized lists, and they tend to recall those words in 'clusters' from the same category – even when the input list contained the words in random order. If grammatical classes are 'meaningful' cognitive categories, should not they also provide a basis for clustering and improved recall? Cofer and Bruce (1965) presented lists in which words could be categorized into the form classes nouns, verbs, and adjectives, but were otherwise unrelated. They found no effects of the categories on either accuracy or clustering in recall. (See Cofer, 1965, for a discussion of some of the complex issues involved in recall of categorized lists.)

A second effect of semantic categories on memory arises in the type of task in which subjects must try to remember an item (such as a number, word, or nonsense syllable) for short periods of time while performing an interfering task, such as counting backwards. In such experiments, ability to remember becomes rapidly poorer with each succeeding item, generally attributed to interference from preceding items. If all of the items up to some point have belonged to one semantic class and the experimenter switches suddenly to another class (e.g. switches from letters of the alphabet to numbers, from animals to plants, or from words with a 'good' connotation to words with a 'bad' connotation), subjects regain their ability to remember the items. However, switching from one grammatical class to another (e.g. from verbs to adjectives) has no such effects (Wickens, 1970). So, at least in these memory tasks, grammatical class seems to be more like a dead metaphor than like a psychologically real classification of reality. . .

Overt language classifications: Vocabulary

According to Whorf, language affects thought basically by means of the kinds of classifications it 'lays upon' reality. Whorf focused on classifications of a general and abstract nature – the covert 'metaphysics' and 'cryptotypes' embedded in language. However, we have seen the difficulty of demonstrating that classifications on that level are actually related to meaningful cognitive units. There is another level of language, however, in which semantic classifications are quite overt, the level of the lexicon (vocabulary). If the same Hopi word refers to what English codes with the three words 'airplane', 'insect', aviator', or if the language of the Eskimo uses three words to refer to that thing coded by the one English word 'snow', these are overt semantic differences in the way the world is 'cut up' and coded.

In fact, it is not unreasonable to suppose that there are concrete and identifiable aspects of the lexical code that affect identifiable and measurable aspects of thought. It is well-established that there are human limitations in the capacity to process and retain information. How much information can be retained, however, is dependent on the way in which it has been 'coded'. Normally, for example, only about seven digits can be remembered, even for very brief periods (Miller, 1956). However, if a string of 0 and 1 digits is recoded by a subject into octal (a system by which groups of three digits are 'named' by a single number), he can remember almost three times as many. Here is a prototypical case in which a classificatory aspect of vocabulary (the number of digits named by a single number in a particular code) can be shown directly related to an aspect of cognition (amount of information stored in memory).

Octal is an 'artificial' code developed for particular purposes within our culture. The Whorfian hypothesis on the level of the lexicon might be considered to contain an additional assertion, namely that *natural* languages as they are spoken by the world's speakers contain differences in codes (analogous, perhaps, to recoding groups of digits into octal) which affect cognitive processes such as perception, classification, and memory.

The bulk of the empirical work on linguistic relativity has involved language at the lexical level, and the rest of this paper will be concerned with work at this level. . . . It is apparent that many factors are necessary in order to have a real test of the effect of a natural language lexicon on thought. (a) We must have at least two natural languages whose lexicons differ with respect to some domain of discourse – if languages are not different, there is no point in the investigation. (b) The domain must be one which can be measured by the investigator independently of the way it is encoded by the languages of concern (for example, colour may be measured in independent physical units such as wavelength) – if that is not the case (as, for example, in such domains as feelings or values), there is no objective way of describing how it is that the two languages differ. (c) The domain must not itself differ grossly between the cultures whose languages differ – if it does, then it may be differences in experience with the domain, and not language, which are affecting thought. (d) We must be able to obtain measures of specific aspects of cognition – such as perception, memory, or classification – having to do with the domain which are independent of, rather than simply assumed from, the language. (e) We must have a cross-culturally meaningful measure of differences in the selected aspects of cognition – preferably we should be able to state the hypotheses in terms of an interaction between the linguistic and cognitive variables, rather than in terms of overall differences between speakers of the languages.

One domain only has appeared to researchers to be ideal for such research – colour. Colour is a continuous physical variable which can easily be designated by objective measures which are independent of the colour terms in any given language (for example, wavelength). Many reports in the anthropological literature have described differences in colour terminologies between languages – that is, differences in the way in which colour terms appear to classify the physically invariant colour space. The physical aspects of colour, the domain of colours as such, is the same in every part of the world – although, of course, the colours most frequently viewed may differ ecologically. Colour discrimination, memory, and classification can be readily measured independently of colour names, rather than simply inferred from the colour terminology of the culture. And, finally, colours lend themselves readily to hypotheses stated in terms of interactions – as has already been illustrated by the preceding examples.

It may seem a long way from the initial introduction of linguistic relativity as an assertion about differences in 'world view' to a study of the possible cognitive effects of differences in colour terms. The transition was made necessary by the requirement that assertions be made in the form of empirically testable hypotheses. Much of the remainder of this paper will trace the history of language-cognition research in the domain of colours, the primary domain in which such research has been carried out.

Colour

Colour is perceived when the human visual system interprets certain aspects of the physical properties of light. Sensory psychologists describe colour with a solid using three psychological dimensions: hue (roughly, the dominant wavelength of the light), brightness (loosely speaking, an intensity dimension), and saturation (the apparent degree of dominance of the dominant wavelength, the 'purity' of the light).[2] The colour solid is divisible into literally millions of perceptually just noticeable differences. There is no evidence that human populations differ in the physiology of the visual system, nor that there are any cultures which differ in actual ability of their members to perceive and discriminate colours (Lenneberg, 1967). In fact, there is evidence that the old world primates, whose colour physiology is similar to that of humans, are not different from humans in colour perception and discrimination (De Valois and Jacobs, 1968). There are far fewer colour names in any language than there are discriminable colours, and fewer still commonly used colour names. Thus, it appears that cultural differences are to be found on the level of categorization rather than perception of colour.

A seminal study on the effects of language on cognition was performed by Brown and Lenneberg (1954). Brown and Lenneberg reasoned that cultures, perhaps because of differing colour 'ecologies' should differ with respect to the areas of the colour space to which they paid the most attention. 'Culturally important' colours should tend to be referred to often in speech and, thus, their names should become highly 'available' to members of the culture. 'Availability' of a name should have three measurable attributes: as Zipf (1935) has shown, words used frequently tend to evolve into shorter words (for example, automobile becomes auto or car); thus, the length of colour words should be an index of their availability. Secondly, a more available word should be one which a speaker can produce rapidly when asked to name the thing to which the word refers. Finally, words frequently used in communication should come to have meanings widely agreed upon by speakers of the language. These three indices of availability are *linguistic* measures; for a measure of cognition, Brown and Lenneberg chose recognition memory, the ability of subjects to recognize a previously viewed colour from among an array of colours. The hypothesis relating the linguistic and cognitive variables was similar to the case, described previously, of the effectiveness of octal as a code for digits; names which are more available should be more efficient codes for colours (you can hang on to them better in memory) – thus, people should be able to retain them longer.

Brown and Lenneberg's actual experiment was in two stages. They first had a sample of English-speaking American undergraduates name a sample of coloured chips. Because the three linguistic measures were found to correlate highly (the same chips tended to be given short, rapid, agreed-upon names), the measures were combined into a composite measure which Brown and

[2] Colour plates illustrating what these dimensions actually look like are printed in many standard introductory psychology text books.

Lenneberg named 'codability'. Other subjects performed a memory task; they were shown either one or four colours, waited a predetermined length of time during which the colours were not visible, and then attempted to pick out which colour(s) they had seen from an array of many colours. The hypothesis was that the more codable colours would also be the best remembered. That is exactly the result which was obtained. Furthermore, the advantage of the more codable colours increased as the number of colours and the length of time they had to be remembered increased. This study is the classic demonstration of an effect of language on memory.

In fact, another variable, 'communication accuracy', was found to correlate with memory more generally than codability (Lantz and Stefflre, 1964; Stefflre, Castillo Vales, and Morely, 1966). However, because this line of research is more relevant to the relation between interpersonal and intrapersonal communication than it is to the relation between a linguistic domain and the non-linguistic domain which it encodes (Lenneberg, 1967), it will not be pursued further here.

The Brown and Lenneberg study used only speakers of a single language. However, its logic can easily be extended to a cross-cultural comparison. Which particular colours are most codable would be expected to vary between languages, but the lawful relationship between memory and codability should remain true – those colours which are most codable should be better remembered by speakers of that language than the less codable colours. That this would be the case seemed so obviously true that it was not tested for many years. Is it obvious?

The first, almost trivial requirement for testing the Whorfian hypothesis which we listed previously was that there be at least two natural languages whose terminologies with respect to some domain were different. The anthropological literature contains many reports of such differences in colour names – for example, cultures which have only one word to describe the colours which English distinguishes as 'green' and 'blue', or cultures whose word for 'orange' includes much of what we would classify as 'red'. From this kind of evidence, it appeared that languages could arbitrarily cut up the colour space into quite different categories. Recently, two anthropologists have challenged this assumption.

Berlin and Kay (1969) first looked at the reported diversity of colour names linguistically, and claimed that there were actually a very limited number of basic – as opposed to secondary – colour terms in any language. 'Basic' was defined by a list of linguistic criteria: for example, that a term be composed of only a single unit of meaning ('red' as opposed to 'dark red'), and that it name only colour and not objects ('purple' as opposed to 'wine'). Using these criteria, Berlin and Kay reported that no language contained more than eleven basic colour names: three achromatic (in English, 'black', 'white', and 'grey') and eight chromatic (in English, 'red', 'yellow', 'green', 'blue', 'pink', 'orange', 'brown', and 'purple').

Berlin and Kay next asked speakers of different languages to identify the colours to which the basic colour names in their language referred. Their initial group of subjects were twenty foreign students whose native language was not English. Subjects saw a two-dimensional array of coloured chips – all of the hues at all levels of brightness (all at maximum saturation) available in the Munsell Book of Color (Munsell Color Company, 1966). The students performed two tasks: (a) they traced the boundaries of each of their native language's basic colour terms, and (b) they pointed to the chip which was the *best example* of each basic term. As might have been expected from the anthropological literature, there was a great deal of variation in the placement of boundaries of the terms. There was not, however, *reliable* variation. Speakers of the same language disagreed with each other in placement of the boundaries as much as did speakers of different languages; and the same person, when asked to map boundaries a second time, was likely to map them quite differently from the way he had at first. It is, thus, likely that even anthropological reports of differences in the boundaries of colour terms are confounded by this unreliability. Surprisingly, in spite of this variation, the choice of best examples of the terms was quite similar for the speakers of the twenty different languages. Berlin and Kay called the points in the colour space where choices of best examples of basic terms clustered 'focal points', and argued that the previous anthropological emphasis on cross-cultural differences in colour names was derived from looking at boundaries of colour names rather than at colour-name focal points.

Brown and Lenneberg's results had been interpreted as a demonstration of the effect of codability on memory. However, Berlin and Kay's focal points suggested a disturbing alternative. Suppose that there are areas of the colour space which are perceptually more 'salient' to all peoples and that these areas both become more codable and can be better remembered as the direct result of their salience? The present author (Heider, 1972c) tested this possibility. If codability is the result of salience, the same colours should be the most codable in all languages; specifically, focal colours should be universally more codable than nonfocal colours. A focal colour representing each of the eight basic chromatic terms was chosen from the centre of each of the best-example clusters produced by Berlin and Kay's subjects; nonfocal colours were chosen from the 'internominal' areas of the colour space, areas which were never picked as the best example of any basic colour name.[3] The chips were mounted on cards and shown, one at a time, in scrambled order, individually, to twenty-three people whose native language was not English. A subject's task was to write down what he would call each colour in his language. The results of the study were clear: the focal colours were given shorter names and named more rapidly than

---

[3] These may not actually be the 'best' chips to represent focal and nonfocal colours. Neither Berlin and Kay's linguistics nor their research methods are above reproach (cf. Hickerson, 1971). Berlin and Kay may have included some colours in their basic name list which should be considered secondary names, or may have assigned secondary status to legitimate basic terms; or they may have systematically skewed the location of their best-example clusters by the use of bilinguals as subjects. All such 'errors' would only contribute to 'noise' in the present author's research design and make it more difficult to demonstrate significant differences between focal and nonfocal colours.

were the nonfocal colours. Thus, in twenty-three diverse languages, drawn from seven of the major language families of the world, it was the same colours that were most codable.

There was a second part to the hypothesis. If memory were the direct result of salience rather than of codability focal colours should be better remembered than nonfocal, even by speakers of a language in which these colours were not more codable. Berlin and Kay's claim about the number of basic colour terms was that there were never more than, but could be fewer than, eleven terms; in fact, they argued that colour terms entered languages in a specific evolutionary order. The Dani of West Irian (Indonesian New Guinea) are a Stone Age, agricultural people who have a basically two-term colour language (K. G. Heider, 1970; Heider, 1972b; Heider & Olivier, 1972). Colour systems of that character have been reported for other cultures as well and form stage I, the first and simplest stage, of Berlin and Kay's proposed evolutionary ordering of colour systems. For Dani, the eight chromatic focal chips were not more codable than the internominal chips (established by having forty Dani name all of the colour chips in the Berlin and Kay array). Would Dani, nevertheless, better remember the focal colours? To find out, Heider (1972c) administered, to a sample of Dani and a sample of Americans, a colour memory test very similar to Brown and Lenneberg's. Subjects were shown focal and nonfocal colours, individually in random order, for five seconds, and after a thirty-second wait, were asked to recognize the colour they had seen from an array of many colours. The mean number correctly recognized by people of each culture for each kind of chip is shown in table 1. The main results were clear: Dani, as well as Americans, recognized the focal colours better than the nonfocal.

This study also illustrates a point about method which was emphasized earlier. A striking aspect of table 1 is that Dani memory performance as a whole was poorer than American. If the hypothesis had been in terms of absolute differences between cultures, we would have noted that Dani both had fewer colour terms and poorer memory for colours than Americans, and might have claimed that linguistic relativity was thereby supported. However, it must be remembered that the Dani are a preliterate people, living in face-to-face communities, probably without need for or training in techniques for coping with the kind of overloads of information which this unfamiliar memory test required. All of those extraneous factors undoubtedly affected Dani memory performance as a whole. Our hypothesis, however, concerned differential memory for different types of colour within culture and, therefore, was not negated by general cultural differences in 'test taking'.

Colour initially appeared to be an ideal domain in which to demonstrate the effects of lexical differences on thought; instead, it now appears to be a domain particularly suited to an examination of the influence of underlying perceptual factors on the formation and reference of linguistic categories. Certain colours appear to be universally salient. There are also universals in some aspects of colour naming. How (by what mechanism) might the saliency be related to the naming? What we are asking for is an account of the development (both in the sense of individual learning and the evolution of languages) of colour names which will specify the precise nature of the role played by focal colours in that development.

Table 1. Accuracy of Colour Memory: mean number of correctly recognized colours

Culture	Stimulus colours	
	Focal	Internominal
US	5·25	3·22
Dani	2·05	0·47

Such an account is related to issues more general than that of linguistic relativity alone. Learning theories in psychology tend to be designed primarily to account for connections formed between initially arbitrary stimuli and responses. The concepts learned in typical concept formation tasks (cf. Bourne, 1966; Bruner, Goodnow, and Austin, 1956) are also arbitrary; what a subject learns when he learns such a concept is a clear-cut rule, usually stated in terms of combinations of the discrete attributes of artificial stimuli, which define the boundaries of membership in the experimenter-determined 'positive subset' (for example, 'anything which is square and has two borders around it' is a member of the 'concept'). Colour categories, however, appear to be concepts with a very different kind of structure.

Rosch (1973b) proposed the following account of the development of colour names: there are perceptually salient colours which more readily attract attention (even of young children – Heider, 1971) and are more easily remembered than other colours. When category names are learned, they tend to become attached first to the salient stimuli (only later generalizing to other, physically similar, instances), and by this means these 'natural prototype' colours become the foci of organization for categories. How can this account be tested? In the first place, it implies that it is easier to learn names for focal than for nonfocal colours. That is, not only should focal colours be more easily retained than nonfocal in recognition over short intervals (as has already been demonstrated), but they should also be more readily remembered in conjunction with names in long-term memory. In the second place, since a colour category is learned first as a single named focal colour and second as that focal colour plus other physically similar colours, colour categories in which focal colours are physically central stimuli ('central' in terms of some physical attribute, such as wavelength) should be easier to learn than categories structured in some other manner (for example, focal colours physically peripheral, or internominal colours central, and no focal colours at all).

A test of these hypotheses obviously could not be performed with subjects who already knew a set of basic chromatic colour terms provided by their language. This brings us to another important possible method for cross-cultural research which has seldom been applied – a learning paradigm. Many cultures lack codes (or a full elaboration of codes) for some domain. If an investigator has theories about that domain, instead of framing his hypotheses in terms of deficits in performance resulting from the lack of codes (with attendant problems in interpreting absolute differences between cultures), he can frame hypotheses in terms of *learning* the codes for that domain. Codes can then be taught – the input stimuli precisely specified and controlled within the context of the experiment in accordance with the relevant hypotheses. Since the variations are within culture, any general difficulty which the people may have with the learning task *per se* will not influence the conclusions. The Dani, with their two-term colour language, provided an ideal opportunity to teach colour names.

Three basic types of colour category were taught. In type 1, the physically central (i.e. of intermediate value in wavelength or brightness) chip of each category was the focal colour, and the flanking chips were drawn from the periphery of that basic name area. In type 2, central chips lay in the internominal areas between Berlin and Kay's best-example clusters; flanking chips, thus, tended to be drawn from the basic colour name areas on either side. Since two different basic colour name chips were included in the same type 2 categories, these categories 'violated' the presumed natural organization of the colour space. Type 3 categories were located in the same spaces as type 1; however, instead of occupying a central position, the focal colour was now to one side or the other of the three-chip category.

Subjects learned the colour names as a paired–associate task, a standard learning task in which subjects learn to give a specific response to each of a list of stimuli. In the present case, colours were the stimuli, and the same Dani word was the correct response for the three colours in a category. Finding suitable 'names' for the colours at first seemed a serious obstacle to the study since Dani would not learn nonsense words, even those constructed according to the rules of the Dani language. Here is an example of a case in which it was necessary to make the task culturally meaningful if it was to be performed at all. Eventually, it was found that there was a set of kin groups called *sibs* (something like clans) whose names were all well known to the Dani and which the Dani could readily learn as names for the colour categories. (*Sibs* did not have particular colours associated with them in Dani culture.) The task was described to each subject as learning a new language which the experimenter would teach him. The subject was told the 'names' for all of the colour chips, then presented with each chip and required to respond with a name. Chips were shown in a different random order each run, five runs a day, with feedback after each response, until the criterion of one perfect run was achieved.

The results of the learning supported Rosch's account of the role of focal colours in the learning of colour names. In the first place, the focal colours were learned with fewer errors than other colours, even when they were peripheral members of the categories. In the second place, the type 1 categories in which focal colours were physically central were learned as a set faster than either of the other types. The type 2 categories, which violated the presumed natural organization of the colour space, were the most difficult of all to learn. Thus, the idea of perceptually salient focal colours as 'natural prototypes' (rather like Platonic forms) for the development and learning of colour names was supported.

We have been speaking of focal colours as 'perceptually' salient. Is this just a metaphor, or is there an actual mechanism of colour vision which could be responsible for the salience? The answer is 'both'. There is a theory of colour perception (Hering, 1964) supported by both psychophysical and physiological data (De Valois and Jacobs, 1968; Hering, 1964), which claims that the primary colours red, green, yellow, and blue correspond to physiologically 'unique hues'. To get some notion of the meaning of unique hues, imagine that there are two 'opponent' colour-coding systems in the primate nervous system (in actual fact, in the lateral geniculate), each of which can respond positively or negatively. One system is responsive to red and green wavelengths of light, the other to yellow and blue wavelengths. Think of the probabilities of stimulation of each system distributed over wavelengths. There will be four points (particular wavelengths) at which one system responds uniquely; that is, a point at which the yellow–blue system is neutral and the red–green system positive, a point at which yellow–blue is neutral and red–green negative, and points at which red–green is neutral and yellow–blue positive and negative.

Do the wavelengths of the proposed four unique hue points correspond to 'focal' colours? They cannot correspond exactly because physiological and psychophysical visual research tends to be performed with monochromatic light (radiant light of a single wavelength), whereas Munsell chips are 'broadband' light (reflected light containing many wavelengths). However, the dominant wavelength of each Munsell chip has been calculated (Munsell Color Company, 1970). It is, in fact, the case that the dominant wavelengths of focal red, yellow, green, and blue correspond reasonably well to the proposed unique hue points. Evidence of an even more direct match of focal yellow, green, and blue to unique hue points (red was not tested) is provided in McDaniel (1972). While unique hue points are not presently an unchallenged physiological theory, and while the theory fails to account for the other four proposed basic chromatic colour terms (pink, orange, brown, and purple), it does lend considerable concreteness to the supposition that focal colours are physiologically, rather than mysteriously, salient.

At this point, the reader may well feel a sense of discontent. We appear to have concluded that colour terminology is entirely universal. But what of colour term boundaries, and what of the degree of elaboration of secondary colour terms? If colour terms make no difference to perception, cognitive processes, communication, or life, why should languages have any colour terms at all, much less differences in terms?

What are colour terms used for? One theory is that we have them in order to communicate about objects which are the same except for colour. All of the cultures which have fewer than the full complement of eleven basic terms are also technologically not at an industrial level. According to this theory, colour terms only become necessary for communication when manufactured objects can be produced in multitudes, and colouring agents are available for imparting different colours to the otherwise identical objects. A paradigmatic situation for using colour terms in this context would be to say 'Bring me the orange bowl', thereby specifying which of several, otherwise indistinguishable, bowls was desired.

But why should anyone want to specify the 'orange bowl'? Think about the contexts in which you actually pay attention to subtle differences in colour. They are probably activities such as deciding what articles of clothing to wear simultaneously, decorating houses, landscaping gardens, and producing and appreciating works of art.

There is one study which bears on this point. Greenfield and Childs (1974) studied the effect of knowing how to weave certain patterns in cloth upon pattern conception among the Zinancantecos of Chiapas, Mexico. The patterns consisted of simple groups of red and white threads. Subjects were asked to 'copy' the pattern by placing sticks into a frame. They were given their choice of various widths and colours of sticks. While some subjects used only the red and white sticks to copy the red and white patterns, others freely substituted pink for white and orange for red. A separate test determined that all subjects could discriminate the differences between red, orange, pink, and white sticks equally well. The important point for our argument is that it tended to be subjects who named the red, pink, orange, and white sticks with different names who adhered strictly to the red and white sticks for copying the patterns; subjects who used only a single term for white and pink and a single term for red and orange were the ones who tended to make the substitutions. It may well be that it is in little understood domains such as aesthetic judgment that the use of colour terms will be found to 'make a difference'. (Of course, the Zinancantecos who used differentiating terms may have done so because they were the more sensitive to aesthetic differences.) What difference terms do make can now be explored against our background of knowledge of what is universal in colour.

We began with the idea of colour as the ideal domain in which to demonstrate the effects of the lexicon of a language on cognition, thereby supporting a position of linguistic determinism. Instead, we have found that basic colour terminology appears to be universal and that perceptually salient focal colours appear to form natural prototypes for the development of colour terms. Contrary to initial ideas, the colour space appears to be a prime example of the influence of underlying perceptual–cognitive factors on linguistic categories.

Other natural categories

Is colour the only domain structured into 'natural categories'? It seems unlikely. Colour may, in fact, provide a better model for the nature of human categorizing than do the artificial concepts used by psychologists in concept formation research. In the first place, there are other domains in which perceptually salient natural prototypes appear to determine categories; geometric forms and facial expression of emotion are cases in point. In the second place, categories not based on biologically 'given' prototypes may also obey psychological laws for the perception and segmentation of experience, thereby yielding naturally structured categories.

That there is something particularly 'well formed' about certain forms, such as circles and squares, was long ago proposed by the Gestalt psychologists. Rosch (1973b) tested the hypothesis that such forms act as natural prototypes in the formation of form categories just as focal colours do for colour categories. The Dani also do not have a terminology for two-dimensional geometric forms, and some pilot studies showed that they neither possessed usable circumlocutions for referring to forms in a communication task nor did they tend to sort forms by form type. Thus, it was reasonable to teach Dani form concepts just as they had been taught colour concepts. The logic of the form learning experiment was the same as that of the colour learning. Circle, square, and equilateral triangle were taken as the presumed natural prototypes of three form categories. In the 'naturally structured' categories, these 'good forms' were physically central to a set of distortions (such as gaps in the form or lines changed to curves). In other categories, a distorted form was the central member, the good forms peripheral. The results mirrored those for colour. The good forms themselves were learned faster than the distorted forms, and the sets of forms in which the good forms were central were learned faster than sets in which they were peripheral. Furthermore, for the forms (though not for the colours), Dani were willing, at the conclusion of learning, to point to which stimulus they considered the best example of the name they had just learned. The good forms tended to be designated as the best examples even when they were actually peripheral to the set; it was as though subjects were trying to structure the categories around the good forms even when the actual sets were structured otherwise.

Facial expressions of emotion are a surprising addition to the class of natural categories. Not only were they once not considered universal; but there was considerable doubt that, even within one culture, emotion could be judged better than chance from the human face (Bruner and Tagiuri, 1954). As had been the case with colours, such judgments seemed to stem from the unsystematic employment of miscellaneous facial expressions in judgment experiments. Ekman (1972) claimed that there are six basic human emotions (happiness, sadness, anger, fear, surprise, and disgust) and that each is associated with a quite limited range of facial muscle movements constituting a pure expression of that emotion; other expressions tend to be blends of emotions, or ambiguous or nonemotional expressions which could not be expected to receive reliable judgments. When Ekman put together sets of pictures of pure expressions of the proposed basic emotions, he found that these pictures were judged correctly by Americans, Japanese, Brazilians, Chileans, and Argentinians. Furthermore, two preliterate New Guinea groups with minimal contact with Caucasian facial expression, the Fore and the Dani, were able to distinguish which of the expressions was meant on the basis of stories embodying the appropriate emotion. Like colour, universality was discovered in facial expressions of emotion only when an investigator thought to ask, not about all possible stimuli, but about the prototypes (best examples) of categories. As is the case for colour terms, there appears to be a residual function of emotion names themselves. In a communication task in which one subject attempted to communicate verbally to another which one of a set of pictures of faces was intended. Americans performed far better with pictures of the pure emotions than with ambiguous expressions; Dani, however, who lack a set of emotion terms, showed no difference in performance between the two types of pictures (Rosch, unpublished data).

It is unreasonable to expect that humans come equipped with natural prototypes in all domains. Dogs, vegetables, and Volkswagens, for example, are probably culturally relative. Yet such categories may also possess an 'internal structure' which renders them more similar to colour than to artificial categories. That is, the colour, form, and emotional expression categories were composed of a 'core meaning' (the clearest cases, best examples) of the category, 'surrounded' by other category members of decreasing similarity to the core meaning. Think about the common semantic category 'dog'. Which is a better example of your idea or image of what that word means (which is doggier?): a German Shepard or a Dachshund? Rosch (1973b) had college students rate members of a number of semantic categories as to their prototypicality and found high agreement in judgment between subjects. Evidence has since been obtained, in a variety of tasks, that such categories seem to be 'stored mentally', not as a list of logical criteria for category membership, but rather seem to be coded in a 'shorthand' form consisting of a fairly concrete representation of the prototype (for further explanation, see Heider, 1972a, and Rosch, 1973b).

If internal structure and prototypes, whether 'given' or learned, are important aspects in the learning and processing of semantic categories, the fact has implications for cross-cultural research. Present anthropological linguistic techniques (for example, componential analysis) tend to emphasize discovery of the minimal and most elegant, logical criteria needed to determine membership in, and distinctions between, classes. Analysis of the best-example prototypes of categories may provide us with a new, psychologically real, and fruitful basis for comparison of categories across cultures.

Even completely aside from internal structure, given any collection of stimuli or cultural environment, it is unreasonable to expect that categories will be formed randomly. For example, there are undoubtedly psychological rules for perceiving 'clusters' of stimuli and 'gaps' between stimuli. Such factors as frequency of particular objects, order of encounter with the objects, 'density' of nonidentical but similar stimuli, and the extent to which objects in one 'cluster' are distinctively different from objects in other 'clusters' are examples of the kinds of factors which might determine psychological grouping. Of course, categories of all types probably not only have labels, but also have some rationale which makes them not purely arbitrary but rather natural categories.

Conclusions

We began with the notion of linguistic relativity defined in terms of insurmountable differences in the world view of cultures brought about by differences in natural languages. Because of the variety of requirements for specificity and cross-cultural controls in testing such assertions, we were reduced to the far less sweeping claim that colour names affect some aspects of thought. However, we discovered that colours appeared to be a domain suited to demonstrate just the opposite of linguistic relativity, namely, the effect of the human perceptual system in determining linguistic categories. Very similar evidence exists in the domains of geometric form and emotion categories. Furthermore, psychological principles of categorization may apply to the formation of all categories, even in culturally relative domains.

At present, the Whorfian hypothesis not only does not appear to be empirically true in any major respect, but it no longer even seems profoundly and ineffably true. Why has it been so difficult to demonstrate effects of language on thought? Whorf referred to language as an instrument which 'dissects' and categorizes 'nature'. In the first part of the paper, we saw that it has not been established that the categorizations provided by the grammar of the language actually correspond to meaningful cognitive units. From the latter part of the chapter, we can now see that for the vocabulary of language, in and of itself, to be a moulder of thought, lexical dissections and categorizations of nature would have to be almost accidentally formed, rather as though some Johnny Appleseed had scattered named categories capriciously over the earth. In fact, the 'effects' of most lexical linguistic categories are probably inseparable from the effects of the factors which led initially to the formation and structuring of just those categories rather than some others. It would seem a far richer task for future research to investigate the entire complex of how languages, cultures, and individuals come, in the first place, to 'dissect', 'categorize', and 'name' nature in the various ways that they do.

Part VII

Imagery and Internal Representation

Part VII
Imagery and Mental Representation

Introduction to imagery and internal representation

A thought is generally interpreted as something expressed in words, and so it is natural to assume that its underlying representation must be in a verbal form. But words and propositions are not the only kinds of thing of which individuals are consciously aware when they are thinking. They also experience imagery; they 'see' pictures in their mind's eye with varying degrees of intensity. Do words and pictures exhaust the possible candidates for thought? The followers of Freud postulate unconscious determinants of thought, and even unconscious fantasy; and Chomsky has postulated very abstract structures in the mind which underlie the use of language and other cognitive operations. Traditionally, however, the main candidates have been words and images.

The topic of imagery has a long history, and the main concern of psychologists used to be to show in what way one individual differs from another with respect to its exercise. Large individual differences were first observed by Fechner (1860) and by Galton (1928). Galton found initially that scholars and scientists, when asked to form an image of their breakfast table, often failed to do so and even failed to understand the question – they attributed the capacity to form images in the mind's eye as a pure invention of poets. Later, however, other individuals experienced no difficulty: 'I can see my breakfast table or any equally familiar thing with my mind's eye quite as well in all particulars as I can do if the reality is before me.'

Another question which interested early investigators was whether individuals could tell the difference between a percept and a visual image. Perky (1910) asked her subjects to project the visual image of a banana on a screen. At the same time an assistant projected a very faint image of a banana on the screen, and gradually increased its intensity until the subjects reported that they had a good image. All twenty-eight subjects mistook the picture for their own image. This result has been partially replicated by Segal and Nathan (1964). But the main interest remained the question of individual differences, and a variety of ingenious techniques (e.g. Binet, 1894) were developed to investigate how the 'visualist' differed in his powers from the 'nonvisualist' (Woodworth, 1938, ch.

2). Much more recently some extreme, pathological cases of thinking in imagery alone have been recorded (Luria, 1969).

Imagery began to be investigated more systematically in the 1960s. Holt (1964) in his paper, 'Imagery: the return of the ostracized', pointed out a variety of situations in which individuals spontaneously reported the occurrence of imagery. These ranged from the practical experience of pilots, radar operators and astronauts to the clinical experience of the effects of hallucinogenic drugs. But there were two main differences in the way in which imagery came to be studied by psychologists. First, there was an interest, not so much in individual differences, but in the function of imagery, and whether it constituted an alternative code to the prevailing assumption of a verbal code. Second, the method of investigation changed radically; it no longer relied on introspective report, and it no longer even stressed conscious experience as a criterion. For example, Bower (1970) reported an experiment in which a series of pairs of objects (concrete words) had to be imagined under two conditions: either 'as far apart in the visual field as possible', or 'as vividly interacting with each other'. The latter condition produced more efficient learning. Paivio (1975) required his subjects to state which of two objects, e.g. 'whale' and 'mouse' was conceptually larger. Two main variables were involved: (a) the portrayed size of the two objects, and (b) whether they were represented pictorially, or in words (see figure 1).

The results showed that response was significantly faster to pictures than to words, and that pictorial size influenced reaction time. When there was incongruence between portrayed size and memory size, e.g. a small picture of a zebra, and a large picture of a lamp, a conflict was inferred by significantly slower reaction times. This effect was not found at all when the names of the two objects were printed in different size. Paivio inferred that response to pictorial stimuli involves visual analogue representations in long-term memory. These results were strengthened by a further experiment in which the subjects had to judge which object was further away. As predicted, the opposite results were obtained. It took longer to say that the pictorially large zebra was further away than the pictorially small lamp. In general, incongruent pictures facilitated performance because of the inverse relation between retinal size and distance.

Studies such as these suggest that visual imagery is an isomorphic analogue to perception. This assumption leads to a number of problems. As Pylyshyn (1975) points out, the postulation of a 'picture-in-the-head' does not suffice as a representation of cognitive internal representation; it merely implies that the representation is equivalent to a perceived datum. This, in turn, risks an infinite regress because it makes no claims about how such knowledge can be used. It comes close to the old idea of an 'homunculus'. 'We need to have some internal representation of the world in order to think about it. . . But if this internal representation is too similar to the world itself it cannot help us to apprehend it since it merely moves the same problem inside' (Pylyshyn, 1975).

However, as we shall see in the subsequent discussion of chess thought, imagery has a conceptual (as well as a perceptual) component. But to assert that imagery is not necessarily pictorial is still to evade the question of its conceptual status. Indeed, Shepard (1975), in discussing the theoretical implications of his research, proposes five negative criteria for the designation of internal representations. At least we can say that there is now cumulative evidence that internal representations are localized in the right hemisphere of the brain, just as analytic and verbal functions are localized in the left hemisphere. The reader is referred to Nebes (1974) for a review of this evidence, and to Kosslyn and Pomerantz (1977) for a vigorous defence of imagery against Pylyshyn's critique.

Figure 1. Examples of congruent (top of figure) and incongruent (bottom of figure) physical-size–memory-size relations between pictures (from Paivio, 1975)

Instead of trying to define imagery, it may be more profitable to consider what can be done with it. The reading we have selected by Shepard and Metzler describes an experiment which uses an ingenious technique for tracking the process of imagery when the subject is instructed to transform objects mentally in a variety of ways. The time required to recognize two perspective drawings of three dimensional 'nonsense objects' is shown to be a linearly increasing function of the angular difference in the portrayed orientation of the objects. A study by Shepard and Feng (cited in Shepard, 1975) provides further direct evidence that subjects do carry out particular operations on internal representations. The task was to transform mentally letters of the alphabet which were named but not presented as stimuli. For example, an instruction to 'reflect about the vertical (or horizontal) axis' of the letter N produces the configuration И, and an instruction to 'rotate it 90° to the left' produces the configuration Z. Both of these operations took (on average) about 2·00 to 2·38 seconds to perform. But an instruction to rotate the letter N 180° to the left took about 3·00 seconds, and an instruction 'to reflect it about the vertical and then about the horizontal axis' took about 4·00 seconds. The remarkable point is that these two latter instructions yield identical images to the original N. Shepard stresses the preliminary character of these data, but they suggest that the reaction times depend upon the particular trajectory of the subjects' internal processes, and not just on the relation between the initial and terminal states.

Do such mental operations have any limitations? One can imagine more complex operations in which the individual may fail to project his imagery. Geoffrey Hinton (personal communication), in analysing Shepard's rotation tasks with cubes, has pointed out one very interesting limitation. The reader may care to try Hinton's task. First imagine a cube standing flat upon a horizontal surface. Most people with any capacity for forming visual images have little difficulty with this task. Second, imagine a cube with one corner only touching the horizontal surface and the diametrically opposed corner vertically above it. This task is very much harder, but should you have succeeded, try now to indicate where the other corners of the cube are in relation to the two diametrically opposed ones. It is almost impossible unless you have considerable experience with cubes. Indeed, many subjects consider that there are only four other corners. The actual configuration is illustrated in figure 2(a). Hinton also observes that the effects of distorting the cube in such an orientation are relatively negligible, as figure 2(b) illustrates.

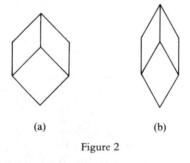

(a)   (b)

Figure 2

However, if the same distortion is made when the cubes are in their normal orientation, then a very marked contrast is apparent between them, as shown in figure 3.

Shepard's research on the mental rotation of objects is compelling evidence for the ways in which internal representations can be manipulated, but it could be argued that they are restricted and highly abstract. Fortunately, there is also a wealth of nonexperimental, 'real life', evidence for such processes. The reading we have selected by Oatley (specially written for this volume) records a variety of ways in which the Polynesians have used their world to navigate between islands without instrumentation. Such (so-called) primitive people are apparently able to accomplish accurate voyages by the use of an elegant system of 'dead reckoning'. They conceive of the boat as stationary with islands 'moving' past it, and the stars wheeling overhead. This internal representation plays a key role in their navigational system. According to Oatley, the natives do not think the islands really move during the course of a voyage, but they are insistent that, in order to navigate, the idea of a 'moving island' must be grasped. The most important aspect of the system (for our purposes) is that it is no mere visual image. It is a dynamic 'cognitive map', a representation of the world from which spatial inferences can be made. Internal representations of the world are often analogical, capturing certain key relations, and they may thus be readily modified as a result of intellectual processes. In this way, a representation may play a crucial part in thinking and problem solving.

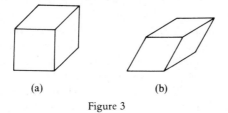

(a)   (b)

Figure 3

Certain intellectual games, such as chess and Go, provide an ideal tool for the study of representations in thinking because they combine a spatial component with an element of problem solving. Chess, in particular, is suitable for the study of nonverbal thought because of its extreme difficulty and the vast amount known about its theory. The psychology of master chess has been studied with the aid of introspection by Binet (1966) and by Cleveland (1907). There is a consensus of opinion that the master's representation of a chess position is based on 'dynamic perception', in terms of chess experience, rather than on the perception of proximal stimuli. Thus, Tarrasch (quoted by Binet) states: 'the player absorbed in the strategy of the game does not see a piece of wood with a horse's head but a piece that follows the course presented for the knight'. Similarly, in blindfold chess, Goetz (again quoted by Binet) reports: 'Thus, to the inner eye, a bishop is not a uniquely shaped piece, but an oblique force.' But is there any objective evidence for such subjective reports?

One source of evidence is the study of eye movements (see Introduction to Part I). However, a specific 'chess representation' has been systematically investigated by De Groot (1965, 1966). He exposed a chess position for five seconds, and then gave the subject time to concentrate on it with his eyes closed. The pieces are then removed from the board, and the subject attempts to replace them on their original squares. Any wrongly placed pieces are then removed, and the subject is invited to replace them. The results discriminated chess ability. Masters experienced little difficulty, but weaker players performed much less well. However, when the pieces do not constitute a position taken from a chess game, but are placed at random, there was no difference in performance between the two classes of player. It would seem that chess masters are able to extract information from a chess position with great rapidity, and encode it in terms of their knowledge. A similar organizational factor was observed by Eisenstadt and Kareev in Reading 33 (specially written for this volume) as a function of whether the position derives from the game of Go, or the much simpler Gomoku, which uses the same pieces but less complex rules. As they point out: 'Perceptual organization refers to internal representation, which can differ for different analyses of the same scene.' One of us (P.C.W., a chess player) experienced considerable difficulty in rapidly identifying the squares on the 9 × 9 Go board. For example, the square G6 on the Go board was repeatedly seen as the square f6 which seemed the square it 'ought to be' on the 8 × 8 chess board. The studies of De Groot and of Eisenstadt and Kareev, demonstrate that experience and ability in games like chess derive, not so much from calculating powers, but from a perceptual–organizational ability specific to the game in question. But it would obviously be untrue to suppose that chess players never calculate. Of course they do, but the point is to know when to calculate and what to calculate. This knowledge, which has been called 'positional instinct' is the internal representation of chess. And the disparity between these two modes of thought provides a crux for the designer of chess programs.

A consideration of chess programs raises two different questions: (1) Do they play chess in the same way that chess masters play chess?, and (2) Will they ever play chess as well as chess masters do? The answer to the first question is an unqualified 'no'. The answer to the second question arouses two sorts of prejudice. These range from the optimism of Simon (Simon and Newell, 1958) who predicted that within ten years a digital computer would be the World Champion 'unless the rules bar it from competition', to the claims of some members of the chess fraternity that a program will never defeat a master. At present the best programs are nowhere near master strength; they are weaker than a 'strong amateur' but they might well defeat the mere social player. Since this question arouses two opposite dogmatisms it is hardly profitable to pursue. The first question is more interesting.

All chess programs involve both some form of look-ahead ('tree-searching') procedure, and an 'evaluation function' i.e. a means of assessing an advantage such as a rook on the seventh rank. The necessity for an evaluation function, first pointed out by Shannon in 1950, becomes obvious when one considers that tree-searching alone would rapidly lead to an exponential explosion. Even if all games are restricted to forty moves, it has been estimated that the number of possible games is far more than the number of atoms in the universe. It is a popular misconception of the nonplayer to suppose that strength in chess is determined by the answer to the question: 'How many moves can you see ahead?' (The chess master, Reti (1923) replied: 'As a rule not a single one.')

Indeed, the mathematician, I. J. Good, has estimated that the average number of moves considered in each position by a chess master lies between 1·6 and 1·9. De Groot puts the figure at 1·48.

The designers of chess programs have concentrated on tree-searching procedures; apart from any merit such procedures may possess, they clearly do not play chess in the way in which a person is capable of playing chess. The Russian program, KAISSA (the current computer world champion) examined 2,877,000 positions before making its seventeenth move in a game against the collective readership of a Soviet newspaper. (It lost the game.) Similarly, the 'Advice-Taking Program' (Zobrist and Carlson, 1973) typically creates, weights and stores some 1,500 attack and counter-attack 'snapshots' before making a move. The idea is sensible. It is an attempt to make the program learn general principles, profit from its mistakes, and thus acquire some of the 'positional instinct' which we have seen underlies master performance. This program is unique in that it first calculates an internal representation of the position, then applies advice from its store of 'snapshots', and finally performs a look-ahead using 'snapshots' to evaluate board positions before reporting its move. But, at the time of writing, its performance has been very poor in computer chess tournaments.

Berliner (a former correspondence world champion), in Reading 34, points out several ways in which chess programs fall well below master chess standards. One of them is that anything that is not detectable at evaluation time does not exist as far as the program is concerned. This is illustrated in the following game between CHECKMO II and P.C.W. This particular program searches to a depth of six 'half-moves' (three for White and three for Black), and then performs an evaluation. After White's 8th move any reasonable club player would have found the elementary tactics by which Black wins an important pawn (see figure 4). But this manoeuvre occurs on Black's 11th move which exists at a depth of 8–ply (eight half-moves), and hence 'does not exist' for the program.

Figure 4. Position after 8. P–K4?? (a blunder)

White: CHECKMO II. Black: P.C.W. 1. P–Q4, N–KB3; 2. B–B4, P–KN3; 3. N–KB3, B–N2; 4. N–B3, P–Q4; 5. Q–Q3? (better is 5. Q–Q2), P–B3; 6. N–K5, QN–Q2; 7. NXN, BXN; 8. P–K4??, PXP; 9. NXP, NXN; 10. QXN, B–B4; 11. Q–B3, QXP; and wins easily.

Black obviously did not need to play particularly well; the program was a victim of its own limited vision. But, as Berliner points out, a master program needs to incorporate 'global goals' (strategy) if it is to make headway. What such a program will have to capture is the way in which heuristic rules, which provide the basis of the evaluation function, become transformed into the chess knowledge which enables a master to grasp the salient features and potentialities of a position.

Existing programs are based on the evaluation of tactics (sequences of forcing moves) rather than strategy. A former world champion, Emanuel Lasker (1932), describes the difference between the two:

The methods followed in the analysis of a given position by combination [tactics] and by the creation of plans [strategy] are differentiated by the direction of the underlying thought. . . In looking for a combination the given position is the essential thing, in the conceiving of plans the intended position is the root of my thinking. When following the former process I seek to find out whether among the positions that I can derive from the present position by a succession of forceful moves I may not be able to detect one desirable to me and to envisage it; with the latter process I hope to be able to attain a position that I have in mind and try to find out whether ways leading up to that conceived position may not start from the given position.

It is precisely this capacity to conceive positions, as opposed to the evaluation of forceful moves, which would seem to be lacking in existing programs. As Levy (1976) has put it:

I have often asked chess programmers the question, 'If I gave you a routine that played perfect tactical chess, that saw every trick and every combination, that never lost material through a trap and never overlooked a possibility to win material by force, how would you set about writing a master strength chess program?' So far no-one has yet been able to offer me any kind of answer.

Although most programs seem rather vulnerable in the end-game, KAISSA is an exception, and has even contributed to the theory of this most difficult part of the game. Authorities, such as Botvinnik, have been uncertain about the theoretical status of the notorious ending, Queen and Knight's pawn versus Queen, but (according to Levy) KAISSA plays it perfectly. When it reaches a won position it prints out: 'I will win in 34 moves', and if its human opponent makes an error it prints out: 'That was a mistake – now I shall win in 17 moves.' Its virtuosity in the ending, compared with its relative weakness in the opening and middle-game, is presumably due to the fact that the very small number of pieces left on the board renders tree-searching a more effective procedure.

The aesthetics of chess have even been discerned in KAISSA's end-game play. This is all the more remarkable when one realizes that computers play, not only poor chess, but also dull chess. According to Levy (1976), Grandmaster Bronstein reached the above ending in a tournament, and at the second adjournment telephoned the KAISSA programmers for the appropriate procedure for his position. 'And they gave me a plan that was so beautiful I would never have found it myself.' Unfortunately, his opponent soon went wrong and Bronstein won. It was only later that it was discovered that at the critical variation the program had made a mistake, overlooking a stalemate possibility. 'But probably there is still a win', Bronstein said a few months later.

Goethe called chess the touchstone of the intellect. But nonplayers may be forgiven for deeming it 'artificial' like some other kinds of artistic expression in which abstract patterns predominate (e.g. music, dance). A game which has been so intensively investigated, but in which counter-examples often refute general principles, and in which master play eludes a verbal prescription, is a convincing testimony to the reality of internal representations.

31. Mental rotation of three-dimensional objects[1]

R. N. Shepard and J. Metzler

Human subjects are often able to determine that two two-dimensional pictures portray objects of the same three-dimensional shape even though the objects are depicted in very different orientations. The experiment reported here was designed to measure the time that subjects require to determine such identity of shape as a function of the angular difference in the portrayed orientations of the two three-dimensional objects.

This angular difference was produced either by a rigid rotation of one of two identical pictures in its own picture plane or by a much more complex, nonrigid transformation, of one of the pictures, that corresponds to a (rigid) rotation of the three-dimensional object in depth.

This reaction time is found (i) to increase linearly with the angular difference in portrayed orientation and (ii) to be no longer for a rotation in depth than for a rotation merely in the picture plane. These findings appear to place rather severe constraints on possible explanations of how subjects go about determining identity of shape of differently oriented objects. They are, however, consistent with an explanation suggested by the subjects themselves. Although intro-spective reports must be interpreted with caution, all subjects claimed (i) that to make the required comparison they first had to imagine one object as rotated into the same orientation as the other and that they could carry out this 'mental rotation' at no greater than a certain limiting rate; and (ii) that, since they perceived the two-dimensional pictures as objects in three-dimensional space, they could imagine the rotation around whichever axis was required with equal ease.

In the experiment each of eight adult subjects was presented with 1,600 pairs of perspective line drawings. For each pair the subject was asked to pull a right-hand lever as soon as he determined that the two drawings portrayed objects that were congruent with respect to three-dimensional shape and to pull a left-hand lever as soon as he determined that the two drawings depicted objects

[1] This paper first appeared in *Science*, **171** (1971), 701–3. © 1971 by the American Association for the Advancement of Science.

of different three-dimensional shapes. According to a random sequence, in half of the pairs (the 'same' pairs) the two objects could be rotated into congruence with each other (as in figure 1(A) and (B)) and in the other half (the 'different' pairs) the two objects differed by a reflection as well as a rotation and could not be rotated into congruence (as in figure (C)).

The choice of objects that were mirror images or 'isomers' of each other for the 'different' pairs was intended to prevent subjects from discovering some distinctive features possessed by only one of the two objects and thereby reaching a decision of noncongruence without actually having to carry out any mental rotation. As a further precaution, the ten different three-dimensional objects depicted in the various perspective drawings were chosen to be relatively unfamiliar and meaningless in overall three-dimensional shape.

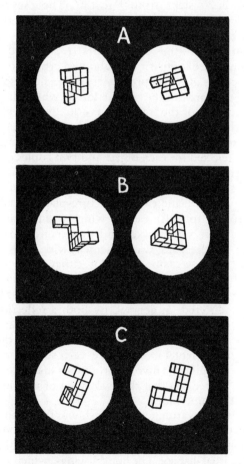

Figure 1. Examples of pairs of perspective line drawings presented to the subjects. (A) A 'same' pair. which differs by an 80° rotation in the picture plane; (B) a 'same' pair which differs by an 80° rotation in depth; and (C) a 'different' pair, which cannot be brought into congruence by *any* rotation.

Each object consisted of ten solid cubes attached face-to-face to form a rigid armlike structure with exactly three right-angled 'elbows' (see figure 1). The set of all ten shapes included two subsets of five: within either subset, no shape could be transformed into itself or any other by any reflection or rotation (short of 360°). However, each shape in either subset was the mirror image of one shape in the other subset, as required for the construction of the 'different' pairs.

For each of the ten objects, eighteen different perspective projections – corresponding to one complete turn around the vertical axis by 20° steps – were generated by digital computer and associated graphical output. Seven of the eighteen perspective views of each object were then selected so as (i) to avoid any views in which some part of the object was wholly occluded by another part and yet (ii) to permit the construction of two pairs that differed in orientation by each possible angle, in 20° steps, from 0° to 180°. These seventy line drawings were then reproduced by photo-offset process and were attached to cards in pairs for presentation to the subjects.

Half of the 'same' pairs (the 'depth' pairs) represented two objects that differed by some multiple of a 20° rotation about a vertical axis (figure 1(B)). For each of these pairs, copies of two appropriately different perspective views were simply attached to the cards in the orientation in which they were originally generated. The other half of the 'same' pairs (the 'picture-plane' pairs) represented two objects that differed by some multiple of a 20° rotation in the plane of the drawings themselves (figure 1(A)). For each of these, one of the seven perspective views was selected for each object and two copies of this picture were attached to the card in appropriately different orientations. Altogether, the 1,600 pairs presented to each subject included 800 'same' pairs which consisted of 400 unique pairs (twenty 'depth' and twenty 'picture-plane' pairs at each of the angular differences from 0° to 180°), each of which was presented twice. The remaining 800 pairs, randomly intermixed with these, consisted of 400 unique, 'different' pairs each of which (again) was presented twice. Each of these 'different' pairs corresponded to one 'same' pair (of either the 'depth' or 'picture-plane' variety) in which, however, one of the three-dimensional objects had been reflected about some plane in three-dimensional space. Thus the two objects in each 'different' pair differed, in general, by both a reflection and a rotation.

The 1,600 pairs were grouped into blocks of not more than 200 and presented over eight to ten one-hour sessions (depending upon the subject). Also, although it is only of incidental interest here, each such block of presentations was either 'pure', in that all pairs involved rotations of the same type ('depth' or 'picture-plane'), or 'mixed', in that the two types of rotation were randomly intermixed within the same block.

Each trial began with a warning tone, which was followed half a second later by the presentation of a stimulus pair and the simultaneous onset of a timer. The lever-pulling response stopped the timer, recorded the subject's reaction time and terminated the visual display. The line drawings, which averaged between 4 and 5 cm in maximum linear extent, appeared at a viewing distance of about 60 cm. They were positioned, with a centre-to-centre spacing that subtended a visual angle of 9°, in two circular apertures in a vertical black surface (see figure 1(A)–(C)).

The subjects were instructed to respond as quickly as possible while keeping errors to a minimum. On the average only 3·2 per cent of the responses were incorrect (ranging from 0·6 to 5·7 per cent for individual subjects). The reaction-time data presented below include only the 96·8 per cent correct responses. However, the data for the incorrect responses exhibit a similar pattern.

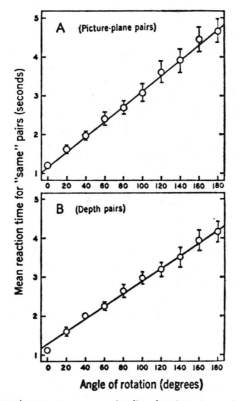

Figure 2. Mean reaction times to two perspective line drawings portraying objects of the same three-dimensional shape. Times are plotted as a function of angular difference in portrayed orientation: (A) for pairs differing by a rotation in the picture plane only; and (B) for pairs differing by a rotation in depth (The centres of the circles indicate the means and, when they extend far enough to show outside these circles, the vertical bars around each circle indicate a conservative estimate of the standard error of that mean based on the distribution of the eight component means contributed by the individual subjects)

In figure 2, the overall means of the reaction times as a function of angular difference in orientation for all correct (right-hand) responses to 'same' pairs are plotted separately for the pairs differing by a rotation in the picture plane (figure 2(A)) and for the pairs differing by a rotation in depth (figure 2(B)). In both cases, reaction time is a strikingly linear function of the angular difference between the two three-dimensional objects portrayed. The mean reaction times for individual subjects increased from a value of about 1 second at 0° of rotation for all subjects to values ranging from 4–6 seconds at 180° of rotation, depending upon the particular individual. Moreover, despite such variations in slope, the *linearity* of the function is clearly evident when the data are plotted separately for individual three-dimensional objects or for individual subjects. Polynomial regression lines were computed separately for each subject under each type of rotation. In all sixteen cases the functions were found to have a highly significant linear component ($p < 0.001$) when tested against deviations from linearity. No significant quadratic or higher-order effects were found ($p < 0.05$, in all cases).

The angle through which different three-dimensional shapes must be rotated to achieve congruence is not, of course, defined. Therefore, a function like those plotted in figure 2 cannot be constructed in any straightforward manner for the 'different' pairs. The *overall* mean reaction time for these pairs was found, however, to be 3·8 seconds – nearly a second longer than the corresponding overall means for the 'same' pairs. (In the postexperimental interview, the subjects typically reported that they attempted to rotate one end of one object into congruence with the corresponding end of the other object; they discovered that the two objects were *different* when, after this 'rotation', the two free ends still remained noncongruent.)

Not only are the two functions shown in figure 2 both linear but they are very similar to each other with respect to intercept and slope. Indeed, for the larger angular differences the reaction times were, if anything, somewhat shorter for rotation in depth than for rotation in the picture plane. However, since this small difference is either absent or reversed in four of the eight subjects, it is of doubtful significance. The determination of identity of shape may therefore be based, in both cases, upon a process of the same general kind. If we can describe this process as some sort of 'mental rotation in three-dimensional space', then the slope of the obtained functions indicates that the average rate at which these particular objects can be thus 'rotated' is roughly 60° per second.

Of course the plotted reaction times necessarily include any times taken by the subjects to decide how to process the pictures in each presented pair as well as the time taken actually to carry out the process, once it was chosen. However, even for these highly practised subjects, the reaction times were still linear and were no more than 20 per cent lower in the 'pure' blocks of presentations (in which the subjects knew both the axis and the direction of the required rotation in advance of each presentation) than in the 'mixed' blocks (in which the axis of rotation was unpredictable). Tentatively, this suggests that 80 per cent of a typical one of these reaction times may represent some such process as 'mental rotation' itself, rather than a preliminary process of preparation or search. Nevertheless, in further research now underway, we are seeking clarification of this point and others.

32. Inference, navigation, and cognitive maps[1]

Keith G. Oatley

It was probably about 3,500 years ago that the islands of the Pacific Ocean began to be explored and settled (Emory, 1959). By 1,000 years ago, islands far away from the central groups, Hawaii to the north, Easter Island to the east, and New Zealand to the south-west were peopled by Polynesians. To reach these out-lying islands required long open sea voyages of 1,000 to 2,000 miles.

Navigation of all kinds is a complex cognitive skill, but as practised by the seafarers of Oceania, it is a skill which is entirely mental and perceptual, using no instruments of any kind. It is based on processes of inference within the structure of a cognitive map.

In contrast to the Polynesian colonizations, the period of European world exploration began only during the Renaissance (see e.g. Taylor, 1971). From our viewpoint it was Captain Cook in an era of developing navigational instrumen-tation who opened up the Pacific only about 200 years ago. To Europeans it seemed unthinkable that Polynesians who were without writing, and who had only a stone age technology could have deliberately explored and colonized such a vast area. . . . One type of theory, widely espoused until recently, was that Polynesian voyages were accidental one-way drifts by coastal fisherman blown helplessly out to sea (e.g. Sharp, 1964). But recently, adding to the archaeolo-gical evidence of the dates and directions of colonization, two new kinds of evidence have appeared in the literature. One is a computer simulation of drift voyages in the Pacific made on the basis of statistics of winds and currents throughout the area at different times of year (Levison, Ward, and Webb, 1973). This work alone makes it highly unlikely that the major voyages could have been made by drifting. Secondly, various accounts have appeared, particularly Gladwin (1970) and Lewis (1972), of the surviving oral traditions and practices of indigenous Pacific Ocean seafarers. These methods, which are of considerable psychological interest, are capable of supporting deliberate exploration, as well as long sea voyages between known islands. The conclusion that these methods, practised entirely without instruments of any kind, were superior to anything

[1] This paper has been specially written for this volume.

developed elsewhere in the world (until recently) is a matter of some surprise to the Eurocentric mind.

In this paper I shall describe some of the inferential processes of human navigation (particularly navigation without instruments) and in so doing try to explore some of the structure of spatial reasoning.

Spatial reasoning is an activity that Helmholtz (1866) called unconscious inference. It also seems to be the basis of many perceptual processes, locomotor activities and motor skills. Spatial inference even seems to be a preferred mode into which the human mind casts all kinds of conceptual problems in order to make them tractable and transparent. From the rather mystical propositions of Pythagoras, that proportions somehow activate the universe, through the Renaissance theories of art, architecture, and magic, one can range to the adage that a picture is worth a thousand words, or the way in which in the natural sciences people try to cast concepts and problems into spatial forms, so that the functional relationships of physical laws are expressed typically in terms of spatial relationships.

Navigation out of sight of land is just one form of analogical reasoning in a spatial frame. Part of its interest is that it seems very basic to spatial thinking, and both the objectives and the components of the task seem fairly clear (even though its detailed mental mechanisms might not be). To reason within a spatial model or analogue seems to involve the following: (a) employing a mental model in which elements, relationships and processes of the task are represented; (b) setting up, or recognizing, correspondences between 'real world' cues, such as objects or places, and their symbolic equivalents in the map or model; (c) using the map or model to make inferences; and (d) on the basis of these inferences acting appropriately in the real world.

These processes are not dissimilar to Craik's (1943) propositions on the nature of thought in general. In the case of navigation the mental model can be called a cognitive map, and this map is, among other things, a theory about the traveller's trajectory and relation to observable and invisible elements of the navigational task.

Elements in navigation

Expanding somewhat on the above, and in the particular context of the spatial thinking required for navigation out of sight of known landmarks, the following seem to be some of the elements of the task.

(1) The traveller locates his or her current position on the earth's surface symbolically within the cognitive map. There is, in other words, some concept of 'here' and its relation to other places. One does not, in the words of a well-known mountaineering joke announce after considering the situation intently that 'we must be on that mountain over there'. The current position can take various forms however: simply a starting point, a home base, or some more remote point on a journey related within the map to other known places.

(2) A traveller must identify within the map a destination, or if exploring, simply a direction of travel.

(3) Again within the map the traveller must compare the necessary direction of travel toward the destination with the reference orientation of the map, if any.

(4) The next task is to start travelling over the earth's surface in a direction corresponding to the required heading within the map. For efficiency this requires (a) being able to travel in a straight line, and (b) orienting this straight path to some external reference direction. Clearly, if the map and the external world can be assigned the same reference direction, the task is easier. North is a standard reference direction for most modern navigation. This was not always so. Though the phrase 'to orient oneself' is a relatively recent usage, it seems that the rising of the sun in the east defined a basic reference direction before the introduction of the magnetic compass.

(5) The traveller then travels an appropriate distance estimated from the map. Then, because errors of estimation or execution are likely to have intruded, he or she must look for signs of the destination. If the voyage is successful and such signs are discerned, the course can be altered towards the destination if necessary. From this point, navigation can be more 'direct' rather than within the map.

(6) During the voyage the estimated distance and heading are conceptualized as movement, or change of position, within the map, so that at any time the traveller can estimate distance and direction to known points such as the starting point.

This structure and its psychological implications can best be explored by considering several different navigational systems, formal and informal, instrumental, and non-instrumental.

Informal navigation within a cognitive map

This kind of navigation is well illustrated by a person travelling in an unknown town. Assuming the traveller has no external map, and disregarding for the moment the presence of landmarks and constraining pathways (like roads), the traveller will be able to retain a sense of direction, and keep heading in a general direction irrespective of twists and turns. He or she will be able to make a circular tour of some kind, and furthermore be able to infer continually the approximate direction and distance of the starting point. This intuitive sense of direction is a basis for most navigational systems. Elaborations either by instruments or cues from the outside world, are typically made to supplement the ability to keep travelling in a straight line. This and the accompanying ability to update one's position within the cognitive map while travelling seem to be part of our basic psychological equipment.

An experimental demonstration of this ability was made by Worchel (1951). Subjects were required to walk blindfolded in a triangular path. They were either led along one side (the hypotenuse), or along the other two sides of right-angled isosceles triangles of different sizes, and their task was to walk unaided and without any external cues back to their starting point. Sighted (but blindfolded) subjects were able to do this to an accuracy of about 15 per cent of the total path length of the triangle.

One interesting result of this experiment was that it made little difference to their accuracy whether subjects were led along two sides of the triangle and had to make their own way back along the hypotenuse, or whether they were led along the hypotenuse and had to walk back along the other two sides, making a right-angled turn at the appropriate point. Evidently, since the task in both cases involves keeping the same track of one's paths, it makes little difference to accuracy whether the right-angled turn is made under guidance or not.

A second result was that blind subjects (who were also blindfolded) did considerably worse at this task than sighted (but blindfolded) subjects. Blind people typically do worse on spatial conceptualization tasks. Counter-intuitive as this may seem if one considers that blind people have a lot of practice at finding their way about without being able to see, it seems that the process of seeing is intimately connected with spatial conceptualization. Perhaps even spatial conceptualization is part of the visual process. In this case the idea of reasoning spatially within a cognitive map is an apt metaphor: there may be something characteristic about 'seeing' spatial interrelationships.

Formal navigation: dead reckoning

The term 'dead reckoning' means deduced reckoning, and is the process whereby a navigator keeps an account of a ship's position by drawing with a pencil and ruler a scaled picture of the ship's track on a nautical chart. It is, in other words, exactly like the process of keeping an intuitive track of one's path as in Worchel's experiment, but with the account of one's track externalized on to a paper map.

A navigator using this method need make no explicit calculations, but simply lays out angles and scaled down distances. If no allowances have to be made for drifts and currents (unfortunately a rare situation) the process is both practically and conceptually straightforward. All that is necessary is for a record to be kept of distances travelled by the ship on various headings. These records, scaled and drawn on to the chart in sequence, give a direct estimate of the ship's current position. The process of 'deducing' the current position from the data of distances and headings is carried out simply by mapping the course travelled on to a smaller-scale version of a similiar two-dimensional space, in which the same logic of spatial relationships is maintained.

It is tempting to think that the processes of spatial inference, as represented in the informal version of the dead reckoning task, is somehow basic to mental functioning, and different from (say) syllogistic reasoning. (Similar cases for analogical reasoning being different from purely verbal or logical reasoning have been made elsewhere, e.g. by Sloman, 1971.)

The unfortunate fact from the analytical point of view is that though we can give an account of spatial intuitions and inferences, and even gain a strong impression of their importance, it is not easy to give a formal account of how they are carried out. The system of formal dead reckoning navigation though it fulfils the same task, and utilizes the same information, does not constitute such an account. Though comparison with drawing lines on an external map makes clearer the elements of the task, we presumably do not wish to argue that spatial inferences within mental structures take place on some kind of two-dimensional sheet laid out in the brain.

Components of the process do become clearer. The ship's log, trailed in the water to give a running estimate of distance travelled, is the analogue of the traveller's necessary ability to judge how far he or she has gone. The compass provides an orientation frame relating both to chart and the outside world, and we find in noninstrumental navigation similar orientation frames. Universally, in any reasonably developed system there are methods for maintaining constant headings, the picking up of cues from natural phenomena (e.g. wind and wave directions, directions of celestial bodies), or even the deliberate creation of such cues. For instance, to walk in Indian file is to have a minimum of three people walking in a straight line so that the one at the back can sight along the other two and shout directions to the one at the front if a deviation from course occurs (Gatty, 1958).

Formal celestial navigation

The development of celestial navigation accompanied European world exploration. One way of thinking about the method is that it involves (a) measuring the angle of elevation above the horizon of two celestial bodies (stars, planets, moon or sun) whose positions relative to earth at the moment of observation are known, (b) making some trigonometric calculations from these measured angles, and (c) drawing two lines on a map in positions derived from these calculations, and reckoning the ship's position as the point at which the lines cross. The method involves a conceptualization of a spherical earth at the centre of a larger rotating celestial sphere on the surface of which the stars are fixed, and on which the sun, moon and planets move rather slowly. It also involves very accurate instruments, such as chronometers and sextants, carefully compiled tables of the positions of celestial bodies, and rather elaborate formulae for how the position lines drawn on to the chart are to be inferred from the sextant sights, chronometer and table readings.

In the development of celestial navigational practice we see a typical course of Western thought, with instrumentation based on the latest technology (navigation nowadays being carried out by computers and satellites). Even from its beginnings, chronometry involved the use of an externalized model of the rotation of the earth (the clock). The taking of sights required accurately machined sextants, and the inferences as to how the ship's position related to the cues, or data of the instrument and table readings, needed a quite elaborate theory of spherical trigonometry. This theory expressed the spatial relationships of points on the earth's surface to the positions of heavenly bodies.

The flavour of the method can be grasped by imagining oneself standing on a beach in (say) the Scilly Islands, and measuring with a sextant the angle of the sun above the horizon at local noon, at the time of the vernal or autumnal equinox. The sextant reading would be about 40°, and from this the latitude can be calculated by subtracting the reading from 90°. This allows one to infer that one's position is somewhere along an east–west line on the chart at 50° north latitude. A further line, crossing this latitude line, is needed to fix the positon, and clearly at other times (with the observation of other celestial bodies) further elements enter into the calculations.

In normal practice dead reckoning is carried out between the taking of celestial sights. But the beauty of celestial navigation is that it enables one to establish one's position anywhere on the earth's surface to an accuracy of a mile or so. (Even where no sea horizon is visible sextants can be made with internal artificial horizons consisting of a small quantity of liquid.)

Although there is some suggestion (e.g. Matthews, 1951) that pigeons use information from the height of the sun, and various indications that early seafarers guaged the height of heavenly bodies as part of their navigational practice, the complete theory of celestial navigation is quite far from the main structure of almost all noninstrumental navigational practices, which are based on dead reckoning.

Formal navigation: Indigenous systems in Oceania

Celestial navigation capitalized on the European virtues of mathematical theory and on instruments of high technological sophistication. In contrast, navigation in Oceania emphasized the deliberate refinement of people's intuitive sense of direction and the learning of direct perceptual cues from the natural environment. For the seaman of Oceania, making a voyage is conceptualized as being within a pattern of islands, the positions of which are represented in his cognitive map. While travelling he thinks of himself as the fixed centre of two moving frames of reference. One frame is the pattern of invisible islands which moves past him at the same speed as his craft through the water, but in the opposite direction. The other frame which provides the main anchoring for his own orientation frame, is the pattern of stars which wheels overhead from east to west.

Figure 1 is an attempt to depict this conceptual structure as described by Gladwin (1970) for Caroline Island navigational practice. The boat, an outrigger sailing canoe, is stationary in the centre, heading in this imaginary voyage in a north-easterly direction, conceptualized in the system as being towards the rising point of the star Vega. Over the period of the voyage, the islands in the cognitive map are thought of as moving with respect to the vessel almost as if they are on a conveyor belt. Throughout the voyage one particular island, off to one side of the ship's track and well beyond the horizon, is used as a reference, and continually kept in mind. As the voyage proceeds this reference, or Etak island, moves successively under (in figure 1) the setting positions of Vega, the

Pliades and Aldebaran. Thus the navigator sees his task partly as the problem of keeping a straight course towards the rising point of Vega. The course is divided up into sections corresponding to the Etak island coming to lie under the setting positions of a succession of stars. The task is somewhat like walking in a straight line between two chairs in a large room with one's eyes shut, while continually pointing to a third chair off to one side of the path. In this way, by a process of continuous mental triangulation the voyager knows his position within the cognitive map. The voyage depicted in figure 1 is between imaginary islands. For an illustration of a real voyage in the Carolines see Alkire (1970) or Oatley, (1974).

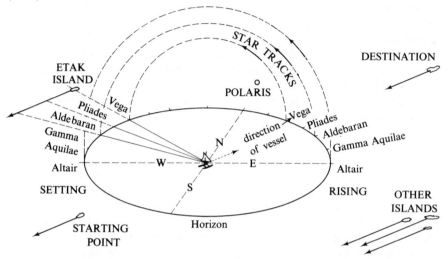

Figure 1. Pictorial representation of the Carolinian voyager's articulation of the moving spatial frames of islands and stars during an (imaginary) voyage

I will now consider in more detail some of the elements in the Carolinian system, relating them to the earlier section on 'Elements in navigation'.

(1) The cognitive map

A competent navigator will know the positions of perhaps 50 to 100 islands in his archipelago, the courses in terms of star rising or setting points between each pair, and sailing directions including information about currents, sea marks, and the characteristics of destination islands for each voyage. Tupaia, the exiled navigator-chief whom Captain Cook took aboard the *Endeavour* in 1769 on his visit to Tahiti, knew of all the major island groups in Polynesia, excluding Hawaii and New Zealand. His geographical knowledge extended from the Marquesas in the east to Fiji in the west, a span of some 2,600 miles, and the map he helped Cook to draw included seventy-four islands (see Beaglehole, 1955). The area of geographical knowledge of present-day Carolinian navigators is comparable, but not so extensive. They are one of the few surviving groups who still practise the navigational skills. With the decline of voyaging the amount of geographical knowledge in the oral traditions of island navigational schools has presumably declined.

Part of the extensive and exacting apprenticeship of a navigator involves learning this information. He would be helped by instructional charts made with pebbles on the sand, in the Marshall Islands by charts made out of sticks, and perhaps most interestingly by mnemonics. These take various forms, one of which, described by Riesenberg (1972) involves the projection of a pattern of (diamond shaped) trigger fish lying in a row. Islands are seen as located at some of the corners of the fish. This device imposes a memorable symmetrical arrangement on a pattern of islands, and the device recalls the patterns 'projected' on to stellar constellations in early European astronomy. The existence in navigational lore of 'sea life', in which phenomena such as 'two sooty terns making cries', are said to be observed at particular places on the sea (even when they could evidently have no such fixed existence) may be related to the mnemonic devices, for instance as dummy positions which occupy empty nodes of mnemonic projection patterns.

(2, 3) Destinations, Courses and Distances

The major problems here are of defining within the map a system of directions. As mentioned above, the direction frame is given by a 'compass' of rising and setting positions of stars, and the Carolinian version, described by Goodenough (1953), is shown as figure 2. As in the Western mariners' compass there are thirty-two principal points, but here the intervals are somewhat unequal. Whether on a voyage any particular star is visible is not important, as the compass is mainly a conceptual one, which also has the advantage of being coordinated with the external cues of real stars rising or setting. All bearings, headings, and directions are thought of in terms of this star compass. Within the map all the islands need to be mentally triangulated with one another, so that the navigator has a spatial conception of their positions, and the relative bearings are labelled by appropriate star directions. In an entirely oral tradition this clearly serves an important function of giving a fixed form to the knowledge in the cognitive map of the island pattern. Distances in the map, and in sailing, are conceptualized in terms of times required for making the voyage.

(4) Making a voyage on a specific course

Navigators basically use all the possible types of information available to allow them to sail straight on given courses. The star compass defines the principal directions, and when visible, stars are cues used for orientation. In the Carolines, between about 5° and 10° north of the equator, stars rise almost vertically, and hence the rising or setting points can be estimated quite accurately up to a couple of hours after or before the actual rising or setting. Moreover navigators know the whole succession of stars rising and setting in the same directions. Even if only a small patch of sky is visible, a group of stars, or, during the day, the sun, is sufficient to anchor the orientation frame. This means that the navigator needs to have a good Gestalt conceptualization of the whole moving structure of the heavenly bodies across the sky. Presumably part of the utility of conceptualizing the craft as stationary during a voyage, is that star and sun movements are the same everywhere in the archipelago, and the important thing is to have a concept of them, defining a set of fixed directions despite their daily movements.

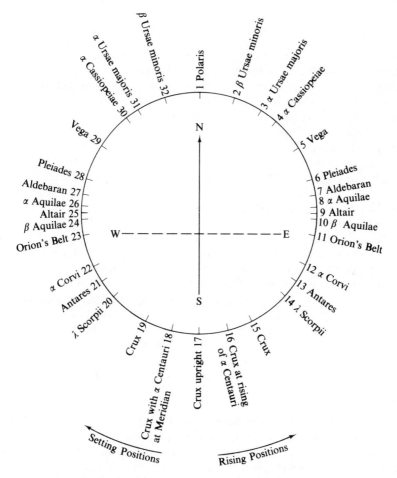

Figure 2. The Carolinian star compass (after Goodenough, 1953)

While voyaging, cues which have relative rather than absolute stability are also used. In particular the boat is sailed with a constant orientation to wind and waves, both of which are felt and so are equally useful at night. There are several types of swells which navigators can discriminate. As well as the waves due to the local wind, one useful cue often available is a low frequency swell set up by trade winds in a distant part of the ocean. Learning to perceive these swells is evidently quite a difficult matter.

Using the various cues to keep the orientation frame stable, navigators contrive to steer courses with an accuracy which compares very favourably with that achieved in small boats steered by compass, Thus even with varying winds and currents Carolinian navigators sail with confidence on courses where the landfall target subtends as little as 5°–7° from this starting point.

(5, 6) Estimation of position and making landfall

As described above, the current position along the course is conceptualized principally in relation to a reference or Etak island. A recommended Etak is given in the sailing directions for each voyage. The development of the skill of knowing one's bearing to an invisible point to one side of the course seems characteristic of navigation in Oceania. For instance during his voyage on Cook's *Endeavour*, Tupaia was at any time able to point (correctly) in the direction of Tahiti.

Among other things, the system of continuous Etak triangulation, allows the navigator to guage when he has arrived in the vicinity of his landfall, where a new set of cues become important, namely those for detecting the presence of land. The visual sighting range of atolls is about 10 miles, but this is reliably extended to about 20 miles by the predictable behaviour of certain birds which fly off the islands at dawn to go and fish, and fly straight back again at dusk. So a voyager, thinking himself to be within a 20-mile range of his destination, might heave to until dawn or dusk to look for these birds. Other indications of land are reflections on the underside of clouds, a slight slowing in the drift of a cloud as it passes over the convection current above an island, reflections and refractions of wave patterns around islands, and patterns of phosphoresence seen deep in the water at night. These and other cues which extend the visual sighting range clearly both expand the landfall target, and allow course to be altered appropriately when land is near.

A few conclusions

It is important to understand that though the term 'cognitive map' is used here, the structure of spatial inference, used by the navigators of Oceania, is not a static one, as in a paper map. Rather it is a dynamic one which continuously relates the navigator's position to the moving celestial frame wheeling overhead, and to the pattern of islands sweeping slowly past as the voyage proceeds. 'Of course,' say the navigators, 'the islands don't really move.' But they are insistent that unless one grasps the concept of the islands moving one would be hopelessly lost. This highlights the sense in which the navigator's cognitive map is a process, not just a picture, another spatial arrangement, from which inferences can be drawn. It also, perhaps, is the reason why, although externalized maplike artifacts are used in teaching navigators, they are not taken to sea.

There now seems to be little doubt that, armed with this sophisticated system of dead (deduced) reckoning navigation, with very efficient fore and aft rigged sailing craft, and the means for provisioning them for long voyages, the Pacific Island navigators were able deliberately to explore and colonize Oceania, continually compiling new sailing directions into their oral traditions and extending their cognitive maps as they did so.

In other areas of the world, e.g. among desert nomads, American Indians, and Australian Aboriginals, there have also been found navigation traditions, or at least the remnants of them, which, although possibly less elaborate than these of Oceania, similarly rely on cognitive maps and cues (particularly of direction) derived from natural phenomena. It also seems sensible to think of navigational abilities of birds and animals in similar terms.

Even for the Westerner living in a populated environment it is possible to practise and extend some of these skills, and Gatty (1958) is a good introduction to this. So as well as celestial orientation cues, television aerials in towns can be used as cues, as they typically have a similar orientation to the local transmitter. In the country several aspects of trees provide orientation cues. Some trees are windblown in the direction of the prevailing wind, others have lichens growing on the side which typically dries least quickly. Some trees with heavy leaf cover, in spots sheltered from strong winds, grow asymmetrically towards the sun. So in Europe and North America such trees have branches on the south side which extend more horizontally, while those on the north have to grow more vertically to reach the light. One can discover more cues of one's own, as well as practising one's intuitive sense of direction and relation to known places.

In many ways, navigation is very like a perceptual task. Cues in the environment are used to address and guide an internal model or representation, within which symbolic inferences are made about the outside world and actions that we might take towards it.

33. Perception in game playing: internal representation and scanning of board positions[1]

Marc Eisenstadt and Yaakov Kareev

Two questions must be addressed by any study of perception in game playing: (a) what is the internal representation of the board position, and (b) how is the board scanned, i.e. how is information extracted from the external display. The two questions are, of course, closely related to one another – internal representations emerge as a result of scanning the board, and scanning is affected by what is already known about the situation on the board.

The problem of internal representation has been addressed by studies of memory for board positions (De Groot, 1965; Chase and Simon, 1973). These studies found that experts performed better than novices when reconstructing meaningful board positions from memory, but were no better than novices when the board positions contained the same pieces in a random configuration. This led to the hypothesis that people segment the board position into a number of chunks. These chunks are configurations which correspond to already known patterns stored in long-term memory. Better players presumably know more of such patterns (and the patterns they know may sometimes consist of more pieces), hence they can extract more chunks out of a given board position. The study by Chase and Simon also demonstrated that pieces on a chess board belonging to the same chunk are very likely to be related to each other by relations of attack and defence, whereas pieces belonging to different chunks are much less likely to have such relations between them.

Simon and Barenfeld (1969) devised a program that simulated the way in which board configurations are scanned. The program used chess relationships to attract attention and to direct the scan, and it was fairly successful in simulating the intial eye movements made by expert players studying a chess position for the first time.

Taken together, these studies suggest that the internal representation of a board configuration consists of meaningful chunks and that the meaningfulness

[1] This paper has been specially written for this volume.

548

of groups of pieces largely depends on what the player already knows about the game; they also suggest that scanning behaviour is largely determined by the same kind of knowledge. The studies to be described in the first half of this paper were designed to explore in further detail the factors affecting internal representation and scanning behaviour. These studies led to a model which is described in the second half of the paper.

The experiments

Our studies involved two board games – Go and Gomoku. Both games are traditionally played with black and white stones on a 19 × 19 board, but the rules of the two games are quite different. In Gomoku, the players alternate placing one of their pieces at a time on the board; the first one to get five of his pieces in a row (in any direction) wins [see a previous psychological study of this game: Rayner, 1958]. Go is a more sophisticated game of territorial control, the rules of which need not be described here in order for the reader to follow our discussion. To simplify both games a 9 × 9 board was used throughout the studies reported. To have a constant opponent for our subjects to play against, we wrote computer programs to play Go and Gomoku (the Go program was specially tailored for the 9 × 9 board). Both programs played a fair game, and could easily beat beginners. For some of the studies, we used X's and O's instead of black or white stones, and played on the square instead of on the grid intersections. (as the games are normally played), but these isomorphic variations still preserve the essential features of both games. Specific details of the experimental set-up are presented with each study.

Internal representation

While the configuration of pieces on the game board clearly does exist in an objective sense, the player plays according to his subjective perception of the board. The subjective perception of board positions does not necessarily correspond perfectly with the actual positions.

Our first experiment used a board reconstruction task to demonstrate the effect of knowledge of which game is being played on the subjective organization of a single objective configuration of black and white stones.

Eight subjects participated in this study. We created two board positions (shown in figure 1) to be used as problems to be solved by the subjects. Position B is actually position A transformed by rotating it counter-clockwise 90°, then forming its mirror image across the vertical axis, and then reversing the colours of the pieces. This transformation enabled us to use a given configuration of pieces in two different experimental conditions.

In the first condition, subjects were asked to analyse one of the positions by making the best move for one of the players. The positions were designed to be ambiguous, i.e. they could have been reached either in the course of a Gomoku game or in a Go game. Half of the subjects were told that their configuration was taken from a Gomoku game, and half were told that it was a Go game. After the subjects performed their analysis and an intervening task, they were asked (without advance warning) to reconstruct the original board configuration from memory. Then the subject solved a 'dummy' problem (which did not involve a reconstruction) and finally entered the second experimental condition: in the second condition, the subjects were presented with the *transformed* version of the original board position and told it was taken from the complementary game (Go rather than Gomoku, or *vice versa*). They performed the same type of analysis required in the first condition, then an intervening task, then a surprise reconstruction.

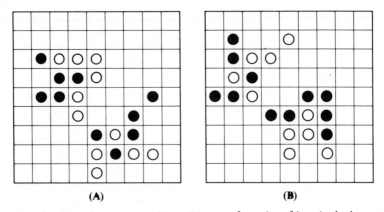

(A)   (B)

Figure 1. Board problem shown to our subjects. B is a transformation of A, arrived at by rotating A counter-clockwise 90° reflecting it across the vertical axis, and reversing the colours of the pieces. The subjects were told one position was taken from a Gomoku game, the other from a Go game (after Eisenstadt and Kareev, 1975)

In order to compare the reconstructions we identified six pieces that were crucial to the Gomoku analysis and six pieces that were crucial to the Go analysis, and labelled these pieces 'Gomoku template' and 'Go template', respectively. Accuracy of the reconstructions was scored by noting how many of these crucial pieces the subject placed correctly.

If context affects what is perceived and stored, then one would expect an interaction between the game played and accuracy of memory of different types of pieces – subjects solving the Gomoku problem should remember more Gomoku-related pieces than Go-related pieces, whereas the reverse should be true when the same subjects solve the Go problem. The results obtained are presented in figure 2, and they fully supported the prediction of an interaction between problem and type of pieces remembered.

Perceptual factors

The preceding study suggests that people usually encode the external elements of the game display in a manner relevant to the game they are playing. The question of how the display is scanned remains unanswered, however. The model of Simon and Barenfeld (1969) suggests that game-specific relationships are the main factor determining scanning behaviour, and the performance of their simulation program indicates that such relationships are indeed very important. However, it seemed to us that other factors also play an important role in directing scanning of the board. Foremost among those factors are the 'purely perceptual' principles suggested by Gestalt psychologists: those of proximity, continuity, and similarity (Koffka, 1935). Proximity should affect the scanning of the board in the following manner: given a certain piece which is looked at, pieces closer to that piece are more likely to be perceptually grouped together with it than pieces farther away from it. Continuity would dictate that straight lines consisting of contiguous pieces are easy to detect. Similarity would operate by making groups of similar pieces (typically pieces of the same colour) easier to detect than groups consisting of different pieces.

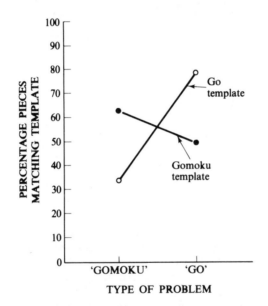

Figure 2. Percentage of crucial Go and Gomoku pieces (labelled 'Go template' and 'Gomoku template', respectively) which were remembered as a function of which game the subjects were told the problem represented (after Eisenstadt and Kareev, 1975)

The game of Gomoku is well suited for studying the effects of Gestalt principles since its basic game-specific patterns are straight lines, which also happen to be primitive Gestalt configurations. In particular, the pattern known as an 'open-three' is very important, because a failure to respond to it results in the loss of the game. This pattern has two forms, continuous and non-continuous, as shown in figure 3 (the reader should convince himself that failure to block an open-three leads to a loss). Each of these two forms may occur either along a diagonal (thus having relatively low proximity) or along a nondiagonal (thus having relatively high proximity), and thus there are four types of open-three (high-proximity + high-continuity; low-proximity + low-continuity; etc). Gestalt theory predicts that low proximity and lack of continuity would each decrease the likelihood of detecting an open-three. We can test the above prediction by looking at the 'detectability' of the four different types of open-threes. (We assume that any open-three which leads to a win for the computer is an open-three which has not been 'detected' by the subject). In ninety-seven games played by five new subjects, the computer established an open-three 317 times. In sixty-three of these cases (20 per cent) the pattern was not responded to by the subjects, so the computer won the game.

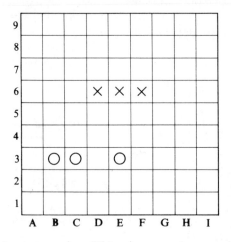

Figure 3. A continuous open-three (X's) and a noncontinuous open-three (O's)

Table 1 presents the percentage of games lost as a function of proximity and continuity of the critical open-threes. A least-squares analysis of variance revealed that both variables had a significant effect. The probability of responding to an open-three was lower for diagonal strings than for nondiagonal strings (0·73 vs. 0·88, respectively). Similarly, the probability of responding to a non-continuous open-three was lower than that of responding to a continuous open-three (0·71 vs. 0·83). The interaction between the two variables was not significant. These results indicate that the Gestalt principles of proximity and continuity do affect the scanning of the board.

To show that the effect of proximity is not merely an artifact of 'diagonality', we replaced the normally square board with a rectangular one which had a ratio of $\sqrt{2}$ to 1 between the two sides (on this board the distances along the diagonal are still longer than those along the long or the short axis). Twelve new subjects took part in this study.

Subjects were expected to lose more games on the longer of the two main axes, and the results fully supported this prediction. Of the losses which occurred along the horizontal and vertical axes, 81 per cent occurred along the longer of the two. Most losses overall (69 per cent), of course, still occurred on a diagonal.

Table 1. Probability of responding to an open-three as a function of proximity and continuity (number of occurrences shown in parentheses)

| Proximity | Continuity | | Mean |
	Continuous Open-threes	Noncontinuous Open-threes	
Nondiagonal strings	0·91 (105)	0·82 (44)	0·88
Diagonal strings	0·77 (142)	0·54 (26)	0·73
Mean	0·83	0·71	0·80

We also rotated a square board 45° (to form a diamond) and replaced the grid by dots to eliminate any possible effects caused by the presence of lines on the board. Nine new subjects played on these rotated boards. Of the games lost, 59 per cent were on the former 'diagonals' that were now running horizontally and vertically. This value is significantly greater than the 36 per cent expected by chance.

These results indicate that Gestalt principles have a strong effect on the way people scan the board; any model of scanning behaviour should have these principles as part of it.

Scanning behaviour

The object of the study reported in this section was to observe directly the scanning behaviour of subjects in the midst of playing actual games. Instead of collecting eye movements, we decided to restrict the players to viewing the board through a movable one-by-one window. This method enabled us to collect simultaneous verbal protocols, and to have a good idea of what the subjects were attending to (since they had no peripheral vision). Since the subjects were involved in their own actual games we were also able to look at the effects of prior memory on scanning.

For this particular study the subjects played their games on a computer-generated video display. The subjects were allowed to view the contents of only one square at a time. A light pen allowed the subjects to indicate which square they wanted to be exposed. The contents of the exposed square remained on display until some other square was pointed to with the light pen, at which time this latest square would become exposed to the player, while the previous one would go blank.

The computer monitored where the subject pointed and how much time had elapsed since he last pointed to the screen. The subjects had unlimited time to scan the board and to make their moves. Three subjects participated in the study. All three played both Go and Gomoku.

The subjects' scanning behaviour was analysed by dividing the window movements into episodes based upon natural breaks in the verbal protocols. Where there was no protocol, pauses greater than two seconds in between two window movements defined the boundary between episodes. The use of a two-second boundary cutoff is based on Chase and Simon (1973).

Four major types of scanning are evident in the behaviour of the subjects:

(a) *confirmatory scan*. The subject has a hypothesis about the existence of certain pieces (or blank squares) on the board, and looks directly at the squares in question in order to confirm (or refute) his hypothesis. One subject, for instance, says 'I think this gives 0 an open-three', while pointing with the light pen to the relevant squares.

(b) *Exploratory scan*. The subject has no explicit hypothesis in mind, but simply looks at various squares in order to see what they contain. A typical protocol which accompanies such a scan is the following: 'Hmm, let's see what X has around here.' Exploratory scans may, upon the discovery of something interesting, lead to new hypotheses which *interrupt* the exploratory scan in favour of a new confirmatory scan (actually, *any* type of scan may be interrupted if it uncovers unexpected findings).

(c) *Revival scan*. The subject looks again at a square which he has just recently examined, and whose contents he must therefore be fairly certain of. This type of scan is essentially a 'rehearsal' mechanism. One subject says 'I must block this string of 0's', and simultaneously points to the very string in question. The distinction between a revival scan and a confirmatory scan is a subtle one, since it really depends on the subject's degree of certainty that a particular configuration exists (if he is positive, then it is a revival scan; if he is unsure, then it is a confirmatory one).

(d) *Imaginary scan*. The subject is planning a move, and points to one of the squares where he has mentally 'placed' a hypothetical piece as part of his planning. For example, one subject says 'If I go here', while pointing with the light pen to the appropriate square.

Let us look in a little more detail at the window movements of one subject in one situation. This particular example occurred in the course of a Gomoku game. The actual board configuration (hidden from the subject except for one exposed square at a time) is shown in figure 4, along with the window movements which constitute the first episode of the subject's scanning. The computer (playing 0) has just moved to F4, creating an open-three. Square F4 is initially exposed to the subject's view, but its contents disappear from view as soon as another square is exposed. The entire series of window movements which precede the subject's move (he finally moves to C4) are shown in table 2. These episodes are labelled according to the types of scan they exhibit – note that one episode may contain a mixture of several types of scan. We shall only discuss episode 1 (but see Eisenstadt, 1974, for a detailed analysis of the other episodes).

During the first episode, the subject confirms the fact that 0's move has given him both an open-three and a diagonal open-two (running from D2 through G5). The confirmatory nature of this episode is supported by the fact that the subject looks precisely at the crucial squares necessary to identify the two relevant strings of 0's on the board.

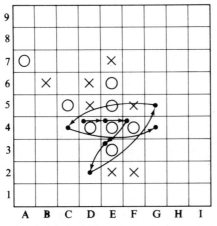

Figure 4. Gomoku game taken from the window-movement experiment. The subject's window-movements from episode 1 are shown superimposed on the board position (which is actually hidden from the subject's view). The computer, playing 0, has just moved to F4 (after Eisenstadt and Kareev, 1975)

Notice that the empty squares C4 and G4 are not looked at immediately following the line of 0's at D4, E4, and F4. Instead, the subject looks first at the three 0's then at the diagonal string, and finally at the two vacant squares surrounding the horizontal group. The important point here is that the precise sequence of window movements is not necessarily as revealing as those same movements looked at in terms of their role within a given episode. This holistic approach to the analysis of window movements allows for idiosyncratic sequences. It thus avoids some of the problems encountered in the analyses of Chase and Simon (1973) and Simon and Barenfeld (1969), which depended upon relations between pairs of pieces. On the basis of such relations alone, it is extremely difficult to account for the window movement from G5 to C4 in episode 1. When looked at as parts of an entire episode, however, it is clear that C4 need not be related to G5 at all. The delay of 1,567 milliseconds in between G5 and C4 also helps discount their interrelatedness. Analysing window movements at the level of episodes takes advantage of the subject's capacity to interrelate and chunk together (within working memory) window movements which seem naturally to belong together but which do not occur sequentially (e.g. F4 and G4).

This analysis is highly intuitive, but illustrates the explanatory convenience of dividing the scanning behaviour of the subjects into episodes. The four types of scanning we observed place important constraints on any model of scanning

Table 2. Window movements from Gomoku game of one subject at move 15, showing episode boundaries and types of scanning involved

Latency (msec.) (elapsed time since last window movement)	Location	Episode number	Type(s) of scan
599	D4		
900	E4		
698	F4		
835	E3	1	Confirmatory
666	D2		
927	G5		
1,567	C4		
990	G4		
2,657	F5		
834	E6		
840	G4		
851	C4	2	Imaginary,
1,270	C5		Exploratory
586	C6		
975	C3		
729	D3		
2,510	E4		
405	D4	3	Revival
479	F4		
3,166	F5		
918	F3		
1,456	E4		
725	D5	4	Imaginary,
1,233	F3		Exporatory
343	E3		
773	E2		
740	F2		
3,052	E4		
359	D4	5	Revival
2,695	C4	6	Imaginary

and internal representation, as we shall see in the next section. A complete model of the subject's scanning behaviour would have to include his precise knowledge of the contents of the board at any given instant since it is otherwise extremely difficult to distinguish between exploratory and confirmatory scans. A model which took account of the subject's knowledge of the board position would also be able to explain why the subject did not look at certain squares during his scan of the board. The model we describe in the next section does not go this far, but rather attempts to incorporate the major features of scanning and internal representation demonstrated by our subjects.

The model

Our experimental results provide a useful set of constraints and guidelines for the construction of a model of scanning and internal representation:

(a) The board reconstruction experiment indicates that internal representations must be composed of meaningful (i.e. game-specific) constituents.

(b) The experiments on perceptual factors indicate that the scanning of the board must be sensitive to the Gestalt principles of continuity and proximity.

(c) The four types of scanning we observed in the window movement experiment provide four additional guidelines: (1) internal representations may be constructed as the result of an active, or goal-driven, scan for constituents of a board configuration (confirmatory scan); (2) internal representations may also be constructed as the result of a passive, or data-driven, 'discovery' of constituents of a board configuration (exploratory scan); (3) internal representations are subject to decay, presumably within working memory (revival scan); (4) the planning of new moves interacts directly with both scanning and internal representation (imaginary scan).

The model described below attempts to take these guidelines into account. Our original model (Eisenstadt and Kareev, 1975) relied heavily on the memory representation outlined in Norman, Rumelhart, and the LNR Research Group (1975). That representation provided a natural and powerful way of thinking about the details of the model, as well as a straightforward way of constructing a computer implementation. Here we give a more general and implementation-independent overview of the model's main features.

Major components

The model consists of three parts: a 'fovea', a working memory and a long-term memory. The fovea, for the purpose of simulating window movements, is simply a 1 × 1 window which indicates where on the board the model is currently looking (the actual board position is of course stored symbolically on another part of the computer, since our model does not have a true hardware 'eye').

Working memory is conceived as being a homogenous list of processes waiting to be executed and data waiting to be processed. The processes involved are responsible for either (a) scanning the board, (b) examining the contents of working memory, or (c) adding new items to working memory. Data, on the other hand, correspond to descriptions of various characteristics of the board positions. The distinction between process and data is deliberately subtle in our model, because processes themselves may serve as data for other processes. To illustrate what an item of data looks like, consider how a simple configuration is stored in working memory: a board configuration is represented in working memory as a list which contains certain details about the configuration. For example, a very simple configuration consisting only of a black piece at board location E4 would be represented by the following list:

$$[PIECE\ BLACK\ (E,4)]$$

In this case, the first element of the list tells us the kind of configuration involved (i.e. PIECE), whereas the second element indicates the colour (i.e. BLACK), and the third element specifies the x and y coordinates[2] which correspond to the board position E4. Working memory contains, at any given moment, lists comparable to this one. It is called a *specific* list because it is a specific instance of the general *class* of lists of the form: [PIECE colour (x,y)]. Such a 'schema', a class of lists, serves as a general-purpose description, with variables indicated in lower-case letters. It is stored in long-term memory, and represents general knowledge about what characteristics (e.g. colour) are relevant to different kinds of configurations. The difference between a specific instance and a class of lists should be clear: if we had a 9 × 9 board filled entirely with eighty-one white pieces, then we could represent those pieces in working memory by using eighty-one specific lists – [PIECE WHITE (A,1)] [PIECE WHITE (A,2)], . . . [PIECE WHITE (I,9)]. All of these would be instances of the class [PIECE colour (x,y)]. Lists can represent arbitrary properties or characteristics. For instance the general class of lists of the form [NEIGHBOURS (x, y) (x', y') orientation] represents the property of two squares being next to one another in a particular orientation. A specific instance of this class would be [NEIGHBOURS (D,5) (E,5) HORIZONTAL], which indicates that squares D5 and E5 on the board are horizontal neighbours.

Pattern rules

Long-term memory consists of a set of *pattern rules,* which show how different classes of list are interrelated (i.e. how large board configurations are made up of smaller ones), and a set of *processing rules,* which specify how to use the pattern rules to construct internal representations of the board within working memory. Here is an example of a typical pattern rule:

$$\left\{ \begin{array}{l} [PIECE\ colour\ (x,y)] \\ \qquad \& \\ [PIECE\ colour\ (x',y')] \\ \qquad \& \\ [NEIGHBOURS\ (x,y)\ (x',y') \\ \quad orientation] \end{array} \right\} \longleftrightarrow [PAIR\ colour\ (x,y)\ (x',y')\ orientation]$$

Reading from the left side of the double-arrow to the right side, the rule says that if we have found two pieces of the same colour which are neighbours in some

---

[2] [The program actually represents both co-ordinates as numbers.]

orientation, then we can think of them as forming a pair in that orientation. Reading from the right side of the double-arrow to the left side, the rule says that a pair of pieces of a given colour in some orientation can be thought of as two neighbouring pieces of the appropriate colour which are neighbours in the approriate orientation. The differences between the two readings is this: the left-to-right reading represents an interpretation of some particular perceptual data (a 'bottom-up' analysis), while the other reading represents a prediction about what should be in the data on the basis of some hypothesis (a 'top-down' analysis). That is, reading from left to right, the rule captures the idea of the automatic discovery of the larger configuration (described on the right side) after having noticed the configurations and characteristics shown on the left side. Reading from right to left, the rule captures the idea of 'seeking out' the subparts of a configuration – i.e. if we wanted to find an adjacent pair, then the components on the left side of the rule tell us what we should look for. These bi-directional rules allow us to capture both the confirmatory (goal-driven) and exploratory (data-driven) aspects of our subjects' scans in the window movement experiment.

A partial set of pattern rules for the game of Gomoku is given in table 3. FEATURE 1 and FEATURE 2 are just arbitrary names for primitive properties which distinguish black pieces from white pieces, and which enable the model to recognize a piece in the first place. If the model's fovea is pointed at a location on the board where one of these features happens to be present, then its appropriate value is added to working memory. For instance, if there were a white piece at F5, and if the fovea were pointed at F5 as well, then the list such as [PIECE WHITE (F,5)] would be added to working memory.

Processing rules

All specific lists in working memory are tagged with a 'status', which has one of three values: PRESENT, ABSENT, or UNKNOWN. PRESENT means that the list in question is known to correspond precisely to an actual configuration of pieces on the board. Thus, if the list [PIECE WHITE (D,5)] has the status PRESENT, then there is (to the best of the model's knowledge) a white piece on board location D5. The status ABSENT means that, to the best of the model's knowledge, there is no configuration on the board corresponding to the list in question. UNKNOWN means that the model does not yet have enough information to decide whether the status is PRESENT or ABSENT. For simplicity, we assume that the model's noticing of features on the board is error-free, and thus a noticed feature on the board automatically results in the addition of a list of the class [FEATURE 1 (x,y)] or [FEATURE 2 (x,y)] with the status PRESENT.

In addition to a status, all lists are tagged with a game-dependent *priority*, which is either HIGH or LOW. For the Gomoku lists shown in table 3 those marked with an asterisk are HIGH priority, while all others are LOW priority. Priority is simply a way of representing 'importance' for a particular game.

When an instance of a HIGH priority list is added to working memory, it is processed *immediately,* according to the rules presented below (that is, it interrupts any other processing). LOW priority lists, on the other hand, are simply added to working memory, and wait their turn to be processed.

The following processing rules are applied, in order, to all specific lists within working memory:

1. (*Top-down confirmation rule.*) If the status of a specific list is UNKNOWN, and its priority is HIGH, an attempt is made to confirm its presence on the board in the following way:
The pattern rules are used (reading from right to left) to identify the subparts of the list in question. A list acquires the status PRESENT if all of its subparts are known to have the status PRESENT. On the other hand, if one of its subparts is known to have the status ABSENT, then it too acquires the status ABSENT. If the status of subparts is UNKNOWN, then this same confirmation process is applied recursively to subparts of subparts, etc., until the most elementary pattern (i.e. FEATURE 1 or FEATURE 2) is sought. At this lowest level, a fovea movement to the appropriate square is made, and the status of all the subparts (and hence the list in question) is eventually determined.

2. (*Bottom-up discovery rule.*) If the status of a list is PRESENT, and this has not previously been the case, then a check is made to see whether this list now completes the left side of any of the pattern rules in long-term memory. If it does, then a new specific list is created by filling in the values of the variables on the *right* side of the pattern rule, and this newly created list is added into working memory as a *discovery* (i.e. with the status PRESENT).

3. (*Bottom-up suggestion rule.*) If a newly PRESENT list completes only *part* of the left side of a pattern rule, but a 'major part' – that is, the first list on the left side of a rule – then a new list is created by filling in the values of the variables on the *right* side of the rule. The actual values which the variables may acquire are constrained in advance by an explicit check of the spatial relations in the board configuration (e.g. [NEIGHBOURS. . .], [IN-LINE. . .], etc). Finally, this newly created list is added to working memory as a *suggestion* (i.e. with the status UNKNOWN).

4. (*Exploration rule.*) If, after processing all the lists according to the above three processing rules, there are no HIGH priority lists with an UNKNOWN status, then a special list [LOOKAROUND], is added to working memory. When it is processed, it causes the model's fovea to move to squares adjacent to the one it is currently fixated on (in the hope that new discoveries will be added to working memory).

Notice that a list can designate an arbitrary process to be preformed, as in the last rule above. In effect, a list class serves as the definition of a procedure, while a specific instance of it in working memory is a procedure in a state of 'suspended animation', waiting either to be reactivated (if its status is UNKNOWN), or else to serve as data (if its status is known to be either PRESENT or ABSENT).

Table 3. Some pattern rules for Gomoku. Lists marked with an asterisk are regarded as having high priority for the game of Gomoku

[FEATURE 1 (x,y)] ⟶ [PIECE WHITE (x,y)]

[FEATURE 2 (x,y)] ⟶ [PIECE BLACK (x,y)]

[PIECE colour (x,y)] & [PIECE colour (x', y')] & [NEIGHBOURS (x,y) (x',y') orientation] ⟶ [PAIR colour (x,y) (x',y') orientation]

[PAIR colour (x, y) (x',y') orientation] & [PIECE colour (x'',y'')] & [IN-LINE (x,y) (x', y') (x'', y'') orientation] ⟶ [TRIO colour (x,y) (x',y') x'',y'') orientation]*

[TRIO colour (x,y) (x',y') (x'',y'') orientation] & [PIECE colour (x''',y''')] & [IN-LINE (x,y) (x',y') (x'',y'') (x''',y''') orientation] ⟶ [FOUR colour (x,y) (x',y')(x'',y'')(x''',y''') orientation]*

[TRIO colour (x,y) (x'',y'') (x''',y''') orientation] & [BLANK (a,b)] & [BLANK (c,d)] & [SURROUND ((a,b) (c,d)) ((x',y') (x'',y'') (x''',y'''))] ⟶ [SUB-OPEN-THREE ((x,y) (x'',y'')(x''',y'')) ((a.b)(c,d))]

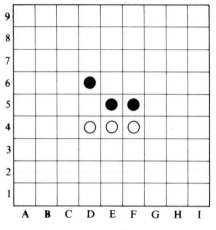

Figure 5. Gomuku board position used for simulators of scanning. White has just moved to F4

1. OK, WE HAVE A WHITE PIECE AT F4.	/bottom–up discovery
2. LET'S SEE WHAT'S HAPPENING AROUND F4 . . .	/exploration
3. (LOOKING AT F5) . . .	/exploration
4. OK, WE HAVE A BLACK PIECE AT F5.	/bottom–up discovery
5. WHAT ELSE? . . .	/exploration
6. (LOOKING AT G4) . . .	/exploration
7. (LOOKING AT F3) . . .	/exploration
8. (LOOKING AT E4) . . .	/exploration
9. OK, WE HAVE A WHITE PIECE AT E4.	/bottom–up discovery
10. WHICH GIVES US A HORIZONTAL WHITE PAIR AT F4 E4.	/bottom–up discovery
11. HMM . . . THERE MIGHT BE A HORIZONTAL WHITE TRIO AT F4 E4 D4 . . .	/bottom–up suggestion followed by top–down confirmation
12. (LOOKING AT D4) . . .	/top–down confirmation
13. YES!	/top–down confirmation
14. HMM . . . THERE MIGHT BE A HORIZONTAL WHITE FOUR AT F4 E4 D4 C4 . . .	/bottom–up suggestion followed by top–down confirmation
15. (LOOKING AT C4) . . .	/top–down confirmation
16. NO!	/top–down confirmation
17. BUT WE HAVE A HORIZONTAL WHITE SUB-OPEN-THREE	/bottom–up discovery

The four processing rules are applied repeatedly to the contents of working memory. The overall structure of the model, particularly processing rule 2, has much of the flavour of a production system (Newell and Simon, 1972; Newell, 1973a; see also Readings 3 and 4 in this volume). However, the model places greater emphasis on the use of special processing rules (i.e. rules 1, 3, and 4) to obtain a smooth mixture of goal-driven and data-driven processing.

The functioning of the model is best explained by means of an example. Figure 5 shows part of a board configuration presented to our model. 0 has just moved to F4, but the model has no knowledge about the overall progress of the game so far (unlike our window movement subjects). The numbered lines below, shown in upper-case letters, are the output of our computer implementation of the model (items in parentheses indicate 'fovea movements'). Following the slash (/) on each line, we indicate in lower case letters which of the four processing rules was responsible for that particular output.

Three points deserve special mention:

(a) The model's exploratory scan (statements 2, 3, 5, 6, 7, 8) proceeds outwards in expanding concentric circles, which guarantees that it will notice horizontal and vertical neighbours of a square before it notices diagonal neighbours. As this happens, the appropriate instances of [NEIGHBOURS (x,y) (x',y') orientation] are added to working memory. If a horizontal or vertical neighbour happens to lead to a hypothesis about an important configuration on the board, then diagonal strings will be overlooked, and the model will make the same kind of blunders we found in our Gomoku-playing subjects (i.e. failing to notice open-threes on diagonals).

(b) At statement 11, processing rule 3 (bottom-up suggestion) uses the constraints provided by the list [IN-LINE . . .] to add an instance of [TRIO . . .] into working memory, and since TRIOs are known to have HIGH priority, all processing is immediately interrupted in favour of a confirmatory scan for this TRIO, using processing rule 1.

(c) An analogous situation occurs at statement 14. This time, however, the hypothesis is refuted (statement 16). The movement of the fovea to C4 (statement 15) resulted in the discovery of a blank square, and now processing rule 2 (bottom-up discovery) becomes applicable, since the list for a blank square completes the left-hand-side of a pattern rule (statement 17). In this case, it is the rule describing three pieces surrounded by a blank on either side.

The model vs. the constraints

How well does the model satisfy the constraints we outlined at the beginning of this section?

(a) Game-specific internal representations are built into the model from the start, since the pattern rules (and the priorities) are specifically tailored to a particular game (Gomoku, in the examples used here). Nontrivial configurations can also be described with these rules (e.g. recursive pattern rules for groups of Go pieces; hierarchically chunked configurations for Gomoku).

(b) Gestalt principles: the principle of proximity is built in via the [NEIGHBOURS. . .] and [LOOKAROUND] lists, which guarantee noticing the nearest pieces first. The principle of continuity is captured by the [IN-LINE . . .] list. Since configurations and their subparts are required to have the same value for the colour variable, the Gestalt principle of similarity is also built into the model.

(c) Four types of scan are built into the model:

1. *Confirmatory scan*. This is explicitly incorporated in the form of processing rule 1 (top-down confirmation).

2. *Exploratory scan*. Different aspects of this are embodied in the remaining processing rules. Processing rule 2 (bottom-up discovery) captures the passive discovery aspect of this type of scan, while processing rule 3 (bottom-up suggestion) captures the manner in which the existence of potentially important configurations can be hinted at (and can interrupt the current processing). Processing rule 4 (exploration), of course, allows the model to 'see what's happening' when it has nothing better to do – another apparent function of our subjects' exploratory scans.

3. *Revival scan*. If we restrict the capacity of working memory (either by limiting the number of lists it can contain or else by assigning lists a strength value which is decremented after each processing cycle) then a new confirmatory scan could be requested whenever a list is dangerously close to being 'kicked out' of working memory. We have in fact restricted working memory by using a simple strength decay, and thus the newly requested confirmatory scans essentially fulfil the role of a revival scan.

4. *Imaginary scan*. This can be dealt with by additional pattern rules which result in the addition of planning processes to working memory. These planning processes add lists representing hypothetical pieces to working memory, and provide for a smooth interaction between scanning and planning within a single processing framework. The nature of these planning processes is described in Kareev (1973) and Eisenstadt and Kareev (1975).

34. Some necessary conditions for a master chess program[1]

Hans J. Berliner

Introduction

Since 1967 chess programming has again been an interesting subject for Artificial Intelligence researchers. At that time Greenblatt (1967) developed a program which soon proved to play nearly as well as the mid-range of registered human players in America.

The basic structure of Greenblatt's program derives from the work of Shannon (1950b). Since then there have been several other programs of this type developed. Of these only the Northwestern University program has achieved a human class C rating, which places it in a unique position along with the Greenblatt program.

Briefly, the type of program being discussed searches to a depth of five ply[2] under tournament conditions (in end-games with very few legal moves they may search from one to three ply deeper). They do not investigate every legal move, but restrict themselves to a subset at each node. Moves are selected for further search on the basis of a scoring function which attempts to rank order the legal moves according to their goodness. The number of moves selected for further examination is usually a function of the depth at which the node occurs. In special situations there are mechanisms which allow the search to be expanded beyond this pruned set, in order to attempt to meet unanticipated problems.

Programs of this type typically evaluate between 5,000 and 50,000 bottom nodes in the trees they generate. They do this by applying a static evaluation function, which, since it must be invoked so many times in the course of the three minutes allowed for a tournament move, must of necessity be restricted to a few milliseconds of computation.

Because programs exist which can compete in human tournaments, and

[1] Excerpts from the paper in *Third International Joint Conference on Artificial Intelligence* (Stanford: Stanford Research Institute, 1973), pp. 77–85. Used by permission of the Third International Joint Conference on Artificial Intelligence.
[2] ['Five ply' means five 'half-moves'. In this case, three for White and two for Black.]

because of the annual computer competitions, there now exists considerable interest all over the world in the future of computer chess. In fact, there is a detectable expectancy in the AI community that a master level chess program will exist before the end of the decade.

It is the purpose of this paper to show that a program with the structure of today's most successful programs cannot be extended to play master chess. When one considers that much effort by several groups has only succeeded in raising the 1968 standard of performance of the Greenblatt program by a hardly measurable amount, there is some reason to believe that the present design is already near the assymptote of its potential. We will show that the domain in which a master level program has to operate could never be subsumed in any domain to which the above programs could be extended. We will also show that certain features in the evaluation procedure used by current programs lead to basic errors that cannot be tolerated in master play. Finally, the outline of a model of chess that could perform as required is presented.

We will draw examples from both human and machine play. In order to minimize the chess knowledge required of the reader, the examples have been chosen to be as obvious as possible, and we have endeavoured to remove all considerations from these, except those pertinent to the discussion. We consider it extremely likely that the phenomena being considered here, are also artifacts in other types of Artificial Intelligence programs.

Analysis of evidence

When branches in a tree-search must be terminated prior to a legal termination point (according to the rules of the game), it is necessary to assign a value (an interim value other than win, lose, or draw) to the terminal node, which then allows comparison with other terminal nodes. This is usually done by invoking a static evaluation function. In games where a search to legal termination is not possible, no other recourse appears possible. An interesting phenomenon arises from the interaction of the artificial termination of the search and the fact that all the terms in the static evaluation function are evaluated at this terminal point. The result of this combination is that for the game playing program, reality exists in terms of the output of the static evalutation function, and *anything that is not detectable at evaluation time does not exist* as far as the program is concerned. This interesting fact is present in all tree-searches in any chess program that we know of, and causes interesting aberrations in program behaviour.

The class of aberrations defined above, we call the Horizon Effect. The complete phenomenon has never received a name in the literature nor have its causes and effects been properly catalogued. The regimen of insisting on evaluation at a prespecified point in the search causes the following effects which seem peculiar to human observers. When the Horizon Effect results in creating diversions which ineffectively delay an unavoidable consequence or make an unachievable one appear achievable, we call it an instance of the Negative Horizon Effect. This is the phenomenon previously reported in the literature. It can best be shown by a typical example.

In figure 1 it is White's turn to play, and for the sake of this example let us suppose the search is to be limited to three ply (we realize that the search usually goes deeper; however it is relatively easy to construct examples at any given depth, and we are choosing our examples for their expository simplicity). What will happen in the above position is that the program will try to play 1. B–N3 and after P–B5, 2. Anything, it is time to do a static evaluation. . . Now at the end of the above three-ply sequence, the program will come to the conclusion that it will lose the Bishop on N3, and will continue its search for something better. It will eventually come upon 1. P–K5 and recognize that if now PXB, then 2. PXN is good for White. Therefore it will consider as best for Black to play PXP, after which White plays 2. B–N3. Since we are now at maximum depth, this position will be evaluated using the standard procedure. The analysis will show that White has saved his Bishop since there is *no sequence of captures* which will win the Bishop. Alas, it is only after the next move that the program finds out that the *non-capture* threat of P–B5 has not been met by this diversion, and it then looks for other ways of parting with material worth less than a Bishop in order to postpone the inevitable day when the Bishop will finally be trapped and captured. In this case 2. RXB would no doubt be tried next since after NXB, 3. B–N3, 'saving' the Bishop by giving up the Rook for the Black Bishop is preferred to losing it. We have seen programs indulge in this type of folly for five to six successive moves, resulting in going from a position in which they are well ahead to one in which they are hopelessly behind.

Figure 1. White to play

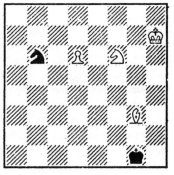

Figure 2. White to play

A clever device to prevent this behaviour was invented by Greenblatt and is also used by the Northwestern University group. This consists essentially of extending a new principal variation for another two ply, to see whether the reason it was considered superior will continue to obtain. In the above example, this will result in finding that the threat of P–B5 does not go away, and thus a potential sequence of blunders is averted. However extending a principal variation two ply can only discover whether a one move threat has or has not been dissipated. Threats requiring two or more moves cannot be dealt with effectively in this manner. This is usually not noticed, since today's best programs perform at a level of skill where two move threats are rare and far from the major cause of concern for their developers.

The Positive Horizon Effect is different in that instead of trying to avert some unavoidable consequences, the program grabs much too soon at a consequence that can be imposed on an opponent at leisure, frequently in a more effective form. Figure 2 shows a flagrant example of the Positive Horizon Effect.

In this position it is White to play and the search is again to a depth of three ply. The program notices that it can play 1. P–Q7 and, if Black does not now play NXP, 2. NXN, then it would get a new Queen. It sees that in this way it can increase its material superiority. It may or may not notice that it will then have to face the formidable task of mating with a Bishop and Knight. The interesting thing about this position is that the manocuvre 1. B–K5 followed by 2. B–Q4 cannot be prevented and results in forcing the Pawn through to a Queen without letting Black give up the Knight for it, thus simplifying the win greatly. Here the important point is that there is a consequence on the horizon, and the program insists on realizing it within the horizon of the search as otherwise *it does not exist*. As a result, a consequence which could have turned out to be very beneficial, turns out only to have a small benefit. It is possible to find examples where wins are 'thrown away' by such a premature cashing in. In fact, the main reason for the demonstrated lack of tolerance of complexity of today's chess programs is that their evaluation function insists on maximizing, in terms of a preconceived set of evaluation terms, anything that it detects within the search horizon, and thus all too frequently destroys an advantageous situation before it really has a chance to bloom.

An example of the Positive Horizon Effect illustrating a throwing away of a positional advantage is shown in figure 3. Here, if the evaluation function is aware of the beneficial effect of controlling an open file, and if the search is again being conducted to three ply, the most likely continuation will be 1. PXP ch, PXP, 2. R–KR1 with control of the open file and 'some advantage'. The fact that on the next move Black can answer R–KR1, after which White's advantage has largely evaporated is not recognized. Neither is the key fact that Black can do absolutely nothing to prevent White from opening the file whenever he likes (for human players there is the dictum 'do not open a file until you are ready to use it'). However today's programs would almost certainly reject the correct 1. R–KR1 since after Black plays R–KR1 and White plays 2. PXP ch, it is time to invoke the procedure which produces PXP. Now in contrast to the earlier variation, White does not control the open file. Nor would he if any other 2nd move were played. Clearly, a program could recognize the value of playing 1. R–KR1 before 1. PXP ch, only if it were secure in the knowledge that the file can be opened at a later time by PXP, and that if Black plays PXP, he will merely incur an equally difficult problem in defence of the KRP as he has now in defence of the KR file. In fact having once played 1. R–KR1 and getting the answer R–KR1, a program that has reasoned thus far should have little difficulty in now playing 2. R–R2 since opening the file at the present moment is not advantageous and making room for the other Rook could help. It should be noted that incorporating the human players' dictum appears extremely difficult as the issue of 'ready to use it' is one requiring dynamic judgments, in which even good human players make mistakes at times . . .

Figure 3. White to play   Figure 4. White to play

Another basic problem, the need for a global strategy, is shown in figure 4. Here every one of today's programs would conduct a five-ply search and then play 1. K–K3. A summary of its findings during this tree-search might run as follows: it decided that P–B7 would lose the Pawn to K–K2, and therefore decided to move the King to the most central location available (this is a quantity recognized by the evaluation function). On the next move, having already achieved its 'optimum' position, the program would be faced with a problem that all hill climbers face when they reach the top: How to back down as little as possible? Accordingly there would occur either K–Q2 or K–B3. The point of this whole example is to show the hopeless hill-climbing characteristics of the present program design. In the given position, even a poor human player would recognize that there is nothing to be gained by the above manoeuvres. The real problem is that today's programs mix their strategical and tactical objectives during the search. Thus the above position could be handled effectively if a tactical search were first done and this came to the conclusion that P–B7 only resulted in losing the Pawn. There being no other tactical tries, control would then revert to a strategical module which would try to improve the position of any and all pieces. Since, in this simplified situation, we only have the King as a candidate, the next step would be to try to find an optimum or near optimum position for the King and determine if it could get there. Here we must not rely solely on a static, preconceived notion of centrality, although that certainly is a part of the picture, but more importantly we seek a functional optimum. This can be found by noting that the Black KNP and KP are not defended by Pawns and could possibly be attacked by the King, and also that our own KBP could possibly benefit from having our King near it. Next, a null move analysis could be carried out, consisting of moving the White King around without looking at intervening moves, to see if we can find the optimum path to any of the desired squares. This will then eventually yield the correct idea of infiltrating with the White King via QR3, which wins easily. Admittedly the control structure that could evoke such behaviour would present some problems. Most of the problems in chess are tactical (immediate) problems and for this reason, the lack of global ideas is frequently obscured in today's programs. However, it is absolutely necessary to be able to generate global goals.

We have above touched only on the relatively simple problem of finding the correct way to proceed. A far more difficult problem, which would also have to be faced by the master strength program, is to judge whether the position can be won or is a draw. A simple 'Pawn ahead' judgment is not enough. There may be other end-games from which to choose, in which the program is also a Pawn ahead. In the position being discussed, for instance, if a further White Pawn were at QN4, and a Black Pawn at its QN4, the position would be a draw. Clearly dynamic judgments of this type are absolutely necessary.

In figure 5, we see a much better understood problem than any of the above. It is the problem of calculating in depth. Here White can execute a mating combination requiring an initial Queen sacrifice and nine further moves, a total of nineteen ply as follows: 1. Q–R5 ch, NXQ, 2. PXP ch, K–N3, 3. B–B2 ch, K–N4, 4. R–B5 ch, K–N3, 5. R–B6 ch, K–N4, 6. R–N6 ch, K–R5, 7. R–K4 ch, N–B5, 8. RXN ch, K–R4, 9. P–N3, Any, 10. R–R4 mate. This combination was played by a former world champion [Alekhine] while playing a total of twenty games simultaneously. The reason no program that looks at ten to twenty alternatives at every node can play the correct move is that the principal variation to justify the initial Queen sacrifice extends much, much further than the five-ply depth that is about all that is possible with a program that gets buried in the exponential explosion of investigating ten sprouts from every node. Now it is quite possible to play master level chess without playing such long combinations. However, in the author's experience one must, at least once a game, be able to look fourteen or more ply ahead. As far as the above example goes, we believe that 99 per cent of all masters would solve it as well as a high percentage of experts and class A players. What is really difficult about the example is not the simple unravelling of the main line, which having few branches is fairly linear, but the conception of the position, and that such a solution involving chasing the King up the board might exist in it.

One could argue that just because good players can solve such problems, this does not show the requirement for the program to see to such depths in order to play at the master level. What this would mean is that the program would have to rely almost exclusively on static, nontree-search computations for its moves. But we have already shown in examples 2 and 3 that static notions must be combined with dynamic tests in depth in order to yield correct results. So a program that could not look ten ply ahead would be subject to any five move threat that comes along. Even though the main thrust of most such threats could no doubt be muted, it would be inevitable that some concession would have to be made. This type of thrust and parry is at the heart of master play. Even more importantly, a program that cannot look ten ply ahead could never conceive a five move threat of its own which is dependent on adverse action. The evidence is quite overwhelming.

Another interesting phenomenon, that of reality or illusion, that afflicts all of today's best programs can be seen in figure 6. Here it is White's turn to play. The first thing that the evaluation function will discover is that White has both of his Rooks *en prise* (capturable by the opponent under favourable conditions). If this position has occurred at some node which is eligible for sprouting, then moves that move either of the Rooks to a 'safer' place will receive good recommendations. If the node is a terminal node, then it will be considered as not satisfactory for White, as it is presumed that at least one of the Rooks will be lost.

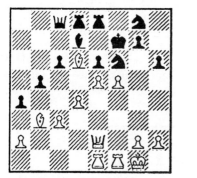

Figure 5. White to play

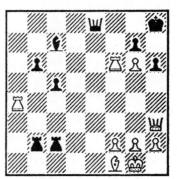

Figure 6. White to play

In actuality, neither of the Rooks is in danger. If Black plays QXR then R–B8 mate, and if PXR, then QXP ch, K–N1, Q–R7 ch, K–B1, P–N7 ch followed by P–N8 = Q ch wins quickly. Even stranger is the fact that if this position occurs somewhere in the tree below the top node, and if, say, two ply earlier White had played RXP(KB6) as a sacrifice which it turns out could not have been accepted, then in today's programs there would now be no knowledge of the sacrifice at KB6 when the position is tendered for evaluation two ply later. Rather the Rook would be considered *en prise*. Indirect defences of this type are seen all the time in master chess. Clearly, if a program aspires to this level it must be able to handle such problems. Part of the solution consists in noting the functional overloading of the pieces that are thought of as doing the capturing. Here the Black Queen is guarding a check on the back rank apart from attacking the White Rook. Also the Black KNP is guarding a Pawn and a check, while attacking the White Rook. However this is not enough, since it is quite possible that the checks that are being defended against are quite harmless, and it would be folly to try to determine, without further searching, the exact potency of every check on the board.

Another problem, that of dynamic evaluation of material, is depicted in figure 7. Here, with either side to play, White's Pawn cannot be stopped from queening, while Black's Pawns are going nowhere fast. Yet there is no doubt that every one of today's programs, if playing Black, would refuse a draw in this position, and it is also very clear that only a very weak human player would offer a draw with White. The programs' rationale is that three passed Pawns are better than one. The problem here is one of recognizing the dynamic potential of the White passed Pawn which cannot be caught. It is true that in this case the job can be done statically by merely noting the distances of the White Pawn and the Black King from the queening square; however, if the Black Pawns were all advanced three squares, the computation would have to be done dynamically, since there is a possibility they may arrive first. Similar dynamic ideas, which no program can at present handle well, are the notion of a defenceless King by reason of no surrounding men of his own to help defend him, and the notion of cooperation among various men rather than only assessing the goodness of their individual positions. Such notions require dynamic exploration to determine the degree of their applicability in a given position. However, in a program where terminal evaluation must be done very quickly because of the large number of nodes that must be evaluated, such luxuries are not possible. We are here directly confronted with a basic limitation of the generate and test approach, when it does not allow enough time to do a detailed evaluation of the nodes visited.

Figure 7

Our last two examples deal with situations that present-day programs can handle. However, the method by which they do this is terribly inefficient and could not be used if one wanted to do tree-searches which could extend even a little deeper than the current five ply. The first of these problems is the problem of defence. It is relatively easy to recognize attacks and develop criteria for judging the value of most attacks. However, this is not so with defence. The problem is that in order for a defence to exist, a threat must first be known. All threats are not of the simple type such as threatening a capture, and it is precisely this other type of threat, which shows up in the backed up value of the current variation, that is not easy to counter because we only know the magnitude of its effect. Figure 8 shows a position of this type. Here it is Black's turn to play and the search is being conducted to a depth of five ply. If Black plays a normal aggressive move such as 1. . P–R7, he will find that after 2. Q–K8 ch, RXQ, 3. RXR he is mated. The search will then eventually revert to the point where Black played P–R7. Now in most of today's programs we would be armed with the killer heuristic (which says that against any new proposed move try the 'killer' Q–K8 ch first). This would indeed result in the efficient dismissal of the next fifteen or so moves likely to be tested. However the fact remains that each of these alternatives is being served up in a generate and test mode, and the program can consider itself fortunate if it discovers the only defence (Q–K5) before it has exhausted half the legal moves.

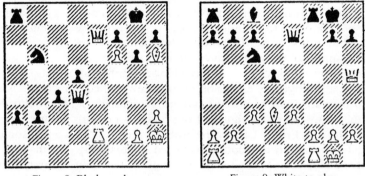

Figure 8. Black to play   Figure 9. White to play

Our final example in figure 9 shows another subtle consideration. In this position, programs that look five ply deep have an excellent chance of finding the mate in three moves: 1. BXP ch, K–R1, 2. B–N6 ch, K–N1, 3. Q–R7 mate. If such a program, due to the fact that White is behind in material, were only to look at captures of pieces of greater or equal value to the current deficit, and checks (an assumption which requires some preprocessing) and to stop at five ply depth (for which it would be difficult to establish a logical reason), there would still be about 100 positions to examine before the mate is found. Here any tournament calibre human player would recognize the situation immediately as one of a set of Queen and Bishop mates. He would only have to determine the functional need to guard the King escape square at KB2, to determine what the correct sequence is and that it does lead to mate. The critical thing here is not that a program could not find the mate once the diagrammed position is reached, but that in advanced chess play such situations occur frequently in deep parts of a tree as a reason why some other move fails. If a program spends 100 nodes investigating such a well-known pattern, then there is a definite limit on the amount of work the program can be expected to do. The answer here quite obviously is to have a repertoire of frequently occurring patterns available to the program together with some guidance to determine the exact applicability of any particular pattern. In the above case, recognition of the Queen and Bishop functionally bearing on the undefended KR7 square, together with the position of the Black King hemmed in by some of its own pieces, is the basic pattern. The dynamic analysis reveals that the King could escape over KB2 if this were not kept under continued guard. With these constraints, the number of variations to be examined are very few.

Some conclusions

Let us examine some potential models of computer chess. All the complete models are clearly too time or space consuming. Therefore, the most reasonable course appears to be to rely upon models that construct trees of possibilities but with some limitations imposed upon the growth of the trees. Now, depending upon how we define these limits, we have a tractable problem. The real question, and that addressed by this paper, is how these limits can be defined and implemented in order to include the range of performance exhibited by chess masters while still keeping the problem tractable.

Let us summarize the requirements noted earlier:

(1) In examples 1–3 we have seen the Horizon Effect in operation. We have also seen that the two-ply extension of each new principal variation is only a stop-gap measure, which prevents one move debacles (anyone who doesn't believe this is invited to try figure 11 out on his program). What can be done about the Horizon Effect? Clearly the problem is due to the fact that some term in the static evaluation function is evaluated 'prematurely'. Prematurely here means that a noticeable change in the value of the term can be forced, without any compensatory change in any other term(s). From this, one can deduce that there can be no arbitrary depth limit imposed on the search. The decision as to whether to terminate the search at a node or continue, has to be a function of the information that exists at that node and how this relates to each and every term in the evaluation function. For instance, if we have an evaluation function that would consider it bad to have a Bishop blocked in by its own Pawns, then some effort must be expended to determine the permanency of such situations . . .

(2) From example 4 we see the need for having global goals and being able to determine something about the feasibility of such proposed goals. This may involve procedures of considerable complexity in order to answer basic questions about the value of any node. All of which adds to the potential evaluation time required at a node.

(3) From example 5, the program must on occasion be able to calculate precise variations to a depth of fourteen and possibly more. This in no way means that every move should be calculated to this depth nor that, when a move is, every branch would go to this depth also. However, the basic facility to allow probing to at least this depth must exist.

(4) From example 6 we see the need to diagnose certain dynamic properties of positions, and the requirement to communicate such data to other nodes in the tree. This need exists in order to avoid faulty interpretation and the necessity of otherwise 'discovering America' over and over again.

When conditions are detected that make a statically calculated decision incorrect (in this case that a Rook is *en prise*), the variation that discovers this fact must during tree back-up assemble the conditions which are necessary for this contradiction to remain true. This new truth should then be stored as applicable to all nodes in the tree below any node for which it is discovered to be true. . .

It is interesting to note that a key to detecting that something may not be as it appears statically, is the use of a functional analysis. In example 6, the initial indication that neither of the Rooks is capturable is that each of their attackers is also defending something of importance. Sometimes it is possible to resolve such function conflicts statically by noting that another piece can assume the required functional role without itself becoming overburdened. When this is not possible, the validity of a potential function conflict must be established dynamically by tree-searching. A general discussion of the use of functional relations in chess perception and reasoning can be found in Newell and Simon (1972). A good discussion of paths and their obstruction can be found in Botwinnik (1970).

(5) From the defence problem in example 7, we see a need for some similar communication within a search-tree. A proper description of a set of undesirable consequences can save tremendous effort in finding problem solutions if such exist, or moving on to more fruitful endeavours if not. Again, the adequacy of the language is important as it must be used to test whether the set of consequences were caused by the latest move, and to provide an input to move generators that could find an appropriate answer to the problem. For this purpose, functional relations which describe attacks that occurred, and path information which describes paths traversed by moving pieces and paths over which threats occurred, appear to be required elements of the language.

(6) The functional relations mentioned in the previous examples are in a sense patterns involving two pieces or a piece and a square. Certain clues can be gained by searching these patterns when they focus about a common square or piece. However, from example 9 we can see the need for a still higher level of pattern abstraction. Here we are looking for groups of pieces which form a pattern around some interesting focus. In the example cited, the KR7 square with the White Queen and Bishop attacking it, and the Black King are the focal points which should suffice to index into the correct pattern, which will then produce a pointer to a routine for deciding if we are confronted with an exploitable instance of the pattern in question.

Above, we have assembled the beginning of a set of requirements for a program that could have the power to play master level chess. It does not take long to dismiss the possibility of extending the current generation of chess programs to meet the above requirements. It is quite enough to realize that such a program requires about a factor of twenty of additional time for each additional two ply of depth that it searches.

In 1958 Newell, Shaw, and Simon argued that 'As analysis deepens, greater computing effort per position soon pays for itself, since it slows the growth in number of positions to be considered.' (1958a). This is well substantiated in the ACM tournaments which have convincingly shown the superiority of programs that search a subset of legal moves and evaluate a moderate amount, over programs that search all legal moves and evaluate little. Clearly it is time to move again, and more substantially, in the direction of more evaluation and less search. The requirements demonstrated in this paper show a need to do possibly ten or more times as much processing at a node than is currently done. This means that, for equivalent computing power, we are faced with generating trees of at most 5,000 nodes distributed throughout the search space. . .

. . . The conditions and the model we have set forth appear to be necessary for master chess. However, they are almost certainly not sufficient. Masters know a great deal of chess knowledge which has as yet not been encoded in any program, and would probably have to be placed in long-term memory for occasional reference. We have avoided discussing what a minimum quantity of such data might look like, since until the necessary mechanisms for its use are in place, so that it would be possible to do some experimentation, there would be little scientific validity in such speculation. There is also the problem of doing at least some learning in order to avoid repeating obvious errors in identical situations. However, an organization which takes account of the conditions noted here is almost certainly necessary to make significant progress beyond the present state of the art, and the model appears extendable to the problems of learning and further pattern encodings, as those prove necessary. In the immediate future, the major problem appears to be how to produce a search of the economy of that proposed while retaining at least the same reliability as evidenced by today's programs which use a more complete search strategy.

Figure 10. White to play

Figure 11. Black to play

Figure 12. White to play

For those who feel that our simple examples would not challenge their program design, we include figures 10–12 which are moderately more difficult. In figure 10 it is White to play and win. In figure 11 it is Black to play and not do something foolish; and we are not thinking of the obviously foolish (1) QXR, but of other foolishness derived from this by the Horizon Effect. In figure 12 it is White to play and win. We expect that a human class B player would have no difficulty with any of these.

Progress to date

Since July 1972 the author has had a program, whose general objectives are those outlined above, running at Carnegie-Mellon University. In this section we wish to report the progress that has been made. As yet the program only concerns itself with tactical (material) issues; however, it is felt that the techniques being developed are general and applicable to the other dimensions of chess evaluation. The program notes, among others, the relations of attack, defence, blocking functions and paths along which such activities occur. Thus, it has a language which is considerably more powerful than the notions of a legal move, which is the analytical element of most of today's programs. Each chessboard is described in this language. This characterization greatly facilitates finding good 'sacrificial' moves and moves which disturb the defence relations among pieces, while not hindering the evaluation of other types of moves. The program has an expectation level associated with every search it conducts, and there are mechanisms for raising and lowering this when results outside a range of acceptability from the expectation can be forced. There is a general causality facility which is used both for defence and improving attacking ideas. This facility can always detect whether a given set of consequences were not caused by the last move tried and thus constitute a problem inherited from higher in the tree. It does this by comparing a description of the consequences with a description of the move tried. However, it is not nearly as adept at detecting causality relations as an experienced chess player. Still, the facility never deduces causality when causality does not exist, and deduces noncausality about 60 per cent of the time that this is appropriate, putting it well ahead of contemporary programs. No dynamic re-evaluations have been implemented as yet, but these are planned for the near future. Higher level patterns are planned for a still later stage.

The program is at present able to investigate an average position for tactical quiescence to a depth of nine ply, generating from 100 to 2,000 nodes. The tactical reliability of such searches is somewhat better than that of the average program that participates in tournaments. Most of our effort in tree-searching has been in an attempt to improve the likely correctness of a proposed move. . . We occasionally grow a tree of 20,000 nodes because the program gets sidetracked in an inconsequential part of the tree. However, there are still several tree control algorithms we plan to implement, which should prevent such behaviour by selective jumping around in the tree. We expect in the not too distant future to extend the depth limit of the program significantly beyond its present nine ply. Even at its present depth, it is less affected by the Horizon Effect than programs with less deep searches. For instance, it has no trouble at all in figure 11, deciding that there are no diversions which can lead to an ultimate capture of the White Rook.

When the program is confronted with the defensive problem of figure 8, after the initial variation starting with 1. . P–R7 is tried, a description of what happened is backed up along with the value of the position at branch termination. At each successive node during backup, if the result is unsatisfactory, the backed-up description is compared with the description of the move made. This is done to see if what happened could have been caused by the latest move tried at that node. If not, a defensive move generator then generates the moves that can do something about the description. The description contains such information as the names of the pieces involved in the action, the path (if any) that they traversed, targets attacked when they arrived at their destinations, etc. If no defensive moves are generated and if no worthwhile aggressive moves remain to be investigated, it is assumed that the problem cannot be solved at this node of the tree. When the search reverts to the point where 1. . P–R7 was tried initially, an examination of the description reveals that the threat could possibly be countered by moving the King, guarding the K8 square, blocking the path of the Rook from K2 to K8, capturing the Rook or the Queen, or blocking or getting ready to block the KB8 square across which the check passes. From this description six moves are generated: K–R1, N–Q2, R–KB1, Q–K5, Q–K4 ch, and Q–K6. It then does not take the program very long to determine that Q–K5 is the only defence (which in fact leaves Black in a winning position).

The program has been tested extensively on positions which one finds in chess books which teach how to play good tactical chess. In such positions a more or less 'hidden' series of moves allows the player to move to achieve a decisive advantage. In working on the first 200 examples in the book *Win at Chess* (Reinfeld, 1958), the program solves about 60 per cent of the middle game problems in times ranging from a fraction of a second to eight minutes, with an average of about eighty seconds. This is despite the fact that the principal variation sometimes extends to nine ply. Occasionally the program finds forced mates in the absolute minimum number of nodes. It also has found improvements on the analysis contained in the book, which the experimenter himself did not notice. The main reason that the program is not able to solve 100 per cent of these problems is that several functional relations and many analytical routines are not yet implemented.

On the basis of tests to date, we find that the language of functions, paths, etc. is very useful for passing messages of the kind described above. We expect that it will also serve for the characterization of thematic relationships which would mitigate against a move being tried when it is 'out of context' with previous moves. However, there seems to be little doubt that more powerful languages are possible. Further, we conjecture that continuing progress in chess will be dependent on the invention of even higher level languages in which chess concepts can be expressed. Each such language level would then have an assymptote, defined by the power of the language, beyond which it would not be possible to improve the strength of the program, given that only a certain amount of time was available to compute a move. Also as concepts are agglomerated into ever higher level concepts, we expect that they would get to be more fuzzy and would require a more complex control structure than used at present in order to produce the same level of reliability as can be obtained with less fuzzy concepts. We feel that this increased conceptualization is evident in the history of chess, and should make it possible ultimately to equal and exceed the performance of the best human players.

Bibliography
(and citation index)

Bibliography
(and citation index)

Abelson, R. P. (1973). The structure of belief systems. In Schank, R. C. and Colby, K. M. (eds.) *Computer Models of Thought and Language*. San Francisco: Freeman. *pp*. 421, 424

Abelson, R. P. (1975a). Concepts for representing mundane reality in plans. In Bobrow, D. and Collins, A. (eds.) *Representation and Understanding: studies in cognitive science*. New York: Academic. *pp*. 421, 423, 429

Abelson, R. P. (1975b). Does a Story Understander need a point of view? In Schank, R. C. and Nash-Webber, B. L. (eds.) *Theoretical Issues in Natural Language Processing*. Preprints of a conference at MIT (June 1975). *p*. 430

Abelson, R. P. and Reich, C. M. (1969). Implication modules: a method for extracting meaning from input sentences. *First International Joint Conference on Artificial Intelligence*. Washington, D.C. *p*. 141

Adamson, R. E. (1952). Functional fixedness as related to problem solving: a repetition of three experiments. *Journal of Experimental Psychology*, **44**, 288–91. *p*. 17

Albert, E. (1964). 'Rhetoric', logic and poetics in Burundi: culture patterns of speech behaviour. In Gumperz, J. and Hymes, D. (eds.) *The Ethnography of Communication*. Washington, D.C.: American Anthropological Association. *p*. 472

Alkire, W. H. (1970). Systems of measurement on Woleai Atoll, Caroline Islands. *Anthropos*, **65**, 1–73. *p*. 543

Allport, D. A. (1975). The state of cognitive psychology. Review of Chase, W. G. (ed.) *Visual Information Processing. Quarterly Journal of Experimental Psychology*, **27**, 141–52. *p*. 10

Allport, G. W. (1937). *Personality: a psychological interpretation*. New York: Holt. *p*. 452

Anderson, J. R. (1976). *Language, Memory and Thought*. Hillsdale, N. J.: Erlbaum. *p*. 23

Anglin, J. (1976). The child's first terms of reference. In Ehreich, S. and Tulving, E. (eds.) *La mémoire semantique*. Paris: *Bulletin de psychologie. pp*. 221, 250, 252

Anisfeld, M. (1968). Disjunctive concepts. *Journal of General Psychology*, **78**, 223–8. *p*. 177

Aristotle (1930). Physics. In *The Works of Aristotle*, trans. R. P. Hardie and R. K. Gaye. Oxford: Clarendon. *pp*. 278, 279, 285

Aristotle (1963). Prior analytics. In Jager, R. (ed.) *Essays in Logic*. Englewood Cliffs, N. J.: Prentice Hall. *p*. 498

Asch, S. E. (1961). The metaphor: a psychological inquiry. In Henle, M. (ed.) *Documents of Gestalt Psychology*. Berkeley: University of California Press. *p*. 443

Austin, J. L. (1962). *How to Do Things with Words*, (ed.) J. O. Urmson, Cambridge, Mass.: Harvard University Press. *p. 350*

Bacon, F. (1855). *Novum Organum*. Oxford: Oxford University Press. (First published 1621.) *pp. 257, 258*

Bakan, D. (1967). *On Method*. San Francisco: Jossey-Bass. *p. 263*

Barclay, J. R. (1973). The role of comprehension in remembering sentences. *Cognitive Psychology*, **4**, 229–54. *pp. 389, 497*

Bartlett, F. C. (1932). *Remembering: a study in experimental and social psychology*. Cambridge: Cambridge University Press. *pp. 5, 344, 353, 371, 379, 432*

Bartlett, F. C. (1958). *Thinking*. London: Allen and Unwin. *p. 15*

Beaglehole, J. L. (1955). *The Journals of Captain James Cook on his Voyages of Discovery*, I. Cambridge: Cambridge University Press. *p. 543*

Beckner, M. (1959). *The Biological Way of Thought*. New York: Columbia University Press. *pp. 190, 464*

Begg, I. and Denny, J. P. (1969). Empirical reconciliation of atmosphere and conversion interpretations of syllogistic reasoning errors. *Journal of Experimental Psychology*, **81**, 351–4. *p. 84*

Bellman, B. (1969). Some constitutive factors of secrecy among the Fala Kpelle of Sucrumu, Liberia. Paper delivered at the meeting of the Liberian Research Association, Stanford, Calif. *p. 472*

Bereiter, C. and Englemann, S. (1966). *Teaching Disadvantaged Children in the Pre-School*. Englewood Cliffs, N. J.: Prentice-Hall. *p. 444*

Berlin, B. (1971). Speculations on the growth of ethnobotanical nomenclature. *Language-Behavior Research Laboratory Paper No. 39*. University of California, Berkeley. *pp. 214, 215, 216, 221, 222*

Berlin, B., Breedlove, D. E., and Raven, P. H. (1966). Folk taxonomies and biological classification. *Science*, **154**, 273–5. *pp. 185, 190*

Berlin, B., Breedlove, D. E., and Raven, P. H. (1974). *Principles of Tzeltal Plant Classification*. New York: Academic. *p. 185*

Berlin, B. and Kay, P. (1969). *Basic Color Terms: their universality and evolution*. Berkeley and Los Angeles: University of California Press. *pp. 443, 464, 506, 510*

Bernstein, B. (1961). Social class and linguistic development: a theory of social learning. In Halsey, A., Floyd, J., and Anderson, C. (eds.) *Education, Economy, and Society*. Glencoe, Ill.: Free Press. *p. 471*

Bernstein, B. (1973). *Class, Codes and Control*, I, *Theoretical Studies Towards a Sociology of Language*. St Albans: Paladin. *p. 443*

Berry, J. W. (1971). Ecological and cultural factors in spatial perceptual development. *Canadian Journal of Behavioral Science*, **3**, 324–36. *p. 478*

Beth, E. W. (1959). *The Foundations of Mathematics*. New York: Harper Torchbooks. *p. 34*

Beth, E. W. and Piaget, J. (1966). *Mathematical Epistemology and Psychology*. Dordrech: Reidel. *pp. 79, 151*

Bever, T. G. (1970). The cognitive basis for linguistic structures. In Hayes, J. R. (ed.) *Cognition and Development of Language*. New York: Wiley. *p. 349*

Beveridge, W. I. B. (1950). *The Art of Scientific Investigation*. London: Heinemann. (Paperback, 1961.) *p. 24*

Bierwisch, M. (1967). Some semantic universals of German adjectivals. *Foundations of Language*, **3**, 1–36. *p.* 100

Binet, A. (1894). *Psychologie des grands calculateurs et joueurs d'echecs*. Paris: Hachette. *p.* 523

Binet, A. (1966). Mnemonic virtuosity: a study of chess players. *Genetic Psychology Monographs*, **74**, 127–62. (First published 1893.) *p.* 527

Black, M. (1959). The views of Benjamin Lee Whorf. *Philosophical Review*, **68**, 228–38. *p.* 504

Black, M. (1963). Reasoning with loose concepts. *Dialogue*, **2**, 1–12. *p.* 463

Black, M. (1970). The *raison d'être* of inductive argument. In Black, M. (ed.) *Margins of Precision*. Ithaca: Cornell University Press. *p.* 453

Bloom, L. (1973). *One Word at a Time: the use of single-word utterances before Syntax*. The Hague: Mouton. *pp.* 242, 244

Blumenthal, A. L. (1970). *Language and Psychology*. New York: Wiley. *pp.* 389, 393

Boas, F. (1965). *The Mind of Primitive Man*. New York: Free Press. (First published 1911.) *p.* 436

Bobrow, D. (1975). Dimensions of representation. In Bobrow, D. and Collins, A. (eds.) *Representation and Understanding: studies in cognitive science*. New York: Academic. *p.* 421

Bobrow, D. and Raphael, B. (1974). New programming languages for Artificial Intelligence research. *Association for Computer Machinery Computing Surveys*, **6**, no. 3. *p.* 66

Bochenski, I. M. (1970). *A History of Formal Logic*. Notre Dame, Indiana: University of Notre Dame Press. *p.* 498

Bohr, N. (1928). The quantum postulate and the recent development of atomic theory. *Atti del Congresso Internazionale dei Fisici, 11—20 Settembre 1927*, II. Bologna. *p.* 274

Boring, E. G. (1953). A history of introspection. *Psychological Bulletin*, **50**, 169–89. *p.* 2

Botwinnik, M. M. (1970). *Computers, Chess and Long-range Planning*. Berlin: Springer Verlag. *p.* 525

Bourne, E. (1976). Agreement in the perception of personality. Ph.D. dissertation, Department of Behavioral Sciences, University of Chicago. *p.* 452

Bourne, L. E. Jr (1966). *Human Conceptual Behavior*. Boston, Mass.: Allyn and Bacon. *pp.* 175, 213, 513

Bourne, L. E. Jr and Restle, F. (1959). Mathematical theory of concept identification. *Psychological Review*, **66**, 278–96. *p.* 175

Bowen, E. (1954). *Return to Laughter*. New York: Doubleday. *p.* 439

Bower, G. H. (1970). Analysis of the mnemonic device. *American Scientist*, **58**, 496–501. *p.* 524

Bower, G. H. and Trabasso, T. (1964). Concept identification. In Atkinson, R. C. (ed.) *Studies in Mathematical Psychology*. Stanford: Stanford University Press. *p.* 175

Bowerman, M. (1976). Semantic factors in the acquisition of rules for word use and sentence construction. In Morehead, D. and Morehead, A. (eds.) *Directions in Normal and Deficient Child Language*. Baltimore: University Park Press. *pp.* 243, 245

Bracewell, R. J. (1974). Interpretation factors in the four card selection task. Paper read at the Trento conference on the selection task (unpublished). *p.* 153

Bracewell, R. J. and Hidi, S. E. (1974). The solution of an inferential problem as a function of stimulus materials. *Quarterly Journal of Experimental Psychology*, **26**, 480–8. *p.* 153

Braithwaite, R. B. (1953). *Scientific Explanation*. Cambridge: Cambridge University Press. *p.* 287

Bransford, J. D., Barclay, J. R., and Franks, J. J. (1972). Sentence memory: a constructive versus interpretive approach. *Cognitive Psychology*, **3**, 193–209. *pp*. 386, 497

Bransford, J. D. and Franks, J. J. (1971). The abstraction of linguistic ideas. *Cognitive Psychology*, **2**, 331–50. *p*. 389

Bransford, J. D. and Johnson, M. K. (1972). Contextual prerequisites for understanding: some investigations of comprehension and recall. *Journal of Verbal Learning and Verbal Behavior*, **11**, 717–26. *p*. 389

Bransford, J. D. and Johnson, M. K. (1973). Considerations of some problems of comprehension. In Chase, W. G. (ed.) *Visual Information Processing*. New York: Academic. *pp*. 389, 392

Bransford, J. D. and McCarrell, N. S. (1972). A sketch of a cognitive approach to comprehension: some thoughts about understanding what it means to comprehend. Paper presented at the Conference on Cognition and the Symbolic Processes, Pennsylvania State University, October 1972. *p*. 141

Brée, D. S. and Coppens, G. (1976). The difficulty of an implication task. *British Journal of Psychology*, **67**, 579–86, *p*. 153

Bricker, V. R. (1975). The ethnographic context of some traditional Mayan speech genres. In Bauman, R. and Sherzer, J. (eds.) *Explorations in the Ethnography of Speaking*. London: Cambridge University Press. *p*. 498

Brown, R. (1956). Language and categories. In Bruner, J. S., Goodnow, J. J., and Austin, G. A. *A Study of Thinking*. New York: Wiley. *p*. 223

Brown, R. (1958). *Words and Things*. New York: Free Press. *pp*. 377, 398, 503

Brown, R. (1965). *Social Psychology*. New York: Free Press. *p*. 244

Brown, R. (1973). *A First Language*. Cambridge, Mass.: Harvard University Press. *p*. 221

Brown, R. and Lenneberg, E. H. (1954. A study in language and cognition. *Journal of Abnormal and Social Psychology*, **49**, 454–62. *p*. 509

Bruner, J. S. (1957). Going beyond information given. In *Contemporary Approaches to Cognition: a symposium held at the University of Colorado*. Cambridge, Mass.: Harvard University Press. *p*. 473

Bruner, J. S., Goodnow, J. J., and Austin, G. A. (1956). *A Study of Thinking*. New York: Wiley. *pp*. 172, 173, 174, 175, 182, 233, 237, 481, 513

Bruner, J. S. and Olver, R. R. (1963). Development of equivalence transformations in children. In Wright, J. and Kagan, J. (eds.) *Basic Cognitive Processes in Children*. Monographs of the Society for Research in Child Development, **28**, no. 2. *p*. 237

Bruner, J. S., Olver, R. R., and Greenfield, P. M. (1966). *Studies in Cognitive Growth*. New York: Wiley. *pp*. 216, 220, 224, 237, 439, 478

Bruner, J. S. and Tagiuri, R. (1954). The perception of people. In Lindzey, G. (ed.) *Handbook of Social Psychology*, II. Cambridge, Mass.: Addison-Wesley. *p*. 517

Burke, K. (1969). *A Grammar of Motives*. Berkeley: University of California Press. *p*. 454

Burt, C. (1919). The development of reasoning in school children. *Journal of Experimental Pedagogy*, **5**, 68–77, 121–7. *pp*. 98, 107

Burton, R. (1970). Validity of retrospective reports assessed by the multitrait-multimethod analysis. *Developmental Psychology*, 311–15. *p*. 452

Campbell, D. T. (1960). Blind variation and selective retention in creative thought as in other knowledge processes. *Psychological Review*, **67**, 380–400. *pp*. 260, 268

Campbell, D. T. (1969). Prospective: artifact and control. In Rosenthal, R. and Rosnow,

R. L. (eds.) *Artifact in Behavioral Research*. New York: Academic Press. *p.* 454

Campbell, D. T. and Fiske, D. W. (1959). Convergent and discriminant validation by the multitrait-multimethod matrix. *Psychological Bulletin*, **56**, 81–105. *p.* 452

Campbell, R., Donaldson, M., and Young, B. (1976). Constraints on classificatory skills in young children. *British Journal of Psychology*, **67**, 89–100. *p.* 171

Carelman, J. (1971). *Catalog of Fantastic Things*. New York: Ballantine. *p.* 182

Carmichael, L., Hogan, H. P., and Walters, A. A. (1932). An experimental study of the effect of language on visually perceived form. *Journal of Experimental Psychology*, **15**, 73–86. *p.* 442

Carnap, R. (1936). Testability and meaning. *Philosophy of Science*, **3**, 420–71. *p.* 287n

Carnap, R. (1937). Testability and Meaning. *Philosophy of Science*, **4**, 2–40. *p.* 287

Carpenter, P. A. and Just, M. A. (1975). Sentence Comprehension: a psycholinguistic processing model of verification. *Psychological Review*, **82**, 45–73. *p.* 77

Carroll, J. B. and Casagrande, J. B. (1958). The function of language classification in behavior. In Maccoby, E. E., Newcomb, T. M., and Hartley, E. L. (eds.) *Readings in Social Psychology*. 3rd edn. New York: Holt, Rinehart, and Winston. *p.* 505

Casagrande, J. B. and Hale, K. L. (1967). Semantic relationships in Papago folk-definitions. In Hymes, D. (ed.) *Studies in Southwestern Ethnolinguistics*. The Hague: Mouton. *pp.* 448, 464

Cattell, R. B. (1957). *Personality and Motivation Structure and Measurement*. Yonkers-On-Hudson: World Book Co. *p.* 452

Cellérier, G. (1972). Information processing tendencies in recent experiments in cognitive learning – theoretical implications. In Farnham-Diggory, S. (ed.) *Information Processing in Children*. New York: Academic. *p.* 293

Ceraso, J. and Provitera, A. (1971). Sources of error in syllogistic reasoning. *Cognitive Psychology*, **2**, 400–10. *pp.* 84, 129

Chafe, W. (1972a). *First Technical Report, Contrastive Semantics Project*. Berkeley: University of California, Department of Linguistics. *p.* 365

Chafe, W. (1972b). Discourse structure and human knowledge. In Carroll, J. B. and Freedle, R. O. (eds.) *Language Comprehension and the Acquisition of Knowledge*. Washington: Winston. *p.* 415

Chapman, L. J. (1967). Illusory correlation in observational report. *Journal of Verbal Learning and Verbal Behavior*, **6**, 151–5. *p.* 446

Chapman, L. J. and Chapman, J. P. (1959). Atmosphere effect re-examined. *Journal of Experimental Psychology*, **58**, 220–6. (Reprinted in Wason and Johnson-Laird, 1968.) *pp.* 84, 129, 135

Chapman, L. J. and Chapman, J. P. (1967). Genesis of popular but erroneous psychodiagnostic observations. *Journal of Abnormal and Social Psychology*, **72**, 193–204. *pp.* 334, 446

Chapman, L. J. and Chapman, J. P. (1969). Illusory correlation as an obstacle to the use of valid psychodiagnostic signs. *Journal of Abnormal and Social Psychology*, **74**, 271–80. *p.* 446

Charniak, E. (1972). Towards a model of children's story comprehension. MIT AI Laboratory Memorandum AI–TR–266. *pp.* 368, 421, 422

Charniak, E. (1973). Jack and Janet in search of a theory of knowledge. *Third International Joint Conference on Artificial Intelligence*. Stanford: Stanford Research Institute. *pp.* 141, 353

588 BIBLIOGRAPHY (AND CITATION INDEX)

Chase, W. G. and Simon, H. A. (1973). Perception in chess. *Cognitive Psychology*, **4**, 55–81. *pp.* 548, 554, 555

Chomsky, N. (1957). *Syntactic Structures*. The Hague: Mouton. *p.* 364

Chomsky, N. (1965). *Aspects of the Theory of Syntax*. Cambridge, Mass.: MIT Press. *pp.* 4, 98, 99

Chomsky, N. (1968). *Language and Mind*. New York: Harcourt, Brace, and World. *p.* 449

Church, J. (1961). *Language and the Discovery of Reality*. New York: Random House. *p.* 270

Clacett, M. (1959). *The Science of Mechanics in the Middle Ages*. Madison, Wis. *pp.* 279n, 280

Claparède, F. (1934). *La genèse de l'hypothèse*. Geneva: Kundig. *p.* 306

Clark, E. (1973). What's in a word? On the child's acquisition of semantics in his first language. In Moore, T. E. (ed.) *Cognitive Development and the Acquisition of Language*. New York: Academic. *pp.* 183, 239, 244, 249, 506

Clark, E. (1974). Some aspects of the conceptual basis for first language acquisition. In Schiefelbusch, R. L. and Lloyd, L. L. (eds.) *Language Perspectives: acquisition, retardation, and intervention*. Baltimore: University Park Press. *p.* 239

Clark, E. (1975). Knowledge, context, and strategy in the acquisition of meaning. In Dato, D. (ed.) *Developmental Psycholinguistcs: theory and applications* (26th Annual Georgetown University Roundtable). Washington, D.C.: Georgetown University Press. *pp.* 240, 249

Clark, H. H. (1969a). The primitive nature of children's relational concepts. In Hayes, J. R. (ed.) *Cognition and the Development of Language*. New York: Wiley. *p.* 110

Clark, H. H. (1969b). The influence of language in solving three-term series problems. *Journal of Experimental Psychology*, **82**, 205–15. *p.* 111

Clark, H. H. (1974). Semantics and comprehension. In Sebeok, T. A. (ed.) *Current Trends in Linguistics*, XII, *Linguistics and Adjacent Arts and Sciences*. The Hague: Mouton. *pp.* 77, 398

Clark, H. H. and Haviland, S. E. (1974). Psychological processes as linguistic explanation. In Cohen, D. (ed.) *Explaining Linguistic Phenomena*. Washington: Hemisphere. *p.* 412

Clark, H. H. and Haviland, S. E. (in press). Comprehension and the Given–New Contract. In Freedle R. (ed.) *Discourse Production and Comprehension*. Hillsdale, N. J.: Erlbaum. *p.* 412

Cleveland, A. A. (1907). The psychology of chess. *American Journal of Psychology*, **18**, 269–308. *p.* 527

Cofer, C. N. (1965). On some factors in the organizational characteristics of free recall. *American Psychologist*, **20**, 261–72. *p.* 507

Cofer, C. N. and Bruce, D. R. (1965). Form-class as the basis for clustering in the recall of nonassociated words. *Journal of Verbal Learning and Verbal Behavior*, **4**, 386–9. *p.* 506

Cole, M., Gay, J., Glick, J., and Sharp, D. (1971). *The Cultural Context of Learning and Thinking*. New York: Basic Books. *pp.* 473, 475, 477, 484, 486, 487, 488

Cole, M. and Scribner, S. (1974). *Culture and Thought: a psychological introduction*. New York: Wiley. *pp.* 439, 483

Collins, A. M. and Quillian, M. R. (1972). How to make a language user. In Tulving, E. and Donaldson, W. (eds.) *Organization of Memory*. New York: Academic. *pp.* 141, 398

Craik, K. J. W. (1943). *The Nature of Explanation*. Cambridge: Cambridge University Press. *pp.* 6, 7, 538

D'Andrade, R. G. (1965). Trait psychology and componential analysis. *American Anthropologist*, **67**, 215–28. *pp.* 446, 451

D'Andrade, R. G. (1973). Cultural constructions of reality. In Nader, L. and Maretzki, T. W. (eds.) *Cultural Illness and Health*. Washington: American Anthropological Association. *p.* 446

D'Andrade, R. G. (1974). Memory and the assessment of behavior. In T. Blalock (ed.) *Measurement in the Social Sciences*. Chicago: Aldine-Atherton. *pp.* 446, 455, 457

Dascal, M. and Margalit, A. (1974). A new 'revolution' in linguistics? 'Text-grammars' vs. 'Sentence-grammars'. *Journal of Theoretical Linguistics*, **1**, 195–213. *p.* 351

Dasen, P. R. (1972a). Cross cultural Piagetian research: a summary. *Journal of Cross Cultural Psychology*, **3**, 23–9. *pp.* 440, 448, 478, 479, 483

Dasen, P. R. (1972b). The development of conservation in aboriginal children: a replication study. *International Journal of Psychology*, **7**, 75–86. *pp.* 478, 479

Davey, A. and Longuet-Higgins, C. (1977). A computational model of discourse production. In Smith, P. T. and Campbell, R. N. (eds.) *Proceedings of the Stirling Conference on Psycholinguistics*. London: Plenum (in press). *p.* 352

de Bono, E. (1967). *The Five-day Course in Thinking*. Harmondsworth, Middx.: Penguin. *p.* 6

De Groot, A. D. (1965). *Thought and Choice in Chess*. The Hague: Mouton. *pp.* 308, 527, 548

De Groot, A. D. (1966). Perception and memory versus thought. In Kleinmuntz, B. (ed.) *Problem Solving: research, method and theory*. London: Wiley. *p.* 527

De Soto, C.B., London, M., and Handel, S. (1965). Social reasoning and spatial paralogic. *Journal of Personality and Social Psychology*, **2**, 513–21. (Reprinted in Wason and Johnson-Laird, 1968.) *pp.* 77, 96, 97, 98

De Valois, R. L. and Jacobs, G. H. (1968). Primate color vision. *Science*, **162**, 533–40. *pp.* 509, 515

Deutsch, M. *et al.* (1976). *The Disadvantaged Child*. New York: Basic Books. *p.* 469

Dewey, J. (1963). *How We Think*. Portions published in Hutchins, R. M. and Adler, M. J. (eds.) *Gateway to the Great Books*, x. Chicago: Encyclopedia Britannica, Inc. (Originally published by Heath, 1933, 1961.) *p.* 379

Donaldson, M. (1959). Positive and negative information in matching problems. *British Journal of Psychology*, **50**, 235–62. (Reprinted in Wason and Johnson-Laird, 1968,) *p.* 77

Donaldson, M. (1963). *A Study of Children's Thinking*. London: Tavistock. *pp.* 98, 108, 109, 480

Donaldson, M. and Wales, R. (1970). On the acquisition of some relational terms. In Hayes, J. (ed.) *Cognition and the Development of Language*. New York: Wiley. *pp.* 110, 230, 232

Doob, L. (1960). *Becoming More Civilized*. New Haven, Conn.: Yale University Press. *p.* 474

Dooling, D. J. and Lachman, R. (1971). Effects of comprehension on retention of prose. *Journal of Experimental Psychology*, **88**, 216–22. *p.* 344

Doran, J. E. and Hodson, F. R. (1966). A digital computer analysis of palaeolithic flint assemblages. *Nature*, **210**, 688–9. *p*. 190

Dreyfus, H. L. (1972). *What Computers Can't Do*. New York: Harper and Row. *p*. 9

Dugas, R. (1950). *Histoire de la mécanique*. Neuchâtel: Editions du Griffon. *p*. 306

Duncker, K. (1945). On problem solving. *Psychological Monographs*, **58**, whole no. 270, 1–113. *pp*. 15, 16, 17, 61

Duthie, J. (1963). A further study of overlap error in three-term series problems. In Donaldson, M. *A Study of Children's Thinking*. London: Tavistock. *pp*. 109, 110

Egan, D. E. and Greeno, J. G. (1974). Theory of rule induction: knowledge acquired in concept learning, serial pattern learning, and problem solving. In Gregg, L. W. (ed.) *Knowledge and Cognition*. New York: Wiley. *p*. 177

Einstein, A. (1905). Zur Elektrodynamik bewegter Körper. *Annalen der Physik*, **17**, 891–921. *p*. 274n

Einstein, A. (1916). *Ueber die spezielle und allgemeine Relativitätstheorie (Gemeinverständlich)*. Braunschweig. *pp*. 274n

Eisenstadt, M. (1974). Blitz planning: the construction and use of internal representations for rapid problem solving. Unpublished doctoral dissertation, Department of psychology, University of California, San Diego. *p*. 554

Eisenstadt, M. and Kareev, Y. (1975). Aspects of human problem solving: the use of internal representations. In Norman, D. A., Rumelhart, D. E., and the LNR Research Group, *Explorations in Cognition*. San Francisco: Freeman. *pp*. 551, 555, 557, 564

Ekman, P. (1972). Universals and cultural differences in facial expressions of emotion. In Cole, J. K. (ed.) *Nebraska Symposium on Motivation*. Lincoln, Nebr.: University of Nebraska Press. *pp*. 219, 517

Elkind, D. (1969). Conservation and concept formation. In Elkind, D. and Flavell, J. (eds.) *Studies in Cognitive Development*. New York: Oxford University Press. *p*. 230

Emory, K. P. (1959). Origin of the Hawaiians. *Journal of the Polynesian Society*, **68**, 29–35. *p*. 537

Endler, N. S. and Hunt, J. M. (1968). S-R inventories of hostility and anxiousness. *Journal of Personality and Social Psychology*, **9**, 309–15. *p*. 452

Erickson, J. R. (1973). A set analysis theory of behavior in formal syllogistic reasoning tasks. Paper presented to the Loyola Symposium on Cognition, Chicago, May 1973. *pp*. 85, 129, 134

Ernst, G. W. and Newell, A. (1969). *GPS: A case study in generality and problem solving*. New York: Academic. *p*. 23

Ervin, S. (1962). The connotations of gender. *Word*, **18**, 248–61. *p*. 503

Evans, J. St. B. T. (1972a). Deductive reasoning and linguistic usage (with special reference to negation). Unpublished Ph.D. thesis, University of London, *pp*. 115, 116, 117

Evans, J. St. B. T. (1972b). Reasoning with negatives. *British Journal of Psychology*, **63**, 213–19. *p*. 116

Evans, J. St. B. T. (1972c). Interpretation and 'matching bias' in a reasoning task. *Quarterly Journal of Experimental Psychology*, **24**, 193–9. *pp*. 80, 154

Evans, J. St. B. T. and Lynch, J. S. (1973). Matching bias in the selection task. *British Journal of Psychology*, **64**, 391–7. *p*. 154

Evans, J. St. B. T. and Wason, P. C. (1976). Rationalization in a reasoning task. *British Journal of Psychology*, **67**, 479–86. *p.* 155

Evans-Pritchard, E. E. (1937). *Witchcraft, Oracles and Magic among the Azande*. Oxford: Clarendon. *pp.* 436, 446

Evans-Pritchard, E. E. (1963). Sanza, a characteristic feature of Zande language and thought. In *Essays in Social Anthropology*. New York: Free Press. *pp.* 471, 472

Fechner, G. T. (1860). See Woodworth, R. S. *Experimental Psychology*, ch.2. New York: Holt, 1938. *p.* 523

Feynman, R. P., Leighton, R. B., and Sands, M. (1963). *The Feynman Lectures on Physics*. Reading, Mass.: Addison-Wesley. *p.* 261

Fillenbaum, S. (1968). Recall for answers to 'conducive' questions. *Language and Speech*, **11**, 46–53. *p.* 112

Fillmore, C. J. (1968). The case for case. In Bach, E. and Harms, R. T. (eds.) *Universals in Linguistic Theory*. Chicago: Holt, Rinehart and Winston. *p.* 367

Fillmore, C. J. (1971). Types of lexical information. In Steinberg, D. D. and Jakobovits, L.A. (eds.) *Semantics: an interdisciplinary reader in philosophy, linguistics and psychology*. Cambridge: Cambridge University Press. *p.* 395

Fillmore, C. J. (1975). An alternative to checklist theories of meaning. *Proceedings of the First Annual Meeting of the Berkeley Linguistics Society*, 123–31. *pp.* 250, 252

Fisher, S. C. (1916). The process of generalizing abstraction; and its product, the general concept. *Psychological Monographs*, **21**, no. 2 (whole no. 90). *p.* 182

Fiske, D. W. (1974). The limits for the conventional science of personality. *Journal of Personality*, **42**, 1–11. *pp.* 451, 452

Flavell, J. (1970). Concept development. In Mussen, P. (ed.) *Carmichael's Manual of Child Psychology*, I. New York: Wiley. *p.* 224

Flavell, J. H. (1977). *Cognitive Development*. Englewood Cliffs, N.J.: Prentice Hall. *p.* 440

Flavell, J. H. and Wohlwill, J. (1969). Formal and functional aspects of cognitive development. In Elkind, D. and Flavell, J. H. (eds.) *Studies in Cognitive Development: essays in honor of Jean Piaget*. New York: Oxford University Press. *p.* 480

Fodor, J. A. (1972). Some reflections on L. S. Vygotsky's Thought and Language. *Cognition*, **1**, 83–95. *pp.* 178, 179

Fodor, J. A. (1976). *The Language of Thought*. Hassocks, Sussex: Harvester Press. *pp.* 87, 179, 445

Frase, L. T. (1969). Depth of processing text: application of graph theory to recall changes induced by the logical analysis of text. *Proceedings of the 77th Annual Convention, American Psychological Association*, 617–18. *p.* 344

Frase, L. T. (1972). Maintenance and control in the acquisition of knowledge from written materials. In Carroll, J. B. and Freedle, R. O. (eds.) *Language Comprehension and the Acquisition of Knowledge*. Washington, D.C.: Winston. *p.* 344

Fredericksen, C. H. (1972). Effects of task-induced cognitive operations on comprehension and memory processes. In Carroll, J. B. and Freedle, R. O. (eds.) *Language Comprehension and the Acquisition of Knowledge*. Washington, D.C.: Winston. *p.* 345

Freud, S. (1925). Negation. In *Complete Psychological Works of Sigmund Freud*, trans. J. Strachey, XIX. London: Hogarth. *p.* 77

Fries, C. C. (1952). *The Structure of English: an introduction to the construction of English sentences*. New York: Harcourt, Brace. p. 503

Furth, H., Youniss, J., and Ross, B. (1970). Children's utilization of logical symbols. *Developmental Psychology*, **3**, 36–57. p. 223

Galanter, E. H. and Gerstenhaber, M. (1956). On thought: the extrinsic theory. *Psychological Review*, **63**, 218–27. p. 13

Galanter, E. H. and Smith, W. A. S. (1958). Some experiments on a simple thought-problem. *American Journal of Psychology*, **71**, 359–66. p. 13

Galbraith, R. C. and Underwood, B. J. (1973). Perceived frequency of concrete and abstract words. *Memory and Cognition*, **1**, 56–60. p. 334

Galileo (1946). *Dialogues concerning Two New Sciences*, trans. H. Crew and A. de Salvio. Evanston and Chicago. p. 286n

Galileo (1953). *Dialogue concerning the Two Chief World Systems*, trans. S. Drake. Berkeley: University of California Press. p. 280

Galton, F. (1928). *Inquiries into Human Faculty and its Development*. London: Dent. (First published 1880.) p. 523

Garner, W. R. (1966). To perceive is to know. *American Psychologist*, **21**, 11–19. p. 383

Garner, W. R. (1974). *The Processing of Information and Structure*. Potomac, Md.; Erlbaum. p. 212

Garner, W. R. (1976). Interaction of stimulus dimensions in concept and choice processes. *Cognitive Psychology*, **8**, 98–123. p. 179

Garrod, S. and Sanford, A. J. (1977). Interpreting anaphoric relations: the integration of semantic information while reading. *Journal of Verbal Learning and Verbal Behavior* (in press). p. 348

Gatty, H. (1958). *Nature is your Guide*. London: Collins. pp. 541, 547

Gatty, T. (1961). Further investigations into the failure to eliminate hypotheses, with special reference to personality and set. Unpublished paper. p. 313

Gay, J. and Cole, M. (1967). *The New Mathematics and an Old Culture*. New York: Holt, Rinehart, and Winston. p. 469

Geertz, C. (1973a). *The Interpretation of Cultures*. New York: Basic Books. p. 454

Geertz C. (1973b). Thick description: toward an interpretive theory of culture. In *the Interpretation of Cultures: selected essays by Clifford Geertz*. New York: Basic Books. p. 438

Gelernter, H. (1963a). Realization of a geometry-theorem proving machine. In Feigenbaum, E. and Feldman, J. (eds.) *Computers and Thought*. New York: McGraw-Hill. p. 48

Gelernter, H. (1963b). Machine-generated problem-saving graphs. In *Proceedings of the Symposium on Mathematical Theory of Automata*. New York: Polytechnic Press. p. 49

Gellner, E. (1973). The savage and the modern mind. In Horton. R. and Finnegan, R. (eds.) *Modes of Thought*. London: Faber and Faber. p. 466

Getzels, J. W. and Jackson, P. W. (1962). *Creativity and Intelligence*. New York: Wiley. p. 6

Gibson, E. J. (1969). *Principles of Perceptual Learning and Development*. New York: Appleton-Century-Crofts. p. 378

Gibson, J. J. (1966). *The Senses considered as Perceptual Systems*. New York: Houghton Mifflin. pp. 378, 383

Gilhooly, K. J. and Falconer, W. A. (1974). Concrete and abstract terms and relations in testing a rule. *Quarterly Journal of Experimental Psychology*, **26**, 355–9. p. 153

Gilmour, J. S. L. (1951). The development of taxonomic theory since 1851. *Nature*, **168**, 400–2. *p.* 191

Gladwin, T. (1970). *East is a Big Bird*. Cambridge, Mass.: Harvard University Press. *pp.* 480, 537, 542

Goffman, E. (1974). *Frame analysis: an essay on the organization of experience*. New York: Harper and Row. *p.* 454

Golding, W. (1955). *The Inheritors*. London: Faber and Faber. *p.* 435

Goldman, N. (1975). Conceptual generation. In Schank, R. C. (ed.) *Conceptual Information Processing*. Amsterdam: North Holland. *p.* 427

Goldstein, I. P. (1974). Understanding simple picture programs. MIT AI Laboratory Memorandum AI–TR–294. *pp.* 25, 375

Good, I. J. (ed.) (1962). *The Scientist Speculates: an anthology of half-baked ideas*. London: Heinemann. *p.* 190

Goodenough, W. H. (1953). Native astronomy in Micronesia: a rudimentary science. *Scientific Monthly*, **73**, 105–10. *p.* 544

Goodwin, R. Q. and Wason, P. C. (1972). Degrees of insight. *British Journal of Psychology*, **63**, 205–12. *pp.* 153, 155

Goody, J. and Watt, I. (1962). The consequences of literacy. *Comparative Studies in Sociology and History*, **5**, 304–45. *p.* 474

Gordon, W. J. J. (1961). *Synectics: the development of creative capacity*. New York: Harper and Row. *p.* 6

Gough, P. B. (1965). Grammatical transformations and speed of understanding. *Journal of Verbal Learning and Verbal Behavior*, **4**, 107–11. *pp.* 105, 111, 112

Gough, P. B. (1966). The verification of sentences: the effects of delay on evidence and sentence length. *Journal of Verbal Learning and Verbal Behavior*, **5**, 492–6. *pp.* 105, 111, 112

Greenberg, J. H. (1966). *Language Universals*. The Hague: Mouton. *p.* 100

Greenblatt, R. D. (1967). The Greenblatt chess program. *Proceedings of the 1967 Fall Joint Computer Conference*, 801–10. *p.* 565

Greene, J. M. (1970). Syntactic form and semantic function. *Quarterly Journal of Experimental Psychology*, **22**, 14–27. *p.* 115

Greenfield, P. M. (1966). On culture and conservation. In Bruner, J.S., Olver, R. R. and Greenfield, P. M. (eds.) *Studies in Cognitive Growth*. New York: Wiley. *p.* 479

Greenfield, P. M. and Bruner, J. S. (1966). Culture and cognitive growth. *International Journal of Psychology*, **1**, 89–107. *pp.* 474, 478

Greenfield, P. M. and Childs, C. (1974). Weaving, color terms, and pattern representation: cultural influences and cognitive development among the Zinacantecos of southern Mexico. In Dawson, J. and Lonner, W. (eds.) *Readings in Cross-Cultural Psychology: Proceedings of the First International Conference of the International Association for Cross-Cultural Psychology*. Hong Kong: University of Hong Kong Press. *pp.* 480, 481, 516

Greenfield, P. M., Nelson, K., and Saltzman, E. (1972). The development of rulebound strategies for manipulating seriated cups: a parallel between action and grammar. *Cognitive Psychology*, **3**, 291–310. *p.* 26

Greenfield, P. M. and Smith, J. H. (1976). *The Structure of Communication in Early Language Development*. New York: Academic. *p.* 242

Greeno, J. G. (1974). Hobbits and Orcs: acquisition of a sequential concept. *Cognitive Psychology*, **6**, 270–92. *p.* 23

Gregg, L. (1967). Internal representation of sequential concepts. In Kleinmuntz, B. (ed.) *Concepts and the Structure of Memory*. New York: Wiley. *p.* 61

Gregory, R. L. (1970). *The Intelligent Eye*. London: Weidenfeld and Nicolson. *p.* 341

Grice, H. P. (1975). Logic and conversation. William James Lectures, Harvard University, 1967. In Cole, P. and Morgan, J. L. (eds.) *Studies in Syntax*, III. New York: Academic. *pp.* 352, 411

Gruber, H. E. (1974). *Darwin on Man: a psychological study of scientific creativity*. London: Wildwood House. *pp.* 6, 259, 304

Gumperz, J. and Hymes, D. (1972). *Directions in Sociolinguistics: the ethnography of communication*. New York: Holt, Rinehart, and Winston. *p.* 480

Guzman, A. (1968). Decomposition of a visual scene into three-dimensional bodies. *AFIPS Proceedings of Fall Joint Computer Conference*, **32**, 291–304. *p.* 357

Hadamard, J. (1945). *The Psychology of Invention in the Mathematical Field*. New York: Dover. *p.* 6

Halliday, M. A. K. (1967). Notes on transitivity and theme in English: II. *Journal of Linguistics*, **3**, 199–244. *p.* 99

Halliday, M. A. K. (1973). Linguistic function and literary style: an inquiry into the language of William Golding's *The Inheritors*. In Halliday, M. A. K. *Explorations in the Functions of Language*. London: Edward Arnold. *p.* 435

Halliday, M. A. K. and Hasan, R. (1976). *Cohesion in English*. London: Longman. *p.* 351

Handel, S., De Soto, C., and London, M. (1968). Reasoning and spatial representations. *Journal of Verbal Learning and Verbal Behavior*, **3**, 351–7. *p.* 98

Hanson, N. R. (1958). *Patterns of Discovery*. Cambridge: Cambridge University Press. *p.* 290n

Harman, H. H. (1967). *Modern Factor Analysis*. 2nd edn. Chicago: University of Chicago Press. *p.* 197

Harris, E. (1970). *Hypothesis and Perception*. London: Allen and Unwin. *p.* 261

Haviland, S. E. and Clark, H. H. (1974). What's new? Acquiring new information as a process in comprehension. *Journal of Verbal Learning and Verbal Behavior*, **13**, 512–21. *p.* 412

Haygood, R. C. and Bourne, L. E. Jr (1965). Attribute- and rule-learning aspects of conceptual behavior. *Psychological Review*, **72**, 175–95. *p.* 176

Heidbreder, E. (1924). An experimental study of thinking. *Archives of Psychology*, **73**, *p.* 259

Heider, E. R. (1971). 'Focal' color areas and the development of color names. *Developmental Psychology*, **4**, 447–55. *pp.* 506, 513

Heider, E. R. (1972a). Nature of the mental code for natural categories. Paper presented at the meeting of the Psychonomics Society, St Louis, November 1972. *p.* 518

Heider, E. R. (1972b). Probabilities, sampling, and ethnographic method: the case of Dani color names. *Man*, **7**, 448–66. *p.* 512

Heider, E. R. (1972c). Universals in color naming and memory. *Journal of Experimental Psychology*, **93**, 10–20. *pp.* 511, 512

Heider, E. R. and Olivier, D. C. (1972). The structure of the color space in naming and memory for two languages. *Cognitive Psychology*, **3**, 337–54. *p.* 512

Heider, K. G. (1970). *The Dugum Dani: a Papuan culture in the Highlands of West New Guinea*. Chicago: Aldine. *p.* 512

Heine, T. T. (1925). *Simplicissimus*, **30**, no. 181. *p.* 193

Heisenberg, W. (1927). Ueber den anschaulichen Inhalt der quantentheorischen Kinematik und Mechanik. *Zeitschrift für Physik*, **43**, 172–98. *p.* 274n

Helmholtz, H. (1962). *Treatise on Physiological Optics*, III, ed. J. P. C. Southall. New York: Dover. (First published 1866.) *p.* 538

Helmholtz, H. (1963). *Handbook of Physiological Optics*. Reprint. New York: Dover. *p.* 341

Hempel, C. G. (1952). *Fundementals of Concept Formation in Empirical Science*, II, no. 7. In *International Encyclopedia of Unified Science*. Chicago. *p.* 287n

Henle, M. (1962). On the relation between logic and thinking. *Psychological Review*, **69**, 366–78. (Reprinted in Wason and Johnson-Laird, 1968.) *pp.* 84, 494

Hering, E. (1964). *Outlines of a Theory of the Light Sense*, trans. L. M. Hurvich and D. Jameson. Cambridge, Mass.: Harvard University Press. *p.* 515

Heron, A. (1971). Concrete operations, 'g' and achievement in Zambian children. *Journal of Cross-Cultural Psychology*, **2**, 325–36. *p.* 478

Hewitt, C. (1972). Description and theoretical analysis of PLANNER. MIT AI Laboratory Report MIT–AI–258. *p.* 66

Hickerson, N. P. (1971). Review of 'Basic color terms: their universality and evolution'. *International Journal of American Linguistics*, **37**, 257–70. *p.* 511

Hill, S. in Suppes, P. (1965). On the behavioral foundations of mathematical concepts. In Morrisett, L. N. and Vinsonhaler, J. (eds.) *Mathematical Learning*, Monographs of the Society for Research in Child Development, **30**, 60–96. *p.* 80

Hintikka, J. (1973). *Logic, Language-games and Information: Kantian themes in the philosophy of logic*. Oxford: Clarendon. *p.* 135

Holt, J. (1969). *How Children Fail*. Harmondsworth, Middx.: Penguin, *p.* 14

Holt, R. R. (1964). Imagery: the return of the ostracized. *American Psychologist*, **19**, 254–64. *p.* 524

Horton, R. (1967). African traditional thought and Western science. *Africa*, **37**, 50–71 (Part 1); 159–87 (Part 2). *p.* 466

Horton, R. (1968). Neo-Tylorianism: sound sense or sinister prejudice? *Man*, **3**, 625–34. *p.* 466

Hovland, C. I. and Hunt, E. B. (1960). Computer simulation of concept attainment. *Behavioral Science*, **5**, 265–7. *p.* 176

Hovland, C. I. and Weiss, W. (1953). Transmission of information concerning concepts through positive and negative instances. *Journal of Experimental Psychology*, **45**, 175–82. *p.* 171

Huddleston, R. D. (1967). More on the English comparative. *Journal of Linguistics*, **3**, 91–102. *p.* 101

Hudson, L. (1966). *Contrary Imaginations*. London: Methuen. *p.* 6

Hudson, L. (1968). *Frames of Mind*. London: Methuen. *p.* 444

Hudson, L. (ed.) (1970). *The Ecology of Human Intelligence*. Harmondsworth, Middx.: Penguin. *p.* 6

Huey, E. B. (1968). *The Psychology and Pedagogy of Reading*. Cambridge, Mass.: MIT Press. *p.* 377

Hughes, G. E. and Cresswell, M. J. (1968). *An Introduction to Modal Logic*. London: Methuen. *p.* 76

Hughes, M. A. M. (1966). The use of negative information in concept attainment. Unpublished Ph.D. thesis, University of London. *p.* 146

Hull, C. L. (1920). Quantitative aspects of the evolution of concepts. *Psychological Monographs*, **28**, whole no. 123. *pp.* 170, 171

Humphrey, G. (1951). *Thinking*. London: Methuen. *p.* 2

Hunt, E. B. (1962). *Concept Learning: an information processing problem*. New York: Wiley. *pp.* 176, 177

Hunt, E. B., Marin, J., and Stone, P. J. (1966). *Experiments in Induction*. New York: Academic. *pp.* 176, 178

Hunter, I. M. L. (1957). The solving of three-term series problems. *British Journal of Psychology*, **48**, 286–98. *pp.* 77, 84, 98, 107

Hunter, I. M. L. (1977a). An exceptional memory. *British Journal of Psychology*, **68**, 155–64. *p.* 44

Hunter, I. M. L. (1977b). Imagery, comprehension and mnemonics. *Journal of Mental Imagery*, **1** (in press). *p.* 44

Huttenlocher, J. and Strauss, S. (1968). Comprehension and a statement's relation to the situation it describes. *Journal of Verbal Learning and Verbal Behavior*, **7**, 527–30. *pp.* 90, 110

Huttenlocher, J., Eisenberg, K., and Strauss, S. (1968). Comprehension: relation between perceived actor and logical subject. *Journal of Verbal Learning and Verbal Behavior*, **7**, 300–4. *pp.* 91, 92, 110

Hymes, D. (1974). Ways of speaking. In Bauman, R. and Sherzer, J. (eds.) *Explorations in the Ethnography of Speaking*. London: Cambridge University Press. *pp.* 497, 499

Ingram, E. (1971). The requirements of model users. In Huxley, R. and Ingram, E. (eds.) *Language Acquisition: models and methods*. New York: Academic. *p.* 474

Inhelder, B. (1972). Information processing tendencies in recent experiments in cognitive learning – empirical studies. In Farnham-Diggory, S. (ed.) *Information Processing in Children*. New York: Academic. *p.* 293

Inhelder, B. and Piaget, J. (1958). *The Growth of Logical Thinking from Childhood to Adolescence*. New York: Basic Books. *pp.* 79, 87, 151, 224, 225, 293, 296, 297, 305, 447

Inhelder, B. and Piaget, J. (1964). *The Early Growth of Logic in the Child*. New York: Harper. *pp.* 224, 225

Inhelder, B., Sinclair, H., and Bovet, M. (1974). *Learning and the Development of Cognition*. Cambridge, Mass.: Harvard University Press. (French edn, Paris: Presses Univers France, 1946.) *p.* 293

Istomina, Z. M. (1963). Perception and naming of color in early childhood. *Soviet Psychology and Psychiatry*, **1**, 37–46. *p.* 506

Jackendoff, R. (1972). *Semantic Interpretation in Generative Grammar*. Cambridge, Mass.: MIT Press. *p.* 130

Jakobson, R. and Halle, M. (1956). *Fundamentals of Language*. The Hague: Mouton. *p.* 436

James, W. (1890). *The Principles of Psychology*. New York: Holt. *pp.* 77, 341

Janik, A. and Toulmin, S (1973). *Wittgenstein's Veinna*. London: Weidenfeld and Nicolson. *p.* 441

Jardine, N. and Sibson, R. (1971). *Mathematical Taxonomy*. London: Wiley. *pp.* 186, 187, 195

Jenkins, H. and Ward, W. (1965). Judgements of contingency between responses and outcomes. *Psychological Monographs*, **79**, whole no. 594. *pp*. 437, 447

Jennings, H. S. (1906). *The Behavior of the Lower Organisms*. New York: Columbia University Press. *p*. 267

Jensen, A. (1969). How much can we boost IQ and scholastic achievement? *Harvard Educational Review*, **39**, 162–70. *p*. 444

Johansson, G. (1971). Visual perception of biological motion and a model for its analysis. Department of Psychology Report 100, University of Uppsala. *p*. 343

Johnson, E. S. (1964). An information processing model of one kind of problem solving. *Psychological Monographs*, whole no. 581. *p*. 61

Johnson, M. K., Bransford, J. D., and Solomon, S. (1973). Memory for tacit implications of sentences. *Journal of Experimental Psychology*, **98**, 203–5. *p*. 388

Johnson-Laird, P. N. (1969). Reasoning with ambiguous sentences. *British Journal of Psychology*, **60**, 17–23. *p*. 141

Johnson-Laird, P. N. (1970). The interpretation of quantified sentences. In Flores d'Arcais, G. B. and Levelt, W. J. M. (eds.) *Advances in Psycholinguistics*. Amsterdam: North-Holland. *p*. 130

Johnson-Laird, P. N. (1972). The three-term series problem. *Cognition*, **1**, 57–82. *p*. 78

Johnson-Laird, P. N. (1977). Psycholinguistics without linguistics. In Sutherland, N. S. (ed.) *Tutorial Essays in Psychology*, I. Hillsdale, N. J.: Erlbaum (in press). *p*. 346

Johnson-Laird, P. N., Legrenzi, P., and Sonino Legrenzi, M. (1972). Reasoning and a sense of reality. *British Journal of Psychology*, **63**, 395–400. *pp*. 152, 316

Johnson-Laird, P. N. and Tagart, J. (1969). How implication is understood. *American Journal of Psychology*, **82**, 367–73. *pp*. 80, 146

Johnson-Laird, P. N. and Tridgell, J. (1972). When negation is easier than affirmation. *Quarterly Journal of Experimental Psychology*, **24**, 87–91. *p*. 117

Johnson-Laird, P. N. and Wason, P. C. (1970). Insight into a logical relation. *Quarterly Journal of Experimental Psychology*, **22**, 49–61. *pp*. 146, 155, 156

Jones, E. E. and Nisbett, R. E. (1972). The actor and the observer: divergent perceptions of the causes of behavior. In Jones, E. E. *et al*. (eds.) *Attribution: perceiving the causes of behavior*. Morristown, N. J.: General Learning Press. *p*. 454

Jones, S. (1970). Visual and verbal processes in problem-solving. *Cognitive Psychology*, **1**, 201–14. *p*. 78

Kagan, J. and Lemkin, J. (1961). Form, color, and size in children's conceptual behavior. *Child Development*, **32**, 25–8. *p*. 238

Kagan, J., Moss, H., and Sigel, I. (1963). Psychological significance of styles of conceptualization. In Wright, J. and Kagan, J. (eds.) *Basic Cognitive Processes in Children*. Monographs of the Society for Research in Child Development, **28**, no. 2. *pp*. 224, 238

Kahneman, D. (1973). *Attention and Effort*. Englewood Cliffs, N. J.,: Prentice-Hall. *p*. 26

Kahneman, D. and Tversky, A. (1972). Subjective probability: a judgement of representativeness. *Cognitive Psychology*, **3**, 430–54. *pp*. 328, 329, 330

Kahneman, D. and Tversky, A. (1973). On the psychology of prediction. *Psychological Review*, **80**, 237–51. *pp*. 327, 331, 332

Kamin, L. J. (1974). *The Science and Politics of I.Q.* Potomac, Maryland: Erlbaum. *p*. 439

Kaplan, I. T. and Schoenfeld, W. N. (1966). Oculomotor patterns during the solution of visually displayed anagrams. *Journal of Experimental Psychology*, **72**, 447–51. *p.* 27

Kareev, Y. (1973). A model of human game playing. Unpublished doctoral dissertation, available as Technical Report no. 36, Center for Human Information Processing, Department of Psychology, University of California, San Diego. *p.* 564

Katz, D. (1937). *Animals and Men*. London: Longman. *p.* 268

Katz, J. J. and Fodor, J. A. (1963). The structure of a semantic theory. *Language*, **39**, 170–210. *p.* 345

Kelley, H. H. (1967). Attribution theory in social psychology. In Levine, D. (ed.) *Nebraska Symposium on Motivation*. Lincoln: University of Nebraska Press. *p.* 454

Kelley, H. H. (1972). Attribution in social interaction. In Jones, E. E. *et al.* (eds.) *Attribution: perceiving the causes of behavior*. Morristown, N.J.: General Learning Press. *p.* 454

Kelley, H. H. (1973). The process of causal attribution. *American Psychologist*, **28**, 107–28. *p.* 353

Kemeny, J. G., Snell, J. L., and Thompson, G. L. (1966). *Introduction to Finite Mathematics*. Englewood Cliffs, N.J.: Prentice-Hall. *p.* 449

Kendler, H. H. and Kendler, T. S. (1962). Vertical and horizontal processes in problem solving. *Psychological Review*, **69**, 1–16. *p.* 175

Kinsbourne, M. (1972). Eye and head turning indicates cerebral lateralization. *Science*, **176**, 539–41. *p.* 26

Kintsch, W. (1972). Notes on the structure of semantic memory. In Tulving E. and Donaldson, W. (eds.) *Organization of Memory*. New York: Academic. *p.* 398

Kintsch, W. (1974). *The Representation of Meaning in Memory*. Hillsdale, N.J.: Erlbaum. *p.* 345

Klahr, D. and Wallace, J. G. (1972). Class inclusion processes. In Farnham-Diggory, S. (ed.) *Information Processing in Children*. New York: Academic. *p.* 179

Klank, L. J. K., Huang, Y. H., and Johnson, R. C. (1971). Determinants of success in matching word pairs in tests of phonetic symbolism. *Journal of Verbal Learning and Verbal Behavior*, **10**, 140–8. *p.* 443

Kneale, W. and Kneale, M. (1962). *The Development of Logic*. Oxford: Clarendon. *p.* 133

Koestler, A. (1964). *The Act of Creation*. London: Hutchinson. *p.* 259

Koffka, K. (1935). *The Principles of Gestalt Psychology*. New York: Harcourt, Brace and World. *p.* 551

Köhler, W. (1957). *The Mentality of Apes*, trans. from 2nd edn by E. Winter. Harmondsworth, Middx.: Penguin. (First German edn pub. 1917.) *pp.* 3, 26

Koslovski, B. and Bruner, J. S. (1972). Learning to use a lever. *Child Development*, **43**, 790–9. *p.* 304

Kosslyn, S. M. and Pomerantz, J. R. (1977). Imagery, propositions, and the form of internal representations. *Cognitive Psychology*, **9**, 52–76. *p.* 525

Krailsheimer, A. J. (trans.) (1966). *Pascal's Pensées*. Harmondsworth, Middx.: Penguin. *p.* 5

Krauss, R. and Rotter, G. (1968). Communication abilities of children as a function of age. *Merrill-Palmer Quarterly*, **14**, 161–73. *p.* 471

Krechevsky, I. (1932). 'Hypotheses' in rats. *Psychological Review*, **39**, 516–32. *p.* 260

Kroeber, A. (1948). *Anthropology*. New York: Harcourt Brace Jovanovich. *p.* 473

Kroeber, T. (1961). *Ishi in Two Worlds: a biography of the last wild Indian in North America.* Berkeley: University of California Press. *p.* 439

Kruskal, J. B. (1964). Multidimensional scaling by optimising goodness of fit to a nonmetric hypothesis. *Psychometrika*, **29**, 1–27. *p.* 197

Kuhn, T. S. (1961a). The function of dogma in scientific research. Paper presented at the Symposium on the History of Science, University of Oxford, 9–15 July 1961. *p.* 289n

Kuhn, T. S. (1961b). The function of measurement in modern physical science. *Isis*, **52**, 161–93. *p.* 289n

Kuhn, T. S. (1962). The historical structure of scientific discovery. *Science*, **136**, 760–4. *p.* 284n

Kuhn, T. S. (1970). *The Structure of Scientific Revolutions.* 2nd. edn. Chicago: University of Chicago Press. (1st edn, 1962.) *pp.* 260, 289n, 290n, 316

Labov, W. (1969). The logic of nonstandard English. *Georgetown Monographs on Language and Linguistics*, **22**, 1–31. Reprinted in Williams, R. (ed.) *Language and Poverty.* Chicago: Markham, *pp.* 444, 472

Labov, W. (1973). The boundaries of words and their meanings. In Bailey, C–J. N. and Shuy, R. (eds.) *New Ways of Analyzing Variation in English*, I. Washington: Georgetown University Press. *p.* 183

Labov, W. and Labov, T. (1974). The grammar of *cat* and *mama*. Paper presented at the Forty-Ninth Annual Meeting of the Linguistics Society of America, New York. *p.* 249

Lakatos, I. (1970). Logic of discovery or psychology of research. In Lakatos, I. and Musgrave, A. (eds.) *Criticism and the Growth of Knowledge.* Cambridge: Cambridge University Press. *p.* 260

Lakoff, G. (1970). Linguistics and natural logic. *Synthese*, **22**, 151–271. *p.* 130

Lakoff, G. (1971). The role of deduction in grammar. In Fillmore, C. J. and Langendoen, D. T. (eds.) *Studies in Linguistics Semantics.* New York: Holt, Rinehart, and Winston. *p.* 419

Lakoff, G. (1972). Hedges: a study in meaning criteria and the logic of fuzzy concepts. *Papers from the Eighth Regional Meeting of the Chicago Linguistic Society.* Chicago: Chicago Linguistic Society. *p.* 183

Lantz, D. and Stefflre, V. (1964). Language and cognition revisited. *Journal of Abnormal and Social Psychology*, **69**, 472–81. *p.* 510

Lashley, K. S. (1929). *Brain Mechanisms and Intelligence.* Chicago: Chicago University Press. *p.* 259

Lasker, E. (1932). *Lasker's Manual of Chess.* London: Printing-Craft. *p.* 530

Leach, E. (1964). Anthropological aspects of language: animal categories and verbal abuse. In Lenneberg, E. H. (ed.) *New Directions in the Study of Language.* Cambridge, Mass.: MIT Press. *p.* 212

Leach, E. (1976). *Culture and Communication: the logic by which symbols are connected.* Cambridge: Cambridge University Press. *p.* 436

Leech, G. N. (1969). *Towards a Semantic Description of English.* London: Longman. *p.* 130

Lees, R. B. (1961). Grammatical analysis of the English comparative construction. *Word*, **17**, 171–85. *p.* 101

Legrenzi, P. (1970). Relations between language and reasoning about deductive rules. In

Levelt, W. J. M. and Flores D'Arcais, G. B. (eds.) *Advances in Psycholinguistics*. Amsterdam: North-Holland. *p.* 150

Lenneberg, E. H. (1967). *Biological Foundations of Language*, New York: Wiley. *pp.* 223, 509, 510

Lenneberg, E. H. and Roberts, J. (1956). The language of experience, a study in methodology. Memoir 13. *International Journal of American Linguistics*, **22**, *p.* 443

Lerman, J. C. (1970). *Les bases de la classification automatique*. Paris: Gauthier-Villars. *p.* 186

Levine, M. (1975). *Hypothesis Testing; a cognitive theory of learning*. Hillsdale, N.J.: Erlbaum. *pp.* 175, 260

Levison, M., Ward, R. G., and Webb, J. W. (1973). *The Settlement of Polynesia: a computer simulation*. Minneapolis: University of Minneapolis Press. *p.* 537

Levi-Strauss, C. (1963). The structural study of myth. In Levi-Strauss, C. *Structural Anthropology*. New York: Basic Books. *p.* 466

Levi-Strauss, C. (1966). *The Savage Mind*. London: Weidenfeld and Nicolson. (First published 1962.) *pp.* 436, 447, 466

Levy, D. (1976). *Chess and Computers*. London: Batsford. *p.* 530

Levy-Bruhl, L. (1966). *How Natives Think*. New York: Washington Square Press. (First published 1910.) *pp.* 436, 487

Lewin, K. (1935). *Dynamic Theory of Personality*. New York: McGraw-Hill. *p.* 34

Lewis, D. (1972). *We the Navigators*. Canberra: National University Press. *p.* 537

Lloyd, B. B. (1972). *Perception and Cognition: a cross-cultural perspective*. Harmondsworth, Middx.: Penguin. *p.* 439

Lorenz, K. (1966). *On Aggression*. London: Methuen. *p.* 266

Lounsbury, F. (1964). The structural analysis of kinship semantics. In Lunt, H. (ed.) *Proceeding of the Ninth International Congress of Linguistics*. The Hague: Mouton. *p.* 462

Luchins, A. S. (1942). Mechanization in problem-solving. Psychological Monographs, **54**, *p.* 313

Luchins, A. S. (1959). *A Functional Approach to Training in Clinical Psychology*. Springfield, Ill.: Thomas. *p.* 33

Luchins, A. S. and Luchins, E. H. (1950). New experimental attempts at preventing mechanization in problem solving. *Journal of General Psychology*, **42**, 279–97. *p.* 18

Lunzer, E. A., Harrison, C., and Davey, M. (1972). The four-card problem and the development of formal reasoning. *Quarterly Journal of Experimental Psychology*, **24**, 326–39. *p.* 152

Luria, A. R. (1966). *Human Brain and Physiological Processes*. New York: Harper and Row. *p.* 108

Luria, A. R. (1969). *The Mind of a Mnemonist*. London: Cape. *pp.* 44, 524

Luria, A. R. (1971). Towards the problem of the historical nature of psychological processes. *International Journal of Psychology*, **6**, 259–72. *p.* 484

Luria, A. R. (1977). *The Social History of Cognition*. Cambridge, Mass.: Harvard University Press. *pp.* 488, 490, 496

Lyons, J. (1963). *Structural Semantics*. Oxford: Blackwell. *p.* 100

Lyons, J. (1968). *Introduction to Theoretical Linguistics*. Cambridge: Cambridge University Press. *p.* 100

McCarthy, J. and Hayes, P. (1969). Some philosophical problems from the standpoint of

Artificial Intelligence. In Meltzer, B. and Michie, D. (eds.) *Machine Intelligence 4*. Edinburgh: Oliver and Boyd. *p*. 64

McDaniel, C. K. (1972). Hue perception and hue naming. Unpublished honors thesis, Harvard College, April 1972. *pp*. 219, 515

McDermott, D. and Sussman, G. (1972). Conniver reference manual. MIT AI Laboratory Report MIT–AI–259. *p*. 66

McFie, J., Piercy, M. F., and Zangwill, O. L. (1950). Visual-spatial agnosia associated with lesions of the right cerebral hemisphere. *Brain*, **73**, 167–90. *p*. 27

McHugh, P. (1968). *Defining the Situation: the organization of meaning in social interaction*. Indianapolis: Bobbs-Merrill. *p*. 480

Mahoney, M. J. (1976). *Scientist as Subject: the psychological imperative*. Cambridge, Mass.: Ballinger. *p*. 262

Maier, N. R. F. (1930). Reasoning in humans, I. On direction. *Journal of Comparative Psychology*, **10**, 115–43. *p*. 17

Maier, N. R. F. (1931). Reasoning in humans. II. The solution of a problem and its appearance in consciousness. *Journal of Comparative Psychology*, **12**, 181–94. *p*. 18

Malcolm, N. (1958). *Ludwig Wittgenstein*. London: Oxford University Press. *p*. 263

Malinowski, B. (1954). *Magic, Science and Religion*. New York: Doubleday. *pp*. 436, 447

Malleson, A. (1973). *Need your Doctor be so Useless?* London: Allen and Unwin. *p*. 437

Maltzman, I. and Morrisett, L. Jr (1953). Effects of task instructions on solution of difference classes of anagrams. *Journal of Experimental Psychology*, **45**, 351–5. *p*. 18

Mandler, J. M. and Mandler, G. (1964). *Thinking: from association to Gestalt*. New York: Wiley. *p*. 2

Markman, E. M. and Seibert, J. (1976). Classes and collections: internal organization and resulting holistic properties. *Cognitive Psychology*, **8**, 561–77. *p*. 179

Marr, D. and Nishihara, H. K. (1976). Representation and recognition of the spatial organization of three-dimensional shapes. MIT AI Laboratory Memorandum 377 (August). *p*. 343

Matte-Blanco, I. (1965). A study of schizophrenic thinking: its expression in terms of symbolic logic and its representation in terms of multi-dimensional space. *International Journal of Psychiatry*, **1**, 91–6. *p*. 85

Matthews, G. V. T. (1951). *Bird Navigation*. Cambridge: Cambridge University Press. *p*. 542

Mayer, D. Y. (1972). Letter to *British Journal of Psychiatry*, **120**, 473. *p*. 350

Mayr, E. (1963). *Animal Species and Evolution*. Cambridge, Mass.: Harvard University Belknap Press. *p*. 185

Mazzocco, A., Legrenzi, P., and Roncato, S. (1974). Syllogistic inference: the failure of the atmosphere effect and the conversion hypothesis. *Italian Journal of Psychology*, **1**, 157–72. *pp*. 84, 132

Medawar, P. B. (1969). *Induction and Intuition in Scientific Thought*. London: Methuen. *p*. 258

Mehler, J. and Bever, T. G. (1967). Cognitive capacity of very young children. *Science*, **158**, 141–2. *pp*. 448, 465

Meltzer, B. (1973). The programming of deduction and induction. In Elithorn, A. and Jones, D. (eds.) *Artificial and Human Thinking*. London: Elsevier. *pp*. 83, 260

Mervis, C. B., Catlin, J., and Rosch, E. (1975). Developent of the structure of color names. *Developmental Psychology*, *p*. 219

Meyer, B. J. F. (1975). *The Organization of Prose and its Effects on Memory*. Amsterdam: North-Holland. *p*. 351

Michotte, A. (1963). *The Perception of Causality*. London: Methuen. *p*. 438

Mill, J. S. (1950). *A System of Logic*. (First published 1843.) In Nagel, E. (ed.) *J. S. Mill's Philosophy of Scientific Method*. New York: Hafner. *p*. 257

Miller, G. A. (1956). The magical number seven, plus or minus two. *Psychological Review*, **63**, 81–97. *p*. 507

Miller, G. A. (1965). Some preliminaries to psycholinguistics. *American Psychologist*, **20**, 15–20. *p*. 377

Miller, G. A. (1966). *Psychology: the science of mental life*. Harmondsworth, Middx.: Penguin. (Originally published 1962.) *p*. 2

Miller, G. A. (1967). Project Grammarama. In *The Psychology of Communication*. New York: Basic Books. *pp*. 262, 316

Miller, G. A. (1969). A psychological method to investigate verbal concepts. *Journal of Mathematical Psychology*, **6**, 169–91. *p*. 169

Miller, G. A., Gallanter, E., and Pribram, K. (1960). *Plans and the Structure of Behavior*. New York: Holt, Rinehart, and Winston. *pp*. 8, 306, 353

Miller, G. A. and Johnson-Laird, P. N. (1976). *Language and Perception*. Cambridge: Cambridge University Press. *pp*. 182, 183, 437

Miller, G. A. and McNeill, D. (1969). Psycholinguistics. In Lindzey, G. and Aaronson, E. (eds.) *Handbook of Social Psychology*, III. Reading, Mass.: Addison-Wesley. *p*. 442

Mineta, F. (1849). *History of the War of 1840–1842*. 5 vols. In Japanese, translated from the Chinese. *p*. 192

Minsky, M. (1967). *Computation: finite and infinite machines*. Englewood Cliffs, N.J.: Prentice-Hall. *p*. 21

Minsky, M. (1970) Form and content in computer science. ACM Turing Lecture. *Journal of the Association for Computing Machinery*, **17**, 197–215. *p*. 375

Minsky, M. (1974). Frame-systems. MIT AI Laboratory Memorandum. (See also Reading 22.) *p*. 421

Mischel, W. (1968). *Personality and Assessment*. New York: Wiley. *pp*. 451, 452

Mischel, W. (1973). Towards a cognitive social learning reconceptualization of personality. *Psychological Review*, **80**, 252–83. *p*. 452

Mitroff, I. I. (1974). *The Subjective Side of Science*. Amsterdam: Elsevier. *p*. 316

Modigliani, V. and Rizza, J. P. (1971). Conservation of simple concepts as a function of deletion of irrelevant attributes. *Journal of Experimental Psychology*, **90**, 280–6. *pp*. 179, 180

Moore, J. and Newell, A. (1973). How can MERLIN understand? In Gregg, L. (ed.) *Knowledge and Cognition*. Hillsdale, N.J.: Erlbaum. *p*. 69

Moore, O. K. and Anderson, S. B. (1954). Modern logic and tasks for experiments on problem solving behavior. *Journal of Psychology*, **38**, 151–60. *p*. 79

Moos, R. H. (1969). Sources of variance in responses to questionnaires and in behavior. *Journal of Abnormal Psychology*, **74**, 405–12. *p*. 452

Morgan, C. L. (1894). *Introduction to Comparative Psychology*, London: Scott. *p*. 267

Munsell Color Company (1966). *The Munsell Book of Color: glossy finish collection*. Baltimore: Munsell Color Company. *p*. 511

Munsell Color Company (1970). *Dominant Wavelength and Excitation Purity for Designated Munsell Color Notation*. Baltimore: Munsell Color Company. *p*. 515

Nebes, R. D. (1974). Hemispheric specialization in commisurotomized man. *Psychological Bulletin*, **81**, 1–14. *p.* 525

Needham, R. (1975). Polythetic classification: convergence and consequences. *Man*, **10**, 349–69. *p.* 464

Neimark, E. D. and Chapman, R. H. (1975). Development of the comprehension of logical quantifiers. In Falmagne, R. C. (ed.) *Reasoning: representation and process.* Hillsdale, N.J.: Erlbaum. *p.* 134

Neisser, U. (1967). *Cognitive Psychology*. New York. Appleton-Century-Crofts. *p.* 377

Neisser, U. and Weene, P. (1962). Hierarchies in concept attainment. *Journal of Experimental Psychology*, **64**, 640–5. *p.* 175

Nelson, K. (1973). *Structure and Strategy in Learning to Talk*. Monographs of the Society for Research in Child Development, 149, **38** (1–2). *pp.* 238, 242, 243

Nelson, K. (1974). Concept, word, and sentence: interrelations in acquisition and development. *Psychological Review*, **81**, 267–85. *pp.* 216, 226, 240, 242, 243, 244

Newcomb, T. M. (1929). The consistency of certain extrovert–introvert behavior patterns in 51 problem boys. *Contributions to Education*, **382**, *pp.* 446, 451, 455

Newell, A. (1973a). Production systems: models of control structures. In Chase, W. G. (ed.) *Visual Information Processing*. New York: Academic. *pp.* 23, 563

Newell, A. (1973b). You can't play 20 questions with nature and win. In Chase, W. G. (ed.) *Visual Information Processing*. New York: Academic. *p.* 10

Newell, A., Shaw, J. C., and Simon, H. A. (1958a). Chess playing programs and the problem of complexity. *IBM Journal of Research and Development*, **2**, 320–35. (Reprinted in E. Feigenbaum, and J. Feldman (eds.) *Computers and Thought*. New York: McGraw-Hill, 1963). *pp.* 49, 575

Newell, A., Shaw, J. C., and Simon, H. A. (1958b). Elements of a theory of human problem-solving. *Psychological Review*, **65**, 151–66. *pp.* 8, 143

Newell, A., Shaw, J. C., and Simon, H. A. (1963). Empirical explorations with the Logic Theory Machine. In Feigenbaum, E. and Feldman, J. (eds.) *Computers and Thought*. New York: McGraw-Hill. *p.* 49

Newell, A. and Simon, H. A. (1963). GPS, a program that simulates human thought. In Feigenbaum, E. and Feldman, J. (eds.) *Computers and Thought*. New York: McGraw-Hill. *p.* 57

Newell, A. and Simon, H. A. (1965a). Programs as theories of higher mental processes. In Stacy, R. W. and Waxman, B. (eds.) *Computers in Biomedical Research*, II. New York: Academic. *p.* 57

Newell, A. and Simon, H. A. (1965b). An example of human chess play in the light of chess playing programs. In Weiner, N. and Schade, J. P. (eds.) *Progress in Biocybernetics*, II. Amsterdam: Elsevier. *p.* 57

Newell, A. and Simon, H. A. (1972). *Human Problem Solving*. Englewood Cliffs, N.J.: Prentice-Hall. *pp.* 21, 23, 563, 575

Norman, D. A. (1972). Memory, knowledge, and the answering of questions. Center for Human information Processing Memorandum CHIP–25. University of California, San Diego. *p.* 421

Norman, D. A., Rumelhart, D. E., and the LNR Research Group (1975). *Explorations in Cognition*. San Francisco: Freeman. *p.* 557

Norman, W. T. (1963). Toward an adequate taxonomy of personality attributes: replicated factor structure in peer nomination personality ratings. *Journal of Abnormal and Social Psychology*, **66**, 574–83. *pp.* 452, 458

Noton, D. and Stark, L. (1971a). Scanpaths in eye movements during pattern reception. *Science*, **171**, 308–11. *p.* 194

Noton, D. and Stark, L. (1971b). Eye movements and visual perception. *Scientific American*, **224** (June), 34–43. *p.* 194

Oatley, K. (1974). Mental maps for navigation. *New Scientist*, **64**, 863–6. *p.* 543

Ogden, C. K. (1935). *Basic English: a general introduction with rules and grammar*. 5th edn. London: Kegan Paul, Trench, and Trubner. *p.* 441

Olson, D. (1970). Language and thought: aspects of a cognitive theory of semantics. *Psychological Review*, **77**, 257–73. *p.* 223

Olver, P. and Hornsby, R. (1966). On equivalence. In Bruner, J. S., Olver, R. R., and Greenfield, P. M. (eds.) *Studies in Cognitive Growth*. New York: Wiley. *p.* 246

Orne, M. (1970). Hypnosis, motivation, and the ecological validity of the psychological experiment. In Arnold, W. and Page, M. (eds.) *Nebraska Symposium on Motivation*. Lincoln: University of Nebraska Press. *p.* 480

Orwell, G. (1949). *Nineteen Eighty-Four*. London: Secker and Warburg. *p.* 441

Orwell, G. (1970a). New words. In *The Collected Essays, Journalism and Letters of George Orwell*, II, *My Country Right or Left 1940–1943*, ed. Sonia Orwell and Ian Angus. Harmondsworth, Middx.: Penguin. *p.* 441

Orwell, G. (1970b). Politics and the English language. In *The Collected Essays, Journalism and Letters of George Orwell*, IV, *In Front of Your Nose 1945–1950*, ed. Sonia Orwell and Ian Angus. Harmondsworth, Middx.: Penguin. *p.* 441

Osgood, C. E., Suci, G. J., and Tannenbaum, P. H. (1957). *The Measurement of Meaning*. Urbana, Ill.: University of Illinois Press. *pp.* 278n, 504

Paivio, A. (1975). Perceptual comparison through the mind's eye. *Memory and Cognition*, **3**, 635–47. *pp.* 524, 525

Palmer, F. and Rees, A. (1969). Concept training in two-year-olds: procedures and results. Paper presented at the Biennial Meeting of the Society for Research in Child Development, 27 March 1969. *p.* 230

Papert, S. (1972). Teaching children to be mathematicians vs. teaching about mathematics. *International Journal of Mathematical Education and Science Technology*, **3**, 249–62. *p.* 375

Papert, S. (1973). Theory of knowledge and complexity. In Dalenoort, G. J. (ed.) *Process Models for Psychology: lecture notes of the Nuffic Conference International Summer Course, 1972*. Rotterdam University Press. *p.* 24

Parsons, D. (1969). *Funny Amusing and Funny Amazing*. London: Pan. *p.* 351

Passini, F. T. and Norman, W. T. (1966). A universal conception of personality structure? *Journal of Personality and Social Psychology*, **4**, 44–9. *p.* 452

Penrose, J. (1962). An investigation into some aspects of problem solving behaviour. Unpublished Ph.D. thesis, University of London. *p.* 312

Perky, C. W. (1910). An experimental study of imagination. *American Journal of Psychology*, **21**, 422–52. *p.* 523

Phillips, J. L. (1969). *The Origins of Intellect: Piaget's theory*. San Francisco: Freeman. *p.* 87

Piaget, J. (1921). Une forme verbale de la comparaison chez l'enfant. *Archives de psychologie*, **18**, 141–72. *p.* 107

Piaget, J. (1926). *The Language and Thought of the Child*. London: Routledge and Kegan Paul. *p.* 471

Piaget, J. (1928). *Judgment and Reasoning in the Child*. London: Kegan Paul. *p.* 107

Piaget, J. (1946). *Les notions de mouvement et de vitesse chez l'enfant*. Paris: Presses Universe France. *p.* 276

Piaget, J. (1950). *The Psychology of Intelligence*, trans. M. Piercy and D. E. Berlyne. London: Routledge and Kegan Paul. *p.* 178

Piaget J. (1952). *The Origins of Intelligence in Children*. New York: International Universities Press. *pp.* 216, 224, 379, 448

Piaget, J. (1954). *The Construction of Reality in the Child*. New York: Basic Books. *p.* 224

Piaget, J. (1967). *Six Psychological Studies*. New York: Random House. *p.* 448

Piaget, J. (1970). *Structuralism*. New York: Basic Books. *p.* 449

Piaget, J. (1972). *The Principles of Genetic Epistemology*. London: Routledge. *pp.* 87, 151

Piaget, J. (1973). *La formation de la notion de force*. EEG, xxix. Paris: Presses Univers France. *p.* 296

Piaget, J. (1974a). *La prise de conscience*. Paris: Presses Univers France. *p.* 306

Piaget, J. (1974b). *Réussir et comprendre*. Paris: Presses Univers France. *p.* 306

Piaget, J. and Garcia, R. (1974). *Understanding Causality*. New York: Norton. (French edn, 1971.) *p.* 296

Piaget, J. and Inhelder, B. (1956). *The Child's Conception of Space*. New York: Humanities Press. *p.* 360

Platt, J. R. (1964). Strong inference. *Science*, **146**, 347–53. *p.* 315

Polanyi, M. (1958). *Personal Knowledge*. Chicago: Chicago University Press. *p.* 290n

Polya, G. (1957). *How to Solve It*. 2nd edn. New York: Doubleday. *p.* 19

Popper, K. R. (1959). *The Logic of Scientific Discovery*. London: Hutchinson. *pp.* 144, 258, 315

Popper, K. R. (1963). *Conjectures and Refutations*. London: Routledge. (American edn, New York: Basic Books, 1962.) *pp.* 265, 315

Popper, K. R. (1972). *Objective Knowledge*. Oxford: Clarendon. *p.* 258

Posner, M. I. (1973). *Cognition: an introduction*. Glenview, Ill.: Scott, Foresman. *p.* 250

Postal, P. (1964). Underlying and superficial linguistic structure. *Harvard Educational Review*, **34**, 246–66. *p.* 98

Potts, G. (1971). A cognitive approach to the encoding of meaningful verbal material. Unpublished doctoral dissertation, University of Indiana. *p.* 389

Potts, G. R. and Scholz, K. W. (1975). The internal representation of a three-term series problem. *Journal of Verbal Learning and Verbal Behavior*, **14**, 439–52. *p.* 78

Power, R. (1974). A computer model of conversation. Ph.D. dissertation, University of Edinburgh. *p.* 352

Price-Williams, D. (1967). Towards a systematics of cross-cultural psychology. *Memorias del XI Congresso Interamericano de Psicologia, Mexico City*. *p.* 479

Price-Williams, D. (1969). A study concerning concepts of conservation of quantities among primitive children. In Price-Williams D. (ed.) *Cross-Cultural Studies*. Harmondsworth, Middx.: Penguin. *pp.* 448, 479

Price-Williams, D., Gordon, W., and Ramirez, M. (1969). Skill and conservation: a study of pottery-making children. *Developmental Psychology*, **1**, 769. *pp.* 479, 481

Putnam, H. (1975a). Is semantics possible? In Putnam, H. (ed.) *Mind, Language, and Reality*. Cambridge: Cambridge University Press. *p.* 464

Putnam, H. (1975b). 'The Innateness Hypothesis' and explanatory models in linguistics. In Putnam, H. (ed.) *Mind, Language, and Reality*. Cambridge: Cambridge University Press. *p.* 449

Pylyshyn, Z. W. (1975). Representation of knowledge: non-linguistic forms. In Schank, R. C. and Nash-Webber, B. Z. (eds.) *Theoretical Issues in Natural Language Processing*. Mimeo. Cambridge, Mass.: MIT. *p.* 524

Quillian, M. R. (1968). Semantic memory. In Minsky, M. (ed.) *Semantic Information Processing*. Cambridge, Mass.: MIT Press. *p.* 70

Quine, W. V. O. (1952). *Methods of Logic*. London: Routledge. *p.* 114

Quine, W. V. O. (1953). Two dogmas of empiricism. In *From a Logical Point of View*. Cambridge, Mass. *p.* 287

Rapaport, D. (1945). *Diagnostic Psychological Testing*. Chicago: Year Book Publications. *p.* 33

Raush, H. L., Dittmann, A. T., and Taylor, T. J. (1959). Person, setting and change in social interaction. *Human Relations*, **12**, 361–77. *p.* 452

Raven, P. H., Berlin, B., and Breedlove, D. E. (1971). The origins of taxonomy. *Science*, **174**, 1210–13. *p.* 185

Rayner, E. H. (1958). A study of evaluative problem solving. Part I. Observations on adults. *Quarterly Journal of Experimental Psychology*, **10**, 155–65. (Reprinted in Wason and Johnson-Laird, 1968.) *p.* 549

Rees, H. J. and Israel, H. C. (1935). An investigation of the establishment and operation of mental sets. *Psychological Monographs*, **46**, whole no. 210. *p.* 18

Reichenbach, H. (1954). *The Rise of Scientific Philosophy*. Berkeley: University of California Press. *p.* 260

Reid, J. W. (1951). An experimental study of 'analysis of the goal' in problem solving. *Journal of General Psychology*, **44**, 51–69. *p.* 17

Reinfeld, F. (1958). *Win at Chess*. New York: Dover Books. *p.* 578

Riesenberg, S. H. (1972). The organization of navigational knowledge on Puluwat. *Journal of the Polynesian Society*, **81**, 19. *p.* 544

Reitman, W. R. (1965). *Cognition and Thought*. New York: Wiley. *p.* 143

Restle, F. (1962). The selection of strategies in cue learning. *Psychological Review*, **69**, 329–43. *p.* 175

Reti, R. (1923). *Modern Ideas in Chess*. London: Bell. *p.* 528

Revlis, R. (1975). Syllogistic reasoning: logical decisions from a complex data base. In Falmagne, R. C. (ed.) *Reasoning: representation and process*. Hillsdale, N.J.: Erlbaum. *pp.* 85, 129, 134

Ricciuti, H. (1965). Object grouping and selective ordering behavior in infants 12–24 months old. *Merrill-Palmer Quarterly*, **11**, 129–48. *p.* 225

Ricklefs, R. E. (1973). *Ecology*. Newton, Mass.: Chiron. *p.* 185

Rieger, C. (1975). Conceptual memory. In Schank, R. C. (ed.) *Conceptual Information Processing*. Amsterdam: North-Holland. *p.* 422, 429

Riesbeck, C. (1975). Conceptual analysis. In Schank, R. C. (ed.) *Conceptual Information Processing*. Amsterdam: North-Holland. *p.* 422

Riessman, D. (1962). *The Culturally Deprived Child*. New York: Harper and Row. *p.* 469

Rips, L. J., Shoben, E. J., and Smith, E. E. (1973). Semantic distance and the verification of semantic relations. *Journal of Verbal Learning and Verbal Behavior*, **12**, 1–20. *p.* 219

Roberge, J. J. (1976). Reasoning with exclusive disjunction arguments. *Quarterly Journal of Experimental Psychology*, **28**, 419–27. *pp.* 116, 117

Robinson, J. A. (1965). A machine-oriented logic based on the resolution principle. *Journal of Association for Computing Machinery*, **12**, 23–41. *p.* 82

Rokeach, M. (1950). The effect of perception time upon rigidity and concreteness of thinking. *Journal of Experimental Psychology*, **40**, 206–16. *p.* 18

Rokeach, M. (1960). *The Open and Closed Mind*. New York: Basic Books. *p.* 18

Rosch, E. (1973a). Natural categories. *Cognitive Psychology*, **4**, 328–50. *p.* 250

Rosch, E. (1973b). On the internal structure of perceptual and semantic categories. In Moore, T. (ed.) *Cognitive Development and the Acquisition of Language*. New York: Academic. *pp.* 218, 219, 250, 251, 513, 517, 518

Rosch, E. (1975a). Universals and cultural specifics in human categorization. In Brislin, R., Bochner, S., and Lonner, W. (eds.) *Cross-Cultural Perspectives on Learning*. New York: Sage/Halsted. *pp.* 218, 219, 464

Rosch, E. (1975b). Cognitive representations of semantic categories. *Journal of Experimental Psychology: General*, **104**, 192–233. *p.* 219

Rosch, E. (1975c). The nature of mental codes for color categories. *Journal of Experimental Psychology, Human Perception and Performance*, **1**, 303–22. *p.* 219

Rosch, E. and Mervis, C. B. (1975). Family resemblances: studies in the internal structure of categories. *Cognitive Psychology*, **7**, 573–605. *pp.* 219, 250, 252, 253

Rosch, E., Mervis, C. B., Gray, W. D., Johnson, D. M., and Boyes-Braem, P. (1976). Basic objects in natural categories. *Cognitive Psychology*, **8**, 382–439. *pp.* 214, 217, 218, 220, 221

Rosenhan, D. L. (1973). On being sane in insane places. *Science*, **179**, 250–8. *p.* 198

Rosenthal, R. and Gaito, J. (1963). The interpretation of levels of significance by psychological researchers. *Journal of Psychology*, **55**, 33–8. *p.* 263

Ross, J. R. (1970). On declarative sentences. In Jacobs, R. A. and Rosenbaum, P. S. (eds.) *Readings in English Transformational Grammar*. Waltham, Mass.: Ginn. *p.* 350

Rugg, H. (1963). *Imagination*. London: Harper. *p.* 259

Rulifson, J. F., Waldinger, R. J., and Dirksen, J. A. (1968). QA4 – A language for writing problem-solving programs. *International Federation for Information Processing Proceedings*. *p.* 66

Rumelhart, D. E. (1975). Notes on a schema for stories. In Bobrow, D. G. and Collins, A. (eds.) *Representation and Understanding: Studies in Cognitive Science*. New York: Academic. *p.* 351

Rumelhart, D. E. and Abrahamson, A. A. (1973). A model for analogical reasoning. *Cognitive psychology*, **5**, 1–28. *p.* 24

Rumelhart, D. E., Lindsay, P. H., and Norman, D. A. (1972). A process model for long-term memory. In Tulving, E. and Donaldson, W. (eds.) *Organization of Memory*. New York: Academic. *p.* 398

Rumelhart, D. E. and Norman, D. A. (1973). Active semantic networks as a model of human memory. *Third International Joint Conference on Artificial Intelligence*. Stanford: Stanford Research Institute. *p.* 70

Russell, B. (1900). *A Critical Exposition of the Philosophy of Leibniz*. Cambridge: Cambridge University Press. p. 441

Russell, B. (1927). *An Outline of Philosophy*. London: Allen and Unwin. pp. 3, 76

Ruud, J. T. (1954). Vertebrates without erythrocytes and blood pigment. *Nature*, **173**, 848–50. p. 190

Rycroft, C. (ed.) (1968). *Psychoanalysis Observed*. Harmondsworth, Middx.: Penguin. p. 439

Ryle, G. (1963). Formal and informal logic. In Jager, R. (ed.) *Essays in Logic*. Englewood Cliffs, N.J.: Prentice-Hall. p. 499

Sachs, H., Schegloff, E. A., and Jefferson, G. (1974). A simplest systematics for the organization of turn-taking for conversation. *Language*, **50**, 696–735. p. 351

Salmon, W. (1967). *The Foundations of Scientific Inference*. Pittsburgh: University of Pittsburgh Press. p. 315

Sandewall, E. (1973). Conversion of predicate-calculus axioms, viewed as non-deterministic programs, to corresponding deterministic programs. *Third International Joint Conference on Artificial Intelligence*. Stanford: Stanford Research Institute. p. 64

Sapir, E. (1944). Grading: a study in semantics. *Philosophy of Science*, **11**, 93–116. p. 100

Savin, H. B. (1973). Meanings and concepts: a review of Jerrold J. Katz's *Semantic Theory*. *Cognition*, **2**, 213–38. p. 346

Schachter, S. and Singer, J. E. (1962). Cognitive, social and physiological determinants of emotional state. *Psychological Review*, **69**, 379–99. p. 454

Schank, R. C. (1972). Conceptual dependency: a theory of natural language understanding. *Cognitive Psychology*, **3**, 552–631. pp. 399, 423

Schank, R. C. (1973a). Identification of conceptualizations underlying natural language. In Schank, R. C. and Colby, K. M. (eds.) *Computer Models of Thought and Language*. San Francisco: Freeman. p. 421

Schank, R. C. (1973b). Causality and reasoning. Technical Report no. 1. Istituto per gli studi Semantici e Cognitivi. Castagnola, Switzerland. p. 424

Schank, R. C. (1975a). The role of memory in language processing. In Cofer, C. N. (ed.) *The Structure of Human Memory*. San Francisco: Freeman. p. 421

Schank, R. C. (1975b). The structure of episodes in memory. In Bobrow, C. and Collins, A. (eds.) *Representation and Understanding: studies in cognitive science*. New York: Academic. p. 423

Schank, R. C. (1975c). Using knowledge to understand. In Schank, R. C. and Nash-Webber, B. L. (eds.) *Issues in Natural Language Processing*. Preprints of a conference at MIT, June 1975. p. 429

Schank, R., Goldman, N., Rieger, C. J., and Riesbeck, C. (1973). MARGIE: memory, analysis, response generation, and inference on English. *Third International Joint Conference on Artificial Intelligence*. Stanford: Stanford Research Institute. pp. 141, 422, 426, 430

Scheerer, M. (1963). Problem-solving. *Scientific American*, **208**, (April), 118–28. p. 17

Schegloff, E. A. (1972). Notes on conversational practice: formulating place. In Sudnow, D. (ed.) *Studies in Social Interaction*. Glencoe, Ill.: Free Press. p. 351

Schegloff, E. A. and Sachs, H. (1973). Opening up closings. *Semiotica*, **8**, 289–327. p. 351

Schütze, C. (ed.) (1963). *Simplicissimus Album*. Bern: Scherz. p. 193

Scribner, S. (1974). Developmental aspects of categorized recall in a West African society. *Cognitive Psychology*, **6**, 475–94. *p.* 483

Scribner, S. (1975). Recall of classical syllogisms: a cross-cultural investigation of error on logical problems. In Falmagne, R. J. (ed.) *Reasoning: representation and process.* Hillsdale, N.J.: Erlbaum. *pp.* 484, 486, 487, 494

Scribner, S. and Cole, M. (1974). Research program on Vai literacy and its cognitive consequences. *Cross-Cultural Psychology Newsletter*, **8**, 2–4. *pp.* 484, 486, 489, 493

Sears, R. R. (1963). Dependency motivation. In Jones, M. R. (ed.) *Nebraska Symposium on Motivation.* Lincoln: University of Nebraska Press. *p.* 452

Segal, S. J. and Nathan, S. (1964). The Perky effect. *Perceptual and Motor Skills*, **18**, 385–95. *p.* 523

Segall, M., Campbell, D., and Herskovits, M. (1966). *The Influence of Culture on Visual Perception.* Indianapolis: Bobbs-Merrill. *p.* 478

Seligman, M. E. P. and Hager, J. L. (1972). *The Biological Boundaries of Learning*: New York: Appleton-Century-Crofts. *p.* 448

Sells, S. B. (1936). The atmosphere effect: an experimental study of reasoning. *Archives of Psychology*, **29**, 3–72. *p.* 131

Serpell, R. (1969). The influence of language, education and culture on attentional preferences between colour and form. *International Journal of Psychology*, **4**, 183–94. *p.* 505

Seuren, P. A. M. (1969). *Operators and Nucleus: a contribution to the theory of grammar.* Cambridge: Cambridge University Press. *p.* 130

Shaffer, L. H. (1961). Concept formation in an ordering task. *British Journal of Psychology*, **52**, 361–9. *p.* 259

Shannon, C. E. (1950a). A chess-playing machine. *Scientific American*, **182**, 48–51. *p.* 528

Shannon, C. E. (1950b). Programming a computer to play chess. *Philosophy Magazine*, **41**, 256–75. *p.* 565

Sharp, A. (1964). *Ancient Voyagers in Polynesia.* London: Angus and Robertson. *p.* 537

Sharp, D. W. and Cole, M. (1975). The influence of educational experience on the development of cognitive skills as measured in formal tests and experiments. Final report to Office of Education. New York: Rockefeller University. Mimeo. *pp.* 484, 486, 487, 489, 493

Shaver, P., Pierson, L., and Lang, S. (1974/5). Converging evidence for the functional significance of imagery in problem solving. *Cognition*, **3**, 359–75. *p.* 79

Shepard, R. N. (1975). Form, formation, and transformation of internal representations. In Solso, R. L. (ed.) *Information Processing and Cognition: the Loyola symposium.* Hillsdale, N.J.: Erlbaum. *p.* 525

Shepard, R. N. and Feng, C. (1972). A chronometric study of mental paper folding. *Cognitive Psychology*, **3**, 228–43. *p.* 525

Shepard, R. N., Hovland, C. I., and Jenkins, H. M. (1961). Learning and memorization of classifications. *Psychological Monographs*, **75**, whole no. 517. *p.* 213

Shepard, R. N., Romney, A. K., and Nerlove, S. B. (eds.) (1972). *Multidimensional Scaling.* New York: Seminar Press. *pp.* 169, 195

Shneidman, E. and Farberow, N. L. (1957). *Clues to Suicide.* New York: McGraw-Hill. *p.* 176

Shweder, R. A. (1972a). Aspects of cognition in Zinacanteco Shamans: experimental results. In Lessa, W. and Vogt, E. Z. (eds.) *Reader in Comparative Religion.* New York: Harper and Row. *p.* 446

Shweder, R. A. (1972b). Semantic structures and personality assessment. Ph.D. dissertation, Department of Social Relations, Harvard University. University Microfilms, Ann Arbor, Michigan. Order no. 72–29, 584. *pp.* 446, 452, 455, 465

Shweder, R. A. (1973). The between and within of cross-cultural research. *Ethos*, **1**, 531–43. *p.* 452

Shweder, R. A. (1975a). How relevant is an individual difference theory of personality? *Journal of Personality*, **43**, 455–84. *pp.* 446, 455

Shweder, R. A. (1975b). Interpretation of intellectual diversity (a review of *Culture and Thought*, by M. Cole and S. Scribner, and *Modes of Thought*, edited by R. Horton and R. Finnegan). *Science*, **188**, 855–8. *p.* 446

Shweder, R. A. (1976). Comment on K. E. Rosengren's, Malinowski's magic: the riddle of the empty cell. *Current Anthropology*, **17**, 681–2. *p.* 463

Shweder, R. A. (in press a). Culture and thought. In Wolman, B. B. (ed.) *International Encyclopedia of Neurology, Psychiatry, Psychoanalysis, and Psychology*. New York: Van Nostrand Reinhold (forthcoming). *pp.* 446

Shweder, R. A. (in press b). Illusory correlation and the M.M.P.I. controversy. *Journal of Consulting and Clinical Psychology* (forthcoming). *pp.* 446, 455

Shweder, R. A. (in press c). Illusory correlation and the M.M.P.I. controversy: a reply to some of the allusions and elusions in Block's and Edward's Commentaries. *Journal of Consulting and Clinical Psychology* (forthcoming). *p.* 446

Shweder, R. A. and LeVine, R. A. (1975). Dream concepts of Hausa children: a critique of the 'doctrine of invariant sequence' in cognitive development. *Ethos*, **3**, 209–30. *p.* 448

Simmons, R. (1973). Semantic networks: their computation and use for understanding English sentences. In Schank, R. and Colby, C. (eds.) *Computer Models of Thought and Language*. San Francisco: Freeman. *p.* 70

Simon, H. (1975). The functional equivalence of problem solving skills. *Cognitive Psychology*, **7**, 268–88. *p.* 23

Simon, H. A. and Barenfeld, M. (1969). Information-processing analysis of perceptual processes in problem solving. *Psychological Review*, **76**, 473–83. *pp.* 27, 548, 551, 555

Simon, H. A. and Newell, A. (1958). Heuristic problem solving: the next advance in operations research. *Operations Research*, **6**, 6–10. *p.* 528

Simon, H. A. and Newell, A. (1964). Information processing in computer and man. *American Scientist*, **53**, 281–300. *p.* 57

Simpson, G. G. (1961). *Principles of Animal Taxonomy*. New York: Columbia University Press. *p.* 187

Sloman, A. (1971). Interactions between philosophy and artificial intelligence: the role of intuition and non-logical reasoning in intelligence. *Artificial Intelligence*, **2**, 209–25. *p.* 540

Slovic, P. and Lichtenstein, S. (1971). Comparison of Baysian and regression approaches to the study of information processing judgement. *Organizational Behavior and Human Performance*, **6**, 649–744. *p.* 335

Smalley, N. S. (1974). Interpreting sentences and relating them to possible instances. Paper read at the Trento conference on the selection task (unpublished). *pp.* 153, 155

Smedslund, J. (1963). The concept of correlation in adults. *Scandinavian Journal of Psychology*, **4**, 165–73. *pp.* 446, 447, 449, 450

Smith, C. S. (1961). A class of complex modifiers. *Language*, **37**, 342–65. *p.* 101

Smith, E. E., Shoeben, E. J., and Rips, L. J. (1974). Structure and process in semantic memory: a featural model for semantic decisions. *Psychological Review*, **81**, 214–41. *pp.* 219, 250, 252

Smith, G. M. (1967). Usefulness of peer ratings of personality in educational research. *Educational and Psychological Measurement*, **27**, 967–84. *p.* 458

Smoke, K. L. (1932). An objective study of concept formation. *Psychological Monographs*, **42**, whole no. 191. *p.* 181

Smoke, K. L. (1933). Negative instances in concept learning. *Journal of Experimental Psychology*, **16**, 583–8. *p.* 181

Sneath, P. H. A. and Sokal, R. R. (1973). *Numerical Taxonomy*. San Francisco: Freeman. *pp.* 186, 190, 191, 195, 196

Staudenmayer, H. (1975). Understanding conditional reasoning with meaningful propositions. In Falmagne, R. C. (ed.) *Reasoning: representation and process*. Hillsdale, N.J., Erlbaum. *p.* 81

Steedman, M. J. and Johnson-Laird, P. N. (1977). A programmatic theory of linguistic performance. In Smith, P. T. and Campbell, R. N. (eds.) *Proceedings of the Stirling Conference on the Psychology of Language*. London: Plenum (in press). *p.* 10

Stefflre, V., Castillo Vales, V., and Morely, L. (1966). Language and cognition in Yucatan: a cross cultural replication. *Journal of Personality and Social Psychology*, **4**, 112–15. *p.* 510

Stenning, K. (1977). Articles, quantifiers, and their encoding in textual comprehension. In Freedle, R. O. (ed.) *Discourse Production and Comprehension*. Hillsdale, N.J.: Erlbaum (in press). *pp.* 347, 351

Stone, V. (1977). Chern's decision. *Bulletin of the British Psychological Society*, **30**, 17. *p.* 258

Sudnow, D. (ed.) (1972). *Studies in Social Interaction*. Glencoe, Ill.: Free Press. *p.* 350

Sussman, G. J. (1973). A computational model of skill acquisition. MIT AI Laboratory Memorandum AI–TR–297. *pp.* 25, 26, 375

Sussman, G., Winograd, T., and Charniak, C. (1972). MICRO-PLANNER reference manual. MIT AI Laboratory Report MIT-AI-203A. *p.* 66

Sutherland, N. S. (1976). *Breakdown: a personal crisis and a medical dilemma*. London: Weidenfeld and Nicolson. *p.* 437

Tambiah, S. J. (1973). Form and meaning of magical acts: a point of view. In Horton, R. and Finnegan, R. (eds.) *Modes of Thought*. London: Faber and Faber. *pp.* 446, 447, 466

Taylor, E. G. R. (1971). *The Haven Finding Art*. London: Hollis and Carter. *p.* 537

Thomas, J. C. Jr (1974). An analysis of behavior in the Hobbits-Orcs problem. *Cognitive Psychology*, **6**, 257–69. *p.* 23

Thompson, B. (1962). The effect of positive and negative instruction on a simple 'find the rule' task. Unpublished paper. *p.* 312

Thorndike, E. L. (1911). *Animal Intelligence: experimental studies*. New York: Macmillan. *pp.* 3, 259

Thorndyke, P. W. (1976). The role of inferences in discourse comprehension. *Journal of Verbal Learning and Verbal Behavior*, **15**, 436–46. *p.* 345

Tichomirov, G. K. and Posnyanskaya, E. D. (1966). An investigation of visual search as a means of analyzing heuristics. *Voprosy Psikhologii*, **12**, 39–53. *p.* 27

Titchener, E. B. (1909). *Lectures on the Experimental Psychology of the Thought processes*. New York: Macmillan. *p.* 3

Tolman, E. C. (1932). *Purposive Behavior in Animals and Men*. New York: Appleton-Century-Crofts. *p*. 260

Toulmin, S. (1959). Criticism in the history of science: Newton on absolute space, time and motion, I. *Philosophical Review*, **68**, 1–29. *p*. 286n

Toulmin, S. (1972). *Human Understanding*. Oxford: Clarendon. *p*. 261

Toulmin, S. and Goodfield, J. (1966). *The Fabric of the Heavens*. New York: Harper Torchbooks. *p*. 34

Trabasso, T. (1972). Mental operations in language comprehension. In Carroll, J. B. and Freedle, R. O. (eds.) *Language Comprehension and the Acquisition of Knowledge*. Washington: Winston. *p*. 399

Trabasso, T., Rollins, H., and Shaughnessy, E. (1971). Storage and verification stages in processing concepts. *Cognitive Psychology*, **2**, 239–89. *p*. 77

Tryon, R. C. and Bailey, O. E. (1970). *Cluster Analysis*. New York: McGraw-Hill. *p*. 195

Tulving, E. and Donaldson, W. (eds.) (1972). *Organization of Memory*. New York: Academic. *p*. 212

Turing, A. (1950). Computing machinery and intelligence. *Mind*, **59**, 433–60. *p*. 8

Tversky, A. and Kahneman, D. (1971). Belief in the law of small numbers. *Psychological Bulletin*, **76**, 104–10. *pp*. 330, 446

Tversky, A. and Kahneman, D. (1973). Availability: a heuristic for judging frequency and probability. *Cognitive Psychology*, **5**, 207–32. *pp*. 334, 446, 465

Tyler, S. A. (1969). *Cognitive Anthropology*. New York: Holt, Rinehart, and Winston. *p*. 448

Tylor, E. B. (1964). *Researches into the Early History of Mankind and the Development of Civilization*. Edited reprint. Chicago: University of Chicago Press. (First published 1865.) *p*. 436

Van Dijk, T. A. (1972). *Some Aspects of Text Grammars*. The Hague: Mouton. *p*. 351

Van Duyne, P. C. (1974). Realism and linguistic complexity. *British Journal of Psychology*, **65**, 59–67. *p*. 153

Van Duyne, P. C. (1976). Necessity and contingency in reasoning. *Acta Psychologica*, **40**, 85–101. *p*. 153

Vendler, Z. (1967). *Linguistics in Philosophy*. Ithaca, N.Y.: Cornell University Press. *pp*. 346, 347

Vendler, Z. (1968). *Adjectives and Nominalizations*. The Hague: Mouton. *p*. 100

Vernon, P. E. (ed.) (1970). *Creativity: selected readings*. Harmondsworth, Middx.: Penguin. *p*. 6

Vince, M. (1977). Bartlett's birds. Letter to the *Bulletin of the British Psychological Society*, **30**, 82. *p*. 259n

Vinh Bang (1968). Le rapport inversément proportionnel entre le poids *P* et la distance *D* dans l'équilibre de la balance. In Piaget, J., Grize, J. B., Szeminska, A., and Vinh Bang, *Epistémologie et psychologie de la fonction*. Paris: Presses Univers France. *pp*. 296, 297

Von Domarus, E. (1944). The specific laws of logic in schizophrenia. In Kasinin, J. S. (ed.) *Language and Thought in Schizophrenia*. Berkeley: University of California Press. *p*. 85

Vygotsky, L. S. (1962). *Thought and Language*, ed. and trans. E. Hanfmann and G. Vakar, Cambridge, Mass.: MIT Press. *pp*. 171, 224, 244, 246, 250

Wallas, G. (1926). *The Art of Thought*. New York: Harcourt. *p.* 259

Wang, H. (1960). Toward mechanical mathematics. *IBM Journal of Research and Development*, **4**, 2–22. *p.* 8

Ward, W. C. and Jenkins, H. M. (1965). The display of information and the judgment of contingency. *Canadian Journal of Psychology*, **19**, 231–41. *pp.* 447, 449, 450, 451

Warrington, E. K. and Taylor, A. M. (1973). The contribution of the right parietal lobe to object recognition. *Cortex*, **9**, 152–64. *p.* 344

Wason, P. C. (1959). The processing of positive and negative information. *Quarterly Journal of Experimental Psychology*, **11**, 92–107. *p.* 77

Wason, P. C. (1960). On the failure to eliminate hypotheses in a conceptual task. *Quarterly Journal of Experimental Psychology*, **12**, 129–40. *pp.* 307, 316, 323

Wason, P. C. (1961). Response to affirmative and negative binary statements. *British Journal of Psychology*, **52**, 133–42. *pp.* 105, 112

Wason, P. C. (1962). Reply to Wetherick. *Quarterly Journal of Experimental Psychology*, **14**, 250. *p.* 313

Wason, P. C. (1964). The effect of self-contradiction on fallacious reasoning. *Quarterly Journal of Experimental Psychology*, **16**, 30–4. *pp.* 117, 126

Wason, P. C. (1965). The contexts of plausible denial. *Journal of Verbal Learning and Verbal Behavior*, **4**, 7–11. (Reprinted in Oldfield, R. C. and Marshall, J. C. (eds.) *Language*. Harmondsworth, Middx.: Penguin, 1968). *pp.* 77, 115

Wason, P. C. (1966). Reasoning. In Foss, B. (ed.) *New Horizons in Psychology*, I. Harmondsworth, Middx.: Penguin. *pp.* 119, 120, 143, 145

Wason, P. C. (1968). Reasoning about a rule. *Quarterly Journal of Experimental Psychology*, **20**, 273–81. *pp.* 119, 121, 144, 145, 146, 316, 324

Wason, P. C. (1969). Regression in reasoning? *British Journal of Psychology*, **60**, 471–80. *pp.* 121, 144, 145, 147

Wason, P. C. (1977). The theory of formal operations – a critique. In Geber, B. (ed.) *Piaget and Knowing*. London: Routledge. *p.* 151

Wason, P. C. and Evans, J. St B. T. (1974/5). Dual processes in reasoning? *Cognition*, **3**, 141–54. *pp.* 121, 154, 156, 157

Wason, P. C. and Golding, E. (1974). The language of inconsistency. *British Journal of Psychology*, **65**, 537–46. *p.* 125

Wason, P. C. and Johnson-Laird, P. N. (eds.) (1968). *Thinking and Reasoning*. Harmondsworth, Middx.: Penguin. *pp.* 9, 307n

Wason, P. C. and Johnson-Laird, P. N. (1969). Proving a disjunctive rule. *Quarterly Journal of Experimental Psychology*, **21**, 14–20. *pp.* 150, 154

Wason, P. C. and Johnson-Laird, P. N. (1970). A conflict between selecting and evaluating information in an inferential task. *British Journal of Psychology*, **61**, 509–15. *pp.* 121, 122, 125, 144, 145, 147, 153

Wason, P. C. and Johnson-Laird, P. N. (1972). *Psychology of Reasoning: structure and content*. London: Batsford. *pp.* 81, 86, 88, 114, 117, 151, 154, 306, 316, 476, 494

Wason, P. C. and Jones, S. (1963). Negatives: denotation and connotation. *British Journal of Psychology*, **54**, 299–307. *pp.* 111, 112

Wason, P. C. and Shapiro, D. (1971). Natural and contrived experience in a reasoning problem. *Quarterly Journal of Experimental Psychology*, **23**, 63–71. *p.* 152

Weaver, H. E. and Madden, E. H. (1949). 'Direction' in problem solving. *Journal of Psychology*, **27**, 331–45. *pp.* 18, 19

Weiner, S. L. and Ehrlichman, H. (1976). Ocular motility and cognitive process. *Cognition*, **4**, 31–43. *p.* 27

Weizenbaum, J. (1976). *Computer Power and Human Reason: from judgment to calculation.* San Francisco: Freeman. *pp.* 8, 9

Werner, H. (1948). *Comparative Psychology of Mental Development.* New York: Science Editions. *pp.* 244, 439

Werner, H. and Kaplan, B. (1956). The developmental approach to cognition: its relevance to the psychological interpretation of anthropological and ethnolinguistic data. *American Anthropologist*, **58**, 866–80. *p.* 436

Wertheimer, Max. (1961). *Productive Thinking.* Enlarged edn, ed. Michael Wertheimer. London: Tavistock. *p.* 14

Wetherick, N. E. (1962). Eliminative and enumerative behaviour in a conceptual task. *Quarterly Journal of Experimental Psychology*, **14**, 246–9. *pp.* 307, 312, 313

Whitfield, J. W. (1951). An experiment in problem solving. *Quarterly Journal of Experimental Psychology*, **3**, 184–97. *p.* 172

Whorf, B. L. (1956). *Language, Thought and Reality.* New York: Wiley. *pp.* 287, 441, 501, 504

Wickens, D. D. (1970). Encoding categories of words: an empirical approach to meaning. *Psychological Review*, **77**, 1–15. *p.* 507

Wilkins, M. C. (1928). The effect of changed material on the ability to do formal syllogistic reasoning. *Archives of Psychology*, **16**, no. 102. *pp.* 86, 131

Wilkinson, A. (1976). Counting strategies and semantic analysis as applied to class inclusion. *Cognitive Psychology*, **8**, 64–85. *p.* 179

Wilson, D. (1972). Presuppositions II. Mimeo, University College London. *p.* 141

Wing, H. and Bevan, W. (1969). Structure in the classification of stimuli differing on several continuous attributes. *Perception and Psychophysics*, **6**, 137–41. *p.* 213

Winograd, T. (1972). *Understanding Natural Language.* New York: Academic. (First published in *Cognitive Psychology*, **3** (1972), 1–191.) *pp.* 349, 352, 399, 421

Winograd, T. (1973). The processes of language understanding. In Benthall, J. (ed.) *The Limits of Human Nature.* London: Allen Lane. *p.* 25

Winograd, T. (1975). Frame representations and the declarative/procedural controversy. In Bobrow, D. and Collins, A. (eds.) *Representation and Understanding: studies in cognitive science.* New York: Academic. *p.* 421

Wittgenstein, L. (1958). *Philosophical Investigations.* 2nd edn, trans. G. E. M. Anscombe. Oxford: Blackwell. *pp.* 169, 219, 373, 441, 464

Wood, D. and Shotter, J. (1973). A preliminary study of distinctive features in problem solving. *Quarterly Journal of Experimental Psychology*, **25**, 504–10. *p.* 78

Woods, W. A. (1975). What's in a link: foundations for semantic networks. In Bobrow, D. G. and Collins, A. (eds.) *Representation and Understanding: studies in cognitive science.* New York: Academic. *p.* 71

Woodworth, R. S. (1938). *Experimental Psychology.* New York: Holt. *pp.* 129, 483, 523

Woodworth, R. S. and Sells, S. B. (1935). An atmosphere effect in formal syllogistic reasoning. *Journal of Experimental Psychology*, **18**, 451–60. *pp.* 84, 129, 131

Worchel, P. (1951). Space perception and orientation in the blind. *Psychological Monographs*, **65**, no. 332. *p.* 539

Ziff, P. (1972). *Understanding Understanding*. Ithaca: Cornell University Press. *pp*. 454, 463, 464

Zipf, G. K. (1935). *The Psycho-biology of Language*. Boston: Houghton-Mifflin. *p*. 509

Zobrist, A. L. and Carlson, F. R. (1973). An advice-taking chess computer. *Scientific American*, **228**, 92–105. *p*. 529